# Standard
## LESSON COMMENTARY®

# 2007–2008

### International Sunday School Lessons

Edited by

**Ronald L. Nickelson**

Published by

**Standard Publishing**

Jonathan Underwood, Senior Editor

*Fifty-fifth Annual Volume*

# In This Volume

## Fall Quarter 2007 (page 1)
### God Creates
#### Writers

LESSON DEVELOPMENT ............................ Mark S. Krause (1, 3-5), Mark Mangano (2), Walter D. Zorn (6),
................................................................John Nugent (7-9), Wesley Paddock (10-13)
VERBAL ILLUSTRATIONS ........................................................................................Charles R. Boatman
LEARNING BY DOING................................................... Ronald G. Davis (1-9), Bob & Charlotte Mize (10-13)
LET'S TALK IT OVER .........................................................A. Eugene Andrews (1-9), Ted Simonson (10-13)

## Winter Quarter 2007–2008 (page 113)
### God's Call to the Christian Community
#### Writers

LESSON DEVELOPMENT ...............Kenny Boles (1-5), James & Mandy Smith (6-9), Mark S. Krause (10-13)
VERBAL ILLUSTRATIONS .......................................................................................... James B. North
LEARNING BY DOING................................................................... Ronald G. Davis (1-5), Alan Weber (6-13)
LET'S TALK IT OVER .................... Vicki Edwards (1-5), David Marvin (6-9), A. Eugene Andrews (10-13)

## Spring Quarter 2008 (page 225)
### God, the People, and the Covenant
#### Writers

LESSON DEVELOPMENT .................................................................Walter D. Zorn (1-5), John Nugent (6-9),
.......................................................................Joe Sprinkle (10, 11), Aaron Prohs (12, 13)
VERBAL ILLUSTRATIONS ........................................................................................Charles R. Boatman
LEARNING BY DOING.....................................................Richard A. Koffarnus (1-5), Ronald G. Davis (6-13)
LET'S TALK IT OVER .....................Vicki Edwards (1-5), A. Eugene Andrews (6-9), Chad Summa (10-13)

## Summer Quarter 2008 (page 337)
### Images of Christ
#### Writers

LESSON DEVELOPMENT ....................... Lee M. Fields (1, 2), Mark S. Krause (3-5), Larry Chouinard (6, 7),
....................................................................... Rick Allbee (8, 9), William R. Baker (10-14)
VERBAL ILLUSTRATIONS ......................................................................................... James B. North
LEARNING BY DOING............................... Ronald G. Davis (1-5), Alan Weber (6-9), Charlotte Mize (10-14)
LET'S TALK IT OVER ..... A. Eugene Andrews (1-5, 8, 9), Truitt F. Evans, Sr. (6, 7), Vicki Edwards (10-14)

#### Artist
TITLE PAGES: James E. Seward
Cover design by DesignTeam
Lessons based on International Sunday School Lessons © 2005 by the Lesson Committee.

## CD-ROM AVAILABLE

The *Standard Lesson Commentary*® is available separately in an electronic format. This compact disk contains the full text of the King James *Standard Lesson Commentary*® and *The NIV Standard Lesson Commentary*®, a variety of preparation resources powered by the Libronix Digital Library System, and a collection of presentation helps that can be projected or reproduced as handouts. Order #06008.

*System Requirements: Windows Vista/XP/2000; Pentium 133 MHz processor (300MHz recommended), 64 Meg RAM (128 recommended); 60 Meg Available Hard Drive Space; 2x or better CD-ROM drive.*

# Index of Printed Texts, 2007–2008

*The printed texts for 2007–2008 are arranged here in the order in which they appear in the Bible. Opposite each reference is the number of the page on which it appears in this volume.*

# Cumulative Index

A cumulative index for the Scripture passages used in the STANDARD LESSON COMMENTARY for the years September 2004–August 2008 is provided below.

V

# Musings of a Repentant Technophobe

## Using Modern Teaching Tools

### *by Chuck Terrill*

Technology scares me. I don't like it. When 8-track tape players became popular, I stuck with my record player. When cassette players became popular, I traded my record player for an 8-track tape player. When CDs became fashionable, I bought a cassette player. It seems that I have always managed to stay about a decade behind in the area of technological advance.

I have repented, albeit begrudgingly. I exchanged my typewriter for a computer just a few years ago. I don't know much of anything about what makes a computer work, but the computer has changed my life.

In our media driven age, the way we present our lessons is important. You know that you have been faithful in your responsibilities as a teacher. You've studied hard, and God has given you a message to present. You know what the Bible says and what it means. How can you help your students apply biblical truth to their lives?

Start by going to www.standardlesson.com. Then click on the "In the World" link. Once you land on that page, you can bookmark it or put it in your Internet browser's *favorites* file. That way you can return easily time and time again. I assure you, it is well worth the effort! This resource will give you timely insight into how the message of the Bible relates to us for the week at hand.

There is little relevance in using illustrations or applications that are long outdated. Our students aren't overly concerned about how mankind perceived God one hundred years ago. They are asking, "What is God doing now? How does the Word of God apply to me today?" You will find that "In the World" is always timely and relevant in this regard. You will receive insight and direction that will help apply Scripture to the lives of your students in a meaningful way.

Now here's the best news: "In the World" is free. This is just one of many ministry resources that Standard Publishing makes available to you to help you faithfully teach the Word of God. While you are visiting www.standardpub.com, review their other valuable resources. You might want to read the Daily Devotion or sign up for the free eNewsletter. All of these free resources are made available for your personal growth and development.

Something else that had me scared was the use of multimedia in the presentation of my Sunday school lessons. Maybe you, also, experimented with creating Microsoft PowerPoint® slides at one time, but you determined that the result just really wasn't worth the extra effort. But what if you had your own assistant, who would design and construct a PowerPoint® presentation for you every week? That sounds good, doesn't it?

Standard Publishing is your own, personal PowerPoint® design assistant! If you purchase the *Standard Lesson eCommentary*, the slide presentations are on the CD. You will also find the PowerPoint® presentation on the CD that accompanies the Standard Lesson Quarterly *Adult Resources* packet.

These presentations are skillfully done and are ready to present or project just as they are. If your computer has the full version of the PowerPoint® program, you have the option of editing the presentation. Even if you don't have the full version of PowerPoint®, you can download the free PowerPoint® "reader" at www.microsoft.com/downloads. It will enable you to use (but not edit) Standard Publishing's dynamic presentations.

Statistically, we remember much more of what we both hear and see as opposed to only hearing or only seeing. That's the main reason to use the PowerPoint® presentations. The extra effort will be well worth it.

Standard Publishing has a wealth of resources for teachers of the International Sunday School Lessons. The student book, *Adult Bible Class*, will help your learners to retain more knowledge as they study in advance. The *Adult Resources* packet contains posters as well as take-home papers that are relevant to the lesson of the day. You might also want to use the on-line lesson at www.christianstandard.com in your preparation time.

Don't be a technophobe. You'll be glad you went online to discover the valuable resources that Standard Publishing has to offer. Your students will rejoice as well.

# Fall Quarter 2007

## God Creates

### (Genesis)

### Special Features

### Lessons

#### Unit 1: God Creates a People

#### Unit 2: God's People Increase

#### Unit 3: God's People Re-created

## About These Lessons

Everyone knows the frustration of trying to follow the plot of a movie after missing the first ten minutes. Beginnings are vitally important! The Bible itself has a grand "plotline," so to speak. A proper understanding of Christianity has its start with the book of Genesis—the beginning.

Sep 2
Sep 9
Sep 16
Sep 23
Sep 30
Oct 7
Oct 14
Oct 21
Oct 28
Nov 4
Nov 11
Nov 18
Nov 25

# Two Bridges

DURING A U.S. PRESIDENTIAL CAMPAIGN, one candidate declared his intention to build "a bridge to the past." His opponent quickly replied that what was really needed was "a bridge to the future." The truth: you can't have the latter without the former, since our view of the past affects how we live out our futures.

This and every year's lessons press this truth into action. We begin by exploring Genesis, which reconnects us with our origins, both as created beings and as God's people. You can't build a bridge any farther into the past than that! Our Genesis lessons demonstrate how that bridge to the distant past directs (or should direct) our walk on the bridge that leads to our eternal future.

The same holds true for the lessons for winter, spring, and summer as they explore various points along the timeline of God's dealings with humans. During our exploration, we will discover anew that the bridge that takes us forward to our glorious eternity is none other than Christ and His cross. To Him be the glory!  —R. L. N.

## International Sunday School Lesson Cycle
## September 2004—August 2010

| YEAR | FALL QUARTER (Sept., Oct., Nov.) | WINTER QUARTER (Dec., Jan., Feb.) | SPRING QUARTER (Mar., Apr., May) | SUMMER QUARTER (June, July, Aug.) |
|---|---|---|---|---|
| 2004-2005 | The God of Continuing Creation (Bible Survey) | Called to Be God's People (Bible Survey) | God's Project: Effective Christians (Romans, Galatians) | Jesus' Life, Ministry, and Teaching (Matthew, Mark, Luke) |
| 2005-2006 | "You Will Be My Witnesses" (Acts) | God's Commitment— Our Response (Isaiah; 1 & 2 Timothy) | Living in and as God's Creation (Psalms, Job, Ecclesiastes, Proverbs) | Called to Be a Christian Community (1 & 2 Corinthians) |
| 2006-2007 | God's Living Covenant (Old Testament Survey) | Jesus Christ: A Portrait of God (John, Philippians, Colossians, Hebrews, 1 John) | Our Community Now and in God's Future (1 John, Revelation) | Committed to Doing Right (Various Prophets, 2 Kings, 2 Chronicles) |
| 2007-2008 | God Creates (Genesis) | God's Call to the Christian Community (Luke) | God, the People, and the Covenant (1 & 2 Chronicles, Daniel, Haggai, Nehemiah) | Images of Christ (Hebrews, Gospels, James) |
| 2008-2009 | The New Testament Community (New Testament Survey) | Human Commitment (Character Studies) | Christ in Creation (Ezekiel, Luke, Acts, Ephesians) | Call Sealed with Promise (Exodus, Leviticus, Numbers, Deuteronomy) |
| 2009-2010 | Covenant Communities (Joshua, Judges, Ezra, Nehemiah, Mark, 1 & 2 Peter) | Christ the Fulfillment (Matthew) | Teachings on Community (Jonah, Ruth, New Testament) | Christian Commitment in Today's World (1 & 2 Thessalonians, Philippians) |

| "Creation" | "Call" | "Covenant" | "Christ" | "Community" | "Commitment" |

# Our Heritage

*by Walter D. Zorn*

EVERY CHRISTIAN should become well acquainted with Genesis, the first book of the Bible. Why? Because it is a divine revelation about the beginning of all that we observe—our universe and the people who live on the earth.

Genesis also reveals to us the beginnings of the Hebrew people, who were chosen by God to precede the Messiah. As Christians we trace our spiritual ancestry back to Abraham, who "is the father of us all" (Romans 4:16). This makes the study of Genesis imperative for Christians who wish to be informed about the beginning of our faith. Our beginning as Christians is found not only at Pentecost (Acts 2) but also with Abraham (Genesis 12–25), and before him, with the first human beings, Adam and Eve.

This quarter's emphasis will be on the covenant people whom God created; but first He had to create a universe that could sustain people made in His image. While the fallen state of humanity is not discussed in this series, it is part of the backdrop as we observe how God chose one man and his wife to be in special covenant relationship with him. Somehow God, through this one family, would create a new people, a nation that would bring redemption to the world.

## Unit 1: September
## God Creates a People

**Lesson 1** begins with the creation of the universe. But the focus of Genesis 1 is not the entire universe as such. Rather, the focus is on this earth, as God fashioned it and its inhabitants: all kinds of living creatures. Humanity was the crown and climax of creation.

This creation of an inhabitable and inhabited earth occurred within a six-day period, with the last three days paralleling the first three days. Not until humanity was created as male and female did God pronounce all His creation to be "very good." Humans were given stewardship responsibility for God's good creation. Believers should experience nothing but awe and wonder in the presence of all creation.

**Lesson 2** emphasizes the meaning and importance of humanity having been created in the image of God. There are many opinions as to what this word *image* means, but it clearly relates to the fact that humanity is God's representative on earth and has stewardship over it. With the use of such words as *subdue* and *have dominion*, it seems that we are to function as "kings" and "queens" over God's good creation. It is imperative for us to take care of the earth that God has given us.

**Lesson 3** is about God's promise to Abram and Sarai (who were later renamed Abraham and Sarah) that they were to have a son in their old age. It is through this son that a new nation was to be born. That nation was to bring blessing and salvation to all the peoples of the world.

Would God keep His promise? How could an old man and woman, past the age for bearing children, have such a child of promise? But God did keep His promise. Nothing is too hard for God! Eventually Abraham trusted God and "[God] counted it to [Abraham] for righteousness" (Genesis 15:6). Sarah's initial laugh of derision was turned into a laugh of joy. Isaac (meaning "laughter") became, in a sense, God's joke on the world. Abraham did indeed become a "father of many nations" through this one son.

**Lesson 4** recounts the story of how Ishmael was born to Hagar, Sarah's handmaid. It really is a story of lack of trust on the part of Abraham and Sarah. They thought they would never have children of their own, despite God's promises. Time was running out, they thought, and so they did the only "natural" thing to do: they produced a child through a surrogate mother, Hagar.

In spite of the resulting conflict, God blessed Hagar and Ishmael; thus was born an estrangement between two great peoples—Jews and Arabs. We can learn an important lesson from God's care and concern for Hagar and Ishmael.

The continuation of the covenant promises depended on Isaac's marrying the "proper" wife and having "proper" children. **Lesson 5** is the story of that selection process. Through prayer, a test, and spiritual discernment, Abraham's servant found Rebekah, a member of Abraham's family. Rebekah's kindness proved her to be God's choice for Isaac. Through her the promised seed of Abraham continued.

## Unit 2: October
## God's People Increase

**Lesson 6** continues the story about Rebekah's marriage to Isaac. They finally had children—twin sons who struggled with each other from before birth. The sibling rivalry created a bitter struggle between two peoples from which the older (Esau = Edom) would serve the younger (Jacob = Israel).

Parental favoritism fostered the rivalry, and the results were disastrous. Things worsened when Esau rashly sold his birthright to Jacob. In spite of Jacob's taking advantage of Esau, God worked through Jacob to fulfill His promises.

**Lesson 7** examines Jacob's dream at Bethel. This involved a ladder that led to Heaven, with angels descending and ascending on it and God above it. In this vision God restated to Jacob the covenant promises as they were originally given to Abraham. In God's sovereign care, Jacob was promised a land, numberless "seed," and God's own divine presence and assurance of fulfillment. Thus, Bethel ("house of God") became a place of worship, where Jacob committed himself to Yahweh God.

In **Lesson 8** Jacob-the-deceiver was deceived by his uncle Laban. Jacob had been given Leah as a wife instead of Rachel, and he had to agree to work seven more years to earn the right to have the younger daughter as his second wife. God used the deception as an opportunity to expand Jacob's family as promised. God is able to work in disappointing situations to bring about good.

**Lesson 9** is the story of a great family reunion and reconciliation. It involved two brothers who had been bitter enemies (see Lesson 6). Although Jacob expected a battle, Esau greeted him with hospitality and signs of forgiveness.

## Unit 3: November
## God's People Re-created

**Lesson 10** is the continuing saga of how parental favoritism can wreak havoc on sibling relationships (see Lesson 6). The fact that Joseph revealed his dreams (which he had a moral obligation to do) made things worse. His brothers reacted by selling him into slavery. Joseph's brothers thus set in motion a series of actions that cascaded in a direction they could not possibly have imagined. Joseph's dreams were his divine calling. But the fulfillment of the calling would come in unusual and mysterious ways that only a sovereign God could bring about.

**Lesson 11** continues to unfold the mysterious ways of God in the account of Joseph. Joseph not only dreamed, he also interpreted dreams. His interpretation of Pharaoh's dream caused Pharaoh to elevate Joseph to a position of high power. God was the source of the dreams and thus He, ultimately, was the one who elevated Joseph to his position.

The story of Joseph crescendos with **Lesson 12.** The years of famine had brought many peoples to Egypt to obtain grain. Joseph's wisdom and oversight over the granaries of Egypt preserved many people, including his own family, the family of promise. Thus, Joseph partially fulfilled the promise to Abraham, for Joseph was blessed to be a blessing.

All this made Joseph a life-figure and deliverer for the world of his day. We can say that Joseph was thus a "type" of Christ in that (1) those closest to him betrayed him and (2) God used the experience to bring about a deliverance.

**Lesson 13** draws the patriarchal stories to a close, with Jacob's blessing of Joseph's sons. The uniqueness of this blessing was in the way Jacob crossed his arms and placed his right hand on Ephraim, the younger son, thus giving him the chief blessing. Jacob himself had experienced something similar in the declaration that "the older will serve the younger" in God's plan. Jacob's legacy continued through his sons as well as through his grandsons from Joseph, who were each given full tribal allotments.

## From the Past to the Future

God created a universe out of nothing. He placed planet Earth within it. Upon that planet He put the crown of His creation: humanity, created in the image of God.

Then sin intervened. To redeem a fallen world, God planned to send His Messiah through a new people created (seemingly out of nothing) just for that purpose. Today, we have a heritage of sin from Adam and a heritage of faith from Abraham. We feel the effects of these two legacies constantly. Through Christ, we know which one wins out in the end!

### Answers to Quarterly Quiz
### on page 8

**Lesson 1**—1. waters. 2. false. 3. Seas. **Lesson 2**—1. true. 2. false. 3. every herb bearing seed, plus fruit of a tree yielding seed. **Lesson 3**—1. stars. 2. 100. **Lesson 4**—1. false. 2. true. **Lesson 5**—1. his servant. 2. Rebekah. **Lesson 6**—1. false. 2. true. 3. red pottage. **Lesson 7**—1. Haran. 2. the Lord. **Lesson 8**—1. Laban. 2. true. **Lesson 9**—1. four. 2. false. **Lesson 10**—1. sheaves and stars. 2. Dothan. **Lesson 11**—1. seven, seven. 2. true. **Lesson 12**—1. five. 2. true. **Lesson 13**—1. true. 2. Ephraim and Manasseh.

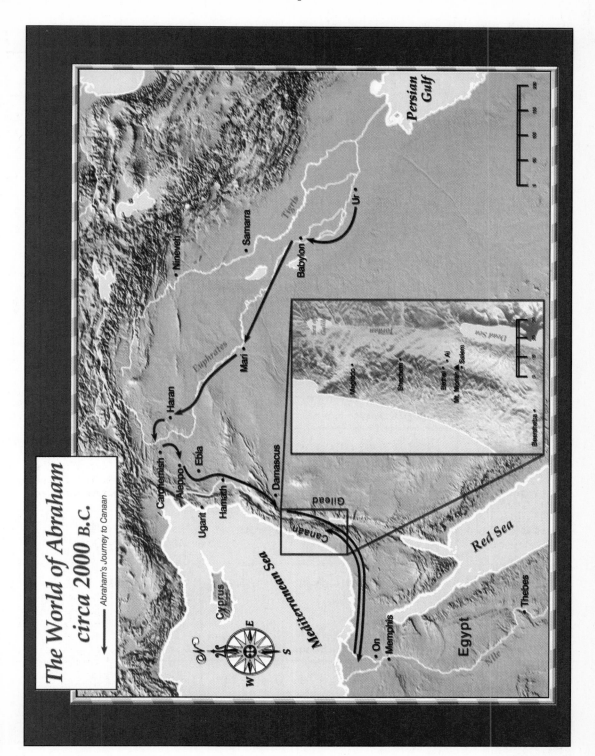

The World of Abraham
circa 2000 B.C.
→ Abraham's Journey to Canaan

# Chronology of Genesis
## From the Call of Abraham to the Death of Joseph

| | | |
|---|---|---|
| 2167 BC | Abram born | |
| 2092 BC | Call of Abram | Genesis 12:1-5 |
| 2081 BC | Ishmael born (Lesson 4) | Genesis 16:15, 16 |
| 2067 BC | Isaac born (Lesson 3) | Genesis 21:1-3 |
| 2050 BC | Abraham offers Isaac | Genesis 22:1-19 |
| 2007 BC | Jacob and Esau born (Lesson 6) | Genesis 25:24-26 |
| 1992 BC | Abraham dies at age 175 | Genesis 25:7 |
| 1930 BC | Jacob flees to Haran (Lesson 7) | Genesis 28:10 |
| 1916 BC | Joseph born | Genesis 30:22-24 |
| 1899 BC | Joseph sold into slavery in Egypt at age 17 (Lesson 10) | Genesis 37:2, 28 |
| 1887 BC | Isaac dies at age 180 | Genesis 35:28 |
| 1886 BC | At age 30, Joseph interprets Pharaoh's dream (Lesson 11) | Genesis 41:46 |
| 1877 BC | Jacob goes to Egypt *Beginning of the Israelites' 430-year stay in Egypt (Exodus 12:40, 41), leading to the exodus in 1447 BC (Lesson 12)* | Genesis 46:5, 6 |
| 1860 BC | Jacob dies at age 147 (Lesson 13) | Genesis 47:28 |
| 1806 BC | Joseph dies at age 110 | Genesis 50:26 |

# It's Their Story Too!

## Making Genesis Come Alive

### by Eleanor A. Daniel

I LOVE STORIES! Most people do. Stories excite the imagination and stimulate thinking. Your challenge is to use stories in such a way that your learners travel with you on a progressive journey to see God at work.

This quarter's lessons are from Genesis. They involve great narratives that demonstrate an unfolding drama of God in relation to His creation and His people. These narratives invite us to adopt them as a part of our own faith story. Your success as a teacher in this regard will help prevent your learners from approaching the studies as a mere series of facts.

You will do more than tell stories, of course. But don't ignore the fact that adults respond well to them. Part of your task is to ask questions that engage learners in their own involvement in the story line. Consider the following story development ideas and questions.

**Lesson 1.** Don't get bogged down in theoretical discussions of cosmology that cannot be adequately addressed during your brief class. Instead, begin where the text does: "In the beginning God." *Questions:* Reflecting on the creation account in Genesis, what does it tell you about God and yourself for humans to have been created in His image? Adding Psalm 8 to your reflection, what response is appropriate to the creative God?

**Lesson 2.** Pick up the story from last week and expand on the nature of humankind as created in God's image. Emphasize God's intention to create those who could interact with Him. *Question:* Though marred by sin, what glimpses do we see of people expressing the image of God?

**Lesson 3.** Connect today's narrative with the original covenant with Abraham in Genesis 12:2, 3. Paint the agony of waiting for a promise that no longer seemed to be fulfillable. *Question:* In what ways did Abraham's responses make him a model—or perhaps not a model at all—for you as you wait upon God in your own life?

**Lesson 4.** Return to the story for last week and show how Abraham tried to resolve his wait for a son. Then cast the story to show the consequences that result from trying to solve problems on our own terms. *Questions:* How was Abraham shaped by the choices he made? How are you shaped by the choices you make?

**Lesson 5.** Check out marriage customs of the patriarchs! Emphasize the importance of finding a spouse in the larger clan to allow for a continuity that would please God. Stress that marriage is a sacred, spiritual contract. The choice we make has profound implications for our relationship with God. *Questions:* How do you see these facts demonstrated in this story? in the lives of those you know?

**Lesson 6.** Emphasize how differences among siblings can create rivalry, especially when parents express disappointment or delight with a child. *Questions:* How can sibling rivalries affect a person's future? How have you seen this develop?

**Lesson 7.** Emphasize how Jacob was invited into the same covenant as Abraham. *Questions:* Why was it important for God to confirm to Jacob his place in the covenant? Why is an understanding of *covenant with God* important for any believer?

**Lesson 8.** Shape the story to emphasize Jacob's deep love for Rachel. *Question:* What does Jacob teach us (positively or negatively) about response to disappointment?

**Lesson 9.** Focus on reconciliation and how to achieve it. *Question:* What does this account teach us about reconciliation?

**Lesson 10.** Examine how rivalry can result in mistreatment. *Question:* If you had been 17-year-old Joseph, what would have been your thoughts as you were sold into Egypt?

**Lesson 11.** Continue to emphasize Joseph's profound disappointments and God's continuing affirmation of him. *Question:* What difference do you think it made to Joseph's character to endure the difficulties he experienced?

**Lesson 12.** Emphasize Joseph's part in protecting God's people. *Question:* How was Joseph able to maintain a perspective about God's work in his life?

**Lesson 13.** Provide an overview of the waning days of Jacob's (Israel's) life. *Questions:* What legacy did Jacob consider to be most important to his sons? What do you think is important for your own family in this regard?

Enjoy the great narratives of God's work that are set forth in Genesis. More importantly, make them your own (and your learners') narratives as well!

# Quarterly Quiz

*The questions on this page may be used in several ways: as a pretest at the beginning of the quarter; as a review at the end of the quarter; or as a review after each lesson. The questions are based on the Scripture text of each lesson* (King James Version). ***The answers are on page 4.***

### Lesson 1

1. At the beginning of creation, the Spirit of God moved upon the face of the ____. *Genesis 1:2*
2. God created animals before He created light. T/F *Genesis 1:3, 20*
3. What did God call the gathering together of the waters? (Seas, Rain, Glaciers?) *Genesis 1:10*

### Lesson 2

1. God created humans in His own image. T/F *Genesis 1:27*
2. God told humans to be careful not to try to subdue the earth. T/F *Genesis 1:28*
3. What did God give the first humans permission to eat? (seafood only; every herb bearing seed, plus fruit of a tree yielding seed; anything they wanted?) *Genesis 1:29*

### Lesson 3

1. God's promise of descendants to Abraham was in comparison to the number of what? (stars, birds, fish?) *Genesis 15:5*
2. Abraham was ____ years old when Isaac was born. *Genesis 21:5*

### Lesson 4

1. Abraham sent Hagar and Ishmael away even though Sarah objected. T/F *Genesis 21:10, 14*
2. After being sent away, Hagar and her son wandered in the wilderness of Beersheba. T/F *Genesis 21:14*

### Lesson 5

1. Whom did Abraham send on a mission to find a wife for his son? (his servant, a Canaanite, Sarah?) *Genesis 24:34-38*
2. "_____ came forth with her pitcher of water on her shoulder." *Genesis 24:45*

### Lesson 6

1. Isaac, Esau, and Jacob were born as triplets to Rebekah. T/F *Genesis 25:19-26*
2. Esau was born red and hairy, ending up being "a cunning hunter, a man of the field." T/F *Genesis 25:25, 27*
3. Esau sold his birthright in exchange for what? (red pottage, green apples, purple grapes?) *Genesis 25:30-34*

### Lesson 7

1. After leaving home, Jacob went toward what? (Haran, Egypt, Rome?) *Genesis 28:10*
2. Who stood above the ladder in Jacob's dream? (the angel Gabriel, Satan, the Lord?) *Genesis 28:12, 13*

### Lesson 8

1. It was ____ who tricked Jacob into marrying Leah. *Genesis 29:21-23*
2. Jacob loved Rachel more than he loved Leah. T/F *Genesis 29:30*

### Lesson 9

1. Esau approached Jacob with ____ hundred men. *Genesis 33:1*
2. Before they reconciled, Esau slapped Jacob when they met. T/F *Genesis 33:4*

### Lesson 10

1. Joseph's dreams involved what things? (sheep and goats, birds and bread, sheaves and stars?) *Genesis 37:7, 9*
2. The brothers were near the town of _____ when they conspired against Joseph. *Genesis 37:17, 18*

### Lesson 11

1. Joseph told Pharaoh that there would be ___ years of plenty, followed by ___ years of famine. *Genesis 41:29, 30*
2. Joseph ended up being second in command in Egypt. T/F *Genesis 41:40, 41*

### Lesson 12

1. When Joseph revealed his identity to his brothers, there were ____ years of famine yet to go. *Genesis 45:1-6*
2. Joseph wanted his father and brothers to live in the land of Goshen. T/F *Genesis 45:9, 10*

### Lesson 13

1. Israel (Jacob) did not give the primary blessing to Joseph's firstborn son. T/F *Genesis 48:14*
2. The names of Joseph's sons whom Jacob (Israel) blessed were what? (Reuben and Judah; Zebulun and Issachar; Ephraim and Manasseh?) *Genesis 48:20*

# The Beginning

DEVOTIONAL READING: **Psalm 8.**

BACKGROUND SCRIPTURE: **Genesis 1:1-25.**

PRINTED TEXT: **Genesis 1:1-6, 8, 10, 12-15, 19, 20, 22, 23, 25.**

Genesis 1:1-6, 8, 10, 12-15, 19, 20, 22, 23, 25

1 In the beginning God created the heaven and the earth.

2 And the earth was without form, and void; and darkness was upon the face of the deep. And the Spirit of God moved upon the face of the waters.

3 And God said, Let there be light: and there was light.

4 And God saw the light, that it was good: and God divided the light from the darkness.

5 And God called the light Day, and the darkness he called Night. And the evening and the morning were the first day.

6 And God said, Let there be a firmament in the midst of the waters, and let it divide the waters from the waters.

. . . . . . . . . .

8 And God called the firmament Heaven. And the evening and the morning were the second day.

. . . . . . . . . .

10 And God called the dry land Earth; and the gathering together of the waters called he Seas: and God saw that it was good.

. . . . . . . . . .

12 And the earth brought forth grass, and herb yielding seed after his kind, and the tree yielding fruit, whose seed was in itself, after his kind: and God saw that it was good.

13 And the evening and the morning were the third day.

14 And God said, Let there be lights in the firmament of the heaven to divide the day

from the night; and let them be for signs, and for seasons, and for days, and years:

15 And let them be for lights in the firmament of the heaven to give light upon the earth: and it was so.

. . . . . . . . . .

19 And the evening and the morning were the fourth day.

20 And God said, Let the waters bring forth abundantly the moving creature that hath life, and fowl that may fly above the earth in the open firmament of heaven.

. . . . . . . . . .

22 And God blessed them, saying, Be fruitful, and multiply, and fill the waters in the seas, and let fowl multiply in the earth.

23 And the evening and the morning were the fifth day.

. . . . . . . . . .

25 And God made the beast of the earth after his kind, and cattle after their kind, and every thing that creepeth upon the earth after his kind: and God saw that it was good.

---

GOLDEN TEXT: In the beginning God created the heaven and the earth.—Genesis 1:1.

*God Creates*
Unit 1: God Creates a People
(Lessons 1-5)

## Lesson Aims

After participating in this lesson, each student will be able to:

1. List elements of the days of creation.
2. Summarize the method and design of God's creation as presented in Genesis 1.
3. Make a plan for greater stewardship toward one aspect of God's created resources.

## Lesson Outline

INTRODUCTION
  A. The Debate over Intelligent Design
  B. Lesson Background
I. GOD AT THE BEGINNING (Genesis 1:1, 2)
  A. Beginning, God, Heaven, Earth (v. 1)
  B. Earth, Darkness, Spirit, Waters (v. 2)
II. CREATION, DAYS 1–3 (Genesis 1:3-6, 8, 10, 12, 13)
  A. First Day of Creation (vv. 3-5)
  B. Second Day of Creation (vv. 6, 8)
    *Furnishing a New World*
  C. Third Day of Creation (vv. 10, 12, 13)
III. CREATION, DAYS 4–6 (Genesis 1:14, 15, 19, 20, 22, 23, 25)
  A. Fourth Day of Creation (vv. 14, 15, 19)
    *Heavenly Bodies*
  B. Fifth Day of Creation (vv. 20, 22, 23)
  C. Sixth Day of Creation (v. 25)
CONCLUSION
  A. "All Creation Waits"
  B. Prayer
  C. Thought to Remember

## Introduction

### A. The Debate over Intelligent Design

I recently spoke to a friend I had not seen for years. I knew that he had been adopted as a child, but I did not know that for several years he had been seeking his birth parents. He eventually found he had another "family" of brothers and sisters; he has developed relationships with them. His comment about this to me was, "When I found out more about where I came from, I began to understand much better who I am." We are intuitively curious about our origins!

The book of Genesis is a book of origins, although it speaks of our origins in a much more profound way than the "origins" my friend was concerned with. As we read Genesis, several questions come to mind: Does this book provide reliable scientific data? Should believing Christians engage in scientific research and debate? Is there any room in the public classroom for the story of creation that Genesis provides?

Many people today (even some Christians) would answer *no* to all three questions. Others have long been engaged in the pursuit of *creation science,* an approach that sees Genesis as a certain guide to the origins of the universe and life itself. Creation science, however, has difficulty gaining a wide hearing in the mainline scientific community. Creation science is dismissed as being tied too closely to what is viewed as a premodern, superstitious, unscientific worldview.

Recently, a variation of creation science has gained notice: *the theory of Intelligent Design.* This effort is supported by scientists having solid academic credentials. Michael J. Behe, a leading proponent of Intelligent Design, has pointed out that many scientific investigations lead to the observation of "irreducible complexity" in natural phenomena. Behe claims that the physical characteristics of living organisms are too complex to be explained by mindless processes such as natural selection and mutation—thus the necessity of a designer.

There is no conflict between the foundational assumptions of the theory of Intelligent Design and the book of Genesis. Intelligent Design demands that we understand a master intellect behind the order of the universe, a designer or creator. This is clearly taught in Genesis.

Yet the theory of Intelligent Design by itself is unable to understand God as more than a master artisan, a superior being who turns out an amazing series of inventions from His workshop. The theory of Intelligent Design cannot lead us fully to the God of the Bible, who not only made us but also continues to have a personal relationship with His creatures. For the fullest understanding of who God is and how we can relate to Him, we must turn to the Bible.

### B. Lesson Background

Genesis in not merely the first book in the Bible. It stands as the first book in a five-book section of the Old Testament we call the *Pentateuch* or the *Books of Moses* (Genesis, Exodus, Leviticus, Numbers, Deuteronomy). This collection was finished long before the end of the Old Testament period; it was already in use during the times of the kingdoms of Israel and Judah, many centuries before Christ.

The overall purpose of the Pentateuch is to tell the story of the origins of the nation of Israel. With this purpose in view, we can understand that Genesis serves as an introduction to the great events of nation-birthing found in Exodus. Genesis provides us with the place to start: the beginning, with God's creation of the heaven and the earth. What better place to start could there be?

Included in this account is the creation of humanity, the first man and woman. They are the ancestors of all people, not just the nation of Israel. The tragedy of Genesis is that humanity rebelled against its creator. Sin flourished. Later, the story focuses on Abraham, father of the nation of Israel. He was chosen because God planned to use one of his descendants (Jesus) to redeem humanity from the bondage of sin.

And so we begin the greatest story ever told. It is the drama of human origins and humanity's eventual deliverance from its self-caused alienation from the creator of the universe. The stage could be no bigger, the stakes no higher.

## I. God at the Beginning
### (Genesis 1:1, 2)

Where did God come from? You will not find the answer in Genesis. God is uncreated, separate and apart from any created thing. The existence of an uncreated creator is the reason there can be anything instead of nothing. The universe is not self-explanatory. It exists because God upholds it by His powerful word (see Hebrews 1:3).

### A. Beginning, God, Heaven, Earth (v. 1)

**1. In the beginning God created the heaven and the earth.**

The opening of Genesis has no comment on *God* other than to place Him at *the beginning*. However far back in time we can imagine, God was there! This is an understated, yet striking, testimony to God's eternality: *In the beginning,* **God**.

The text sketches God's creation in broad terms. The use of *heaven* and the *earth* together may refer simply to the totality of the physical universe. Some think, however, that *heaven* as used here refers to the realm of God and the created angelic beings. That is a domain not normally accessible to humans. [See question #1, page 16.]

### B. Earth, Darkness, Spirit, Waters (v. 2)

**2. And the earth was without form, and void; and darkness was upon the face of the deep.**

**And the Spirit of God moved upon the face of the waters.**

At this point in creation, the future home of humanity is characterized four ways. First, it is *without form* or unfinished; God has yet to mold it into final state. Second, it is *void* or empty; the living creatures who will inhabit it have yet to be created. Third, it is dark; this is not a limiting factor for God (see Psalm 139:12), but the condition must be changed in order for earth to be a suitable habitation for humans. Fourth, it is watery; there is no solid ground to stand upon. This too is a condition that must be modified in order to give human life a chance for survival.

The text notes the presence of the *Spirit of God*. This is not a separate being from God of verse 1. God's ability to be present is not limited by conditions that allow for His presence. This is an indirect affirmation of the doctrine of God's omnipresence (His presence everywhere).

While this spiritual presence of God is not referred to as the Holy Spirit, the concept is there in part. Holiness refers to more than moral purity. The Bible also understands being holy as being separate. At this point, God clearly is separate from His creation. The created world is not part of God, and He is not part of the created world. They are distinct. [See question #2, page 16.]

## II. Creation, Days 1–3
### (Genesis 1:3-6, 8, 10, 12, 13)

The work proceeds in an orderly fashion. God does not leave the world void and uninhabitable. He has a plan that leads to the final creation of human beings in His image.

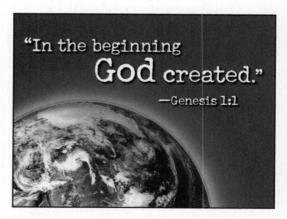

Visual for Lesson 1. *Start a discussion by pointing to this visual as you ask, "Why is it important to acknowledge this truth?"*

This part of Genesis does not describe any creative method of God beyond speaking. The mechanics of this are not revealed to us in any scientific way. We must believe that the word of God is powerful and creative (see Psalm 33:6; Hebrews 11:2, 3). In the New Testament, this creative Word of God is identified with His Son (see John 1:3; Hebrews 1:3).

## A. First Day of Creation (vv. 3-5)

**3-5. And God said, Let there be light: and there was light. And God saw the light, that it was good: and God divided the light from the darkness. And God called the light Day, and the darkness he called Night. And the evening and the morning were the first day.**

God's first day of creation concerns not living creatures but *light.* It is difficult to conceive of life without light, for it is a necessary component of life as we generally understand it. If there were no light, it would be a blind universe. [See question #3, page 16.]

Notice that *darkness* is not created. Light is separated from darkness, but there is no sense of God "making darkness." This is because darkness has no real existence. It is simply an absence, a lack of light. Darkness is a "without." This is why darkness is an apt metaphor for moral evil and sin, which is living "without God" (our moral light).

Verse 5 establishes the pattern for the days of creation. Each section ends with the statement *the evening and morning were the . . . day,* indicating a creative cycle has been completed. This is also the source of the Bible way of reckoning days. For most of the Jews of Bible times, the new day does not begin at sunrise but at sundown, because that signals the end of the old day.

## B. Second Day of Creation (vv. 6, 8)

**6, 8. And God said, Let there be a firmament in the midst of the waters, and let it divide the waters from the waters. . . . And God called the firmament Heaven. And the evening and the morning were the second day.**

### VISUALS FOR THESE LESSONS

The visual pictured in each lesson (example: page 11) is a small reproduction of a large, full-color poster included in the *Adult Resources* packet for the Fall Quarter. The packet is available from your supplier. Order No. 192.

The word *firmament* is difficult for us to understand, because we don't use this term in daily conversation. What the text is describing, however, is easy to understand: it is the separation of "ground waters" (rivers, lakes, oceans) from "sky waters" (clouds). The term *Heaven* here probably does not refer to the dwelling place of God and His angels. Rather, it is the sky and atmosphere above the earth, the place where birds fly. This is an essential step in transforming the watery void (v. 2) into a place fit for human habitation.

### FURNISHING A NEW WORLD

America's space probes to Mars early in this century revealed a barren world. Mars had water on it sometime in the ancient past, although not as much as on the primeval Earth that Genesis describes. Nevertheless, a Florida company called 4Frontiers Corporation has announced plans to establish a high-tech human colony on Mars by the year 2025.

The company plans to begin by developing a replica of the proposed Mars settlement here on Earth and charging admission to tourists (see www.sliceofscifi.com and www.4frontiers.com). Backers say it is necessary to colonize Mars in case disease or a collision with an asteroid should wipe out the human race or if we happen to make Earth uninhabitable through war or pollution.

The 4Frontiers plan sounds only slightly like God's activity in preparing the Earth for human habitation. There are significant differences: God's presence was everywhere in His creation; He had a plan that could see beyond the next 20 years; and He had the power to make His plan work regardless of whatever technical difficulties there were to overcome.

It is good to remember that we humans are creatures, not the creator. In this light we should frame even our most grandiose plans with appropriate humility.
—C. R. B.

## C. Third Day of Creation (vv. 10, 12, 13)

**10. And God called the dry land Earth; and the gathering together of the waters called he Seas: and God saw that it was good.**

The organization of the earth continues. Now *the waters* are no longer allowed to dominate, but are confined to appropriate areas. This allows for *dry land,* a prerequisite for plant life. [See question #4, page 16.]

**12, 13. And the earth brought forth grass, and herb yielding seed after his kind, and the tree yielding fruit, whose seed was in itself, after his kind: and God saw that it was good. And the evening and the morning were the third day.**

Various kinds of plant life appear. This continues the preparation of the earth for human habitation, for now there is renewable sustenance for humankind and for the necessary animals.

The author notes a remarkable thing about the vegetation: it produces *seed* after its own *kind*. In other words, the seed from an apple produces apple trees, not watermelons. Modern science has explained the mechanics of this, but it was very mysterious to people in the ancient world. If we pause to consider the consistency of this pattern, it is still remarkable today. God makes plant life that is capable of reproduction, and therefore that plant life is not dependent upon His direct creative action for each succeeding generation.

## III. Creation, Days 4–6 (Genesis 1:14, 15, 19, 20, 22, 23, 25)

The author now moves on to describe the creation of the patterns of the earth in relation to other heavenly bodies.

### D. Fourth Day of Creation (vv. 14, 15, 19)

**14, 15, 19. And God said, Let there be lights in the firmament of the heaven to divide the day from the night; and let them be for signs, and for seasons, and for days, and years: and let them be for lights in the firmament of the heaven to give light upon the earth: and it was so. . . . And the evening and the morning were the fourth day.**

The author's interest is not in astrophysics or the possibility of space travel. Rather, he is explaining how *days* and *seasons* came into being, thus allowing for the growing cycles that result in crop production from the plant life (food) that came in day three. [See question #5, page 16.]

It is astounding for us to contemplate the perfection and intricacy of God's system! Consider that water can exist in its liquid form only within a very narrow temperature range, namely from 32 to 212 degrees Fahrenheit. This is a tiny slice of the range of temperatures found in our solar system, from the inferno of the sun (27 million degrees Fahrenheit at its core) to the temperature of absolute zero of the outer planets (approaching –459 degrees Fahrenheit).

Yet, because of the precise distance that the earth is positioned from the sun as well as various other factors, water is able to remain liquid over most of our planet. There could be no life as we know it without this precious liquid. Modern scientific knowledge does not negate the majesty of these verses, but only makes them more astounding.

---

### How to Say It

ABRAHAM. *Ay*-bruh-ham.
DEUTERONOMY. Due-ter-*ahn*-uh-me.
HEBREWS. *Hee*-brews.
JUDAH. *Joo*-duh.
LEVITICUS. Leh-*vit*-ih-kus.
OMNIPRESENCE. *ahm*-nih-*prez*-ence (strong accent on *prez*).
PENTATEUCH. *Pen*-ta-teuk.

---

### HEAVENLY BODIES

NASA's Deep Impact space probe of 2005 was made to collide intentionally with the comet Tempel 1. The mission's purpose was to create a cloud of comet debris that could be photographed and analyzed by the mother craft orbiting the comet. The debris cloud gave scientists clues about how the solar system was formed at the time of creation that Genesis tells us about.

However, Marina Bai, a Russian astrologer, brought a lawsuit for $300 million against NASA to compensate her for what she called her "moral sufferings." Bai claimed that the experiment deformed her horoscope and violated her life and spiritual values. Bai said that the comet was important to her life because her grandfather had wooed her grandmother by showing her the comet.

While the astrologer's claims can appropriately be ridiculed as silly, her belief in the power of heavenly bodies to control human destiny is a common one today. Even some Christians have an unwarranted, unholy respect for this pseudoscience. Genesis establishes that God put the heavenly bodies in their places as signs of His power, to give light to His creation, and to establish the seasons by which the earth brings forth our food. Other interpretations go beyond (or against) what Scripture teaches.                —C. R. B.

### E. Fifth Day of Creation (vv. 20, 22, 23)

**20. And God said, Let the waters bring forth abundantly the moving creature that hath life, and fowl that may fly above the earth in the open firmament of heaven.**

On the fifth day God begins to supply the earth with animal *life*. This day is devoted to "nonland" creatures: birds and aquatic life. Today, we have developed the capabilities to fly and to live underwater. But for most of history, neither of those was feasible. Thus the birds and aquatic life are creatures that ancient people understand to be fundamentally different from humans. To appreciate these marvels is to begin to understand the wonder of God's created world that permeates this beautiful Genesis account.

**22, 23. And God blessed them, saying, Be fruitful, and multiply, and fill the waters in the seas, and let fowl multiply in the earth. And the evening and the morning were the fifth day.**

At the time of the writing of Genesis, the total human population of the earth was a tiny fraction of what it is today. Even so, the rivers and oceans of Genesis are full of fish, and the skies are full of a marvelous variety of birds. The few urban varieties of birds that most people are familiar with today are but a small fraction of the avian creatures.

The Lewis and Clark expedition explored the Pacific Northwest of the U.S. some 200 years ago. On that expedition the explorers observed such a heavy migration of salmon that it seemed as if one could walk across the river on the backs of the fish! This abundance now has been reduced, but we can still appreciate God's original provision for *the earth*.

### F. Sixth Day of Creation (v. 25)

**25. And God made the beast of the earth after his kind, and cattle after their kind, and every thing that creepeth upon the earth after his kind: and God saw that it was good.**

God's last stage of preparation of the earth for the coming of humanity is to create land animals. The term *cattle* has the larger meaning of range animals that eat plant life. Later, the author differentiates between domesticated and wild animals of this class (Genesis 3:14).

The creeping animals are probably reptiles and small rodents. Such animals are later considered unclean and generally forbidden as a food source for the Israelites (see Acts 10:12-14, where Peter objects to eating "creeping things").

The stage is now fully set for the creation of men and women. This will be covered in next week's lesson.

## Conclusion

### A. "All Creation Waits"

Violin players are taught from the first day of lessons that their violins must be tuned every time they play. The longer the violinist waits to retune, the worse the instrument sounds. After Adam and Eve's disobedience, creation ended up being "out of tune" because of sin. The one who created our earth and its heavens intends to return and "retune" it according to His perfect will.

Paul teaches that all creation is anticipating the revelation of God's ultimate purpose (see Romans 8:19-23). Paul even speaks of creation groaning in pain as it waits for its creator (Romans 8:22). The one who created will re-create, and there will be "new heavens and a new earth, wherein dwelleth righteousness" (2 Peter 3:13). What a glorious day that will be! Then sin will be no more, and "he shall reign for ever and ever" (Revelation 11:15).

As wonderful as this promise is, however, we do not know when God's re-creation of the universe will be. It could be tomorrow. It could be 10,000 years from now. Until that day, this present universe is what we have. Although it is marred by human sin, it retains the pattern and intention of the master designer.

That fact should bring praise to our lips. When science discovers some new intricacy or complexity in nature, we should marvel. When we see the vivid colors of the sunrise on a stately peak, we should stop to ponder the artistry of the maker. When we are high in the mountains on a clear night and see the uncountable stars in all their majesty, we should stand in awe of their creator, for "the heavens declare the glory of God" (Psalm 19:1).

### B. Prayer

Mighty and loving creator, the all-wise and all-powerful God, may we stand in awe of Your master design and plan for the universe. May we live daily in appreciation of the marvels of Your creation, our world, which exists and is sustained through the word of Your power. In Jesus' name, amen.

### C. Thought to Remember

It was God who created.

## Home Daily Bible Readings

**Monday, Aug. 27**—God the Creator (Psalm 8)

**Tuesday, Aug. 28**—The First Day (Genesis 1:1-5)

**Wednesday, Aug. 29**—The Sky (Genesis 1:6-8)

**Thursday, Aug. 30**—The First Harvest (Genesis 1:9-13)

**Friday, Aug. 31**—The Sun and Moon (Genesis 1:14-19)

**Saturday, Sept. 1**—The Birds and Sea Creatures (Genesis 1:20-23)

**Sunday, Sept. 2**—The Animals (Genesis 1:24, 25)

# Learning by Doing

*This page contains an alternative lesson plan emphasizing learning activities.*
*Classes desiring such student involvement will find these suggestions helpful.*

## Into the Lesson

Put up a sign reading *Unintelligent Design* before class begins. As class begins ask, "What are examples of what has proven to be 'unintelligent design' in the modern world of products and businesses?"

Allow time for response. If the group needs examples, suggest such products as the Edsel, New Coke, and Betamax video. (Be prepared for the argument that the problem with some of these was marketing rather than product design.) Draw upon the lesson's introductory comments to make a transition to the study of the Word.

*Alternative:* Have one of your learners do a sentence diagram Genesis 1:1 on the board. This should come out as *subject:* God; *action:* created; *object:* the heavens and the earth; *qualifier:* in the beginning (adverbial prepositional phrase). Note both the simplicity of the expression and the profundity of the thought.

## Into the Word

Divide the class into six groups (or pairs). Give each a piece of poster board and a broad-point felt-tip marker for writing. One piece of poster board should be labeled "Day One," another "Day Two," etc. Ask each group first to identify what God created on the day listed on its poster board. When they finish, each group is to make a quick list of what needed to be in place for that created entity (or entities) to exist and sustain itself (or themselves). After a few minutes, collect the sheets and post them in numerical order for class viewing.

With a tone of mock arrogance, say, "I just don't think these look good in that order, so I'm going to rearrange them." Then switch two of the sheets and make an appropriate comment. For example, you can switch day two and day five, then ask, "Now, don't you think that will work better?" Wait for a learner to say something like, "Well, that won't work because the flying creatures of day five would have no home without the firmament and sky created on day two."

Make other impossible switches as time allows. Then comment, "The order of God's creation is second in importance only to the actual creative acts themselves. In the succession of days, we can see God making preparations for the creative work that follows." (You can also add, "And everything has to be in place and functioning in full unity before God can reach the peak of His work: the creation of humans. But that's next week's study.")

Next, give each learner a sheet of paper. Ask each to number his or her paper from 1 to 16 (or refer your learners to the student books, if you use that resource). Say, "I am going to read a number of truths affirmed in today's lesson text. For each truth, you are to identify a verse number that reveals it. Some truths may be in more than one verse." Then read the following:

1. Oceans are God's way of collecting water to allow dry land to appear. 2. The earth changed in form, at God's directive and control. 3. God announced that an element of His creation was good. 4. There was a beginning for all material elements. 5. Grasses, herbs, and trees were created with reproductive abilities. 6. Water covered the earth at its beginning. 7. When light appeared, darkness was no more. 8. Animals were God's last creation before humans. 9. Eternal God was present when time began. 10. Flying creatures were made on the fifth day. 11. Though God is light, the earth began in darkness. 12. The first things God named were *day* and *night*. 13. Sea creatures were God's first creation of life forms for the earth. 14. The heavens were created to contain some of earth's water. 15. Sun, moon, and stars were created to establish seasons and seasonal markers for the earth. 16. The Spirit of God sustained the earth and held it in place until all creation was complete.

After taking responses to all truths, allow time for follow-up comments. These comments may include objections to the manner in which some of the truths are worded.

## Into Life

Distribute the words of the hymn, "I Sing the Mighty Power of God," by Isaac Watts (easy to find in a hymnal or on the Internet). Suggest that class members use the stanzas for daily devotions in the week ahead. As they do, they can renew their commitments to being good stewards of God's creation. Reflecting on two lines of the hymn per day will offer real challenge and opportunity for praise and submission.

# Let's Talk It Over

*The questions on this page are designed to promote discussion of the lesson by the class and to encourage application of the lesson Scriptures. The answers provided are only discussion starters. Let your class talk it over from there.*

**1. What should our acceptance of the fact that God created the world mean in our lives on a day-to-day basis?**

Humans think of themselves as rulers and owners of the world. But the truth is that the world belongs to God. God provided the world to meet our needs, but also to demonstrate His glory. Therefore, it is our role to be caretakers of the earth, not abusers. Instead of treating the world as our disposable possession, we are to view it as something for which we are to be responsible stewards.

This realization affects our understanding of ecology and environment (although "environmental extremism" is to be avoided, as it tends to see the earth itself as something almost to be worshiped). How we care for the earth is an indicator of what we think of the things of God. As stewards of this world, we are to be faithful.

**2. How has your belief in God as creator helped you in the difficult times of life?**

At times, life just does not seem to make sense. Often it seems that life is void and without form, as at the beginning. It is in these tough times that we remember that the same God who created this world out of nothing is still with us today. He can take the lifeless lumps of clay of our lives and mold them into something special for Him.

The power that brought the world into being is the same power that can bring order out of the chaos of life. It is our responsibility to be moldable so that He can work His will in our lives.

**3. How can the ancient recurring phrase *And God said* speak to our lives today?**

In the first chapter of Genesis, the creative phrase *And God said* is used in verses 3, 6, 9, 14, 20, 24, and 26. There is power in the word of God. When God speaks, things happen. His word has the power to give life (see Ezekiel 37:4-10). His word is convicting (see Hebrews 4:12).

The word of God is also a source of hope (see Romans 15:4). The written Word of God gives us examples to follow (1 Corinthians 10:11) and to avoid (1 John 3:12). It gives us knowledge of eternal life (1 John 5:13). God's Word is a lamp for our feet and a light for our path (Psalm 119:105).

**4. When God looked at His creation, He said that it was good. How should that influence our attitude toward this world and toward our work?**

There seems to be a tendency to find fault and see deficiencies with everything. People are often dissatisfied with the things that they have. Thus many work seven days per week (when God himself only worked six) to improve their lot in life and "get more stuff."

Many people also have an attitude of perfectionism, always striving to make things just a little better. This makes for great material for the TV sit-coms, but in real life it ruins people. In the final analysis, we end up dwelling on all that was not accomplished or how we could have done something better.

Instead, it would be better for us to take a lesson from God: at the end of the day, look back and rejoice in what was accomplished and concentrate upon the good that the day held. Our work cannot be perfect, as God's is. But we can still rejoice in our service to Him.

**5. What significance does (or should) the fact that God divided night from day have on your life?**

The separation of day from night, seas from dry land, etc., introduces us to the idea of *boundaries*. Humans seem to have a knack for modifying or erasing boundaries that God has created. Think about New York City, for instance. For many decades, she has had the reputation of being "the city that never sleeps." The idea is that she is a city of perpetual illumination, a city that never grows dark (except during power outages, of course!).

What a dangerous concept! God created day (with its presence of bright light) to be separate from night (with its absence of bright light) for some very good reasons. Humans need a certain amount of sleep each night for optimum health and productivity; too much light works against this. This is not to suggest that we turn off all streetlights between the hours of 10:00 PM and 5:00 AM out of respect for God. Rather, the concern is we remember that God Almighty established various boundaries for good reasons.

# In the Image of God

DEVOTIONAL READING: Isaiah 40:25-31.

BACKGROUND SCRIPTURE: Genesis 1:26–2:3.

PRINTED TEXT: Genesis 1:26-31.

### Genesis 1:26-31

26 And God said, Let us make man in our image, after our likeness: and let them have dominion over the fish of the sea, and over the fowl of the air, and over the cattle, and over all the earth, and over every creeping thing that creepeth upon the earth.

27 So God created man in his own image, in the image of God created he him; male and female created he them.

28 And God blessed them, and God said unto them, Be fruitful, and multiply, and replenish the earth, and subdue it: and have dominion over the fish of the sea, and over the fowl of the air, and over every living thing that moveth upon the earth.

29 And God said, Behold, I have given you every herb bearing seed, which is upon the face of all the earth, and every tree, in the which is the fruit of a tree yielding seed; to you it shall be for meat.

30 And to every beast of the earth, and to every fowl of the air, and to every thing that creepeth upon the earth, wherein there is life, I have given every green herb for meat: and it was so.

31 God saw every thing that he had made, and, behold, it was very good. And the evening and the morning were the sixth day.

GOLDEN TEXT: God said, Let us make man in our image, after our likeness: and let them have dominion over . . . all the earth.—Genesis 1:26.

## God Creates
### Unit 1: God Creates a People
### (Lessons 1-5)

## Lesson Aims

After participating in this lesson, each student will be able to:

1. Recite Genesis 1:27 from memory.

2. Explain the significance the "image of God" has in terms of his or her relationship to other created things and to other people.

3. Suggest one way for his or her church to treat those of other races with the respect due them as beings created in the image of God.

## Lesson Outline

INTRODUCTION
    A. Family Resemblance?
    B. Lesson Background
 I. GOD CREATES (Genesis 1:26, 27)
    A. Image, Part 1 (v. 26a)
    B. Dominion (v. 26b)
      *The Two Sides of Dominion*
    C. Image, Part 2 (v. 27)
 II. GOD BLESSES (Genesis 1:28)
    A. Family (v. 28a)
    B. Dominion (v. 28b)
III. GOD PROVIDES (Genesis 1:29, 30)
    A. Humanity (v. 29)
    B. Land Animals (v. 30)
IV. GOD APPRAISES (Genesis 1:31)
    A. Great Creation! (v. 31a)
      *Part of What Makes Us "Very Good"*
    B. Great Day! (v. 31b)
CONCLUSION
    A. A Final Thought
    B. Prayer
    C. Thought to Remember

## Introduction

### A. Family Resemblance?

Many people seem to be enthralled with detecting "resemblances." They look at a baby's picture and can't help exclaiming, "He has his father's eyes" or "She has her mother's nose." Some people are able to hire themselves out as celebrity look-alikes for parties. Late-night comedians occasionally even amuse their audiences with pictures of people who look like their dogs!

We may have two eyes, two ears, one nose, etc. as dogs do, but that and any other kind of resemblance between them and us is ultimately superficial. The being we most closely resemble is God. We are created in His image. Parts of the Bible can be thought of as a kind of mirror in this regard. When we look into its pages, we can see descriptions of God—His love, His holiness, etc. As we see those descriptions, we realize that they should be reflected in our own character as well (example: 1 Peter 1:15, 16).

We hasten to add that there are many ways that God is not like us. He is all-knowing and all-powerful, but we are not. His divine nature is not ours. He is ever the creator while we are ever the creature.

Attempts to "be as gods" in these ways is Satanic (Genesis 3:5). Yet through Christ we put off the old man of sin and "put on the new man, which after God is created in righteousness and true holiness" (Ephesians 4:22-24). That is where the ideal family resemblance lies! When that renewal in Christ happens, the image of God from Genesis 1:27 shines brightly in our lives.

### B. Lesson Background

God formed light on the first day of creation. God then waited until the fourth day to fill the cosmos with sources of that light. On the second day of creation, God formed the sky and established terrestrial waters. God waited until the fifth day to fill that sky with birds and those waters with living creatures. On the third day of creation, God formed the dry land. He waited until the sixth day to fill that land with animals and people.

In six creative days, then, God formed and filled this world to be the theater of His glory. Psalmist and prophet alike proclaim that God's glory is revealed and praised from the east to the west (Psalms 50:1; 113:2, 3; Isaiah 45:6; 59:19; Malachi 1:11). If everything that is exists by the command of God, then the whole creation must give glory to God.

Taking center stage in this theater is humanity, the pinnacle of God's creative activity. The verb *created* occurs three times in Genesis 1:27. This makes clear that here the goal has been reached toward which all of God's creativity from verse 1 onward was directed. Only after the creation of mankind does God judge His work to be "very good" (1:31). Up to that point, He had found all that He had made merely "good" (1:4, 10, 12, 18, 21, 25). The most striking feature of the creation of mankind is that both male and female are created "in the image of God" (Genesis 1:26, 27).

# I. God Creates
# (Genesis 1:26, 27)

## A. Image, Part 1 (v. 26a)

**26a. And God said, Let us make man in our image, after our likeness.**

Genesis 1:26 is the initial verse in the narration of humanity's creation. The shift from *Let there be* to *Let us make* is clue enough that something momentous is being narrated.

But what does God really mean when He says *Let us make man in our image, after our likeness*? Our lesson introduction notes that we "resemble" God in certain ways. Yet we are also very different from Him. We have physical bodies and are subject to death; God, on the other hand, is Spirit (John 4:24; 1 Timothy 1:17; 6:16). Furthermore, He does not originate or decay in time (Psalms 90:2, 4; 102:24-28; Isaiah 44:6; 48:12).

Over the centuries, theologians have explored our "resemblance" to God in terms of a group of spiritual qualities. Note how human behavior is based on (or should be based on) the following divine characteristics: *compassion* (2 Corinthians 1:3, 4), *forgiveness* (Colossians 3:13), *holiness* (Leviticus 19:2; 1 Peter 1:14-16; 1 John 3:3), *humility* (Philippians 2:3-11), *kindness* (2 Samuel 9:3), *love* (Ephesians 5:2; 1 John 4:7-21), *mercy* (Luke 6:36), *peacemaking* (Matthew 5:9), and *righteousness* (Ephesians 4:24).

These passages strongly suggest that we resemble (or should resemble) our creator in some vital ways. Let us not forget that as His image-bearers, we represent Him. In the ancient world images of "gods" or kings were viewed as representatives of deity or royalty. Mankind, created in the image of God, is the representative or viceroy of God. We are not God, but other people should be able to see Christ in us. Our holy living should reflect God's majesty.

At this point, we should pause to consider how sin has affected the image of God in us. Has humanity's decision to sin defaced God's image in us or caused the loss of that image altogether? The answer to this question is supplied by three biblical references: Genesis 9:6; 1 Corinthians 11:7; and James 3:9. All three speak of humanity after the fall into sin in terms of humanity before that fall. This suggests that the image of God in us is not lost through sin.

A claim that fallen humanity no longer bears the image of God would compromise our uniqueness. On this view, sinful humans would no longer have unique moral, rational, or religious capacities. Our Bible and our experiences tell us otherwise!

Sin clearly does, however, hinder our relationship with God. Sin hinders God's desire that we represent His interests. Accordingly, the New Testament points us to one who can restore our relationship to God. As the sinner turns to God through faith in Jesus Christ, he or she begins to live for the glory of God, not for self and sin. Upon following the biblical plan of salvation, he or she becomes a member of a different kingdom—the kingdom of God. As such, this person begins to represent the concerns of his or her new king. What a privilege!

## B. Dominion (v. 26b)

**26b. And let them have dominion over the fish of the sea, and over the fowl of the air, and over the cattle, and over all the earth, and over every creeping thing that creepeth upon the earth.**

This half-verse reflects the priorities of creation. It shows the hierarchy of God's attention and intention. God gives us *dominion* over the earth, and we exercise that dominion (both wisely and not so wisely) every day. That is not to say that we rule over every aspect of existence on earth. No one can predict the exact course of a hurricane or the time of the next earthquake, let alone control them. Being the dominant species on earth has not resulted in the defeat of AIDS or even the common cold. Dominion has limitations.

Having dominion also has implications for ecology. Although the environmental movement often errs on the side of fanaticism, we still have a responsibility for stewardship of the earth's resources. That responsibility is a clear reflection of our mandate to have dominion *over all the earth*. Rulers bear responsibility in the eyes of God for that over which they rule. As we rule the earth, we will answer to God for our deeds (or lack of deeds) in that role.

Being created in God's image is God's acknowledgment that He puts more value on humans than on other elements of creation. Yet this fact does not negate the value of the rest of creation. Our concern for the creation is driven by our love

***

## How to Say It

COLOSSIANS. Kuh-*losh*-unz.
EPHESIANS. Ee-*fee*-zhunz.
EZEKIEL. Ee-*zeek*-ee-ul or Ee-*zeek*-yul.
ISAIAH. Eye-*zay*-uh.
PATRIARCHS. *pay*-tree-arks.
PHILIPPIANS. Fih-*lip*-ee-unz.
TAURINE. *to*-reen.

for the creator. We look forward to the day when the ideal of Psalm 8 and Genesis 1:26 will be realized fully (compare Revelation 21:4, 5).

The text before us describes the extent of human dominion. Obviously, domesticated animals such as *cattle* are ruled by people. There is no question about that. But what about the other creatures listed?

Birds and *fish* in ancient times are not particularly subject to humans in any practical sense. Apart from limited hunting and fishing techniques, ancient people had little impact upon such creatures. Perhaps the confidence expressed in this verse is a kind of prophetic hint—a God-given awareness that humanity's future reach will extend to the depths of the oceans and beyond the heights of the atmosphere.

King David was one who was well acquainted with the idea of human dominion, particularly in light of what he wrote in Psalm 8:6-8: "Thou madest [humanity] to have dominion over the works of thy hands; thou hast put all things under his feet: all sheep and oxen, yea, and the beasts of the field; the fowl of the air, and the fish of the sea, and whatsoever passeth through the paths of the seas."

Years before he became king himself, David was a regular in King Saul's presence. David knew that kings may rule countries, but their personal impact on the day-to-day lives of their subjects was often quite limited. Many of a king's subjects lived their lives without ever seeing the king. Yet a king's influence can be felt profoundly through taxation, conscription into military service, etc. A king's dominion is extensive, but it also has limits.

We may draw a similar parallel concerning our dominion over the earth and her creatures. We do not influence directly the daily lives of every bottle-nosed porpoise, sparrow hawk, or giant anteater. Yet human ability that is exercised improperly can result in eventual extinction of various species. As those with dominion over creation, we need to use care.

### THE TWO SIDES OF DOMINION

The human race has condemned itself for despoiling nature, allegedly causing global warming, and abuse of our planet's resources. Some of the accusations are valid. For example, widespread use of DDT and other pesticides almost brought the noble bald eagle and other avian species to extinction. Strip mining once left vast tracts of land as wastelands upon which nothing could grow. Chemical spills poisoned the ground, and oil spills polluted the oceans.

But there is also good news: DDT was outlawed and the bald eagle has made a spectacular comeback. Reforestation, restoration of landforms, and pollution controls on automobiles and industry are all part of a concerted effort to undo the damage done in an earlier, less informed era. A specific example of this turnaround is the whooping crane. Only about 20 were left in 1941; now there are about 475.

There are indeed two sides to our dominion over creation: to be responsible and to be irresponsible. The Bible calls on us to be stewards who use the earth's resources properly, resisting the temptation either to abuse the creation or to worship it. We glorify God when we are good stewards.
                                                    —C. R. B.

### C. Image, Part 2 (v. 27)

**27. So God created man in his own image, in the image of God created he him; male and female created he them.**

All humans are stamped with God's *image*. *Male and female*, old and young, rich and poor—it doesn't matter. Possessing this image means that God expects us to treat each other with the respect and dignity that that image calls for. Yet so often respect is not what we see. The problem is sin.

The New Testament teaches us how sin must be handled: God's image in us must be transformed into conformity with the God-Man, Jesus Christ. The challenge is "to be conformed to the image of his Son, that he might be the firstborn among many brethren" (Romans 8:29).

Our conformity to Christ should grow day by day. Full and final conformity to Christ comes

Visual for
Lesson 2

God said, "Let us make man in our image."

*Point to this visual as you ask, "How do we get into trouble when we forget this truth?"*

at our own death and resurrection. Paul writes, "That I may know him, and the power of his resurrection, and the fellowship of his sufferings, being made conformable unto his death; if by any means I might attain unto the resurrection of the dead" (Philippians 3:10, 11).

Paul also tells us that, "Ye have put off the old man with his deeds; and have put on the new man, which is renewed in knowledge after the image of him that created him" (Colossians 3:9, 10; compare Ephesians 4:22-24). Could there be any greater privilege than this? [See question #1, page 24.]

## II. God Blesses
## (Genesis 1:28)
### A. Family (v. 28a)

**28a. And God blessed them, and God said unto them, Be fruitful, and multiply, and replenish the earth.**

God gives people the power to reproduce themselves. This mandate should also be seen as a blessing and gift from God. The mandate carries an unspoken promise that God will enable us to fulfill it.

This mandate is repeated to Noah (Genesis 9:1). The patriarchs are reminded of God's part in this divine promise (Genesis 17:2, 20; 28:3; 35:11). The book of Genesis rejoices in the fruitfulness of the human race. [See question #2, page 24.]

### B. Dominion (v. 28b)

**28b. And subdue it: and have dominion over the fish of the sea, and over the fowl of the air, and over every living thing that moveth upon the earth.**

We discussed the meaning of *dominion* earlier. [See question #3, page 24.] Here we may add that the Hebrew root behind the verb *have dominion* is elsewhere in the Old Testament applied to a king's rule (Isaiah 14:6), to Messiah's rule (Numbers 24:19; Psalms 72:8; 110:2), and to God's rule (Isaiah 41:2). In Genesis 1 the dignity of royal rule is granted to the multitude of humanity. Ezekiel 34:4 implies that proper rule includes strengthening the weak, healing the sick, binding up the injured, and searching for the lost.

The Hebrew verbal root behind the word *subdue* occurs 15 times in the Old Testament. This verb carries the idea of some sort of coercion— for example, the subjection of a country through war (Numbers 32:22, 29). It follows, then, that creation will not easily oblige humanity's domin-

ion, especially after sin enters the picture. Humans will have to bring creation into submission through strength or force.

## III. God Provides
## (Genesis 1:29, 30)
### A. Humanity (v. 29)

**29. And God said, Behold, I have given you every herb bearing seed, which is upon the face of all the earth, and every tree, in the which is the fruit of a tree yielding seed; to you it shall be for meat.**

Here we see how God made provision for humanity. People are to have as food the *seed* and *fruit* of plants. God's original intent is for humans to exist on a vegetarian diet. In Genesis 9:3, after the fall and the flood, people will be given permission to eat literal *meat:* "Every moving thing that liveth shall be meat for you; even as the green herb have I given you all things."

Much later, the prophet Isaiah's expectation will be that one day "the lion shall eat straw like the ox" (Isaiah 11:7; compare Isaiah 65:25). This prophecy suggests that a return to the paradise that originally existed in the Garden of Eden is to come. [See question #4, page 24.]

### B. Land Animals (v. 30)

**30. And to every beast of the earth, and to every fowl of the air, and to every thing that creepeth upon the earth, wherein there is life, I have given every green herb for meat: and it was so.**

God also provides for the animals and birds in the form of *every green herb*. This can imply that there is not yet a predator-prey relationship among the animals at this point in the biblical narrative.

Some students of the Bible propose, however, that to give the animals *every green herb* to eat doesn't necessarily exclude the possibility that the animals also ate each other. If they did, then Adam and Eve certainly would have known what the phrase, "thou shalt surely die," meant because they actually would have seen death among the animals (Genesis 2:17).

Today, we know that felines (cats) need a substance called *taurine* to survive. This is an amino acid that is found in animal tissue. (You can see taurine listed as an ingredient on a can of cat food.) Did the felines that were created before humans need taurine? If so, did they get it by eating other animals before humans chose to sin and thus bring about their own deaths? No one knows—the Bible doesn't say.

## IV. God Appraises
## (Genesis 1:31)

### A. Great Creation! (v. 31a)

**31a. And God saw every thing that he had made, and, behold, it was very good.**

We discussed in the Lesson Background what it means for God to appraise His creation as *very good*. The strong implication is that the creation of mankind is indeed the ultimate purpose of God's creative week. Humanity is not an afterthought in the creation, but is the result of God's intention and good pleasure. [See question #5, page 24.]

#### PART OF WHAT MAKES US "VERY GOOD"

When God had finished His creative work, capped by creation of man and woman, he pronounced it "very good." Part of what made it "very good" was the character of life itself that enables us to overcome adversity and see beyond ourselves. We can excel at this trait at times.

An example is Jessica Esquivel. In 1990 she contracted chickenpox when she was six years old. She became gravely ill, with streptococcus bacteria shutting down her organs and cutting off the flow of blood to her extremities. Surgeons eventually had to amputate her legs and arms below the knees and elbows (www.chsd.org).

Twelve years later, her indomitable spirit demonstrated itself as she prepared for her high school prom. Jessica showed off her new "high-heeled feet" that allowed her to wear dressy shoes that evening. Now, as an adult, she works in a hotel chain and aspires to write profiles of people like herself to encourage others to accept the challenge of overcoming life's adversities.

### Home Daily Bible Readings

**Monday, Sept. 3**—The Creator of All (Isaiah 40:25-31)

**Tuesday, Sept. 4**—Created in God's Image (Genesis 1:26, 27)

**Wednesday, Sept. 5**—God Provides (Genesis 1:28-31)

**Thursday, Sept. 6**—A Hallowed Day (Genesis 2:1-3)

**Friday, Sept. 7**—God's Glory in Creation (Psalm 19:1-6)

**Saturday, Sept. 8**—Thanksgiving for God's Greatness (Psalm 103:1-14)

**Sunday, Sept. 9**—Remember God's Commandments (Psalm 103:15-22)

It is this character trait of "getting outside one's self" that reflects God's self-sacrificing nature. It is part of what makes the human spirit "very good." We are indeed "fearfully and wonderfully made" (Psalm 139:14).          —C. R. B.

### B. Great Day! (v. 31b)

**31b. And the evening and the morning were the sixth day.**

The expression *the sixth day* is also fascinating. The previous five days of creation were all referred to indefinitely; translated literally from the Hebrew, they would come out as "day, first," "day, second," etc. However, *the sixth day* in Hebrew is definite—it is "day, the sixth" (as is also the seventh day). Our English translations add the definite article *the* to all the days, but in the Hebrew the definite article is attached only to days six and seven. Days six and seven are thus intended to stand apart from the other five. Day six is the day on which God created us!

## Conclusion

### A. A Final Thought

There is no idea more sinister than philosophical naturalism. Its explanation of human origins devalues us, it leaves us without meaning, it results in despair and misery. Parents, teachers, and preachers should take every opportunity to teach that human value, dignity, purpose, and hope are based first of all in the biblical teaching of creation.

To connect the "created . . . created . . . created" of Genesis 1:27 with the "Holy, holy, holy" of Isaiah 6:3 is tempting! The uniqueness of the latter suggests significance in the former. As the Lord is the super-superlatively holy one, so the human is the super-superlative creature. We stand in a unique relationship with the holy one, who is in our midst!

### B. Prayer

Loving Father, we praise You that we are fearfully and wonderfully made. We thank You for the right to represent You and Your kingdom. We ask that the Holy Spirit will empower us to reflect You before a watching world.

We thank You for the relationship we have with You through Jesus Christ our Lord. May we be true sons and daughters of You, the creator. In the name of Jesus, the one into whose image we are being transformed, we pray, amen.

### C. Thought to Remember

Live up to God's image in you.

# Learning by Doing

*This page contains an alternative lesson plan emphasizing learning activities.*
*Classes desiring such student involvement will find these suggestions helpful.*

## Into the Lesson

Write the following six phrases/clauses on separate slips of paper: "So God created man," "in his own image," "in the image of God," "created he him," "male and female," "created he them." Repeat each as necessary for every learner to have one slip. Hand the slips out randomly as learners arrive.

As class begins, say, "I want you to circulate until you find other class members who have phrases and clauses that form Genesis 1:27—the key verse of today's study. The verse has been divided into six sections." (If the multiples do not work for the number of students typically in attendance, combine some of the segments of Genesis 1:27 to make fewer slips.) Say, "When you have the verse complete, sit together as a group."

## Into the Word

Once the groups for the previous activity have formed, give each group a sheet with the following questions. Direct them to read and consider today's text before they answer.

1. In what sense are we made in God's image and likeness?

2. In what sense do we have dominion over sea creatures, birds, and land animals?

3. What is the significance of the phrase, "male and female," in its emphatic placement in verse 27?

4. Why would the command to be fruitful and multiply be essential to fulfilling the second part of verse 28?

5. A vegetarian diet for us is the plan of God in verse 29. Why do you think that there is no indication at first for what will later be permitted: people could be meat eaters? (See Genesis 9:3.)

6. Why does God conclude His evaluation of His creation with "very good" rather than the simpler "good" that He had earlier stated?

Your groups will need a significant amount of time to respond; be sure to allow enough time for each group to report its answers. There may be some significantly different conclusions, but a discussion of those differences will be an important part of the study.

Next, say, "Unbiblical views of the nature of humanity are taught both inside and outside the church. Let's see if we can think of four diverse views of people as represented by various worldviews." Give each learner a piece of white paper folded into four equal segments. Provide instructions and scissors for cutting this folded sheet into four connected figures of people; have them do so.

Next, direct your learners (who may be in groups or working individually) to write into the four figures the four diverse views. If they need a start, suggest the view that humans have evolved from apes or a view such as Nazism, which saw one group of humans superior to another.

When students have had time to write down some ideas, ask for the ways in which the views identified contradict the concept of humans being created in the image and likeness of God. For example, the evolutionary view sees no distinction "in kind" between people and the animals that God created for our benefit.

After this activity, suggest that your students carry their cutouts with them for the week ahead. As they do, they can listen and look for inadequate, irresponsible, and unbiblical views of human nature. Tell your learners that the simple cutouts are as inadequate a representation of people as are the views noted on them.

## Into Life

Make a transition by saying, "Churches sometimes seem to ignore certain segments of the population in their surrounding community. We almost act as if some individuals and groups are not made in the image of God. Are there groups or types of individuals in our community that our congregation seems to be ignoring? What strategy will help our congregation see that these folks are made in God's image and are worthy of His love?" Allow time for response.

Next, give the following assignment: "As you cross paths with people this week—from family members to people on the street—quickly think this thought: 'You are made in the image of God, in His likeness!' Then consider how any interaction with someone should be tempered by that truth." Then say, "Possibly some of you will have some interesting reflections next Sunday on the impact of that thought on your interpersonal relations. Be prepared to share!" Next Sunday, remember to ask for volunteers to report on how your challenge turned out.

# Let's Talk It Over

*The questions on this page are designed to promote discussion of the lesson by the class and to encourage application of the lesson Scriptures. The answers provided are only discussion starters. Let your class talk it over from there.*

**1. In what ways does being created in the image of God affect your daily living? In what area are you best in this regard? In what area do you need the most improvement?**

The lesson writer mentions various ideas of what being created in the image and likeness of God means. Since we are created in the image of God, Christians are to reflect His image and His nature in the world. This includes forgiveness of others, since God has forgiven us.

When we look to the world, we should see the world as God sees it: a place in need of redemption. A day for judgment is coming. As we live, we can view each day as the day of salvation for someone! That motivates us to share the message of forgiveness and hope to the world. Being in the image of God encourages us to live lives of holiness (see 1 Peter 1:15, 16). Use the lists in Galatians 5:19-26 to enhance your discussion in this regard.

**2. God could have filled the earth with people all by His own direct, creative power. So why do you think God chose instead to create just two people and tell them to be fruitful and multiply?**

When God chose procreation to be the means of multiplying people on earth, He allowed us, in a sense, to take part in the creation of new life. People also get just a glimpse of what it means for God to be *Father* as they learn parenting roles. Those who are parents learn what it means for God to be patient with them as they patiently deal with stubborn and rebellious children. By trusting us with children, God also demonstrates His confidence in us.

**3. What does it mean to you personally to have dominion over God's creation? What cautions do you (or should you) take in this role?**

Humans sometimes have been known to take the idea of dominion to an extreme. When that happens, the result is *domination* rather than *dominion.* The former demonstrates itself in an abuse of what we have. Sometimes this takes the form of a reckless disregard of ecology. Polluting the environment and justifying it by saying we have control over these things is not what God meant for us to do when He gave us dominion.

By extension, *domination* may be seen in the verbal or physical abuse of family members. We should be careful not to abuse those things or people God has placed in our care!

**4. How has God been the provider for your life and your church?**

God has the wisdom and power to provide what is needed in just the right way at just the right time. He did this for Abraham in Genesis 22. Abraham had been told to sacrifice his son Isaac, but at just the right time God stopped Abraham and provided a ram instead. Abraham named that place (translated) "God provides."

Christians often face financial crises, health issues, family or work problems, etc. But at just the right time God provides what is needed. At a time when He didn't *seem* to provide, it may be because a longer-term part of His plan was at work.

The nature of God's bounty applies also to the situations of churches. Many churches have been embroiled in bitter controversies and debates. But at just the right time God provided the answers and peace that were so greatly needed! In some situations where peace wasn't forthcoming, the longer-term result may have been a multiplication of God's work, as in Acts 15:36-41.

**5. Why do you think God created us last?**

We often speak of "saving the best for last." Although everything that God made was *good,* the addition of man and woman was *very good.* The other parts of creation needed to be in place first to form a suitable habitat for us, the pinnacle of God's creation.

God has a special place in His heart for that which is in His image: us. In views that reject creation by God, people are often seen as just another part of the evolutionary process. Under that idea, we really have no place of distinction from the rest of creation other than being the top monkey.

The sanctity of human life is diminished in this attempt to place all of creation on the same plane. When we recognize the special place of humanity in God's plan of creation, we will then respect human life and battle against things such as abortion and euthanasia (mercy killing).

# Abraham, Sarah, and Isaac

**DEVOTIONAL READING: Isaiah 51:1-5.**

**BACKGROUND SCRIPTURE: Genesis 15:1-6; 18:1-15; 21:1-8.**

**PRINTED TEXT: Genesis 15:5, 6; 18:11-14a; 21:1-8.**

### Genesis 15:5, 6

5 And he brought him forth abroad, and said, Look now toward heaven, and tell the stars, if thou be able to number them: and he said unto him, So shall thy seed be.

6 And he believed in the LORD; and he counted it to him for righteousness.

### Genesis 18:11-14a

11 Now Abraham and Sarah were old and well stricken in age; and it ceased to be with Sarah after the manner of women.

12 Therefore Sarah laughed within herself, saying, After I am waxed old shall I have pleasure, my lord being old also?

13 And the LORD said unto Abraham, Wherefore did Sarah laugh, saying, Shall I of a surety bear a child, which am old?

14 Is any thing too hard for the LORD?

### Genesis 21:1-8

1 And the LORD visited Sarah as he had said, and the LORD did unto Sarah as he had spoken.

2 For Sarah conceived, and bare Abraham a son in his old age, at the set time of which God had spoken to him.

3 And Abraham called the name of his son that was born unto him, whom Sarah bare to him, Isaac.

4 And Abraham circumcised his son Isaac being eight days old, as God had commanded him.

5 And Abraham was a hundred years old, when his son Isaac was born unto him.

6 And Sarah said, God hath made me to laugh, so that all that hear will laugh with me.

7 And she said, Who would have said unto Abraham, that Sarah should have given children suck? for I have born him a son in his old age.

8 And the child grew, and was weaned: and Abraham made a great feast the same day that Isaac was weaned.

GOLDEN TEXT: Is any thing too hard for the LORD?—Genesis 18:14a.

## God Creates
### Unit 1: God Creates a People
### (Lessons 1-5)

## Lesson Aims

After participating in this lesson, each student will be able to:

1. Retell the facts of God's promise to Abraham for offspring.

2. Explain the significance of the miraculous conception of Isaac.

3. Identify one area in his or her life to trust in God's care more fully.

## Lesson Outline

INTRODUCTION
  A. Genealogy
  B. Lesson Background
  I. COUNTING STARS (Genesis 15:5, 6)
  A. Unfathomable Heavens (v. 5)
  B. Faithful Abraham (v. 6)
    *Amazing Statistics*
 II. COUNTING YEARS (Genesis 18:11-14a)
  A. Abraham and Sarah Limited (vv. 11, 12)
  B. The Lord Not Limited (vv. 13, 14a)
III. COUNTING BLESSINGS (Genesis 21:1-8)
  A. Promised Son Is Born (vv. 1, 2)
  B. Promised Son Is Named (vv. 3-5)
  C. Promised Son Brings Joy (vv. 6-8)
    *Laughing for Joy*
CONCLUSION
  A. The Importance of Abraham
  B. Abraham and You
  C. Prayer
  D. Thought to Remember

## Introduction

### A. Genealogy

Genealogical research attracts much attention these days. Many people yearn to know more about their ancestors and thus their origins. Countries such as the U.S. and Canada are heavily populated by people whose ancestors immigrated. Such folk may try to reconstruct lost information about their family trees from the country of their ancestors' origin.

The quest to regain a connection with the past often yields fascinating stories and details. The resources now available on the Internet have allowed people to do armchair research without visiting courthouses to look at records or tramping through cemeteries to squint at gravestones.

Genealogy is an important subject in the Bible because God's promises often extend over many generations. This week's lesson studies a genealogy that almost ended before it really began.

### B. Lesson Background

Perhaps the most important ancestor in human history other than Adam is Abraham. Jewish people trace their ancestry back to him through his son Isaac. Many Arabic people see Abraham as their father through his son Ishmael (next week's lesson). While the combined numbers of the Jewish and Arabic people are impressive, Paul taught that Abraham is the father of all Christian believers (Romans 4:16). The book of Genesis tells the story of how God chose Abraham and his wife Sarah to be the ancestor couple for His covenant people.

It is difficult to date the time of Abraham exactly, and even more difficult to understand what society was like in his time. We describe these times as the period of the patriarchs. Abraham was the father/leader of an extended family and household that included several hundred people. They tended large flocks of animals for their livelihood. This forced them to be seminomadic, as they periodically had to move operations to new grazing areas. The Bible tells us that Abraham lived 175 years—an unusually long life by today's expectations (Genesis 25:7). One educated guess is that he lived 2167–1992 BC.

Abraham first appears in Genesis as *Abram*, the son of Terah (Genesis 11:31). They were citizens of Ur, a large, sophisticated city in Mesopotamia. Terah, Abram, and their families left that life to travel westward to Canaan. Terah died in Haran, about halfway to the final destination (Genesis 11:32).

At that time, the Lord called Abram to continue the trek to Canaan, giving him a list of promises and blessings. Two of the most important were (1) that Abram would be the father of "a great nation" and (2) that through him would "all families of the earth be blessed" (Genesis 12:2, 3). This was the beginning of what we call *the Abrahamic covenant*.

The key to God's covenant with Abraham was his descendants: those who would prepare the way for God's chosen Messiah, Jesus. Yet Genesis records that Abraham and Sarah were not blessed with a child for many, many years. How this major problem was overcome is the marvelous story of this week's lesson.

## I. Counting Stars
## (Genesis 15:5, 6)

Genesis records six occasions during which God appeared to Abraham in order to make or reinforce covenantal promises. These are Genesis 12:1-3, 7; 13:14-18; 15:4, 5, 13-18; 17:1-8; 18; and 22:1-18. Genesis 15, which records the third of the six occasions, begins with God's appearance to Abraham in a vision. Abraham is reminded that the Lord is his "shield" and "exceeding great reward" (Genesis 15:1).

Abraham is troubled by this because he is childless and part of God's promise to him involve a large number of descendants. He sees no alternative but to leave his considerable wealth to his chief employee, Eliezer of Damascus (see Genesis 15:2, 3). Yet he quickly learns that this is not God's plan.

### A. Unfathomable Heavens (v. 5)

**5a. And he brought him forth abroad, and said, Look now toward heaven, and tell the stars, if thou be able to number them.**

Abraham does not have a telescope. Even so, about 5,000 *stars* are visible to the naked eye. But just try counting them as you look at the night sky! It is almost impossible since it's hard to remember which ones you've already counted and which ones you haven't as you *number them* off.

Modern technology doesn't seem to make the job much easier. Some researchers estimate that our galaxy, the Milky Way, has 400 billion stars. One educated guess is that the total number of stars in the universe is something like the numeral 1 followed by 22 zeros.

These numbers boggle the mind, and the estimates are just that—estimates. We would not be able to count accurately the stars on a very clear night by hand and naked eye, and scientists come up with estimates that are rounded off in the billions. They cannot count the stars either. (That 400 billion estimate of the number of stars in the Milky Way used to be 200 billion!)

The bottom line is that the number of stars is uncountable. It is a figure known only by the creator of the stars.

**5b. And he said unto him, So shall thy seed be.**

The *seed* of Abraham is his descendants. This is not just his own, immediate offspring, but is the many generations that will proceed from them. All of these are considered as Abraham's seed. Abraham undoubtedly considers this to be a great gift. God promises a marvelously open-ended blessing to his chosen vessel, Abraham.

### B. Faithful Abraham (v. 6)

**6. And he believed in the LORD; and he counted it to him for righteousness.**

Abraham's earlier attitude could be expressed as, "Don't tell me about thousands of descendants; just show me one!" He undoubtedly has difficulty imagining a large progeny when he does not have even a single child. Yet when God illustrates His promise by means of uncountable stars, Abraham no longer questions. He believes. He trusts that God will keep His promise.

This is a simple act of faith, but it has enormous consequences. Because of his faith, God considers Abraham to be a righteous man. This is the first clear statement in the Bible of the principle of justification by faith. Abraham does not earn God's favor by his deeds. To the contrary, he is given the status of a righteous person by his faith.

As we will see, this is the faith coming from (and resulting in) an obedient heart. Abraham is willing to trust God and follow His directions. The affirmation of this verse is so important that it is repeated in Romans 4:3, 9, 22; Galatians 3:6; and James 2:23.

### How to Say It

ABRAHAM. *Ay*-bruh-ham.
ABRAM. *Ay*-brum.
DAMASCUS. Duh-*mass*-kus.
ELIEZER. El-ih-*ee*-zer.
HARAN. *Hair*-un.
ISAAC. *Eye*-zuk.
ISHMAEL. *Ish*-may-el.
MESOPOTAMIA. *Mes*-uh-puh-*tay*-me-uh (strong accent on *tay*).
PATRIARCHS. *pay*-tree-arks.
TERAH. *Tair*-uh.
UR. Er.

### AMAZING STATISTICS

If you're a baseball fan, you may know the name of Fernando Tatis, but few others do. In the history of Major League Baseball, only 12 players have hit two "grand slam" (bases loaded) home runs in a single game, and Tatis is one of them. But Tatis stands alone in the record books as the only player to hit two grand slams *in the same inning*!

It happened in the third inning of a game played on April 23, 1999. The first three batters got on base, and Tatis came to the plate and hit a home run. Later, two batters walked and another got on base on an error, loading the bases. After

Mark McGwire flied out with the bases loaded, Tatis came to bat and hit his second grand slam of the inning, gaining for himself a unique place in the record book. This obviously was not a good day for the opposing pitcher!

Abraham's place in the record book of history is also unique. He stands alone as the common (or claimed) spiritual ancestor of billions. Abraham casts his shadow across 4,000 years of history. Ballplayers sometimes say, "You gotta believe!" That, in essence, was the secret of Abraham's greatness: "He believed in the Lord; and [the Lord] counted it to him for righteousness." It is still as true now as it was 4,000 years ago: without faith, we cannot please God.　　　—C. R. B.

## II. Counting Years
## (Genesis 18:11-14a)

We noted earlier that the Lord appears to Abraham six times in Genesis. The setting now before us is the fifth of those six. Abraham's heart of obedient faith is now to be put to the test. God does not make Abraham's son appear out of thin air. The appearance of a son will involve both Abraham and his wife, Sarah.

### A. Abraham and Sarah Limited (vv. 11, 12)

**11. Now Abraham and Sarah were old and well stricken in age; and it ceased to be with Sarah after the manner of women.**

At this time *Abraham* is about 100 years *old,* and Sarah is 90 (see Genesis 17:17). Physical change has affected their bodies. Sarah has stopped her monthly cycles *(after the manner of women)*. People of the ancient world knew, as we know today, that a woman in this stage of her life no longer becomes pregnant. [See question #1, page 32.]

**12. Therefore Sarah laughed within herself, saying, After I am waxed old shall I have pleasure, my lord being old also?**

Sarah has been a woman of faith, having followed Abraham when he left Haran (Genesis 12:4, 5). At this point, however, her faith falters. Not only does she doubt her body's ability to achieve pregnancy, she doubts her husband's ability to impregnate her.

So Sarah laughs the laugh of derision in her heart. Her chuckle is not from happiness. It is from lack of faith.

### B. The Lord Not Limited (vv. 13, 14a)

**13. And the LORD said unto Abraham, Wherefore did Sarah laugh, saying, Shall I of a surety bear a child, which am old?**

This skeptical laugh in Sarah's heart does not go unnoticed by God. *The Lord* is well aware of the seeming impossibility of a pregnancy for *Abraham* and *Sarah.* [See question #2, page 32.]

**14a. Is any thing too hard for the LORD?**

The reader of Genesis 1 knows that God created *heaven* and *earth.* Thus to read that God can give a child to an elderly couple seems a small matter compared with what we already know to be true. If we have believed what we read, we can easily answer the question *Is any thing too hard for the Lord?* by responding, "No, nothing is too hard for the Lord to accomplish" (compare Jeremiah 32:17, 27).

We are reminded of another woman, a very young woman, who will be confronted with a miraculous pregnancy many centuries after the time of Abraham. She will question this too, because of her virginity. She will then be reminded that nothing is impossible with God (Luke 1:37). She will give a simple response of obedient faith: "Behold the handmaid of the Lord; be it unto me according to thy word" (Luke 1:38).

## III. Counting Blessings
## (Genesis 21:1-8)

Sarah's laugh of derision eventually gives way to faith, since Hebrews 11:11 tells us that, "Through faith also Sarah herself received strength to conceive seed, . . . because she judged him faithful who had promised."

### A. Promised Son Is Born (vv. 1, 2)

**1, 2. And the LORD visited Sarah as he had said, and the LORD did unto Sarah as he had spoken. For Sarah conceived, and bare Abraham a son in his old age, at the set time of which God had spoken to him.**

God is present in Sarah's life to fulfill His promise, and the result is a miraculous pregnancy. This is not a virginal conception, for that is a unique event in human history. But this is still a supernatural event—a conception, gestation, and birth that science cannot explain.

Somehow, God reverses the effects of aging on *Sarah.* Thus a woman who is some 40 or 50 years past the natural childbearing state is allowed to be as fertile as a 20-year-old wife for the case of this single pregnancy. [See question #3, page 32.]

### B. Promised Son Is Named (vv. 3-5)

**3. And Abraham called the name of his son that was born unto him, whom Sarah bare to him, Isaac.**

In a wonderful bit of irony, the boy is named *Isaac,* which means, "he laughs." This is no longer the laugh of derision or doubt. It is now a laugh of joy.

In this case, God's promise-keeping has the providential side effect of giving an elderly childless couple the joy of their hearts. They have the son they must have asked for in prayer for many years.

**4, 5. And Abraham circumcised his son Isaac being eight days old, as God had commanded him. And Abraham was a hundred years old, when his son Isaac was born unto him.**

God previously had established the circumcision of all the males in Abraham's household to be the primary sign of his covenant with *Abraham.* Accordingly, Abraham had applied the circumcision knife to all the men and boys, including his son Ishmael and himself (Genesis 17:23, 24).

We can imagine the joy that Abraham now feels. He is able to apply this sign of the covenant to the one who will fulfill the promise of a multitude of descendants for him.

### C. Promised Son Brings Joy (vv. 6-8)

**6. And Sarah said, God hath made me to laugh, so that all that hear will laugh with me.**

We see a side of *Sarah* here that should endear her to us. Her original laughter of contempt is reevaluated, and now she is able to see the humor of her situation. She has abandoned any bitterness she may have harbored for her years of childlessness. She is not embarrassed to *laugh* out loud so anyone who hears can share with her, for her laughter springs from a deep joy that God has given to her. [See question #4, page 32.]

#### LAUGHING FOR JOY

"Did you hear the one about . . . ?" So goes the opening line of countless jokes. Most of us enjoy a good joke, and if the story is told well, it doesn't even have to be plausible to make us laugh. Some people like side-splitting, belly-laugh-producing jokes; others prefer subtle humor. Whatever our preference, laughter is good medicine.

In recent years science has established that laughter is good for our physical, mental, and emotional health. A good laugh relaxes muscles, reduces stress, lowers blood pressure, and enhances the function of the immune system. It even reduces pain.

Sarah's decision to name her child *Isaac*— meaning "he laughs"—was especially poignant. At first, Sarah laughed at God's "ridiculous" announcement. That was a laugh of derision, and it's hard to see any "good medicine" in it. It was a scornful laugh that originated in the pain of barrenness.

But by the time her child was born, Sarah was laughing for joy. This was a laugh of thanksgiving for a promise fulfilled. If we see God as Sarah came to see Him, we will also find our lives filled with joyful delight. Think about it: When was the last time you laughed with joy over something marvelous that God did in your life? —C. R. B.

**7. And she said, Who would have said unto Abraham, that Sarah should have given children suck? for I have borne him a son in his old age.**

Sarah's situation is startling: an elderly woman nursing a baby who has an *old* man as the father. It is absurd from a worldly standpoint, but marvelous from the standpoint of faith. Sarah's joy for having *a son* is mingled with her pleasure at giving her faithful husband this child.

**8. And the child grew, and was weaned: and Abraham made a great feast the same day that Isaac was weaned.**

The rate of infant mortality in the ancient world is very high. Perhaps 25 percent of live-born babies do not live to see their first birthday. There is nothing more tragic than the death of a baby, but many societies have done things to protect parents from part of the pain this loss can bring. In some cultures, for instance, babies are not named until they are several years old. The idea in that practice is to lessen attachment to the infant in case of early death.

**Chronology of Genesis**
*From the Call of Abraham to the Death of Joseph*

| | | |
|---|---|---|
| 2167 BC | Abram born | |
| 2092 BC | Call of Abram | Genesis 12:1-5 |
| 2081 BC | Ishmael born (Lesson 4) | Genesis 16:15, 16 |
| 2067 BC | Isaac born (Lesson 5) | Genesis 21:1-3 |
| 2050 BC | Abraham offers Isaac | Genesis 22:1-19 |
| 2007 BC | Jacob and Esau born (Lesson 6) | Genesis 25:24-26 |
| 1992 BC | Abraham dies at age 175 | Genesis 25:7 |
| 1930 BC | Jacob flees to Haran (Lesson 7) | Genesis 28:10 |
| 1916 BC | Joseph born | Genesis 30:22-24 |
| 1899 BC | Joseph sold into slavery in Egypt at age 17 (Lesson 10) | Genesis 37:2, 28 |
| 1887 BC | Isaac dies at age 180 | Genesis 35:28 |
| 1886 BC | At age 30, Joseph interprets Pharaoh's dream (Lesson 11) | Genesis 41:46 |
| 1877 BC | Jacob goes to Egypt (Beginning of the Israelites' 430-year stay in Egypt (Exodus 12:40), leading to the exodus in 1447 BC) (Lesson 12) | Genesis 46:5, 6 |
| 1860 BC | Jacob dies at age 147 (Lesson 13) | Genesis 47:28 |
| 1806 BC | Joseph dies at age 110 | Genesis 50:26 |

Visual for Lesson 3

*Keep this chart posted all quarter to give your learners a chronological perspective.*

In Abraham and Sarah's world, it is a time for celebration when a baby is *weaned*. This is because weaning is a fairly reliable sign that a child will live to adulthood and not become a casualty of a childhood disease or birth defect.

So they celebrate! The first step in becoming the father of a large nation has now been taken. God has kept His promise, and Abraham's faith has not been in vain. [See question #5, page 32.]

## Conclusion

### A. The Importance of Abraham

The promises to Abraham focused on two points: (1) Abraham's posterity was to be made a great nation and be given the land of Canaan as a possession (see Genesis 17:8), and (2) in Abraham (and through Christ) all the families of the earth were to be blessed (see John 8:56-58; Galatians 3:16).

In this light, Genesis 12:2, 3 can be seen as the theme of the entire Bible: God would make a great nation of Abraham, and God would bring blessing to the nations through Abraham and his offspring. We as Christians believe that Abraham is the "father of the faithful" and that Jesus is the true child of Abraham. Everyone in Christ is part of the offspring of Abraham.

Paul's writings are very important for forming our self-understanding as Christians. Paul was a Jewish Christian, and he was extremely knowledgeable about the Jewish Scriptures, our Old Testament. Paul was a "Hebrew of the Hebrews" (Philippians 3:5). We may be surprised, then, when we learn who Paul thought was the primary hero of the Old Testament. We may expect this person to have been Moses, the great lawgiver and founder of the nation of Israel. In-deed, Paul had great respect for Moses. But Paul's "leading man" was Abraham. This is because Paul understood Abraham to be the primary example of the person of faith.

In the fourth chapter of Romans, Paul lays out a devastating argument against the necessity of circumcision for Christians. This amounts to a repudiation of the whole idea of being considered righteous because of keeping the Jewish law, an idea that was being debated in the first-century church.

Paul notes that Abraham was reckoned as righteous because of his faith (Romans 4:3-5; compare Genesis 15:6). But in a nice piece of detective work, Paul also notes that this reckoning occurred *before* Abraham was circumcised (Romans 4:10-12; compare Genesis 17:24). Abraham's right standing with the Lord was not the result of works, but the result of his faith.

This may seem like a complicated argument from the ancient world that has little relevance for us today. But such a conclusion would be to miss Paul's point. It is because of this system of "righteousness through faith" (as opposed to "righteousness through works") that all Christians are saved.

We cannot earn our salvation. It is a gift, given freely by God to those who believe in His Son, Jesus Christ, as they follow the biblical plan of salvation. It is this mighty truth that allows Paul to say, "they which are of faith, the same are the children of Abraham" (Galatians 3:7).

### B. Abraham and You

To be a Christian means to be a person of faith. Today's lesson teaches the story of two faithful people, Abraham and Sarah, and how they acted faithfully in spite of various "facts of life." Abraham's heart trusted that God would provide a son even when his mind told him this was impossible. May we examine our own lives and be resolved to live as people of faith, fully trusting God for our current lives and for our eternal future.

### C. Prayer

God of Abraham, Sarah, and Isaac, we trust in You to be our shield and our protector. We trust in you to be our rewarder and the guide for our future. May we, like Abraham, be counted as righteous in Your eyes because of our faith. We pray this in the name of your Son, Jesus Christ, amen.

### D. Thought to Remember

Abraham is still a model of faith.

## Home Daily Bible Readings

**Monday, Sept. 10**—Listen! (Isaiah 51:1-5)

**Tuesday, Sept. 11**—Abraham Believed (Genesis 15:1-6)

**Wednesday, Sept. 12**—Abraham Doubted (Genesis 17:15-22)

**Thursday, Sept. 13**—Abraham the Host (Genesis 18:1-8)

**Friday, Sept. 14**—Sarah's Laughter (Genesis 18:9-15)

**Saturday, Sept. 15**—Sarah's Joy (Genesis 21:1-8)

**Sunday, Sept. 16**—The Faith of Abraham (Hebrews 11:8-12)

# Learning by Doing

*This page contains an alternative lesson plan emphasizing learning activities.*
*Classes desiring such student involvement will find these suggestions helpful.*

## Into the Lesson

As learners arrive, tie a piece of yarn or string into a bow on a finger of each one. As class begins, have someone recall the meaning of the old practice of tying a string around one's finger as a reminder of something to be done.

Then say, "Today's study is about an occasion to be anticipated with hope and remembered with joy." Have learners keep the strings on their fingers through the Into the Word segment.

*Alternative:* Buy or borrow one of the large foam hands with the pointed index fingers displayed by sports fans who consider their teams to be "Number 1." Tie a large ribbon into a bow around the finger. Display it and say, "Today's lesson text describes an occasion of which the Bible challenges us over and over, *remember!*"

Assign the following texts (or a sampling of them) to individual readers; all are related to today's lesson text and God's promises to Abraham: Genesis 26:3; 28:4; Exodus 2:24; 6:2-4, 8; 32:13; Leviticus 26:42; Numbers 32:11; Deuteronomy 1:8; 6:10; 9:5; 29:12, 13; 30:20; 34:4; Joshua 24:2-4; 2 Kings 13:23; 1 Chronicles 16:15-18; Nehemiah 9:7, 8; Isaiah 51:2; Ezekiel 33:24; Luke 1:72, 73; Acts 3:25; 7:1-5; Romans 4:18; Galatians 3:6, 7, 29; Hebrews 6:13-15.

Have learners read their verses aloud. Say, "God's promises to Abraham became the watchword of His people. When the church began, the apostles affirmed that Abraham's covenant was fulfilled in Christ's covenant. Christians are children of Abraham, blessed by God's grace."

## Into the Word

Call the following activity *Ask Abraham.* Say, "If we could ask Abraham some questions about the occasion of today's lesson text, the answers would be clear. Read the text and then 'be Abraham' as I ask him some questions."

Give the class opportunity to read the lesson text silently, and then ask this series of questions. Remind your learners to "be Abraham" as they respond (answers are in parentheses after each question): 1. When the Lord came to you the third time, where did he tell you to look? *(toward heaven)*; 2. Was it day or night? *(night)*; 3. How many stars could you see? *(too many to count)*; 4. How many offspring did you have at the time?

*(none)*; 5. How many offspring did God say you would have? *(as many as the stars)*; 6. Did you believe God's Word? *(yes)*; 7. How did God respond to your belief? *(called me righteous even though I was a sinner)*; 8. At what stage of life were you when God reiterated His promise to give you a son? *(too old to have children; Sarah too!)*; 9. How did your wife Sarah react to this latest promise? *(she laughed)*; 10. Did God notice Sarah's lack of faith? *(yes, He asked me about it)*; 11. Is anything too hard for God? *(no, Sarah and I experienced the "impossible")*; 12. How do you account for Sarah's being able to become pregnant? *(the Lord enabled it)*; 13. When did this son arrive? *(just when God said he would; about a year after Sarah laughed)*; 14. How old were you when Isaac was born? *(100 years old)*; 15. Why did you circumcise Isaac? *(because God established that as part of the covenant)*; 16. What difference did you see in Sarah's attitude when her son was born? *(her laughter was from joy)*; 17. What did you do on the occasion that Isaac was weaned? *(we held a great celebration feast)*; 18. What have you learned from all this, Abraham? *(let learners respond openly)*.

Then ask one further open-ended question: "How does Abraham's faith apply to today?"

## Into Life

Copy and distribute the following checklist (if you do not use the student books, where this activity also is found). Say, "Look at these life situations and check off the ones that convict you most. At the bottom of the page, write your commitment to trusting God more in the one area for which you have the greatest difficulty."

___ I barely make ends meet financially, but nonetheless God expects me to be generous with His church and those in need.

___ My schedule is overcrowded and hectic, but nonetheless God wants me to make time for study, worship, and service.

___ I'd much rather spend time with godly friends and family, but nonetheless God wants me to cultivate relationships with the ungodly, as a witness to them.

___ Spiritually, I know God has assured me of His presence and a glorious future, but nonetheless my anxieties about the here-and-now often run amok.

# Let's Talk It Over

*The questions on this page are designed to promote discussion of the lesson by the class and to encourage application of the lesson Scriptures. The answers provided are only discussion starters. Let your class talk it over from there.*

**1. What are some ways that you have you seen God use elderly people to accomplish His will and advance His kingdom?**

Some cultures revere the elderly. In others, however, age is disdained and youth is glorified. Immaturity marks the landscape of those cultures, from entertainment to business to sports.

This glorification of youth to the exclusion of the aged contradicts the teaching of Scripture. Various passages speak of the honor that is to be given to those who are older (see Exodus 20:12; Proverbs 23:22; 1 Timothy 5:1, 2; 1 Peter 5:5). Those whom God chooses to provide leadership for the church are referred to as *elders.*

Those who have the wisdom of age have kept many of us from making costly mistakes, whether financially, relationally, or spiritually. Those with the wisdom of age provide a needed balance of patience and grace in the midst of the sometimes misguided exuberance of youth. However, old age is no guarantee of wisdom (see 1 Kings 11:4; Ecclesiastes 4:13).

**2. What was a time when you doubted the promises or provisions of God and even laughed at the seeming absurdity of the situation? How did things turn out? How did you grow spiritually as a result?**

We can be guilty of limiting the power of God. We may doubt the likelihood of the salvation of someone we know has been caught in the web of some big sin. Yet it is not God's desire that anyone should perish. He sent His Son to die for all, even the vilest of sinners.

At other times we may take the word of a physician as "gospel" instead of trusting the power of God, the great physician, to bring healing in a seemingly impossible situation. We may snicker inwardly when someone shares a big dream concerning a ministry idea, only to see God bless that faith and that ministry.

**3. How does Genesis 21:1, 2 help ensure a proper view about God and time?**

The concept of *time* is important to us because for us time runs out. But time never runs out for God. God is not bound by time. He has always existed, and He will always exist.

Though God exists above time, He chooses to work within time. We see that with Abraham and Sarah. We also see it with Jesus: "But when the fulness of the time was come, God sent forth his Son" (Galatians 4:4). We can be sure that God is working in our time and will provide for our needs at the right time, in the right way.

**4. What was a time when you experienced an "Isaac moment," a time of joyous laughter at God's provisions? What led up to that moment, and how did things turn out? How was your faith increased?**

The birth of Isaac was a time of joy for Abraham and Sarah. God had done the humanly impossible. God can continue to bring joyous laughter to His people, if we let him. The spiritual new birth of a person baptized into Christ provides a time of great joy for God's people, particularly if that person's acceptance of Christ seemed very unlikely.

Even at the time of the death of one of God's saints, there can be joy and even laughter as we remember the life and influence of this departed brother or sister in Christ. It is God's desire that His people experience joy and laughter. "A merry heart doeth good like a medicine: but a broken spirit drieth the bones" (Proverbs 17:22).

**5. What are some appropriate and inappropriate ways we can respond when we see God fulfilling promises and working His will?**

When God fulfilled the promise to give a son to Abraham and Sarah, Abraham's response was that of celebration and feasting. Scripture says, "joy shall be in heaven over one sinner that repenteth, more than over ninety and nine just persons, which need no repentance" (Luke 15:7).

In the church we can be guilty of feeling inconvenienced when someone responds to an invitation and desires baptism. Instead of rejoicing, we may inwardly groan about the delay in getting out of church. Even when we have fellowship meals, there sometimes is little mutual rejoicing and celebration. We may eat as quickly as possible so we can leave and get on with other things of life. Learning to take time to celebrate God's working can be a spiritual discipline.

# Abraham, Hagar, and Ishmael

DEVOTIONAL READING: **Genesis 16.**

BACKGROUND SCRIPTURE: **Genesis 21:9-21.**

PRINTED TEXT: **Genesis 21:9-21.**

### Genesis 21:9-21

9 And Sarah saw the son of Hagar the Egyptian, which she had borne unto Abraham, mocking.

10 Wherefore she said unto Abraham, Cast out this bondwoman and her son: for the son of this bondwoman shall not be heir with my son, even with Isaac.

11 And the thing was very grievous in Abraham's sight because of his son.

12 And God said unto Abraham, Let it not be grievous in thy sight because of the lad, and because of thy bondwoman; in all that Sarah hath said unto thee, hearken unto her voice; for in Isaac shall thy seed be called.

13 And also of the son of the bondwoman will I make a nation, because he is thy seed.

14 And Abraham rose up early in the morning, and took bread, and a bottle of water, and gave it unto Hagar, putting it on her shoulder, and the child, and sent her away: and she departed, and wandered in the wilderness of Beer-sheba.

15 And the water was spent in the bottle, and she cast the child under one of the shrubs.

16 And she went, and sat her down over against him a good way off, as it were a bowshot: for she said, Let me not see the death of the child. And she sat over against him, and lifted up her voice, and wept.

17 And God heard the voice of the lad; and the angel of God called to Hagar out of heaven, and said unto her, What aileth thee, Hagar? fear not; for God hath heard the voice of the lad where he is.

18 Arise, lift up the lad, and hold him in thine hand; for I will make him a great nation.

19 And God opened her eyes, and she saw a well of water; and she went, and filled the bottle with water, and gave the lad drink.

20 And God was with the lad; and he grew, and dwelt in the wilderness, and became an archer.

21 And he dwelt in the wilderness of Paran: and his mother took him a wife out of the land of Egypt.

---

GOLDEN TEXT: [God said to Abraham,] And also of the son of the bondwoman will I make a nation, because he is thy seed.—Genesis 21:13.

---

*God Creates*
Unit 1: God Creates a People
(Lessons 1-5)

## Lesson Aims

After participating in this lesson, each student will be able to:

1. Outline the facts regarding Abraham's dismissal of Hagar and Ishmael.

2. Summarize the significance of God's promise in Genesis 21:13.

3. Suggest some ways for his or her church to reach out to Muslims or other non-Christians with the gospel.

## Lesson Outline

INTRODUCTION
    A. Outsiders and Insiders
    B. Lesson Background
 I. HAGAR AND ISHMAEL DISMISSED (Genesis 21: 9-13)
    A. Conflict in the Household (vv. 9, 10)
    B. Conflict for Father Abraham (vv. 11-13)
II. HAGAR AND ISHMAEL SUSTAINED (Genesis 21: 14-19)
    A. Abandoned by Family (v. 14)
    B. Abandoning Hope (vv. 15, 16)
    C. Saved by God (vv. 17-19)
       *Taking a Gamble . . . or Not*
III. HAGAR AND ISHMAEL BLESSED (Genesis 21: 20, 21)
    A. Ishmael Becomes a Man (v. 20)
    B. Ishmael Takes a Wife (v. 21)
       *Unwelcome, but Still Loved*
CONCLUSION
    A. Children of the Free Woman
    B. Prayer
    C. Thought to Remember

## Introduction

### A. Outsiders and Insiders

"Call me Ishmael." So begins the famous novel *Moby-Dick,* by Herman Melville. Melville employs many biblical names and images to tell a story of self-destruction of the obsessive Captain Ahab. Ishmael, the narrator, is always the outsider, not quite part of the main drama unfolding around him. His namesake, the Ishmael of Genesis, also ended up being an outsider.

Today, Muslims see Abraham as their father in the faith, much like Jews and Christians do (compare Romans 4:16). Muslims, however, trace their spiritual lineage back to Abraham through Ishmael, the son who was cast out of Abraham's household. According to the Qur'an (or Koran), the holy book of the religion of Islam, Abraham was told by God to take Ishmael and his mother, Hagar, to a far land. They traveled many days until they came to a deserted place.

Unbeknownst to them, so the story goes, this was the spot where Adam had built the first place to worship God. Abraham left Hagar and Ishmael there. When Hagar and Ishmael were near death from lack of water, the Qur'an claims that the youngster began to kick in the sand, and a well sprang up. This became the well Zamzam, and the city that grew around it is known today as Mecca. Muslims falsely believe that a descendant of Ishmael named Mohammed restored true worship of God at this site in the seventh century AD.

Unrest and violence in the Middle East today are partly fueled by different ideas concerning how people are connected to Abraham and his sons. Jews claim the side of Isaac, the child of promise according to Genesis. Muslims believe that their ancestor Ishmael was the primary child of promise blessed by God. Each side sees itself as the "insider" and the other as the "outsider."

This religious rivalry, combined with politics and nationalism, has led to instability and war, disrupting the lives of many innocent people. The fundamentalist brand of Islam believes there is no room for accommodation with infidels, those who don't believe as they do and who don't follow the teachings of Mohammed to the letter.

This week's lesson looks at the story of Abraham, Hagar, and Ishmael from the Bible's point of view. It is a sad story of a family broken apart because of foolish behavior and bitterness. We grieve with Abraham as he is forced to choose between his two sons. Many of those studying this lesson have experienced the pain of family fighting and break-up. Today's text offers hope to us in that we see that God did not curse one side of a family squabble while blessing the other side.

### B. Lesson Background

Last week's lesson focused on how Abraham and Sarah were able to have a son in spite of advanced age. Regarding Sarah specifically, we learned of many admirable qualities: her faith, her courage, and her sense of humor and joy.

Yet there was another side to Sarah that was not so admirable. Today we see a headstrong woman, who could be jealous and scheming. In the end one of her schemes backfired, and her jealousy caused her to act with cruelty.

Sarah and Abraham lived in a world where it was common for households to include slaves. One of their slaves was an Egyptian girl named Hagar (Genesis 16:3). Hagar was Sarah's personal attendant. When Abraham and Sarah's attempts to produce a child were unsuccessful, Sarah hatched a scheme to remedy the problem: she offered to let Abraham have Hagar as a type of slave-wife, hoping this union would yield a child.

Sarah's logic in this seems strange to us. Why would a wife willingly allow her husband to have an intimate relationship with another woman? This seems to be a recipe for disaster! But the logic of this practice, common at the time, went something like this: "If my slave produces a child, that child will be mine, just like his mother is my property." Sarah thought she could have a son by a secondary way, and thus please her husband.

This plan "worked" (if we can use that word!), and Abraham and Hagar conceived the baby that was to become Ishmael. But the plan backfired on Sarah in two ways. First, becoming pregnant had an unanticipated effect on Hagar: she began to think that she was better than Sarah (Genesis 16:4). Hagar had been successful at becoming pregnant, something Sarah had failed in; this ruined the relationship between the two women and ensured that Ishmael would never be accepted by Sarah. Second, Ishmael himself displayed his own arrogance after Isaac was born. This is where today's lesson begins.

# I. Hagar and Ishmael Dismissed (Genesis 21:9-13)

Many people today live in "blended" households. Typically, this involves a woman with one or more children marrying a man with one or more children—the children from previous marriages. Those familiar with blended families will testify that theirs is not an easy situation. There is often conflict, perceived slights, and favoritism.

Now imagine a blended family that involves more than one wife! That explosive combination is what we find in Abraham's household.

## A. Conflict in the Household (vv. 9, 10)

**9. And Sarah saw the son of Hagar the Egyptian, which she had borne unto Abraham, mocking.**

Ishmael, *the son of Hagar the Egyptian*, is recorded as *mocking*. We don't really know what

or why he is mocking. He may be mocking *Sarah* for her old age, or he may be mocking Isaac. This is probably learned behavior, copied from his mother. We also don't know exactly how old the boy is at this time, although Genesis 17:25 indicates that he is at least 13. We can see that he is old enough to poke fun and immature enough not to know that this is a dangerous practice.

**10. Wherefore she said unto Abraham, Cast out this bondwoman and her son: for the son of this bondwoman shall not be heir with my son, even with Isaac.**

Ishmael's unwise display of haughtiness is the final straw for Sarah. So she demands that Hagar and Ishmael be expelled from the household, where she rules as the supreme mistress. She had once used Hagar as a tool to satisfy her husband's desire for a *son*. That purpose is no longer valid, for Sarah now has her own son, namely *Isaac*.

In her anger, Sarah decides to jettison this embarrassing mistake once and for all. She does this both to soothe her own wounded pride and to protect the rights of the younger Isaac as Abraham's rightful heir. [See question #1, page 40.]

## B. Conflict for Father Abraham (vv. 11-13)

**11. And the thing was very grievous in Abraham's sight because of his son.**

This is not so easy for Abraham. Sarah is rejecting his true, biological *son* by another woman. *Abraham's* blood flows in Ishmael's veins. Abraham, however, was a willing accomplice in the unwise impregnation of Hagar. The fact that he tried to "push" God's timetable in trying to obtain a son now brings him grief.

**12. And God said unto Abraham, Let it not be grievous in thy sight because of the lad, and because of thy bondwoman; in all that Sarah hath said unto thee, hearken unto her voice; for in Isaac shall thy seed be called.**

---

### How to Say It

ABRAHAM. *Ay*-bruh-ham.
BEER-SHEBA. Beer-*she*-buh.
CANAAN. *Kay*-nun.
DEUTERONOMY. Due-ter-*ahn*-uh-me.
HABAKKUK. Huh-*back*-kuk.
HAGAR. *Hay*-gar.
ISHMAEL. *Ish*-may-el.
ISHMAELITES. *Ish*-may-el-ites.
ISHMEELITES. *Ish*-me-el-ites.
KORAN or QUR'AN. Kuh-*ran*.
NEGEV. *Neg*-ev.
PARAN. *Pair*-un.

In this moment of great distress, *God* does not abandon *Abraham*. God instructs Abraham to go ahead and do what *Sarah* wishes, as curious and cruel as it may seem. God's promises will still be fulfilled through *Isaac*.

Families can be horribly dysfunctional. They can bear the scars of abuse, betrayal, and tragedy. However, God does not abandon us, even in the darkest days. Yet, while God is at work, He does not always restore a family to an earlier state that seemed to be better. The mess that had been created in Abraham's family by several factors is not going to be fixed by God as we may think of *fix* or *repair* in human terms. Instead, we will see God unfailingly love each family member and do what is best to care for him or her. [See question #2, page 40.]

**13. And also of the son of the bondwoman will I make a nation, because he is thy seed.**

This word of the Lord must surely be a surprise to Abraham. God has plans for Ishmael too! His descendants will become *a nation* also. He too shares in the blessings of being a *son* of Abraham. However, Abraham will experience little firsthand joy in the successes of Ishmael's life, for the expulsion is to proceed.

## II. Hagar and Ishmael Sustained (Genesis 21:14-19)

Abraham ultimately is driven by his obedient faith. He has been tested many times before. Now he is about to be tested again.

### A. Abandoned by Family (v. 14)

**14a. And Abraham rose up early in the morning, and took bread, and a bottle of water, and gave it unto Hagar, putting it on her shoulder, and the child, and sent her away.**

It seems that Abraham's greatest tests are acted out when he rises *up early in the morning*. This is the way he had witnessed the horrific destruction of Sodom and Gomorrah (Genesis 19:27). In the next chapter, it will be the setting of his supreme trial: the sacrifice of his son Isaac (Genesis 22:3). We can imagine the grief at this early-morning drama, perhaps so early that no one else in the household is a witness.

**14b. And she departed, and wandered in the wilderness of Beer-sheba.**

We should remember that the land of Canaan is largely undeveloped at this time. Hagar has no place to go, and she heads into the unpopulated *wilderness of Beer-sheba*. This is in the southern part of Canaan, the beginning of the cruel Negev desert. Abraham later sees Beer-sheba as a place

of worship (Genesis 21:33). Centuries later, it will be the southern extremity of Israel (Judges 20:1).

### B. Abandoning Hope (vv. 15, 16)

**15, 16a. And the water was spent in the bottle, and she cast the child under one of the shrubs. And she went, and sat her down over against him a good way off, as it were a bowshot.**

Hagar has lost hope and is preparing to die. Her location is desolate, but it has enough vegetation to provide *shrubs* that are large enough to provide a measure of shade from the relentless sun. The distance of a *bowshot* is about 100–150 yards, still within hearing distance.

**16b. For she said, Let me not see the death of the child. And she sat over against him, and lifted up her voice, and wept.**

Hagar cannot bear to watch her son die. The teenage boy does not follow her, so we assume he is incapacitated from lack of water. Now alone, Hagar weeps bitterly. She pours out all her feelings of abandonment. The text describes this as a lifting *up*, a prayer. God has allowed her to reach the utter depths of human despair, but He has not given up on her.

### C. Saved by God (vv. 17-19)

**17, 18. And God heard the voice of the lad; and the angel of God called to Hagar out of heaven, and said unto her, What aileth thee, Hagar? fear not; for God hath heard the voice of the lad where he is. Arise, lift up the lad, and hold him in thine hand; for I will make him a great nation.**

*God* now conveys a message to *Hagar.* We can imagine that the last thing she expects to hear in the desert is a voice *out of heaven*! Interestingly, *the angel* doesn't say that God has heard her prayer, but that God has been moved by *the voice of the lad.* [See question #3, page 40.]

Hagar herself will share Ishmael's blessings. She is thus made privy to the promise Abraham has been given: Ishmael too will be the father of *a great nation.* Hagar's life has not been in vain. Her life has great purpose in the overall plans of God.

**19. And God opened her eyes, and she saw a well of water; and she went, and filled the bottle with water, and gave the lad drink.**

The rare watering place in the desert (oasis) is highly prized by the seminomadic shepherd people of Abraham's day. *Water* is life. "No water" means rapid death. Hagar and Ishmael are saved by God's miraculous provision of water where there should be no water, a *well* in the wilderness. [See question #4, page 40.]

### TAKING A GAMBLE . . . OR NOT

A California couple decided to spend a few days in Las Vegas on a gambling vacation. The thoughtful pair arranged for a dog-sitter. However, they left their two sons—a nine-year-old and an autistic five-year-old—by themselves at home. The boys' grandmother began to suspect the nature of the situation and called police.

The couple was charged with two felony counts of child endangerment. The emotional charge by the older boy was, "They shouldn't leave us alone. I didn't know who I could call in an emergency. I thought they loved [the puppies] more than they loved us." The boys had reason to question their parents' care for them. A similar event had taken place a few months earlier.

Abraham didn't abandon his son so he could go to Las Vegas in search of a good time. Even so, some may think that Abraham took a gamble on his son's life. But we must not overlook one crucial fact: Abraham acted at God's direction. To follow God's leading is never a gamble. To *believe* that statement is probably fairly easy for most; to have the godly courage to *live it out* may be another matter entirely!           —C. R. B.

## ⫶III⫶ Hagar and Ishmael Blessed (Genesis 21:20, 21)

Being saved from death-by-dehydration is not the end of the story for Hagar and Ishmael. With a secure water supply, they begin to prosper. Later, there is a measure of reconciliation between the two sides of Abraham's clan, for we are told that Isaac and Ishmael together bury their father (Genesis 25:9). Ishmael lives to the ripe old age of 137 and has a large family (25:12-17).

### A. Ishmael Becomes a Man (v. 20)

**20. And God was with the lad; and he grew, and dwelt in the wilderness, and became an archer.**

To be *an archer* implies that Ishmael rejects the life of a tender of flocks of animals. He is now a hunter, living off the wild game of the *wilderness*. In this he prefigures a future rejected relative: Esau (Genesis 25:27). One occupation is not superior to another, for God blesses both. [See question #5, page 40.]

### B. Ishmael Takes a Wife (v. 21)

**21. And he dwelt in the wilderness of Paran: and his mother took him a wife out of the land of Egypt.**

It is difficult to be certain about this location, but ancient *Paran* is probably located near the site

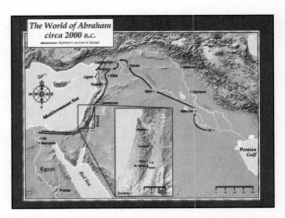

Visual for Lesson 4. *Point to this visual as you ask, "What kind of call from God would cause you to be willing to make a move of this magnitude?"*

of modern Elat on the northern tip of the Gulf of Aqaba. *The wilderness of Paran* is the extremely inhospitable region to the west, still largely uninhabited today. The name *Paran* has a rich biblical history. (See Genesis 14:6; Numbers 10:12; 12:16; 13:3, 26; Deuteronomy 33:2; Habakkuk 3:3.)

Since Ishmael's father is not a part of his life, it is up to *his mother* to find him a *wife*. Hagar does so, and the unnamed wife is from her people, the Egyptians. Elsewhere we learn that Ishmael ends up with 12 successful sons (see Genesis 25:12-16). Some of these descendants later figure into other Bible stories as the Ishmaelites (or Ishmeelites). See Genesis 37:25-28; Judges 8:24.

God keeps His promise to Abraham and to Hagar concerning Ishmael and his descendants. While our family structures differ from those of Abraham's time, we learn important lessons about God's care for families in conflict.

### UNWELCOME, BUT STILL LOVED

A couple was evicted from their home of many years on Fifth Avenue in New York City. "Pale Male" and "Lola" are red-tailed hawks that had built a nest on a window ledge of an apartment house. Some residents of the building had complained about the carcasses of rats and pigeons that fell from the nest onto the sidewalk below. Thus the eviction.

However, the hawks were invited to return just three weeks later. After the original nest was removed, bird lovers raised a fuss. So an architect designed a new nest to prevent the overflow of uneaten prey that had caused the trouble. The birds were soon back home, raising a family.

Hagar and Ishmael had been evicted from Abraham's home because their presence was distasteful to at least one of the residents (Sarah). Then God befriended them and saw to it that they were blessed with the safety and family that followed. Today, those who trace their spiritual descent through Abraham and Ishmael are the Muslims. Many of them have declared Christians to be their enemies. In reaction, at least some Westerners would like to "evict" Muslims and send them somewhere else. How can we demonstrate the truth and grace of Christ to people whom we may find hard to love?    —C. R. B.

## Conclusion

### A. Children of the Free Woman

The apostle Paul uses the life and person of Abraham to illustrate the truths of the gospel and its application to the people of the church. In Galatians 4, Paul employs the family troubles of the patriarch to explain our freedom in Christ. You must know the story of today's lesson to make sense of his powerful argument.

Paul's primary agenda in Galatians is to refute the idea that Christians are required to keep the Jewish law. For Paul, this obligation would negate the freedom we have in Christ. One way Paul makes his point is to use a story from the first book of the law (Genesis) to illustrate the importance of freedom in God's plan of redemption.

Paul begins with a contrast of Hagar and Sarah (Galatians 4:22). Hagar is a "bondmaid"; Sarah is a "free woman." Paul points out that the child Abraham produced with Hagar was "born after the flesh," that is, through natural impregnation and birth. The child produced with Sarah

was "by promise," that is, through supernatural provision to allow the elderly woman to become pregnant (4:23).

Paul goes on to equate the slave woman and her son with the bondage of the law as symbolized by the Jerusalem of his day (Galatians 4:25). This is his way of talking about the stifling, restrictive legalism that some Jewish Christians were trying to impose upon Paul's Gentile converts. To force the law upon these non-Jews would be to bind them by the old covenant and ignore the blessings of the new covenant.

Paul contrasts this with the free woman and her son, whom he equates with the heavenly Jerusalem (Galatians 4:26). His final point in this section is "we are not children of the bondwoman, but of the free" (4:31). In other words, why would you exchange the marvelous freedom from sin that is possible through faith in Christ for the bondage of the Jewish law? (See 5:1.)

Paul's foundational point here is not directly tied to the teaching points of the Hagar/Ishmael story as found in Genesis (today's lesson), but that should not worry us. Our study of Genesis allows us to see this crucial doctrine of Christian freedom in a striking way. We are free in Christ! Not free to sin, but free to live our lives for the glory of God and in His service.

There is a larger doctrinal point that lies behind both the Galatians illustration and the Genesis account, however. That is that God is a God of promises, and He always keeps His promises. He did not abandon His promise to Abraham when Abraham attempted to keep his line going by having a child with a slave woman. The Lord was still faithful to provide through both Isaac and Ishmael, despite Abraham's foibles.

Likewise, God will not abandon us, even when our families—either our physical family or our spiritual family—are in shambles. God's love for us is proven through His gift of His only Son, Jesus. Even when the animosity among the members of a fractured family runs very high, God's love is constant and unchangeable. In times of personal adversity, we are well reminded to "keep yourselves in the love of God" (Jude 21).

### B. Prayer

Father, You show us unity in Your very person; we show You division in our lives and families. May You continue to heal our rifts and calm our conflicts. We pray this in the name of Your only Son, Jesus, amen.

### C. Thought to Remember

God can work in the midst of conflict.

## Home Daily Bible Readings

**Monday, Sept. 17**—Sarah Deals Harshly with Hagar (Genesis 16:1-6)
**Tuesday, Sept. 18**—God Protects Hagar (Genesis 16:7-16)
**Wednesday, Sept. 19**—Abraham's Offspring (Genesis 21:9-13)
**Thursday, Sept. 20**—Waiting for Death (Genesis 21:14-16)
**Friday, Sept. 21**—Water from God (Genesis 21:17-19)
**Saturday, Sept. 22**—Ishmael Grows Up (Genesis 21:20, 21)
**Sunday, Sept. 23**—Ishmael's Descendants (Genesis 25:12-18)

# Learning by Doing

*This page contains an alternative lesson plan emphasizing learning activities.*
*Classes desiring such student involvement will find these suggestions helpful.*

## Into the Lesson

Display one or more Muslim (Islamic) symbols around your classroom for learners to see as they arrive. Inexpensive flags with the Muslim crescent moon may be available locally. A copy of the Qur'an by the door should stir interest. Also display a modern map of the Arabic world (Middle East), with Mecca highlighted.

The lesson writer in the Introduction has a good summary on Ishmael's relationship to Islamic belief. Read that section of the introduction, beginning with the sentence. "Today, Muslims see Abraham as their father in the faith" and ending with "Muslims falsely believe that a descendant of Ishmael named Mohammed restored true worship of God at this site in the seventh century AD." The reading will take only about a minute, but it will offer a valuable background to today's study and a valuable insight into the current world situation.

## Into the Word

Make and distribute copies of the following word-search puzzle. If your class uses the optional student books, you will also find it there.

```
S S A R A H H A G A R F
A U B R Y S U O L A E J
S H P A M E I S A I C C
S A C E I L S H R M A O
E A E C R F L G S A R M
R R A N D I I H H A G P
T G A A R S O A A B A A
S R E E A H H R R N A S
I R M G I N S A I A C S
D I S N H E M C A T E I
L S A E R S A H H A Y O
G L O V E S A R A B R N
```

To introduce the puzzle, say, "The story in today's lesson text in Genesis 21 describes intense emotions. Look in the puzzle for words that characterize deep feelings. As you find these words, look at the lesson text for verses in which such an emotion must have been felt passionately." The words to be found are: *compassion, distress, dread, grace, grief, jealousy, love, panic, selfishness, superiority,* and *vengeance.*

Allow some latitude for learners' identification of related verses. For example, compassion could characterize Abraham in his providing some sustenance for Hagar and Ishmael as he dismisses them (v. 14); some will see God's compassion as Ishmael cries out (vv. 17, 18).

Note that every study of the Scriptures is directly or indirectly a study of the nature of God. Read aloud the following statements about God. Ask class members to decide what each of the following statements reveals about God's nature. The statements are drawn from events of both today's and last week's lessons.

1. By grace God chose Abraham, a sinner, to be the father of God's special people.
2. God had a plan for Abraham's life that He revealed to Abraham.
3. Even those chosen by God can still go the way of their own will.
4. God sometimes allows bad things to happen in order to realize His will fully.
5. God keeps His promises, even when they appear to have been forgotten.
6. God is everywhere, even in the wilderness.
7. God even loves people who are lost in their own pride.
8. God hears and answers prayers.
9. God sustains, sometimes miraculously.
10. God may do more than He promises, but He never does less.

If the class needs a stimulus, suggest this for the first statement: "God can do as He pleases; He has chosen to use sinners to accomplish His redemptive will."

## Into Life

Say, "Paul uses Isaac and Ishmael as figures of those born free and those born to bondage, respectively (Galatians 4:22-31). If Ishmael is a figure for those who are still caught in slavery to law and sin, let's make an 'Ishmael pact' in which we commit to speaking on behalf of Christ to those who are lost in the wilderness of unrighteousness."

Distribute "Hello, my name is . . . " peel-and-stick labels. Ask each to write *Ishmael* on the label and wear it. When asked what the label means, each can respond: "**I S**peak **H**ow **M**y **A**lmighty Expresses **L**ove! John 3:16!" Or your class can make an acronym from the word *Isaac* instead.

# Let's Talk It Over

*The questions on this page are designed to promote discussion of the lesson by the class and to encourage application of the lesson Scriptures. The answers provided are only discussion starters. Let your class talk it over from there.*

**1. What was a wrong-headed (or even sinful) way that you tried to deal with a mistake you made? How did things turn out? What should you have done instead?**

The mistake Abraham and Sarah made by trying to "push" God's timeline by conceiving Ishmael was only compounded by sending Hagar and Ishmael away. The saying, "out of sight, out of mind," is not a reality when it comes to sin. A man who insists his girlfriend have an abortion lives with that decision for the rest of his life. The unwed woman who aborts a child deals with two sins: the promiscuous sex that led to the pregnancy and the abortion.

These and other sins affect future relationships. Instead of hiding sins, we must do the biblical thing and confess them. David discovered this truth after his sin with Bathsheba (Psalm 51). Though we still have a memory of the sin, we have the promise of forgiveness when we confess (1 John 1:9).

**2. What was a time when God worked amazing things in your family life when the situation seemed hopeless? How did you honor Him for His provision?**

It is an amazing and humbling thing to realize that God can and does work through our mistakes and our sins to accomplish His purpose. Many people repent and start fresh after being convicted by God because of their sins. Good can come out of bad situations when our recognition of the love and grace of God motivates us to serve Him in greater ways.

When those opposed to God seem to be winning battles, it is important to remember that God wins the war. God will work through the seeming defeats to accomplish His purpose. This was demonstrated in the life of Joseph, a product of a very dysfunctional family (see Genesis 45:5, 7; 50:20).

**3. What was a time when God answered you in a way that you weren't expecting? What did this teach you about how God likes to work?**

Though Hagar was crying out to God, verse 17 reveals that the answer to Hagar was given because of the cry of Ishmael. The combined cries and prayers of Christians are vital. Yet we remember that even though God is able to "hear" all prayers, that doesn't necessarily means He always "listens" (Lamentations 3:44; John 9:31).

God is pleased when His people's many prayers and cries are lifted with a unified spirit. The answers to our prayers are not always as we expect or hope them to be. But the answers are always in line with accomplishing God's will.

**4. In what ways have you seen God provide for His people when all seemed hopeless? Why do you think that God sometimes waits until the need is very severe before He intervenes?**

Things that seem to be impossible for us are not so for God. God is able to work through the obstacles of our lives and use them as opportunities to reveal His power. This is seen time and again in His meeting the needs of His people.

The nation of Israel appeared helpless and hopeless in the wilderness. Yet He never neglected the needs of His people (see Deuteronomy 2:7). Once during the ministry of Jesus, a large crowd was with Him. It was time to eat, so Jesus challenged His apostles to feed the crowd. They considered this to be an impossible request, but Jesus provided (see Matthew 14:15-21). The God who performed such miracles certainly can provide for our daily needs in non-miraculous ways! Sometimes God provides for others through our hands (Mark 9:41).

**5. What can the phrase, "God was with the lad," teach us about God's presence during wilderness times in our lives?**

Ishmael dwelt in the wilderness—a wild place, a deserted place. Yet God was still with him. We may feel we have been left on our own when we are in times of emotional and spiritual distress; these are times when we feel as though we are wandering in a wilderness. But in these barren places of life God is still there.

Many of the effective servants of God spent time in a physical wilderness or a secluded place (see Luke 4:1, 2, 42; 5:16; Galatians 1:17; and Revelation 1:9). God can use a wilderness experience to prepare us for a task (Exodus 2:15; 3:1). God uses those times to shape us.

# Isaac and Rebekah

DEVOTIONAL READING: **Psalm 100.**

BACKGROUND SCRIPTURE: **Genesis 24.**

PRINTED TEXT: **Genesis 24:34-45, 48.**

### Genesis 24:34-45, 48

34 And he said, I am Abraham's servant.

35 And the LORD hath blessed my master greatly, and he is become great: and he hath given him flocks, and herds, and silver, and gold, and menservants, and maidservants, and camels, and asses.

36 And Sarah my master's wife bare a son to my master when she was old: and unto him hath he given all that he hath.

37 And my master made me swear, saying, Thou shalt not take a wife to my son of the daughters of the Canaanites, in whose land I dwell:

38 But thou shalt go unto my father's house, and to my kindred, and take a wife unto my son.

39 And I said unto my master, Peradventure the woman will not follow me.

40 And he said unto me, The LORD, before whom I walk, will send his angel with thee, and prosper thy way; and thou shalt take a wife for my son of my kindred, and of my father's house:

41 Then shalt thou be clear from this my oath, when thou comest to my kindred; and if they give not thee one, thou shalt be clear from my oath.

42 And I came this day unto the well, and said, O LORD God of my master Abraham, if now thou do prosper my way which I go:

43 Behold, I stand by the well of water; and it shall come to pass, that when the virgin cometh forth to draw water, and I say to

her, Give me, I pray thee, a little water of thy pitcher to drink;

44 And she say to me, Both drink thou, and I will also draw for thy camels: let the same be the woman whom the LORD hath appointed out for my master's son.

45 And before I had done speaking in mine heart, behold, Rebekah came forth with her pitcher on her shoulder; and she went down unto the well, and drew water: and I said unto her, Let me drink, I pray thee.

· · · · · · · · · · ·

48 And I bowed down my head, and worshipped the LORD, and blessed the LORD God of my master Abraham, which had led me in the right way to take my master's brother's daughter unto his son.

---

GOLDEN TEXT: I bowed down my head, and worshipped the LORD, and blessed the LORD God of my master Abraham, which had led me in the right way to take my master's brother's daughter unto his son.—Genesis 24:48.

---

## God Creates
### Unit 1: God Creates a People
### (Lessons 1-5)

## Lesson Aims

After participating in this lesson, each student will be able to:

1. Tell how God continued the promises to Abraham by providing a wife for his son Isaac.

2. Use the story of Isaac and Rebekah to suggest how God may be guiding his or her life choices today.

3. Seek God's guidance in a particular area through prayer and obedience to His will.

## Lesson Outline

INTRODUCTION
    A. How to Choose a Spouse—or Not!
    B. Lesson Background
 I. MISSION EXPLAINED (Genesis 24:34-41)
    A. God's Blessings (vv. 34-36)
    B. Abraham's Desire (vv. 37, 38)
    C. Servant's Oath (vv. 39-41)
II. WOMAN IDENTIFIED (Genesis 24:42-45)
    A. Servant Sets Conditions (vv. 42-44)
    B. Conditions Are Met (v. 45)
      *Right Person, Right Place, Right Time*
III. GOD WORSHIPED (Genesis 24:48)
    A. Remembering God (v. 48a)
    B. Acknowledging Divine Leading (v. 48b)
      *Praising God in Good News and Bad*
CONCLUSION
    A. Hearing God's Voice, Accepting His Lead
    B. Prayer
    C. Thought to Remember

## Introduction

### A. How to Choose a Spouse—or Not!

When I was in graduate school, students were surprised when one of our classmates made plans to return to her home country rather suddenly. When asked what the reason was, she said, "My parents have found a husband for me, and I am going to marry!" She was very happy.

To us, this seemed strange. She had never met her future husband and had only a picture of him. Yet she trusted her parents and the process of arranged marriage. Thus she looked forward to becoming the wife of someone she did not know.

Arranged marriage is still practiced in some places in the world today, but it is becoming rarer. For example, all marriages in Japan were once arranged, but today this has slipped to no more than 10 percent. Western influences have convinced young people all over the world that they should be able to choose their own marriage partners and that marriage should be based on love, not the perceived standards of parents.

A key figure in some societies is the matchmaker, the marriage arranger. This person suggests marriage combinations that will be satisfying and successful. Ironically, a more recent variation of this is online matchmaking services. In this system men and women seeking marriage undergo testing to develop a personality profile. These profiles are matched by a computer, supposedly yielding a higher probability of compatibility. Therefore, we have come full circle and may be returning to arranged marriages, but with a machine doing the arranging rather than parents or tribal elders!

No matter what system is used, there is no "sure thing" when it comes to selecting a marriage partner. People change over time, and circumstances arise that can be allowed to destroy a commitment. The story of Isaac and Rebekah is the record of God's special provision for a blessed marriage. We should not expect God to control our marriage choices today at the same level. But the match of Isaac and Rebekah also involved their parents. Isaac was not left to wander around looking for a wife, dating and hoping. Abraham guided the process.

### B. Lesson Background

Sarah, Abraham's wife, died at age 127 (Genesis 23:1, 2). Since she was 90 years old when Isaac was born, we assume that Isaac was nearing age 40 when Abraham began the search for that son's future wife (25:20). Sarah's death probably caused Abraham to realize that his own passing was coming, and that he must see to the marriage of his son before it was out of his hands.

This week's lesson is about an arranged marriage that was crucial to the history of Israel. God's promise to Abraham was that he would be followed by many descendants (Genesis 12:2), and that one of those descendants would be a blessing to "all families of the earth" (Genesis 12:3). We know that this later "seed" of Abraham was Jesus Christ (Galatians 3:16). God had provided Abraham with Isaac. But there would be no descendants unless Isaac had a wife and they produced children. How that wife was provided is the focus of this lesson.

## I. Mission Explained
## (Genesis 24:34-41)

Abraham decided that Isaac should not marry a Canaanite woman (Genesis 24:3). The wisdom of this decision was borne out later in the Old Testament, for marriage to foreign women often resulted in the introduction of paganism into Israel (see Judges 3:6). That led to various disasters.

So in the first part of Genesis 24, Abraham directs a trusted servant to return to Abraham's kindred to find a wife for his son. This is not a small matter! The servant takes 10 camels loaded with goods and provisions for this lengthy trip of approximately 500 miles. When the servant leaves his master, Abraham probably does not expect him to return in less than a year.

The text tells us that the purpose of the journey is fulfilled relatively quickly, as the future wife of Isaac is identified and negotiations for her begin. She is Rebekah, the granddaughter of Abraham's brother Nahor (Genesis 24:15, 48). She is pictured as a beautiful, chaste, and obedient young woman, the perfect wife for Isaac (24:16-18).

We should pause to consider the importance of that name *Nahor.* This is both a personal name and a place name in Genesis. Nahor was the name of Abraham's grandfather (Genesis 11:23-26) and of his brother (11:27). While we know little about this brother, Genesis tells us that Nahor worshiped God as Abraham did (31:53). This means that Nahor and his family practiced the worship of one God as opposed to the worship of multiple gods of the Canaanites and other surrounding peoples. This was undoubtedly a central factor in Abraham's desire to find a wife for Isaac from his own family (24:1-4).

Nahor is also the name of a city in northern Mesopotamia (Genesis 24:10). Although the exact location of this city is unknown today, there is frequent mention of a city called *Nakhur* in the ancient Mari tablets (discovered in 1935, dated eighteenth century BC). This leads us to understand that the extended family of the Nahor clan is well known, prosperous, and influential in this region.

### A. God's Blessings (vv. 34-36)
**34. And he said, I am Abraham's servant.**

We do not know the name of this *servant.* Some believe it is Eliezer, mentioned as the steward of Abraham's household in Genesis 15:2. This reference to Eliezer, however, is 40 to 50 years prior to the text in front of us. It is thus likely that he has already died.

The unnamed servant of this story is probably in a similar position to Eliezer's, the senior servant (Genesis 24:2). He is presented as a person whom Abraham trusts without reservation. He is a man of prayer and integrity (see 24:12-14). He is speaking to Laban, Rebekah's brother, shortly after arriving at the town of Nahor (24:10, 11, 28-33).

**35. And the LORD hath blessed my master greatly; and he is become great: and he hath given him flocks, and herds, and silver, and gold, and menservants, and maidservants, and camels, and asses.**

Abraham's wealth is measured in the number of animals he owns, the number of servants he has, and the amount of precious metals he has accumulated. In all of these things, God has richly *blessed* Abraham. When the servant said that Abraham has *become great,* he means that he has become wealthy and recognized in his community (compare the description of Isaac's wealth in Genesis 26:14).

**36. And Sarah my master's wife bare a son to my master when she was old: and unto him hath he given all that he hath.**

Abraham's servant provides another important piece of information. Abraham has only one *son* considered to be an heir, and this son will inherit *all* of Abraham's wealth. This means that the servant is searching for a woman to marry a man who will be very wealthy when his father dies. The fact that Isaac was born in the time of *old* age of his parents implies that Isaac should receive his inheritance in the near future.

### B. Abraham's Desire (vv. 37, 38)
**37, 38. And my master made me swear, saying, Thou shalt not take a wife to my son of the daughters of the Canaanites, in whose land I dwell: but thou shalt go unto my father's house, and to my kindred, and take a wife unto my son.**

Although Abraham has prospered in the land *of the Canaanites,* he has been unwilling to assimilate into their culture. This is largely a religious

---

### How to Say It

ABRAHAM. *Ay*-bruh-ham.
CANAANITE. *Kay*-nun-ite.
ELIEZER. El-ih-*ee*-zer.
ISAAC. *Eye*-zuk.
LABAN. *Lay*-bun.
MESOPOTAMIA. *Mes*-uh-puh-*tay*-me-uh
    (strong accent on *tay*).
NAHOR. *Nay*-hor.
REBEKAH. Reh-*bek*-uh.

issue. Abraham and his family have a tradition of worship of the one true God. The Canaanite people, on the other hand, practice fertility cults. These involve ritual, temple prostitution and other abominations to the Lord. The conquest of the promised land of Canaan that occurs later, as described in the book of Joshua, indicates that such abominations are still being practiced in Canaan long after Abraham's time (compare Deuteronomy 7:22-26). [See question #1, page 48.]

### C. Servant's Oath (vv. 39-41)

**39, 40. And I said unto my master, Peradventure the woman will not follow me. And he said unto me, The LORD, before whom I walk, will send his angel with thee, and prosper thy way; and thou shalt take a wife for my son of my kindred, and of my father's house.**

The servant is frank about the providential circumstances surrounding this quest for *a wife*. Abraham has lived by faith his entire life (see Hebrews 11:8, 9, 17). The servant has carried out his master's will confidently, believing that God's *angel* has prepared his *way*.

**41. Then shalt thou be clear from this my oath, when thou comest to my kindred; and if they give not thee one, thou shalt be clear from my oath.**

The servant is also practical in his negotiations. He does not know what type of reception he will receive from Abraham's kin. They may not be open to sending one of their young women away with an unexpected stranger. If this happens, then the servant's obligation is fulfilled, and he is set free from his *oath* to Abraham.

## II. Woman Identified (Genesis 24:42-45)

Abraham's servant now recounts for Laban the events that have just happened. The story the servant tells about how he encountered Rebekah must sound very strange to those listening. It seems strange to us too, unless we understand the ways of God. God's promise to Abraham requires that Isaac become a father, and God is ensuring that this will happen.

### A. Servant Sets Conditions (vv. 42-44)

**42. And I came this day unto the well, and said, O LORD God of my master Abraham, if now thou do prosper my way which I go.**

The long journey of Abraham's servant ended at *the well* that is mentioned in Genesis 24:11. There the servant expected to meet a suitable woman, as women are the ones who come to draw water. The servant did not leave this to his own discernment, however, but prayed to *God* for the right match.

**43, 44. Behold, I stand by the well of water; and it shall come to pass, that when the virgin cometh forth to draw water, and I say to her, Give me, I pray thee, a little water of thy pitcher to drink; and she say to me, Both drink thou, and I will also draw for thy camels: let the same be the woman whom the LORD hath appointed out for my master's son.**

The servant was looking for a young, unmarried woman, all of whom normally would be virgins in that culture. The servant had devised a little test for any woman who might come to *the well*. He wanted to see if he could find a *woman* who would be willing to show generous hospitality to a stranger.

To pass the test, however, she needed to go beyond the bare minimum of giving a *drink* to the thirsty man. Abraham's servant wanted someone who would volunteer to lift enough *water* out of the well to satisfy his entire entourage (Genesis 24:14). [See question #2, page 48.]

This is many gallons for thirsty *camels*! It is estimated that a camel can drink 25 gallons of water in a few minutes. The woman the servant wanted thus would be committing herself to hoisting perhaps 200 to 250 gallons of water out of the well. At one or two gallons a dip, this would be a commitment to raising and lowering her pitcher for an hour or more.

### B. Conditions Are Met (v. 45)

**45. And before I had done speaking in mine heart, behold, Rebekah came forth with her pitcher on her shoulder; and she went down unto the well, and drew water: and I said unto her, Let me drink, I pray thee.**

Abraham's servant had come much too far not to carry out his plan. Even though he had arrived at a new place and knew no one, he boldly had proceeded to ask *Rebekah* for a *drink*. She responded just as he envisaged. Now he knows that God has directed him to the right woman to be Isaac's wife. [See question #3, page 48.]

RIGHT PERSON, RIGHT PLACE, RIGHT TIME

Which statement do you think has greater validity: "The times make the person" or "The person makes the times"? Sometimes it's hard to tell. Sometimes it's a little of both as one reinforces the other.

Take the case of Rosa Parks. It was December 1, 1955, in Montgomery, Alabama, when she refused to give up her seat on a bus to a white man. She was African-American, and she was tired of the injustices inflicted on people of her race through segregation laws.

Parks was arrested, convicted, and fined. In response, African-Americans boycotted the bus system for 381 days. In 1956, the U.S. Supreme Court banned segregation on public transportation. Parks was just a private person trying to better the lot of her people in a small way. But that day she was the proverbial "right person in the right place at the right time." History was made because of it.

When Abraham's servant approached the well in Nahor, he met a young woman who would do what she could under the circumstances that confronted her. As a result, Rebekah's name has become known to devout people ever since.

The text doesn't tell us how aware Rebekah may have been of God's leading, but she did what was right in the circumstance. As such, she became a vital link of the blessings that come to us today from the God of Abraham, Isaac, and Jacob. What small thing will you do today that may set in motions ripples through history?    —C. R. B.

## III. God Worshiped
## (Genesis 24:48)

In Genesis 24:46, 47 (not in today's text), Abraham's servant recounts Rebekah's generosity. The servant is able to taste success for his long mission! God has blessed his efforts and has granted the desires of Abraham.

### A. Remembering God (v. 48a)

**48a. And I bowed down my head, and worshipped the LORD, and blessed the LORD God of my master Abraham.**

Abraham's servant continues to recount the events that have just happened. It is curious that the servant does not say that he approaches God as his own Lord, but as *the Lord God of my master Abraham*. This shows that while he is confident, capable, and entrusted with a large, expensive expedition, he is still a humble, devoted man. As he begins to see Abraham's quest fulfilled, he takes joy for his master. His first impulse is to thank God for the success.

We can certainly learn a lesson from this. Prayer is every bit as appropriate in our times of victory and success as in our times of desperation and need. [See question #4, page 48.]

### B. Acknowledging Divine Leading (v. 48b)

**48b. Which had led me in the right way to take my master's brother's daughter unto his son.**

### Chronology of Genesis
*From the Call of Abraham to the Death of Joseph*

| | | |
|---|---|---|
| 2167 BC | Abram born | |
| 2092 BC | Call of Abram | Genesis 12:1-5 |
| 2081 BC | Ishmael born (Lesson 4) | Genesis 16:15, 16 |
| 2067 BC | Isaac born (Lesson 5) | Genesis 21:1-3 |
| 2050 BC | Abraham offers Isaac | Genesis 22:1-19 |
| 2007 BC | Jacob and Esau born (Lesson 6) | Genesis 25:24-26 |
| 1992 BC | Abraham dies at age 175 | Genesis 25:7 |
| 1930 BC | Jacob flees to Haran (Lesson 7) | Genesis 28:10 |
| 1916 BC | Joseph born | Genesis 30:22-24 |
| 1899 BC | Joseph sold into slavery in Egypt at age 17 (Lesson 10) | Genesis 37:2, 28 |
| 1887 BC | Isaac dies at age 180 | Genesis 35:28 |
| 1886 BC | At age 30, Joseph interprets Pharaoh's dream (Lesson 11) | Genesis 41:46 |
| 1877 BC | Jacob goes to Egypt *Beginning of the Israelites' 430-year stay in Egypt (Exodus 12:40, 41), leading to the exodus in 1447 BC (Lesson 12)* | Genesis 46:5, 6 |
| 1860 BC | Jacob dies at age 147 (Lesson 13) | Genesis 47:28 |
| 1806 BC | Joseph dies at age 110 | Genesis 50:26 |

Visual for Lesson 5

*Keep this chart posted all quarter to give your learners a chronological perspective.*

The servant does not take credit for the success. He understands that he has been *led* to Rebekah. While we may take this for granted, we can feel a sense of wonder at what has been accomplished. Abraham has been largely out of touch with his relatives "back in the old country." He took a risk in sending his servant to reconnect with his family and find a wife for Isaac.

This mission could have been thwarted in many ways. The servant could have run away with the camels and their precious loads, and Abraham never would have been able to find him. The caravan could have been attacked by bandits and wiped out. The servant might have been unable to find Abraham's kin in the vast territory of Mesopotamia. The servant could have schemed and conspired with a woman to pose as the right kind of wife for Isaac, thus deceiving Abraham.

Finding Rebekah is something along the lines of finding the proverbial needle in a haystack. From a human standpoint, the odds that this quest would be successful must have been very low. Yet God, who always keeps His promises, works to ensure Isaac gets the right wife. God thus ensures that the line of Abraham will be continued through the birth of God's Son, Jesus Christ. [See question #5, page 48.]

PRAISING GOD IN GOOD NEWS AND BAD

On January 2, 2006, an explosion in a coal mine near Sago, West Virginia, trapped 13 miners deep underground. The eyes of the world had been on the situation for nearly two days when the first hint of good news came at 11:50 PM on January 3.

CNN cautiously reported that 12 miners had been found alive. CNN then reported that news as fact some 15 minutes later. Newspapers started printing their morning editions with the good news. The headline of the *Atlanta Journal Constitution* was typical: "Miracle in Mine." As church bells rang, the families waiting at the Sago Baptist Church that night changed their prayers from petition to thanksgiving. They began singing praise songs.

Three hours later the thanksgiving and praise turned to anger when news arrived of a miscommunication. Only one miner was alive. We can understand the feelings of those relatives and friends whose hearts were torn by that terrible mistake in communication.

It's easy to praise God when the news is good. Abraham's servant demonstrated this fact as he praised God for the way his quest was concluded. This is not hard to understand. But the real test of our faith in God is when the news is bad. What do we say then? Can we still thank God for His care even when things do not go the way we want?       —C. R. B.

## Conclusion

### A. Hearing God's Voice, Accepting His Lead

Many believers have thought that life's decisions would be simpler if they could just hear an audible word from God telling them what to do. If only God were like a magic mirror on the wall, which could speak directly into our situation and unambiguously tell us what to do!

But if God were to speak this way, would we listen and heed His voice? We all have been given solid advice by our parents that we ig-

nored. As acts of rebellion and as assertions of independence we shunned this advice.

God has given us loads of "advice" in the form of His Word, the Holy Scriptures. Yet we often disregard this form of divine guidance and think that our way is better. This is to our detriment and loss. We learn hard lessons. We come back to God, ask for forgiveness, and admit that His ways are best for us. Do we really believe that an audible voice of God would keep us from ignoring His direction? On the contrary, just as we heard Mother's warnings and still did the wrong thing, we would be found guilty of disobeying God's direct, personalized counsel.

This has bearing when it comes to finding a marriage partner. It is unrealistic to expect a return to a system of arranged marriages today, but we can learn from this process. The young person would be well served to trust the opinions of his or her parents and other wise family members. The parents would be prudent to consider the best interests and happiness of their son or daughter before they attempt to veto a potential partner.

And all sides would be sensible to act as people of faith, praying fervently for God's guidance and blessing. For parents, such prayer should begin when the son or daughter is very young. That will make it more likely that a pending marriage will be the cause of great celebration and joy, as it was for the servant of Abraham in this lesson.

God's Word should be the guide to the one seeking a spouse and to the parents who provide counsel. While we should not expect to hear God's voice pointing us to marriage partners, we can easily use God's standards to "narrow the field," so to speak (see 1 Corinthians 7; 2 Corinthians 6:14). We can pray persistently that God will lead us to the right person. We can ask others to pray for us. And in all things, whether married or unmarried, we can resolve to be used by God and be joyful in His service.

### B. Prayer

Ageless and timeless God, You are always faithful and merciful. We acknowledge that You guide Your people if they follow Your lead. We know that You will never abandon us if we trust in You.

May we be resolved to seek Your will and follow Your paths in all our decisions, small or great. We pray this in the name of the author of our salvation, Jesus Christ, amen.

### C. Thought to Remember

God still wants to guide our decisions.

## Home Daily Bible Readings

**Monday, Sept. 24**—Wanted: A Wife (Genesis 24:1-9)

**Tuesday, Sept. 25**—A Drink for the Camels (Genesis 24:10-21)

**Wednesday, Sept. 26**—The Daughter of Bethuel (Genesis 24:22-27)

**Thursday, Sept. 27**—A Show of Hospitality (Genesis 24:28-32)

**Friday, Sept. 28**—The Errand (Genesis 24: 33-41)

**Saturday, Sept. 29**—A Wife for Isaac (Genesis 24:42-51)

**Sunday, Sept. 30**—God's Steadfast Love (Psalm 100)

# Learning by Doing

*This page contains an alternative lesson plan emphasizing learning activities.*
*Classes desiring such student involvement will find these suggestions helpful.*

## Into the Lesson

Decorate your learning space with wedding reception items such as bells and flowers. Offer wedding cake as learners arrive. Have a "Congratulations" banner displayed.

If your budget allows, send wedding invitations to class members prior to class. One of your learners may enjoy creating these invitations on his or her computer. Consider using an e-mail chain if your class has one set up.

Use today's lesson text for the information on the invitation: bride and groom's parents' names, bride and groom's names, location (your classroom), and time (class time and date). For a bit of humor, add the note, "Sheep and goat gifts only, please."

## Into the Word

As learners walk into class, give each a slip labeled either "bride" or "groom"; in this light, have learners sit either on the "bride" or "groom" side of the classroom, as their slips indicate. Then say, "Today's story is of an arranged marriage between families hundreds of camel-miles apart. What made the marriage untypical was the fact that God was the matchmaker. It was He who intervened and enabled the marriage.

"Nevertheless, there had to be certain qualms, anxieties, and questions for the parents of both Isaac and Rebekah. You have a slip that identifies which perspective I want you to ponder. Here's your task: ask questions you think may well have been in the minds of the parents you are 'thinking for.' I'll write them down as we go. Begin by reading through the entirety of today's lesson text."

Write on the board the headings "Bride's Parents" and "Groom's Parents" to prepare for a two-column list. If groups need examples to get them started, give these: For the bride's parents, "Will we ever see our daughter again?" For the groom's parents, "Will my servant actually bring a bride back?" (If you use the student books, you will find other questions listed there as examples.)

Tell your learners that the questions do not necessarily need biblically precise answers. Learners are free to use their "sanctified imaginations" as long their answers are consistent with human emotions.

Allow a brief time for discussion as you add each item to your two-column list. At an appropriate point, caution your learners that we should not expect God to intervene in our lives in the same way that He did for Isaac. Say, "Isaac had a critical, unique role to play in God's plan to redeem the world through Abraham's lineage. But if you look at how God was able to intervene in the life of Isaac to accomplish God's will, you may see that God has the power to work in your life as well, if you allow Him."

Next ask, "How do you see God guiding your own life choices?" If responses come slowly, offer such stimulus questions as, "How may God's hand have been at work in leading you to the job you now have?" "How have you seen God answer your prayers for direction in a specific matter?" "How do your prayers reflect the fact that you are inadequate for some tasks and must depend on God's power and grace?"

Let class members respond freely. Their witness to one another here may have the same effect the servant's testimony had on Rebekah and her family: conviction!

## Into Life

Display the phrase, "My next big decision is . . ." Ask your learners to finish that idea, either audibly or in their own minds. Suggest that they ponder such areas as family, job, health, service, and finances. After allowing a moment or two for learners to ponder this issue, dramatically edit your phrase to read, "God's role in my next big decision is . . ." Say, "We are not always careful to consider how God is involved. Look at Abraham's confidence that his decision was being guided by God. Abraham's confidence even rubbed off on his servant."

Provide each learner with a strip of paper 1" wide by 8" long. Ask class members to write on their strips the phrase, "God's role in my next big decision," leaving an exaggerated space between the words *in* and *my*. Make one yourself and then demonstrate a point by holding the strip in view of all and tearing it slowly between the *in* and *my*. Say, "Every decision is made with God either attached or detached. Which will it be for you? Take the slip with you to help you think about your next big decision."

# Let's Talk It Over

*The questions on this page are designed to promote discussion of the lesson by the class and to encourage application of the lesson Scriptures. The answers provided are only discussion starters. Let your class talk it over from there.*

**1. Isaac was not to marry outside of his culture, his people. How can this ancient principle speak to the people of God today, if at all?**

Christians are to marry those who are spiritually related through the blood of Christ. Second Corinthians 6:14 exhorts Christians, "Be ye not unequally yoked together with unbelievers: for what fellowship hath righteousness with unrighteousness? and what communion hath light with darkness?" Although the passage was not necessarily written with marriage in view, the principle is valid in that context. There is no greater "yoking together" of people than marriage!

Some Christians violate this principle, thinking that they will influence the unbeliever for Christ. Too often it is the Christian who is influenced away from Christ by the unbeliever. Teaching this principle is vital for the youth in the church.

**2. What can we learn from the prayer of Abraham's servant that can apply to the way we pray?**

Abraham's servant made a very specific prayer to God for guidance in the task he was called to do. Often our own prayers are very general in nature. We make requests such as, "Lord, keep all of our troops in Iraq safe," or, "Lord, bless all the missionaries." But greater specificity in our prayer life demonstrates to God greater concern, deeper thought, and passion on our part. He wants to hear the specific requests, praises, and pleas of His people.

Instead of praying for "all the sick," we can maintain prayer lists and lift these people by name before God. The same should be true of prayers we offer for those outside of Christ. God honors the faithful prayers of His people (James 5:16; 1 Peter 3:12).

**3. What are some ways to respond when God answers our prayers?**

We can be very long on asking God for things, yet very short on thanking God when He provides! We may even live as if we are responsible for what we receive. Sometimes when God grants a blessing to us, we consider it a coincidence, with no thanks offered to God.

Humility and praise is to mark the prayer life of the Christian. A helpful way to be sure God gets the praise is to maintain a journal in which you write out the things for which you pray. Then you can go back through the journal on a regular basis to see how God has answered your prayers. This will prompt you to thank God for His goodness.

**4. What lessons for Christian servanthood do we learn from the servant of Abraham?**

The first thing the servant does is to bow his head, which is a sign of humility. When we receive blessings from God, it is a time of celebration. But it is also a time for humility. We do not deserve God's provisions, especially in the abundance with which He gives them.

In his state of humility, Abraham's servant worshiped the Lord. In our case, perhaps the first thing we do to celebrate our victories is to have a big party—a promotion party for a job, a housewarming for a new house, etc. Abraham himself hosted a great feast after the birth of Isaac (Genesis 21:8). Yet undoubtedly a heartfelt bowing in quiet praise is the best initial response.

The servant also expressed an attitude of "others first" in his response. He was filled with joy for his master, Abraham. When we realize that it is not "all about me," we will see the benefit others receive from the blessings of God. We can rejoice with them and for them.

**5. In what ways do you need to honor God for His personal leading in your life?**

God never leaves His children. Instead, He always leads them. One of the most popular passages in all of Scripture is Psalm 23, which reminds us of the leading of God. He leads beside the quiet waters and even through the valley of the shadow of death.

As God led the children of Israel through their 40 years of wandering in the desert, so He leads us through our wilderness experiences of life. Our difficult times may be financial crises, rebellious children, job loss, or death of loved ones. Through all of these times, God continues faithfully to lead His people. Our task is to be faithful followers.

# Esau and Jacob as Rivals

DEVOTIONAL READING: 1 Corinthians 1:26-31.

BACKGROUND SCRIPTURE: Genesis 25:19-34.

PRINTED TEXT: Genesis 25:19-34.

**Oct 7**

### Genesis 25:19-34

19 And these are the generations of Isaac, Abraham's son: Abraham begat Isaac:

20 And Isaac was forty years old when he took Rebekah to wife, the daughter of Beth-uel the Syrian of Padan-aram, the sister to Laban the Syrian.

21 And Isaac entreated the LORD for his wife, because she was barren: and the LORD was entreated of him, and Rebekah his wife conceived.

22 And the children struggled together within her; and she said, If it be so, why am I thus? And she went to inquire of the LORD.

23 And the LORD said unto her, Two nations are in thy womb, and two manner of people shall be separated from thy bowels; and the one people shall be stronger than the other people; and the elder shall serve the younger.

24 And when her days to be delivered were fulfilled, behold, there were twins in her womb.

25 And the first came out red, all over like a hairy garment; and they called his name Esau.

26 And after that came his brother out, and his hand took hold on Esau's heel; and his name was called Jacob: and Isaac was three-score years old when she bare them.

27 And the boys grew: and Esau was a cunning hunter, a man of the field; and Jacob was a plain man, dwelling in tents.

28 And Isaac loved Esau, because he did eat of his venison: but Rebekah loved Jacob.

29 And Jacob sod pottage: and Esau came from the field, and he was faint:

30 And Esau said to Jacob, Feed me, I pray thee, with that same red pottage; for I am faint: therefore was his name called Edom.

31 And Jacob said, Sell me this day thy birthright.

32 And Esau said, Behold, I am at the point to die: and what profit shall this birthright do to me?

33 And Jacob said, Swear to me this day; and he sware unto him: and he sold his birthright unto Jacob.

34 Then Jacob gave Esau bread and pottage of lentils; and he did eat and drink, and rose up, and went his way. Thus Esau despised his birthright.

---

GOLDEN TEXT: The LORD said unto her, Two nations are in thy womb, and two manner of people shall be separated from thy bowels; and the one people shall be stronger than the other people; and the elder shall serve the younger.—Genesis 25:23.

## God Creates
### Unit 2: God's People Increase
### (Lessons 6-9)

## Lesson Aims

After participating in this lesson, each student will be able to:

1. Describe the early rivalry between Jacob and Esau.

2. Compare and contrast the rivalry between Jacob and Esau with rivalries within families and/or churches today.

3. Create a plan for his or her church to help people recognize and defuse destructive tensions that threaten families and/or the church.

## Lesson Outline

INTRODUCTION
  A. Sibling Rivalry
  B. Lesson Background
 I. SIBLINGS STRUGGLE BEFORE BIRTH (Genesis 25:19-26)
  A. Family Background (vv. 19, 20)
  B. Barren Wife (v. 21)
  C. Inquiry of the Lord (vv. 22, 23)
    *Differing Personalities*
  D. Birth of Twin Sons (vv. 24-26)
 II. SIBLINGS STRUGGLE AFTER BIRTH (Genesis 25: 27-34)
  A. Differences (v. 27)
  B. Preferences (v. 28)
  C. Disdainfulness (vv. 29-34)
    *Instant Gratification*
CONCLUSION
  A. Rivalry, God's Choice, and Consequences
  B. Prayer
  C. Thought to Remember

## Introduction

### A. Sibling Rivalry

I have a sister who is one year and one month younger than I. We were bitter rivals growing up. One might say we fought like cats and dogs! There were no holds barred.

As we grew to be teenagers, I could no longer physically fight my sister, but we continued our battles with our tongues. I felt that Dad preferred my sister; I received several punishments for things I never did.

However, there was one time my sister took my side. I climbed a tree after being told not to, and then I fell and nearly killed myself. I had actually broken my left arm close to the shoulder. I asked my sister not to tell Mom or Dad lest I receive certain punishment. She obliged and "protected" me, helping me hide my broken arm for two weeks. The pain became unbearable, and I had to reveal my predicament.

When I finally confessed, I was taken to the doctor. Despite the fact that my sister went along with my request, I think she enjoyed my agony more than ever. The rivalry persisted even when one was doing the other a favor; each was gleeful at the other's suffering. Such is sibling rivalry.

### B. Lesson Background

Today's lesson is the opening story of the struggle between close relatives—Jacob and Esau, the twin sons of Isaac. We should not be surprised to read of such a struggle, because Genesis records similar animosities leading up to today's text: between brothers Cain and Abel (4:1-16); within Noah's family (9:18-27); between Abraham and Lot, his nephew (chapter 13); and between half-brothers Ishmael and Isaac (chapters 16, 17, 21). This kind of rivalry did not cease with Esau and Jacob, but continued among Jacob's sons, namely Joseph and his brothers (chapters 37–50).

Barrenness is also part of our lesson's background. This was a key issue for the story of Abraham and Sarah, as we saw previously. Only God was able to open Rebekah's womb, but not as she expected or perhaps wanted!

Isaac and Rebekah were living somewhere near Beer-lahai-roi (translation: "well of the living one who sees me"; Genesis 25:11). This was between Kadesh and Bered, somewhere south of Beersheba in the Negev (see Genesis 16:14).

## I. Siblings Struggle Before Birth (Genesis 25:19-26)

### A. Family Background (vv. 19, 20)

**19. And these are the generations of Isaac, Abraham's son: Abraham begat Isaac.**

The word *generations* (or the singular *generation*) describes an important framework. If a narrative follows, this word is best understood as "account," "family history," or perhaps "story." If a genealogical list follows, the word is best understood as "descendants."

After the initial introduction of creation in Genesis 1:1–2:3, there are ten generations given. These are the heavens and the earth (Genesis

2:4–4:26), Adam (5:1–6:8), Noah (6:9–9:29), Ham and Japheth (10:1–11:9), Shem (11:10-26), Terah (11:27–25:11), Ishmael (25:12-18), Isaac (25:19–35:29), Esau (36:1–37:1), and Jacob (37:2–50:26). We note that the rest of Genesis is taken up with the stories of Esau and Jacob in this regard, primarily with the latter.

The phrase *these are the generations of Isaac, Abraham's son* is the title of the eighth of these generational segments in Genesis. The next phrase is so abrupt as to be somewhat amusing: *Abraham begat Isaac.* He certainly did, but not without great agony, fretting, and even laughter (Genesis 15:2; 16:1-4; 17:17; 18:12-15).

In fact, *Isaac* means "he laughs" in Hebrew. We could say that the conception and birth of Isaac revealed God's sense of humor to the world: only a sovereign God could bring about this birth, because Abraham and Sarah were 100 and 90 years old, respectively, when Isaac was born (Genesis 17:17; 21:5)!

**20. And Isaac was forty years old when he took Rebekah to wife, the daughter of Bethuel the Syrian of Padan-aram, the sister to Laban the Syrian.**

Verse 20 gives us more family background. The mention of *Laban* provides hints at the future adventures of Jacob, who will be one of Isaac's sons. The fact that the text informs us that Isaac is *forty years old* when he marries *Rebekah* implies the unusual lateness of Isaac's marriage.

Rebekah, for her part, is *the daughter of Bethuel;* he is a son of Nahor, a brother to Abraham (Genesis 22:20-24; 24:15). Laban is Rebekah's brother, a *Syrian* (or Aramean). That family lives in *Padan-aram,* located in northwest Meso-

potamia (part of modern-day Syria). The name *Padan-aram* means "Plain of Aram" (see Genesis 28:2-7; 31:18; 35:9, 26; 46:15).

### B. Barren Wife (v. 21)

**21. And Isaac entreated the LORD for his wife, because she was barren: and the LORD was entreated of him, and Rebekah his wife conceived.**

A *barren* wife is socially despised in ancient times (compare 1 Samuel 1:1-7; Psalm 113:9; Isaiah 54:1). Yet great men are born to mothers who previously had been barren and were desperate for God's help (see Judges 13:2-5 regarding Samson and 1 Samuel 1:11 regarding Samuel the prophet).

The original text suggests a very strong request by stating the verb in two forms: *Isaac entreated the Lord* and *the Lord was entreated of him.* God is willing to listen to the entreaty and thus respond to it. The answer follows: *and Rebekah his wife conceived.* Only by God's will and purpose are the sons—soon to be known as Jacob and Esau—begotten.

On the surface it seems that God answers Isaac's prayer of supplication immediately. But one must remember that Isaac and Rebekah have been married 20 years by this point (compare Genesis 25:26b with 25:20). Couples in ancient times usually expect children very soon after marriage; thus Isaac and Rebekah have been anticipating children for some 20 years!

Isaac's plea to God thus may cover a rather long period of time—perhaps 15 or more years of pleading. This should teach us to wait on God and be content in His timing. The prayers are answered. God's sovereignty over His creation and creatures is demonstrated in this conception. [See question #1, page 56.]

### C. Inquiry of the Lord (vv. 22, 23)

**22. And the children struggled together within her; and she said, If it be so, why am I thus? And she went to inquire of the LORD.**

In this case there are twins—surely unexpected. Just as the case of Isaac brought the laughters of disbelief and joy, so now Rebekah is overwhelmed with the struggle going on within her *womb!* She is happy for the pregnancy but disturbed about the turmoil within.

The Hebrew word for *struggle* usually comes with the idea "to oppress, crush, suppress, smash." The form of the Hebrew in this text means "to struggle together," that is, to kick and shove one another. Rebekah is concerned about what is happening to her: *If it be so, why am I*

---

### How to Say It

ABRAHAM. *Ay*-bruh-ham.
ADONIJAH. Ad-o-*nye*-juh.
ARAMEAN. *Ar*-uh-*me*-un (strong accent on *me*).
BEER-LAHAI-ROI. *Bee*-er-luh-*hi*-roy (strong accent on *hi*).
BEERSHEBA. Beer-*she*-buh.
BETHUEL. Beh-*thew*-el.
EPHRAIM. *Ee*-fray-im.
JAPHETH. *Jay*-feth.
LABAN. *Lay*-bun.
MANASSEH. Muh-*nass*-uh.
MESOPOTAMIA. *Mes*-uh-puh-*tay*-me-uh (strong accent on *tay*).
PADAN-ARAM. *Pay*-dan-*a*-ram.
REUBEN. *Roo*-ben.

*thus?* Just as Isaac had turned to Yahweh God because of his wife's barrenness, so now Rebekah turns to Yahweh God concerning her difficult pregnancy. So she makes an inquiry *of the Lord.* [See question #2, page 56.]

Exactly how and where she does this we do not know. The use of mechanical means, such as the priest's Urim and Thummim for *yes* or *no* answers, is not yet available (see Exodus 28:30). There is no mention of a prophet, priest, or angel to deliver the message. Yet God does respond. As God answered Isaac's prayer, so now He answers Rebekah's inquiry.

**23. And the LORD said unto her, Two nations are in thy womb, and two manner of people shall be separated from thy bowels; and the one people shall be stronger than the other people; and the elder shall serve the younger.**

Verse 23 lays out the answer in poetic form. The response addresses the destiny of the sons as *nations,* one to be *stronger than the other.* The statement *the elder shall serve the younger* suggests that it is the younger who will be the stronger, but not necessarily. At this point, it is possible that the stronger, elder son will indeed serve the weaker, younger son. However, as nations later on, the stronger will be Israel/Judah over the weaker Edom. These are the two nations at issue.

Variations of the theme *the elder shall serve the younger* are found throughout Genesis. Note the Lord's acceptance of Abel over Cain (Genesis 4:4, 5), Isaac over Ishmael (17:17-21), Joseph over his brothers (37:5-11), Ephraim over Manasseh (48:17-20), and Judah over Reuben (49:3, 4, 8-10). We could add David over his older brothers (1 Samuel 16:1-13) and Solomon over Adonijah (2 Samuel 3:2-5; 1 Kings 1).

"The law of primogeniture" is in effect at this time, and Moses will articulate it more fully centuries later (Deuteronomy 21:15-17). This law requires that every father give his firstborn son a double share as an inheritance. This double share is in line with the eldest son's responsibilities as the family's new patriarch. Yet at times God seems to delight in reversals. Consider that the "first shall be last; and the last shall be first" (Matthew 19:30). God has a specific purpose in mind when He notes that *the elder shall serve the younger* (see Romans 9:10-12).

### DIFFERING PERSONALITIES

Nicola and Stuart Richardson tried for six years to have children. Fertility treatments finally succeeded. At seven weeks a nurse saw two heartbeats on the ultrasound scan. After further scanning, the nurse told Nicola that she could see *four* heartbeats! On January 21, 2002, Nicola gave birth to three boys and a girl. The children have personalities that differ from one another. As their mother describes them, Harry is active, Matthew loves music, Ben charms everyone with his smile, and Anna is content to play alone.

The Richardsons discovered what every parent of more than one child knows: children are different! Rebekah certainly was aware of this, even before her children were born. Her alarm at the struggles of her preborn babies was so great that she felt compelled to ask God, *Why?* The Lord explained the situation in terms of her sons' future relationship with each other, including the lives of their descendants.

Parents today should not expect direct revelations from God concerning their children's future or their relationships with one another. The parents' task is to recognize differing personalities as a fact of life, then shape those personalities so God may be glorified in their lives.   —C. R. B.

### D. Birth of Twin Sons (vv. 24-26)

**24. And when her days to be delivered were fulfilled, behold, there were twins in her womb.**

The story is narrated as if it is a surprise to Rebekah when she discovers she has *twins in her womb.* The surprise is indicated by the use of the word *behold.*

**25. And the first came out red, all over like a hairy garment; and they called his name Esau.**

But the fact that she is bearing twins is not the only surprise. These boys are as different as night and day—they are definitely not identical twins! The first son born comes out *red* (which sounds like *Edom* in the Hebrew). His appearance is somehow *like a hairy garment.* The parents name him *Esau,* which sounds like the word for *hairy,* though it does not mean the same. Thus, Esau is named for his appearance (compare Genesis 25:30; 36:1, 8).

**26. And after that came his brother out, and his hand took hold on Esau's heel; and his name was called Jacob: and Isaac was threescore years old when she bare them.**

While one son is named for his appearance, the other is named for his action: *his hand* takes *hold* of *Esau's heel.* The name *Jacob* sounds like the word *heel* in Hebrew. The verb form means "to defraud." It carries the idea of sneaking up behind someone to betray, hamper, hinder, or even supplant. Figuratively, it means "to deceive." This "heel grabber" will be a deceiver who himself will often be deceived (see Genesis 27:36; 29:25; 31:7, 26, 27).

Jacob will indeed live up to his name. Jacob's pattern of deceit will cause conflict. These brothers are in conflict even before birth. Conflict will follow them and their descendants. [See question #3, page 56.]

## II. Siblings Struggle After Birth (Genesis 25:27-34)

### A. Differences (v. 27)

**27. And the boys grew: and Esau was a cunning hunter, a man of the field; and Jacob was a plain man, dwelling in tents.**

*Esau* and *Jacob* are not only born in conflict, they live in conflict. One indication is their differing occupations; this difference ties in to parental preferences (see below). Esau becomes *a cunning hunter, a man of the field*. He loves the outdoors, especially the hunting of wild game. He certainly looks the part, having a hairy body and perhaps a reddish color to either his hair or skin or both.

By contrast, Jacob is not a man of the fields. He is, rather, *a plain man, dwelling in tents*. The word *plain* used to describe Jacob probably means "complete" or "self-contained." Thus he is able to live quietly and self-sufficiently. Perhaps he follows the herds as he dwells in the tents. [See question #4, page 56.]

### B. Preferences (v. 28)

**28. And Isaac loved Esau, because he did eat of his venison: but Rebekah loved Jacob.**

Not only are the boys different in abilities and interests, they are also treated differently by their parents. *Isaac* loves *Esau* for his ability to provide wild game (*venison*) from the countryside. Apparently this is the main reason Isaac prefers Esau. *Rebekah*, on the other hand, prefers *Jacob*, but no reason is given. Rebekah may have God's response of Genesis 25:23 in mind as she sides with the younger son.

Psychologically, all this makes for a profound difference in the ways the boys react to circumstances and life in general. Such preferential treatment is bound to cause ongoing conflict within the family. And it does.

### C. Disdainfulness (vv. 29-34)

**29, 30. And Jacob sod pottage: and Esau came from the field, and he was faint: and Esau said to Jacob, Feed me, I pray thee, with that same red pottage; for I am faint: therefore was his name called Edom.**

It is ironic that a mighty hunter would come in from the field famished and weak. Yet, there

Visual for Lesson 6. *Use this visual to start a discussion on conflict resolution. Ask, "What's a good first step to take toward resolving conflicts?"*

*Esau* stands, vulnerable before his brother, who apparently has been preparing a stew of lentils that looks *red* (see v. 34, below).

As we have already noted, Esau was "red" when he was born; now he begs for some "red" stuff. Thus, his descendants will be called *Edom*, which means "red." These words look and sound alike in Hebrew. The play on words emphasizes the foolishness of Esau's action (see Hebrews 12:16, 17).

**31. And Jacob said, Sell me this day thy birthright.**

*Jacob* takes advantage of his brother's vulnerability and immediately tells him what he wants in exchange for the soup: *Sell me this day thy birthright*. No "please" or "I pray thee," just the outright desire of the birthright.

**32. And Esau said, Behold, I am at the point to die: and what profit shall this birthright do to me?**

There is no doubt that Esau greatly exaggerates his own condition of being *at the point* of death. But haven't we all said at some time, "I am so hungry I could die" or "I'm dying of thirst"? The point is that Esau despises his birthright as firstborn in order to gratify an immediate felt need of hunger

**33, 34. And Jacob said, Swear to me this day; and he sware unto him: and he sold his birthright unto Jacob. Then Jacob gave Esau bread and pottage of lentils; and he did eat and drink, and rose up, and went his way. Thus Esau despised his birthright.**

*Jacob* makes *Esau* swear an oath, thus securing the *birthright* permanently. The older is beginning to serve the younger!

Before bringing our lesson to a conclusion, it is useful to pause and consider verses 29-34 as a whole. The story is told in an "X-shaped" manner to emphasize the fact in the middle statement. The flow goes something like this, with statement D in that important middle position:

$A^1$: *Esau came from the field* (v. 29).
  $B^1$: *Feed me . . . with that . . . pottage* (v. 30).
    $C^1$: *Sell me . . . thy birthright* (v. 31).
      D: *I am at the point to die:*
        *and what profit shall this*
        *birthright do to me?* (v. 32).
    $C^2$: *He sold his birthright* (v. 33).
  $B^2$: *Esau . . . did eat and drink* (v. 34a).
$A^2$: *[Esau] rose up, and went his way* (v. 34b).

Notice that statements $A^1$ and $A^2$ are similar or parallel to each other in a certain way. The same is true for statements $B^1$ and $B^2$ as well as statements $C^1$ and $C^2$. So what does the middle statement D emphasize? The foolish logic people can use to talk themselves into doing the dumbest things! [See question #5, page 56.]

### INSTANT GRATIFICATION

Too bad Esau didn't live in the twenty-first century! When his brother demanded that high price for a bowl of soup, Esau merely could have gunned his SUV down to the ATM, grabbed a quick $40, then gone around the corner to the McTaco-in-the-Box drive-up window. He thus could have satisfied his hunger in a couple of minutes with little fuss and bother.

But on second thought, that hypothetical sequence still may may not have been fast enough for Esau. Think about your computer. In the last two decades, processing speed has increased exponentially. Yet which of us hasn't complained when it doesn't respond as rapidly as we wish?

This mind-set affects us even at church. Some churches have started putting the Sunday sermons on CDs, but to have to wait for a week to pick it up has become too tedious. So some churches now have the CDs ready as churchgoers walk out the door!

Movie actress Carrie Fisher sarcastically noted that "instant gratification takes too long." Esau is an easy target for his impatience as well as his deeper problem: his willingness to trade something of long-term value for the instant gratification of his need for food. But in this way Esau is a very modern person. How often in the past month have you trapped yourself with this same immature attitude? —C. R. B.

# Conclusion

## A. Rivalry, God's Choice, and Consequences

The rivalry between Jacob and Esau yielded bitter fruit for many years. Their two peoples (the Israelites and the Edomites) would forever be known as enemies (see 1 Samuel 14:47, 48; 2 Samuel 8:13, 14; Jeremiah 49:7-22; Ezekiel 25:12-14; 35; Obadiah; Malachi 1:2-5).

But today's story is really about God's choice —His purpose and will being worked out through the life of a young man who was chosen in spite of himself. The deceiver would be deceived often enough that one day he would learn how to struggle not only with others but with God and prevail (Genesis 32:28). The consequences would change his name (*Jacob* to *Israel*) and his life forever.

Sometimes when God chooses a person, it may not be pleasant—it may be for a life of struggle rather than one of contentment. God sees to it that we all must struggle with Him before we can make a significant contribution to His kingdom.

Incidentally, my sister and I have reconciled our bitter rivalry from years past.

### B. Prayer

O Sovereign Lord, may Your purposes and will for us be realized in spite of our weaknesses and desires. Teach us to desire Your will above all felt needs that beg for instant gratification. Lead us to resolve all conflicts within our families as well as within our church families to Your honor and glory. In Christ's name, amen.

### C. Thought to Remember

Struggles today can yield much fruit tomorrow
—either good or rotten.

---

## Home Daily Bible Readings

**Monday, Oct. 1**—God Chose the Least (1 Corinthians 1:26-31)
**Tuesday, Oct. 2**—Rebekah Agrees to Marry Isaac (Genesis 24:50-61)
**Wednesday, Oct. 3**—Isaac Takes Rebekah as His Wife (Genesis 24:62-67)
**Thursday, Oct. 4**—Rebekah's Twins Struggle in the Womb (Genesis 25:19-23)
**Friday, Oct. 5**—The Birth of Jacob and Esau (Genesis 25:24-28)
**Saturday, Oct. 6**—Esau Sells His Birthright (Genesis 25:29-34)
**Sunday, Oct. 7**—Esau's Lost Blessing (Genesis 27:30-40)

# Learning by Doing

*This page contains an alternative lesson plan emphasizing learning activities.*
*Classes desiring such student involvement will find these suggestions helpful.*

## Into the Lesson

Display this fictitious word and its definition as class begins: "sibble (*verb*, 2007): to quibble with a sibling over who is 'number one.'"

Introduce two men (whom you have recruited in advance) to present the following dual monologues representing Jacob and Esau. With a bit of dramatic flair, say, "Now here are Jacob and Esau, the siblings who sibble."

Give your two actors copies of the following script ahead of time to allow each to become familiar with it. Explain the process to them: simply alternating lines, as given.

ESAU: Mother always did like my brother best.
JACOB: Father always did like my brother best.
ESAU: Mine was the birthright; I *was* born first.
JACOB: Mine was the birthright . . . by hook or by crook.
ESAU: I became a manly man, a hunter. Un-h-h!
JACOB: I was a bit of a Mama's boy, hanging around the tent.
ESAU: Well, we were twins, but we didn't look alike. They called me the hairy one. And we certainly didn't act the same.
JACOB: Well, we were twins, but we hardly acted like twins . . . or looked like twins. My brother's red hair set him apart.
ESAU: I was a man of food. I loved to eat meat from the animals I hunted, as did my father!
JACOB: I was the sensitive one. I learned to cook from my mother. My specialty was bean soup.
ESAU: We were special children, conceived by God's grace. It's simply that I was more special than my brother. Just ask Dad.
JACOB: We were special children, born by God's intervention, just as our father had been. It's simply that God wanted me to be the leader.
ESAU: Did not! JACOB: Did too! ESAU: Did not!
JACOB: Did too! ESAU: Did not! JACOB: Did too!

Interrupt your actors, and ask them to be seated. They can continue to growl and snipe at one another as they are seated.

## Into the Word

Because today's study is about family division and rivalry, designate half of your class as *US* and the other half as *THEM*. (Simply draw an invisible line down the middle.) Say, "In this next activity it's going to be '*Us* versus *Them*,' so hold your animosities and your elbows in! We don't want this to turn into a 'Jacob versus Esau' conflict."

Give the learners time to read through today's text in Genesis 25:19-26. Then say, "The US group can answer my questions with a word or phrase beginning with either *U* or *S*. The THEM group can answer my questions with a word or phrase beginning with either *TH* or *EM*."

Alternate asking the following questions to US and THEM. Keep score, as an additional source of group rivalry. Give questions one and two as samples. Award points for reasonable answers that are not listed within parentheses.

1. US, what was Rebekah's relationship to Laban? *(sister)*; 2. THEM, how old was Isaac when he married? *(thirty plus ten)*; 3. US, how do you suppose Isaac and Rebekah felt about being childless after 20 years of marriage? *(sad, unhappy)*; 4. THEM, how could one characterize the lengthy state of Rebekah's womb? *(empty)*; 5. US, how does God characterize the "one people" in Rebekah's womb in relationship to the other? *(stronger)*; 6. THEM, which of the two does God say will serve the other? *(the elder)*; 7. US, what does the word *behold* in verse 24 imply? *(surprise)*; 8. THEM, how old was Isaac when the twins were born? *(threescore)*; 9. US, how might one describe Esau's newborn appearance? *(unusual)*; 10. THEM, what's another word that could be used to describe the boys' birth other than "came out"? *(emerged)*; 11. US, what kind of hunter was Esau? *(skillful)*; 12. THEM, rather than describe Jacob as plain or quiet, how else might one characterize him? *(thoughtful)*; 13. US, how might you say the parents loved the boys? *(unequally)*; 14. THEM, how could you characterize Esau's claim he was close to death? *(theatric)*.

## Into Life

Tell your learners that you want them to suggest principles of "A Parenting Curriculum." It will note elements that must be a part of an effective parenting course of study to be offered by the church. Of course, they will want to consider the successes and mistakes of Isaac and Rebekah. Once you have the list, pass it along to church leadership for consideration. Perhaps your class can sponsor and/or lead such a class.

# Let's Talk It Over

*The questions on this page are designed to promote discussion of the lesson by the class and to encourage application of the lesson Scriptures. The answers provided are only discussion starters. Let your class talk it over from there.*

**1. What are some ways that people react when God delays granting answers to prayers that they know are in His will? How can we comfort people during those times?**

There are things we know are God's will because of what is written in Scripture, yet they may not come to pass in a (to us) timely manner. That situation is much like what happened when Isaac and Rebekah were unable to have a child. For them to have a child was God's will because it was to be through Isaac that the Abrahamic covenant was to be fulfilled.

Some situations call for perseverance in prayer (Luke 18:1-8). It is during these times that the Lord may be teaching us patience and trust. To fret and fuss may only intensify the sense of delay as God continues to try to work His will in our lives. Delays in the answers also demonstrate to us that we are not in charge; life events do not always take place on our timetables.

**2. What are some areas in your life where you have questioned God because of your own frustrations and uncertainties? Where did your questioning lead you?**

There are times in our lives when God does not seem to be a just God. In our families, as in Isaac's family, there are struggles. We know God's desire is for families to be united in Him, yet it often does not seem to happen.

We may feel that if we have faithfully prayed for the needs in our families, then everything should go well. But this is not the reality. In bad times we can remember that families in the Bible and throughout history have had difficulties. As much as it rests with us individually, we can keep the peace and remain faithful. But we also realize that others, even those within our families, are responsible for their own walks of faith. And sometimes they will walk away from God.

**3. What is the meaning and significance of your name? Should you care? Why, or why not?**

Names in the Bible often have meanings. *Moses* means "to draw out"—a reminder that he was drawn out of the water as a baby. From a previous lesson, we remember that *Isaac* refers to laughter—a reminder of Sarah's reaction.

You can easily look up the meaning of your own name on the Internet. But few pay much attention to those meanings. Rare are the parents, for example, who would name their baby girl *Susan* because a Web site said that *Susan* means "lily," and that's the meaning they were after.

Much more important is the name we gain when we are born into the family of God. That name is *Christian*. It is a family name, meaning we are "of Christ." Wearing this name challenges us to consider how Jesus would have us respond to situations in life. Wearing this name means we do not live for self but for Christ.

**4. What family principles do we learn from the differences between Esau and Jacob?**

Two children of the same parents growing up in the same environment can be totally different. Children are not "blank slates" that merely take on the personalities of their parents.

This is true not only in families, but in the church as well. Being born again through the blood of Jesus Christ makes us brothers and sisters in the family of God. But we are different. God has given us differing spiritual gifts and abilities (see 1 Corinthians 12:4-7). There is nothing wrong with such differences. In fact, there are benefits in them (1 Corinthians 12:12-31). Just as we don't force our children all to be the same, so in the church we respect the diversity of gifts and abilities. In so doing, we allow God to use each of us differently for His glory.

**5. Christians sell their spiritual birthright when they turn from God and go back to their former, sinful way of life (see Galatians 4:8-11; 2 Peter 2:20). Was there a time when you were in danger of "selling" your Christian birthright? What corrective measures did you take?**

Christians, by definition, are born again in Christ. Failing to heed God's Word puts us in danger of selling out (compare 2 Chronicles 36:16). We maintain our spiritual birthright when we seek God's kingdom first (see Matthew 6:33). Applying that principle in daily situations can be quite a challenge! One key is to avoid being a "lone ranger" Christian. We draw strength from one another.

# Jacob's Dream at Bethel

DEVOTIONAL READING: Psalm 105:1-11.

BACKGROUND SCRIPTURE: Genesis 27:41–28:22.

PRINTED TEXT: Genesis 28:10-22.

### Genesis 28:10-22

10 And Jacob went out from Beer-sheba, and went toward Haran.

11 And he lighted upon a certain place, and tarried there all night, because the sun was set; and he took of the stones of that place, and put them for his pillows, and lay down in that place to sleep.

12 And he dreamed, and behold a ladder set up on the earth, and the top of it reached to heaven: and behold the angels of God ascending and descending on it.

13 And, behold, the LORD stood above it, and said, I am the LORD God of Abraham thy father, and the God of Isaac: the land whereon thou liest, to thee will I give it, and to thy seed;

14 And thy seed shall be as the dust of the earth; and thou shalt spread abroad to the west, and to the east, and to the north, and to the south: and in thee and in thy seed shall all the families of the earth be blessed.

15 And, behold, I am with thee, and will keep thee in all places whither thou goest, and will bring thee again into this land; for I will not leave thee, until I have done that which I have spoken to thee of.

16 And Jacob awaked out of his sleep, and he said, Surely the LORD is in this place; and I knew it not.

17 And he was afraid, and said, How dreadful is this place! this is none other but the house of God, and this is the gate of heaven.

18 And Jacob rose up early in the morning, and took the stone that he had put for his pillows, and set it up for a pillar, and poured oil upon the top of it.

19 And he called the name of that place Beth-el: but the name of that city was called Luz at the first.

20 And Jacob vowed a vow, saying, If God will be with me, and will keep me in this way that I go, and will give me bread to eat, and raiment to put on,

21 So that I come again to my father's house in peace; then shall the LORD be my God:

22 And this stone, which I have set for a pillar, shall be God's house: and of all that thou shalt give me I will surely give the tenth unto thee.

---

GOLDEN TEXT: Behold, I am with thee, and will keep thee in all places whither thou goest, and will bring thee again into this land; for I will not leave thee, until I have done that which I have spoken to thee of.—Genesis 28:15.

## *God Creates*
### Unit 2: God's People Increase
### (Lessons 6-9)

## Lesson Aims

After participating in this lesson, each student will be able to:

1. Recount the contents of Jacob's dream and his reaction to it.

2. Compare and contrast Jacob's dream with "normal" dreams.

3. Explain how he or she will be sensitive to God's leading, balancing clear direction from Scripture with analysis of external circumstances.

## Lesson Outline

INTRODUCTION
  A. Second-Generation Believers
  B. Lesson Background
I. JACOB'S JOURNEY (Genesis 28:10, 11)
  A. Heading Toward Haran (v. 10)
  B. Layover in Luz (v. 11)
    *"Nowhere"*
II. JACOB'S DREAM (Genesis 28:12-15)
  A. What Jacob Sees (v. 12)
  B. What God Says (vv. 13-15)
III. JACOB'S RESPONSE (Genesis 28:16-22)
  A. With Awe (vv. 16, 17)
  B. With a Memorial (vv. 18, 19)
    *Remembering*
  C. With a Vow (vv. 20-22)
CONCLUSION
  A. Responding to God's Promises
  B. Prayer
  C. Thought to Remember

## Introduction

### A. Second-Generation Believers

Many of us have been challenged by evangelistic sermons claiming that "Christianity is only one generation from extinction." By this, preachers usually mean no one is automatically born a believer. Although many people have been brought up in Christian homes, this favorable environment is not enough to make one a Christian. At some point each person must respond to the gospel through personal decision, not the decision of the parents. This is why Christians must spread the good news to the next generation.

Our Jewish forefathers also had to make personal decisions. Abraham accepted God's call, Isaac accepted God's call, and in today's passage even Jacob—the deceiver—is invited to continue the faith of his father and grandfather. How does his response apply to us today?

### B. Lesson Background

Isaac and Rebekah had been living prosperously in Beer-sheba since Isaac made peace with the Philistines (Genesis 26). Like her mother-in-law Sarah, Rebekah was unable to conceive. So God intervened to keep the promise alive. Unlike her mother-in-law, however, Rebekah gave birth to twin sons. This complicated matters since only one son could be the child of promise.

God foretold that Jacob was to be that child, but Jacob did not wait patiently for God to fulfill this prophecy. Instead, he lived up to (or down to!) his name, which can mean "heel-grabber": he manipulated his brother into surrendering his birthright, and he deceived his father in order to get the blessing that was intended for Esau.

Esau, of course, was furious about his brother's deception—so much so that he plotted to kill him as Cain did Abel. Aware of these plans, Rebekah arranged for Jacob to escape his brother's fury and marry a woman from Abraham's kin. It was important that the child of promise maintain a pure bloodline by not marrying a Canaanite. So Jacob went to Haran, the hometown of Rebekah's brother Laban.

## I. Jacob's Journey
## (Genesis 28:10, 11)

### A. Heading Toward Haran (v. 10)

**10. And Jacob went out from Beer-sheba, and went toward Haran.**

*Haran* is located north of the promised land, approximately 550 miles from Jacob's home in *Beer-sheba*. This puts plenty of needed distance between Jacob and his brother's wrath, but it is also a risky move in light of family history.

In Genesis 11:31 we are told that Abraham's father, Terah, left his homeland of Ur of the Chaldees with the intention of arriving in Canaan, the land of promise. Was he called by God to do this? We know that God was recognized as Terah's God (Genesis 31:53), yet Terah also worshiped false gods (Joshua 24:2). The Bible is silent about why he set out for Canaan and why Terah did not complete the trip. He went as far as Haran (about 600 miles northwest of Ur) and settled there. It was up to his son Abram (later renamed Abraham) to finish what he had begun.

Perhaps Abraham remembered his father's failure. So when arranging a wife for his son Isaac, Abraham deliberately sent his servant—not Isaac personally—to Haran to find a wife (Genesis 24:6-8; see Lesson 5). This move ensured that Isaac would not be tempted to stay in Haran as his grandfather had. Rebekah, on the other hand, could not afford to keep her son Jacob nearby. The threat posed by Esau was too great; so Jacob's risky journey began.

### B. Layover in Luz (v. 11)

**11. And he lighted upon a certain place, and tarried there all night, because the sun was set; and he took of the stones of that place, and put them for his pillows, and lay down in that place to sleep.**

Jacob at this point is about 60 miles into his journey. He has run out of sunlight and thus stops for the *night*. We learn in verse 19 that this *certain place* is called *Luz*, a region located 20 miles northwest of the Dead Sea.

What is most notable about this place is that it is *not* noteworthy. Other travelers in Jacob's day may intentionally set up camp near a temple or other holy place in hopes of gaining the favor of their god(s). Jacob, on the other hand, stops at no place in particular. This underscores the fact that Jacob does not attempt to engineer or manipulate the divine blessing he is about to receive, as was the case with the blessing he received in dealing with Esau. The revelation he is about to receive is entirely due to God's gracious initiative.

Christians need to hear this message today. We have not been instructed to orchestrate a divine word from God. It is not a matter of praying the right prayer, meditating the right way, or assuming the right bodily posture. God is not like a vending machine that yields goods automatically when we push the right buttons.

Instead, God speaks to whom He will, when He will, and how He will. In Scripture God sometimes reveals himself to those who have petitioned Him with fervent prayer and fasting, but often He does so when humans least expect it. [See question #1, page 64.]

#### "Nowhere"

"Where are you going?" "Nowhere."
"What are you going to do?" "Nothing."
"Whom are you going to do it with?" "Nobody."

That conversation (or a variation of it) has taken place countless times between parents and teens. Actually, there are lots of places that can be classified as *nowhere* or *nowhere in particular.* As one moves westward across the North Ameri-

can continent, one can find vast expanses of prairie and desert that qualify as *nowhere.*

Even places that used to be *somewhere* are now *nowhere.* Towns that were once thriving now may be hanging on by a thread; or they may have turned into ghost towns, slowly disintegrating as sun and weather beat upon them.

The place where Jacob stopped was *nowhere*—just a convenient place to sleep. But God met him there. We may think that the great experiences of life must happen in special places. Yet such events often happen in ordinary places that become special because of what happens there. Wherever we meet God is somewhere special! That's what Jacob came to discover.      —C. R. B.

## II. Jacob's Dream (Genesis 28:12-15)
### A. What Jacob Sees (v. 12)

**12. And he dreamed, and behold a ladder set up on the earth, and the top of it reached to heaven: and behold the angels of God ascending and descending on it.**

While sleeping, Jacob dreams of *a ladder* that spans the gap between *heaven* and *earth.* This ladder is not there, however, for Jacob to climb. The one who reached to grab his brother's heel, his brother's birthright, and his father's blessing will not climb this ladder to reach and grab God.

Neither will God descend to meet Jacob face to face. Only God's *angels* ascend and descend. God is above; Jacob remains on earth. There is a necessary gap between the two. This distance may be for Jacob's protection, or God may simply be teaching him a lesson about holiness.

### B. What God Says (vv. 13-15)

**13a. And, behold, the LORD stood above it, and said, I am the LORD God of Abraham thy father, and the God of Isaac.**

God's speech to Jacob is a monologue. Jacob is not invited to converse with God; he is required to hear what God has to say.

God says three things. First, God introduces himself as the *God of Abraham* and *Isaac.* Will He be Jacob's God as well? At this point, it is not clear that Jacob will follow the footsteps of his fathers. The decision to find a wife from Abraham's kin is an important step in the right direction, but Jacob's journey is also driven by his desire to survive Esau's wrath. Yet the way that Jacob responds to this gracious initiative of God will be decisive for how many will come to know God: as the God of Abraham, Isaac, and Jacob (Exodus 3:15).

**13b, 14. The land whereon thou liest, to thee will I give it, and to thy seed; and thy seed shall be as the dust of the earth; and thou shalt spread abroad to the west, and to the east, and to the north, and to the south: and in thee and in thy seed shall all the families of the earth be blessed.**

Second, God affirms that the promise He made to Abraham and Isaac is now extended to Jacob. Using language similar to Genesis 13:14-16, God promises to give Jacob and his descendants the very land that Jacob is in the process of leaving, to multiply Jacob's offspring like *the dust of the earth*, to spread his family in all four directions, and to bless all the earth's *families* through them. [See question #2, page 64.] Despite Jacob's past, despite the threat to his life, and despite his self-imposed exile from the land of promise, God assures Jacob that he is indeed God's chosen man.

**15. And, behold, I am with thee, and will keep thee in all places whither thou goest, and will bring thee again into this land; for I will not leave thee, until I have done that which I have spoken to thee of.**

Third, God recognizes Jacob's insecurities as one heading for unfamiliar territory. Thus God commits to be *with* Jacob, to protect him in his travels, and to return him to the *land* of promise. [See question #3, page 64.]

## III. Jacob's Response (Genesis 28:16-22)

### A. With Awe (vv. 16, 17)

**16, 17. And Jacob awaked out of his sleep, and he said, Surely the LORD is in this place; and I knew it not. And he was afraid, and said, How**

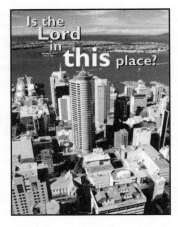

Visual for
Lesson 7

*Start a discussion by asking, "How do you associate God's presence with the places you frequent?"*

**dreadful is this place! this is none other but the house of God, and this is the gate of heaven.**

Abraham and Isaac each had a chance to obey. Now it is Jacob's turn. How will he respond?

Upon waking from his dream, Jacob reacts to God's threefold speech with a threefold affirmation: (1) *the Lord is in this place*, (2) *this is none other but the house of God*, and (3) *this is the gate of heaven*. We will point out the importance of each of these three below. An important fact to be noticed at this point is that Jacob's threefold affirmation is couched in fear. He had gone to sleep on common turf, but he awakens on holy ground.

Although God's message to Jacob is full of comfort, the awe-inspiring nature of the vision also sounds a clear message: God is no human to be trifled with or manipulated. He stands on high with angels to do His bidding. God proclaims His word; humans must listen and respond. This recognition on Jacob's part is vital in his development as God's man, the man of the promise.

In our day of undisciplined speech about God, we need to be reminded of the healthy fear exemplified by our forefathers in the faith. Men like Jacob, Moses, Elijah, Isaiah, Ezekiel, and Daniel truly respected God's awe-inspiring presence. God is still a consuming fire (Hebrews 12:28, 29). The apostle Paul deems it appropriate to describe God as dwelling in unapproachable light, unable to be seen with human eyes (1 Timothy 6:15, 16). [See question #4, page 64.]

### B. With a Memorial (vv. 18, 19)

**18. And Jacob rose up early in the morning, and took the stone that he had put for his pillows, and set it up for a pillar, and poured oil upon the top of it.**

Rather than immediately resuming his journey, Jacob lingers to commemorate the place where God has met him. He selects the *stone* that functioned as his pillow, sets it upright, and anoints it with *oil*. We should not associate this act with idol worship, as if Jacob believes the stone itself possesses magical, dream-inducing powers. Such a practice will later be condemned as detestable to God (Deuteronomy 16:22).

We should view this instead as an act of reverence, an acknowledgement that Jacob has received God's message loud and clear. Anointing with oil is a common way to set apart particular persons or objects in ancient times. By anointing kings, priests, altars, and garments, the Israelites who come after Jacob will set apart people and things for service on behalf of the one true God.

So Jacob does not regard this rock as special in and of itself. Rather, he considers this particular place to be sacred because God has chosen it for His unique purposes. It is God who gives it meaning—a meaning that Jacob wishes never to forget. This is part one of Jacob's threefold response.

It is fitting for Jacob to use a stone for this purpose. In ancient times, stones serve as witnesses to agreements between parties, especially agreements concerning property boundaries. Years later Jacob will erect another stone to commemorate a boundary agreement between himself and his future father-in-law (Genesis 31:46-53). In setting up this first stone, Jacob may be communicating to God that he accepts God's will for his life, including the boundary lines to the land that God has promised to Jacob's descendants.

### REMEMBERING

Sixteen million U.S. citizens served in America's armed forces during World War II. More than 400,000 of them died.

Surprisingly, it took nearly 60 years for a monument to be built in Washington, D.C., to honor those who served in what has been called "the defining event of the twentieth century." Nevertheless, there is now a monument for those who fought in that war. These were common people called upon to make uncommon sacrifices and save the world from tyranny.

Erecting memorials is nothing new. This practice is seen in many cultures of many eras. Centuries ago, Jacob erected a stone memorial as a tribute to the God who turned his life in a new direction. Most war memorials today are constructed at sites far removed from where the events they commemorate took place. Not so with Jacob; he raised his stone at the very site where his life took its turn. It was a reminder of Jacob's vow that his life would be different from that point onward.

Today, God has already done the work of setting up "spiritual remembrance stones," if we can use that terminology. The Lord's Supper provides a frequent reminder of the work of Christ. Baptism is a tangible reminder of a person's decisive turn toward Him. How do you use these two "spiritual remembrance stones" to draw ever closer to Him?                                    —C. R. B.

**19. And he called the name of that place Beth-el: but the name of that city was called Luz at the first.**

In parallel with the second part of Jacob's threefold affirmation of verses 16, 17, he renames Luz to be Beth-el. The new name means "house of God."

### How to Say It
ABRAHAM. *Ay*-bruh-ham.
BEER-SHEBA. Beer-*she*-buh.
BETH-EL. *Beth*-ul.
CANAAN. *Kay*-nun.
CHALDEES. *Kal*-deez.
ESAU. *Ee*-saw.
HARAN. *Hair*-un.
LABAN. *Lay*-bun.
LUZ. Luzz.
TERAH. *Tair*-uh.
UR. Er.

The name sticks. Future Israelites will remember its significance. Even God, when He later reappears to Jacob, identifies himself as "the God of Beth-el" (Genesis 31:13).

Unfortunately, not all future Israelites will learn the lesson that Jacob learns there. Instead, they will set up idols and establish Bethel as a worship center to compete with Jerusalem. This will gain for Bethel a reputation of transgression (1 Kings 12:28-32; Hosea 10:15; Amos 4:4). How easy it is for later generations to forget! The fear is lost, the awe subsides, and another gift to God degenerates into an agent of idolatry.

### C. With a Vow (vv. 20-22)

**20-22. And Jacob vowed a vow, saying, If God will be with me, and will keep me in this way that I go, and will give me bread to eat, and raiment to put on, so that I come again to my father's house in peace; then shall the LORD be my God: and this stone, which I have set for a pillar, shall be God's house: and of all that thou shalt give me I will surely give the tenth unto thee.**

Jacob's *vow* is part three of his threefold affirmation of verses 16, 17. This vow may be interpreted in a wholly positive or somewhat negative way. Positively, we notice that Jacob officially accepts his father's God as his own and pledges to *give* Him a *tenth* of all he will acquire, as Abraham did (Genesis 14:18-20). Negatively, Jacob seems to place conditions on his allegiance, saying *if* God does what He has promised (and more), then Jacob will worship Him.

We see Jacob specifying the elements of food and clothing along with God's already generous offer of continued blessing. One could construe Jacob's response as a desire to turn God's gracious gift—which is meant to be accepted and appreciated on God's terms—into a negotiation, with two parties jockeying for position.

Such jockeying, if that is indeed what is going on here, would hark back to Jacob's strained relations with Esau and would point forward to Jacob's strained relations with Laban. Indeed, God's later encounter with Jacob will be that of a wrestling match, after which Jacob is renamed *Israel*, meaning "one who wrestles with God."

So—is Jacob's vow the initial round of that wrestling match? Or is it a promising start to a committed, though imperfect, relationship? When Jacob finally arrives at his destination, God certainly uses Laban to teach Jacob a much-needed lesson about Jacob's cunning ways. But should we see that lesson as a response to Jacob's former life before Bethel or to his entire life, including his desire to strike a deal at Bethel?

It is not necessary for us to answer such questions with full confidence. But it is helpful to consider possible answers in light of God's future reflection on the Bethel encounter. Many years later, when it is time for Jacob to leave Haran and return home, God will remind Jacob of the vow he made and the rock he anointed at Bethel (Genesis 31:13). This will remind Jacob of a time of hope and a symbol of promises made and things to be fulfilled. So while it is possible to see Jacob's conditional vow as a symptom of flawed character, one may also see it as a turning point in his life. It is a time when he not only accepts God's gracious invitation but also takes concrete steps to apply it to his own situation.

Today we don't expect direct revelations from God in dreams. Even so, many Christians have had "Bethel-like moments." These are times when God awakens us to His claim upon our lives. Can you identify moments like this in your own life? [See question #5, page 64.]

## Home Daily Bible Readings

**Monday, Oct. 8**—Remember God's Works (Psalm 105:1-6)

**Tuesday, Oct. 9**—An Everlasting Covenant (Psalm 105:7-11)

**Wednesday, Oct. 10**—The Conflict Deepens (Genesis 27:41-45)

**Thursday, Oct. 11**—To Seek a Wife (Genesis 27:46—28:5)

**Friday, Oct. 12**—Esau Takes Another Wife (Genesis 28:6-9)

**Saturday, Oct. 13**—God's Covenant with Jacob (Genesis 28:10-17)

**Sunday, Oct. 14**—The Place Named Bethel (Genesis 28:18-22)

# Conclusion

## A. Responding to God's Promises

Jacob was born into an important family that was chosen by God to do great things. Jacob knew from an early age that the day would come when he would be called to continue his family's legacy. Yet Jacob was far from perfect. At his best he listened, waited, and obeyed. At his worst he tried to force events along paths of his own choosing via human ingenuity and deceit.

Yet God was able to work through Jacob's worst moments. God showed His love for Jacob at Bethel by extending to him a promise that he did nothing to deserve. Jacob could have responded in all sorts of negative ways. Instead, Jacob recognized that the call was from God and responded with that fact in view.

Through Jesus Christ our Lord, God's invitation to join the people of promise—the church—has been extended to all. It matters not whether we are male or female, slave or free, Jew or Gentile. It matters not whether we grew up in a solid Christian home, in a "Christmas-and-Easter-only" religious environment, or in the belly of paganism. It matters not whether we were a respectful youth, raucous teen, or greedy business person. God's invitation confronts us where we are, regardless of where we have been.

Our past cannot stand in for us, whether good deeds, ideal parents, or worldly achievements. God lays claim to our present life and calls us to an eternity with Him. Despite Jacob's imperfections, he responded to that call and took the necessary first step forward. God was certainly not finished working on him, but Jacob welcomed Him in to begin that work. So must we.

## B. Prayer

"O God of Bethel, by Whose hand / Thy people still are fed, / Who through this weary pilgrimage / Hast all our fathers led.

"Our vows, our prayers, we now present / Before Thy throne of grace; / God of our fathers, be the God / Of their succeeding race.

"Through each perplexing path of life / Our wandering footsteps guide; / Give us each day our daily bread / And raiment fit provide.

"O spread Thy covering wings around / Till all our wanderings cease, / And at our Father's loved abode / Our souls arrive in peace" (Philip Doddridge, 1737).

In Jesus' name, amen.

## C. Thought to Remember

Respond to God today.

# Learning by Doing

*This page contains an alternative lesson plan emphasizing learning activities. Classes desiring such student involvement will find these suggestions helpful.*

## Into the Lesson

Set up a 5' or 6' stepladder at the front of your class's space. On the rungs, set or attach the following objects: an EXIT sign, an angel figurine or doll, a pillow, a rock, a packet of seeds, a small replica of a crowd of people, a loaf of bread, a candle pillar/pedestal, a garment.

On the top step set a card that says, "Genesis 28:10-22." Say, "All the items here relate in some way to today's text. As the text is read, see whether you can make the associations."

## Into the Word

Recruit in advance one of your better readers to read the lesson text aloud. If possible, also recruit someone proficient in American Sign Language to sign the words as they are read; the text is graphically rich and will show itself well in signs.

After the reading, let your learners identify representations they see between the objects and the text. If there are any they cannot relate, use this list to help them: *EXIT sign,* verse 10 (as Jacob leaves his home); *pillow,* verse 11; *ladder,* verse 12; *angel figure,* verse 12; *seed,* verses 13b and 14 (Jacob's seed spread abroad); *crowd of people,* verse 17 (the house of God); *bread,* verse 20; *candle pillar/pedestal,* verse 22 (the stone pillar set up); *a garment,* verse 20 (expressing Jacob's trusting God for clothes).

Explain, "One basic principle of biblical interpretation is that we must not quickly generalize or spiritualize when reading a Bible story and seeing God's intervention. I am going to make several generalizations related to today's text. I want you to decide whether each generalization is justifiable. Give me your reasoning."

Read each of the following generalizations and allow learners to react positively or negatively. (The activity is included in the optional student book.) 1. Having godly grandparents and godly parents does not make one godly. 2. When God has a special revelation to give, He will give it to you personally in a dream. 3. Angels ascending and descending on a ladder is a picture of Jesus coming to earth. 4. The land of Israel, which Jacob was leaving, was given perpetually to Jacob's descendants. 5. God could speak no sweeter words to a person than "I am with thee, and will keep thee." 6. When one realizes that God is some-

how meeting him or her, it is both dreadful and delightful. 7. Setting up and dedicating a shrine to God is the right thing to do when one feels especially touched by Him. 8. It is OK to bargain with God in a "something for something" *(quid pro quo)* manner, as Jacob did. 9. Jacob's example of committing a tenth of all that he had to God is a validation of the tithe as the required expectation in Christian giving. 10. God's faithfulness to His promises is never in doubt; ours always is.

## Into Life

Say, "The instructions for the direction that our lives should take comes to us in a manner different from God's direction for Jacob. How does God give us direction and assurance for our lives?" Let learners respond, assuming they will mention the Scriptures' primary role, plus open and closed doors of opportunity as secondary.

Comment on the answers. Then say, "Jacob's revelation was a divine intervention that came to him in words and images. In what way or ways is God's revelation to us today similar and dissimilar?" Learners should take note of the priority of God's written Word.

Distribute copies of the following personal-response list (also included in the optional student book). Suggest that learners use it for a time of self-evaluation sometime in their devotional lives in the coming week.

* *Often I find myself running away, as Jacob did, from the consequences of my behavior.*
* *Sometimes my sleep is restless because of conflicts in my interpersonal relationships.*
* *I am always glad to receive reassurances from God's Word regarding my future.*
* *Occasionally, I act as if I were not aware of God's presence where I am.*
* *I need to establish a "pillar" that reminds me of God's presence and blessing.*
* *I need to think of every place as Bethel, the house of God.*
* *I have full confidence that God will provide my daily needs for food, clothing, and housing.*
* *I am committed to returning a significant portion of God's material blessings for use in the work of His kingdom.*

Close with a prayer for deeper commitment.

# Let's Talk It Over

*The questions on this page are designed to promote discussion of the lesson by the class and to encourage application of the lesson Scriptures. The answers provided are only discussion starters. Let your class talk it over from there.*

**1. How does Jacob's situation in verse 11 compare and contrast with the times we seek God in the comfort of our worship centers?**

When we enter a worship center or church sanctuary, we do so with the intent of seeking God. That's why we go there. But there is no indication that Jacob stopped at "a certain place" because he desired to find God there. Yet an encounter took place nonetheless!

As Jacob discovered, God is not necessarily encountered in comfortable surroundings or at our own initiative. We may think that it is easier to worship God in sanctuaries that have climate control, plush carpeting, and padded pews. But God is not bound by our comfort. It is in the uncomfortable situations of life that we may draw closest to God. Soldiers in foxholes know this. People lying in hospital beds know this. We shouldn't be surprised if God uses uncomfortable situations to draw us closer to Him, the God who comforts.

**2. What part will you and your church have in helping fulfill God's intent to bless the world?**

God blesses the world through His Son, but also through His people. It is God's people who fulfill the Great Commission of Matthew 28:19, 20. God sends out His church as a body, and Christians individually, to accomplish that work.

Instead of looking at the world and seeing it in all its corruption—and thereby seeking to avoid involvement in the world—we are to recognize our role of making a holy difference as we are wholly different. The corruption of the world is lessened as the church takes seriously its mission to go into the world and be a blessing to the world. This requires courage, faith, and conviction to implement on a Christian-by-Christian basis.

**3. What do we learn about God as He identifies himself in Genesis 28:13-15? How does this knowledge of God help us?**

God is spoken of as standing above. That is God's position. From this vantage point He sees all. We know we can never get out of God's sight (see Psalm 139:7-12). This can be both comforting and convicting: comforting in knowing that He is an ever-present help, but convicting as we know that He sees us as we sin.

As the God of Abraham and Isaac, we know that God is God of the past. He has always existed. His promise to Jacob to "keep thee in all places whither thou goest" means that God is God of the future as well. He is faithful never to leave nor neglect His children. It has been so for centuries without fail.

**4. Is Jacob's response to God's presence a model for us today? Why, or why not?**

Being in the presence of God should evoke a feeling of reverence and awe toward Him. That should never change! An old cliché is that "familiarity breeds contempt." Becoming comfortable and "familiar" with God may result in losing a sense of awe toward Him. Instead of fearing God, we may end up looking on Him as a kind of cosmic vending machine who meets whims.

We have seen much emphasis in recent years on the celebration of God's presence. This has manifested itself through worshiping Him with exuberance and abandon in worship assemblies. For balance, it may be good for us also to worship God in quietness and submission. One of the words for worship means, "to bow or prostrate oneself before another." Hopefully, we always do this in a spiritual sense; it can be appropriate to do this also in a physical sense in private or corporate worship.

**5. Do you have your own sacred place—your own, private Bethel—where you meet God on a regular basis? What is it like? If you don't have one, what can you do to set one up? Or should you let God take the initiative in this regard?**

We teach that God is not confined to a place. Christians may talk about the fact that they can worship God anywhere at anytime. Both of these observations are true. But it is not wrong to have that special place to meet God.

For some, the place where they go to meet God may be a kind of "prayer closet," either within a church building or at home. Others prefer an outdoor setting for their special place, perhaps a quiet spot on the porch, beside a lake, or in the woods.

# Jacob and Rachel

**DEVOTIONAL READING: Psalm 91.**

**BACKGROUND SCRIPTURE: Genesis 29.**

**PRINTED TEXT: Genesis 29:21-35.**

### Genesis 29:21-35

21 And Jacob said unto Laban, Give me my wife, for my days are fulfilled, that I may go in unto her.

22 And Laban gathered together all the men of the place, and made a feast.

23 And it came to pass in the evening, that he took Leah his daughter, and brought her to him; and he went in unto her.

24 And Laban gave unto his daughter Leah Zilpah his maid for a handmaid.

25 And it came to pass, that in the morning, behold, it was Leah: and he said to Laban, What is this thou hast done unto me? did not I serve with thee for Rachel? wherefore then hast thou beguiled me?

26 And Laban said, It must not be so done in our country, to give the younger before the firstborn.

27 Fulfil her week, and we will give thee this also for the service which thou shalt serve with me yet seven other years.

28 And Jacob did so, and fulfilled her week: and he gave him Rachel his daughter to wife also.

29 And Laban gave to Rachel his daughter Bilhah his handmaid to be her maid.

30 And he went in also unto Rachel, and he loved also Rachel more than Leah, and served with him yet seven other years.

31 And when the LORD saw that Leah was hated, he opened her womb: but Rachel was barren.

32 And Leah conceived, and bare a son; and she called his name Reuben: for she said, Surely the LORD hath looked upon my affliction; now therefore my husband will love me.

33 And she conceived again, and bare a son; and said, Because the LORD hath heard that I was hated, he hath therefore given me this son also: and she called his name Simeon.

34 And she conceived again, and bare a son; and said, Now this time will my husband be joined unto me, because I have borne him three sons: therefore was his name called Levi.

35 And she conceived again, and bare a son; and she said, Now will I praise the LORD: therefore she called his name Judah; and left bearing.

**Oct 21**

---

GOLDEN TEXT: Jacob served seven years for Rachel; and they seemed unto him but a few days, for the love he had to her.—Genesis 29:20.

---

*God Creates*

Unit 2: God's People Increase

(Lessons 6-9)

## Lesson Aims

After participating in this lesson, each student will be able to:

1. Describe Jacob's family life.

2. Compare and contrast marriage customs of Jacob's time with those of today.

3. Write a prayer committing some disappointing circumstance in life into God's hand and seeking guidance for dealing with the situation in a positive manner.

## Lesson Outline

INTRODUCTION

    A. Actions and Consequences

    B. Lesson Background

I. JACOB'S DECEPTION RETURNED (Genesis 29:21-27)

    A. Jacob's Intent (vv. 21, 22)

    B. Laban's Deception (vv. 23-25)

    *"It Served Him Right"*

    C. Laban's Justification (v. 26)

    *Bound by Tradition?*

    D. Laban's Concession (v. 27)

II. JACOB'S FAVORITISM BACKFIRES (Genesis 29:28-35)

    A. Laban's Action (vv. 28, 29)

    B. God's Intervention (vv. 30, 31)

    C. Leah's Sons (vv. 32-35)

CONCLUSION

    A. Learning from Divine Discipline

    B. Prayer

    C. Thought to Remember

## Introduction

### A. Actions and Consequences

If you want to spark an interesting discussion among Christians, ask people to share testimonies of discipline that may have been divine in origin. I have done this in various settings, and the results are both amusing and instructive.

The essential storyline often goes something like this: "When my coworkers, neighbors, or schoolmates engage in various 'low-profile' sins, whether speeding, shoplifting, or cheating on their taxes, they seldom get caught and often ap-

pear to benefit from their choices. For the most part, I resist such practices due to my faith and convictions. But the one time I decided to join their iniquity, I was caught red-handed and had to bear the shame."

I know this to be true in my own life. The one time I lied to my boss, I was exposed. The one time I joined my friends in an act of theft, we all got busted. The one time I drag-raced my buddies, the radar gun nailed me. It is not like I engaged in these activities all the time only to have my actions finally catch up with me. No, these were flukes. They were one-time acts of rebellion, and without fail, I never got away with them—and it's a good thing too!

Scripture teaches that God disciplines those whom He loves (Hebrews 12:5, 6). God loves us so much that He will not allow us to avoid consequences (immediately or eventually) when we tread sinful paths. We should not be alarmed when we do not escape cleanly from sinful endeavors. We should be deeply concerned, however, if we *do* continue to get away easily.

If discipline is a sign of divine love (and it often is), then God certainly loved Jacob. In today's lesson, God allows Jacob to suffer twice in order to straighten his crooked path.

### B. Lesson Background

Last week we saw God shower His grace on Jacob by meeting him at Bethel. There God extended the promise He had made to Jacob's grandfather Abraham. Despite Jacob's legacy of deception, God gave him the honor of being the father of the chosen people through whom God would bless all nations. Jacob accepted this offer. Then he continued his northward journey to escape Esau and to acquire a wife from his mother's household.

In Genesis 29 we learn that Jacob arrived safely in Haran and was graciously welcomed into the household of his uncle Laban. Since Jacob would be staying for a while, working arrangements had to be made. Jacob had fallen for Rachel, the younger and more attractive of Laban's two daughters. So he offered to work seven years in exchange for Rachel's hand in marriage. Typically, the groom was obligated to offer some kind of "bride price" to the bride's family. This would offset the work production the family would be losing by giving their daughter in marriage. In this case, seven years of labor was an agreeable arrangement to both parties, so a deal was made.

Jacob was so enamored with Rachel that the years seemed to fly by (Genesis 29:20). Jacob was then ready to claim his bride, pack his bags, and head back home to the promised land. Things could not have been going better for Jacob, but God was not finished with him. Jacob's character was about to be forged in the fire of divine discipline.

# I. Jacob's Deception Returned (Genesis 29:21-27)

## A. Jacob's Intent (vv. 21, 22)

**21. And Jacob said unto Laban, Give me my wife, for my days are fulfilled, that I may go in unto her.**

After Jacob's years of service pass, he seems to demand that his *wife* be given to him. There are at least three ways this abruptness may be understood. First, the author may be summarizing concisely what was actually a much more pleasant exchange. Second, *Jacob* may be showing his eagerness to finally consummate his long-awaited marriage. Third, Jacob's tone may reflect tension that has somehow arisen between him and *Laban.* Perhaps the two of them do not have a healthy working relationship. Whatever the case, the ruse that Laban is about to pull on Jacob certainly indicates that the relationship between the two is about to get worse!

Jacob calls Rachel his *wife* not simply because they are about to be married. In Jacob's day, a woman has the legal status of "wife" during the betrothal period.

**22. And Laban gathered together all the men of the place, and made a feast.**

Ancient Near Eastern weddings are not one-day events. They often involve a week of feasting, attended by the two families being brought together in the marriage.

There is no evidence to indicate that Jacob's family back in Canaan is able to attend the wedding or that they even know of the event. This is important. Were Isaac and Rebekah present,

Jacob would not be as vulnerable to the deception that Laban is plotting. Thus far, however, Jacob is oblivious to Laban's scheme.

## B. Laban's Deception (vv. 23-25)

**23. And it came to pass in the evening, that he took Leah his daughter, and brought her to him; and he went in unto her.**

How, we may wonder, is Laban able to pass off *Leah* for Rachel? Would not Jacob know the truth simply by looking at her?

Two factors may account for Jacob's oversight. The first factor is lighting—or lack thereof. We are told that Laban brought Leah to Jacob *in the evening.* In an age before electricity, the darkness of evening is much more pronounced than what we experience today.

The dim lighting is only compounded by the fact that women often wear veils on their wedding day. In Genesis 24:65 we see Rebekah (Laban's sister) veiling herself lest she be seen prematurely by her groom-to-be, Isaac.

**24. And Laban gave unto his daughter Leah Zilpah his maid for a handmaid.**

It is customary for parents, especially those who are wealthy, to give wedding gifts to their daughters. A *maid* is certainly a generous gift! This indicates that whatever tension may exist between Laban and Jacob, Laban still loves *his daughter* and seeks to bless her. Our introduction to *Zilpah* is important because Leah later gives her to Jacob for the purposes of bearing additional children (Genesis 30:9-13). Leah's handmaid thus becomes mother to two of the twelve tribes of Israel—no small role for a servant.

**25. And it came to pass, that in the morning, behold, it was Leah: and he said to Laban, What is this thou hast done unto me? did not I serve with thee for Rachel? wherefore then hast thou beguiled me?**

The next *morning* Jacob discovers that he has been tricked. Naturally, he is appalled. But the reader has a hard time feeling sorry for him. We remember from Genesis 27 that it was Jacob who took advantage of his father's inability to see clearly in pretending to be Esau. The one who had deceived his own father is the one who is now *beguiled* himself.

Although we cannot approve of the deception practiced by Laban, and we rightly recognize that two wrongs don't make a right, perhaps we see the divine hand at work: God allows Jacob to be deceived. This brings consequences on Jacob in a "what goes around comes around" kind of way. Is this divine payback for Jacob's past behavior? [See question #1, page 72.]

---

### How to Say It

ABRAHAM. *Ay*-bruh-ham.

BILHAH. *Bill*-ha.

ESAU. *Ee*-saw.

JUDAH. *Joo*-duh.

LABAN. *Lay*-bun.

LEVI. *Lee*-vye.

NAPHTALI. *Naf*-tuh-lye.

REUBEN. *Roo*-ben.

SIMEON. *Sim*-ee-un.

ZILPAH. *Zil*-pa.

### "IT SERVED HIM RIGHT"

"What goes around comes around." "He had it coming to him." "It served him right." People have various ways of acknowledging the repayment of evil when they think they see it.

But what if you wish to help out with the revenge? Lucky you! A psychic web site offers a "Get Even Voodoo & Revenge Spell" to pay back someone who has done you wrong—all for a mere $39 (plus $7.25 for shipping). Of course, for those times when someone is trying to do the same to you, there is a "Self-Protection Voodoo & Revenge Spell" for the same price.

All of this is based on the faulty assumptions that life is subject to the various whims of forces ruling the universe and that all one needs is a little cash to employ or survive their onslaught. That's quite a stretch from the biblical view of God! It is He who works (or allows) what will ultimately be the best for us. Laban's deception may have "served Jacob right," but it wasn't fictitious karma at work.
—C. R. B

### C. Laban's Justification (v. 26)

**26. And Laban said, It must not be so done in our country, to give the younger before the firstborn.**

The irony continues! Jacob, who disrespected the significance of birth order by manipulating Esau into handing over his birthright (Genesis 25:27-33), is now manipulated by *Laban* into honoring the order of birthright. We are not told that Laban knows about Jacob's earlier misdeeds, but here Laban attempts to justify his own actions.

Laban informs Jacob that birth order must not be violated in his land. He is almost saying to Jacob, "Maybe you do that kind of thing down in your country, but up here we keep to our principles." If that's the case, then Laban is tacitly admitting that birth order takes precedence over honesty. In any case, we cannot resist thinking that Jacob recognizes that he is "reaping what he sowed" for deceiving his father and taking advantage of his brother. [See question #2, page 72.]

### BOUND BY TRADITION?

One of the vices of each younger generation is the compulsion to try everything that is new. However, one of the vices of each older generation is the refusal to try *anything* new! Someone has said that the seven last words of the church are, "We've never done it that way before." Many congregations shrivel up and die because they refuse to consider any new way of doing things.

Tradition can be a good thing. It can keep us from hastily jumping on the bandwagon of every new idea that comes along. But tradition becomes the deadly weight of *traditionalism* when we allow it to anchor us in the past. That can prevent us from following God in new paths where He may want us to walk. For example, traditionalism can keep us from singing new music. On the other hand, always doing something different just because it is different results in a kind of traditionalism in and of itself!

Unfortunately for Jacob (and Leah!), Laban allowed a cultural tradition to sacrifice the principle of honesty. Couldn't Laban have mentioned to Jacob the birth-order tradition up front, before Jacob's seven years of service started? Whether we keep traditions or break them, God expects us to base our actions on principles of integrity and holiness.
—C. R. B.

### D. Laban's Concession (v. 27)

**27. Fulfil her week, and we will give thee this also for the service which thou shalt serve with me yet seven other years.**

Laban now makes a slight concession to Jacob. He could demand that Jacob serve him an additional *seven years* first and be allowed to have Rachel only afterward. Instead, he allows Jacob to marry Rachel immediately after Leah's weeklong marital celebration is concluded, with the seven additional years of work to follow. (See Judges 14:12, 17 for an example of another weeklong wedding feast.) This plan may satisfy Jacob's longing for Rachel, but it severely strains Jacob's marital relationships, as future events will demonstrate.

## II. Jacob's Favoritism Backfires (Genesis 29:28-35)

### A. Laban's Action (vv. 28, 29)

**28, 29. And Jacob did so, and fulfilled her week: and he gave him Rachel his daughter to wife also. And Laban gave to Rachel his daughter Bilhah his handmaid to be her maid.**

Laban's deception reveals a flaw in his character, regardless of how he justifies his decision. He does not have to choose between honoring birthright priorities and being forthright with Jacob up front. He could have both (1) informed Jacob of the birthright principle and (2) required him to honor them. Be that as it may, Laban does honor this second agreement with Jacob.

As with Leah, Laban gives a *handmaid* to *Rachel. Bilhah*, like Zilpah, is more than a generous wedding gift. She will also become mother of two tribes of Israel, namely Dan and Naphtali (Genesis 30:1-8).

## B. God's Intervention (vv. 30, 31)

**30. And he went in also unto Rachel, and he loved also Rachel more than Leah, and served with him yet seven other years.**

Jacob keeps his part of the bargain by serving *seven* more *years*. [See question #3, page 72.] Jacob's marriage to *Rachel* becomes official with both the arrangement by Laban and the act of sexual intercourse *(he went in also unto Rachel)*. Jacob knows that sexual intercourse is the event chosen by God for the two to become one flesh (Genesis 2:24; Matthew 19:4-6).

This means that ideally there is no such thing as premarital or extramarital sex for our forefathers of the faith. All sex is intended to be marital. This is why Paul insisted that the young men in Corinth not sleep with prostitutes. Such men thought they were simply meeting physical needs or desires. But Paul reminded them of the issue of becoming one flesh (1 Corinthians 6:15, 16).

We also see in this verse that Jacob clearly favors Rachel above *Leah*. On the one hand, we cannot blame him for this. He did not choose Leah, but was tricked into marrying her.

On the other hand, however, we recall that the favoritism of his parents contributed to the feuding between Jacob and his brother, Esau (Genesis 25:28). Had Isaac not favored Esau and had Rebekah not favored Jacob—had the two parents loved both children equally—then perhaps Jacob would not be exiled from his homeland while Esau's temper cools. So Jacob continues the unhealthy pattern of favoritism set by his parents. That poor choice warrants divine attention.

**31. And when the LORD saw that Leah was hated, he opened her womb: but Rachel was barren.**

*Leah* may be the firstborn daughter, but she is second place in Jacob's eyes. She is not loved by her husband, and her physical appearance is somehow inferior to that of her sister (Genesis 29:17). Yet God sometimes chooses to exalt those of whom little is expected. In the case at hand, His intervention favors Leah.

We see this pattern of intervention on God's part again later in Moses, the man who could not speak very well. We also see intervention with Gideon, the least in his family. God does not need "great" people to do His work, and that gives hope to ordinary folks like us.

God's method of blessing in the case at hand is simple: He ensures that Leah is fertile and *Rachel* is *barren*. [See question #4, page 72.] Jacob may prefer Rachel as a companion, but he also needs a wife who will give him sons. His future liveli-

Visual for Lesson 8. *Ask for volunteers to explain why the statement on this visual is true. Follow their response by asking for examples.*

hood depends on it, as does the promise that God gave him.

## C. Leah's Sons (vv. 32-35)

**32. And Leah conceived, and bare a son, and she called his name Reuben: for she said, Surely the LORD hath looked upon my affliction; now therefore my husband will love me.**

*Reuben* is the first of six *sons* that God will give *Leah*. This is all that a woman in her time and situation can ask for. When God's blessings rain down, they pour!

Notice, however, that the first three sons are given names that reflect her husband's continued neglect. The name *Reuben* is made from two words that mean, "to see" and "a son." With this name she highlights how God has seen her affliction and how she hopes that her *husband* will begin to appreciate her because of this son. [See question #5, page 72.]

**33. And she conceived again, and bare a son; and said, Because the LORD hath heard that I was hated, he hath therefore given me this son also: and she called his name Simeon.**

Apparently Jacob does not show Leah his appreciation, because she names her next son *Simeon*. This name is built from the word meaning "to hear." This name thus reflects her acknowledgment that God has heard about how her husband continues to disregard her.

**34. And she conceived again, and bare a son; and said, Now this time will my husband be joined unto me, because I have borne him three sons: therefore was his name called Levi.**

The second son, Simeon, also is not enough to gain Jacob's favor. So Leah names her third son

*Levi,* meaning "joined." By this she expects that her husband will now join himself more fully to her emotionally.

**35. And she conceived again, and bare a son: and she said, Now will I praise the LORD: therefore she called his name Judah; and left bearing.**

With Leah's fourth *son* comes an important shift in tone. Leah feels no longer compelled to name her sons with reference to Jacob's disfavor. Instead, she turns her attention to God's favor. She realizes that although she may never receive her husband's emotional affection, she is clearly loved by God. For this reason, she names her fourth son *Judah,* meaning "praise."

Leah's childbearing days do not end at this point (see Genesis 30:17-21). But this particular phase, marked by the words *and left bearing,* ends on a high note. God is praised, and the tribe that descends from Judah will become Israel's royal line from which will come David and Jesus. In retrospect we now see that Jesus descended from a fourth-born son of a neglected wife of a swindling man (Jacob) of a second-born son (Isaac) of a wandering pilgrim (Abraham). Praise God for His marvelous deeds!

## Conclusion

### A. Learning from Divine Discipline

One may assume—based on the dream at Bethel, the warm reception at Haran, and the immediate identification of a worthy spouse—that Jacob had the world by the tail. All he had to do was wait a few years for Esau to drop his grudge. Meanwhile Jacob would marry the woman of his dreams and return home to claim Abraham's promise.

## Home Daily Bible Readings

**Monday, Oct. 15**—Assurance of God's Protection (Psalm 91)

**Tuesday, Oct. 16**—The Kiss That Brought Tears (Genesis 29:1-12)

**Wednesday, Oct. 17**—Seven Years of Labor (Genesis 29:13-20)

**Thursday, Oct. 18**—The Trickster Is Tricked (Genesis 29:21-25a)

**Friday, Oct. 19**—Seven More Years (Genesis 29:25b-30)

**Saturday, Oct. 20**—Four Sons Born to Leah (Genesis 29:31-35)

**Sunday, Oct. 21**—Rachel's Sons (Genesis 30:22-24; 35:16-21)

But just when it seemed that Jacob was free and clear, God allowed events to take an unexpected course. With a level of deception equal only to Jacob's own, Laban taught Jacob a lesson in integrity (although lesson-teaching probably was not Laban's intent). Jacob eventually had to reckon also with the legacy of his parents: the favoritism he inherited from them, which he assimilated into his own marital relationships.

We wish we could say that Jacob "learned his lesson" fully. We wish we could say that he never again deceived or stooped to divisive favoritism. But he did. He later tricked Laban out of livestock (Genesis 30:37-43) and played favorites with Rachel's oldest son (37:3, 4).

But God still refused to abandon Jacob. Instead, He allowed Jacob's bad decisions to blow up in his face (sometimes called *natural consequences* today). Jacob and Laban parted company after a dangerous encounter (Genesis 31). Jacob was forced to bow before the brother who was supposed to serve him (33:3). Jacob's favorite wife died in childbirth (35:16-20). Eleven of his sons deceived him into thinking that his favorite son, Joseph, was dead (37:12-35). Indeed, Jacob lived a long, hard life of wrestling with God and people—thus God's new name *Israel* for him, meaning, "he struggles with God" (32:22-28).

To struggle with God is a gift of grace to us all. It means that God has not abandoned us; He is still there for us to struggle with. It means that despite our imperfections God continues to guide and shape us. Divine discipline may not be our preferred means of relating to God, but at least it means the relationship is active.

We should not, however, intentionally provoke divine discipline. Our God is still a consuming fire (Hebrews 12:29); He will not be toyed with. Furthermore, Jacob would not wish his struggles on anyone else. I suspect he would much rather we learn from his mistakes, submit to God, and enjoy more of the blessings that God showers on those who seek to please Him.

### B. Prayer

God of Abraham, Isaac, and Jacob, we come to You humbly and thank You for Your discipline. It can be terribly uncomfortable to be on the receiving end of that discipline, yet there is no place more valuable to be. Thank You for not abandoning us. May we submit to Your discipline when You bring it, lest in resisting it we find ourselves resisting You. In Jesus' name, amen.

### C. Thought to Remember

Receive the Lord's discipline as a gift.

# Learning by Doing

*This page contains an alternative lesson plan emphasizing learning activities.*
*Classes desiring such student involvement will find these suggestions helpful.*

## Into the Lesson

Display this old saying for learners to see as they arrive: "What goes around comes around." Underneath, have these choices displayed: (A) a universal truth, without question; (B) wishful thinking, for the vindictive; (C) an observation of farmers having livestock in corrals or pens; (D) a simple description of seasons and weather patterns, based on Earth's spherical shape and orbital path; (E) a matter of divine discipline, both in this life and the next.

Ask your learners to choose which of those labels they think best fits the old saying. After they defend their answers, say, "Today's study is a 'what goes around comes around' story. In this story, the deceiver Jacob is thoroughly deceived by his kinsman Laban. Let's see if there's any legitimate use of the old expression."

Say, "To understand the story in today's text of Genesis 29:21-35, one must know the beginning, found in verses 1-20 of the chapter." Recruit in advance readers for each of these parts: narrator, Jacob, shepherds (one may represent), and Laban. Give them labels to wear around their necks.

Each may stand as he reads his part.

> Narrator reads verses 1-3.
> Jacob reads verse 4a.
> Shepherd reads verse 4b.
> Jacob reads verse 5a.
> Shepherd reads verse 5b.
> Jacob reads verse 6a.
> Shepherd reads verse 6b.
> Jacob reads verse 7.
> Shepherd reads verse 8.
> Narrator reads verses 9-13.
> Laban reads verse 14a.
> Narrator reads verse 14b.
> Laban reads verse 15.
> Narrator reads verses 16-18a.
> Jacob reads verse 18b.
> Laban reads verse 19.
> Narrator reads verse 20.

## Into the Word

Next, say, "Now we're ready for today's text. It's a text that has two key players, both of whom were known to play fast and loose with the truth.

But first of all, we want to make sure that we ourselves don't play fast and loose with the truths of the story." Give each learner a copy of the statements below. Tell them that these statements include factual errors that they are to find and correct. (Work in teams, if desired.)

1. Jacob asked Laban to give him his wages and health insurance, as he wanted to marry Leah.

2. Laban gathered together all the men of the city and declared a fast.

3. After dark, Laban took Leah, his daughter, and brought her to Jacob with Jacob's full knowledge and consent.

4. In the daylight, Jacob saw that Laban had played a trick, so Jacob reminded Laban that he had served nine years for Rachel.

5. Laban told Jacob that his country never gave the older before the younger.

6. Jacob promised to serve Laban for seven more months.

7. Jacob loved Rachel just as much as Leah, and served Laban for the seven additional months.

8. When the Lord saw that Rachel was loved, he opened her womb, but Leah had to wait.

As learners note the additions, deletions, and changes, you will have opportunity to make teaching points from the lesson commentary.

## Into Life

Gather empty 7-Up® cans for the following application activity, one per learner. Asking around in advance may identify someone who will save the cans for you. Also provide slips of paper that can be rolled and passed through the openings on the tops of the can.

Say, "Jacob worked seven years for the hand of Rachel. He was 'up, up, up' the whole time, because of his deep love for her. Imagine how far 'down, down, down' he fell on the morning he awoke to find Leah beside him. Then he had to think, 'Seven years down, seven years to go' when Laban offered him Rachel.

"Use your 7-Up® can this week to remind you of today's study. For some major disappointment you have had, consider writing it on the slip, rolling it up, putting it in the can, standing the can upside down, and saying, 'Lord, this disappointment has kept me down too long. Help me up by Your Spirit.'"

# Let's Talk It Over

*The questions on this page are designed to promote discussion of the lesson by the class and to encourage application of the lesson Scriptures. The answers provided are only discussion starters. Let your class talk it over from there.*

**1. What was a time when an old sin came back to haunt you? How did God's love and grace see you through that situation?**

We may replace the warning, "What goes around comes around" with, "whatsoever a man soweth, that shall he also reap" (Galatians 6:7).

Our old sins can come back on us in various ways. It is not that God is in the business of relentless, tit-for-tat payback; sometimes what seems like divine payback is really just natural consequence. Someone who has abused alcohol or drugs may suffer ill effects later. But forgiveness and spiritual renewal is always available, even if the physical consequences are permanent. Many Christians have marvelous testimonies about how God brought good out of a sinful situation. What's yours?

**2. Were you ever guilty of manipulating circumstances or people to achieve selfish desires? How did God enable you to put this kind of sinful practice in the past?**

There are times when Christians are guilty of trying to get their way in the church through devious means. People have been known to threaten to withhold—or actually withhold—their financial gifts because something was not to their liking. One woman was known to use 1 Corinthians 8:9 as a club to get her way; whenever something in church wasn't to her liking, she would say, "We have to stop doing such and such because it's a stumbling block to me."

Some try to manipulate others through guilt trips. Sadly, some church leaders have used this technique to recruit workers for various projects. Also, using the old "soft soap" routine to flatter someone into agreeing to a project is a form of manipulation.

To confront the sin of manipulation, we must realize that this is not the way of holiness. We ourselves do not want to be manipulated; thus, following the Golden Rule will help us to overcome such tendencies.

**3. Seven more years! In what areas has love for Christ driven you to go the second mile (or the second year)? What was a time when someone else went the second mile with you or for you?**

Love is what causes a parent to stay up all night with a sick child. Love for a spouse will cause one to stay faithful through times of extreme sickness, not even considering breaking the vow of "till death shall separate us." A Christian's desire to see a friend come to Christ will cause him or her never to give up, but to continue to pray and share Christ as opportunities present themselves.

A second-mile Sunday school teacher continues to be present week after week even when it seems no progress is being made with some undisciplined children. Many of us realize that had it not been for such people, we might not be in Christ today.

**4. How does God continue to show His concern for those the world looks down on? What is your part in meeting the needs of those considered to be "the downtrodden"?**

The world looks down on people who don't measure up to cultural norms and trends in the areas of belief, wealth, physical appearance, etc. Christians certainly are not immune from being disparaged or ridiculed in any of these areas!

Sometimes we feel as if we are fighting a losing battle in the culture wars. But God continues to love those who uphold His principles. God delights in working through weakness, and He often chooses to use the "least" of this world to advance His name (1 Corinthians 1:25-29).

**5. What was a time when God blessed you in a time of affliction? What has His blessing meant to you since that time?**

We can often be disappointed with ourselves, our loved ones, or our situations. This disappointment may or may not be due to personal sin, the sin of others, sickness, or mere human error. But God is faithful and sees us through. God's faithfulness often is clearest in hindsight.

Sometimes our affliction takes the form of a significant loss. This may be the loss of a job or the death of a loved one. Seeing God work during such times strengthens our faith and the faith of others who witness God's work in our lives. The apostle Paul wasn't immune to times of affliction, and neither are we.

# Esau and Jacob Reconciled

**DEVOTIONAL READING: Psalm 133.**

**BACKGROUND SCRIPTURE: Genesis 33.**

**PRINTED TEXT: Genesis 33:1-11.**

### Genesis 33:1-11

1 And Jacob lifted up his eyes, and looked, and, behold, Esau came, and with him four hundred men. And he divided the children unto Leah, and unto Rachel, and unto the two handmaids.

2 And he put the handmaids and their children foremost, and Leah and her children after, and Rachel and Joseph hindermost.

3 And he passed over before them, and bowed himself to the ground seven times, until he came near to his brother.

4 And Esau ran to meet him, and embraced him, and fell on his neck, and kissed him: and they wept.

5 And he lifted up his eyes, and saw the women and the children, and said, Who are those with thee? And he said, The children which God hath graciously given thy servant.

6 Then the handmaidens came near, they and their children, and they bowed themselves.

7 And Leah also with her children came near, and bowed themselves: and after came Joseph near and Rachel, and they bowed themselves.

8 And he said, What meanest thou by all this drove which I met? And he said, These are to find grace in the sight of my lord.

9 And Esau said, I have enough, my brother; keep that thou hast unto thyself.

10 And Jacob said, Nay, I pray thee, if now I have found grace in thy sight, then receive my present at my hand: for therefore I have seen thy face, as though I had seen the face of God, and thou wast pleased with me.

11 Take, I pray thee, my blessing that is brought to thee; because God hath dealt graciously with me, and because I have enough. And he urged him, and he took it.

**Oct 28**

GOLDEN TEXT: Esau ran to meet him, and embraced him, and fell on his neck, and kissed him: and they wept.—Genesis 33:4.

## Lesson Aims

After participating in this lesson, each student will be able to:

1. Describe the reunion of Jacob and Esau.
2. Identify the facts of Jacob's humility in the reunion story.
3. Make a plan for reconciliation to one person estranged from him or her.

## Lesson Outline

INTRODUCTION
   A. Stories of Estrangement
   B. Lesson Background
  I. JACOB APPROACHES ESAU (Genesis 33:1-3)
   A. Jacob Sees Esau (v. 1a)
   B. Jacob Prepares to Meet Esau (vv. 1b, 2)
   C. Jacob Bows Before Esau (v. 3)
      *Folly of Pride, Wisdom of Humility*
 II. ESAU RECEIVES JACOB (Genesis 33:4-7)
   A. Brothers Embrace (v. 4)
   B. Jacob Introduces (v. 5)
   C. Family Bows (vv. 6, 7)
III. JACOB AND ESAU RECONCILE (Genesis 33:8-11)
   A. Peace Offering Explained (v. 8)
   B. Peace Offering Declined (v. 9)
   C. Peace Offering Accepted (vv. 10, 11)
      *Bringing Gifts for Peace . . . or Pieces?*
CONCLUSION
   A. A Story of Reconciliation
   B. Prayer
   C. Thought to Remember

## Introduction

### A. Stories of Estrangement

A man and his wife have not spoken in days. One too many times she embarrassed him in public, and one too many times he responded harshly. Even though they share the same bed, a cold gap remains between them.

Two coworkers communicate only indirectly through other employees. One too many times an idea was stolen, and one too many times others were recruited to take sides. Though they occupy adjacent offices, genuine collaboration is out of the question.

Tales of wounded pride are all too common. Each of us is familiar with a close relationship that was threatened by an unfortunate conflict caused by one party's lapse of judgment and another party's defensive retaliation. Scripture does not teach us that following Jesus means that Christians will live lives free of conflict. It does show us, however, a way to overcome.

Matthew 18 and other New Testament passages provide principles and procedures for seeking genuine reconciliation. The Old Testament furnishes stories of success and failure that bring these principles to life. Today we consider one such story.

### B. Lesson Background

The feud between Jacob and Esau began at an early age. Even in the womb, these boys jockeyed for position. The struggle was so intense that their mother, Rebekah, thought it was necessary to ask God for an explanation.

God informed her that two "nations" were in her womb and that the older would serve the younger (Genesis 25:23). This jockeying for position continued at their birth. Although Esau emerged as the firstborn, Jacob was clutching at his heel even as he left the womb. This prenatal rivalry was later compounded by parental favoritism (Genesis 25:27, 28).

As the boys grew older, the tension mounted. On one occasion, Jacob manipulated Esau into trading his birthright for stew (Genesis 25:29-34). On another, Jacob and Rebekah tricked Isaac into conferring his fatherly blessing on Jacob instead of Esau (27:1-40). This was the breaking point in the brothers' relationship. Having been tricked twice, Esau planned to kill Jacob after their father passed away (27:41).

This prompted Jacob to flee northward. His relocation gave Esau the time and space he needed to cool off (Genesis 27:42-45). But the plan took much more time than Jacob had anticipated. Laban, his father-in-law, tricked him into staying twice as long as he had planned. Then Jacob stuck around for several more years to gain enough wealth to head back home. So after 20 years of self-exile (31:38), Jacob finally began his perilous journey home.

The first obstacle he faced was Laban. The two of them had a falling out, and it took divine intervention for Laban to allow Jacob to leave in peace (Genesis 31:29). Then, upon reaching the border of the promised land, Jacob encountered a second obstacle: an angelic messenger who wrestled with him all night (32:22-32). Before leaving, this wrestling angel blessed Jacob by renaming him *Israel*, which means "one who struggles with God." Surviving this heavenly opponent prepared Jacob for his most intimidating human foe: a potentially vengeful Esau.

# I. Jacob Approaches Esau (Genesis 33:1-3)

## A. Jacob Sees Esau (v. 1a)

**1a. And Jacob lifted up his eyes, and looked, and, behold, Esau came, and with him four hundred men.**

By this point, *Jacob* has taken two precautionary measures to increase his chances of surviving the encounter with *Esau*. First, Jacob has sent messengers ahead with gifts of appeasement (Genesis 32:3-5). Second, he has divided his group into two camps (32:7); should those in one camp die by the sword, the others might escape.

The sight Jacob now sees must be terrifying. He undoubtedly wonders why Esau is bringing along such a large escort. This is certainly not a typical homecoming party! Is Esau trying to protect himself, or is he planning to attack Jacob? As readers, we experience this episode much like Jacob: we have no clue what Esau will do next.

## B. Jacob Prepares to Meet Esau (vv. 1b, 2)

**1b, 2. And he divided the children unto Leah, and unto Rachel, and unto the two handmaids. And he put the handmaids and their children foremost, and Leah and her children after, and Rachel and Joseph hindermost.**

Again Jacob divides his camp, this time according to preference. Those he loves least head the procession.

In Genesis 29:30-35 we saw Jacob's greater love for *Rachel* despite Leah's status as first wife and mother of his first sons. This ranking, then, appears to be for protection, since it provides Jacob's favored family members with a head start in case a battle breaks out (32:8). It can also, however, be a matter of protocol: as Jacob introduces his loved

---

### How to Say It

ABRAHAM. *Ay*-bruh-ham.
COLOSSIANS. Kuh-*losh*-unz.
CORINTHIANS. Ko-*rin*-thee-unz (*th* as in *thin*).
ESAU. *Ee*-saw.
GALATIANS. Guh-*lay*-shunz.
HOSEA. Ho-*zay*-uh.
LABAN. *Lay*-bun.
PENIEL. Peh-*nye*-el.

---

ones to Esau, perhaps he wishes "to save the best for last." [See question #1, page 80.]

## C. Jacob Bows Before Esau (v. 3)

**3. And he passed over before them, and bowed himself to the ground seven times, until he came near to his brother.**

Here we see that Jacob is no coward. He could remain with Rachel and Joseph at the end of the procession, but instead he places himself on the front line.

More importantly, however, Jacob bows before *his brother*, Esau. This action is doubly significant. On the one hand, it stands out as a model for those seeking to initiate reconciliation. Jacob has deeply wounded Esau in the past. Realizing this, Jacob comes humbly to his brother, begging forgiveness. Even though Jacob may feel justified in his past actions, and even though 20 years have elapsed, Jacob still comes humbly as if he had committed the offense only the day before. He sets aside pride to prostrate himself before Esau—not just once, but *seven times*. His bowing is not a perfunctory, superficial act, but is an act of complete contrition and submission.

On the other hand, Jacob's bowing stands out in this story because the blessing Jacob stole from Esau seemed to indicate that Esau would be the one bowing before Jacob (Genesis 27:29). To be sure, the Edomites, who descend from Esau, will have to submit (bow) to the Israelites, who descend from Jacob. But between Esau and Jacob personally, this apparently doesn't happen in their lifetimes. Only Jacob does the bowing.

This teaches Jacob (and us) an important lesson about divine promises: the promises God makes concerning His people are not always experienced firsthand by the initial recipients of the promise. Abraham was told that he would become a great nation, that he would inhabit the promised land, and that all nations of the earth would be blessed through him. Yet Abraham did not see this promise realized in his own lifetime.

God knows that Jacob's descendants will become *Israel*, God's special people. God also knows that Esau's descendants will become *Edom*, a less powerful nation that will be made subject to Jacob's descendants (especially David, 2 Samuel 8:14). So, in the long run, the blessing will come to fruition, as will the promise to Abraham. But Jacob "jumped the gun" and tried to force matters down a path of his own choosing. The result of his antics? Jacob bows before Esau.

God's purposes will not be thwarted despite human shenanigans. After 20 difficult years, God brings Jacob and Esau's relationship back into proper alignment. Now that Jacob is "at the bottom," God can use him to do great things.

This verse teaches us three lessons. First, humility may be central to reconciliation. It's not always about who is more right or wrong—it often is about swallowing our pride so God may bring peace. Second, it is dangerous to personalize God's promises strictly. God has made many promises to the church, but not all of us will experience all of them in our lifetimes. Third, those who exalt themselves will be humbled by God (compare Luke 14:11; 18:14). We are to be patient and faithful until God elevates us in His own timing. [See question #2, page 80.]

### FOLLY OF PRIDE, WISDOM OF HUMILITY

In 1980, Robert Graham created the Repository for Germinal Choice—what some came to call the Nobel Prize sperm bank. Graham, the inventor of shatterproof plastic eyeglasses, believed the repository could improve the human race. Women could choose the father of their babies from the genius-level contributors to the repository. However, not many women were interested. In 19 years, only 215 children were born through the repository's efforts.

One outspoken donor and supporter was William Shockley, who had won a Nobel Prize in 1956 for his work on the transistor. He was reputed to be a racist who promoted the idea of tampering with genetics to accomplish his vision. His loud advocacy of both the repository and his racist views brought derision to the organization. It closed in 1999.

Pride—whether in one's accomplishments, genes, or wealth—is evidence of misplaced values. Pride fosters arrogance. Humility is a much better way to relate to God and to others. After pride had forced Jacob and Esau apart, Jacob's humble approach to his brother initiated the reconciliation process. Is there an area of your relationships where a humble approach could work in a similar way?                    —C. R. B.

## II. Esau Receives Jacob
## (Genesis 33:4-7)

### A. Brothers Embrace (v. 4)

**4. And Esau ran to meet him, and embraced him, and fell on his neck, and kissed him: and they wept.**

Like the father in the story of the prodigal son (Luke 15:11-32), *Esau* runs to embrace his "prodigal brother." Jacob cannot imagine a warmer greeting. Emotions pour from them both. We see tears of joy and reconciliation.

But is it all too good to be true? The last man who ran out, embraced, and *kissed* Jacob was Laban (Genesis 29:13). Laban then proceeded to deal with Jacob in a less-than-honest fashion for 20 years. Jacob certainly appreciates this warm reception from Esau, but the reconciliation is not yet complete.

### B. Jacob Introduces (v. 5)

**5. And he lifted up his eyes, and saw the women and the children, and said, Who are those with thee? And he said, The children which God hath graciously given thy servant.**

Esau is the first to speak. He is likely aware that these people are Jacob's family, thus his question is rhetorical. The question gives Jacob an opportunity to introduce his family properly.

Note that Jacob refers to himself as Esau's *servant.* This reinforces his own humility.

### C. Family Bows (vv. 6, 7)

**6, 7. Then the handmaidens came near, they and their children, and they bowed themselves. And Leah also with her children came near, and bowed themselves: and after came Joseph near and Rachel, and they bowed themselves.**

Not only does Jacob bow before Esau, the members of his entire entourage humble themselves in this manner. This reinforces the completeness of Jacob's contrition.

## III. Jacob and Esau Reconcile
## (Genesis 33:8-11)

### A. Peace Offering Explained (v. 8)

**8. And he said, What meanest thou by all this drove which I met? And he said, These are to find grace in the sight of my lord.**

Esau is still in the driver's seat, thus he asks all the questions. Of course, he already knows why Jacob sent the gifts; the envoys Jacob sent ahead relayed that message previously (Genesis 32:4, 5). But Esau also knows it is necessary that he and Jacob have this conversation—a conversation that must take place face to face.

Jacob not only submits to this line of questioning, he also defers to Esau as *my lord.* Jacob's intentions are clear: he seeks *grace,* which, in this case, means forgiveness of past wrongs. [See question #3, page 80.]

### B. Peace Offering Declined (v. 9)

**9. And Esau said, I have enough, my brother; keep that thou hast unto thyself.**

It is difficult to gauge Esau's response. At face value, it appears that he declines the offering because he does not need it and prefers that Jacob use it to meet his own family's needs.

But for Jacob, it is crucial that Esau accept it. This is Jacob's attempt to clear his conscience and set things right. He has stolen from Esau, and the two will not be reconciled fully until repayment is made. That being the case, Esau's initial denial is either (1) an effort to keep the power he now holds over Jacob, or (2) a sincere act of generosity, or (3) a cultural practice somewhat along the lines of Genesis 23:7-16. Regardless, Esau's initial response is not acceptable to Jacob.

### C. Peace Offering Accepted (vv. 10, 11)

**10. And Jacob said, Nay, I pray thee, if now I have found grace in thy sight, then receive my present at my hand: for therefore I have seen thy face, as though I had seen the face of God, and thou wast pleased with me.**

*Jacob* desperately needs Esau to accept the peace offering. So he begins to apply pressure. Esau has presented himself as the gracious older brother. He ran to Jacob, hugged him, and kissed him. But for his act of *grace* to be complete, he must set Jacob free from the debt. Esau must allow Jacob a concrete way to express his gratitude for the grace he has received. [See question #4, page 80.]

To deny Jacob the means to do this will be to withhold forgiveness and subject Jacob to a different form of bondage. It is almost as if Jacob is saying, "If you are truly the gracious man I think you are, and if you are truly pleased with me, then you need to accept these gifts. If not, this is all just a sham and the real Esau is the bitter Esau I left behind who doesn't know how to let go of a grudge."

It is also important to discuss why Jacob compares seeing Esau's face to seeing *the face of God.* There are a few ways we can understand this. One way highlights Esau's graciousness. God is known for His grace, and in this encounter Esau's response to Jacob rises to a level that is pleasing to God. Put differently, Esau receives Jacob so warmly that it is like Heaven smiling down.

Another interpretation highlights Esau's position of judgment. Jacob could be acknowledging that Esau occupies the position of judge—and Esau knows that Jacob is guilty. Esau has heard Jacob's pleas for mercy, and at this point Esau can either grant or withhold pardon for Jacob's sin.

A third interpretation stresses language parallel to that of the previous chapter. Jacob spent all night wrestling with a mysterious, extraordinary man (Genesis 32:24); this man is identified in Hosea 12:4 as an angel. After surviving the fight,

Visual for Lesson 9. *Point to this visual as you ask, "Why is unity important to the church?" Explore the difference between* unity *and* uniformity.

Jacob renamed the place *Peniel,* meaning "face of God," because he believed he had seen God face-to-face and lived (Genesis 32:30). So Jacob simply may be comparing the experience he just had with the angel to the experience he is now having with Esau.

As Jacob had doubts about surviving the encounter with the angel, so also he now has doubts about surviving the encounter with Esau (although in neither case did Jacob actually see God himself). Under this interpretation, it is almost as if Jacob is saying, "I have stared death in the face and have lived to talk about it" concerning both encounters.

It is difficult to tell which of these interpretations is right. It may be some combination of them.

**11. Take, I pray thee, my blessing that is brought to thee; because God hath dealt graciously with me, and because I have enough. And he urged him, and he took it.**

Like the situation of Abraham's purchase of a burial plot in Genesis 23, Jacob knows he has to pay. He cannot remain indebted to Esau, so he urges Esau until he complies.

We see here that genuine reconciliation requires responsibility of both parties. Jacob has to be willing to humble himself, and Esau has to let go of a long-held grudge. This applies to Christians today. Christ has taught us to forgive others' debts as we have been forgiven (Matthew 6:12; 18:21-35). Hanging on to resentment is unhealthy for both parties.

Sometimes reconciliation is a matter of verbal confession and verbal forgiveness. At other times, restitution may need to be made so both parties may truly experience closure. In such cases the party that was wronged must, with a sincere heart, imitate Esau's willingness to accept an offer that has been made, even though he or she may prefer not to.

Notice also the language Jacob uses in this verse. Until this point in the conversation, he has not referred to himself as being "blessed," perhaps in order to avoid digging up painful memories of blessing theft (Genesis 27:35, 36). But he approaches Esau and beseeches him to receive *my blessing* that Jacob is offering him. It is almost as if Jacob is saying, "Take your blessing back. I don't want it anymore. It wasn't mine for the taking."

If this is so, then the Jacob and Esau saga has come full circle. Jacob surrenders, as best he can, that which he had stolen. Thus he can move forward with only that which God provides for him. Jacob learns to trust in God alone, and that is sufficient to carry him the rest of his journey. He indeed "hast prevailed" in his struggle "with God and with men" (Genesis 32:28). [See question #5, page 80.]

### BRINGING GIFTS FOR PEACE . . . OR PIECES?

On March 9, 2004, a psychology professor at Claremont McKenna College offered a "gift" of an unusual sort to her campus community. After speaking at a forum on racial tolerance, she filed a police report alleging that her car had been vandalized. It apparently was a hate crime, since racist epithets had been spray-painted on her car. What a perfect gift of an illustration concerning the subject the professor had addressed in her forum!

The next day, administrators gave a "gift" to the students by calling off classes for the day.

---

### Home Daily Bible Readings

**Monday, Oct. 22**—Jacob's Prayer (Genesis 32:3-12)

**Tuesday, Oct. 23**—Jacob's Presents to Esau (Genesis 32:13-21)

**Wednesday, Oct. 24**—The Brothers Wept Together (Genesis 33:1-4)

**Thursday, Oct. 25**—The Gift of Reconciliation (Genesis 33:5-11)

**Friday, Oct. 26**—Their Separate Ways (Genesis 33:12-15)

**Saturday, Oct. 27**—An Altar to God (Genesis 33:16-20)

**Sunday, Oct. 28**—The Blessedness of Unity (Psalm 133)

---

Thousands of students gladly received the gift of a day free from classes in order to bring their own "gifts" to campus: demonstrations against such a terrible act of racial intolerance.

However, it was soon discovered that the professor had damaged her own car in order to call attention to the issue of racial prejudice. The court then had a "gift" for the manipulative professor: a one-year prison sentence. What the professor hoped to accomplish in terms of fostering racial peace ended up merely shredding her own reputation into pieces (www.sfgate.com).

Jacob had a history of being a manipulator. But when he brought gifts to Esau, they were offered in a genuine spirit. Too often what people bring to resolve relationship problems is not so much a peace offering as it is an attempt to prove themselves right. The frequent result is not peace, but relationships that are in pieces.          —C. R. B.

## Conclusion

### A. A Story of Reconciliation

Christians can learn valuable lessons from the account of Jacob and Esau. We may find ourselves in the shoes of one or the other at different points, sometimes the offender and sometimes the offended. Our culture encourages us to respond with extremes. At one extreme is inflicting payback. At the other extreme is a kind of quietism, meaning "just try to forget about it and move on with life."

Our Savior, however, does not give us either of those options. He calls us to seek reconciliation actively with those who have offended us (see Matthew 5:23, 24; 18:15; compare 2 Corinthians 5:18-21; Galatians 6:1, 2; Colossians 3:13; and James 5:16).

Those of us who share the blame for being estranged from another person must humble ourselves like Jacob. Those of us who have held grudges against someone who has wronged us need to embrace the offending party, like Esau, as we accept genuine confession, forgiving truly as God in Christ Jesus has forgiven us.

### B. Prayer

We thank You, Father, for reconciliation through Christ. It is tempting, Lord, to hoard reconciliation, to accept it for ourselves but fail to extend it to others. Prepare us to accept with joy the ministry of reconciliation that You have entrusted to us. In Jesus' name, amen.

### C. Thought to Remember

Reconciliation requires humility and acceptance.

# Learning by Doing

*This page contains an alternative lesson plan emphasizing learning activities.*
*Classes desiring such student involvement will find these suggestions helpful.*

## Into the Lesson

Recruit a pair of learners and ask them to walk back and forth in front of the class, crossing paths. As they do, they are to greet one another in ways typical to a variety of cultures and contexts. Suggest such greetings as (1) a hearty handshake, (2) a simple hug, (3) a bowing of the head to each other, (4) a tip of the hat (which you'll need to provide), (5) an elaborate handshake and hug, (6) a kiss on each cheek, (7) a snappy salute, (8) a friendly wave, (9) a slight nod accompanied by hands positioned palm-to-palm, finger-tips-to-the-lips (10) a sign-language "I love you," and/or (11) others of your choosing and description. Ask the pair simply to cross back and forth quickly, demonstrating the greetings as they use few, if any, words.

When they finish, ask, "What determines the type of greeting you offer and receive?" Expect answers dealing with time and place, the intimacy of the relationship, and culture.

## Into the Word

Now ask the pair to demonstrate the manner of Jacob's greeting to his brother Esau according to Genesis 33:3. Ask the class, "What called for that elaborate greeting, and what did it signify?"

To complement your learners' responses to the previous questions, be sure they understand the causes and the depth of the estrangement between the Jacob and Esau. The passage of time (20 years) could have allowed a hardening of hearts and deepening of animosities—or the opposite!

Make two cutouts of biblical men (robed figures) in profile. Set them on a chalkboard rack or attach them to a wall in a nose-to-nose position. Distribute cutout arrows with the following words/phrases on them: *Parental Favoritism, Different Interests and Abilities, Childhood Rivalries, Lying, Cheating, Threats of Murder, Miles and Years, Prosperity.*

Ask those holding the arrows to bring them up and attach them between the brother figures. As they do, they are to move the figures apart the distance of the arrow being used—thus creating a visual of the estrangement of the two.

As each arrow is added, ask, "What specifically does this represent that can cause an alienation, a distance between the two brothers?"

This will offer an opportunity for a review of the brothers' relationship all the way back to Genesis 25 and Lesson 6.

Now ask seven class members, by name, to come to the front, bow, and remove the arrows one by one, consequently moving the two brother-figures closer together. After seven are moved, one item will be left, with the brothers close, but not "kissably close." Ask, "After looking at today's text, what else is there in Jacob's (or Esau's) behavior that can remove this last barrier to brotherly kindness and closeness?"

Someone will likely say, "Jacob's gift of many animals," "Esau's running, embracing, kissing, and weeping," or "the kind, reconciling words of either brother." If need be, suggest they look at Genesis 32:9-11 or 32:13-15 or 33:4.

Let the class continue to list and explain elements of Jacob's plan to meet Esau in a context of humility, grace, and blessing. As they do, make a list entitled, "Steps and Prerequisites to Reconciliation."

Expect elements such as *giving significant gifts* (Genesis 32:13-15); *setting aside the fears that are intrinsic in estrangement* (32:11); *"wrestling with God" a bit* (32:24, 25); *using intermediary ambassadors to break the ice* (32:16-21); *praying* (32:9-12); *demonstrating personal humility* (33:3); *being willing to show true emotion* (33:4); *affirming the presence of God's grace* (33:5, 11); *having witnesses present* (33:5-7); and *offering hospitality* (33:12). (A similar activity is included in the optional student book.)

## Into Life

To move to application, hand each learner a wedge-shaped piece of paper. Say, "All of us have experienced wedges between ourselves and others. Sometimes we create the wedge; sometimes others create it. Some of us give the wedge a kick to make sure it is firmly fixed! Is there someone from whom you are estranged—either in your family, church, or at work—with whom you can begin a process of reconciliation? Which of the ideas from our 'Steps' list can you use?"

Direct learners to write down a reconciliation technique they will use to try to remove their "wedge." Indicate that once the wedge is removed, they should tear up the paper.

# Let's Talk It Over

*The questions on this page are designed to promote discussion of the lesson
by the class and to encourage application of the lesson Scriptures. The answers
provided are only discussion starters. Let your class talk it over from there.*

**1. What motives do people have for placing some things or certain family members at greater risk? How can we improve our motives and strengthen our faith in this regard?**

It is highly unlikely that any of us will ever face a situation like Jacob's, where we end up placing some family members at greater risk. Even so, we might act in a similar way with "things."

This can be bad or good, depending on our motives. Sometimes Christians hold back their giving in the hope that the needs of a church or a ministry will be provided by others—then they can keep what they have for themselves. On a more positive note, we might save our best for God. There are many things we are called upon to be involved in, many causes to take up. But we may say no to several of them, wanting to reserve the best of our time and talents for God.

**2. In what areas of your life do you need to come humbly before another, seeking forgiveness? What responsibility do offended parties have to express their hurt?**

We live in close relationships in the church. When two or three are gathered together, not only is God in their midst, but the possibility for misunderstanding and disagreement is present as well. We sometimes say things that hurt another's feelings. We can slip (or jump) into gossip or backbiting (Galatians 5:15).

We may fail to exhibit a proper concern for people when they are hurting. Demonstrating impatience with those who are struggling with sin erects barriers between Christians. We then compound the problem when our pride keeps us from asking for forgiveness.

**3. Why do we sometimes fail to seek reconciliation? What benefits are there when we do?**

Pride undoubtedly heads the list of reasons people don't seek reconciliation. The solution is to come to grips with the nature of God's grace. God took the initiative to reconcile us to Him, although He is the one who has been offended. God does not attempt to sell us His forgiving grace—it is a free gift.

But God's grace is not a gift that is forced upon us. And it is a gift we can reject. Failing to be reconciled to God is a rejection of His grace. Accepting His grace but then not extending forgiveness to others puts us in the position of being the unmerciful servant in Matthew 18:21-35.

A church in which people have failed to forgive and be reconciled to one another is a church that will be filled with internal struggles. This will make the church mostly ineffective in fulfilling the Great Commission (Matthew 28:19, 20).

**4. What principle can we apply to modern life from Jacob's insistence that Esau accept his gift? Or is that an ancient cultural practice that we can safely disregard? Explain.**

God's grace is a gift freely given—that's truth. But our response is at least somewhat analogous to that of Jacob toward Esau: we offer our lives to God (the offended party) as living sacrifices to Him (Romans 12:1).

We should be careful, however, to make sure we don't think that our service is somehow purchasing God's grace. That's where the analogy with Jacob and Esau breaks down. Jacob's giving of gifts can be seen as an attempt to gain Esau's favor; our gifts and service to God are responses to the favor that God already has shown us.

In modern person-to-person situations, gifts may or may not be appropriate, depending on the setting. We probably cannot make a hard and fast rule in that regard.

**5. What does Esau's acceptance of Jacob's gift teach us?**

Sometimes we don't want to be the recipients of others' services or gifts. This can create a mind-set of "being in someone's debt." Some Christians seem always to want to be on the giving end but never on the receiving end.

If you think about it, that is an arrogant, almost selfish, attitude. Refusing to receive gifts and blessings from others can hurt those who want to do good for you. They feel blessed and want to be a blessing to others. If someone offers a gift as a peace offering after a time of estrangement, our knee-jerk response may be to say, "That's not necessary." But the one offering the gift may feel like the matter is still not resolved if there is a refusal to accept the gift.

# Joseph Is Mistreated

DEVOTIONAL READING: Psalm 70.

BACKGROUND SCRIPTURE: Genesis 37.

PRINTED TEXT: Genesis 37:5-11, 19-21, 23, 24a, 28.

### Genesis 37:5-11, 19-21, 23, 24a, 28

5 And Joseph dreamed a dream, and he told it his brethren: and they hated him yet the more.

6 And he said unto them, Hear, I pray you, this dream which I have dreamed:

7 For, behold, we were binding sheaves in the field, and, lo, my sheaf arose, and also stood upright; and, behold, your sheaves stood round about, and made obeisance to my sheaf.

8 And his brethren said to him, Shalt thou indeed reign over us? or shalt thou indeed have dominion over us? And they hated him yet the more for his dreams, and for his words.

9 And he dreamed yet another dream, and told it his brethren, and said, Behold, I have dreamed a dream more; and, behold, the sun and the moon and the eleven stars made obeisance to me.

10 And he told it to his father, and to his brethren: and his father rebuked him, and said unto him, What is this dream that thou hast dreamed? Shall I and thy mother and thy brethren indeed come to bow down ourselves to thee to the earth?

11 And his brethren envied him; but his father observed the saying.

. . . . . . . . . . .

19 And they said one to another, Behold, this dreamer cometh.

20 Come now therefore, and let us slay him, and cast him into some pit, and we will say, Some evil beast hath devoured him; and we shall see what will become of his dreams.

21 And Reuben heard it, and he delivered him out of their hands; and said, Let us not kill him.

. . . . . . . . . . .

23 And it came to pass, when Joseph was come unto his brethren, that they stripped Joseph out of his coat, his coat of many colors that was on him;

24 And they took him, and cast him into a pit.

. . . . . . . . . . .

28 Then there passed by Midianites merchantmen; and they drew and lifted up Joseph out of the pit, and sold Joseph to the Ishmaelites for twenty pieces of silver: and they brought Joseph into Egypt.

---

GOLDEN TEXT: They . . . sold Joseph to the Ishmaelites for twenty pieces of silver: and they brought Joseph into Egypt.—Genesis 37:28.

## God Creates
### Unit 3: God's People Re-created
### (Lessons 10-13)

## Lesson Aims

After participating in this lesson, each student will be able to:

1. Describe the early relationship of Joseph with his brothers and parents.

2. Explain why Joseph had to tell about his dreams.

3. Make a commitment to share the gospel in a situation where it may not be welcome, and be prepared for the potentially difficult result.

## Lesson Outline

Introduction
  A. The Butterfly Effect
  B. Lesson Background
 I. Dreamer Dreams (Genesis 37:5-9)
  A. Sheaves in the Field Bow Down (vv. 5-8)
  B. Sun, Moon, and Stars Bow Down (v. 9)
    *Delusions of Grandeur*
 II. Family Reacts (Genesis 37:10, 11)
  A. Jacob Rebukes (v. 10)
  B. Brothers Envy (v. 11)
III. Plot Develops (Genesis 37:19-21, 23, 24a, 28)
  A. First Plan: Murder (vv. 19-21, 23, 24a)
  B. Second Plan: Slavery (v. 28)
    *The Tangled Web*
Conclusion
  A. Can We See the Hand of God?
  B. Prayer
  C. Thought to Remember

## Introduction

### A. The Butterfly Effect

Have you ever noticed that something that seemed to be small or insignificant at one point can have a major effect over a longer period of time? One theory of forecasting changes in the weather and the stock market says that small variations in initial conditions can bring about large variations in the long-term behavior of a system.

The idea was originally expressed by Edward Lorenz in 1963 in a paper he wrote for the New York Academy of Sciences. Initially, he referred to the effect as being like the flap of a seagull's wings, but later would use the more picturesque phrase *butterfly effect*. Simply stated, the idea is that the flap of a butterfly's wing in one part of the world could eventually result in a hurricane in another part. (A more scientific description for *butterfly effect* is "sensitive dependence on initial conditions.")

The lesson today about Joseph is a portion of the greater narrative that describes God's movement to bring salvation to the world. Whether or not butterflies can cause hurricanes can be debated. But one thing is certain: the reach through history of the things done to and by Joseph is profound indeed!

### B. Lesson Background

Jacob eventually returned to Canaan from living in Padan-aram, where he had married and where most of his children were born (last week's lesson). The livelihood of the family was based on raising livestock. In this relatively dry region, it was necessary to move the flocks and herds around to provide them with daily food. Sometimes the shepherds would have to go long distances to find that food.

Jacob was a very successful shepherd, and apparently he intended for Joseph, his favorite son, to follow in his footsteps. To that end, we see Joseph learning the family operation. The biblical record tells us that Joseph had eleven brothers and one sister. The nature and significance of Joseph's interaction with his brothers is a vital part of the Genesis account.

## I. Dreamer Dreams (Genesis 37:5-9)

As we enter into the story of Joseph, around the year 1900 BC, we find a boy at age 17 (Genesis 37:2). Immediately we are introduced to a love-hate triangle consisting of Joseph, his brothers, and their father, Jacob. Joseph's father loved him more than he loved his other sons. This created a burning resentment toward Joseph.

Three things aggravated the situation. First, Joseph had brought a bad report about his brothers to his father, Jacob (also known as Israel; Genesis 37:2). Second, Joseph received preferential treatment in terms of a special coat, a colorful one perhaps with long sleeves (37:3, 23). Third, Joseph had been having dreams of personal grandeur. That's where our story opens today.

### A. Sheaves in the Field Bow Down (vv. 5-8)

**5. And Joseph dreamed a dream, and he told it his brethren: and they hated him yet the more.**

For the most part, we discount the possibility of receiving information through dreams today. It is comparatively rare even in the Bible for people to receive revelations from God in dreams. Dreams in the Bible can refer to the normal dreams of sleep (Isaiah 29:7, 8), the imaginary dreams of false prophets (Jeremiah 23:25-32; 27:9, 10), or dreams of revelation (Genesis 41:17; Daniel 2:28).

The dreams of revelation are found primarily in Genesis and Daniel. *Joseph* is one of the few to whom God speaks in this manner. Equally important is the fact that Joseph will later demonstrate the God-given ability to interpret the dreams of others (Genesis 40:12, 13, 18, 19; 41:25-32). This ability will open doors for the family of Jacob to come to Egypt.

As we are introduced to Joseph's dreams, we are also introduced to his brothers' response. For them the dream represents an intolerable attitude of superiority.

**6, 7. And he said unto them, Hear, I pray you, this dream which I have dreamed: for, behold, we were binding sheaves in the field, and, lo, my sheaf arose, and also stood upright; and, behold, your sheaves stood round about, and made obeisance to my sheaf.**

We are introduced to the style of grain harvest in Joseph's day. Men and women go out with hand sickles and cut the grain. As they do, they gather the cut stalks into *sheaves*. The sheaves are stacked in the field to await transport to the place of threshing. (A fuller picture of the process of grain harvesting in Bible times is found in the book of Ruth.)

To make *obeisance* means to bow down in an act of great respect or worship. Here *obeisance*

---

## How to Say It

CANAAN. *Kay*-nun.
DOTHAN. *Doe*-thun (*th* as in *thin*).
ELISHA. E-*lye*-shuh.
ESAU. *Ee*-saw.
HAGAR. *Hay*-gar.
ISHMAEL. *Ish*-may-el.
ISHMAELITES. *Ish*-may-el-ites.
ISRAEL. *Iz*-ray-el.
KETURAH. Keh-*too*-ruh.
MIDIAN. *Mid*-ee-un.
MIDIANITES. *Mid*-ee-un-ites.
OBEISANCE. oh-*bee*-sense.
PADAN-ARAM. *Pay*-dan-*a*-ram.
POTIPHAR. *Pot*-ih-far.
SHECHEM. *Shee*-kem or *Shek*-em.

---

signifies that someone else has (or will have) power over those who are doing the bowing.

**8. And his brethren said to him, Shalt thou indeed reign over us? or shalt thou indeed have dominion over us? And they hated him yet the more for his dreams, and for his words.**

Joseph's suggestion that his brothers will bow down to him infuriates them. As far as they are concerned, Joseph will never rule or *have dominion* over them. [See question #1, page 88.]

Though the Bible is silent on this matter, it is very possible that the brothers have already discussed killing Joseph as soon as Jacob is dead (compare Esau's idea in Genesis 27:41). Whether they have or not, Joseph's dream adds fuel to the already burning fire. It is bad enough to have to accept the fact that Joseph is their father's favorite. But the suggestion that they will bow down before him is too much. The stage is being set for terrible happenings.

We may note at this point that we have a prediction that will be fulfilled in the later years of Joseph. "Joseph's brethren came, and bowed down themselves before him with their faces to the earth. . . . And Joseph remembered the dreams which he dreamed of them" (Genesis 42:6, 9; compare 43:26, 28; 44:14).

### B. Sun, Moon, and Stars Bow Down (v. 9)

**9. And he dreamed yet another dream, and told it his brethren, and said, Behold, I have dreamed a dream more; and, behold, the sun and the moon and the eleven stars made obeisance to me.**

Some time after the first *dream*, Joseph dreams again. For Joseph, the two dreams provide absolute verification that the message is true, since the two dreams concern the same subject. We may compare this with Pharaoh's two dreams in the same night; those dreams had different images but the same meaning (Genesis 41:25).

Joseph's second dream has implications as serious as the first. It predicts that Joseph's father (Jacob), his mother, and his 11 brothers will bow down to him. The number 11 leaves no doubt about whom these images signify!

### DELUSIONS OF GRANDEUR

Jackie Gleason starred as bus driver Ralph Kramden of *The Honeymooners* in the early years of television. Ralph lived with his wife, Alice, in a run-down apartment in the city. He was a blustering big-mouth—a self-appointed "king of his castle"—who went through scheme after scheme in which he dreamed of becoming great, rich, and successful.

Ralph's best friend, Ed Norton, worked for the sewer department. Ed was a more down-to-earth kind of person, yet he also had dreams of grandeur. One observer noted that the men had more ambition than aptitude.

Part of the appeal of these fictional characters was that they represented the mind-set of many watching. Ralph was "every man," the frustrated plodder whose life was dull despite his daydreams. Joseph also had dreams of grandeur, but these were of a far different type from those of Ralph Kramden and "every man"! Joseph didn't create his dreams; they came from God. Joseph's dreams were not daydreams, whipped up out of whims of fantasy; they were God's revelation of assured future events.

Some Christians have been known to muse about all the grandiose things they could do for God if only they could win the lottery or some such. Much more productive and pleasing to God would be efforts to strengthen our character and integrity. As time would tell, those were to become hallmarks of Joseph's life. They can be ours as well. —C. R. B.

## II. Family Reacts
## (Genesis 37:10, 11)

Joseph usually is the one who can do no wrong in his father's eyes. But this dream offends even his father. The implications are incredible, even to Jacob.

### A. Jacob Rebukes (v. 10)

**10. And he told it to his father, and to his brethren: and his father rebuked him, and said unto him, What is this dream that thou hast dreamed? Shall I and thy mother and thy brethren indeed come to bow down ourselves to thee to the earth?**

It is possible that Joseph's *father* (Jacob) does not know about the first dream regarding the sheaves. Jacob certainly wants his son to be the leader of the family, but to hear Joseph now declare his authority in this fashion is too much. Is Joseph really arrogant enough to think that his father and *mother* and 11 brothers will *bow down* to him? (The mother in view here is not Rachel, who is dead by this time, but Joseph's stepmother, Leah.)

At this moment it appears that Joseph is alone: his brothers hate him, and his father has rebuked him. We should keep in mind, however, that Joseph is being honest about what he experienced. The Bible makes it clear that these dreams are not fabrications on Joseph's part.

### B. Brothers Envy (v. 11)

**11. And his brethren envied him; but his father observed the saying.**

The idea that the brothers envy Joseph suggests a stronger and more significant passion than even hatred. The emotion of envy magnifies the possibility that their feelings will spill over into violence. This is another signal that the brothers are plotting revenge. [See question #2, page 88.]

The phrase *his father observed the saying* tells us that Jacob recognizes that this dream does have potential for revelation. Jacob's reaction is similar to that of Mary in the New Testament: "But Mary kept all these things, and pondered them in her heart" (Luke 2:19). [See question #3, page 88.]

In any case, Jacob seems unaware of the danger that Joseph is in. This is seen by the fact that Jacob is willing to send Joseph to check on his brothers one more time (Genesis 37:12, 13, not in today's text).

## III. Plot Develops
## (Genesis 37:19-21, 23, 24a, 28)

It is only a matter of time until Joseph is again alone with his brothers. Supposedly they are tending flocks near Shechem, so Joseph goes there first. But a resident of the area tells him that his brothers have moved to Dothan, about 14 miles north of Shechem (Genesis 37:12-17) and perhaps 60 miles from home.

Dothan is a major city in the area, important to two people in the Bible: Joseph and Elisha. Whereas God allows Joseph to be taken to Egypt in slavery from near Dothan, He will miraculously deliver Elisha from the Syrian army in that locale centuries later (2 Kings 6:13-17). The brothers may have moved on to there in order to find better grass for the flocks and herds or because more water is available. There is no suggestion that they are trying to hide from their father.

### A. First Plan: Murder (vv. 19-21, 23, 24a)

**19, 20. And they said one to another, Behold, this dreamer cometh. Come now therefore, and let us slay him, and cast him into some pit, and we will say, Some evil beast hath devoured him; and we shall see what will become of his dreams.**

*Behold, this dreamer cometh* indicates that Joseph has gained a new nickname that is intended to be an unveiled insult. The brothers' first plan is to kill Joseph outright. That will put an end to his dreams and free them from this pesky brother! [See question #4, page 88.]

**21. And Reuben heard it, and he delivered him out of their hands; and said, Let us not kill him.**

*Reuben* is the oldest of the brothers. He is the one who accepts responsibility as the firstborn son to save Joseph by suggesting that they cast him into a pit (Genesis 37:22, not in today's text). For reasons unknown, Reuben apparently leaves Joseph in the care of the other brothers (v. 29, not in today's text). [See question #5, page 88.]

**23, 24a. And it came to pass, when Joseph was come unto his brethren, that they stripped Joseph out of his coat, his coat of many colors that was on him; and they took him, and cast him into a pit.**

The offensive *coat* has to be removed. The coat symbolizes all the things the brothers hate about *Joseph*. Its existence demonstrates that he is privileged. Stripping Joseph of this article of clothing provides a first taste of revenge. Humiliating this 17-year-old boy brings the brothers cynical pleasure.

The next stage of their revenge is throwing Joseph into *a pit,* meaning a dry cistern. It is impossible for him to climb out of it without assistance from outside.

### B. Second Plan: Slavery (v. 28)

**28. Then there passed by Midianites merchantmen; and they drew and lifted up Joseph out of the pit, and sold Joseph to the Ishmaelites for twenty pieces of silver: and they brought Joseph into Egypt.**

After casting Joseph into the pit, it is time for lunch (see v. 25, not in today's text). Before the *Midianites* arrive, the brothers may enjoy special delicacies that Joseph has brought from their father. It is doubtful that they share any with their captive!

As they eat, they spot a camel caravan on its way to *Egypt.* Dothan is close to one of the major trade routes to that country. The brothers recognize the opportunity to solve their problem while keeping their hands free of their brother's blood.

It is at the suggestion of Judah that Joseph be sold to the *merchantmen* (see vv. 26, 27, not in today's text). Reuben planned to save Joseph somehow, but failed. Instead, Judah is the one to step forward and provide a solution that keeps Joseph alive.

We will see this failure-success pattern again. When famine later comes to Canaan and the brothers return from Egypt with food, Reuben will try to convince his father to allow Benjamin to go along on a follow-up trip. That offer will

| Comparison of Joseph and Jesus | | |
| --- | --- | --- |
| Joseph | | Jesus |
| Genesis 30:22-24 | Conceived under miraculous circumstances | Luke 1:26-38 |
| Genesis 37:28 | Taken to Egypt under stressful circumstances | Matthew 2:13-15 |
| Genesis 37:5 | Rejected by brothers | John 7:5 |
| Genesis 37:11 | Hated because of envy | Matthew 27:18 |
| Genesis 37:23 | Stripped by enemies | Matthew 27:28 |
| Genesis 37:28 Leviticus 27:5 | Sold for the price of a slave | Matthew 26:15 Exodus 21:32 |
| Genesis 39:6b-12 | Resisted strong temptation | Matthew 4:1-17 |
| Genesis 39:13-20 | Suffered undeserved punishment | Mark 15:25-32 |
| Genesis 40 | Associated with two criminals, one who was blessed and one who was not | Luke 23:39-43 |
| Genesis 41:46 | Began most important work at age 30 | Luke 3:23 |

Visual for Lesson 10

*After exploring these comparisons, ask your learners if they can think of others.*

be rejected (Genesis 42:37, 38). Judah then will demonstrate leadership qualities once again by stepping forward to accept personal responsibility for the life of Benjamin. His offer will be accepted (43:8-15).

We may pause to consider the two designations *Midianites* and *Ishmaelites.* One opinion is that these are different designations for the same group. In favor of this idea, we may compare Genesis 37:36 with 39:1; the former says it is the Midianites who sell Joseph to Potiphar while the latter says it is the Ishmaelites who do so. Much later we find Gideon fighting against "the Midianites" (Judges 7:24, 25; 8:1); we are told they wore "golden earrings, because they were Ishmaelites" (Judges 8:24).

On the other hand, some scholars see the caravan as made up of Midianite merchants who act as "middlemen" for the Ishmaelites. Both groups are relatives of Abraham. Ishmael was Abraham's son born to Hagar, Sarah's Egyptian maidservant. Midian was one of the sons of Keturah, Abraham's second wife (Genesis 25:1, 2). Both the Midianites and Ishmaelites are thus blood relatives of Jacob and his family.

The relative value of 20 *pieces of silver* is uncertain. Weighing a total of about 8 ounces, 20 pieces of silver (or shekels) seems to be the going price for slaves in the time of Joseph. Compare Exodus 21:32, where servants (slaves) later are to be valued at 30 shekels of silver. Jesus' life will also valued at 30 pieces of silver when He is betrayed centuries later (Zechariah 11:12, 13; Matthew 26:15; 27:9, 10).

In any case, the sale of Joseph brings monetary profit to the brothers as well as providing the means by which they can be rid of him. The brothers confidently assume that they will never see their brother again. *Now* what will become of his dreams (Genesis 37:20)? Time will tell!

### THE TANGLED WEB
*Oh, what a tangled web we weave,*
*When first we practise to deceive!*
Those are the words of the Scottish poet Sir Walter Scott (1771–1832). The truth of the sentiment is seen in the frequency of its quotation in commentary on a wide range of subjects. For example, an Internet search of the phrase *what a tangled web we weave* will return scores of "hits" on subject matters as diverse as teaching botany to grade-school children, digital library practices, shady bookkeeping techniques, political shenanigans, misleading advertising, and falsified scientific research.

Joseph's brothers had a hard time trying to decide upon the most expedient way to get rid of their pesky younger sibling. Whatever method they chose, they knew they would have to deceive their father, who loved Joseph more than any of them. Whether to kill him outright or sell him into slavery, they still had to concoct a story.

Their deception would ultimately be exposed. Isn't that still true? Is there one of us who has not seen (or caused) the sad effects of "the tangled web"?
—C. R. B.

# Conclusion

## A. Can We See the Hand of God?
When the news of Joseph's "demise" reached Jacob, he cried out in his grief (Genesis 37:33-35). He already had lain his dear wife Rachel to rest. Then he (apparently) lost the most precious of his sons as well. Yet unbeknownst to all parties, a great plan was beginning to unfold. The brothers in their haste to dispose of Joseph had no idea of the chain of events that they had set in motion.

God in His foreknowledge was aware of what was to come. God had already promised through Abraham that his family would sojourn in Egypt for 400 years (Genesis 15:13). That sojourn would result in a group of people large enough to be a nation.

Joseph was being sent ahead as a kind of "point man" for his family to this end. At the place where today's lesson ends it is almost certain that he could see only the slavery that lay ahead. The brothers later remembered Joseph's state of mind at this point in time: "We saw the

anguish of his soul, when he besought us, and we would not hear" (Genesis 42:21).

Because we can look back on the entire story, it is easy for us to see the hand of God at work in all of this. But what about Joseph when he first began to have dreams of great significance? Did he see the hand of God working in his life? At the age of 17 it is more likely that he simply knew that he was having dreams that amazed even him.

Joseph may or may not have understood that his dreams pointed to his being a leader. Of much greater importance was the fact that Joseph determined to maintain his personal integrity regardless of what happened. His brothers thought him to be positioning himself to take over the family. The life of Joseph demonstrated that he primarily sought to work with integrity no matter what position of life he was in. God, the unseen mover in this story, had chosen the right man for the job!

It can be very difficult to see God's hand during our trials today. Yet God remains as the unseen mover in our lives and indeed in all of history. This fact leads us to today's prayer.

## B. Prayer
Our Father in Heaven, we ask that You help us to use the story of Joseph to inspire us to be patient as we await the outcome of events we experience. In our waiting, we pray that we would conduct ourselves with all holiness, even during—especially during!—the toughest times. In the name of Christ, amen.

## C. Thought to Remember
God is still the unseen mover.

# Home Daily Bible Readings

**Monday, Oct. 29**—The Favored Son (Genesis 37:1-4)

**Tuesday, Oct. 30**—The Jealous Brothers (Genesis 37:5-11)

**Wednesday, Oct. 31**—The Messenger (Genesis 37:12-17)

**Thursday, Nov. 1**—The Dreamer (Genesis 37:18-24)

**Friday, Nov. 2**—Sold into Slavery (Genesis 37:25-28)

**Saturday, Nov. 3**—A Father's Distress (Genesis 37:29-36)

**Sunday, Nov. 4**—A Prayer for Deliverance (Psalm 70)

# Learning by Doing

*This page contains an alternative lesson plan emphasizing learning activities. Classes desiring such student involvement will find these suggestions helpful.*

## Into the Lesson

Locate a display of real butterflies pinned to a presentation board or under glass. If this is not available, a large poster showing a variety of butterflies can be substituted. Images can be found on the Internet.

Have the butterfly display visible to learners as they arrive. This will stimulate discussion and curiosity before and at the beginning of class. You as the teacher should not dominate the discussion, but from time to time feel free to add "fascinating facts" about butterflies (which you have researched in advance).

Begin the class proper by asking, "Has anyone had a butterfly land on your bare skin?" Have class members describe how the butterfly felt on their skin. Then ask, "Does it seem possible that so small a creature could affect weather?" Wait for a response. Then say, "Some scientists theorize that the motion of a butterfly's wings can influence air movement over a larger area." Draw upon the Lesson Introduction for further comments regarding "the butterfly effect."

Next ask, "What other small movements may have a larger effect on the environment?" Answers might include a small snow slide resulting in an avalanche, a pebble dropped into a lake creating a widening circle of waves, a seed falling into fertile ground developing into a tree that eventually produces more trees.

Ask the class to tell of individuals who began a Christian work that has blossomed into a much bigger effort for God. Some examples may include missionaries, someone who began a ministry within the congregation, or national ministries such as Focus on the Family.

## Into the Word

Have a class member describe Joseph's two dreams, giving all the details listed in Genesis 37:5-9. Ask how those dreams related to the lifestyle of Jacob's family. Have the class talk about the importance of (even worship of) the sun, moon, and stars to early civilization. Recruit, in advance, someone to describe farming methods for harvesting wheat in Joseph's day.

Next, select one class member to play the part of Jacob and another to act as Joseph. Select several individuals to represent the brothers.

The actors are to role-play the discussion that occurred when Joseph told his dreams to his family. Instruct your actors to use some imagination as to how the conversation probably unfolded.

When the actors finish, ask the entire class to identify what part of the drama was spelled out in Scripture and what part was "sanctified imagination." Then ask them to discuss whether the imagined conversation fits into what is known of Joseph and his family from the scriptural record.

Ask, "Why do you think Joseph told of his dreams rather than keeping them a secret?" Probe for different points of view. If no one brings it up, mention Joseph's young age as a possible factor. Then summarize the sequence of events that led to the sale of Joseph into slavery. Using a Bible-times map, locate the area where Joseph's brothers put him into a pit and where the caravan took him after he was sold. Note the approximate distance of 250 to 300 miles that Joseph traveled with them.

Begin a discussion about whether or not Joseph had even an inkling at this time that he was destined to do something great for God and for his family. Challenge your learners to back up their conclusions with Bible facts from the lesson.

## Into Life

Ask, "What barriers keep you from telling others about the gospel of Jesus Christ?" Allow time for several to answer.

Give each person an index card. Say, "Across the top of the card, write, 'God has saved me through Jesus, and I should tell another person about it!'" Then explain, "First, write the name of the person with whom you intend to share the gospel. Then write what you need to say and when you will say it. Finally, sign your name as a commitment to follow up on your resolve." Allow a few minutes of silence for this exercise to be completed. Tell your learners to keep their cards visible throughout the week ahead as a reminder.

When the written assignment is completed, pause for silent prayer. Each should pray for the courage to complete this task. After one minute, the teacher should close the prayer audibly, asking God to strengthen class members to tell someone of His work in their lives.

# Let's Talk It Over

*The questions on this page are designed to promote discussion of the lesson by the class and to encourage application of the lesson Scriptures. The answers provided are only discussion starters. Let your class talk it over from there.*

**1. What was a time when you saw speaking the truth cause resentment? How do you handle such a reaction in a godly way?**

Our Lord's truth-statements about himself aroused much opposition. A primary reason was that those statements challenged vested interests (John 11:48). Opposition to Christianity is common on the mission field, where the testimony of missionaries is often taken as a challenge by the leaders of established pagan religions. Again, vested interests become threatened (compare Acts 16:16-19).

We can expect opposition as well when we stand for righteousness. Political passions often run strong and distort moral issues, especially at election time. Remember that Jesus said, "If they have persecuted me, they will also persecute you" (John 15:20). A humble response is important (Luke 6:27-36).

**2. What was a time when you had to tell a truth that turned out to be very unpopular? How did you handle the situation?**

Most of us are familiar with the concept of "shooting the messenger." This is the idea that if a certain message is unpopular, then people may react by attacking the one who is bringing the message rather than coming to grips with the truth of the message itself. This can take the form of character assassination. When Jesus' enemies could not refute His truth, they said, "He hath a devil, and is mad; why hear ye him?" (John 10:20). The result may be physical confrontation, as in Acts 14:19.

Maintaining poise and coolness under fire is important. "A soft answer turneth away wrath: but grievous words stir up anger" (Proverbs 15:1). This is not a skill learned overnight! Humility is always called for. An arrogant presentation of the truth will not be persuasive.

**3. Was it inconsistent for Jacob to rebuke Joseph but keep the matter in mind anyway ("observed the saying")? Why, or why not?**

Jacob—of all people!—had learned in his life that God works in mysterious ways. Jacob too had been given a dream in which God made mighty promises about his descendants (Genesis

28:12-15). Jacob may have wondered if God was behind Joseph's dream as well.

While we don't want to go overboard in "spiritualizing" things, it is a mistake to look at every incident in life merely from a flesh-and-blood point of view (see Ephesians 6:12). God may be intending for a certain situation to bring Him glory in some way. It is always wise to pray, "Lord, what do You want me to do in this situation?"

**4. Does it surprise you that Joseph's brothers conspired to kill him? Why, or why not? What does this situation teach us about dealing with human nature in a godly manner?**

There are obvious reasons why the brothers would be angered by their father's favoritism and Joseph's dreams. But for them to cook up a plan to murder a family member seems extreme!

This is a striking example of the lengths people will go to when frustrated. Compare this incident with other biblical murder plots: Haman's plot to kill Mordecai, David's plot to kill Uriah, the plot to kill Paul, and the plot to kill Jesus. The devil's intention is to kill and destroy (John 10:10). He will use jealousy, anger, lust, and ambition to accomplish his purpose. Anger is one of his favorite tools. Learning to control one's temper honors God—and may prevent a life from being taken (Proverbs 15:1, 18; Ephesians 4:31).

**5. Why do half-hearted attempts to do right usually fail?**

Reuben joined his brothers in his hatred of Joseph. But then Reuben seems to have lost his nerve (or his conscience partly got the better of him) when he suggested leaving the boy in a pit instead of killing him outright. This incident, along with Genesis 35:22, gives us a picture of a man who does not have a firm moral compass.

The other brothers may have had a hunch that Reuben would not "rat them out" to their father when they decided to sell Joseph into slavery. If so, they were right! If we try to take a moral stand but are not living with clean hands ourselves, others know it. People will ignore our moral stand if that stand is inconsistent with the way we live our lives. We may also become a target of derision for our inconsistency.

# Joseph Is Exalted

DEVOTIONAL READING: **Psalm 105:16-22.**

BACKGROUND SCRIPTURE: **Genesis 41:25-45.**

PRINTED TEXT: **Genesis 41:25-40.**

### Genesis 41:25-40

25 And Joseph said unto Pharaoh, The dream of Pharaoh is one: God hath showed Pharaoh what he is about to do.

26 The seven good kine are seven years; and the seven good ears are seven years: the dream is one.

27 And the seven thin and ill-favored kine that came up after them are seven years; and the seven empty ears blasted with the east wind shall be seven years of famine.

28 This is the thing which I have spoken unto Pharaoh: What God is about to do he showeth unto Pharaoh.

29 Behold, there come seven years of great plenty throughout all the land of Egypt:

30 And there shall arise after them seven years of famine; and all the plenty shall be forgotten in the land of Egypt; and the famine shall consume the land;

31 And the plenty shall not be known in the land by reason of that famine following; for it shall be very grievous.

32 And for that the dream was doubled unto Pharaoh twice; it is because the thing is established by God, and God will shortly bring it to pass.

33 Now therefore let Pharaoh look out a man discreet and wise, and set him over the land of Egypt.

34 Let Pharaoh do this, and let him appoint officers over the land, and take up the fifth part of the land of Egypt in the seven plenteous years.

35 And let them gather all the food of those good years that come, and lay up corn under the hand of Pharaoh, and let them keep food in the cities.

36 And that food shall be for store to the land against the seven years of famine, which shall be in the land of Egypt; that the land perish not through the famine.

37 And the thing was good in the eyes of Pharaoh, and in the eyes of all his servants.

38 And Pharaoh said unto his servants, Can we find such a one as this is, a man in whom the Spirit of God is?

39 And Pharaoh said unto Joseph, Forasmuch as God hath showed thee all this, there is none so discreet and wise as thou art:

40 Thou shalt be over my house, and according unto thy word shall all my people be ruled: only in the throne will I be greater than thou.

GOLDEN TEXT: Pharaoh said unto Joseph, Forasmuch as God hath showed thee all this, there is none so discreet and wise as thou art: thou shalt be over my house, and according unto thy word shall all my people be ruled: only in the throne will I be greater than thou.—Genesis 41:39, 40.

---

## *God Creates*
### Unit 3: God's People Re-created
### (Lessons 10-13)

---

## Lesson Aims

After participating in this lesson, each student will be able to:

1. Explain how God elevated Joseph to a position of power in Egypt.

2. Compare Joseph's experience of hardship resulting in blessing with other biblical or modern examples.

3. Give thanks to God for working all things together for good in his or her own life.

## Lesson Outline

INTRODUCTION
    A. Rising Above Adversity
    B. Lesson Background
I. DREAMS' EXPLANATION, PART 1 (Genesis 41: 25-27)
    A. God Is Revealing (v. 25)
    B. Famine Is Coming (vv. 26, 27)
II. DREAMS' EXPLANATION, PART 2 (Genesis 41: 28-32)
    A. Review of the Dreams (vv. 28-31)
    B. Reason for Two Dreams (v. 32)
    *"An Ill Wind . . . "*
III. JOSEPH'S ADVICE (Genesis 41:33-36)
    A. Wise Man Needed (v. 33)
    B. Support Team Needed (v. 34a)
    C. Stockpile Needed (vv. 34b-36)
IV. PHARAOH'S RESPONSE (Genesis 41:37-40)
    A. Total Agreement (v. 37)
    B. Best Choice (v. 38)
    *Wisdom in Listening*
    C. High Position (vv. 39, 40)
CONCLUSION
    A. Victory Through Faithfulness
    B. Prayer
    C. Thought to Remember

## Introduction

### A. Rising Above Adversity

Milos Cols (pronounced Milosh Schultz) is an evangelical minister in Prague, Czech Republic. As a minister there during the Communist era, he experienced a great deal of adversity. The government took away his ordination. He was not allowed to preach in Prague. The intent was to stop his activities by making his life as miserable as possible.

One day Milos was called in by the secret police for questioning. He showed up late, and the interrogator was furious. Milos told him, "I was sleeping so well that I forgot to wake up on time for this meeting." It was a subtle way to say, "You do not frighten me, no matter what you choose to do." The interrogator understood the innuendo and was even more furious. When his tirade ended, he allowed Milos to leave, unharmed.

Communism left Prague in 1989, and Milos is still preaching the Word. God expects his servants to rise above adversity, and He strengthens them to do so. That's just what Milos did.

### B. Lesson Background

When we last saw Joseph, he was on his way to Egypt and into slavery. His chances for a good life appeared to be very bleak. Joseph probably thought he would never see his family again.

Joseph was purchased by Potiphar, the captain of Pharaoh's guard. Joseph proved to be an excellent worker. Soon he was appointed to be manager over all the administrative affairs of Potiphar's household.

This situation lasted as long as Joseph was able to keep his master's wife away from him. Potiphar's wife lusted after Joseph, creating a major temptation for him. One day she waited for the appropriate moment to try once more. Joseph rebuffed her approach, but in revenge she accused him of attempted rape (Genesis 39).

Joseph wound up in prison. There he demonstrated his skills as an administrator, and he was soon running the prison. This position lasted for several years. During that time, Pharaoh's butler (or cupbearer) and baker were thrown into prison. Both had dreams. Joseph interpreted their dreams, and the interpretations proved to be accurate: the butler was restored to his position, and the baker was hanged.

Then Pharaoh had dreams that no one could explain. The butler told Pharaoh about Joseph. Joseph was cleaned up, appropriately dressed, and brought before Pharaoh (Genesis 41:14). [See question #1, page 96.]

The Egyptians believed that revelation from "the gods" could come through dreams. The dreams of Pharaoh thus provided the avenue for Joseph to be released from prison. Joseph himself had had two dreams (Genesis 37:5-7, 9) and two of his fellow prisoners had dreams as well (40:5-23). Then Joseph found himself confronted with two dreams of Pharaoh to interpret.

# I. Dreams' Explanation, Part 1
## (Genesis 41:25-27)
### A. God Is Revealing (v. 25)

**25. And Joseph said unto Pharaoh, The dream of Pharaoh is one: God hath showed Pharaoh what he is about to do.**

We are not able to identify with certainty the *Pharaoh* under whom *Joseph* serves, but we can make an educated guess. Using biblical chronology, we can date Joseph's life to between 1916 and 1806 BC. Joseph enters Pharaoh's service at age 30 (Genesis 41:46). That is about the year 1886 BC. This dating points to Sesostris (also spelled Senusret) II as the Pharaoh in question. His reign occurs during Egypt's Middle Kingdom Twelfth Dynasty (a dynasty that lasts from approximately 1937 to 1759 BC).

This Pharaoh, whoever he is, has had two dreams. Yet *the dream of Pharaoh is one.* That signifies that the two dreams mean the same thing. When dreams come in twos, it shows that God is firm about the matter (see v. 32, below).

Pharaoh does not understand his dreams, but he is certain that the dreams have a divine source. Any lesser explanation will not satisfy him. Joseph confirms his feelings and warns Pharaoh that the dreams contain a serious matter. Joseph does not claim to be the source of the wisdom. Rather, God is the source (see Genesis 41:16). Pharaoh may even be familiar with the name for God of *Elohim,* because the god *el* is well known in the world of that day.

### B. Famine Is Coming (vv. 26, 27)

**26, 27. The seven good kine are seven years; and the seven good ears are seven years: the dream is one. And the seven thin and ill-favored kine that came up after them are seven years; and the seven empty ears blasted with the east wind shall be seven years of famine.**

### How to Say It

ABRAHAM. *Ay*-bruh-ham.
CZECH. Check.
EGYPT. *Ee*-jipt.
EZEKIEL. Ee-*zeek*-ee-ul or Ee-*zeek*-yul.
ISAIAH. Eye-*zay*-uh.
JEREMIAH. Jair-uh-*my*-uh.
NATHAN. *Nay*-thun (*th* as in *thin*).
PHARAOH. *Fair*-o or *Fay*-roe.
POTIPHAR. *Pot*-ih-far.
SENUSRET. Sen-*oos*-ret.
SESOSTRIS. Sis-*os*-tris.

The meaning of the dreams is made known: Egypt is to enjoy *seven years* of great harvests followed by *seven years of famine. Kine* are cows. The *ears* are stalks or heads of grain, not ears of corn as we may think. Corn as we know it does not exist in this region of the world in Bible times.

The idea of plant life being *blasted* signifies God's judgment (compare 2 Kings 19:26; Isaiah 37:27). An *east wind* can also indicate judgment from God (Exodus 10:13; Psalm 48:7; Jeremiah 18:17; Ezekiel 17:10; 19:12; Jonah 4:8).

# II. Dreams' Explanation, Part 2
## (Genesis 41:28-32)
### A. Review of the Dreams (vv. 28-31)

**28, 29. This is the thing which I have spoken unto Pharaoh: What God is about to do he showeth unto Pharaoh. Behold, there come seven years of great plenty throughout all the land of Egypt.**

As Joseph reviews the meaning of the dreams, he assures Pharaoh that the message of the dreams is going to come to pass, and that it will happen very soon (*What God is about to do;* see also v. 32, below). This adds to the urgency of the situation.

Joseph is not some sort of magician or fortune-teller who can explain dreams (compare Daniel 2:1-11). He has already proven that he is God's conduit for explaining this kind of revelation (Genesis 40). Joseph correctly recognizes that he is only a tool in the hands of God (Genesis 41:16). If there is an explanation to Pharaoh's dreams, it will come from God.

**30. And there shall arise after them seven years of famine; and all the plenty shall be forgotten in the land of Egypt; and the famine shall consume the land.**

What Joseph is proposing is almost unbelievable. *Seven years of famine?* Incredible!

A prediction of famine must take into account the fact that rain in *Egypt* is rare anyway. The average rainfall along Egypt's coastline is only about four to eight inches per year. That is not adequate to support crops, even without a famine. The rest of the country, away from the coastline, may get only one or two inches of rainfall annually. Instead, agriculture in Egypt is tied to the Nile River. The Nile floods annually, bringing a new load of rich silt for the coming year's crops.

What all this means is that the powerful Egyptian "gods" of the Nile are going to fail for seven years. Yet Pharaoh believes that the dreams are true messages from the spiritual world, and Joseph provides him with the explanation. Up to this point no one else can even guess what the dreams are about. Pharaoh does not challenge Joseph's interpretations. This undoubtedly is tied in with Joseph's successful track record in interpreting the dreams of the butler and the baker.

**31. And the plenty shall not be known in the land by reason of that famine following; for it shall be very grievous.**

Joseph is in the role of court prophet similar to that of Nathan in 2 Samuel 7. To bring bad news to a ruler is dangerous, but Joseph must tell the truth: the *famine* will be *very grievous*. [See question #2, page 96.]

The famine will affect not only Egypt but surrounding lands as well (Genesis 41:54, 57). The famine will be so severe that people will forget the good years when they had plentiful crops. It was famine that brought Abraham, Joseph's great-grandfather, to Egypt (12:10). It will be famine that will drive Joseph's brothers and father to Egypt as well (42:1-3; 43:1; 47:4).

### B. Reason for Two Dreams (v. 32)

**32. And for that the dream was doubled unto Pharaoh twice; it is because the thing is established by God, and God will shortly bring it to pass.**

The famine to come will be an act of *God*. There is a significant purpose for this famine. Yet even Joseph, with his wisdom and insight, surely is not aware of the primary reason for the upcoming famine.

Remember that *Pharaoh* is not the only one who has had his *dream* repeated or *doubled*. Joseph himself had two dreams that had one and the same meaning (Genesis 37:5-7, 9).

### "AN ILL WIND . . . "

People in many places think their own weather is unique in being highly changeable. They like to say, "If you don't like the weather in _____, just wait five minutes, and it will change." Whether or not such a bold statement is true in every location, the western United States is especially subject to drastically changing weather patterns. The *El Niño* phenomenon of one year can bring record rains; the *La Niña* weather pattern that may follow can result in near drought.

Strong winds are common in *La Niña* years. Those *Santa Ana winds*, as they are called, quickly dry out the vegetation. This often results in horrendous wildfires. Government agencies are trying to get better at predicting weather patterns to improve preparedness.

Even with modern forecasting tools and big budgets, no modern governmental agency can beat Joseph in accuracy of predictions and being prepared for a natural disaster! He listened to God and thus saved the lives of many. Yet our job is even more important than Joseph's was. The book of Revelation predicts disaster after disaster that will befall the sinful people of the world. Will we warn them in time?     —C. R. B.

## III. Joseph's Advice
### (Genesis 41:33-36)
#### A. Wise Man Needed (v. 33)

**33. Now therefore let Pharaoh look out a man discreet and wise, and set him over the land of Egypt.**

Joseph proceeds to give *Pharaoh* advice on how to deal with the coming crisis. This displays boldness on Joseph's part. After all, he is a slave, freshly yanked out of prison. Pharaoh, by contrast, is viewed as a god-king. How dare a mere mortal presume to advise a god-king before that god-king requests him to do so? Yet Joseph plunges forward. [See question #3, page 96.]

The word *now* shows a transition from the stated facts to the moral conclusion. The word *discreet* deals with the ability to show discernment or good judgment. The man for this new position must be skilled in leading people; compassionate, yet firm; and of the highest integrity. Otherwise, the project will fail. [See question #4, page 96.]

#### B. Support Team Needed (v. 34a)

**34a. Let Pharaoh do this, and let him appoint officers over the land.**

The next stage will be for *Pharaoh* to *appoint officers over the land* to assist the new "starvation avoidance director" or perhaps "famine relief director" (if we may call him by either of those titles), and to implement the boss's plan. This will be more than just an advisory committee. It is to be a structured, action organization that is controlled by the government.

#### C. Stockpile Needed (vv. 34b-36)

**34b-36. And take up the fifth part of the land of Egypt in the seven plenteous years. And let them gather all the food of those good years that come, and lay up corn under the hand of Pharaoh, and let them keep food in the cities. And that food shall be for store to the land against the seven years of famine, which shall be in the land of Egypt; that the land perish not through the famine.**

The tax is to be one-fifth of the crops raised in each of *the seven plenteous years*. But if the famine is to be for seven years, then how will collecting only one-fifth per year for seven years be enough for *seven years of famine*? A period of famine doesn't necessarily mean that food production goes all the way down to zero. In any case, Joseph is preparing (under divine guidance) to feed more that just the Egyptians (Genesis 41:53-57). Unknowingly, Joseph is preparing food stores even for his own family.

## IV. Pharaoh's Response (Genesis 41:37-40)

### A. Total Agreement (v. 37)

**37. And the thing was good in the eyes of Pharaoh, and in the eyes of all his servants.**

*Pharaoh* and everyone around him are duly impressed by what they have seen and heard from Joseph. The man before them appears to have no devious agendas. Rather, Joseph is transparent in the whole matter. Joseph has identified the source of the explanation as God, not himself (Genesis 41:15, 16). He has given sound advice as to how to deal with the crisis. Now the matter is in the hands of Pharaoh.

We are not told how long the matter is discussed. No disagreement or debate is noted.

### B. Best Choice (v. 38)

**38. And Pharaoh said unto his servants, Can we find such a one as this is, a man in whom the Spirit of God is?**

The question raised involves whom to appoint to the position of "famine relief director." This will take an unusual person. The most important characteristic will be integrity. The opportunities for graft, bribery, and other misconduct will be enormous. This person will have vast powers and access to great wealth.

*Pharaoh* is aware that many men are not able to handle such a job without being corrupted by it. Pharaoh has never seen Joseph before. But Joseph has already demonstrated his integrity, first in the house of Potiphar (Genesis 39:5-10) and then in the prison (39:20-23). Pharaoh may not be fully aware (or aware at all) of Joseph's integrity in these cases, but God certainly knows.

We need also to remember that Joseph has earned respect by his ability to do what Pharaoh's advisors could not do—namely, interpret the dreams of Pharaoh, the baker, and the cupbearer. For Pharaoh, this is evidence of divine leading in the life of Joseph.

No man could do what Joseph has done if he didn't have divine help. Joseph is thus identified as a man *in whom the Spirit of God is*. The phrase *Spirit of God* is used only twice in Genesis—here

Visual for Lesson 11. *This sobering visual can bring to mind past tragedies. Ask your learners how they draw on God's promises to cope.*

and in 1:2. Pharaoh believes that a divine spirit can empower servants of the deity. Thus Joseph is the ideal man for this important job.

Pharaoh's choice is undoubtedly the result of God's work on his heart. What is happening here is not by chance or coincidence. Pharaoh expected his own advisors to be able to interpret the dreams, but they could not. To their credit, they don't even try to fabricate an interpretation (Genesis 41:8). Now standing before Pharaoh is a man who interprets the dreams without apparent expectation of personal gain.

### WISDOM IN LISTENING

In the spring of 2004, a self-styled "prophet" who had a substantial audience among Christians in the San Diego area announced an impending disaster. "God had told him" that He would send a devastating earthquake upon the coastal regions of California during the second week of September that year. Yet not a single earthquake of any significance occurred anywhere in the world during that period!

The following spring, the same man predicted a major disaster for the western coast of the U.S. for the end of August. It could be prevented only if vast numbers of Christians went to the Pacific shoreline and prayed for God to stop the calamity, he claimed. There was no noticeable increase in prayer activity on California beaches, but no catastrophic event occurred either.

Joseph was a much better prophet than this man in California—fortunately for Pharaoh! Despite the fact that Pharaoh was a pagan ruler, it was to his credit that he listened carefully to what the man of God had to say. Pharaoh undoubtedly had other prophets, but he chose to listen to the one who truly spoke God's message. Are we as wise as Pharaoh in that regard?        —C. R. B.

### C. High Position (vv. 39, 40)

**39, 40. And Pharaoh said unto Joseph, Forasmuch as God hath showed thee all this, there is none so discreet and wise as thou art: thou shalt be over my house, and according unto thy word shall all my people be ruled: only in the throne will I be greater than thou.**

The unbelievable becomes believable. Only a few hours earlier, Joseph had been in prison. He had been there for over two years (Genesis 41:1), with little hope of ever being released.

Yet Joseph had made the best of the situation. Rather than sitting down, folding his arms, and pouting, he had gone to work. As a result, he had risen to become second only to the warden in that prison.

When Joseph left prison to meet Pharaoh, he had no idea what direction his life was going to take. A meeting with Pharaoh! This could have meant either the end of his life, freedom, or merely being thrown right back in prison. It is highly unlikely that the thought of receiving a lifetime appointment to a high government position ever crosses Joseph's mind.

But now he is being made the second most important man in all of Egypt (compare Daniel 2:48; 5:29; 6:1-3). Egypt is one of the most powerful nations in the world at the time. Now Joseph is in charge of *all* of Pharaoh's *people*. Joseph's word is to be the final word in all matters. He is answerable to no one except Pharaoh.

In the text that follows, we find Pharaoh affirming Joseph's high status (Genesis 41:41).

### Home Daily Bible Readings

**Monday, Nov. 5**—In Potiphar's House (Genesis 39:1-6a)

**Tuesday, Nov. 6**—Joseph Refuses (Genesis 39:6b-10)

**Wednesday, Nov. 7**—Revenge (Genesis 39:11-20)

**Thursday, Nov. 8**—Pharaoh's Dreams (Genesis 41:1-8)

**Friday, Nov. 9**—Joseph the Interpreter (Genesis 41:25-36)

**Saturday, Nov. 10**—Second-in-Command (Genesis 41:37-45)

**Sunday, Nov. 11**—God's Wonderful Works (Psalm 105:16-22)

Pharaoh does this by giving his personal signet ring to Joseph (41:42). This kind of ring is used to make wax-seal impressions on official decrees. That seal impression will be as if Pharaoh himself is issuing the decree.

Joseph is also given linen robes and a gold neck chain. He will also ride in a chariot—the limousine of the day. He is given a bodyguard who is to run before him (Genesis 41:43). People will bow down as his chariot passes by.

But that's not all. Joseph also is given a wife from the family of one of the most important religious figures in the country (Genesis 41:45). We cannot resist speculating at this point that Joseph must recall his early dreams, wondering how they will come to pass. He certainly will recall those dreams a few years later (42:9). [See question #5, page 96.]

## Conclusion

### A. Victory Through Faithfulness

Joseph is one of the greatest men of the Old Testament. He started out as the special child of his father, but was hated by his brothers. He was sold into slavery by these brothers. Then he was indicted by a vindictive woman for refusing to be unfaithful to God. He was forgotten in prison for a time by a person whom he befriended and for whom he predicted a return to his former position.

Any one of these events could have been enough to send a person into a permanent depression. Joseph had frequent opportunities to sin. Who would care if he did? Potiphar's wife certainly wouldn't have cared! His father thought he was dead. His brothers were far away and didn't know or care where he was. His peers in Egypt were accustomed to sin and degradation. They would not seek to lead Joseph in the right direction morally.

Through exile, slavery, and abuse, Joseph remained faithful to God. After 13 years (from age 17 to age 30), God honored Joseph's faithfulness.

### B. Prayer

Heavenly Father, give us the determination to persevere when times are difficult. Help us to use those times to draw closer to You. When we do draw closer, help us to remain close. Help us to thank You for the good times and the blessings You bestow. Give us the integrity that Joseph had. In Jesus' name, amen.

### C. Thought to Remember

God never forgets faithfulness.

# Learning by Doing

*This page contains an alternative lesson plan emphasizing learning activities.*
*Classes desiring such student involvement will find these suggestions helpful.*

## Into the Lesson

Prior to class, make a large poster collage depicting recent natural disasters across the world. This can be a combination of headlines and photos from magazines and newspapers. It can be articles and images downloaded from the Internet. A long sheet of butcher paper could be used in place of a poster board, or the display could be put on a bulletin board. Another alternative is to affix the materials to the board or wall one item at a time as each is introduced.

Have the class discuss these events, including whether national and international response was adequate to meet the needs of the victims in specific instances. Then ask if anyone has experienced a natural disaster. Ask that person or persons to tell how they felt, how they survived, how others reacted, etc.

The discussion may include testimonies of how God provided and protected them during these times of crisis. Do not allow this section of the class to extend very long. The testimonies should be short, highlighting God's providential care.

## Into the Word

Have a class member briefly retell the story of how Joseph came to be imprisoned in Egypt. You may wish to call this person early in the week to ask him or her to be prepared. Ask this question for discussion: "Given Joseph's revelatory dreams of leadership, what do you think went through his mind while he was imprisoned?"

Next, divide the class into small groups. Give each group a sheet of paper and ask for drawings of Pharaoh's dreams. Say that you want the drawings to be in comic-strip fashion (stick figures are fine). There should be two series of drawings: one series for the first dream and another series for the second dream.

Call the class back together and ask someone from each group to show and explain their comic strip. Then lead a discussion centered around these questions:

1. Why do you think Pharaoh believed Joseph's interpretation?

2. What *events* in Joseph's past prepared him to head up the effort to store food in view of the coming famine?

3. What *characteristics* of Joseph qualified him for the role of "famine relief director"? (This exercise is in the optional student book.)

Write responses on the board; discuss as appropriate. Then say, "Another interpreter of dreams was Daniel." Have someone read Daniel 2:1-30. Write "Joseph and Daniel" at the top of the board. Ask, "What similarities are there between Joseph and Daniel?" Have a "scribe" list responses on the board. Follow with these questions: "How was God working in each of the two situations to further His plans? Did either man seek this ability or the fame that followed?"

Ask the class to list other Bible characters who suffered while God was working out His plans for both them and others.

## Into Life

Before class, write the following three questions on a poster (large enough to be seen throughout the classroom). Do not show the poster until you come to this part of the lesson.

1. What was a difficult time in your life that turned positive?

2. What situation in your life right now may be the beginning of something that God is doing?

3. Specifically, how will you respond to God in this situation?

Divide the class into groups of four. Appoint one person in each group who will be in charge of keeping the discussion moving. Have each group discuss the questions sequentially. Ask the leaders of each group to encourage (but not force) everyone to participate. State a time limit before starting the discussions; notify the leaders a few minutes before the time is up, so they can be sure that every question is covered.

When time is up, ask for volunteers to offer answers to the class as a whole. Again, do not "put anyone on the spot" to respond. There may be some who were willing to reply in the previous small-group setting, but who would be embarrassed to do so in front of everyone.

Finally, have a time of silent prayer. Each should pray about how God is working right now is his or her life to produce a great harvest in the future. At the end of one minute, the teacher should close the prayer audibly, thanking God for His work in the lives of the learners.

# Let's Talk It Over

*The questions on this page are designed to promote discussion of the lesson by the class and to encourage application of the lesson Scriptures. The answers provided are only discussion starters. Let your class talk it over from there.*

**1. How did Joseph's experiences in Potiphar's house and in prison serve as preparation for his challenge before Pharaoh? How are Joseph's experiences relevant for us today?**

It was no accident that the gift of interpreting dreams should be given to someone like Joseph. He demonstrated godly integrity and character in resisting the temptress. He drew upon his godly integrity and his character to save him during the discouragement of imprisonment. While others may have despaired, Joseph developed a habit of dependence on God for everything, always.

God honored Joseph's devotion. It is valuable to look back over our lives and recognize that God is always busy in our experiences helping us build character—when we allow Him to!

**2. How can we recognize an approaching famine of God's Word? What corrective action can we take to avoid or reverse such a famine?**

As bad as a famine of food for the body is, a famine of food for the soul is worse! Some believe we are heading into a famine of God's Word; some believe we are in the midst of that famine right now.

For example, civil authorities and business leaders in America often seem bent on obliterating any mention of Christianity (witness "Happy Holidays!" instead of "Merry Christmas!"). Some evangelical chaplains in America's armed services feel pressured to omit the name of Christ in public prayers. Some high-school valedictorians have been forbidden to mention the name of Jesus in their commencement addresses.

Avoiding or reversing such a famine begins with prayer. Also, the power of the ballot box is crucial in democratic societies. But most important is to ensure that we don't promote a "voluntary famine" in our own lives by neglecting regular Bible study and devotions.

**3. How can we make Joseph's boldness our own in the twenty-first century?**

Joseph is not our only biblical example of godly boldness. The names Moses, Ruth, Jeremiah, Daniel, Peter, and Paul also come to mind.

All these people had an underlying base of high moral integrity. Godly boldness must have this starting point. We establish and build on such a starting point when we allow the Scriptures to train us in righteousness and to equip us for every good work (2 Timothy 3:16, 17). The stories of Joseph, Moses, Daniel, and others encourage us to be bold and discover in our day that God is just as faithful as He ever was.

**4. In what ways would you say that you are a person of discretion, as Joseph uses the concept? How can you improve?**

We would like to be charitable and say that most people have *discernment* or *good judgment* at least on some level. But when we see the choices that some people make while shopping at the grocery store, we may wonder if that's always true!

Before seeking out or accepting high-visibility leadership roles, we may want to examine those "little areas" of life to see how much good judgment we really have. As Jesus pointed out, "He that is faithful in that which is least is faithful also in much: and he that is unjust in the least is unjust also in much" (Luke 16:10).

Consider also Paul's question: "For if a man know not how to rule his own house, how shall he take care of the church of God?" (1 Timothy 3:5). Joseph honed his leadership skills while performing the lesser tasks of managing Potiphar's house and the prison.

**5. How can you cooperate with God in working out His will for your life? What parallels do you see between Joseph's life and yours?**

The events in Joseph's life illustrate Romans 8:28: "All things work together for good to them that love God, to them who are the called according to his purpose." That promise is just as true today. He will work all things together, both bad and good, in order to bless and protect His own for eternity.

However, we can cooperate in the great working out of God's plan by living lives of daily faithfulness. Joseph showed a hatred of evil when he fled from Potiphar's wife. Joseph cooperated with and assisted the prison warden rather than resisting him. The Lord rewarded Joseph's godly behavior.

# God Preserves His People

DEVOTIONAL READING: **Psalm 85.**

BACKGROUND SCRIPTURE: **Genesis 43:1–45:15.**

PRINTED TEXT: **Genesis 45:1-12.**

### Genesis 45:1-12

1 Then Joseph could not refrain himself before all them that stood by him; and he cried, Cause every man to go out from me. And there stood no man with him, while Joseph made himself known unto his brethren.

2 And he wept aloud: and the Egyptians and the house of Pharaoh heard.

3 And Joseph said unto his brethren, I am Joseph; doth my father yet live? And his brethren could not answer him; for they were troubled at his presence.

4 And Joseph said unto his brethren, Come near to me, I pray you. And they came near. And he said, I am Joseph your brother, whom ye sold into Egypt.

5 Now therefore be not grieved, nor angry with yourselves, that ye sold me hither: for God did send me before you to preserve life.

6 For these two years hath the famine been in the land: and yet there are five years, in the which there shall neither be earing nor harvest.

7 And God sent me before you to preserve you a posterity in the earth, and to save your lives by a great deliverance.

8 So now it was not you that sent me hither, but God: and he hath made me a father to Pharaoh, and lord of all his house, and a ruler throughout all the land of Egypt.

9 Haste ye, and go up to my father, and say unto him, Thus saith thy son Joseph, God hath made me lord of all Egypt: come down unto me, tarry not:

10 And thou shalt dwell in the land of Goshen, and thou shalt be near unto me, thou, and thy children, and thy children's children, and thy flocks, and thy herds, and all that thou hast:

11 And there will I nourish thee; for yet there are five years of famine; lest thou, and thy household, and all that thou hast, come to poverty.

12 And, behold, your eyes see, and the eyes of my brother Benjamin, that it is my mouth that speaketh unto you.

GOLDEN TEXT: God sent me before you to preserve you a posterity in the earth, and to save your lives by a great deliverance.—Genesis 45:7.

## God Creates
### Unit 3: God's People Re-created
### (Lessons 10-13)

## Lesson Aims

After participating in this lesson, each student will be able to:

1. Summarize Joseph's speech to his brothers when he revealed his identity.

2. Articulate the importance of seeing the "bigger picture" when viewing the events of life.

3. Write a prayer that asks for God's strength in resisting temptation to seek revenge when wronged.

## Lesson Outline

INTRODUCTION
    A. A Struggling Young Minister
    B. Lesson Background
  I. JOSEPH'S ANNOUNCEMENT (Genesis 45:1-4)
    A. Joseph Unrestrained (vv. 1a-2)
    B. Joseph Reveals (vv. 3, 4)
      *What Is Least Expected*
  II. GOD'S PURPOSE (Genesis 45:5-8)
    A. What the Brothers Should Not Do (v. 5a)
    B. What God Is Doing (vv. 5b-8)
      *Good News from Bad?*
  III. JOSEPH'S INSTRUCTIONS (Genesis 45:9-11)
    A. Come to Egypt (v. 9)
    B. Dwell in Goshen (v. 10)
    C. Avoid Becoming Destitute (v. 11)
  IV. JOSEPH'S VERIFICATION (Genesis 45:12)
CONCLUSION
    A. Servanthood Wins Out
    B. Prayer
    C. Thought to Remember

## Introduction

### A. A Struggling Young Minister

A young minister found a church about 200 miles from the seminary he planned to attend. The church at first was very glad to have him. But they had one restriction: he could not attend board meetings.

The young minister was not upset by this restriction because he didn't enjoy board meetings anyway. The agreement stipulated that the employment could be terminated by either party by giving a notice of 30 days to the other.

About a year after the young minister was hired, the church held a special board meeting. The major topic of discussion was this new minister. It was concluded at that meeting that they would fire him, but would wait 30 days before telling him he had been fired. Then he would have to leave immediately.

One conscientious elder came to the young man and told him what had happened. Immediately the young man began to look for another church, and he found one. He would be going back to school in just two weeks, and the new church provided a rent-free parsonage, all the utilities, and a raise in salary. The elder who warned the young minister even gave him the money needed for his next semester's tuition. God still can bring good out of bad situations!

### B. Lesson Background

When we last saw Joseph, he had become the second most powerful man in Egypt, an unimaginable height of power. Joseph then had two sons—Manasseh and Ephraim—by his Egyptian wife Asenath (Genesis 41:50-52).

The predicted years of plenty passed, and the famine arrived. The Egyptians survived by buying the grain that was stored up from the years of plenty (Genesis 41:53-56). Canaan experienced famine as well (42:5). Word came to Jacob that grain was available in Egypt (42:1, 2). So 10 of Joseph's 11 brothers came to Egypt to buy grain. Joseph quickly recognized them, but he did not reveal his own true identity (42:6-8). The brothers knew only that they were dealing with an Egyptian official through a translator (42:23).

The brothers revealed that their father was still alive. Joseph had them arrested as spies and thrown in jail for a time. Reuben concluded that this was their punishment for having sold Joseph into slavery (Genesis 42:22). The brothers were released, given their grain, and sent back home. But Simeon had to stay behind as a hostage (42:24-26). Joseph told them they could buy no more grain if they did not bring back the youngest brother with them (42:33, 34; 43:3-5).

Joseph was age 17 when his brothers sold him into slavery (Genesis 37:1). He was age 30 when he entered Pharaoh's service (41:46). By the time Joseph saw his brothers on their return trip to Egypt, there had been 7 years of plenty and 2 years of famine (45:6). This means that Joseph was about age 39 when the brothers saw him in Genesis 42:6. Thus it was some 21 or 22 years since Joseph had seen any of his family members.

As we pick up today's story, the brothers have returned to Egypt, this time with brother Benjamin, who hadn't made the first trip. It is the second year of the famine (Genesis 45:6). The brothers' second trip to Egypt is recorded in Genesis 43. Our text today follows the test that Joseph devised in Genesis 44. Their return home was cut short as they were forced to return to Joseph's presence (44:3-5, 14).

# I. Joseph's Announcement (Genesis 45:1-4)

## A. Joseph Unrestrained (vv. 1a-2)

**1a. Then Joseph could not refrain himself before all them that stood by him; and he cried, Cause every man to go out from me.**

*Joseph* wants to be alone with his brothers for the very personal moment to come. It is not the type of moment that Joseph wants to share with his Egyptian associates. Thus he cries *Cause every man to go out from me.*

Perhaps the Egyptians will consider it a bit strange for Joseph to be associating so intimately with this rag-tag band of foreigners. The Egyptians may also worry that Joseph, their boss, will be more vulnerable. He will have no guards around to protect him if the visitors decide to attack. But privacy will help the brothers respond to Joseph with less fear.

**1b. And there stood no man with him, while Joseph made himself known unto his brethren.**

The first shock comes when *Joseph* begins to speak to his brothers in their native tongue (exactly what he says is in v. 3, below). Up to this time a translator has stood between them (Genesis 42:23). Joseph has understood what they have been saying all along, and they have not realized it. To them, Joseph has been no more than a powerful Egyptian authority with whom they have to deal.

The second shock will be when he reveals to them who he is. The translator may have re-

ferred to Joseph by his Egyptian name, Zaphnath-paaneah. That means something like, "the one who furnishes the sustenance of the land" (Genesis 41:45).

**2. And he wept aloud: and the Egyptians and the house of Pharaoh heard.**

Joseph had *wept* when he first saw his brothers. He also had wept upon seeing his brother Benjamin. But those weepings were done out of sight (Genesis 42:24; 43:30). Joseph is known as a man who is able to exercise great self-control (compare 39:8-10). But now the dam of his emotions bursts. He can suppress his emotions no longer.

Has Joseph waited and prayed for this moment of reconciliation? At this point he has seen his brother Benjamin personally, and he knows his father is still alive. It is a time for tears of joy, a time for great rejoicing.

The weeping is so great that the sound of it penetrates the stone walls; everyone can hear it. This is a moment of raw emotion. This is the third time Joseph weeps for his brothers. He will do so two more times (Genesis 45:14, 15; 50:17). [See question #1, page 104.]

We have no information of any adverse effect this incident has on Joseph's relationship with *Pharaoh.* Quite the opposite seems to be the case (Genesis 45:16-20).

## B. Joseph Reveals (vv. 3, 4)

**3a. And Joseph said unto his brethren, I am Joseph; doth my father yet live?**

The first thing the brothers hear this Egyptian official speak in their native Hebrew is the startling declaration *I am Joseph.* It makes sense for Joseph to reveal his true name first.

But why does Joseph ask if his *father* is still living? Just moments earlier the brothers were expressing their great concern for their father if Benjamin were not to return with them (Genesis 44:29-32). Isn't the issue of the father's being alive already settled? Note that Joseph does not ask about "your father," but *my father.* Joseph is concerned about more than the mere fact that his father is still breathing. He wants more detail.

**3b, 4. And his brethren could not answer him; for they were troubled at his presence. And Joseph said unto his brethren, Come near to me, I pray you. And they came near. And he said, I am Joseph your brother, whom ye sold into Egypt.**

When Joseph reveals who he is, the brothers cannot speak because they are *troubled*—what an understatement! The Hebrew word can mean, "disturbed," "terrified," or "panicked." (This same

---

## How to Say It

ABRAHAM. *Ay*-bruh-ham.
ASENATH. *As*-e-nath.
CANAAN. *Kay*-nun.
EPHRAIM. *Ee*-fray-im.
GOSHEN. *Go*-shen.
ISAAC. *Eye*-zuk.
MANASSEH. Muh-*nass*-uh.
PHARAOH. *Fair*-o or *Fay*-roe.
POTIPHAR. *Pot*-ih-far.
ZAPHNATH-PAANEAH. *Zaf*-nath-*pay*-uh-nee-uh (strong accent on *Zaf*).

Hebrew word is used to describe high degrees of alarm in Judges 20:41; 1 Samuel 28:21; and 2 Samuel 4:1.) In their imaginations they may visualize torture, imprisonment, exile, and death. At one time they had power over Joseph's life to do as they pleased. Now the tables are turned.

Joseph's further statement *whom ye sold into Egypt* is not necessarily said in anger or rebuke. It primarily serves as a reminder of how this whole state of affairs got its start.

### WHAT IS LEAST EXPECTED

Gary Tenen and Randy Tufts came upon a hole in the ground in the Arizona desert in 1974. What they really found was a lot more: it was a seven-acre wet, or "living," cavern right there under the arid Arizona surface. Eventually Tufts and Tenen would discover rooms the size of football fields, smaller chambers, and an underground lake. One of the cave's notable features is the second longest stalactite ever found: one-quarter inch wide and 21 feet long! As Tufts said, "We never expected to find anything like this in our wildest dreams."

The two kept their find secret for as long as possible. Eventually they contacted the owners of the land. The owners in turn sold the land to the Arizona State Park system for the cavern's preservation. Today, Kartchner Caverns is a jewel in the state's park system, bringing delight to thousands of visitors each year.

Joseph's brothers went to Egypt only to buy grain. While there, they discovered what they least expected: their long-lost brother. "I am Joseph," he said. The added words, "whom ye sold into Egypt," left no doubt. Joseph would prove to be an unexpected treasure to them: he would

## Home Daily Bible Readings

**Monday, Nov. 12**—Restoration of God's Favor (Psalm 85)

**Tuesday, Nov. 13**—Food in Egypt (Genesis 42:1-20)

**Wednesday, Nov. 14**—Jacob's Difficult Decision (Genesis 43:1-15)

**Thursday, Nov. 15**—Dining Together (Genesis 43:16-34)

**Friday, Nov. 16**—Joseph Tests His Brothers (Genesis 44:1-13)

**Saturday, Nov. 17**—Judah's Plea (Genesis 44:14-34)

**Sunday, Nov. 18**—Brothers Reconciled (Genesis 45:1-15)

save their lives! God sometimes brings into our lives a treasure (something or someone) we least expect and creates a wonderful blessing. When that happens, will you be able to recognize God to be the true source?
—C. R. B.

## II. God's Purpose (Genesis 45:5-8)

### A. What the Brothers Should Not Do (v. 5a)

**5a. Now therefore be not grieved, nor angry with yourselves, that ye sold me hither.**

Joseph sees no need for self-blame. Nor does he want a feud to erupt in which each brother blames the others for what they had done more than 20 years previously. The reason for Joseph's challenge is given next.

### B. What God Is Doing (vv. 5b-8)

**5b. For God did send me before you to preserve life.**

Joseph comforts the brothers with what is the central issue of the whole drama: *God* has been directing the sequence of events all along. It is God who has now brought them all to this place and point in time.

We do not know when Joseph realizes this bigger picture of preserving *life*. It may have been when he saw his brothers arrive for food the first time. If they are out of food early in the famine, what will happen to them as the famine drags on?

The bigger picture that Joseph sees is not necessarily a revelation from God. It is more likely the insight of a wise, godly man who is able to put the various pieces of the puzzle together.

**6. For these two years hath the famine been in the land: and yet there are five years, in the which there shall neither be earing nor harvest.**

Here we learn how long *the famine* has lasted thus far. Joseph's information that the famine will last for another *five years* is news to the brothers! Who is this man who knows how long a famine will last? This only adds to the brothers' shock. It is important for the brothers to know that this famine is a long-term hardship, not one that will end shortly. That will influence their decision to return to Egypt with their families.

The Hebrew word for *earing* refers to getting the ground ready for planting. (Compare "to ear his ground, and to reap his harvest" in 1 Samuel 8:12.) The bottom line is that agricultural activity is shut down.

**7. And God sent me before you to preserve you a posterity in the earth, and to save your lives by a great deliverance.**

We do not know how much Joseph understands regarding the significance that his extended family will have in the greater plan of *God.* Joseph certainly knows of the promises made to Abraham, Isaac, and Jacob (see Genesis 50:24, where Joseph recites the promise on his deathbed). But it is doubtful that Joseph understands how sweeping and far-reaching God's plans really are!

Abraham's concern was to have a son; Joseph is concerned about placing what family members there are in a place where they will be safe and secure. Security, abundance of food, good living conditions, and a sense of peace may help his extended family to flourish. What is happening to them is all part of a great plan of God. Joseph is simply an instrument in carrying out the plan. [See question #2, page 104.]

**8. So now it was not you that sent me hither, but God: and he hath made me a father to Pharaoh, and lord of all his house, and a ruler throughout all the land of Egypt.**

Joseph is a man with status—so much so that he is considered to be *a father to Pharaoh.* That status came to him by the power of *God.* Joseph does not claim any great achievements as his own.

Even so, it is important for the brothers to know how great his position is. This is not to frighten or threaten them, but to let them know that he has come a long way. He has the power to save them from the famine. When we consider all three descriptors of Joseph's position *(father . . . lord . . . ruler),* we see a powerful person indeed!

This is not merely bluster on Joseph's part, because Pharaoh said much the same things when Joseph was first appointed to his position (Genesis 41:40-43). The brothers are dealing with the man who, more than 20 years earlier, had told them dreams of how he would rule over them. The dreams have come to pass. The brothers end up bowing before Joseph numerous times (42:6; 43:26, 28; 50:18). [See question #3, page 104.]

### GOOD NEWS FROM BAD?

The continent of Africa has long been a cauldron brewing with bad news. In recent years, Zambia, Malawi, and Zimbabwe (among others) have seen millions of people suffer malnutrition and starvation. Chronic drought destroys hope of growing sufficient food. Sometimes one faction will use hunger as a weapon against another. HIV/AIDS has taken so many adults in some countries that few are left to work the farms. Political corruption destroys morale.

Can good come out of such evil? If Joseph's situation is an example, the answer is *yes.* His brothers sought to do evil to him, but God turned it into good—to the saving of many lives. Even today, God may step in and turn evil events into an opportunity for good. The leadership of two people has begun to offer hope to Africa. Bono, lead musician of the band U2, is challenging Western society to help the world's neediest people. And Rick Warren, minister of Saddleback Church in California, has started three foundations to provide aid.

But from God's eternal perspective, saving lives won't mean much unless we save souls as well. If the misery of Africa results in taking the gospel for the spirit along with food and medicine for the body, what good news that will be!

—C. R. B.

## III. Joseph's Instructions (Genesis 45:9-12)
### A. Come to Egypt (v. 9)

**9. Haste ye, and go up to my father, and say unto him, Thus saith thy son Joseph, God hath made me lord of all Egypt: come down unto me, tarry not.**

What we see here is a departure from the patriarchal policy of the Old Testament. No longer is Jacob (Joseph's *father*) making the major decisions for his family. Instead that responsibility has shifted to Joseph. This is not Joseph's plan, but God's. Joseph is not making recommendations; he is giving orders.

Joseph is now occupying the position Jacob had envisioned for him except that Joseph is now in charge of even his own father. Jacob will need to be convinced that this move is the will of God—after all, God had given him and his forefathers the land of Canaan. That "divine convincing" will come in Genesis 46:1-4. The words *haste* and *tarry not* make it clear that this move must be made immediately if the family is to continue to flourish. [See question #4, page 104.]

### B. Dwell in Goshen (v. 10)

**10a. And thou shalt dwell in the land of Goshen.**

All of this information is directed at Jacob, Joseph's father. Jacob needs to know that Joseph has the power to give him and his extended family *land* in Egypt.

It is important that this land be somewhat separated from where most of the Egyptians live. The children of Israel need to flourish on their own and maintain their own way of life. They should not be seen as a threat to their neighbors (compare 1 Chronicles 7:21). They need land that will be useful for their herds (Genesis 47:1-4).

*Goshen* is unknown outside of the Bible. It is also called the "land of Ramses," but that does not help us to know exactly where it is. We believe that it is in the Nile Delta, in the northeast part of Egypt. This gift is from God for His people. Do the travelers know that they and their descendants will be in Egypt for some 400 years (Genesis 15:13)?

**10b. And thou shalt be near unto me, thou, and thy children, and thy children's children, and thy flocks, and thy herds, and all that thou hast.**

Joseph wants his father and his family to be nearby. He has his own wife, children, and Egyptian associates. But that is not the same as having his extended family around. Joseph has strong feelings for his father. Joseph knows his father feels the same about him. It will be important for them to be close to one another.

There is no evidence that Joseph "takes over" the family after Jacob dies. The children of Israel will exist within Egypt as a subsociety without rulers in the traditional sense. That will change when a new king arises in Egypt, a king who will exert authority over the Israelites in a most forceful way (Exodus 1).

### C. Avoid Becoming Destitute (v. 11)

**11. And there will I nourish thee; for yet there are five years of famine; lest thou, and thy household, and all that thou hast, come to poverty.**

Joseph wants his father to know about the *five years of famine* that remain. If they fail to respond to Joseph's request, they could lose every-

thing. Perhaps the veiled warning here is that they could die if they stay in Canaan.

## IV. Joseph's Verification (Genesis 45:12)

**12. And, behold, your eyes see, and the eyes of my brother Benjamin, that it is my mouth that speaketh unto you.**

Joseph has been telling his brothers what he wants them to say to their father Jacob. Now Joseph shifts back to addressing the brothers themselves. Do they really need any more evidence to convince them that it really is Joseph who is in their presence?

## Conclusion

### A. Servanthood Wins Out

The greatest attribute in the character of Joseph is that of *servanthood*. But the important aspect to this is not his service to Potiphar, the prison warden, or even Pharaoh. The important thing is his service to God. Joseph's faithfulness to God resulted in the saving of many lives. These included not only those of Egypt and Joseph's own family, but of many in the countries surrounding Egypt. [See question #5, page 104.]

This is also a special instance of the concept of *the suffering servant* in the Bible. In the early years of his life, Joseph suffered for maintaining his integrity. Those who should have been closest to Joseph were his betrayers; but God used the experience to bring about physical redemption for Jacob's family. In that sense he is a "type" of Christ. Centuries later, God used Christ's obedience to make eternal redemption available to all humanity.

Joseph understood, to some extent, what was happening as part of a larger plan being worked out by God: it was to preserve life. In an even larger sense, God was continuing to fulfill His promises to Abraham that would culminate in the coming of the Messiah.

### B. Prayer

Our heavenly Father, let us ever be mindful that You can work through all events to accomplish Your will. Help us not to be discouraged in the down times. Help us to see them as preparation for greater things ahead. In Jesus' name, amen.

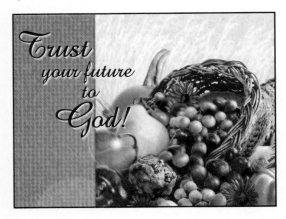

Visual for Lesson 12. *Ask your learners, "How do God's past provisions for you lead you to trust in Him for the year to come?"*

### C. Thought to Remember

God has a plan that is greater than our current situations.

# Learning by Doing

*This page contains an alternative lesson plan emphasizing learning activities.*
*Classes desiring such student involvement will find these suggestions helpful.*

## Into the Lesson

There are many modern stories of how God has worked in adverse circumstances to bring about good. Find someone in your church or town who can give a testimonial that demonstrates God's providential care in his or her life during a very difficult period. Begin class by letting the person tell his or her story.

If you cannot find a person willing to do this, read to the class the story of the fleas in the barracks from *The Hiding Place* by Corrie ten Boom. If you do not have a copy of this book, the excerpt is easy to find on the Internet.

## Into the Word

Have someone (other than the teacher) research the details of how Joseph prepared Egypt for the famine and how the food was distributed when the famine began. Begin this section of the lesson with a report from that individual. Use of visuals such as maps, charts, or drawings will be very helpful in keeping the learners' attention.

Remind the class that Joseph's own family also suffered from the famine. Then ask these questions: "Why did Jacob send only 10 of the 11 brothers to Egypt? Why didn't the brothers recognize Joseph when they arrived in his presence?"

Several answers are possible for the second question. They can include the fact that many years had passed, and Joseph had matured; the brothers were not expecting to find him there, so they would not be looking for him; Joseph was dressed as an Egyptian; Joseph did not speak to them in the Hebrew language; etc.

Ask what Joseph learned from his brothers on this trip. Answers are that his father was still alive as was the younger brother Benjamin (Joseph's full brother). Ask why Joseph imprisoned them before letting them go home and why he kept Simeon when they left. Allow the class to use their "sanctified imaginations" as they think of possible reasons.

Next, assign class members who enjoy drama to play the roles of Jacob and the 11 brothers (or fewer than the 11, depending on your class size). Have them role-play the discussion about returning to Egypt a second time for more supplies. Then ask the class to describe vividly the scene when the brothers came into Joseph's presence after the silver cup was found in Benjamin's bag. What emotions were the brothers feeling before and after Joseph revealed who he was? What clues are there that show the depth of Joseph's emotions?

Then ask, "What was Joseph's summary of the reason for his ordeal in Egypt?" Finally have the class discuss the provisions Joseph made for his family. Explore why Goshen was chosen as a home for Jacob and his sons.

Next divide the class into groups of four (quads). Provide a large sheet of paper for each group. Ask each quad to draw a simple graph showing the progression of Joseph's highs and lows. When groups have completed their charts, draw a composite chart on the board; this will include all the events listed by the groups. There may be some discussion concerning where on the graph to put each event.

## Into Life

Write the following Scripture references on the board: Psalm 94:1-3; Nahum 1:2; Hebrews 10:30. Say, "Joseph had every reason to want revenge inflicted on his brothers; however, he did not succumb to the temptation to respond to them that way."

Then have the class as a whole look up the passages written on the board. Ask, "What do those words teach about vengeance or revenge?" Mention that Joseph triumphed in part because he resisted the desire for revenge. Then say, "Suggest ways that vengeance can be destructive both to the one seeking revenge and one(s) against whom revenge is taken." (This activity is in the optional student book.) Ask for reactions to the old saying, "Revenge is a dish best served cold."

Give each learner a sheet of paper. At the top they should write "Revenge." Have them write "Forgiveness" about one-third of the way down the page and "Prayer" about two-thirds of the way down the page. Give these instructions: "Under *Revenge*, list circumstances where you wanted to strike back; under *Forgiveness* make a list of people whom you need to forgive; under *Prayer* write a prayer asking God to help you to forgive with the same spirit Joseph demonstrated." Allow a few minutes of silent work. Ask for volunteers to share answers.

# Let's Talk It Over

*The questions on this page are designed to promote discussion of the lesson by the class and to encourage application of the lesson Scriptures. The answers provided are only discussion starters. Let your class talk it over from there.*

**1. What do you think was the main thing that prompted Joseph's weeping? What conclusions about our own character can we draw by noting what makes us weep? Explain.**

There before Joseph stood family members he had not seen for many years—the very brothers who had sold him into slavery. And there he was experiencing the fulfillment of his revelatory dreams in which his brothers bowed down to him. The effect of seeing God's hand at work in all their lives was overwhelming.

Solomon teaches us that there is indeed, "A time to weep, and a time to laugh" (Ecclesiastes 3:4). Solomon also notes that, "As the crackling of thorns under a pot, so is the laughter of the fool" (Ecclesiastes 7:6). This seems to indicate that our expression of emotion allows us to evaluate our own character as we note what it is that is bringing forth that emotion.

**2. How do we see in Joseph the meeting of the spiritual and the practical? Can this be a model for us? Why, or why not?**

Joseph had been enabled to interpret Pharaoh's dream and to know how long the famine would last. He also had been enabled to draw up and implement a practical survival plan for both Egypt and his own people. Joseph saw God at work, but also took responsibility for personal action and urged the same of others.

Many unbelievers excel at being practical; they relentlessly strive to figure out what "works." But without a spiritual basis, their practicality inevitably turns into "situation ethics." The first requirement of a Christian is to know God. This means a life of study of His Word. We then live out the practicality of our faith with that basis. Faith in Christ is what "works"!

**3. How did the concepts of faith and luck differ for Joseph? How do they differ for us?**

"So now it was not you that sent me hither, but God" (Genesis 45:8). It is one or the other! For things to turn out the way they did because of the brothers' efforts would have been luck. The brothers themselves had to decide, each of them, whether (1) their crime against Joseph resulted in a lucky turn of events or (2) the great God who runs the universe determined to save His people by working through a devious human plot.

If the brothers chose to believe in luck, they could never rest easy under Joseph's benevolence. If they gave glory to God for His surprising mercies, they could rejoice with Joseph in the wonder of it all! Healings, promotions, gifts—all can be seen as "lucky breaks" or as mercies from above. It is Christians who know about the latter!

**4. How can we benefit from times of waiting? Why doesn't God "speed things up" in ways that we may prefer?**

Our lives seem to consist both of times of waiting and times of action. Often the waiting times seem so long! Children require years to grow before assuming the responsibilities of adulthood. Sometimes it seems like a long wait before choosing a mate. Elderly people, incapacitated by illness and age, find themselves waiting for a visit from loved ones.

Spiritually, it is always beneficial to wait on the Lord before making an important decision. Prayer during a time of waiting is invaluable; snap decisions run the risk of leaving God out of the picture. Character is never formed in a hurry; it requires plenty of time. "I will wait upon the Lord, . . . and I will look for him" (Isaiah 8:17).

**5. Some character qualities of Joseph's servanthood were *godliness, responsibility, wisdom,* and *forgiveness.* Why are these four so necessary in the lives of Christians today? What would life be like if we lacked one particular quality, but still had the other three? Or can they really be separated?**

Joseph demonstrated *godliness* time and again through his strength of moral character. Joseph showed *responsibility* when he looked after his family. Joseph's *wisdom* came to the fore when he suggested and implemented a plan of famine relief. Joseph's spirit of *forgiveness* is not in doubt.

These four qualities are stressed in various ways in the New Testament. Some passages for discussion are Ephesians 4:32; Colossians 1:28; 2:3, 23; 3:13; 1 Timothy 2:2, 10; 5:8; 6:6; Titus 1:1; James 1:5; 3:17; and 2 Peter 1:3, 6, 7; 3:11.

# Jacob Blesses His Family

**DEVOTIONAL READING: Psalm 145:1-13.**

**BACKGROUND SCRIPTURE: Genesis 48:8-21.**

**PRINTED TEXT: Genesis 48:11-19.**

### Genesis 48:11-19

11 And Israel said unto Joseph, I had not thought to see thy face: and, lo, God hath showed me also thy seed.

12 And Joseph brought them out from between his knees, and he bowed himself with his face to the earth.

13 And Joseph took them both, Ephraim in his right hand toward Israel's left hand, and Manasseh in his left hand toward Israel's right hand, and brought them near unto him.

14 And Israel stretched out his right hand, and laid it upon Ephraim's head, who was the younger, and his left hand upon Manasseh's head, guiding his hands wittingly; for Manasseh was the firstborn.

15 And he blessed Joseph, and said, God, before whom my fathers Abraham and Isaac

did walk, the God which fed me all my life long unto this day,

16 The angel which redeemed me from all evil, bless the lads; and let my name be named on them, and the name of my fathers Abraham and Isaac; and let them grow into a multitude in the midst of the earth.

17 And when Joseph saw that his father laid his right hand upon the head of Ephraim, it displeased him: and he held up his father's hand, to remove it from Ephraim's head unto Manasseh's head.

18 And Joseph said unto his father, Not so, my father: for this is the firstborn; put thy right hand upon his head.

19 And his father refused, and said, I know it, my son, I know it: he also shall become a people, and he also shall be great: but truly his younger brother shall be greater than he, and his seed shall become a multitude of nations.

GOLDEN TEXT: Israel said unto Joseph, I had not thought to see thy face: and, lo, God hath showed me also thy seed.—Genesis 48:11.

## God Creates
### Unit 3: God's People Re-created
### (Lessons 10-13)

## Lesson Aims

After participating in this lesson, each student will be able to:

1. Describe Jacob's (Israel's) blessing of Joseph's children.

2. Explain the importance of the heritage passed on from Jacob to his grandchildren.

3. Pass along a spiritual heritage by explaining to someone else his or her own walk with the Lord.

## Lesson Outline

INTRODUCTION
   A. Passing Along a Heritage
   B. Lesson Background
I. UNEXPECTED MEETING (Genesis 48:11, 12)
   A. Israel's Astonishment (v. 11)
   B. Joseph's Reverence (v. 12)
II. SWITCHED BLESSING (Genesis 48:13-16)
   A. Position of Children (v. 13)
   B. Position of Hands (v. 14)
   C. Request of Israel (vv. 15, 16)
     *Telling the Truth Voluntarily*
III. ATTEMPTED CORRECTION (Genesis 48:17-19)
   A. Joseph's Displeasure (vv. 17, 18)
   B. Israel's Refusal (v. 19)
     *Passing the Torch*
CONCLUSION
   A. Leaving a Legacy
   B. Prayer
   C. Thought to Remember

## Introduction

### A. Passing Along a Heritage

Erskine E. Scates, Sr. (1909–1979) was an outstanding church leader. During his various ministries, he planted or reopened churches in Colorado, New Mexico, Utah, and Wyoming. He also planted a Bible college and led in establishing several youth camps.

Many men and women entered the ministry or went to the mission field because of Scates's influence. One of the key contributions he made was the heritage he passed on to his family. Erskine and his wife, Faith, had several sons. One

led successful ministries in New Mexico and Arizona. Two more became career missionaries. Several grandchildren are also involved in ministry, both in the United States and Brazil.

That's what you call leaving a heritage! But as Scates labored in ministry back in the 1930s and 1940s, do you suppose that he had any idea of the kind of heritage he was in the process of passing along?

### B. Lesson Background

Joseph's brothers followed his instructions concerning their move. They took the wagons Pharaoh gave them, returned to Canaan, and brought Jacob (their father) and the rest of the family to Egypt. All together, 70 souls ended up in the land of Egypt. These included Joseph and his children, who were already there (Genesis 46:27; Exodus 1:5).

It was a stirring moment when Jacob and Joseph met. They clung to one another and wept for a long time (Genesis 46:29, 30). Some of the family even were privileged to meet Pharaoh. At this point Jacob (also known as Israel) was 130 years old (47:9); he lived another 17 years (47:28).

Jacob was nearly blind as he approached the time of his death (Genesis 47:29; 48:10). Like his father before him, Jacob sensed the urgency to settle his affairs (compare 27:1-4). A primary task was to bestow blessings on his sons and grandsons. This was an intentional ceremony, not a casual afterthought. Joseph, through his two sons, received the double portion. Judah received the blessing that stated that the line of the Messiah would pass through his tribe (compare Genesis 49:9-12 with Hebrews 7:14; Revelation 5:5).

Our lesson today looks at the blessing given to Manasseh and Ephraim, Jacob's grandsons. The year is about 1860 BC.

## I. Unexpected Meeting
## (Genesis 48:11, 12)

### A. Israel's Astonishment (v. 11)

**11. And Israel said unto Joseph, I had not thought to see thy face: and, lo, God hath showed me also thy seed.**

Let's begin by making sure that we don't get confused by names. *Israel* was the new name given to Jacob after he wrestled the mysterious man at Peniel (Genesis 32:24-30). Thus, Israel and Jacob are one and the same person.

The name *Israel* means "one who struggles with God"; this depicts the entire life of Jacob. Jacob's original name meant something like "heel-grabber" or, figuratively, "manipulator." Jacob's new name, Israel, is a covenant name. The importance of this name is seen in the fact that the designations *Israel* and *Israelite(s)* appear more than 2,500 times in the Bible!

*I had not thought to see thy face* is Israel's admission of the despair in his life at the loss of Joseph years earlier. Israel had assumed that he would never see Joseph again. We are reminded of the depth of pain Israel felt when the brothers concocted the story that Joseph had been killed by a wild animal. It had seemed like the end of the world for Israel (Genesis 37:33-35).

Perhaps a tremor goes through Israel's body as he thinks of the approximately 22 years of pain he experienced because he believed Joseph to be dead. (It's amazing that his other 11 sons were able to keep "their little secret" all those years!) All of that has now changed. Israel can have the joy of passing on a special heritage through his favored son.

The phrase *God hath showed me also thy seed* means that not only does Israel have the joy of seeing his son again, he also becomes acquainted with that son's own offspring. The specific children in view here are Joseph's two sons, Manasseh and Ephraim (Genesis 48:1, 5, not in today's text).

This particular meeting probably is not the first time that Israel has seen these grandchildren. We may assume that he saw them with Joseph when Israel first arrived in Goshen (Genesis 46:28, 29). [See question #1, page 112.]

### B. Joseph's Reverence (v. 12)

**12. And Joseph brought them out from between his knees, and he bowed himself with his face to the earth.**

Reuben is Israel's firstborn. But because he committed a sexual sin, Israel is giving Reuben's blessing rights to Joseph's sons (Genesis 49:1-4;

---

**How to Say It**

BOAZ. *Bo*-az.
CANAAN. *Kay*-nun.
EPHRAIM. *Ee*-fray-im.
ISHMAEL. *Ish*-may-el.
ISRAEL. *Iz*-ray-el.
LABAN. *Lay*-bun.
LEVI. *Lee*-vye.
MANASSEH. Muh-*nass*-uh.
PADAN-ARAM. *Pay*-dan-*a*-ram.
PENIEL. Peh-*nye*-el.
PHARAOH. *Fair*-o or *Fay*-roe.
SHECHEM. *Shee*-kem or *Shek*-em.

---

1 Chronicles 5:1, 2). Those sons are Manasseh and Ephraim; they are the ones whom *Joseph* brings *out from between his knees.*

Elsewhere in Genesis, bowing depicts a greeting to someone worthy of great honor (Genesis 24:52; 33:3; 42:6; 43:26). That is undoubtedly the case here as Joseph shows respect to his father, who is near death. Joseph lives in a world where respect is openly demonstrated. Joseph's respect toward his father is not an act of worship, but of esteem. [See question #2, page 112.]

## II. Switched Blessing
## (Genesis 48:13-16)
### A. Position of Children (v. 13)

**13. And Joseph took them both, Ephraim in his right hand toward Israel's left hand, and Manasseh in his left hand toward Israel's right hand, and brought them near unto him.**

The next stage of the ceremony is about to begin. *Joseph* positions his children in order to receive *Israel's* blessing. Like his father Isaac before him, Israel in his old age is hardly able to see (Genesis 27:1; 48:10). Yet Israel is not depending on touch to determine which boy is which. Israel knows that Joseph will place the older boy under his right hand and the younger under his left. Joseph places the boys in their proper birth order before Israel so that Israel will give the primary blessing to the older son and the secondary blessing to the younger.

### B. Position of Hands (v. 14)

**14. And Israel stretched out his right hand, and laid it upon Ephraim's head, who was the younger, and his left hand upon Manasseh's head, guiding his hands wittingly; for Manasseh was the firstborn.**

Now an amazing thing happens: when *Israel* stretches out his hands, he crosses his arms. In so doing, he chooses *the younger* over *the firstborn.* Israel does this intentionally *(wittingly);* this is no accident. Israel undoubtedly remembers his own experience when he was on the receiving end of the blessing, especially since he received the better blessing through his own deception rather than by his father's freewill choice. Israel knows exactly what he is doing, and no one will be able to deceive him. [See question #3, page 112.]

Perhaps we see a little bit of Israel's former shrewd nature come to the surface one last time. By crossing his arms, Israel may be reminding Joseph that he (Israel) is still the patriarch. Joseph has the highest status possible in Egypt next to Pharaoh. He is accustomed to telling people what to do. When Israel was about to visit Pharaoh, Joseph told him what to say. But the decision as to who will receive the major blessing belongs to Israel, not Joseph.

## C. Request of Israel (vv. 15, 16)

**15. And he blessed Joseph, and said, God, before whom my fathers Abraham and Isaac did walk, the God which fed me all my life long unto this day.**

As Joseph's sons are being blessed, *Joseph* is blessed as well. An important aspect of the blessing is for Israel to recall those whom God led and cared for previously, namely his grandfather, *Abraham*, and his father, *Isaac*. These two walked in the way of the Lord. James even identifies Abraham as "the Friend of God" (James 2:23; compare 2 Chronicles 20:7).

The phrase *fed me all my life* is to be understood as something like "guided me all my life" or "shepherded me all my life." Part of the role of shepherding is to see that the flock is fed, but Jacob is speaking of more than just food here. Sheep are creatures that have no natural defense. This means that they require more care than other animals. For example, water must appear to be still for them to drink. Flowing, rippling water frightens them. Sheep are easily killed by predators.

God has cared for Israel all of his life. God cared for him when he fled to Padan-aram and when he left that place to return home. Had God not intervened, Laban, Israel's uncle and father-in-law, may have killed him (Genesis 31:24, 29). God cared for Israel when he returned to Canaan. God cared for him in his encounter with his brother Esau. God cared for him and his family when Simeon and Levi massacred the men at Shechem (34:25; 35:5).

The last great testimony to that care was when Joseph sent for him to come to Egypt to live. Imagery of God's care is very powerful in the Bible. See Psalm 23 and the picture of Jesus as the good shepherd in John 10:11-18.

**16. The angel which redeemed me from all evil, bless the lads; and let my name be named on them, and the name of my fathers Abraham and Isaac; and let them grow into a multitude in the midst of the earth.**

Putting verses 15 and 16 together, we see a threefold recognition of (1) God in covenant with Israel's *fathers*, (2) God as Israel's own shepherd, and (3) *the angel* who had delivered him.

Many commentators believe that this angel was actually an appearance of God in human form rather being a created angel, as we may normally think. We read of visits by "the angel of the Lord" to various people in the Old Testament. At some point in the narrative the statement may switch from "angel of the Lord" to "Lord." For example, compare Genesis 16:7-12 with 16:13; also compare 22:15 with 22:16. Thus the phrase *angel of the Lord* could be another way of saying *Lord* or *God*. In some cases, however, the angel of the Lord seems to be distinct from God (see 2 Samuel 24:16; Zechariah 1:11-13; Luke 1:11).

With the phrase *bless the lads*, Israel begins the blessing. [See question #4, page 112.] The phrase *which redeemed me* introduces one of the powerful relationship pictures we have in the Old Testament: that of redemption or deliverance. The Hebrew word that is behind this idea occurs more than 100 times in the Old Testament, and its first usage is right here.

One direction that the concept of redemption takes in the Old Testament is that of *kinsman-redeemer*. This is a person who rescues family members who fall into debt or slavery (Leviticus 25:25, 49). The most famous story in the Old Testament regarding a kinsman-redeemer is found in the book of Ruth. As kinsman-redeemer, Boaz takes on the responsibility of marrying Ruth and redeeming the family property.

Israel had no earthly kinsman-redeemer to rescue him from the fury of either his brother or his uncle. Israel recognizes that it was God who had taken on that role, protecting him until he could return again to Canaan. The same could be said about Joseph; indeed, Joseph himself said it (see Genesis 45:5, 8, 9; 50:20). Joseph has no earthly person who stands in for him in times of trouble, but he is delivered again and again by God.

Israel (Jacob) requests two blessings for the boys. The first is an issue of identity: *let my name be named on them, and the name of my fathers Abraham and Isaac*. When Moses encounters God hundreds of years later, God will be the God of Abraham, Isaac, and Jacob (Exodus 3:6, 15, 16; 4:5). This threefold identification with Abraham, Isaac, and Jacob is so important that it carries across hundreds and hundreds of years, right into the New Testament (Luke 20:37; Acts 3:13; 7:32).

The second requested blessing is for the boys to *grow into a multitude in the midst of the earth*. The promise made to Abraham and Isaac (Genesis 22:17; 26:4) is now being passed on to Joseph's sons. Shortly after the exodus begins more than 400 years later, the tribes of Manasseh and Ephraim will number together 72,700 (Numbers 1:32-34)—and that counts only males age 20 and older (Numbers 1:3). Blessings fulfilled!

### TELLING THE TRUTH VOLUNTARILY

James Frey got his proverbial "15 minutes of fame" on October 26, 2005, on *The Oprah Winfrey Show*. But his fame had turned to infamy by January 2006. His best-selling book *A Million Little Pieces* was purportedly the true story of his sensationally wretched life. He claimed to have led a thoroughly despicable existence as an alcoholic, drug addict, and criminal. One of his claims involved having a role in a train crash that killed two young women.

Oprah interviewed Frey on her show and recommended his book to her audience. Sales of the book skyrocketed. But then an investigative Web site poked many holes in his story. Soon Frey had to admit to the deception. The truth became clear.

Israel certainly had committed his share of deception in his life! But Israel's acknowledgment near the end of his days was of a wholly different kind from that of James Frey. The most important distinction is that Israel's confession was self-initiated and voluntary while Frey's admission was forced from him by an investigation.

Israel's acknowledgment reminded Joseph of the real source of his strength and blessings: the God of their fathers. Israel recognized that it was God's messenger who had redeemed him from the evil he had committed. God wants us all to have this attitude, an attitude of voluntary acknowledgment of the truth that our hope lies in Him alone. And it would be a good idea to make this confession before we come anywhere close to reaching Israel's age of 147!          —C. R. B.

Visual for Lesson 13. *How can we make the statement on this visual a daily reality? Ask your learners to list specific ways.*

wish. When Israel crosses his arms (Genesis 48:14), Joseph perhaps thinks that this is just a blind man's mistake.

Joseph undoubtedly is aware that as soon as the blessing is given, it cannot be altered. The finality of the blessing demonstrates how seriously people in Bible times take such pronouncements. In the incident when Israel (Jacob) received the blessing intended for Esau (by this time many decades in the past), no court papers were served, no lawyers were summoned, no one tried to figure out how to overturn the blessing on the grounds of "false pretenses" or "fraudulent conveyance." The blessing of the patriarch is final; it is not changed even by the patriarch himself (compare Esther 1:19; 8:8; Daniel 6:8, 12).

## III. Attempted Correction (Genesis 48:17-19)

### A. Joseph's Displeasure (vv. 17, 18)

**17, 18. And when Joseph saw that his father laid his right hand upon the head of Ephraim, it displeased him: and he held up his father's hand, to remove it from Ephraim's head unto Manasseh's head. And Joseph said unto his father, Not so, my father: for this is the firstborn; put thy right hand upon his head.**

The second half of verse 16 did not reveal any distinction, on the surface, between the blessings given to Manasseh (the older) and *Ephraim* (the younger). Yet Joseph knows the significance of the positioning of *his father's* hands; the *right hand* is the hand of chief blessing.

Joseph is determined that his *firstborn* son will receive the special blessing from Israel. His attempt to move Israel's hands indicates his concern. Joseph may assume that Israel has the same

### B. Israel's Refusal (v. 19)

**19. And his father refused, and said, I know it, my son, I know it: he also shall become a people, and he also shall be great: but truly his younger brother shall be greater than he, and his seed shall become a multitude of nations.**

Using touch, a blind man still can tell the difference between a taller, older child and a shorter, younger one. Israel makes it clear that he knows what he is doing. He considers himself to be still in control. Israel will make this one final decision for the family, not Joseph.

So we have another instance of reversed blessing. Traditionally, the oldest son was to receive the greater honor. But Isaac was chosen over Ishmael, and Jacob over Esau. Now it's Ephraim over Manasseh. [See question #5, page 112.]

*He also shall become a people* indicates that Manasseh still will have tribal status in the land when the Israelites take Canaan. This alone is a great blessing both to Manasseh and to Joseph. There will be no singular "tribe of Joseph" that receives land. But through his sons, Joseph actually will have the share of two tribes.

The words *his seed shall become a multitude of nations* is a figurative expression that establishes that Ephraim's descendants will be of more significance than those of his brother. "And he blessed them that day, saying, In thee shall Israel bless, saying, God make thee as Ephraim and as Manasseh: and he set Ephraim before Manasseh" (Genesis 48:20, not in today's text).

We see here a demonstration of the faith of the aged patriarch. He knows what God wants him to do, and he will do God's will over the protests of even his favorite son. Shortly after the exodus begins hundreds of years later, the tribe of Ephraim will be about 25 percent larger than the tribe of Manasseh (Numbers 1:32, 34).

Shortly after blessing the children of Joseph, Israel gives blessing and benediction to the rest of his sons (Genesis 49). Jacob then breathes his last and his body is embalmed (50:2). His body is carried back to Canaan and placed in a cave (49:29–50:14).

### PASSING THE TORCH

The 2003 *Tour de France* was the centennial event of that famous bicycle race in and around France. Throughout the race, the focus was on Lance Armstrong, who ended up with his fifth consecutive victory. An hour-long celebration of the event's history followed the race. Past winners rode by the cheering crowds.

A poignant moment occurred just before the parade began. An older man on an ancient bicycle was to ride at the head of the parade. By his side was a young boy on a small, modern bike. It was to symbolize the "passing of the torch" from a one generation of cyclists to another. One photograph shows the two riders as they are waiting for the signal to begin the parade. The older man is gently resting his hand on the child's shoulder, as if to encourage him for what was ahead.

Today's lesson allows us to witness part of a passing-of-the-torch ceremony (the rest is in Genesis 49). Sometimes a torch is passed intentionally and voluntarily; sometimes it is forcefully taken; sometimes the passing "just happens" without much thought as people drift through the natural cycle of life. The passing happens in families, in businesses, and in churches. Members of all generations must use godly wisdom as they play out this drama of changing roles. —C. R. B.

## Conclusion

### A. Leaving a Legacy

How important it is to leave a legacy! Israel (Jacob) had received a legacy from his father, who had received it in turn from *his* father. Then it was Israel's turn to leave it to the following generation. Life goes on a generation at a time. Each generation builds upon (or destroys) what the previous generation leaves behind.

A legacy can be thought of as a kind of inheritance. Usually when we think of an inheritance, we think of cash and various physical assets. A much more important inheritance is a spiritual one. What kind of people will live in and lead the next generation? Very often, people follow the example of those who precede them, whether good or bad. So the example set is vitally important.

Church leaders have a great responsibility in this regard (see 1 Timothy 4:12; Titus 2:7). Christian leaders are responsible for the legacy they leave behind in life and teaching. Our legacy includes our sense of humility, the way we interact with others, and a holy lifestyle. We will be remembered longest for what we did, not what we said. The condemnation of those who set a bad example will be severe indeed (Mark 9:42).

### B. Prayer

Our Father in Heaven, continually remind us that we are passing on a heritage, a legacy, a spiritual inheritance. Help us to remember that our lives are the examples of Christ that most people will see. In Jesus' name, amen.

### C. Thought to Remember

Find joy in passing along a godly legacy.

---

## Home Daily Bible Readings

**Monday, Nov. 19**—Bring Your Father (Genesis 45:16-20)

**Tuesday, Nov. 20**—God's Reassurance (Genesis 46:1-4)

**Wednesday, Nov. 21**—The Reunion (Genesis 46:28-34)

**Thursday, Nov. 22**—A Blessing (Genesis 47:7-12)

**Friday, Nov. 23**—Joseph's Promise (Genesis 47:27-31)

**Saturday, Nov. 24**—A Grandfather's Blessing (Genesis 48:8-21)

**Sunday, Nov. 25**—The Greatness and Goodness of God (Psalm 145:1-13a)

# Learning by Doing

*This page contains an alternative lesson plan emphasizing learning activities.*
*Classes desiring such student involvement will find these suggestions helpful.*

## Into the Lesson

Prior to class, contact three or four class members and ask them to bring something that has been passed down in their families. At the beginning of class, have each one tell the story (briefly) of the article he or she brought. Ask why that article is important to its present owner. Make a transition by noting that today's lesson is about a spiritual inheritance or heritage; this is something that is far more important than physical memorabilia.

*Alternative introduction:* Say, "Many people research their genealogies. Genealogies were important to ancient people also. Notice how many times genealogies are included in the Bible. How many of you have someone in your family who has documented a genealogy?" After responses, ask, "Why do you think genealogies are still important—or are they? What about the cautions in 1 Timothy 1:4 and Titus 3:9? Do you consider your own ancestry to be a blessing or a burden? Why?" Allow discussion, but don't let it drag out.

## Into the Word

Bring several Bible times-and-customs books to class. (Find these in your church's library or the public library.) Write on the board the names of Israel's (Jacob's) 12 sons. Next to Joseph's name, write *Manasseh* and *Ephraim*.

Divide the class into small groups. Ask each group to research and write a brief newspaper article about Jacob's blessings on his descendants. Inform your groups that the bulk of the story should focus on the switched blessings of Manasseh and Ephraim (today's text). The story and its headline can be a bit "sensationalized" to recognize how unusual such a switch was.

Inform the groups that they can work in a passing mention of the blessings of Genesis 49 (not part of today's text) at the end of their articles. Distribute the times-and-customs books as resources for details such as traditional rituals regarding the blessings, deviation from tradition, expected family actions and reactions, etc. (If this assignment is too difficult for your class, ask the groups to write only some possible headlines.)

Allow about 10 minutes, then read each group's newspaper articles to the entire class. Discuss. Ask your learners to list the main point

of each son and grandson's blessing (or "anti-blessing," as the case may be!), using today's text along with Genesis 49 as a guide. Write answers beside the names on the board.

Move back to a focused discussion of today's text by pointing out the distinction (or "hierarchy") of blessings of which both Israel and Joseph were aware. Say, "The firstborn normally was to receive the primary or greater blessing. Does this ancient 'hierarchy of blessing' seem like favoritism, or was there good reason for it?"

Point out that Israel (Jacob) certainly had material assets to leave to his descendants, but the blessings focused on issues of a spiritual nature rather than "I leave Ephraim 10 percent of my sheep." Ask your learners to compare and contrast Israel's emphasis in his pronounced blessings with the emphasis we see today on the disposition of material assets in wills. Use this as a transition to the Into Life segment.

## Into Life

Say, "Ancestry is significant, but it is beyond our control. It is what it is; it cannot be changed; we cannot pick our parents. What is still within our control, however, is the legacy or heritage we leave to the generation to follow."

Point out that many people have made financial preparations for their children through wills and trust funds. However, the most important inheritance to leave behind is a spiritual legacy. No more important blessing can be left for our loved ones. However, our legacies can be left to our spiritual children and grandchildren, not just to those related to us by blood or legal adoption.

Give everyone several sheets of paper. Ask them to write a spiritual blessing to each of their children. Those who do not have children will write to someone whom they consider to be a son or daughter "in the faith" (see 1 Timothy 1:2) whom they influence. (Those who do have biological or adopted children can write to spiritual children as well.)

Encourage your learners to give or mail the blessings to the people addressed. The experience may be difficult for those who are estranged from family members or whose children have died. Gently suggest that it can be a healing process for them to write the blessing, even if not mailed.

# Let's Talk It Over

*The questions on this page are designed to promote discussion of the lesson by the class and to encourage application of the lesson Scriptures. The answers provided are only discussion starters. Let your class talk it over from there.*

**1. What was a time in your life when the presence of children drew you closer to God?**

"God hath showed me also thy seed" is a remark by a man surrendered to God. It is the observation of one who knows that the blessing of grandchildren is a special kindness from above.

The presence of children can remind us how quickly the years pass. Adults have been known to exclaim, "My, how you've grown!" upon seeing a child they haven't seen in three or four years. As children, we may have thought such statements meant little—perhaps we even found them to be a little irritating! But those statements can spring from the adults' realization that they are just that much closer to seeing the Lord personally as the growth of children means a passing of generations.

As we grow older, there may be a greater intensity in our prayers that God will enable us to pass along our spiritual wisdom to the next generation. Although nothing is said about the spiritual character of Manasseh and Ephraim, godly children and grandchildren can be a great encouragement in the Lord.

**2. What are some ways to show respect to parents today that may be different from how respect was shown in Bible times? What are some extremes to avoid?**

One of the Ten Commandments required that the ancient Israelites honor their parents (Exodus 20:12). Joseph's actions were in line with this, even though it had not been written when he lived. Although Joseph was prime minister of Egypt, he still showed deference to his father. Jesus had strong words for those who would twist this obligation into something else (Mark 7:9-13).

Ways to honor parents are many. They fall into two categories: things *to do* and things *not to do*. Regarding the latter, one challenge we have is not showing frustration with an elderly parent who is becoming feeble. Frustration can show itself in expressions of contempt such as rolling one's eyes (as in, "Oh, boy—there she goes again!"). It takes a great deal of learned patience not to become frustrated. The list of things *to do* is nearly endless, but it undoubtedly includes making sure the parent has the basic necessities of life.

**3. Is it possible for Christian fathers and grandfathers to bless children today as Israel does here and in Genesis 49? Why, or why not?**

Jacob's blessings are clearly prophetic, so it's not possible for us to bless our children in the same manner. Even without the prophetic element, a fatherly pronouncement of blessing would be decidedly countercultural! The role of the father has been diminished in modern society. TV, films, and the comics often depict him as a clumsy, laughable, clueless figure. Restoring the biblical concept of a father who takes responsibility for his "clan" to pass along a spiritual heritage is a big challenge!

**4. How can we use special occasions in the church to pass along blessings to the generation to follow—that is, to give solemn reminders of and encouragement in the Christian faith?**

Baptisms, weddings, and funerals are "blessable moments," if we may coin that expression. The baptism of a teenager may include an exhortation to parents that they be diligent in rearing their children in the fear of God. The sermon in a wedding ceremony can include the same exhortation. The funeral service for a deceased Christian is an ideal time to remind other family members that there is a spiritual heritage to be embraced and carried forward.

**5. What was a time in your life when "the customary" was set aside as the Lord led in a new and surprising direction? What was the end result?**

Joseph was a devoted believer, but he was mistaken in the case at hand. His father was acting under the direction of the Holy Spirit. The custom of blessing the eldest was not wrong in and of itself. It is simply that God is over all and can change a custom as He wishes.

A tradition can very easily become an unthinking routine. In some cases, this is harmless; decorating the house a certain way for the holidays each year is an example. But other instances are more serious. Refusing to change a procedure or worship practice in the church because "we've never done it that way before" reveals deadly and deadening traditionalism.

# Winter Quarter 2007–2008

## God's Call to the Christian Community
### (Luke)

### Special Features

### Lessons

#### Unit 1: God's Call in Christ

#### Unit 2: Inspired by God's Call

#### Unit 3: Responding to God's Call

### About These Lessons

This quarter we look to the Gospel of Luke to discover how God calls the church to live out her purpose. The requirements are breathtaking in scope! But we have the power of the Holy Spirit to help us put them into action.

Dec 2
Dec 9
Dec 16
Dec 23
Dec 30
Jan 6
Jan 13
Jan 20
Jan 27
Feb 3
Feb 10
Feb 17
Feb 24

# Quarterly Quiz

*The questions on this page may be used in several ways: as a pretest at the beginning of the quarter; as a review at the end of the quarter; or as a review after each lesson. The questions are based on the Scripture text of each lesson* (King James Version). **The answers are on page 120.**

### Lesson 1

1. What was the name of the angel who appeared to Zechariah in the temple? (Michael, Gabriel, Uriel?) *Luke 1:19*

2. How did the people know that Zechariah had seen a vision in the temple? (glowing countenance of Zechariah, loud noises in the temple, Zechariah was unable to speak?) *Luke 1:22*

### Lesson 2

1. Mary was excited and happy to receive a visit from the angel. T/F. *Luke 1:29*

2. What was miraculous about Elisabeth's pregnancy? (she was a virgin, she was very old, she already had many children?) *Luke 1:36*

### Lesson 3

1. The friends and relatives of Zechariah and Elisabeth assumed the name of the son would be _____. *Luke 1:59*

2. Zechariah prophesied that his son would be a prophet. T/F. *Luke 1:67, 76*

### Lesson 4

1. Caesar _____ made the decree that all the world should be taxed. *Luke 2:1*

2. Why did Joseph journey to Bethlehem from Nazareth? (looking for work, directed by an angel, it was the city of his lineage?) *Luke 2:4*

### Lesson 5

1. What had Simeon been promised by God that he would see before his death? (an angel, a vision of Heaven, the Christ?) *Luke 2:26*

2. What sacrifice did Joseph offer to "redeem" his son according to the Law of Moses? (two turtledoves, a lamb, 10 pieces of silver?) *Luke 2:24*

### Lesson 6

1. For what Jewish feast was Jesus taken to Jerusalem at age 12? (Day of Atonement, Passover, Hanukkah?) *Luke 2:41*

2. Jesus was separated from His parents for three days. T/F. *Luke 2:46*

### Lesson 7

1. God is kind to the unthankful and the evil. T/F. *Luke 6:35*

2. What should we do with those who "despitefully use" us? (avoid them, confront them, pray for them?) *Luke 6:28*

### Lesson 8

1. Jesus says that evil fathers always give evil gifts to their children. T/F. *Luke 11:13*

2. The heavenly Father gives "the ____ ____ to them that ask him." *Luke 11:13*

### Lesson 9

1. King Solomon was not clothed as well as what, according to Jesus? (lilies of the field, the heavens, the angels?) *Luke 12:27*

2. What is the "thing which is least," according to Jesus? (growing taller by worrying, getting rich, consuming certain food and drink?) *Luke 12:25, 26*

### Lesson 10

1. When Jesus sent out the 70, what did He tell them to say when they first entered a house? (Grace, Thank you, Peace?) *Luke 10:5*

2. Jesus promised the 70 that they would have the power to walk on scorpions without being hurt. T/F. *Luke 10:19*

### Lesson 11

1. Jesus was told that Pilate had mingled the blood of _____ with their sacrifices. *Luke 13:1*

2. Jesus told a parable about a fig tree that always produced many figs. T/F. *Luke 13:9*

### Lesson 12

1. Jesus advised us to take a place of middle honor when we choose a seat at a wedding banquet. T/F. *Luke 14:10*

2. If we provide for the lowly members of our society, we will be rewarded at the _____. *Luke 14:14*

### Lesson 13

1. In Jesus' example, why would the builder of the tower be mocked? (he couldn't finish it, he didn't need it, it fell down because of cheap construction?) *Luke 14:28-30*

2. Jesus said if we do not "hate" our own lives, we cannot be His disciples. T/F. *Luke 14:26*

# God's Call, Then and Now

*by Mark S. Krause*

WHICH OF THE FOUR GOSPELS is your favorite? If pressed to choose, many would opt for the Gospel of Luke. This book, like the other Gospels, is full of beloved stories about our Savior. But some of our favorite stories are found only in Luke. These include accounts of Mary and Joseph's trip to Bethlehem, the angel choir that appeared to the shepherds, the teaching about the Good Samaritan, and the encounter on the road to Emmaus between the resurrected Jesus and two disciples.

Luke is the longest of the four Gospels and the most comprehensive. He writes like a professional historian, yet with a personal touch. Unlike the other Gospels, Luke continued to write about the church after Jesus' ascension to Heaven. The second volume of Luke's labors is the book of Acts.

This quarter we will look at texts from Luke's Gospel that deal with God's call to His people. One cannot read the Bible without encountering individuals who are called by God to do certain things. Moses heard the voice of God coming from the burning bush (Exodus 3:4). Samuel was called by God while still a child living in the temple (1 Samuel 3:4). Jesus appeared to Paul on the Damascus road to call him to be the apostle to the Gentiles (Acts 26:14-18; compare Galatians 1:15, 16). Paul was even careful to note that the Lord spoke to him in a specific language!

## Unit 1: December
## God's Call in Christ

Several of our lessons are drawn from Luke's opening chapters. These lessons are concerned with events leading up to and including the birth and childhood of Jesus. **Lesson 1** opens our quarter with a study of a supernatural event that preceded the birth of John the Baptist, the Messiah's forerunner. The lesson involves the appearance of the angel Gabriel to the elderly priest Zechariah as he performed his temple service. Zechariah is an important figure because he became the father of John the Baptist.

The call Zechariah received was a call to faith in God's ability in light of the seemingly impossible: Zechariah was expected to believe that he and his wife, both elderly, finally would have a child—a son. We may find it amazing that he expressed his doubt in light of the facts that an angel was delivering the message. Further adding to our amazement is that Zechariah, a well-learned priest, would have known about the Old Testament stories of God granting children to barren couples such as Abraham and Sarah, Isaac and Rebekah, and Elkanah and Hannah.

**Lesson 2** allows us to compare and contrast the faith Mary expressed at her call with the doubt Zechariah expressed at his in Lesson 1. The angel Gabriel appeared to both, in separate incidents that were several months apart. Both Zechariah and Mary were quite startled at the angel's appearance. Each was promised a child. Each was given a hint of his or her child's future greatness. Each was told what the name of his or her child was to be.

Both children could be conceived only through divine intervention, and both Mary and Zechariah were well aware of the hurdles God would have to overcome in their respective situations. Yet the young Mary expressed more belief than the elderly priest Zechariah! An interesting study, indeed.

In **Lesson 3** we examine Zechariah's prophecy concerning his newborn son. With a tongue finally loosened after many months, Zechariah boldly announced that John was to "be called the prophet of the Highest: for thou shalt go before the face of the Lord to prepare his ways" (Luke 1:76). In this regard, John was to have the two prophetic roles of *foretelling* and *forthtelling*, although those functions of his later life are not part of this lesson.

**Lesson 4** takes us to the night of Jesus' birth. Here we will read again the familiar account of how an angel called a group of shepherds to rejoice over the birth of the Christ.

It's difficult to imagine an occupation more humble and lowly than that of shepherd. Yet on this great night it is not to priests or to the Roman emperor that the angel appears. This teaches us something about how God views matters.

In **Lesson 5,** the final study of the quarter, we read of a certain man named Simeon. He had waited a lifetime to see the arrival of God's salvation. As he held the baby Jesus, that is exactly what he saw. Moved by the Holy Spirit, he then acted as a witness to the significance of the Messiah's birth. As we shall see, Simeon has something important to teach us about being a witness.

## Unit 2: January
## Inspired by God's Call

**Lesson 6**, also from Luke's early chapters, allows us to take a fresh look at the single incident we have recorded from the childhood of Jesus. Here we will see that even at age 12 Jesus sensed a strong call to discuss the weighty things of God as He dialogued with the great teachers at the Jerusalem temple.

All of us have questions for which we seek answers. Inquiry within the community of faith can lead to spiritual maturity. Entering into dialogue in the temple, Jesus grew in faith and wisdom. We must grow in these ways as well.

**Lesson 7** takes us to the adult ministry period of Jesus. Here we will be challenged by Jesus' call as to how we are to relate to others. That call is for our actions to be controlled by love, and not by selfishness or the desire for revenge. This is definitely not the way the world approaches things!

Expressing love as Jesus would have us to is not really "natural." Everyone has to learn how to follow Jesus' example and teaching in this regard. That's where this lesson comes in.

We will then shift our attention to Jesus' teaching about prayer in **Lesson 8**. Here we will find ourselves called to practice ongoing conversation with our loving Father.

People long for relationships with others who care enough to listen to and respond to their concerns. To whom can we go? Jesus taught that we have a loving heavenly Father to whom we can persistently present our needs and the desires of our hearts. This lesson will help us clarify some vital issues regarding prayer.

**Lesson 9** recognizes that we all experience pressure and anxiety at times. What can we do to combat anxiety and worry? Jesus says that when we trust in God, we have no need to worry.

This is true even when (or especially when) believers undergo times of great stress and persecution. In such times of distress—even life-threatening distress—it is even more important to heed God's call to trust in Him.

## Unit 3: February
## Responding to God's Call

The final unit of lessons for this quarter focuses on God's personal call to each believer. **Lesson 10** introduces us to Jesus' commission to His 70 disciples. This introduction brings us to consider how Jesus' call to labor for Him applies to us as well.

Now as then, Jesus calls us to struggle for a purpose greater than ourselves. When Jesus appointed 70 disciples to prepare His way, they obeyed despite the probability of hardship and rejection.

Those who engage in missions and evangelism in the twenty-first century will also be subject to hardship and rejection. But we have the strength of God as did the first-century disciples. God will not let His church fail.

**Lesson 11** stresses an issue that is crucial for everyone: the need for ongoing repentance. As we look at our lives honestly, we will see things that we should admit and change. But how do we go about changing in order to become a holy, godly people?

That change starts with repentance. Repentance allows us to ask for and receive God's help in becoming holy. Jesus' call to life-changing repentance is always with us.

**Lesson 12** examines another aspect of Jesus' call on our lives: the call to humility. Modern culture values and rewards people who put themselves forward to be first. That is nothing new. Ancient cultures did it too, as this lesson shows us.

But a life of humility is better. In this lesson Jesus will teach us that true recognition and exaltation come from God, not from our own attempts at seeking glory and honor.

The quarter ends, fittingly, with a sweeping call of Jesus in **Lesson 13** to be His disciples throughout our lives. People look for causes that they can support passionately. What or who is worth supporting so passionately that one may even give up everything for? Jesus!

Being a follower of Jesus has great benefits, but His call also comes with many demands. If we are to be true disciples, we must heed the many aspects of our Savior's call. This lesson will help us come to grips with His call on our lives.

## God's Call, Then and Now

God calls the community of Christian faith (the church) to live out the purpose for which she was created. That purpose has not changed. That purpose is summed up in the Great Commission: "Go ye therefore, and teach all nations, baptizing them in the name of the Father, and of the Son, and of the Holy Ghost: teaching them to observe all things whatsoever I have commanded you" (Matthew 28:19, 20).

The "whatsoever I have commanded you" includes the lessons that God's Word teaches us this quarter. Nothing good can happen without faith, willingness, love, repentance, prayer, and humility.

117

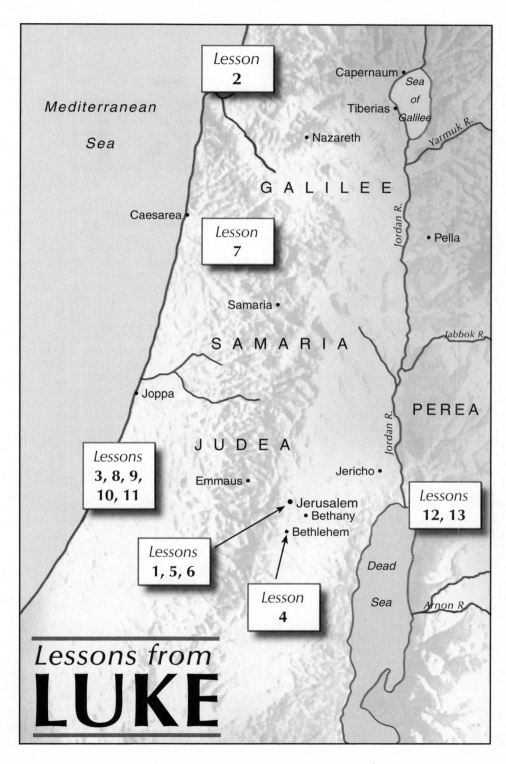

# THE GOSPEL OF LUKE

# "What Can I Learn from History?"

## Lessons from the Gospel of Luke

### by Richard A. Koffarnus

MANY PEOPLE talk about the subject of history in negative terms. "History is more or less bunk," said Henry Ford (1863–1947). "History is little else than a picture of human crimes and misfortunes," complained the French philosopher Voltaire (1694–1778).

Those who study and preserve history are also frequent targets of condemnation. "Historians," one anonymous critic wrote, "fall into one of three categories: those who lie, those who are mistaken, and those who do not know."

Yet without history and the historians who record it, we would be ignorant of the roots of our culture. Without that knowledge, society would have to rediscover its foundations and core principles constantly. For that reason, even the most primitive peoples, often without a written language, employ tribal historians to pass on their oral traditions.

This quarter's lessons are based on the Gospel written by Luke, Paul's traveling companion and coworker. Thanks to Luke, a physician by trade, we have a wonderful perspective on the life of Jesus. Luke also gave us the book of Acts, the inspired historical account of the first 30 years of the church. For the next 13 weeks, you can challenge your learners to broaden their historical knowledge of the New Testament era by studying the work and world of Luke.

## Understanding Historical Context

One way to make history relevant to your learners is to put your lesson material into a historical context. When did the events recorded by Luke actually take place?

Many chronologies of the life of Christ exist. For example, the *Standard Bible Atlas* contains such a chronology, as does *A Harmony of the Gospels* by Robert Thomas and Stanley Gundry. The little pamphlet, "Chronological Outline of the Life of Christ" by Rupert C. Foster is also useful. You can use reference tools such as these to prepare a time line to display each week. That way your class will always know where they are in their study of the life of Christ.

You can also help your learners understand historical context by answering the question, "What was going on in the world at the time of

these events recorded by Luke?" Each week have a different student report on some notable historical event that took place between 5 BC and AD 30, the time period covered in Luke's Gospel. Besides describing the events, each report should answer the question, "What relationship, if any, did this event have to life in first-century Israel?" Check your local library and the Internet for historical information on this time period.

Another way to make history relevant to your learners is to let them "witness" it happening. There are several good video portrayals of the Gospel of Luke available, including *The JESUS Film*. Most have narration taken directly from Luke. They strive to recreate the authentic look and feel of first-century Israel as Jesus experienced it. You can show a relevant clip from the video to introduce each lesson so your learners can form accurate mental pictures of the people, places, and events described by Luke. (Make sure not to violate copyrights.)

## Studying History's Superstars

An approach once commonly used by historians, including Luke, is the so-called "great-man theory" of history. According to this approach, we can discover the causes of the great events of the past by studying the important people of history. Of course, Luke focuses his work on the greatest historical figure of them all, the Lord Jesus.

Still, there are other notables worth learning about who appear in the third Gospel. The Roman Emperor Augustus is mentioned by Luke as part of the background to the birth of Christ in **Lesson 4.** How much do your learners actually know about this powerful ruler and his impact on the Mediterranean world? One way to enlighten them would be to have a class member portray him by delivering a monologue about his life. Another possibility is to have two learners pretend to be angels in conversation about the shocking contrast between the luxurious lifestyle of Augustus and the humble birth of the King of kings.

Later in the quarter, your learners will encounter the familiar figure of Pontius Pilate **(Lesson 11).** Nearly everyone knows the role Pilate played in the crucifixion of Christ, but few know anything else about his life and work in first-century Israel. How did he come to power? What kind of governor was he? What became of him after the resurrection of Jesus?

To enhance a report on Pilate, you can post several pictures of this Roman that are based on his theorized likeness as taken from coins and artwork (easy to find on the Internet). Include the caption, "Have you seen this man?" Pretend that you (or one of your learners) are a TV news reporter presenting a missing-person case to your viewers. Discuss the rise and fall of Pilate in history and legend. Explain what we know and don't know about the fate of the man who executed Jesus.

### Learning About the Less-Than-Greats

In recent years, the "great-man theory" of history has been replaced among historians by other approaches. One of the newer approaches deals with social history. Instead of focusing only on the big shot "movers and shakers" of society, many historians now want to know what the less-than-great people were thinking and doing.

The theory here is that more often than not history's great leaders respond to changes among the masses rather than the other way around. The social historian is interested in why such developments happened when they did and what effects they later had.

Although Luke was not a social historian, he gives us numerous glimpses of first-century Palestinian culture in his story of Jesus. Properly highlighted, these "snapshots" can help your class to understand better the significance of what Jesus was teaching and doing.

For example, in **Lesson 1** we meet John the Baptist's father, a priest named Zechariah. We learn from an appearance of the angel Gabriel that John is to be raised similar to a Nazarite, never tasting wine or strong drink. Your learners will gain a clearer perspective of this if they understand something of the work of a temple priest and the lifestyle and beliefs of a Nazarite. During class, you can "interview" two learners—one portraying a priest and the other a Nazarite—to explain what each one does and why he does it. Some of your learners may enjoy doing the advance research required for such a role play.

The setting for **Lesson 12** is a Sabbath day banquet in the home of a prominent Pharisee. Jesus used the seating customs associated with such a banquet to teach on the nature of true humility. To illustrate this setting, arrange your classroom like a first-century banquet room, with the chairs arranged in the shape of a "U"

or a semi-circle. Reserve one chair in the middle for yourself and two chairs on either side of it for "honored guests." After your learners have seated themselves, move some to places of greater honor and some to lesser places.

Before class, explain the exercise to the learners being demoted so they can pretend to be humiliated. For the most realism, you can use floor cushions (instead of chairs) arranged around a very low table, although this may not be practical for various reasons.

Other customs mentioned by Luke include the presentation of the infant Jesus at the temple **(Lesson 5)** and the celebration of Passover **(Lesson 6)**. To research these topics, you can consult Bible dictionaries and encyclopedias or books devoted to Bible customs. Of course, the Internet is a great research tool as well.

### Twenty-Twenty Hindsight

Modern Christians have the advantage of being able to look back at completed events of salvation-history that the Old Testament prophets could only imagine (1 Peter 1:10-12). History is far from being "bunk"! Most Christians would agree that history is, in reality, "His story"—the workings of God in human affairs.

That being the case, we can only benefit from a greater understanding of the historical context of the New Testament, since that knowledge will help us to interpret and apply God's Word correctly. History thus becomes a window on the present and future work of God. As the French poet and politician Alphonse De Lamartine (1790 –1869) observed, "Providence conceals itself in the details of human affairs, but becomes unveiled in the generalities of history."

### Answers to Quarterly Quiz on page 114

**Lesson 1**—1. Gabriel. 2. Zechariah was unable to speak. **Lesson 2**—1. false. 2. she was very old. **Lesson 3**—1. Zechariah. 2. true. **Lesson 4**—1. Augustus. 2. it was the city of his lineage. **Lesson 5**—1. the Christ. 2. two turtledoves. **Lesson 6**—1. Passover. 2. true. **Lesson 7**—1. true. 2. pray for them. **Lesson 8**—1. false. 2. Holy Spirit. **Lesson 9**—1. lilies of the field. 2. growing taller by worrying. **Lesson 10**—1. Peace. 2. true. **Lesson 11**—1. Galileans. 2. false. **Lesson 12**—1. false. 2. resurrection. **Lesson 13**—1. he couldn't finish it. 2. true.

# Called to Believe

December 2
Lesson 1

DEVOTIONAL READING: **Psalm 66:1-4, 16-20.**

BACKGROUND SCRIPTURE: **Luke 1:5-25.**

PRINTED TEXT: **Luke 1:8-23.**

### Luke 1:8-23

8 And it came to pass, that, while he executed the priest's office before God in the order of his course,

9 According to the custom of the priest's office, his lot was to burn incense when he went into the temple of the Lord.

10 And the whole multitude of the people were praying without at the time of incense.

11 And there appeared unto him an angel of the Lord standing on the right side of the altar of incense.

12 And when Zechariah saw him, he was troubled, and fear fell upon him.

13 But the angel said unto him, Fear not, Zechariah: for thy prayer is heard; and thy wife Elisabeth shall bear thee a son, and thou shalt call his name John.

14 And thou shalt have joy and gladness; and many shall rejoice at his birth.

15 For he shall be great in the sight of the Lord, and shall drink neither wine nor strong drink; and he shall be filled with the Holy Ghost, even from his mother's womb.

16 And many of the children of Israel shall he turn to the Lord their God.

17 And he shall go before him in the spirit and power of Elijah, to turn the hearts of the fathers to the children, and the disobedient to the wisdom of the just; to make ready a people prepared for the Lord.

18 And Zechariah said unto the angel, Whereby shall I know this? for I am an old man, and my wife well stricken in years.

19 And the angel answering said unto him, I am Gabriel, that stand in the presence of God; and am sent to speak unto thee, and to show thee these glad tidings.

20 And, behold, thou shalt be dumb, and not able to speak, until the day that these things shall be performed, because thou believest not my words, which shall be fulfilled in their season.

21 And the people waited for Zechariah, and marveled that he tarried so long in the temple.

22 And when he came out, he could not speak unto them: and they perceived that he had seen a vision in the temple; for he beckoned unto them, and remained speechless.

23 And it came to pass, that, as soon as the days of his ministration were accomplished, he departed to his own house.

---

GOLDEN TEXT: Behold, thou shalt be dumb, and not able to speak, until the day that these things shall be performed, because thou believest not my words, which shall be fulfilled in their season.—Luke 1:20.

---

*God's Call to the
Christian Community*
Unit 1: God's Call in Christ
(Lessons 1-5)

## Lesson Aims

After participating in this lesson, each student will be able to:

1. Describe the meeting between Zechariah and the angel Gabriel.

2. Explain why Zechariah should have believed the angel and why he doubted.

3. Confess one area of life where his or her faith could be stronger.

## Lesson Outline

INTRODUCTION
    A. Tall Tales
    B. Lesson Background
 I. ORDINARY SETTING (Luke 1:8-10)
    A. Faithful Service (vv. 8, 9)
    B. Expectant Moment (v. 10)
 II. EXTRAORDINARY NEWS (Luke 1:11-13)
    A. Startling Appearance (vv. 11, 12)
      *Speaking to an Angel, Responding to God*
    B. Stunning Promise (v. 13)
 III. EXCEPTIONAL SON (Luke 1:14-17)
    A. His Character (vv. 14, 15)
      *"He Shall Be Great"*
    B. His Mission (vv. 16, 17)
 IV. DIVINE CONFIRMATION (Luke 1:18-23)
    A. Human Doubt (v. 18)
    B. Angelic Sentencing (vv. 19, 20)
    C. Divine Proof (vv. 21-23)
CONCLUSION
    A. Zechariah: "God Remembers"
    B. John: "Yahweh Has Been Gracious"
    C. Prayer
    D. Thought to Remember

## Introduction

### A. Tall Tales

The annual Liars' Contest used to be a popular event within the Pennsylvania German community. Each person would tell a story to see who could go the furthest beyond the reach of credibility. It was all in good fun because no one was expected to believe the outlandish tales.

However, when God tells a person something that is frankly incredible, He expects to be believed. When God warned Adam and Eve that eating the fruit of the forbidden tree would result in their deaths, He meant it. When He told Noah, Abraham, and Moses things that seemed totally impossible, they believed Him. Then the time came for Zechariah to take his turn. He was called to believe that God would give him a son and that son would prepare for the coming of the Messiah.

### B. Lesson Background

Through the centuries of the Old Testament, God spoke to the Jewish people through the prophets at many times and in various ways (see Hebrews 1:1). But by the time we reach Luke 1, it had been 400 years since God said anything at all. So when an angel came from Heaven to announce that God was going to raise up a prophet, it was (or should have been) a stunning development for God's people.

On a more personal level, the announcement was stunning to a priest named Zechariah. Although his name means, "God remembers," he and his wife, Elisabeth, could well have thought that God had forgotten them. They were childless because she was barren; in addition, they were well along in years (Luke 1:7). Still, they were wholly devoted to serving their God. [See question #1, page 128.]

As God broke His 400 years of silence, the events would be carefully recorded by Luke, a physician and an associate of the apostle Paul (Colossians 4:14; 2 Timothy 4:11). As Luke explained in the opening verses of his Gospel, he was the recipient of eyewitness testimony and had "perfect understanding of all things from the very first" (Luke 1:3). We can put full confidence in what he wrote. The historical truth of these events teaches us a lesson that Zechariah learned the hard way: we are called to put full confidence in God.

## I. Ordinary Setting
## (Luke 1:8-10)

### A. Faithful Service (vv. 8, 9)

**8. And it came to pass, that, while he executed the priest's office before God in the order of his course.**

On the surface, the day looks ordinary. The priests are performing their usual service, and people are saying their routine prayers. But something quite extraordinary is about to happen. Little does *he* (Zechariah) know what God has planned for him on this "ordinary" day.

Zechariah is a member of the priestly *course* of Abijah (see 1 Chronicles 24:10; Luke 1:5). As one of 24 such divisions of the priesthood (see 1 Chronicles 24:18), his group takes its turn to serve at the temple two weeks of every year. Then they serve with all the other groups during the major festivals.

Zechariah, now an old man (Luke 1:18), can look back over the many years that he has faithfully *executed the priest's office.* In faithful submission to the will of God, he is like the priests who later become believers in Jesus (see Acts 6:7).

**9. According to the custom of the priest's office, his lot was to burn incense when he went into the temple of the Lord.**

When priests and their assistants serve at the temple, their responsibilities include sacrificing animals, filling the oil in the lamp stand, and setting out the "showbread" on the sacred table. At special times they also lead the people in prayer and praise to God. *According to the custom* of their office, the priests cast lots to decide who will do which duty. Casting lots keeps the selection process impartial (compare 1 Chronicles 24:5, 31; 25:8; 26:12-16).

The specific *lot* that falls to Zechariah on this day is *to burn incense* at the altar of incense. This is a wooden box overlaid with gold, standing in front of the Holy of Holies. According to Exodus 30:1-10, incense is to be offered twice daily. Since there are thousands of priests, each is permitted to burn this incense no more than once in his lifetime. Thus Zechariah knows this "ordinary" day is special for him in a certain way. But he does not yet know just how special it will be! [See question #2, page 128.]

### B. Expectant Moment (v. 10)

**10. And the whole multitude of the people were praying without at the time of incense.**

The scene is typical and ordinary: while the priest goes into the Holy Place, the surrounding courtyards are filled with worshipers. But "ordinary" need not imply "unsacred." This is always a sacred moment. The sacredness is about to be enhanced by what God is going to do. A devout priest is serving, the people are praying, and God's silence of 400 years is about to be broken.

## II. Extraordinary News (Luke 1:11-13)

### A. Startling Appearance (vv. 11, 12)

**11. And there appeared unto him an angel of the Lord standing on the right side of the altar of incense.**

*The altar of incense* is next to the giant curtain that separates the Holy Place from the Holy of Holies, the two rooms of the temple (Exodus 30:6; 40:5; 1 Kings 6:22). The fragrance of the burning incense is a sweet aroma in God's presence.

As Zechariah goes about his duties of replenishing the incense, *an angel of the Lord* appears beside the altar. Named later in the narrative as Gabriel (v. 19), this is the same angel who will carry God's message to a young virgin named Mary in a few months.

**12. And when Zechariah saw him, he was troubled, and fear fell upon him.**

The reaction of Zechariah is not surprising except in its understatement! He is *troubled* because he cannot fathom what is happening. In addition, he is afraid since the event is clearly supernatural.

SPEAKING TO AN ANGEL, RESPONDING TO GOD

The title of a syrupy love song from the 1950s asks "How Do You Speak to an Angel?" The point of the song is that a young man has met the perfect girl, but he is tongue-tied.

Obviously, the recording artist was using the word *angel* in a figurative way. But if we take the question of the song title literally, Scripture provides insight. Appearances by angels sometimes cause fear (Daniel 8:15-17; Luke 1:12, 29, 30; Acts 10:1-4). In such cases, the angel may speak words of comfort so the human will be able to respond. In other cases, people react to angelic encounters in a rather human-to-human way. See the cases of Abraham, Lot, and Gideon in Genesis 18:1-5; 19:1, 2; and Judges 6:11-13.

Despite the apparent calmness of Abraham, Lot, and Gideon, knowing that an angel was coming from the presence of God would cause any of us to become a bit "troubled" at the appearance of such a heavenly being! I don't expect to receive a visit from an angel (none of us should), but if it happened I think I would be terrified. I probably would be just as tongue-tied as the young man depicted in the 1950s song.

---

**How to Say It**

AARONIC. Air-*ahn-i*k.

ABIJAH. Uh-*bye*-juh.

ABRAHAM. *Ay*-bruh-ham.

JUDEA. Joo-*dee*-uh.

MALACHI. *Mal*-uh-kye.

MOSES. *Mo*-zes or *Mo*-zez.

NAZARITE. *Naz*-uh-rite.

YAHWEH (Hebrew). *Yah*-weh.

ZECHARIAH. *Zek*-uh-*rye*-uh (strong accent on *rye*).

However, the fact of ultimate importance is that Zechariah and others who received angelic appearances listened and obeyed. God has much to say to us through the pages of His Word. We need not react with dread at His words, but we must indeed listen and obey. —J. B. N.

### B. Stunning Promise (v. 13)

**13. But the angel said unto him, Fear not, Zechariah: for thy prayer is heard; and thy wife Elisabeth shall bear thee a son, and thou shalt call his name John.**

*Zechariah* does not know what is happening, but *the angel* does. Gabriel knows both Zechariah and *Elisabeth* by name; he even knows that the faithful priest has been praying for *a son.* [See question #3, page 128.] Elisabeth is to *bear* a son; *his name* will be *John* (which means, "Yahweh has been gracious").

At certain times in Scripture, God sends angels to deliver news that is simply unbelievable from a human perspective. But people are expected to believe it anyway. Such is the case here. Against the laws of nature, Zechariah is going to have a son! That son will be the one to prepare for the coming of the Christ.

To be childless in the Jewish culture is considered to be a severe misfortune (Luke 1:25). We may assume that Zechariah has prayed year after year for a child, to no (apparent) avail. In his old age he may have begun to pray that prayer less and less often. But God has heard, and God has not forgotten. God answers the prayer on His own timetable (compare Genesis 15:1-5; 21:1-7; 30:1, 22). The son of Zechariah and Elisabeth will go on to be one of the most remarkable men in history: John the Baptist.

## III. Exceptional Son
## (Luke 1:14-17)

### A. His Character (vv. 14, 15)

**14. And thou shalt have joy and gladness; and many shall rejoice at his birth.**

The fear and confusion of Zechariah eventually will be replaced with *joy and gladness.* Like Abraham in his old age, Zechariah is going to have a son!

While the birth of a baby is generally a time of celebration and happiness, this birth will be something more. More than just the family and friends, *many shall rejoice* at John's birth (compare Luke 1:57, 58). The effects of *his birth* bring joy even across the centuries to our own time.

**15. For he shall be great in the sight of the Lord, and shall drink neither wine nor strong drink; and he shall be filled with the Holy Ghost, even from his mother's womb.**

Many movie stars, athletes, and politicians are great in the sight of people. But John will grow up to be *great in the sight of the Lord.* It is, after all, the Lord's evaluation that is important! Jesus will later say of him, "Among them that are born of women there hath not risen a greater than John the Baptist" (Matthew 11:11).

Like those who took the Nazarite vow to separate themselves to the Lord, John will drink nothing intoxicating (compare Numbers 6:1-3; Judges 13:2-5; Amos 2:11, 12). But John is not just another Nazarite; he is far more special. He will be *filled with the Holy Ghost,* even while he is still in *his mother's womb.* Perhaps this is why, three months before he is born, he leaps for joy when Mary comes to see Elisabeth (Luke 1:41).

#### "HE SHALL BE GREAT"

I once knew a man who had a very high opinion of his granddaughter. His view of her was always expressed with highest praise: she was beautiful, smart, and talented. I didn't want to disagree with him, but I thought he overrated her. She was an attractive teenager, but I would not have called her beautiful. She got good grades in school, but I would not have called her exceptionally intelligent. As for her talent, I was equally underimpressed.

As the old saying goes, "Beauty is in the eye of the beholder." I didn't share his estimate of her abilities. But then again, I don't think he had a very wide exposure to people of talent and intelligence with which to compare hers. The girl was outstanding in his eyes. And that's all right; I appreciated his devotion to his granddaughter. Yet if this same estimate had come from an experienced judge of beauty and talent contests, I would have been more inclined to take it at face value.

John was to be "great in the sight of the Lord." The Lord is objective about such things (remember, He is "no respecter of persons"; Acts 10:34). He has wide experience in knowing and judging people. Being judged "great" in the Lord's sight certainly puts John in a special category. May God see each of us as "great" as we do our parts to prepare the world for Christ's return! —J. B. N.

### B. His Mission (vv. 16, 17)

**16. And many of the children of Israel shall he turn to the Lord their God.**

Gabriel's prediction that John's mission will be to call *the children of Israel* to *turn to the Lord* implies that many Israelites have fallen away from *God.* Many eventually will flock to hear John, will repent, and will be baptized by him (Matthew 3; Mark 1:1-8; Luke 3:1-20; John 1:19-28).

**17. And he shall go before him in the spirit and power of Elijah, to turn the hearts of the fathers to the children, and the disobedient to the wisdom of the just; to make ready a people prepared for the Lord.**

John's mission was also predicted at the end of the Old Testament: "Behold, I will send you Elijah the prophet . . . and he shall turn the heart of the fathers to the children, and the heart of the children to their fathers" (Malachi 4:5, 6). In this way John is to prepare the people of Judea for the coming of the Messiah. [See question #4, page 128.] Although John himself may or may not have been aware of his importance as a "type" of Elijah, Jesus understood it perfectly (see Matthew 17:10-13).

It is striking that God's closing words in the Old Testament and some of the first words in the New Testament are about John the Baptist. Although there have been more than 400 years of silence between the times of Malachi and Luke, God's plan has not changed. Now John will have a significant role in helping to make that plan a reality. He will be wholly devoted to preparing the way for the Messiah. John will have no regard for his own importance. Right up to the time of his grisly death, he will live only to answer the call of God.

## IV. Divine Confirmation
## (Luke 1:18-23)

### A. Human Doubt (v. 18)

**18. And Zechariah said unto the angel, Whereby shall I know this? for I am an old man, and my wife well stricken in years.**

What *the angel* has just said is more than *Zechariah* can swallow! In his human weakness, Zechariah is reluctant to believe (compare Genesis 18:12). So Zechariah blurts out the thought of his heart: *Whereby shall I know this?*

Zechariah needs some kind of proof that such things will be so. After all, he is *an old man* and

Visual for
Lesson 1

*Keep this visual posted all quarter as a reminder of how our 13 lessons fit together.*

his wife is *well stricken in years.* The years have taken their toll on them both. While the unbelief of Zechariah is understandable, we should not make excuses for it. [See question #5, page 128.]

### B. Angelic Sentencing (vv. 19, 20)

**19. And the angel answering said unto him, I am Gabriel, that stand in the presence of God; and am sent to speak unto thee, and to show thee these glad tidings.**

*The angel* now identifies himself. In so doing, he shows why Zechariah should believe what he has just been told. *Gabriel* is the same angel who had carried God's message to Daniel five and a half centuries earlier (Daniel 8:16; 9:21). This exalted being, who regularly stands in the very *presence of God,* has come with a message directly from on high. It is God's message, and it is good news. So why shouldn't Zechariah believe it? Zechariah surely knows how God opened the womb of Sarah (Genesis 21:1-7)!

**20. And, behold, thou shalt be dumb, and not able to speak, until the day that these things shall be performed, because thou believest not my words, which shall be fulfilled in their season.**

God, in an act of stern kindness, gives Zechariah both punishment and confirmation: he will be struck *dumb* (meaning *not able to speak*) for the entire period of Elisabeth's pregnancy. Until the day when *these things shall be performed*—and they most certainly will be—Zechariah will suffer the consequence of his unbelief. God has spoken and Zechariah does not believe. Now Zechariah cannot speak further words of unbelief or any other words at all. God will lift the punishment at the time of John's naming (Luke 1:62-64).

## C. Divine Proof (vv. 21-23)

**21. And the people waited for Zechariah, and marveled that he tarried so long in the temple.**

The crowds pray and wait outside in the temple courtyards. On this day, Zechariah is their closest link to the presence of God, so they are eager to see him emerge from the sacred building. Usually the stay of a priest in the Holy Place lasts only a few minutes. Then he comes out and pronounces the familiar Aaronic blessing on the people (see Numbers 6:24-26). When Zechariah delays, taking much longer than a priest usually does, they are concerned. What is happening?

**22. And when he came out, he could not speak unto them: and they perceived that he had seen a vision in the temple: for he beckoned unto them, and remained speechless.**

Zechariah finally emerges. He does not say the expected words of blessing on the people; indeed, he is unable to *speak unto them* at all! Instead, he uses hand signals to explain what has happened. The fact that he is *speechless* is proof that the hand of God is upon him.

**23. And it came to pass, that, as soon as the days of his ministration were accomplished, he departed to his own house.**

When the two weeks of his ministry in the temple are over, Zechariah returns *to his own house* in the hill country of Judea (see Luke 1:39, 40). The chief priests and their important assistants have houses in Jerusalem itself, but lesser priests live out in the countryside. There they farm, keep livestock, or work at a trade.

Zechariah's return home is not the end of the story; it is only the beginning. After four centuries of silence, God has spoken to His people once again. God's plan of salvation is moving forward!

## Home Daily Bible Readings

**Monday, Nov. 26**—Sing God's Praises (Psalm 66:1-4)

**Tuesday, Nov. 27**—Righteous Before God (Luke 1:5-7)

**Wednesday, Nov. 28**—Incense Offering Interrupted (Luke 1:8-13)

**Thursday, Nov. 29**—A Ministry Foretold (Luke 1:14-17)

**Friday, Nov. 30**—Zechariah Sees a Vision (Luke 1:18-23)

**Saturday, Dec. 1**—Elisabeth Conceives (Luke 1:24, 25)

**Sunday, Dec. 2**—God Listened to My Prayer (Psalm 66:16-20)

# Conclusion

## A. Zechariah: "God Remembers"

God tells no tall tales; it is impossible for Him to lie (see Hebrews 6:18). Throughout history, God has required that people listen when He speaks and that they believe what He says.

God's expectation applied to Zechariah, perhaps especially so. Yet even though he was a faithful priest (Luke 1:6), he stumbled at believing God's "impossible" promise. Since we have the advantage of hindsight of the completed New Testament, we may be tempted to excuse Zechariah's failure because we know some things he didn't. But Zechariah also had hindsight to draw on: he undoubtedly knew of the Old Testament accounts of how God intervened to bring sons to elderly, childless couples. Having hindsight is no guarantee that we will always exercise faith!

God did not intend to leave us in the bondage of sin. From the beginning of our disobedience, when God promised that the seed of woman would bruise Satan's head (Genesis 3:15), God had a plan to save us. After many centuries, God still pushes His plan forward. Now we—like Zechariah—are called to believe.

## B. John: "Yahweh Has Been Gracious"

John the Baptist was rightly named. He was living proof of God's graciousness. To Zechariah and Elisabeth in their old age, God extended grace by granting them a son. To the entire human race, God proved His grace by sending His own Son—whose way John the Baptist prepared. As this all unfolded, one thing was clear: Yahweh (God) has been gracious.

As we enter this Christmas season, let us remember again each part of the sacred story. Let us rejoice to hear Gabriel's glad tidings to Zechariah and to Mary; let us echo the multitude of the heavenly hosts praising God. We believe in the baby of Bethlehem; we believe in the Christ of the cross; we believe in the future return of our king. We have been called to believe—and we do!

## C. Prayer

Our Father, we thank You for remembering us in spite of our sins and for opening the door of salvation. Thank You for providing all we need to be able to believe in Your Son Jesus. He is the one by whom we are saved. In His name we pray, amen.

## D. Thought to Remember

God yet calls us to believe.

# Learning by Doing

*This page contains an alternative lesson plan emphasizing learning activities.*
*Classes desiring such student involvement will find these suggestions helpful.*

## Into the Lesson

Cut from poster board seven rectangles of about five by eight inches each. Write the following letter pairs on them, one letter pair per rectangle, front and back: D and B, O and E, U and L, B and I, T and E, E and V, R and E. Be certain that the letter on the back of each rectangle is upside down in relation to the letter on the front.

Affix these seven as "flaps" on the wall, taping each securely at the top. The word *DOUBTER* should be showing. Tell the class that there is a second word on the reverse of the letters showing. Ask the class to guess the letters underneath the letters showing. With each correct guess, lift the flap and tape it up to allow the letter to show.

Once the second word is fully revealed, say, "That's the challenge of today's study: *Doubter, believe!* The doubter today is Zechariah, but the same challenge comes to all of us." Keep the letter flaps in view to refer to later.

## Into the Word

Distribute the following matching activity. Have your learners work in pairs or small teams. Say, "The headings of the lesson outline are given here in alphabetical order. The all-capital headings are the main outline elements; mixed-case headings are subpoints. Use today's text to help you discover the right answer." (This activity is included in the optional student book.)

| | |
|---|---|
| ____ Angelic Sentencing | a. Luke 1:8, 9 |
| ____ DIVINE CONFIRMATION | b. Luke 1:8-10 |
| ____ Divine Proof | c. Luke 1:10 |
| ____ EXCEPTIONAL SON | d. Luke 1:11-13 |
| ____ Expectant Moment | e. Luke 1:11, 12 |
| ____ EXTRAORDINARY NEWS | f. Luke 1:13 |
| ____ Faithful Service | g. Luke 1:14-17 |
| ____ His Character | h. Luke 1:14, 15 |
| ____ His Mission | i. Luke 1:16, 17 |
| ____ Human Doubt | j. Luke 1:18 |
| ____ ORDINARY SETTING | k. Luke 1:18-23 |
| ____ Startling Appearance | l. Luke 1:19, 20 |
| ____ Stunning Promise | m. Luke 1:21-23 |

Give learners a few minutes to work and then call for answers. As segments and titles are correctly matched, have those verses read aloud.

Next, introduce the following Hard-to-Believe activity. Write on the board this question: *How important is this issue to me in believing what someone is stating as truth?* Then ask for a silent response to each of the following 10 items.

The possible responses are a raised fist (that is, with no fingers extended) for *no importance;* index finger up for *very little importance;* two fingers up for *of some importance;* three fingers up for *very important.* 1. Lack of knowledge about the one making the claim. 2. Personal experience. 3. Being outside the realm of empirical science. 4. The time and setting of the affirmation. 5. The lack of confirming witnesses. 6. Inability to prove the claim immediately. 7. The seemingly low confidence of the one affirming. 8. The person's skeptical, even cynical attitude. 9. The likelihood of being scoffed at or laughed at for believing it. 10. The absence of biblical revelation or biblical precedent for the claim.

Quickly run through the list and ask for responses. Then write this question on the board: *How may these factors have had an effect in Zechariah believing or disbelieving the message given to him?*

Repeat each element and ask learners to respond. For example, for #1, did Zechariah know Gabriel personally? For #2, were the years and years of Elisabeth's barrenness reason to believe she could not become pregnant? For #3, how would the physical condition of Zechariah and Elisabeth for becoming parents affect Zechariah's reaction? For #10, would not Zechariah know of the Old Testament examples of Abraham and Sarah, Elkanah and Hannah, and others?

Make your way through the entire list in this manner. This will allow you a thorough examination of why Zechariah should have believed and why he doubted. (A similar exercise is in the optional student book.)

## Into Life

Prepare and give each learner a strip of paper that is printed with seven blocks bearing the letters *D, O, U, B, T, E, R.* Ask each to carry the slip for the week or put it in his or her daily devotional Bible. Learners are to determine a time each day when he or she will write one letter of the word *BELIEVE* on the back. Tell them this is the daily challenge for the godly: *Doubter, believe!* Refer back to the Into the Lesson activity.

# Let's Talk It Over

*The questions on this page are designed to promote discussion of the lesson by the class and to encourage application of the lesson Scriptures. The answers provided are only discussion starters. Let your class talk it over from there.*

**1. Whom do you know whose life reflects a quiet, faithful walk with Jesus? What impact has that example had on you?**

Zechariah and Elisabeth were ordinary people in their community. Yet the Lord blessed and used this humble, devoted couple in a special way. The pattern in Scripture is that God chooses to work through such people. Two are Moses (Numbers 12:3) and Mary (Luke 1:48).

All of us can take heart from Paul's observation: "For ye see your calling, brethren, how that not many wise men after the flesh, not many mighty, not many noble, are called: but God hath chosen the foolish things of the world to confound the wise; and God hath chosen the weak things of the world to confound the things which are mighty" (1 Corinthians 1:26, 27).

**2. What was a time when a certain event or routine in your life proved to be something special for God in a way that was above and beyond your beginning expectation?**

Sometimes we are challenged to decide whether the way something turned out was a co-incidence or was God's intervention. On the one hand, when we recognize that coincidences do happen, we avoid overspiritualizing every little thing. On the other hand, it is impossible to believe in a sovereign God who orders the universe while also believing that impersonal coincidence accounts for 100 percent of events and their effects. Time after time we see God intervening in the lives of people in the Bible to bring about His will.

When the unexpected is interjected into our routine, it may become a source of annoyance. Our irritation can blind us to seeing God's hand at work. Car trouble upsets our schedules, but may result in meeting an automobile mechanic who needs our witness. The cases of Zechariah and others challenge us to live life expectantly— not expecting an angelic appearance, but watching to see God working in and around us.

**3. What was a time when you prayed for something and you were surprised when God answered your prayer? What did you learn about yourself as a result?**

We can conclude from Gabriel's words in verse 13 that Zechariah had been praying for a child. Yet when the angel told Zechariah his prayer was answered *yes*, he found it hard to believe. As a result, Zechariah ended up with nine months of muteness. Perhaps we could say that that was God's "time out" discipline for him! It certainly gave Zechariah a tangible reminder of the power of God.

**4. How does God interact with us today? What are some reasons for failing to notice God working in and around our lives?**

God is sovereign, yet He reacts to and interacts with people. In today's text we see a unique way that He does so. On an ongoing basis, God interacts with us through His Holy Spirit (John 16:5-15; Acts 2:38, 39), through other believers (1 Thessalonians 5:11; James 5:16; 1 Peter 4:10, 11), and through the circumstances in our lives (James 1:2-4). Jesus told us that His Father is always at work (John 5:17). Yet sometimes we don't acknowledge what we see as coming from God. Even though we may be in a situation where nothing seems to be quite right, that does not mean that God is not working around us (Romans 8:28).

**5. Scripture offers us examples of God-fearing individuals who struggled to understand or believe something that God told them. What Bible passages do you struggle to understand or believe? How do you remain faithful in spite of doubt?**

We cannot understand God completely (Isaiah 55:8, 9). Believing in His promises, however, is our source of hope. When we stay with God through our doubts, we grow in the knowledge of His faithfulness (Psalm 34:8; Proverbs 3:5, 6).

Obedience to God's Word will result in oppression by the world (John 15:18-27), and we will struggle to understand why. We may wonder if the oppression is a result of misunderstanding God's Word. Misinterpretations of God's Word can indeed make life more difficult. We can overcome as we study alongside a learned teacher or use a reliable commentary to give us the insight we need to apply a passage properly.

# Called to Be a Vessel

DEVOTIONAL READING: Psalm 40:1-5.

BACKGROUND SCRIPTURE: Luke 1:26-38.

PRINTED TEXT: Luke 1:26-38.

### Luke 1:26-38

26 And in the sixth month the angel Gabriel was sent from God unto a city of Galilee, named Nazareth,

27 To a virgin espoused to a man whose name was Joseph, of the house of David; and the virgin's name was Mary.

28 And the angel came in unto her, and said, Hail, thou that art highly favored, the Lord is with thee: blessed art thou among women.

29 And when she saw him, she was troubled at his saying, and cast in her mind what manner of salutation this should be.

30 And the angel said unto her, Fear not, Mary: for thou hast found favor with God.

31 And, behold, thou shalt conceive in thy womb, and bring forth a son, and shalt call his name JESUS.

32 He shall be great, and shall be called the Son of the Highest; and the Lord God shall give unto him the throne of his father David:

33 And he shall reign over the house of Jacob for ever; and of his kingdom there shall be no end.

34 Then said Mary unto the angel, How shall this be, seeing I know not a man?

35 And the angel answered and said unto her, The Holy Ghost shall come upon thee, and the power of the Highest shall overshadow thee: therefore also that holy thing which shall be born of thee shall be called the Son of God.

36 And, behold, thy cousin Elisabeth, she hath also conceived a son in her old age; and this is the sixth month with her, who was called barren.

37 For with God nothing shall be impossible.

38 And Mary said, Behold the handmaid of the Lord; be it unto me according to thy word. And the angel departed from her.

GOLDEN TEXT: Mary said, Behold the handmaid of the Lord;
be it unto me according to thy word.—Luke 1:38.

## God's Call to the Christian Community
### Unit 1: God's Call in Christ
(Lessons 1-5)

## Lesson Aims

After participating in this lesson, each student will be able to:

1. Retell the story of Gabriel's appearance to Mary.

2. Give examples of other instances in which God chose "lowly" people to carry out His tasks.

3. Write a prayer that asks God to use him or her in a way that seems impossible to human thinking.

## Lesson Outline

INTRODUCTION
  A. Precious Cargo, Fragile Vessels
  B. Lesson Background
I.  GABRIEL'S GREETING (Luke 1:26-30)
  A. In a Real Time and Place (v. 26)
  B. To a Real Person (v. 27)
  C. With Real Grace (vv. 28-30)
    *The Lord Is with Thee*
II.  GOD'S MESSAGE (Luke 1:31-33)
  A. Mary's Son (v. 31)
  B. God's Son (v. 32a)
  C. David's Son (vv. 32b, 33)
    *No End*
III.  MARY'S RESPONSE (Luke 1:34-38)
  A. Reasonable Doubt (v. 34)
  B. Divine Explanation (vv. 35-37)
  C. Humble Acceptance (v. 38)
CONCLUSION
  A. Chosen Vessel, Willing Vessel
  B. Prayer
  C. Thought to Remember

## Introduction

### A. Precious Cargo, Fragile Vessels

New York jeweler Harry Winston bought the famed Hope Diamond from an estate sale in 1949. In 1958, Winston decided to donate the diamond to the Smithsonian Institution in Washington, D.C. Weighing 45.52 carats, the gem was extremely valuable.

So how would the transfer be made? Rejecting armored trucks or elaborate delivery schemes, Winston merely put the diamond in a box and sent it through the U.S. mail! It arrived in good order, without incident.

Are we startled that someone would choose a fragile vessel and an ordinary means of conveyance for such an extraordinary cargo? As we ponder this account, we can recall the fact that God chose a young peasant named Mary to bring His precious Son into the world. When she was called to be a vessel, she agreed. Her willingness to be used by God is the highlight of this week's lesson.

### B. Lesson Background

As we compare last week's lesson with today's, we see interesting parallels in God's plan to bring salvation to humanity. The angel Gabriel appeared to both Zechariah and Mary, in separate incidents. Each was quite startled at Gabriel's appearance. Gabriel instructed each not to be afraid. Each was promised a child. Each was given a hint of his or her child's future greatness. Each was told what the name of his or her child was to be.

Thus the beauty of God's plan for salvation continued to unfold. Zechariah had been called to believe; then Mary was called to be a vessel. Even though we should not expect angelic appearances today, God continues to issue calls to us through His Word.

## I. Gabriel's Greeting
## (Luke 1:26-30)

### A. In a Real Time and Place (v. 26)

**26. And in the sixth month the angel Gabriel was sent from God unto a city of Galilee, named Nazareth.**

Luke's Gospel is careful to locate events in both time and place. The account is definitely not a "once upon a time" fairy tale! In preparing to send His Son into the world, God makes sure that this angelic announcement is documented.

After Gabriel appeared to Zechariah in Jerusalem and announced that Elisabeth would give birth to a son (Luke 1:13), the mute priest returned home to the hill country of Judea (1:23, 39, 40). Elisabeth rejoiced in the knowledge of her pregnancy, but remained in seclusion for the first five months (1:24). Then, *in the sixth month* of her pregnancy, something of even greater importance takes place.

Gabriel, the angel who stands in the presence of God himself (Luke 1:19), is sent to a *city of Galilee* by the name of *Nazareth*. Nazareth is not mentioned anywhere in the Old Testament, but it is situated very close to Sephoris (or Sepphoris), the capital of the district of old Galilee. Nazareth is also close to an important trade route. This city's location is about 17 miles due west of the lower end of the Sea of Galilee (see, for example, www.nazarethvillage.com). A derogatory evaluation of the character of the city comes from Nathanael: "Can there any good thing come out of Nazareth?" (John 1:46).

### B. To a Real Person (v. 27)

**27. To a virgin espoused to a man whose name was Joseph, of the house of David; and the virgin's name was Mary.**

This time Gabriel's message of an unexpected birth is not to an elderly man, but to a very young woman who is a *virgin*. Some reject the idea that a *virgin* can have a child. But Scripture does not shy away from its bold claim: the miracle of the ages is about to happen—to a virgin. If one cannot accept the miraculous, then one cannot accept Jesus.

To be *espoused* means that *Mary* and *Joseph* have already taken the first steps to becoming married. To break the relationship at this point requires a legal divorce (compare Matthew 1:19). Thus an ancient espousal is a much stronger concept than the modern idea of being engaged.

The final step of the extended marriage process takes place in a ceremony where the groom calls for his bride and takes her to his home. In the case of Mary, even after Joseph takes her to his home, she remains a virgin until after Jesus is born (see Matthew 1:24, 25).

We are not entirely sure whether it is to Mary or to Joseph that Luke is referring to as being *of the house of David* at this point. Joseph definitely is of that line according to Matthew 1:20 (compare Luke 3:23, 31). Mary's own descent from David would signify that Jesus is of David's line biologically as well as legally through adoption

by Joseph. For the Messiah to be of the house of David is an important part of the story line (see 2 Samuel 7:12-16; Matthew 1:1; Luke 1:32; 3:31; 18:38, 39; etc.).

### C. With Real Grace (vv. 28-30)

**28. And the angel came in unto her, and said, Hail, thou that art highly favored, the Lord is with thee: blessed art thou among women.**

Since a young woman is usually betrothed in her teens at this time, it is likely that Mary is quite young when *the angel* greets her. Perhaps she is no more than 15. Even so, she is *highly favored* in the eyes of *the Lord*. There is no record that the priest Zechariah, for his part, received such a commendation.

Gabriel continues his greeting with words of assurance. The phrase *the Lord is with thee* means that God is about to do something good for His people (compare Judges 6:12). The phrase *blessed art thou among women* does not appear in the earliest Greek manuscripts at this point. However, it does appear at Luke 1:42, where Elisabeth utters it under the inspiration of the Holy Spirit. Thus we know that the phrase is a genuine blessing from God. [See question #1, page 136.]

#### "THE LORD IS WITH THEE"

I grew up in a midwestern state of the U.S., and my entire family, grandparents included, lived within an 80-mile radius. But when I was 12, my maternal grandparents moved to Florida. That Christmas my mother, my sister, and I went to spend Christmas break with them. While we were there, my grandfather took me fishing. I'm not sure I had ever been fishing before or even had been out in a boat.

The whole experience was rather exciting and intimidating at the same time. But as long as grandpa was with me, I had no fear. The water, the rocking of the small rowboat, the sights and sounds—nothing made me afraid. Grandpa was close by, and I felt secure.

Mary was initially troubled at the appearance of the angel, but she was soon told of the Lord's favor. A message of reassurance is also available to each of us. We have the Lord's promise that He is with us at all times (Matthew 28:20). With this realization, we can be as relaxed and confident as a child out on the water with his grandpa.

          —J. B. N.

---

### How to Say It

EZEKIEL. Ee-*zeek*-ee-ul or Ee-*zeek*-yul.
GABRIEL. *Gay*-bree-ul.
GALILEE. *Gal*-uh-lee.
ISAIAH. Eye-*zay*-uh.
JERUSALEM. Juh-*roo*-suh-lem.
JUDEA. Joo-*dee*-uh.
MICAH. *My*-kuh.
NATHANAEL. Nuh-*than*-yull (*th* as in *thin*).
NAZARETH. *Naz*-uh-reth.
SEPHORIS. *Sef*-uh-ris.
ZECHARIAH. *Zek*-uh-*rye*-uh (strong accent on *rye*).

---

**29. And when she saw him, she was troubled at his saying, and cast in her mind what manner of salutation this should be.**

But Mary is confused and *troubled* at the words of Gabriel. Angelic appearances can have this effect! Dozens of questions probably flash through her mind in an instant. Why has an angel appeared to her? What do these words signify? So far nothing makes sense, because this event is far beyond anything she has ever experienced.

**30. And the angel said unto her, Fear not, Mary: for thou hast found favor with God.**

Gabriel recognizes the obvious signs of distress in Mary's countenance. So he assures her with the words *Fear not.* He also calls her by name, a subtle proof that this is no case of mistaken identity. It is indeed *Mary* who has *found favor with God;* it is she who is the one God has chosen!

The position of women is generally low in the ancient world. But God singles out a woman to be a favored servant. [See question #2, page 136.] He is going to send salvation to the world through His Son—and His Son will not come out of thin air, but will be born of a woman (see Galatians 4:4). Luke's Gospel and his book of Acts tell of women who were significant in God's plan (examples: Luke 2:36-38; 7:36-50; Acts 16:11-15; 18:1-3).

## II. God's Message
## (Luke 1:31-33)
### A. Mary's Son (v. 31)

**31. And, behold, thou shalt conceive in thy womb, and bring forth a son, and shalt call his name JESUS.**

Gabriel's greeting now gives way to God's message for Mary: contrary to all expectation and all human experience, this virgin will *conceive.*

---

## Home Daily Bible Readings

**Monday, Dec. 3**—God's Wonderful Works (Psalm 40:1-5)

**Tuesday, Dec. 4**—An Unexpected Visitor (Luke 1:26-29)

**Wednesday, Dec. 5**—Mary's Son's Future (Luke 1:30-33)

**Thursday, Dec. 6**—The Miraculous Conception (Luke 1:34, 35)

**Friday, Dec. 7**—Nothing Is Impossible! (Luke 1:36-38)

**Saturday, Dec. 8**—Elisabeth Blesses Mary (Luke 1:39-45)

**Sunday, Dec. 9**—Mary Sings to the Lord (Luke 1:46-56)

---

Gabriel knows in advance what the baby's gender will be. He also announces to Mary (as he had to Zechariah) that God has chosen the baby's *name.* That name is to be *Jesus.* This is the Greek equivalent of the Hebrew name *Joshua,* which means, "the Lord is salvation."

This verse is an obvious fulfillment of the prophecy in Isaiah 7:14. The wording is similar, although the designation of the child is expressed differently. In Isaiah the designation is *Immanuel,* which means, "God with us" (see Matthew 1:23). Both designations correctly identify God's Son: *Immanuel* identifies who He is; *Jesus* tells us what He is going to do. Many other names and titles, such as those prophesied in Isaiah 9:6, also apply to Him.

### B. God's Son (v. 32a)

**32a. He shall be great, and shall be called the Son of the Highest.**

God has a special plan for Mary, but the far greater plan is for her child. Every mother wants her children to be *great,* but Jesus will be great in ways that Mary cannot begin to imagine. Although John the Baptist will be called "a prophet of the Highest" (Luke 1:76), Jesus will be called *the Son of the Highest.*

During Jesus' ministry some 30 years later, people will embrace Him gladly as a healer and teacher. The people will shout with excitement at the thought that He is the kind of Messiah for whom they have been waiting. But when Jesus says that God is His own Father, making himself equal with God, they will be angry enough to kill Him (see John 5:18). Can Mary accept what the angel declares before Jesus' birth, that He is to be *the Son of the Highest*?

### C. David's Son (vv. 32b, 33)

**32b. And the Lord God shall give unto him the throne of his father David.**

Centuries earlier, God had promised David that one day a special descendant of his would rule (again, 2 Samuel 7:12-16). God himself is to establish the kingdom for that son of David. *The throne of his father David* that *the Lord God* will give to this child means that the child will be no less than the long-awaited Messiah.

The eager expectation for this Messiah will be seen later in the expressions that people use when they fervently cry out to Jesus: "Have mercy on us, O Lord, thou Son of David" (Matthew 20:30); "Hosanna to the Son of David" (Matthew 21:9); "Blessed be the kingdom of our father David, that cometh in the name of the Lord" (Mark 11:10). Devout Jews of the time know that the Messiah—whenever He is to come and whoever He is—will be a son of David (see Matthew 22:42-46).

**33. And he shall reign over the house of Jacob for ever; and of his kingdom there shall be no end.**

The closest Old Testament expression of *and he shall reign over the house of Jacob for ever* is in 2 Samuel 2:4, where David is anointed to rule "over the house of Judah." God promised David that the kingdom God would establish would be an everlasting kingdom (2 Samuel 7:16; also see 1 Kings 8:25; Micah 4:7). The reign of Jesus will extend not just through earthly years, but also through all eternity. We see Messiah's eternal rule expressed in Ezekiel 37:25.

Furthermore, the good news of the Messiah will be not just for the Jews. As the angel will tell the shepherds on the night when Jesus is born, "I bring you good tidings of great joy, which shall be to all people" (Luke 2:10). God's plan for salvation intends that the inhabitants of Heaven will include those of "every kindred, and tongue, and people, and nation" (Revelation 5:9).

### NO END

A challenge that has attracted countless scientists and inventors over the years is the idea of creating a perpetual motion machine. Perpetual motion refers to "a condition in which an object moves forever without the expenditure of any limited internal or external source of energy" (Wikipedia).

Many designs have been attempted over the years, but none has ever worked "perpetually." Some designs depend on magnetism, some depend on gravity. Some designs are known as "Rube Goldberg"-type inventions—complicated in construction, almost whimsical in nature, and apparently more useful for generating chuckles than anything else. The problem is that there is always enough friction that some of the energy is dissipated, and ultimately the motion of the machine stops.

Only God is the source of perpetual energy. And His angel Gabriel announced to Mary that God's kingdom would never end. The Roman Empire lasted for 1,229 years; the Holy Roman Empire lasted for 1,004 years. As I write this, the U.S. government under its current constitution is the longest-lived government in the world (218 years). No one knows how long the United States of America will endure, but the kingdom of God will last forever! The energy of its king will never be exhausted. Where does your primary allegiance lie?　　　　　—J. B. N.

## III. Mary's Response
## (Luke 1:34-38)
### A. Reasonable Doubt (v. 34)

**34. Then said Mary unto the angel, How shall this be, seeing I know not a man?**

Sometimes when God calls someone to do something, that person raises doubts. Moses felt incompetent (Exodus 3); Gideon felt incapable (Judges 6:15); Zechariah was skeptical (Luke 1:18). Mary herself raises a concern: *How shall this be, seeing I know not a man?*

Mary correctly understands that Gabriel does not mean that she and Joseph will eventually have a son after they are fully married. God's plan calls for her to conceive before that marriage is consummated. Thus Mary's question is one of honest bewilderment. By saying *I know not a man*, Mary states the fact that she has never been sexually intimate. (A similar use of the word *know* is found numerous times in the Old Testament, such as in Genesis 4:1.)

Thus Mary expresses reasonable doubt that what the angel has said can be possible. She knows that she is a virgin, and who can believe that a virgin can bear a child? Yet she readily accepts the explanation she receives (next verse). [See question #3, page 136.]

### B. Divine Explanation (vv. 35-37)

**35. And the angel answered and said unto her, The Holy Ghost shall come upon thee, and the power of the Highest shall overshadow thee: therefore also that holy thing which shall be born of thee shall be called the Son of God.**

God's intention is that His own Spirit, *the Holy Ghost,* will *come upon* Mary. In that way the miracle of the virginal conception can and will happen. Because Jesus is to be born through God's Spirit and God's *power,* He will be *holy,* and He will rightly *be called the Son of God.* Through all the years of His life on earth, Jesus will be holy. He will be tempted in every point, just as everyone is, yet completely without sin.

The virginal conception is a supernatural event. That is to say, it is an event that goes above and beyond what we know to be the normal laws of nature. To be sure, there were cases in the Old Testament of God's miraculous or providential intervention for children to be conceived (Genesis 18:10-14; 25:21; 30:22; Judges 13:3; 1 Samuel 1:19, 20). The fact that no one else is ever conceived in the way Luke 1:35 tells us does not mean that Jesus could not have been. Instead, the virginal conception proves the uniqueness of God's Son.

**36. And, behold, thy cousin Elisabeth, she hath also conceived a son in her old age: and this is the sixth month with her, who was called barren.**

In confirmation of what he is saying, Gabriel tells Mary that God's miraculous plan is already in effect: her elderly *cousin Elisabeth* is already in *the sixth month* of her own pregnancy. These two miracles prove that God is intervening in history in a special way.

**37. For with God nothing shall be impossible.**

What a marvelous truth Gabriel now proclaims! This is an echo of Genesis 18:14. Mortals cannot break the laws of nature, but God can. Mortals cannot walk on water or raise the dead, but God can. Nothing that is necessary to the plan of God can ever be impossible to Him. He who ordains the laws of nature is able to suspend them.

When we reflect on the statement *for with God nothing shall be impossible,* we may ask ourselves, "What about Hebrews 6:18?" That verse says that it is impossible for God to lie. God cannot lie because to do so would violate His holy nature. He can never be divided against himself. But in all that is consistent with truth and holiness, nothing is ever impossible with God.

### C. Humble Acceptance (v. 38)

**38. And Mary said, Behold the handmaid of the Lord; be it unto me according to thy word. And the angel departed from her.**

*Mary* is to be honored for her humble acceptance of God's call. As the *handmaid of the Lord,* she completely yields herself to God's will. In total surrender, she invites the fulfillment of the

Visual for
Lesson 2

*Have this visual on display in the front of the room as you introduce question #1 on page 136.*

angel's message so that everything can take place according to His *word.* With the message delivered and accepted, Gabriel returns to Heaven.

While Scripture does not teach us to worship Mary or pray to her, it is entirely appropriate to honor her purity, her faith, and her submission. She is aware of the difficulties this pregnancy will bring—with Joseph, with her own family, and with the people of Nazareth. [See question #4, page 136.] Yet she willingly accepts her role in God's great drama to prepare for the coming of Jesus, on whom the main attention should be focused. [See question #5, page 136.]

## Conclusion

### A. Chosen Vessel, Willing Vessel

Throughout sacred history, God has chosen men and women to be instruments of His will. He chose Abraham to begin the Jewish nation; He chose Moses to be their lawgiver. He chose the kings to rule them; He chose the prophets to instruct them. All of these were chosen and called to play their significant roles in His plan.

As His plan to save humanity neared a critical point, God chose Mary. He called her to be a chosen vessel, to become the earthly mother of His divine Son. She was young, inexperienced, perhaps naïve. But in her virginal purity she was the right vessel to bring Jesus into the world.

The beauty of Mary's story lies in her willing submission to God's plan. Despite the fact that she could not grasp how everything was to happen, she was willing. Regardless of the physical hardships and the social disgrace she would endure, she was willing. Even though there would be "a problem of explanation" with Joseph, she was willing.

Mary's willing response to God's call is an example for us. God still issues calls to men and women to be used as His holy vessels, and we must respond. He calls us to accept His Son, to become followers, and then to be proclaimers. He calls us to be His vessels—vessels of His love, vessels of His truth, vessels of His power (2 Corinthians 4:7).

### B. Prayer

Father, may it be unto us according to Your will. Help us to follow the example of Mary in humble submission. Most of all, fill us again with joy for the coming of Jesus into the world. In His holy name we pray, amen.

### C. Thought to Remember

God still calls people to be vessels for Him.

# Learning by Doing

*This page contains an alternative lesson plan emphasizing learning activities.*
*Classes desiring such student involvement will find these suggestions helpful.*

## Into the Lesson

Do a *Who Am I?* activity in which you read the following identification statements. Ask your learners to name the Bible person being described as you complete each description.

1. "Though I was of lowly birth, God picked me for an important role in His redemptive scheme. I was born to slaves in a foreign land, but I was raised by royalty. After working as a shepherd, I was used by God to deliver His people from slavery. Who am I?" *(Moses)*

2. "Though I was of lowly birth, God picked me for an important role in His redemptive scheme. My father had eight sons; I was the youngest. We lived in Bethlehem. From shepherd boy to king of Israel—that was my destiny. God's Messiah was one of my descendants. Who am I?" *(David)*

3. "Though I was a lowly shepherd, God picked me for an important role in His plan of redemption. My task was hard and fearful. I had to pronounce doom on Israel's neighbors, including Damascus, Gaza, Tyre, Ammon, and Moab. I even pronounced doom and exile for Israel herself. My visions involved locusts, fire, and a plumb line. I even predicted the death of Israel's king. My name begins with the letter A. Who am I?" *(Amos)*

4. "Though I was of lowly birth, God picked me for an important role in His plan of redemption. I was an obscure maiden in an obscure village. Who would think my name would become known throughout the world? Who would think I would be chosen by God to give birth to His Son? Who am I?" *(Mary)*

At the conclusion, turn to today's text. (See also the optional student book for this activity.)

## Into the Word

Distribute photocopies of the following word-find puzzle (or use the optional student book, where it is also printed). Say, "Find 13 words that can be used of Mary as she is described in today's text in Luke 1:26-38. As you find and circle each word, identify also the verse that states or implies that description of Mary." If you do not want this to be a "silent" activity, have students work in pairs.

```
M A L R E E C N A I F D
Y C H A A L A A L D E E
D T U O Y E B Z I E D S
A V M E L O S A S E E U
L B B I B E R R R H O F
N L L D T F H E E H A N
I A E E A N D N A D A M O
G A I D S L O E N F T C
R H E L I S O G R D C A
I L L W E F E R T I L E
V D E T O L B D E A V E
O B E D I E N T S S E L
```

The 13 words to be found are *angel* (v. 26), *Galilean* (v. 26), *Nazarene* (v. 26), *virgin* (v. 27), *fiancée* (v. 27), *blessed* (v. 28), *confused* (v. 29), *afraid* (vv. 29, 30), *fertile* (v. 31), *royal* (v. 32), *bewildered* (v. 34), *humble* (v. 38), and *obedient* (v. 38). For the last part of the exercise to work, all 13 words must be located.

Next, give this direction: "look at the puzzle's unused letters. Can you find a message there?" (The unused letters in sequence left to right, top to bottom read: "Mary: called to be a vessel; behold the handmaid of the Lord, called to be a vessel.") The message emphasizes the lesson title, theme, and the desired response to this study.

## Into Life

Tell your learners that the next activity is called Impossible Tasks. Ask them to identify the Bible person who—at least implicitly—was given an "impossible" imperative by God. 1. Build a massive boat! 2. Cross the sea without a boat! 3. Destroy the walled city! 4. Kill the giant! 5. Have a baby as a virgin! 6. Evangelize the world! Answers are *Noah, Moses, Joshua, David, Mary,* and *the church.*

Ask the class to identify other "impossible tasks" God demanded of people in the Bible. Ask also for examples of what your learners consider impossibilities that were accomplished through the ages by people empowered by God. Conclude by suggesting that each learner ponder a prayer he or she can utter that includes some petition most would deem impossible. (A similar activity is included in the optional student book.)

# Let's Talk It Over

*The questions on this page are designed to promote discussion of the lesson by the class and to encourage application of the lesson Scriptures. The answers provided are only discussion starters. Let your class talk it over from there.*

**1. God still invites faithful people to assist with His work. What can you do in the coming week to respond? How might you have to rearrange your priorities to serve Him best?**

There is no shortage of challenges to service in the pages of the Bible! Undoubtedly the most significant thing any of us can do is to share with others the good news of God's redemptive love (Matthew 28:19, 20). The Bible specifically mentions that we should care for the neediest (James 1:27). The list goes on.

The problem is not a shortage of ministry opportunities, but a perceived shortage of time. Those who live in Western democracies can find themselves buried under an avalanche of opportunities for entertainment, with little time left for substantive service to God. Correcting this imbalance requires careful reflection on priorities and perhaps even repentance.

**2. What are some limitations that people believe hinder them from serving God? How may God view such limitations?**

Sometimes we may think, "If only I had this or that, I would give it to God." We should recall that God makes clear in the Parable of the Talents that He looks to see who is serving faithfully with what they have. To faithful people He entrusts more (Matthew 25:14-23). The case of Gideon shows us that God may impose severe limitations so that we really know that He is the one who is accomplishing something and not human strength (Judges 7:1-8).

Mary was a poor girl of no social or academic significance. Yet God chose her to be an essential figure in the most pivotal event of human history. God sees us, knows our hearts, and can empower those of us who are devoted to Him (2 Chronicles 16:9). While sin can keep us from achieving God's purposes for our lives, our own frailties cannot (2 Timothy 2:20, 21).

**3. When was a time you struggled to make sense of something that was happening to you? How did your faith grow as a result?**

We may be inclined to think that it's wrong to question God. That may be true at times (see Job 38:2; 40:8; Isaiah 45:9). Yet the Bible reveals many examples of God's interacting with people who struggle to understand Him and His ways. Think of Abraham (Genesis 18:16-33), Moses (Exodus 33:12, 13; Numbers 11:10-15), Gideon (Judges 6:13, 36-40), and Paul (2 Corinthians 12:7-10).

Each of these interactions was unique, but each resulted in God's servant knowing Him better. And knowing God better is the ultimate blessing, no matter what struggle we endure to get there.

**4. What life circumstances have challenged or enhanced your service to God? How have you dealt with the challenges?**

Mary's special assignment came with the challenge of being an unwed mother. This made her an easy target of gossip and ridicule in that culture. Her condition theoretically could have brought death by stoning (Deuteronomy 22:20, 21). Yet she agreed to God's call without knowing how He would work out the details.

Each generation of Christians faces its own challenges. Today, for instance, workplace rules may limit believers in how they express their faith. While we must have respect for our employers, we cannot deny God. Sometimes, however, it is the more subtle things that keep us from serving God. An overly busy schedule is an enemy when God tells us the importance of stillness and quiet time with Him (Psalm 46:10).

**5. The Bible records various responses to God's invitation to join Him in fulfilling His plans. Which one is most like your own response to something God has invited you to do?**

God was patient (up to a point) with Moses' hesitation; God accommodated Gideon's test regarding the fleece; and God was merciful with Jonah's rebellion. We too may find ourselves hesitating, testing God, and running away as He uses scriptural commands, opportunities ("open doors"), and encouragement from mature Christian friends to invite us to serve. We may expect that He will be tolerant of our weaknesses as He was with Moses, Gideon, and Jonah. But God's tolerance has limits (examples: Exodus 4:14; Deuteronomy 6:16; Luke 4:12).

# Called to Proclaim

December 16
Lesson 3

DEVOTIONAL READING: **Malachi 3:1-4.**

BACKGROUND SCRIPTURE: **Luke 1:57-80.**

PRINTED TEXT: **Luke 1:59-64, 67-80.**

### Luke 1:59-64, 67-80

59 And it came to pass, that on the eighth day they came to circumcise the child; and they called him Zecharias, after the name of his father.

60 And his mother answered and said, Not so; but he shall be called John.

61 And they said unto her, There is none of thy kindred that is called by this name.

62 And they made signs to his father, how he would have him called.

63 And he asked for a writing table, and wrote, saying, His name is John. And they marveled all.

64 And his mouth was opened immediately, and his tongue loosed, and he spake, and praised God.

. . . . . . . . . . . . . . .

67 And his father Zacharias was filled with the Holy Ghost, and prophesied, saying,

68 Blessed be the Lord God of Israel; for he hath visited and redeemed his people,

69 And hath raised up an horn of salvation for us in the house of his servant David;

70 As he spake by the mouth of his holy prophets, which have been since the world began:

71 That we should be saved from our enemies, and from the hand of all that hate us;

72 To perform the mercy promised to our fathers, and to remember his holy covenant;

73 The oath which he sware to our father Abraham,

74 That he would grant unto us, that we, being delivered out of the hand of our ene-mies, might serve him without fear,

75 In holiness and righteousness before him, all the days of our life.

76 And thou, child, shalt be called the prophet of the Highest: for thou shalt go before the face of the Lord to prepare his ways;

77 To give knowledge of salvation unto his people by the remission of their sins,

78 Through the tender mercy of our God; whereby the dayspring from on high hath visited us,

79 To give light to them that sit in darkness and in the shadow of death, to guide our feet into the way of peace.

80 And the child grew, and waxed strong in spirit, and was in the deserts till the day of his showing unto Israel.

---

GOLDEN TEXT: His mouth was opened immediately, and his tongue loosed, and he spake, and praised God.—Luke 1:64.

---

<table>
<tr><td>

*God's Call to the*
*Christian Community*
Unit 1: God's Call in Christ
(Lessons 1-5)

</td></tr>
</table>

## Lesson Aims

After participating in this lesson, each student will be able to:

1. List three elements of praise in "Zechariah's song."

2. Compare and contrast John's role as a "prophet of the Highest" with our responsibility to proclaim Christ.

3. Write a short song or poem of praise for the area of service that God has granted him or her.

## Lesson Outline

INTRODUCTION
    A. Religious Phonies
    B. Lesson Background
  I. NAMING THE BABY (Luke 1:59-64)
    A. Usual Procedure (v. 59)
    B. Mother's Protest (vv. 60, 61)
    C. Father's Response (vv. 62-64)
     *"His Name Is . . ."*
  II. PRAISING THE LORD (Luke 1:67-75)
    A. For His Salvation (vv. 67-71)
     *Saved from Our Enemy*
    B. For His Covenant (vv. 72-75)
 III. PREDICTING THE MESSIAH (Luke 1:76-80)
    A. Preparing the Way (v. 76)
    B. Proclaiming Salvation (vv. 77-79)
    C. Getting Himself Ready (v. 80)
CONCLUSION
    A. Called to Proclaim: Then and Now
    B. Prayer
    C. Thought to Remember

## Introduction

### A. Religious Phonies

*The Didache,* a Christian work written in the second century AD, offers advice on how to spot a false prophet: if a prophet comes to your house and tries to stay more than two days or if he asks for money, then he is a false prophet. Regardless of the validity of this advice, there always has been a need for a way to spot religious phonies, including those who falsely claim to speak for God.

In the Old Testament there were false prophets who predicted peace when God said there would

be war and destruction (Jeremiah 14:13-16). In our own times there are those who wrongly predict the time of Christ's second coming. There are also those who prophesy health and wealth—often in exchange for a generous donation. John the Baptist, however, was a true prophet of God. John stands in sharp contrast to false prophets of all eras.

### B. Lesson Background

A genuine prophet of the Old Testament could prove that he spoke for God by being able to predict accurately what would happen. If a self-proclaimed prophet tried to do this and his prediction did not come to pass, he was to be put to death (Deuteronomy 18:20-22). But God's prophet also had the important task of proclaiming God's call to repentance. In the writings of the Old Testament prophets, this call to righteous living comprises the majority of their content.

Thus, *foretelling* and *forthtelling* were the two tasks of the prophet. John the Baptist came as "the prophet of the Highest" (Luke 1:76). In his predictive, foretelling role, John's main task was to proclaim a message of the coming of the Messiah. His message was that "one mightier than I cometh . . . he shall baptize . . . he will thoroughly purge" (Luke 3:16, 17).

In the forthtelling role, John proclaimed God's call to repentance. Like the prophet Nathan rebuking King David (2 Samuel 12) or Elijah condemning King Ahab (1 Kings 21), John confronted King Herod (Matthew 14:4). Like many of the prophets of old, John was finally killed for proclaiming God's truth to someone who did not want to hear it. Jesus said, "Among those that are born of women there is not a greater prophet than John the Baptist" (Luke 7:28).

Unlike the prophets before John, the Bible gives us a tantalizing glimpse of the beginning of his life. Just as the angel Gabriel had promised, Elisabeth gave birth to a son in her old age. The presentation of a newborn child was a community event. So neighbors and relatives gathered in the rural village in the Judean hill country where John's parents lived to rejoice and praise God for this blessing (Luke 1:57, 58).

## I. Naming the Baby
## (Luke 1:59-64)

### A. Usual Procedure (v. 59)

**59. And it came to pass, that on the eighth day they came to circumcise the child; and they called him Zechariah, after the name of his father.**

Circumcision of infant males *on the eighth day* is a sacred duty of Jewish parents (Genesis 17:9-14; Leviticus 12:3; compare Luke 2:21). At this time, those in attendance are determined that the child should be named *Zechariah,* in honor *of his father.* They probably reason that it is an appropriate tribute to the father who finally has a son. The name *Zechariah* fittingly means, "God remembers." Selecting this name for the baby seems the obvious choice!

## B. Mother's Protest (vv. 60, 61)

**60. And his mother answered and said, Not so; but he shall be called John.**

Sometime during the nine months of pregnancy that followed the angelic appearance, Zechariah apparently informed his wife what the angel had said about the child's name. (He would have had to use some means other than audible words to communicate this, since he is mute even up to this point in the narrative.) Therefore when well-meaning friends and relatives propose the name *Zechariah,* Elisabeth has a firm answer: *Not so.* [See question #1, page 144.] Instead of what they suggest, *John* is to be the name. Appropriately enough, the name *John* means, "Yahweh has been gracious."

**61. And they said unto her, There is none of thy kindred that is called by this name.**

The neighbors and relatives cannot understand such a departure from tradition. They know the family trees of both Zechariah and Elisabeth. They know that there is no one named *John* who is related to either of them.

What those in attendance apparently do not know is the content of the angel's message of nine months earlier: "Fear not, Zechariah: for thy prayer is heard; and thy wife Elisabeth shall bear thee a son, and thou shalt call his name John" (Luke 1:13).

---

### How to Say It

BENEDICTUS. *Ben*-eh-*dik*-tus (strong accent on *dik*).
DEUTERONOMY. Due-ter-*ahn*-uh-me.
DIDACHE. *Did*-uh-kay.
ELIJAH. Ee-*lye*-juh.
HEROD. *Hair*-ud.
JEREMIAH. Jair-uh-*my*-uh.
LEVITICUS. Leh-*vit*-ih-kus.
MICAH. *My*-kuh.
YAHWEH (Hebrew). *Yah*-weh.
ZECHARIAH. *Zek*-uh-*rye*-uh (strong accent on *rye*).

---

## C. Father's Response (vv. 62-64)

**62. And they made signs to his father, how he would have him called.**

The people who have gathered to celebrate the circumcision and naming of the baby are puzzled. They can think of no reason why Elisabeth prefers the name *John* to the name of her husband. Therefore, they turn to Zechariah in the expectation that he will have the good sense to overrule his wife.

While the angel had said that Zechariah would be unable to speak (Luke 1:20), the fact that those present make *signs* to him may indicate that he is deaf as well as mute. In any case, those gathered are able to communicate their question to Zechariah.

**63. And he asked for a writing table, and wrote, saying, His name is John. And they marveled all.**

The *writing table* that Zechariah requests is perhaps a wooden slate with a shallow surface of wax. If so, he can use a pointed stylus for writing in the wax. The stylus may be flat on the other end for smoothing out the wax to erase what is no longer needed. Zechariah has had nine months to become proficient with this instrument!

With the writing tablet in hand, Zechariah settles the issue about the name: *His name is John.* In that one short statement, Zechariah demonstrates obedience to God's message as delivered by the angel. All the people gathered for this event, however, are amazed that Zechariah has chosen the same nonfamily name as his wife has. What is going on?

### "HIS NAME IS . . ."

*What's in a name? that which we call a rose*
*By any other name would smell as sweet.*
—*Romeo and Juliet,* Act II, Scene 2

What's in a name? A great deal! The name *George Washington* suggests diplomatic skill, graciousness, and selfless service. The name *Adolf Hitler* does not. The name *Marilyn Monroe* suggests blatant sexuality. The name *Mother Teresa* does not. These are more than "just names"; they carry a great deal of emotive force.

Today we give our children names based on a variety of factors, but normally without any particular realization of, or concern for, the original meaning of the name itself. But this has not always been the case. In biblical times, names were often given to carry special significance. Some even were changed to fit the situation. Thus *Abram* ("exalted father") became *Abraham* ("father of a multitude"). *Naomi* ("pleasant") changed her name to *Mara* ("bitter"). *Jacob* ("grasps the heel," or figuratively, "deceiver") had his name changed to *Israel* ("he who struggles with God").

Both Joseph and Mary were told to call Mary's baby *Jesus* ("savior"). Zechariah was told to name his son *John* ("Yahweh has been gracious"). When we follow the biblical plan of salvation, each of us takes on a new name: *Christian* ("of Christ"). Make sure you don't change this name to something else!     —J. B. N.

**64. And his mouth was opened immediately, and his tongue loosed, and he spake, and praised God.**

Zechariah regains the power of speech as soon as he demonstrates his obedience. When *his tongue* is *loosed*, his first words are words of praise. All the gratitude and wonder that has been bottled up inside of him for nine months comes pouring out. [See question #2, page 144.]

Even after the people return to their homes, they can't stop talking about this special child (Luke 1:65, 66, not in today's text). Everyone who hears the story is amazed. What must the future hold for this child?

## II. Praising the Lord
## (Luke 1:67-75)

### A. For His Salvation (vv. 67-71)

**67. And his father Zechariah was filled with the Holy Ghost, and prophesied, saying.**

Earlier, Zechariah was punished for being doubtful (Luke 1:20). Now God is accepting Zechariah back into service fully as he is *filled with the Holy Ghost* and prophesies. This means that he is enabled by the Holy Spirit to say what he could not say on his own, and the words are of great poetic beauty.

While Zechariah's words came from his heart, they are authored ultimately by God's Spirit. As a result, the words have a literary splendor that is beyond mere spontaneous speech. Often called the *Benedictus* (from the Latin word for *Blessed*), Zechariah's marvelous outpouring has two parts. Verses 68-75 are praise to God for the salvation He is delivering to His covenant people. Verses 76-79 are a pronouncement of the role John will have in preparing for the coming of the Messiah.

**68. Blessed be the Lord God of Israel; for he hath visited and redeemed his people.**

The first words to come from the lips of Zechariah in nine months are spoken with joy. *Blessed be the Lord God* is a statement of recognition that God deserves to be praised. [See question #3, page 144.] The faithful God *of Israel* has not

forgotten His people. Now He has *visited* them, which means that He is stepping into human history in an act of divine power. Now He comes to redeem, rescuing His people from their captivity to sin. The day of God's visitation is a day of deliverance! However, as Jesus would later say about Jerusalem, "Thou knewest not the time of thy visitation" (Luke 19:44).

**69. And hath raised up a horn of salvation for us in the house of his servant David.**

Zechariah's praise for this *horn of salvation* may refer to the horns on the corners of the altar at the temple. A guilty person could cling to them in order to escape death (as in 1 Kings 1:50; 2:28). More likely, however, the *horn* is a symbol of strength and protection (as the horns of an ox). By means of this *horn of salvation*, the enemy will be vanquished and the people will be delivered (compare 2 Samuel 22:3; Psalm 18:2). [See question #4, page 144.]

Zechariah expects this *salvation* to be *for us in the house of his servant David*, meaning the Jewish people (compare 2 Samuel 7:26; 1 Chronicles 17:24). The mention of David is a strong sign that the promise of a Messiah is about to be fulfilled (compare Psalm 132:11, 12, 17). What will be revealed later is that Christ will be the Savior not only of the Jews, but of all who believe.

**70. As he spake by the mouth of his holy prophets, which have been since the world began.**

From the beginning God announced there would be deliverance. To Adam and Eve came the promise of one who would bruise the serpent's head (Genesis 3:15). God demonstrated deliverance to Noah, and He promised the coming Messiah to Abraham. In many different generations, He spoke *by the mouth of his holy prophets*. Zechariah knows these prophecies and is excited that now, at last, they are being fulfilled.

**71. That we should be saved from our enemies, and from the hand of all that hate us.**

In the more than 400 years since the close of the Old Testament, the land of Israel has been subjected to numerous invasions, civil war, and armies of occupation. Israel thus is eager to be *saved* from her *enemies*, especially the occupying armies of Rome. For too long she has suffered at *the hand of all that hate* the people of God. Zechariah, like most of the people of Israel, may be thinking mostly in terms of a Messiah who will deliver the nation from her political, earthly enemies (Psalm 106:10).

When Jesus comes, the cheering crowds will turn against Him when they see that He is not going to be the kind of king they want or expect.

Although Jesus will not provide deliverance from Rome, He will provide deliverance from Israel's more important enemies: the hosts of Satan. This spiritual deliverance is the salvation that ancient Israel needs most of all. It is what we need most as well.

### SAVED FROM OUR ENEMY

The plotline of "alien invasion" is a staple of science-fiction books. This kind of plot goes back a long way.

The granddaddy of this kind of science-fiction theme is H. G. Wells's famous *The War of the Worlds,* published in 1898. This book tells the tale of a Martian invasion of England. The staying power of this story line is amazing. Orson Welles adapted the tale into a fictionalized documentary that aired on radio on October 30, 1938, as a Halloween feature. (For the American audience, the Martians landed in New Jersey.) The story then became a movie in 1953 and again in 2005.

Whenever a book or movie features an "alien invasion" plotline, there is always a sense of relief at the ultimate demise of the invaders. And the more harm the invaders are seen to inflict, the greater that relief is! Now think about it: is there any nonfictional invader that has ever harmed humans more than the one known as *sin*?

"That we should be saved from our enemies" was Zechariah's hope. That God did even better by making it possible for all to be saved from the enemy of sin was the result of the cross. Sin is the ultimate enemy of the human race, and God's grace is what allows us to be saved from this mortal foe.      —J. B. N.

### B. For His Covenant (vv. 72-75)

**72. To perform the mercy promised to our fathers, and to remember his holy covenant.**

God had *promised* in the Old Testament to *perform . . . mercy* for His people (compare Micah 7:20). Zechariah expects that the God of all mercy is going to *remember his holy covenant:* if humans will give God their allegiance, He will be their protector. Just as He did not abandon the children of Israel to their slavery in Egypt, He will not now abandon His children in spiritual captivity. The meaning of Zechariah's own name says it well: "God remembers." Perhaps Zechariah himself is remembering passages such as Genesis 17:7; Leviticus 26:42; and Psalm 105:8, 9 as he praises God.

**73, 74. The oath which he sware to our father Abraham, that he would grant unto us, that we, being delivered out of the hand of our enemies, might serve him without fear.**

Visual for Lesson 3

*Point to this visual as you ask, "How and why will you praise the Lord this Christmas season?"*

*The oath* in question is found in Genesis 22:15-18. There God promised *Abraham* that his seed would become a mighty nation, which would have victory over its *enemies.*

Zechariah may be speaking better than he knows. The promised deliverance is not to be the kind often seen in the Old Testament, where Israel was delivered temporarily from oppressors. By the Messiah's deliverance, God's people will be able fully to *serve Him without fear,* without the specter of further defeat hanging over their head. This will be God's gift to His people, a favor that He will *grant.*

**75. In holiness and righteousness before him, all the days of our life.**

As a devoted priest, Zechariah knows what it means to serve the Lord. All his life he has been "righteous before God, walking in all the commandments and ordinances of the Lord blameless" (Luke 1:6). Now righteous Zechariah eagerly anticipates a day when all God's people will be able to serve Him *in holiness and righteousness.*

This hope will be partially fulfilled when Christ establishes the church, whose members are "a holy priesthood, to offer up spiritual sacrifices" (1 Peter 2:5; compare Titus 2:11-14). The fulfillment will come when we serve Him in full holiness in Heaven (Revelation 22:3).

## III. Predicting the Messiah (Luke 1:76-80)

### A. Preparing the Way (v. 76)

**76. And thou, child, shalt be called the prophet of the Highest: for thou shalt go before the face of the Lord to prepare his ways.**

The second part of the *Benedictus* concerns the role of John the Baptist. Speaking tenderly to the infant, Zechariah prophesies the future of his son. John will be not only *the prophet of the Highest,* he also will be widely recognized and *called* as such. In that role, John's job will be *to prepare* the way for Jesus (Isaiah 40:3; Malachi 3:1; Matthew 3:3). Some 30 years after Zechariah prophesies the words before us, John will tell the people to repent and get ready for Jesus (Matthew 3:11, 12; Mark 1:1-8; Luke 3:1-18; John 1:19-34). The beautiful words of Zechariah echo the prophecy of Isaiah 40:3-5.

### B. Proclaiming Salvation (vv. 77-79)

**77. To give knowledge of salvation unto his people by the remission of their sins.**

After John grows up and begins preaching in the wilderness, he will proclaim a baptism of repentance "for the remission of sins" (Luke 3:3). John's preparatory ministry will be a vital first step for *his people* to learn the *knowledge of salvation.* Through John's ministry the people will learn at least two important things. First, they have sin, of which they must repent. Second, only God can provide *remission of their sins.*

**78, 79. Through the tender mercy of our God; whereby the dayspring from on high hath visited us, to give light to them that sit in darkness and in the shadow of death, to guide our feet into the way of peace.**

When God sends John the Baptist to call people to repentance, it will not be an act of anger. Rather, it will be an act of deepest love, an act of *tender mercy.*

Matthew 4:15, 16 (from Isaiah 9:1, 2) speaks of Jesus as a dawning light (see also Isaiah 58:8, 10; 60:1-3). The promise of the *dayspring* (or dawning of the sun) is a promise that the Messiah will come. What a glorious day when God visits His people! To those who *sit in darkness* (Psalm 107:10), Christ will come as the light of the world (John 8:12). To those *in the shadow of death,* the promise will be that those who believe in Jesus will live, even though dead (John 11:25). To the lost, Christ will come as the way *to guide* their *feet.* To all who do not know the *way of peace,* Christ will come as the prince of peace. Today, the fulfillments of Zechariah's prophecies are facts of history.

### C. Getting Himself Ready (v. 80)

**80. And the child grew, and waxed strong in spirit, and was in the deserts till the day of his showing unto Israel.**

Raised in a godly home, young John grows both physically and spiritually. [See question #5, page 144.] At some point his elderly parents die, and John lives *in the deserts* of Judea. Year by year the time for his public appearance approaches. Captive *Israel* is going to hear the message of redemption!

## Conclusion

### A. Called to Proclaim: Then and Now

John's mother, Elisabeth, stood up against the pressure of popular opinion and insisted that what God said about naming the baby would be carried out. John's father, Zechariah, was faithful as well—once he had learned from nine months of silence. He joyfully proclaimed the praise of God and the salvation of God.

Following in his parents' footsteps, John was faithful to his own call to proclaim. To people who trusted their own goodness and ancestry to save them, John proclaimed repentance. To a nation largely unaware that they sat in darkness, John proclaimed the coming of the Lord. He was the prophet—the spokesman—for God.

We can learn from the example of the godly family of today's lesson. God has called His people to proclaim. Let us be faithful to that call.

### B. Prayer

Our Father, we praise You for Your tender mercy. We thank You for the remission of our sins. Loosen the self-imposed silence of our tongues so we can be bold to proclaim Your wonders. In Jesus' name, amen.

### C. Thought to Remember

John was called to proclaim. So are we.

---

## Home Daily Bible Readings

**Monday, Dec. 10**—A Messenger Is Coming (Malachi 3:1-4)

**Tuesday, Dec. 11**—Elisabeth Births a Son (Luke 1:57-61)

**Wednesday, Dec. 12**—His Name Is John (Luke 1:62-66)

**Thursday, Dec. 13**—God Sends a Powerful Savior (Luke 1:67-75)

**Friday, Dec. 14**—Preparing the Way (Luke 1:76-80)

**Saturday, Dec. 15**—Warnings to the Crowds (Luke 3:7-14)

**Sunday, Dec. 16**—A Powerful One Is Coming (Luke 3:15-20)

# Learning by Doing

*This page contains an alternative lesson plan emphasizing learning activities.*
*Classes desiring such student involvement will find these suggestions helpful.*

## Into the Lesson

Recruit in advance a class member to deliver the following two- to three-minute monologue. Your actor should be dressed as an elderly Jewish priest (Zechariah) of the first century.

"My son. *[dramatic pause]* I never thought I would say those words. God had been good to me and my wife, Elisabeth. We had lived a long time with His blessings. But He had not answered our fervent prayers for a son. In resolute faith we had gone about the service of our God day by day, year by year.

"When I was called from my Judean village to do my regular priestly duties at the temple, I had no idea what God was about to do. He is, indeed, the God of marvelous surprises.

"My temple duty was simple. *[Use hand gestures to illustrate the following.]* I add incense to the fire, to show the prayers of God's people ascending as a sweet aroma to our Father God. All assembled outside pray; the smoke from my incense symbolizes their words rising to Heaven. But on one particular day, suddenly neither the aroma nor the smoke had my attention. For beside me stood God's messenger, Gabriel.

"I was stunned and afraid. I could not believe the angel's words. Elisabeth and I were to have a son, a very special son. My doubt earned my penalty: I became mute until it all came true.

"For nine long, silent months, I could not vocalize my praise nor tell my story. But the day of the naming of my son—ah, the melody of the words *my son*!—I had to write in large letters *HIS NAME IS JOHN* when all my family members were insisting that we name him after me. That was the angel's word . . . God's word. So it had to be mine as well. And the second I lifted my stylus from the writing tablet, I could speak. And I haven't stopped yet . . . as you can readily hear. Glory to God!"

## Into the Word

Have incense burning as learners arrive to direct attention to the context for today's study: the incense-burning duty of Zechariah in the temple. (Do not do this if your class includes anyone who is sensitive to strong aroma, if fire codes forbid it, or if it will set off a smoke detector.) Have two of your good oral readers read Luke 1:5-25, 57-67 aloud to give the whole picture of Zechariah and Elisabeth's story; have your readers alternate reading odd- and even-numbered verses to make it more interesting.

Display the word *PRAISE* written vertically and ask the class to help you prepare an acrostic on the word, based on Zechariah's song in Luke 1:68-79. Suggest the class look for deeds and attributes of God revealed in Zechariah's words. For example, in verse 68, God is **R**edeemer and God **I**nitiates certain actions. From verse 69, God **S**aves. From verse 70, God **S**peaks. From verse 72, God **R**emembers. From verse 74, God **P**rotects. From verse 75, God **E**xpects things of us (holiness and righteousness). From verses 72 and 78, God **A**cts mercifully. From verse 67, God **I**nspires people to speak. From verses 72 and 73, God **P**lans.

Once your class has its acrostic, stop and ask individuals to offer sentence prayers, praising God for the elements Zechariah noted in his prayer. For example, "O God who speaks, help us to listen to Your words." (This acrostic and prayer stimulus activity is also included in the optional student book.)

## Into Life

Make this proposal to your learners: "For Monday through Saturday of this coming week, use Zechariah's praise song for your personal devotional time, two verses each day. For example, on Monday, read verses 68 and 69, personalizing the verses in whatever ways possible, such as substituting *me* for *us* in verse 69."

Prayer thoughts can follow the models of the sentence prayers offered in the preceding activity. For example, Monday's prayer could be something like, "O God of redemption and salvation, thank You for adopting me into the family of Your servant David."

The optional student book includes two sections calling for the learner to compare himself or herself first to the elderly Elisabeth and Zechariah, then to Zechariah's son in the matters of serving the Messiah. You may find those to be useful group procedures.

# Let's Talk It Over

*The questions on this page are designed to promote discussion of the lesson by the class and to encourage application of the lesson Scriptures. The answers provided are only discussion starters. Let your class talk it over from there.*

**1. How would you encourage a person who was experiencing opposition for doing what he or she knew was right? What gives you the courage to say what is right when you're in the minority?**

Elisabeth had to stand her ground against well-meaning people as she acted in obedience to God's direction regarding her son's name. Jesus was misunderstood by those closest to Him (Mark 3:21). Our obedience to God will not always be understood by others. But it is the way we express our love to God (John 14:23).

Of course, we may have times when we experience opposition when we only *think* we are right. It helps to have trusted, God-honoring friends who will be honest with us in such a case—even if it means telling us something we don't want to hear (Proverbs 27:6).

**2. What was a time in your life when you received a clear and immediate blessing as a result of honoring or obeying God? Explain.**

Obedience to Bible precepts may lead quickly to richer, more harmonious relationships with family and friends. Employing God's principles that deal with earning and spending money can have the instant result of keeping us from falling into certain financial predicaments. The list can go on.

Unfortunately, Christianity has many immature believers who neglect to apply the wisdom of God's Word to all areas of their lives. As a result, they suffer broken relationships, money struggles, and the road weariness of unbelievers. In such cases, applying the Word of God may not yield immediate, visible results if there's a "deep hole" that will take some time to climb out of. But in the short or long run, God will bless us when we keep His Word (Luke 11:28).

**3. Praise of God is still appropriate for us 2,000 years later. What avenues do you have for praising God? What tends to prevent you from pouring out praise to Him? How do you overcome this?**

We often think of praise as a corporate activity on Sunday mornings. But we can and should praise God in the privacy of our thoughts as well.

Praising God is a part of our purpose and privilege (1 Peter 2:9).

Even on bad days the redeemed have much to be thankful for. Mother Teresa has been attributed with saying, "In light of Heaven, the worst suffering on earth, a life full of the most atrocious tortures on earth, will be seen to be no more serious than one night in an inconvenient hotel." Jesus offers us abundant, eternal life. In light of this, our proper response is praise (Luke 19:37-40).

Differences in ways people offer praise sometimes create conflict. God cares more about the sincerity of our praise and worship than the style of its expression (Psalm 150; John 4:23, 24).

**4. Quickly think of three things for which to praise God. What do these three things say about your view of what's most important?**

If "family" tops your list, perhaps you need to read Luke 9:61, 62; 14:26 (see Lesson 13). If some material possession is most important, read Luke 12:15-21. If personal comfort is a big deal to you, see Luke 9:58. Notice that "salvation" is high on Zechariah's list. It should be on ours as well.

**5. What are you doing today to live out a life of service to God? How do the seasons of life affect this?**

According to Ephesians 2:10, God has a life of service ready for us to step into! But we should be alert to the nature of our service changing as we move through the seasons of life. Even here, though, God may surprise us. Zechariah and Elisabeth probably thought they were well past the season of rearing a child, but God had definite plans in that regard!

The Bible gives us many ideas as to how to live out a life of service. Some of us may be called, even in middle to late life, to take the gospel to a foreign country (see Lesson 10). Others may assist by supporting those who go (Matthew 28:19, 20). More generally, each of us can follow God's commands to love Him and others, no matter where we live or work (Matthew 22:37-40). To live a holy, peaceful life is more than a casual suggestion (1 Timothy 2:2; Hebrews 12:14).

# Called to Rejoice

DEVOTIONAL READING: **Psalm 96:1-6.**

BACKGROUND SCRIPTURE: **Luke 2:1-20.**

PRINTED TEXT: **Luke 2:1-14.**

## Luke 2:1-14

1 And it came to pass in those days, that there went out a decree from Caesar Augustus, that all the world should be taxed.

2 (And this taxing was first made when Cyrenius was governor of Syria.)

3 And all went to be taxed, every one into his own city.

4 And Joseph also went up from Galilee, out of the city of Nazareth, into Judea, unto the city of David, which is called Bethlehem, (because he was of the house and lineage of David,)

5 To be taxed with Mary his espoused wife, being great with child.

6 And so it was, that, while they were there, the days were accomplished that she should be delivered.

7 And she brought forth her firstborn son, and wrapped him in swaddling clothes, and laid him in a manger; because there was no room for them in the inn.

8 And there were in the same country shepherds abiding in the field, keeping watch over their flock by night.

9 And, lo, the angel of the Lord came upon them, and the glory of the Lord shone round about them; and they were sore afraid.

10 And the angel said unto them, Fear not: for, behold, I bring you good tidings of great joy, which shall be to all people.

11 For unto you is born this day in the city of David a Saviour, which is Christ the Lord.

12 And this shall be a sign unto you; Ye shall find the babe wrapped in swaddling clothes, lying in a manger.

13 And suddenly there was with the angel a multitude of the heavenly host praising God, and saying,

14 Glory to God in the highest, and on earth peace, good will toward men.

GOLDEN TEXT: For unto you is born this day in the city of David a Saviour, which is Christ the Lord.—Luke 2:11.

## God's Call to the Christian Community
### Unit 1: God's Call in Christ
(Lessons 1-5)

## Lesson Aims

After participating in this lesson, each student will be able to:

1. Recite the story of Jesus' birth from Luke's Gospel.

2. List several evidences of joy or reasons for joy that are found in the text.

3. Read today's text aloud at a family or work Christmas celebration.

## Lesson Outline

INTRODUCTION
    A. Close Encounters of a Special Kind
    B. Lesson Background
  I. ROYAL DECREE (Luke 2:1-3)
    A. Caesar's Demand (v. 1)
      *Taxes*
    B. People's Duty (vv. 2, 3)
 II. HUMBLE BIRTH (Luke 2:4-7)
    A. Joseph's Situation (v. 4)
    B. Mary's Situation (vv. 5, 6)
    C. Baby's Situation (v. 7)
III. ANGELIC ANNOUNCEMENT (Luke 2:8-12)
    A. Unsuspecting Shepherds (vv. 8, 9)
    B. Unprecedented News (vv. 10, 11)
      *For All People*
    C. Unlikely Sign (v. 12)
IV. DIVINE PRAISE (Luke 2:13, 14)
    A. Glorious Multitude (v. 13)
    B. Glorious Message (v. 14)
CONCLUSION
    A. Close Encounter in Bethlehem
    B. Close Encounter in Heaven
    C. Prayer
    D. Thought to Remember

## Introduction

### A. Close Encounters of a Special Kind

Thirty years ago, the well-known movie *Close Encounters of the Third Kind* attempted to create the excitement and wonder that would attend the arrival of intelligent creatures from outer space. It is only one of many such movies and TV shows that have tried to imagine an extra-terrestrial visitation.

But what of a close encounter, an actual visitation, from the creator himself? What about such an event in real history, not just in science fiction? What would it be like if the greatest being of all came to our planet? What preparations would we make? What excitement would it cause?

Such a visitation, of course, has actually happened. Jesus Christ, through whom the universe was created (John 1:3; Hebrews 1:2), arrived on our planet just over 2,000 years ago. He did not come in an armada of spaceships, nor was His coming greeted by world leaders. He came in a way that no one could have imagined: He made His close encounter by being born into the human race through the most humble of circumstances.

### B. Lesson Background

Julius Caesar lived from 100 to 44 BC. Before his assassination, he adopted Gaius Octavius as his son. However, the young man had to overcome dangerous foes before he could claim his place as the emperor of Rome. Following the defeat of Antony and Cleopatra in 31 BC, the Roman senate conferred on Octavius the title *Augustus*, meaning "the august one," in 27 BC.

Until his death in AD 14, Caesar Augustus was one of the most powerful of earthly rulers. But earthly glory is fleeting. Jesus' birth was little-noticed when Augustus was famous, but now that birth is world-known while Augustus is all but forgotten.

## I. Royal Decree
## (Luke 2:1-3)

### A. Caesar's Demand (v. 1)

**1. And it came to pass in those days, that there went out a decree from Caesar Augustus, that all the world should be taxed.**

Luke takes special care to show that Jesus is born into human history at a real time, in a real place. Jesus' birth comes about during the reign of *Caesar Augustus,* who serves officially as Roman emperor from 27 BC to AD 14. As ruler of *all the world* (a phrase that signifies the known area around the Mediterranean Sea), Augustus has the power to decree an official census to assist in collecting taxes.

#### TAXES

Benjamin Franklin (1706–1790) is credited with the observation, "In this world nothing is certain but death and taxes." Franklin is normally thought of as a smiling, optimistic entrepreneur. But this famous quotation may strike one as being depressing, fatalistic, and negative.

Taxes do seem to be a constant fact of life. People have complained about taxation for centuries. High taxation rates contributed to civil unrest during the era of the Roman Empire. High taxation was one of the factors that resulted in the French Revolution. High taxation rates contributed to the Whiskey Rebellion in Pennsylvania in 1794. But comparatively speaking, modern America does not have it that bad. Residents in some countries of Europe pay much more in taxes as a percentage of their income. Yet Americans still like to complain about taxes!

Joseph and Mary went to Bethlehem to register for their taxes. We may wonder whether those two griped about their taxes while on the way. Do you think that this event shows us God's sense of humor as He integrates Jesus' birth with the all-too-human chore of dealing with taxes? —J. B. N.

### B. People's Duty (vv. 2, 3)

**2. (And this taxing was first made when Cyrenius was governor of Syria.)**

Luke connects the birth of Jesus to events that are well known to people of the time. Even so, the exact year of Jesus' birth is difficult to determine, and there are various facts to consider. The first is that the birth is during Augustus's four-decade reign (v. 1), but that doesn't narrow things down much! The second fact is that *Cyrenius* is *governor of Syria*. This man had been made "Counsel" in 12 BC, with his governorship coming somewhat later.

A third fact to consider is that the birth of Jesus takes place during the lifetime of Herod the Great (Matthew 2; Luke 1:5). We know from secular history that Herod died just before the Passover of 4 BC. When these and other facts are

---

### How to Say It

BETHLEHEM. *Beth*-lih-hem.
CAESAR AUGUSTUS. *See*-zer Aw-*gus*-tus.
CLEOPATRA. Clee-oh-*pat*-ruh.
CYRENIUS. Sigh-*ree*-nee-us.
DIONYSIUS. Die-oh-*nish*-ih-us.
GAIUS OCTAVIUS. *Gay*-us Ock-*tay*-vee-us.
GALILEAN. Gal-uh-*lee*-un.
GALILEE. *Gal*-uh-lee.
JULIUS CAESAR. *Joo*-lee-us *See*-zer.
MANOAH. Muh-*no*-uh.
MEDITERRANEAN. *Med*-uh-tuh-*ray*-nee-un (strong accent on *ray*).
MICAH. *My*-kuh.
NAZARETH. *Naz*-uh-reth.
SOLOMON. *Sol*-o-mun.

---

combined, a reasonable calculation places the birth of Christ in 5 or 4 BC.

This calculation may seem curious to us. We naturally may suppose that Jesus would be born in "the year zero" (even though there is no "year zero") just by definition, since BC means "before Christ." The problem is traceable to the work of a sixth-century monk named Dionysius. Our modern calendar is based on his calculations, and unfortunately he made an error of several years.

**3. And all went to be taxed, every one into his own city.**

Every Jewish man has to return to the city of his ancestors to be enrolled. For Joseph this means a long journey in support of a despised Roman tax.

# II. Humble Birth
## (Luke 2:4-7)
### A. Joseph's Situation (v. 4)

**4. And Joseph also went up from Galilee, out of the city of Nazareth, into Judea, unto the city of David, which is called Bethlehem, (because he was of the house and lineage of David).**

When *Joseph* first learned that his pledged bride was already pregnant, he decided to give her a quiet divorce (see Matthew 1:18, 19). Only after an angel appeared to him did Joseph agree to keep her as his wife. While Scripture does not state what difficulties he and Mary experienced in *Nazareth*, it is easy to imagine the gossip they endured as Mary began to "show."

Now the decree from Rome gives them an opportunity to leave. Their journey takes them some 70 miles southward. But since they are traveling to an elevation that is about 1,250 feet higher than Nazareth, Scripture says they go *up from Galilee* into *Judea*.

Joseph's ancestral home is *Bethlehem* because he is *of the house and lineage of David*. Bethlehem is the city where David lived as a boy (see 1 Samuel 17:12, 58). Bethlehem means, "house of bread." This is a fitting meaning for the birthplace for the one who will be "the bread of life" (John 6:35, 48)! [See question #1, page 152.]

### B. Mary's Situation (vv. 5, 6)

**5. To be taxed with Mary his espoused wife, being great with child.**

For *Mary* the trip is probably both a bane and a blessing. The trip is naturally quite uncomfortable given the advanced stage of her pregnancy. But at least this trip takes her away from the wagging tongues in Nazareth. The virgin's baby will be born in another town, in welcome privacy.

In obedience to the angel of the Lord, Joseph had taken Mary as his wife. Since he has not yet had intimate relations with her (see Matthew 1:25), Scripture discreetly calls her *his espoused wife*. Mary is now reaching the final days of her pregnancy and so is *great with child*.

Thus by a royal decree issued in far-away Rome, a Galilean peasant and his espoused wife make their way to Bethlehem. By a divine decree issued five centuries earlier in Micah 5:2, the birth of their child is predetermined to be in Bethlehem. Little does Caesar Augustus know that he is helping to carry out the plan of God!

**6. And so it was, that, while they were there, the days were accomplished that she should be delivered.**

Perhaps Joseph and Mary complete the journey to Bethlehem before the ninth month of her pregnancy begins. Scripture simply affirms that while they are there the time comes for the delivery of the baby. By human appearances it will be just another baby. But in divine reality the son of Mary is the Son of God.

### C. Baby's Situation (v. 7)

**7. And she brought forth her firstborn son, and wrapped him in swaddling clothes, and laid him in a manger; because there was no room for them in the inn.**

Thus Mary gives birth to her *firstborn son*. This is not her only child, because there will be other sons and daughters in years to come (see Mark 6:3).

In accordance with the custom of the time, Mary wraps the baby in long strips of cloth that the *King James Version* calls *swaddling clothes*. This procedure is intended to keep the baby

---

## Home Daily Bible Readings

**Monday, Dec. 17**—Sing a New Song (Psalm 96:1-6)

**Tuesday, Dec. 18**—Joseph and Mary (Matthew 1:18b-21)

**Wednesday, Dec. 19**—Traveling to Bethlehem (Luke 2:1-5)

**Thursday, Dec. 20**—Jesus, Firstborn Son (Luke 2:6, 7)

**Friday, Dec. 21**—Angels Proclaim the News (Luke 2:8-14)

**Saturday, Dec. 22**—Shepherds Visit the King (Luke 2:15-20)

**Sunday, Dec. 23**—Judging with God's Truth (Psalm 96:7-13)

---

warm and give him a sense of security. An ancient non-biblical work notes that the baby who would later become King Solomon "was nursed with care in swaddling clothes. For no king has had a different beginning of existence" (Wisdom of Solomon 7:4). The opposite of such care is seen in Ezekiel 16:4.

Various interpretations have been offered regarding *the inn* that has *no room* for this family. Perhaps it is a public stopping place with "no vacancy" in the sleeping quarters that are located around the perimeter of the building; therefore, Joseph and Mary can go only to the open feeding area for animals. A tradition dating back to the second century puts the birthplace in a cave.

Whatever the exact circumstance, it is a humble beginning for the prince from Heaven! The baby Jesus has only a common *manger*, an animal's feed box, for His bed. [See question #2, page 152.]

## III. Angelic Announcement (Luke 2:8-12)

### A. Unsuspecting Shepherds (vv. 8, 9)

**8. And there were in the same country shepherds abiding in the field, keeping watch over their flock by night.**

The scene moves from the manger to the nearby countryside. The focus remains on how humble the setting is. In the surrounding area, there are lowly *shepherds* who camp *in the field* with their sheep. The shepherds are *keeping watch over their flock* that *night* to protect it from predators and thieves.

**9. And, lo, the angel of the Lord came upon them, and the glory of the Lord shone round about them; and they were sore afraid.**

If there ever was a once-in-a-lifetime experience, this is it! Along with *the angel of the Lord* appears the *glory*, or shining majesty, of God to radiate all around. The shepherds, as simple peasant folks at the bottom rung of the social ladder, are less ready than anyone to be in the presence of majesty. Their fear is understandable. Their reaction may be compared with that of Manoah and his wife in Judges 13:22. After the angel of the Lord spoke to them, they said, "We shall surely die, because we have seen God."

### B. Unprecedented News (vv. 10, 11)

**10. And the angel said unto them, Fear not: for, behold, I bring you good tidings of great joy, which shall be to all people.**

An *angel* is literally a "messenger," and this angel has a wonderful message indeed. First, the angel quickly offers the shepherds reassuring words: *Fear not.* Then comes the threefold message: *good tidings . . . great joy . . . all people.* The birth of this child is indeed "good news," the beginning of the gospel. He will bring the world the joy of salvation.

Surprisingly, this salvation will be available not just to those of Israel, but to everyone. Some students restrict the phrase *all people* in this context to mean only the Jews. The reason for this is that other accounts mention salvation of "his people" (Matthew 1:21) as Jesus reigns over "the house of Jacob" (Luke 1:33). The prophecies of Isaiah, Amos, and others, however, support the view that the pronouncements include Gentiles. God intends salvation to be for Jew and non-Jew alike (Acts 10:34, 35; 11:18).

### FOR ALL PEOPLE

The American Civil War was devastating. Approximately 600,000 soldiers died—about 2 percent of the U.S. population. Men fought for various reasons. Some fought to keep slavery; some fought to eliminate it. Some fought for state's rights; some fought to preserve the union. Some fought to protect their families; some fought against their own brothers.

Four months after the pivotal battle of Gettysburg in 1863, U.S. President Abraham Lincoln went to that small Pennsylvania town to dedicate a cemetery for the honored war dead. In his famous address there, he called attention to the fact that the nation "conceived in liberty, and dedicated to the proposition that all men are created equal" was then engaged in a war that was testing whether such a nation could endure. He concluded by urging his hearers to be dedicated to ensuring that government "of the people, by the people, for the people" should "not perish from the earth."

Lincoln's frame of reference was that government belonged to the people—all the people. The ultimate result of that war was that one class of people could not enslave another class. American liberties were to be for everyone. If a human government can choose that ideal as its goal, how much more so when God's will is concerned! God is no respecter of persons and shows no favoritism. The message of the angel to the shepherds was that the good tidings of great joy would be to *all people.* It still is.　　—J. B. N.

**11. For unto you is born this day in the city of David a Saviour, which is Christ the Lord.**

When the angel says *unto you,* he signifies that this event is directed even to lowly shepherds.

The shepherds know that *the city of David* is Bethlehem. This newborn baby will be the rescuer for those who need to be rescued, a *Saviour* for those who need to be saved—meaning everyone! While many Jews hope for a Messiah to deliver them from the Romans, God intends that the Messiah deliver them from their sins.

The Savior will be known as *Christ the Lord.* The title *Christ* comes from a Greek word meaning "the anointed one." In Hebrew the word for "the anointed one" is *Messiah* (John 1:41). Anointing with oil was the Old Testament inauguration ritual for prophets, priests, and kings. As God's anointed, Jesus will fill all three offices. As the Lord, Jesus will be master over everyone.

### C. Unlikely Sign (v. 12)

**12. And this shall be a sign unto you; Ye shall find the babe wrapped in swaddling clothes, lying in a manger.**

A Jewish commentary on Psalm 23 says, "There is no more disreputable occupation than that of shepherd." The religious leaders certainly would consider shepherds to be unlearned and ignorant (compare the reaction of the religious leaders to Peter and John—fishermen—in Acts 4:13). Yet the only invited guests to witness the newborn Jesus on this glorious night are shepherds!

Knowing that the shepherds can hardly believe their ears, the angel voluntarily gives them *a sign:* when they arrive in Bethlehem they will find the baby *wrapped in swaddling clothes, lying in a manger.* The swaddling clothes are to be expected on any newborn baby; the manger as a baby bed is not. The sign is to confirm to them, when they find the baby, that everything the angel says about Him is true. Shortly thereafter, they find Jesus just as the angel predicts (v. 16). [See question #3, page 152.]

## IV. Divine Praise
## (Luke 2:13, 14)

### A. Glorious Multitude (v. 13)

**13. And suddenly there was with the angel a multitude of the heavenly host praising God, and saying.**

No earthly dignitaries are on hand to welcome the arrival of God's Son. Even if there were, would they know what words to say? So God provides His own welcoming party in the form of a *heavenly host.* This happens *suddenly,* as the angel is joined by this *multitude.* In the Old Testament such words typically identify an army of angels, who serve the Lord of Hosts (Psalms 103:21; 148:2). Scripture does not state whether this host fills the sky or stands on the hills that surround the shepherds.

This host has an additional message. Their voices join to praise God for the great thing He has done. What God had planned from the beginning is taking place. What the prophets had prophesied, even without understanding the full import of their own words, is being fulfilled. And what the angels have longed to look into (see 1 Peter 1:10-12) is finally coming about. No wonder the heavenly host is summoned to rejoice!

### B. Glorious Message (v. 14)

**14. Glory to God in the highest, and on earth peace, good will toward men.**

A primary message of that first Christmas is *Glory to God.* To say this is to proclaim that He who dwells "in the light which no man can approach" (1 Timothy 6:16) has sole claim to glory. To God alone belong all majesty, radiance, and splendor. He is the Lord of Heaven and earth; He is God *in the highest.* In Heaven, glory is given to God; on earth, *peace* is extended to us.

Peace is more than the mere absence of conflict; it is the presence of everything that is necessary for one's well-being. This peace will come to the world through the prince of peace. Rome had brought a military peace that would later permit the early Christians to spread the gospel. The peace mentioned here, however, is a peace between God and people. For one of the greatest peace pronouncements in the New Testament, see Romans 5:1. [See question #4, page 152.]

The phrase *good will toward men* indicates that God's favor rests on those who accept His grace.

Visual for
Lesson 4

*Be sure you have this visual on display as you discuss the phrase, "Glory to God in the highest."*

## Conclusion

### A. Close Encounter in Bethlehem

With their words ringing in the ears of the shepherds, the angels departed and returned to Heaven. No heavenly messenger had ever proclaimed such a glad message. To the world had been born a Savior, Christ the Lord. We should join the humble shepherds in their excitement and amazement. This is a message that calls everyone to rejoice. [See question #5, page 152.]

The message of the birth in Bethlehem is far more than the mere sweetness of a baby. The real message of Christmas is the coming of the Son of God to live (and give) His life as the Son of Man. "The Word was made flesh, and dwelt among us" (John 1:14). This is the miracle of the incarnation.

Jesus came to have a close encounter, an intimate participation in our world. He came as a baby, helplessly swaddled in tight strips of cloth. He came as a human to face hunger and thirst, temptation and persecution. He wept real tears; He bled real blood; He died a real death on the cross; He gained a real resurrection.

In all this, "he became the author of eternal salvation unto all them that obey him" (Hebrews 5:9). He "was in all points tempted like as we are, yet without sin" (Hebrews 4:15). Jesus knew what it was to be a man. He came to earth to be Immanuel—"God with us" (Matthew 1:23).

### B. Close Encounter in Heaven

Jesus came to live with us on earth so that one day we can live with God in Heaven. His close encounter with humanity makes possible our close encounter with God in the future. Revelation 21:3 foretells the day when, "He will dwell with them, and they shall be his people, and God himself shall be with them, and be their God."

Because of the messages of Christmas and Easter, we can look forward to the day when we shall join the angel's praise: "Glory to God in the highest." Christmas calls us to rejoice in the coming of our Savior. Christmas calls us to rejoice in the gift of God's grace.

### C. Prayer

Father, we praise You for sending Your Son to bring us salvation. May our hearts rejoice as we hear again the good news. As Jesus came to dwell among us, we long for the day when we shall dwell with You. In Jesus' name, amen.

### D. Thought to Remember

The gospel is still good news of great joy
for all people.

# Learning by Doing

*This page contains an alternative lesson plan emphasizing learning activities. Classes desiring such student involvement will find these suggestions helpful.*

## Into the Lesson

Recruit a person to play the part of a TV news anchorperson. After your opening prayer, this person enters the classroom, sits at a desk in front of the class, faces a pretend TV camera, and makes the following announcement:

Now some breaking news as our last item. By decree of the president, all citizens must return to the place of their birth for a census and taxing enrollment. All must complete this enrollment by the fifth of January in the year 2008. Failure to comply is not an option. Failure to comply is punishable by imprisonment.

The anchorperson then "signs off," briefly shuffles some papers, and leaves.

Ask, "What kind of burden would that requirement place on you, if any? Would you feel resentful?" After a brief time of sharing say, "Of course, that is much like the Roman decree heard in a remote Galilean village by a young couple, newly married and expecting, whose family hometown was a journey of several days away."

If your class uses the optional student book, you may find the Angel Words exercise there to be a good alternative to the above activity.

## Into the Word

Read John 1:14 to your class. In that verse Jesus, the Word become flesh, is said to be full of grace and truth. Point out that Jesus said of himself, "I am . . . the truth" (John 14:6). Distribute paper and pens (or use this activity from the optional student book) and say to your group, "The story in our text today in Luke 2 is a very familiar one, so let's take a true-false quiz on the content. Number your paper from 1 to 15." Then read the following affirmations:

1. The Roman ruler who made the decree requiring Joseph and Mary to travel to Bethlehem was Julius Caesar.

2. The primary purpose of Caesar's enrollment demand was to have an accurate census.

3. The Roman governor of Syria at the time was Brastius.

4. Joseph needed to travel to Bethlehem, David's hometown, for he was of David's family line.

5. Joseph and Mary traveled to Bethlehem when she was in the late stages of pregnancy.

6. While in Bethlehem, Mary delivered her baby.

7. The baby boy born was Mary's first child.

8. The newborn baby was laid in an animal's feeding trough because that was customary, for comfort and a sense of security.

9. Nearby to Bethlehem, God's angel appeared to shepherds in the night to announce the baby's birth.

10. The angel's glow of God's glory severely frightened the shepherds.

11. The angel indicated that the good news was only for the Jews.

12. The angel clearly called the baby Christ.

13. The directions given to the shepherds for finding the child in Bethlehem included the fact that a star would shine brightly over the place as they approached.

14. A large number of angels joined the first angel with praises and a blessing.

15. It appears that Jesus was born at night.

Answers are: *1. F; 2. F; 3. F; 4. T; 5. T; 6. T; 7. T; 8. F; 9. T; 10. T; 11. F; 12. T; 13. F; 14. T; 15. T.*

After moving through the statements and allowing time for silent response, repeat the statements and let students answer aloud. Ask for confirming verses from the text.

## Into Life

Close today's session with an oral reading of Luke 2:1-14. Prepare copies of the text that you have marked for three readers (or groups of readers) to read aloud. For example, consider this division for verse one: (1) "And it came to pass in those days," (2) "that there went out a decree from Caesar Augustus," (3) "that all the world should be taxed." You can simplify the readers' task by putting each segment on its own line.

Next, say, "The biblical texts recording the events surrounding Jesus' birth are read often in this season. Look for an appropriate occasion over the next few days to read today's text aloud in the presence of family, friends, or coworkers."

(The optional student book has an activity entitled Ever Feel Like a Shepherd? If you are able to use that resource, draw your learners' attention to it as time allows.)

# Let's Talk It Over

*The questions on this page are designed to promote discussion of the lesson by the class and to encourage application of the lesson Scriptures. The answers provided are only discussion starters. Let your class talk it over from there.*

**1. Without overspiritualizing things, when have you noticed God working through the "mundane" events in life? How can we get better at noticing His work around us?**

Taxes, travel, accommodation hassles. As God's amazing intervention into history unfolds, the miraculous is hidden within the mundane. Elizabeth Barrett Browning had the right idea when she wrote,

Earth's crammed with heaven,
And every common bush afire with God;
And only he who sees takes off his shoes;
The rest sit round it and pluck blackberries.

What was true in Browning's day (over 100 years ago) is no less true today: alert eyes are needed to acknowledge God's work around us. The first step in doing this is to pause and actually *look* (see Psalm 19).

**2. Jesus set aside great power and majesty to become human. What are some ways we can set aside our own personal power or influence? Under what circumstances should we do so?**

We may be tempted to say that we have no power to give up. But all of us have some level of influence. We exercise that influence, in bad or good ways, through whatever power of persuasion, money, talent, or position we have.

Sometimes we use our power to "make sure" that we get the credit that we think is due to us, to get our own way, or to put someone in his or her place. All these circumstances are prime candidates for deciding *not* to do what we have the power *to* do! Jesus modeled humility for us.

On the other hand, it is wrong to have a talent or spiritual gift and pretend not to have it. That's false humility, used sometimes to avoid certain areas of Christian service.

**3. Should we seek signs today? Why, or why not?**

The truth of the gospel was established by signs (John 20:30, 31). The return of Christ will be preceded by signs (Mark 13:24-27). Even so, there is such a thing as false signs (Mark 13:22; 2 Thessalonians 2:9). Jesus became exasperated with people who sought signs (John 4:48). Paul cautioned, "the Jews require a sign, and the Greeks seek after wisdom: but we preach Christ crucified" (1 Corinthians 1:22, 23).

There is a difference between *seeking* a sign and *being alert for* a sign. It's safe to assume that the shepherds were not out in their fields each night scanning the starry sky to detect every streaking meteorite that might be interpreted as a sign—they had better things to do! But when a sign came, their hearts were ready to receive it. May ours be as well (1 Thessalonians 4:16).

**4. You see in a shopping mall parking lot a festive holiday banner that reads *Peace on Earth*. How does the original context of that phrase help us avoid misinterpreting it?**

As the lesson commentary notes, the peace at issue here is a peace between God and humanity. But the abbreviated phrase *Peace on Earth* can mislead people into thinking in terms of an idealistic desire for the end to earthly wars and strife. As desirable as that is, it is not the primary issue.

This Christmas season, you may be surprised to see how often this phrase is taken the wrong way. For example, your local TV station may feature a story about certain people or groups being reconciled to one another at Christmas, with the reporter finishing the story with the gushy declaration, "After all, it is the season of peace." You can use this as an opportunity to offer the correct meaning to those who may be watching the story with you. Challenge the thinking of those about you by pointing out Matthew 10:34!

**5. What Christmas tradition causes you to rejoice most in the meaning of the Christmas message?**

In Exodus 12, God instituted an annual festival so that Old Testament Israel would remember how He rescued them from bondage. Under the new covenant, the Lord's Supper reminds us that Christ's sacrifice rescued us from bondage to sin (1 Corinthians 11:23-26). Traditions that serve as periodic reminders of God's work are valuable. It is important for us to remember God's goodness to us—how he sent His Son to earth to reconcile us to himself. Christmas can be a valuable time to honor God, as long as we don't let traditions become a ritualistic tradition*alism*.

# Called to Witness

Dec
30

DEVOTIONAL READING: Isaiah 49:5, 6.

BACKGROUND SCRIPTURE: Luke 2:22-38.

PRINTED TEXT: Luke 2:22-35.

### Luke 2:22-35

22 And when the days of her purification according to the law of Moses were accomplished, they brought him to Jerusalem, to present him to the Lord;

23 (As it is written in the law of the Lord, Every male that openeth the womb shall be called holy to the Lord;)

24 And to offer a sacrifice according to that which is said in the law of the Lord, A pair of turtledoves, or two young pigeons.

25 And, behold, there was a man in Jerusalem, whose name was Simeon; and the same man was just and devout, waiting for the consolation of Israel: and the Holy Ghost was upon him.

26 And it was revealed unto him by the Holy Ghost, that he should not see death, before he had seen the Lord's Christ.

27 And he came by the Spirit into the temple: and when the parents brought in the child Jesus, to do for him after the custom of the law,

28 Then took he him up in his arms, and blessed God, and said,

29 Lord, now lettest thou thy servant depart in peace, according to thy word:

30 For mine eyes have seen thy salvation,

31 Which thou hast prepared before the face of all people;

32 A light to lighten the Gentiles, and the glory of thy people Israel.

33 And Joseph and his mother marveled at those things which were spoken of him.

34 And Simeon blessed them, and said unto Mary his mother, Behold, this child is set for the fall and rising again of many in Israel; and for a sign which shall be spoken against;

35 (Yea, a sword shall pierce through thy own soul also;) that the thoughts of many hearts may be revealed.

---

GOLDEN TEXT: Simeon blessed them, and said unto Mary his mother, Behold, this child
is set for the fall and rising again of many in Israel; and for a sign
which shall be spoken against.—Luke 2:34.

## God's Call to the Christian Community
### Unit 1: God's Call in Christ
(Lessons 1-5)

## Lesson Aims

After participating in this lesson, each student will be able to:

1. Explain who Simeon was and why his witness to the coming of the Messiah was so significant.

2. Understand that the promises of God are certain, even when they seem to be delayed.

3. Make a commitment to proclaim to others how he or she has seen God fulfill His promises.

## Lesson Outline

INTRODUCTION
  A. To Witness
  B. Lesson Background
 I. WITNESS BY OBEYING (Luke 2:22-24)
  A. Purification (v. 22a)
  B. Presentation (vv. 22b, 23)
   *Dedicated to the Lord*
  C. Sacrifice (v. 24)
 II. WITNESS BY BELIEVING (Luke 2:25-29)
  A. Lifetime of Waiting (vv. 25, 26)
  B. Moment of Fulfillment (v. 27)
   *He Came by the Spirit*
  C. Words of Benediction (vv. 28, 29)
 III. WITNESS BY PROCLAIMING (Luke 2:30-35)
  A. Good News for All (vv. 30-33)
  B. Bad News for Some (v. 34)
  C. Painful News for One (v. 35)
CONCLUSION
  A. To Witness Is to See
  B. To Witness Is to Tell
  C. Prayer
  D. Thought to Remember

## Introduction

### A. To Witness

When a crime is committed, the police always look for witnesses. When a disaster hits a community, the reporters for the evening news always want to interview a witness on the site. Many times people on the scene can hardly wait to tell what they know. This is a reminder that the verb *witness* has at least two meanings: "to see something" and "to testify about something."

People see and testify not only to crimes and disasters, but also to good things. People who are getting married choose good friends to sign the marriage license in witness. They invite family and friends to witness the happy event. Life has many special moments that are good to witness.

In this lesson we will be introduced to a man who witnessed a great event of history. He was told long in advance of the great day; he spent his life waiting for the moment. The event was the arrival of the Messiah at the temple; the eyewitness was a man named Simeon.

### B. Lesson Background

A striking element of Luke's account of Jesus' birth is the mention of the man Simeon. While he bore the noble name of one of the tribes of Israel, absolutely nothing is known about him outside Luke's few verses. Of the various things this text says about Simeon, the most important is that "the Holy Ghost was upon him" (Luke 2:25).

While the presence of the Holy Spirit was not a common experience in the lives of the people of Israel, the Holy Spirit has been directly involved since the beginning (Genesis 1:2). In the Old Testament the Spirit came upon people whom God selected to do special tasks. To such people the Spirit gave skill in craftsmanship (Exodus 31:3), wisdom in leadership (Judges 3:10), or phenomenal physical strength (Judges 14:6). As king of Israel, David pleaded with God, "Take not thy Holy Spirit from me" (Psalm 51:11). Most importantly, the prophets were enabled to speak "as they were moved by the Holy Ghost" (2 Peter 1:21).

As the Gospel accounts begin, it had been more than 400 years since the last Holy Spirit–inspired Scripture was penned (the book of Malachi). Today we will see that Simeon had received, at some point in his life, Holy Spirit–inspired knowledge of the coming of the Messiah. He had a firsthand privilege of seeing the infant Savior.

## I. Witness by Obeying
## (Luke 2:22-24)

Our opening verses show several of the ways in which God calls people to be witnesses to their faith. The first is by obedience to His Word. Joseph and Mary demonstrate their respect for God by doing what He says. The purification of the mother and the redemption of the firstborn son are acts of submission to God's law.

### A. Purification (v. 22a)

**22a. And when the days of her purification according to the law of Moses were accomplished.**

*According to the law of Moses*, a Jewish woman is ceremonially unclean for 7 days after she gives birth to a son (Leviticus 12:2-4). On day 8 she is to have her baby circumcised (Luke 2:21). Then she is to remain in seclusion for another 33 days. During this period of nearly 6 weeks, she is not to touch any hallowed thing, nor can she go to the temple. When the 40 *days of her purification* are over, it is time for Mary and Joseph to take the baby Jesus to Jerusalem.

## B. Presentation (vv. 22b, 23)

**22b, 23. They brought him to Jerusalem, to present him to the Lord; (as it is written in the law of the Lord, Every male that openeth the womb shall be called holy to the Lord).**

As Luke makes clear, there is more than one requirement of the law that Mary and Joseph deal with. One is Mary's purification (Leviticus 12); the other is the presentation and redemption of their son. The two requirements are closely linked. Devout Jews perform this presentation in Jerusalem if at all possible. Once Joseph and Mary reach the city, they go to the temple so they can *present* their firstborn *to the Lord.*

The *law of the Lord* gives a specific requirement for every firstborn male, that is, for *every male that openeth the womb.* Firstborn males belong to the Lord as His *holy* possession. This applies to both humans and livestock (Exodus 13:2, 12). This law reminds the people that the Lord had brought the Jews out of Egypt by slaying the firstborn of the Egyptians (Exodus 13:15).

The Lord also provided a way by which the newborn male could be redeemed or "bought back" at a price of five shekels (Numbers 18:15, 16). From the very infancy of Jesus, everything in His life is done to fulfill all that the law requires (see also Matthew 3:15; Galatians 4:4).

---

### How to Say It

AUGUSTINE. *Aw*-gus-teen (strong accent on *Aw*) or Aw-*gus*-tin.

CORINTHIANS. Ko-*rin*-thee-unz (*th* as in *thin*).

EGYPT. *Ee*-jipt.

EGYPTIANS. Ee-*jip*-shuns.

GALATIANS. Guh-*lay*-shunz.

ISAIAH. Eye-*zay*-uh.

ISRAEL. *Iz*-ray-el.

LEVITICUS. Leh-*vit*-ih-kus.

SIMEON. *Sim*-ee-un.

ZECHARIAH. *Zek*-uh-*rye*-uh (strong accent on *rye*).

---

## DEDICATED TO THE LORD

I am not a firstborn child. I am the second son (third child) born to the third son (fourth child) in my grandfather's family. Yet when my mother was pregnant with me, my 70-year-old grandmother (a very devout Christian woman) dedicated me to the Lord. That may seem a bit brazen to some. After all, won't the child grow up to make his or her own decisions about religion or anything else?

My grandmother never told my parents what she had done. She never told me either, as she died when I was only a few months old. She told only my aunt. My aunt did not tell me what my grandmother had done until I was 26 years old. At that time I was already engaged in a preaching ministry, and I was taking advanced studies to prepare for a career in Bible college teaching. It was an uncanny feeling to discover that I had been dedicated to the Lord's service even before I was born!

Long before Jesus was born, He had already been dedicated to His task. His presentation in the temple was the formality that confirmed what God had predicted as far back as the Garden of Eden. Today—right now—you have the opportunity to dedicate yourself (or dedicate yourself anew) to serving God. You need not and should not depend on a parent or grandparent to do this for you. What choice will you make?     —J. B. N.

## C. Sacrifice (v. 24)

**24. And to offer a sacrifice according to that which is said in the law of the Lord, A pair of turtledoves, or two young pigeons.**

The parents also *offer a sacrifice* to God. In *the law of the Lord*, the parents are told to offer a lamb as a burnt offering and a turtledove or pigeon as a sin offering (Leviticus 12:6-8). If they cannot offer a lamb because of their poverty, they are permitted to offer *a pair of turtledoves, or two young pigeons.* (One of the pair would take the place of the lamb as the burnt offering; the other would be the sin offering.) [See question #1, page 160.]

The offering of Joseph and Mary serves as a subtle reminder that these people are humble peasants. They do not have the means to offer a lamb as a burnt offering. This fact reminds us that God's Son does not come to live in the palace of a king. He experiences humanity's hardships; He suffers as the Son of Man. "For ye know the grace of our Lord Jesus Christ, that, though he was rich, yet for your sakes he became poor, that ye through his poverty might be rich" (2 Corinthians 8:9).

## II. Witness by Believing
## (Luke 2:25-29)

When God speaks, His people accept what He says as true. Thus we bear witness by believing. Although God's promises may seem unlikely or even impossible, they are steadfast and sure. In these verses Simeon bears witness to God's faithfulness by believing that the Messiah would indeed come in his lifetime.

### A. Lifetime of Waiting (vv. 25, 26)

**25. And, behold, there was a man in Jerusalem, whose name was Simeon; and the same man was just and devout, waiting for the consolation of Israel: and the Holy Ghost was upon him.**

*Simeon* is the name borne by a man who encounters Jesus' family in the temple. This is a famous name, the name of the second son of Jacob by Leah; it is thus the name of 1 of the 12 tribes of Israel.

According to the way the world looks at people, there is little that is noteworthy about Simeon. In God's sight, however, Simeon has an important role in identifying the infant Jesus as the long-awaited Messiah. Simeon is *just,* or righteous. He is *devout* in the practice of his faith. This man is waiting for *the consolation,* or "comforting," *of Israel.* He is part of the faithful remnant of Israel who still expects that God will comfort His people as Isaiah had promised (see Isaiah 40:1, 2; 49:13). *The Holy Ghost,* whom Jesus later will call *the Comforter* (John 14:16), has a special presence in Simeon's life.

**26. And it was revealed unto him by the Holy Ghost, that he should not see death, before he had seen the Lord's Christ.**

*The Holy Ghost* has brought consolation into Simeon's life by revealing a wonderful truth: before Simeon dies, he will see *the Lord's Christ.* The Lord God has promised to send His Christ, His Messiah—His Anointed One. Jesus is the one anointed by God to bring deliverance to humankind. Many thousands of God-fearing Jews have lived and died without seeing the coming of the Messiah. But the Spirit has assured Simeon that he will see this event. How blessed Simeon is!

### B. Moment of Fulfillment (v. 27)

**27. And he came by the Spirit into the temple: and when the parents brought in the child Jesus, to do for him after the custom of the law.**

*The Spirit* previously has rested upon Simeon to reveal the coming of Christ. Now that same Spirit leads Simeon *into the temple.* Today is the day—the great moment has finally arrived!

Guided by the Spirit, Simeon notices a certain young couple who has come to present their child *after the custom of the law.* The Spirit has brought Simeon to this encounter with *the child Jesus.* [See question #2, page 160.]

#### HE CAME BY THE SPIRIT

I am not what I call a subjective person, nor easily moved by warm fuzzies. I tend to think of myself as rational, thoughtful, and methodical. Perhaps that is why I am always a bit skittish when I hear people say, "It was a God thing."

I know what they mean: they believe that God led them to a certain action that turned out to be beneficial to themselves and others. Yet I always struggle with the question, "But did God really do it, or was it just coincidence?" It's not that I don't believe that God works in marvelous ways or that He is incapable of direct intervention in our lives to accomplish His will. I just wish there were some kind of objective test I could apply that would guarantee that the event was indeed "a God thing."

Even so, I cannot deny that God has indeed led people throughout history. Centuries ago, He led Augustine to England to begin the conversion of that people to Christianity. He led Boniface to Germany to begin the conversion of the tribes there. He led Luther through the turmoil of the sixteenth-century Protestant Reformation. He led John Wesley into a significant revival in England in the eighteenth century. He led Dwight Moody into revivalism in the century that followed.

Perhaps I just need to have more faith in God's leading. His leading is always better seen in hindsight than in present tense. Regardless, the Spirit led Simeon to the temple for a glorious experience with the incarnate Christ. Where or to whom might the Spirit lead you today? —J. B. N.

### C. Words of Benediction (vv. 28, 29)

**28. Then took he him up in his arms, and blessed God, and said.**

When Simeon approaches the parents, why do Mary and Joseph release their infant into his arms? Do they see the reverent joy in his eyes? Does the Holy Spirit also reveal the nature of this event to them? We don't know, but there must be something both commanding and reassuring in Simeon's bearing for the young mother to allow a stranger to hold her baby!

Notice that Simeon's blessing is not directed to the child but to God. *Blessed* be the *God* of Israel, for He has brought salvation to His people!

**29. Lord, now lettest thou thy servant depart in peace, according to thy word.**

Simeon's words of blessing form a reverent prayer. After untold years of waiting and believing, now he is ready to *depart in peace.* Apparently he is an older man for whom death is imminent. [See question #3, page 160.] The Christ child has come during Simeon's lifetime, *according to* God's *word.* Everything is just as God said it would be. Following "Mary's Song" (Luke 1:46-55) and "Zechariah's Song" (1:67-79), this begins Luke's third great canticle: "Simeon's Song" (2:29-32). [See question #4, page 160.]

## III. Witness by Proclaiming (Luke 2:30-35)

The ultimate role of a witness is to proclaim what he or she has seen. A witness who sees but fails to speak up has failed to fulfill this function. Simeon gladly speaks out to everyone who will listen: the salvation of the Lord has come!

### A. Good News for All (vv. 30-33)

**30. For mine eyes have seen thy salvation.**

As a faithful witness, Simeon is eager to proclaim what he knows. With his own *eyes* he has seen the Lord's *salvation.* He has seen the child through whom deliverance will come. Indeed, his eyes have seen the glory of the coming of the Lord (Isaiah 40:5; 52:10)!

Still, it must be admitted that Simeon has seen only a baby. There is nothing remarkable in the appearance of this infant. There is no golden halo over His head. But Simeon sees the baby Jesus through the eyes of faith. He believes what God has revealed through His Spirit. It is in this sense that Simeon can say he had seen the Lord's salvation. [See question #5, page 160.]

**31. Which thou hast prepared before the face of all people.**

Simeon knows that the arrival of Jesus somehow advances God's plan of salvation *before the face of all people.* There is important doctrinal truth here: God's salvation is not just for Israel; it is for everyone. God's love is being extended to the whole world. The universality of the gospel is a strong theme in the Gospel of Luke. See the next verse.

**32. A light to lighten the Gentiles, and the glory of thy people Israel.**

Simeon gets more specific. This child will be *a light* that will penetrate the pagan darkness of *the Gentiles,* as Isaiah 42:6 and 49:6 promise. This light will also be the shining *glory* of God's chosen people. For Israel, nothing will be more

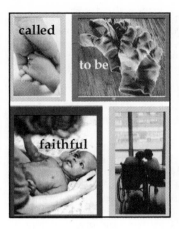

Visual for
Lesson 5

*Point to this visual as you ask, "In what ways will you be a faithful witness this week?"*

to the nation's glory than giving birth to the Messiah (Isaiah 46:13).

Christ does not come, therefore, to cast aside either Jews or Gentiles or to set them against one another. When this light penetrates the darkness, there will be illumination for all. In Christ there is neither Greek nor Jew (Colossians 3:11).

**33. And Joseph and his mother marveled at those things which were spoken of him.**

Simeon has spoken of the child in such glowing terms that *Joseph* and the baby's *mother* are frankly amazed. While they themselves know special truth about Jesus, they are startled by words spoken by a total stranger. How can he know who this child is? How can he know about the salvation God would bring through Him? But Simeon has even more to say!

### B. Bad News for Some (v. 34)

**34. And Simeon blessed them, and said unto Mary his mother, Behold, this child is set for the fall and rising again of many in Israel; and for a sign which shall be spoken against.**

Simeon now blesses *Mary* and Joseph, following with a special message for Mary personally. The coming of Jesus is *set* for both bad news and good. It is the determination of God that it shall be so.

The bad news and good news are expressed in terms of *the fall and rising again of many in Israel.* This points to a division within Israel. God has set Christ as the great divide regarding the destiny of every person. While Jesus is the source of salvation for all who obey Him (see Hebrews 5:9), He is also the point of spiritual collapse for those who reject Him. Though He is himself the *sign* and symbol of God's love, He will be *spoken against* by many of those whom He comes to save. Tragically, such opposition is to be especially true of Simeon's own nation (Isaiah 8:14; 1 Corinthians 1:23; 1 Peter 2:8).

### C. Painful News for One (v. 35)

**35. (Yea, a sword shall pierce through thy own soul also;) that the thoughts of many hearts may be revealed.**

Simeon has yet one more thing to say to Mary. There will be dark moments in her future because of Jesus. The height of her joy at the birth of her son will be matched by the depth of her anguish at the cross. As the nails pierce His hands and feet, and as the spear pierces His side, it will be as if *a sword* were piercing the *soul* of Mary. She will stand at the foot of the cross, staying by Jesus as He dies (see John 19:25).

When Jesus goes to the cross to die, He creates a great moral crossroad. When people see His sacrificial death, *the thoughts* of their *hearts* are *revealed* (Matthew 27:38-43). The idea of the cross is still outright foolishness to many (see 1 Corinthians 1:23). It has been wisely said, "Jesus is the touchstone of human hearts."

## Conclusion

### A. To Witness Is to See

"I was there! I saw it with my own eyes!" Such are the words of a witness. To see, to hear, to feel firsthand—this is what makes a witness. Often a person will take special pride in the fact that he or she was present when some significant event took place. The greater the event, the more important the witness.

## Home Daily Bible Readings

**Monday, Dec. 24**—A Light to All Nations (Isaiah 49:5, 6)

**Tuesday, Dec. 25**—The Presentation to God (Luke 2:21-24)

**Wednesday, Dec. 26**—The Consolation of Israel (Luke 2:25, 26)

**Thursday, Dec. 27**—A Sign from the Spirit (Luke 2:27, 28)

**Friday, Dec. 28**—A Light to the Gentiles (Luke 2:29-33)

**Saturday, Dec. 29**—A Sign of Opposition (Luke 2:34, 35)

**Sunday, Dec. 30**—A Sign of Redemption (Luke 2:36-38)

The birth of Jesus had been awaited with great anticipation. After so many centuries of preparation, God fulfilled the prophecies and promises. The miracle of the ages came to people who were faithful members of God's community. God chose them for their special roles; they became witnesses of what He had done.

Luke demonstrated how the shepherds were called to witness the newborn Messiah. Then he added Simeon, who had waited much of his life to see God's anointed one. In the verses that follow today's text, Luke also related how Anna, an aged prophetess, gave thanks when the holy family came into the temple.

Other people witnessed Jesus at age 12; still more witnessed Him in His ministry. Near the end of the first century, the apostle John would look back and recall Christ, "which we have heard, which we have seen with our eyes, which we have looked upon, and our hands have handled" (1 John 1:1).

### B. To Witness Is to Tell

When people are witnesses to a big event, they are nearly always eager to tell someone about it. To witness is not only *to see;* to witness is also *to tell.* Joseph, Mary, Simeon—all in their own way became witnesses to the greatness of God. They believed what God said, obeyed what God commanded, and gladly proclaimed what God had done.

At the end of Jesus' life on earth He told His disciples, "Ye shall be witnesses unto me." The apostles had been eyewitnesses to all He did, so they could testify to what they had seen. Even in the face of persecution they said, "We cannot but speak the things which we have seen and heard" (Acts 4:20). In the words of the apostle John, "That which we have seen and heard declare we unto you" (1 John 1:3).

Christians are also called to be witnesses today. While we are not eyewitnesses to the life of Jesus, we have experienced firsthand the power of His Word in our lives. Witnessing is a vital part of faith, and the world desperately needs to know what we know about Jesus.

### C. Prayer

Our Father, we praise You for making salvation available to all people. Help us to be as eager as Simeon to tell others that we have met Christ. In the name of Him who is our light and our glory we pray, amen.

### D. Thought to Remember

No silent witnesses!

# Learning by Doing

*This page contains an alternative lesson plan emphasizing learning activities.*
*Classes desiring such student involvement will find these suggestions helpful.*

## Into the Lesson

Purchase inexpensive birth announcement cards (for a boy) for your class members. Put the following information on the cards: "It's a Boy—the Son of God!"; "Born at Bethlehem, Judea"; "Your Presence (not Presents) Is Requested." You may choose to ask a class member to create these with a computer instead of purchasing them.

If you cannot afford to mail the announcements, simply lay them on the chairs before your learners arrive. As learners react, note that Simeon, in today's text, got an even better birth announcement from God: a special invitation from the Spirit to see the young baby in the temple.

Ask a class member to bring a quality dictionary to class and be ready to read the entries for the word *witness*. Ask students to include the notations that it can be a noun and a verb and that it can be both a transitive verb (takes a direct object) and an intransitive verb (doesn't take an object). Point out today's lesson title "Called to Witness" as you can emphasize the necessity both to see the facts of the story and to repeat the story to others as a testimony. Having witnessed, a witness states his or her witness!

## Into the Word

Assign the following Old Testament Scriptures to selected readers: Exodus 13:2, 15; Leviticus 12:2-4; Leviticus 12:6-8; Numbers 3:12; Numbers 18:16. Note the various requirements and conditions as they are read; list them on the board. (These Scriptures are also listed on the activity page of the optional student book in a section titled Birth Rites.) Say, "These passages will help clarify some of the activities of Mary and Joseph in today's text, especially in Luke 2:22-24."

Next, ask your class to prepare an acrostic description of Simeon, as he is seen in Luke 2:25-29. Give each learner a sheet of paper with *SIMEON* written vertically (or direct them to the Simeon Says activity in the optional student book). You can have your learners work in small groups or pairs, depending on class size.

Possible choices (among many) are *S*pirit-filled, *I*sraelite, *M*an, *E*xpectant, *O*ld (as Simeon is assumed to be elderly), *N*oticed (by God). You may wish to tell your class that the words can simply include the relevant letter rather than starting with it (example: dev*O*ut). You may find your learners to be very creative!

*Alternative:* Put Simeon on the witness stand. Have an individual dressed as an elderly first-century Jewish man seated in the front of the group. Start right in: "Well, Mr. Simeon, as the prosecution's chief witness in this matter, do you swear to tell the truth, the whole truth, and nothing but the truth?" Let Simeon answer, "I serve the God of truth, so what I report about His dealings with us will be the absolute truth!"

Continue by asking an assortment of questions related to the text or implied by the circumstances of Christ's birth. Let your actor respond as he believes Simeon would. Consider letting the class join in the questioning. Conclude by saying, "Well, members of the jury, you have heard the witness. The choice is yours. Believe, or do not believe!"

## Into Life

Simeon's witness in his praise incorporates much doctrine that should be a part of each Christian's testimony. Ask your class to look at Luke 2:30-35 and identify key concepts of God's acts of redemption in Christ.

Write the following concepts on the board. Ask the class to explain how the encounter with Simeon revealed each: 1. Salvation belongs to God. 2. Salvation is available for all, no matter one's ethnicity, gender, national origin, or religious history. 3. Salvation is easily likened to light in the midst of darkness. 4. Jesus fulfills the messianic prophecies and thus becomes the glory of all Israel. 5. For incarnation, God provided human parents for His divine Son. 6. Not all will believe the revelation of grace in Christ. 7. Jesus, who brought joy as a newborn, will ultimately bring grief in His death. 8. Jesus will be the great divider of humanity: some will turn their hearts to Him, while others will turn their hearts against Him.

Let the class suggest connections, but if needed, share these possibilities: #1 with verses 30, 31; #2 with verses 31b, 32; #3 with verses 31, 32; #4 with verse 32; #5 with verse 33; #6 with verse 34; #7 with verse 35a; #8 with verses 34, 35. Challenge learners to compose a personal statement of testimony incorporating as many of these ideas as possible.

# Let's Talk It Over

*The questions on this page are designed to promote discussion of the lesson by the class and to encourage application of the lesson Scriptures. The answers provided are only discussion starters. Let your class talk it over from there.*

**1. What inspiration can we gain from the fact that Joseph and Mary faithfully fulfilled their obligations under the Old Testament law, despite having been shown special, miraculous attention by God?**

People who feel that God has shown them special favor sometimes think that it is not that important for them to serve in some basic and ordinary ways in the church. The earthly parents of Jesus seem to have been just as eager to fulfill humbly their responsibilities as they were before. They believed they now had far more reason to praise and honor God because of the ways He had worked in their lives.

The same should be true for us. The more we are blessed, the greater should be our desire to serve God and fulfill our responsibilities to Him.

**2. Simeon received specific communication from the Holy Spirit. How does the Spirit's leading in our own lives compare and contrast with that of Simeon's?**

The New Testament shows us many instances of people being guided or led by the Holy Spirit (Luke 4:1; Acts 13:2, 4; 15:28; 16:6; 20:23). Figuring out *how* that leading occurred and *if* such leadings are to be expected today are the hard parts! But we must try, since the ongoing walk of a Christian revolves around discerning God's direction for life.

We should frankly admit that what we think is the Holy Spirit's leading may at times be nothing more than our own desires and whims at work. This is called *subjectivism*. What we think to be the Holy Spirit's leading should always be tested against Scripture. Will the contemplated action make us more like Jesus? Will the action help the church fulfill the Great Commission (Matthew 28:19, 20)? Will the result be to create more fruit of the Spirit according to Galatians 5:22, 23? If the result of our action will create divisions with others, will it be the godly or the ungodly kind of division (Matthew 10:34; Luke 14:26; Romans 16:17, 18; 1 Corinthians 5; 2 Corinthians 6:14-18; Titus 3:10)?

Asking such questions is an important part of distinguishing the Spirit's leading from the impulses of the flesh.

**3. Simeon is content for his days on earth to end after he meets Jesus. How have you seen people respond to Jesus in their "golden years"?**

Sixty or more years of difficult life experiences can create a very hardened heart! But at any age, a person will not understand his or her need for a redeemer without first being convicted of sin. True conviction of sin is accompanied by a sense of urgency to remedy the problem (Acts 2:37; 8:36; 16:30), no matter what the age. Joy is the proper response for anyone after accepting Jesus as Lord (Acts 8:39).

**4. What was a time when you saw God bring about a blessing after many years of waiting and expecting? What was your reaction?**

Childless Abram (Abraham) was 75 years old when God promised him offspring (Genesis 12:1-7). Isaac was not born, though, until Abraham was 100 years old and Sarah was 90 (Genesis 17:17; 21:5). Then it was Isaac's turn to be childless for a long time (Genesis 25:21, 26). The favorite wife of Isaac's son Jacob was, in turn, barren for many years (Genesis 29:31–30:2, 22). The stories of Abraham, Simeon, and others serve as an important reminder: When it appears that the passage of time has moved something into the category of "won't happen in my lifetime," that's when God may surprise us!

**5. Simeon's delight comes from knowing something about who Jesus is. How did you first react when you realized who Jesus is and what He has done for you?**

Allow your learners—all who are willing—time to relate their experiences in encountering Jesus (what some call *testimonies*). It is important that we share our joy with others in this regard. Not every believer is called to be a preacher, but we can all share about how we came to know Jesus as Savior.

Taking time to let learners answer this question in a safe environment with other believers present may make it easier for them to share later with unbelievers as opportunity arises. Also, we can pray specifically for God to grant us what may be called "divine appointments" when we can share the good news (compare 1 Peter 3:15).

# Inspired to Inquire

DEVOTIONAL READING: **Psalm 148:7-14.**

BACKGROUND SCRIPTURE: **Luke 2:41-52.**

PRINTED TEXT: **Luke 2:41-52.**

### Luke 2:41-52

**41** Now his parents went to Jerusalem every year at the feast of the passover.

**42** And when he was twelve years old, they went up to Jerusalem after the custom of the feast.

**43** And when they had fulfilled the days, as they returned, the child Jesus tarried behind in Jerusalem; and Joseph and his mother knew not of it.

**44** But they, supposing him to have been in the company, went a day's journey; and they sought him among their kinsfolk and acquaintance.

**45** And when they found him not, they turned back again to Jerusalem, seeking him.

**46** And it came to pass, that after three days they found him in the temple, sitting in the midst of the doctors, both hearing them, and asking them questions.

**47** And all that heard him were astonished at his understanding and answers.

**48** And when they saw him, they were amazed: and his mother said unto him, Son, why hast thou thus dealt with us? behold, thy father and I have sought thee sorrowing.

**49** And he said unto them, How is it that ye sought me? wist ye not that I must be about my Father's business?

**50** And they understood not the saying which he spake unto them.

**51** And he went down with them, and came to Nazareth, and was subject unto them: but his mother kept all these sayings in her heart.

**52** And Jesus increased in wisdom and stature, and in favor with God and man.

---

GOLDEN TEXT: After three days they found him in the temple, sitting in the midst of the doctors, both hearing them, and asking them questions.—Luke 2:46.

---

## God's Call to the Christian Community
### Unit 2: Inspired by God's Call
#### (Lessons 6-9)

## Lesson Aims

After participating in this lesson, each student will be able to:

1. Identify the unusual events of Jesus' trip to Jerusalem at age 12.

2. Explain what the story of Jesus as a 12-year-old contributes to our understanding of His life and ministry.

3. Suggest one way to ensure that "being about the Father's business" is of first importance in his or her life.

## Lesson Outline

INTRODUCTION
    A. Parental Challenges
    B. Lesson Background
I. IMPORTANT TRIP (Luke 2:41-44a)
    A. Faithful Family (vv. 41, 42)
    B. Absent Son (vv. 43, 44a)
II. STARTLING DISCOVERIES (Luke 2:44b-47)
    A. Search and Return (vv. 44b-46a)
      *Ignorance Is Bliss?*
    B. Questions and Answers (vv. 46b-47)
III. UNUSUAL DIALOGUE (Luke 2:48-50)
    A. Accusation (v. 48)
    B. Response (vv.49, 50)
      *His Father's Business*
IV. REVEALED CHARACTER (Luke 2:51, 52)
    A. Return and Obedience (v. 51)
    B. Growth and Favor (v. 52)
CONCLUSION
    A. Listening to God
    B. Prayer
    C. Thought to Remember

## Introduction

### A. Parental Challenges

Parents know what a challenge it is to respond appropriately to the developmental stages in their children's lives. This involves understanding a child's needs at given points. For instance, my four-year-old son has rules geared to his age. "You get three books, a kiss, and a prayer at bedtime," and, "You get to dress yourself, but you may ask for help with the shoes" are examples.

Those are good rules for now, but I have to be ready to make adjustments when he turns five. These will be rules such as, "You can go to kindergarten five days a week," and, "You get a one dollar weekly allowance." He may want the rules for five-year-olds now, but I know the time is not right, so I must resist his requests. Such are the challenges of being a parent!

Now let's try to imagine the parenting challenges that faced Mary and Joseph. How difficult was it for them to understand their son Jesus as He grew? How difficult was it for them to anticipate what His calling signified at the various developmental stages of His childhood? In addition to experiencing the normal physical changes of a boy becoming a man, Jesus was coming to grips with what it meant to be the Son of Man. Our own difficult teenage years provide us with only an inkling of the challenges He faced.

### B. Lesson Background

The events we read about in this week's lesson witness Jesus in Jerusalem. This is not the first time He has been there (see Luke 2:21-40; also see last week's lesson). It is interesting that the passages describing the two trips end with the same idea: Jesus continued to grow.

There are two settings for today's lesson. One is the dusty road between Nazareth and Jerusalem (a journey of about 75 miles). The other is the temple in Jerusalem itself. What happened in these two settings will cause us to ask a question that rings true for parents today: What do we make of a child who causes His parents grief when He chooses not to do what He must have known His parents wanted Him to do?

## I. Important Trip
## (Luke 2:41-44a)

### A. Faithful Family (vv. 41, 42)

**41, 42. Now his parents went to Jerusalem every year at the feast of the passover. And when he was twelve years old, they went up to Jerusalem after the custom of the feast.**

Why did God select Mary and Joseph to be Jesus' earthly *parents*? This story reveals a primary reason: Mary and Joseph are faithful people. They love God and rear their children to honor Him. They are exactly the right kind of people to guide Jesus through childhood.

Jesus' parents regularly attend the annual *passover* festival. This is a testimony to their faithfulness. Men are generally expected to attend three major annual feasts in *Jerusalem* (see Exodus 23:14-17; Deuteronomy 16:16). One of these three is the Feast of Unleavened Bread (Exodus 12:17, 18). Although this feast is technically distinct from Passover, the two are right next to each other on the calendar. Thus it is natural to see them as one and the same event (Leviticus 23:5, 6).

It is highly unlikely that each and every Jewish man always attends every major feast annually. But those conscientious in their faith make the effort. That Mary also comes along represents a later development of attendance by women. They attend *after*, or "according to," *the custom* (compare 1 Samuel 1:3, 7, 21). [See question #1, page 168.]

While it is likely that Jesus has been attending Passover with His parents *every year*, this particular one has elevated significance. Jesus is now age 12. Thus He is approaching age 13, when He will take on increased responsibility. The modern ceremony of *bar mitzvah* (literally, "son of the commandment") for Jewish boys who reach age 13 is not practiced in Jesus' day. But as a cultural precursor to that, perhaps Luke tells this story of the 12-year-old Jesus to record the approximate point at which He becomes recognized as having greater status in the religious community.

### B. Absent Son (vv. 43, 44a)

**43, 44a. And when they had fulfilled the days, as they returned, the child Jesus tarried behind in Jerusalem; and Joseph and his mother knew not of it. But they, supposing him to have been in the company, went a day's journey.**

For modern readers, it may be difficult to imagine how Jesus' parents could "lose" Him for a day before realizing it. But let's think through what actually happens on such a pilgrimage. The journey of 75 miles between Nazareth and Jerusalem is at walking pace, thus it is a trip of at least 3 days. For safety and convenience, those who travel to and from Jerusalem for holy festivals go as groups of families and neighbors. Once they are on the road, they are joined by other groups that are traveling as well.

---

### How to Say It

BAR MITZVAH. bar *mits*-vuh.
DEUTERONOMY. Due-ter-*ahn*-uh-me.
HERESY. *hair*-uh-see.
JERUSALEM. Juh-*roo*-suh-lem.
LEVITICUS. Leh-*vit*-ih-kus.
NAZARETH. *Naz*-uh-reth.
RABBIS. *rab*-eyes.

---

In this situation, it is natural for the youngsters of the various families to gravitate toward one another and walk together; the adults likely do the same. (We see the same thing at church picnics: the kids prefer to interact with each other rather than with the adults.) Given Joseph and Mary's world of extended families and village life, they naturally assume that Jesus is with others in their traveling party.

Regardless of the distance *they* cover by foot, we should consider the time of *a day's journey*. Imagine traveling all day in your car only to realize you have to turn around and return to your starting point. Whether the travel is by car or foot, it means extra expense, more time away from work, etc. The extra expense of increased worry is our next consideration.

## II. Startling Discoveries (Luke 2:44b-47)

### A. Search and Return (vv. 44b-46a)

**44b, 45. And they sought him among their kinsfolk and acquaintance. And when they found him not, they turned back again to Jerusalem, seeking him.**

When Joseph and Mary first realize that Jesus is missing, they do not know for certain that He is still back in *Jerusalem*. There is no doubt that they are alarmed by the possibility that something terrible has happened to Him. On the return journey they undoubtedly look in desperation for young Jesus all along the way. Even *their kinsfolk and acquaintance* do not know where He is. It is a frightening situation.

#### IGNORANCE IS BLISS?

An old saying goes, "When ignorance is bliss, 'tis folly to be wise." Ignorance may save us from worry, but it is always best to be informed of actual conditions.

Consider, for example, the case of the Johnstown Flood. Johnstown, Pennsylvania, was built on the flood plain at the juncture of two rivers. A thriving city of 30,000 inhabitants, Johnstown enjoyed the prosperity of the local steel factories. The pressure of its prosperity led the city fathers to narrow the riverbed in order to increase land available for building. Fourteen miles upriver, the South Fork Dam created a large lake on the side of a mountain, 450 feet higher than the city.

On the afternoon of May 31, 1899, following a night of heavy rain, the residents of Johnstown heard a low rumble. The rumble soon turned into a loud roar as the dam broke. A 60-foot wall of water swept downstream, ultimately killing

2,200 people (www.jaha.org). Ignorance of the faulty engineering was not bliss.

Jesus had stayed behind in Jerusalem. Ignorance of that fact definitely did not turn out to be bliss to His parents! Their ignorance of what was happening was accidental, but sadly much ignorance of God's way today is intentional and self-inflicted (Acts 3:17; 17:30; Ephesians 4:18). With the Word of God in our hearts, this need not be so.        —J. B. N.

**46a. And it came to pass, that after three days they found him in the temple.**

The three-day period in question comprises (1) the first day of travel toward Nazareth before Jesus' parents know He is missing, (2) the daylong journey back to Jerusalem, and (3) a day spent looking around Jerusalem in search of Jesus. The population of modern Jerusalem exceeds 600,000. The population of Jerusalem in Jesus' day is much less, of course. One reasonable estimate puts it at 60,000. Even so, this "normal" population can swell greatly during feast days. So finding a child in such a crowded city naturally proves difficult. The temple precincts themselves, the focal point of the festival, cover an area of many acres.

### B. Questions and Answers (vv. 46b, 47)

**46b. Sitting in the midst of the doctors, both hearing them, and asking them questions.**

The scene Jesus' parents come across is, at first glance, not an abnormal one: a group of *doctors* (meaning teachers and rabbis) discussing the law. What is curious is to see a 12-year-old *sitting in* their *midst*! Perhaps Jesus simply has found a group and joined the discussion. Or perhaps His impressive interaction with one teacher has attracted the attention of other teachers.

**47. And all that heard him were astonished at his understanding and answers.**

We shouldn't assume that the people are *astonished* because young Jesus actually is doing the teaching. Rather, what is impressive is the way His understanding of the discussion allows Him to respond and interact. Jesus is clearly performing at a level well above what is normally expected of a child His age. The teachers are genuinely impressed by Jesus, and they naturally are interested in the abilities of a potential pupil. [See question #2, page 168.]

Earlier in Luke we read that Jesus is God's Son, so perhaps we're not terribly surprised by Jesus' proficiency. But consider Him at this point in time. Luke records this story because it marks an important point in Jesus' life. We do not know

how much the young Jesus understands about His divinity at this juncture, but He is at the age when a child's ideas on spiritual matters are beginning to form.

This occasion, therefore, seems to mark the time when Jesus begins to communicate something about His nature and mission. It also marks the occasion when some Jews begin to recognize that there is something special about Him. This is an exceptional moment in history!

## III. Unusual Dialogue (Luke 2:48-50)
### A. Accusation (v. 48)

**48. And when they saw him, they were amazed: and his mother said unto him, Son, why hast thou thus dealt with us? behold, thy father and I have sought thee sorrowing.**

Imagine that a group from your church goes on a short-term mission trip. As that trip draws to a close, your 12-year-old finds the work to be so meaningful that he begs to stay behind as your group prepares to return home. On one level, you would admire your child's desire to work for the Lord. On another level, you would see this for the youthful zeal that it is.

Yet the case of young Jesus must involve more than youthful zeal. He has come to understand, at some level, that He has a special calling. But at His young age He may not yet understand how best to manage this calling. So He assumes He should stay in Jerusalem without His parents' knowledge or consent. There is a delightful innocence to Jesus' desire to cast aside one set of responsibilities to pursue another. Yet, this is not the time, and His parents have to help Him understand this.

So, what do we make of a child who causes His parents grief when He chooses not to do what He must have known His parents wanted Him to do? A certain heresy that developed in the second century proposed that Jesus was not really human. People who held this idea could not imagine that Jesus was "like us." Also, some Christians have a hard time believing that Jesus may have been a difficult child at times, even causing His parents anguish, while remaining sinless (Hebrews 4:15).

But here we have an example of the sinless Jesus causing parental anguish in deciding to remain behind. This 12-year-old has enough knowledge to realize something about His mission, but not yet enough experience and patience to push it forward in the best way possible. Indeed, there will come a time when it will be His mother who pushes Jesus to do something even though He realizes that "mine hour is not yet come" (John 2:4).

We are not told how well Jesus' parents comprehend their son's true nature and role. Mary's Song in Luke 1:46-55 reveals that she is aware that God is going to bring about some kind of fulfillment through her child. Joseph is aware that Jesus somehow is "Immanuel . . . God with us" (Matthew 1:23). When they first took Jesus to the temple, Mary and Joseph heard Simeon's understanding of Jesus to be "the Lord's Christ" (Luke 2:25-35). They also heard Anna's understanding of Him to be an important part of redemption (Luke 2:36-38). But we don't know exactly how Mary and Joseph really interpret all this, even 12 years later.

Thus, the parents' amazement is a little difficult for us to sort out as they see that He is capable of entering into dialogue with the teachers. It appears that this is the first time they see Jesus' abilities in this regard. Yet, Mary is still Jesus' mother, and her concern soon overcomes her wonder. [See question #3, page 168.]

### B. Response (vv. 49, 50)

**49. And he said unto them, How is it that ye sought me? wist ye not that I must be about my Father's business?**

The young Jesus is convinced that He belongs in the temple. His answer reveals no concern about the mental state of His parents. His question *How is it that ye sought me?* expresses surprise that they would wonder where He is. And when He asks *wist ye not that I must be about my Father's business?* He expresses how natural it seems to Him that this is where He belongs.

The reference to being *about my Father's business* is vague in the original Greek. It literally says something like, "about the ___ of my Father." The translator is left to make an intelligent guess regarding what to put in that blank. The use of *business* (meaning, "concerns") in the *King James Version* is a good choice.

Even despite that bit of vagueness, one thing is crystal clear: Jesus has become aware of a personal relationship with God, and it draws Him to the temple. Jesus senses that His role in life is not carpentry, but service to the Lord. When Mary speaks of "thy father" (v. 48), Jesus responds in terms of His heavenly Father.

Jesus seems to be surprised at His parents' surprise. He thinks that they should have known exactly where He was. Jesus' response signals something of a break between himself and His parents as He announces where His ultimate

## Home Daily Bible Readings

**Monday, Dec. 31**—A Horn for God's People (Psalm 148:7-14)
**Tuesday, Jan. 1**—The Passover Feast Instituted (Numbers 9:1-5)
**Wednesday, Jan. 2**—First Passover Observed (Exodus 12:11-14)
**Thursday, Jan. 3**—The Annual Pilgrimage (Luke 2:39-45)
**Friday, Jan. 4**—About the Father's Business (Luke 2:46-50)
**Saturday, Jan. 5**—Growing Up in Nazareth (Luke 2:51, 52)
**Sunday, Jan. 6**—Praise the Lord! (Psalm 148:1-6)

allegiance lies. Does young Jesus expect to stay at the temple (compare 1 Samuel 1:21-28) while His parents go home? The text doesn't say.

### His Father's Business

"Raccoon" John Smith (1784–1868) was one of the famous evangelists on the Kentucky frontier of the early nineteenth century. An outstanding preacher and minister, he learned the value of a disciplined life as he grew up on that wild frontier.

At age 11, he traveled with his father and brother to south central Kentucky. There they laid claim to 200 acres for the family farm. While his dad and brother began the task of clearing trees from the land, John was sent back 100 miles with a packhorse to get a load of corn for seed and meal.

The idea of sending an unescorted 11-year-old out like this would be unthinkable today! But it was not unusual at the time. John completed his assignment in spite of some distractions, arriving back safely with the corn. Nothing dissuaded him from completing the responsibility given to him by his father.

Jesus at age 12 also felt the weight of responsibility. Thus He tarried in Jerusalem at that tender age. Sadly, some folks never seem to feel the weight of much responsibility at any age. Christian responsibility begins to take hold when we acknowledge that we must be about our heavenly Father's business.                    —J. B. N.

**50. And they understood not the saying which he spake unto them.**

The parents have been frantically seeking their son. They've been struck with wonder at His abilities in the temple. And now they're hit with a puzzling statement. Indeed, one wonders whether they've been able to fathom any of this. Except for the events surrounding Jesus' birth 12 years previously, we assume that life has been relatively "normal" up to this point. This incident means that Joseph and Mary suddenly are faced anew with Jesus' uniqueness. Obviously, it is all a little too much for them. So they fail to grasp the significance of Jesus' statement.

## IV. Revealed Character (Luke 2:51, 52)

### A. Return and Obedience (v. 51)

**51. And he went down with them, and came to Nazareth, and was subject unto them: but his mother kept all these sayings in her heart.**

Even though the young Jesus is surprised by His parents' surprise, He remains obedient to them. Jesus realizes that obedience to His heavenly Father means obedience to the parents that His heavenly Father has chosen for Him. Jesus never sins, thus he does not violate Exodus 20:12: "Honor thy father and thy mother."

So He returns with His parents. When we read that Mary *kept all these sayings in her heart,* we see her "filing things away" for future reference (compare Genesis 37:11; Luke 2:19). [See question #4, page 168.]

### B. Growth and Favor (v. 52)

**52. And Jesus increased in wisdom and stature, and in favor with God and man.**

This statement reminds us of Luke's comment in 2:40: "The child grew, and waxed strong in spirit, filled with wisdom; and the grace of God

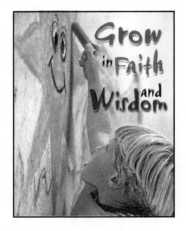

Visual for
Lesson 6

*Point to this visual as you ask, "How do you plan to grow in faith and wisdom this week?"*

was upon him" (compare 1 Samuel 2:26; Proverbs 3:4). It prepares the reader for what is to come, namely, the story of Jesus' baptism and the official beginning of His ministry.

The account we have just read reveals that the young *Jesus* is coming to grips with how He should live up to His responsibilities both to God and to His parents. Jesus understands that choosing to reject the will of His parents while still under their guardianship is not the behavior of an obedient child. Part of increasing *in wisdom and stature, and in favor with God and man* thus involves obedience to His earthly parents. [See question #5, page 168.]

## Conclusion

### A. Listening to God

Jesus had a unique calling. Even so, we can learn some things from His example as we make choices. First, Jesus understood that God would not call Him to go against divine principles in order to fulfill God's will for His life. Thus Jesus realized that God's will for Him could not involve going against the wishes of Joseph and Mary. Parents have been known to demand that their children do things contrary to God's will, but that was not the case here. So Jesus submitted to His parents' authority. Likewise, we should understand that our choices must not conflict with things we know to be true of God's expressed desires as we daily decide how to live.

Second, we see from Jesus' example that sometimes God says, "Wait—the time isn't quite right." It's easy to get excited about a dramatic plan, claiming that it's God's will to "sell all" (Luke 18:22) and go to a foreign mission field. There indeed are times when we must follow God to challenging, exciting places. But often the harder thing is to stay in the current situation and continue to serve Him in an "ordinary" way. After perhaps imagining a life lived in or near the temple, discussing spiritual truths each day, it may have been disappointing for young Jesus to go back to Nazareth and help Joseph carry timber. But that was what God desired at that point in time.

### B. Prayer

Our Father, whether You call us to new grand plans or to continue where we are, help us to be faithful and to submit our desires to Yours, as Jesus did. We pray in Jesus' name, amen.

### C. Thought to Remember

Make sure to listen to God's desires
above your own.

# Learning by Doing

*This page contains an alternative lesson plan emphasizing learning activities.*
*Classes desiring such student involvement will find these suggestions helpful.*

## Into the Lesson

Give each learner a piece of paper that has the outline of a child (photocopy these in advance). Ask each person to identify one of the challenging changes or passages of a child's life and write it on the outline in large letters. If parents are present, they may choose to cite an example from their own child's life experience.

You may find it helpful to offer examples by citing transitions such as potty training, learning to tie shoes, or dealing with peer pressure. After a few moments, ask your learners to share their conclusions and illustrations. In larger classes, ask people to share their conclusions in groups of three or four. After a time of small-group discussion, have groups share their conclusions with the entire class.

Make the transition to Bible study by asking, "Have you ever thought of the boy Jesus experiencing similar childhood transitions? Today's study will focus on one of those transition times in Jesus' life. It will teach us an important lesson about life focus."

## Into the Word

Begin the Into the Word section with a brief lecture from the material in the Lesson Background. As you speak, have the phrase *Keyword: Grow* displayed. Your lecture should emphasize the changes and growth experiences in the life of the boy Jesus.

Next, form teams of two to five people for a scrapbooking exercise. Give each team a sheet of letter-sized paper with five photo-frame boxes drawn down the left side. After reading Luke 2:41-52, the teams should list important snapshots they would include of Jesus' boyhood years in the scrapbook they are assembling. They will list these snapshots in the photo frames provided in the handout.

Next, ask students to note down the right side why they feel each snapshot to be valuable for Jesus' scrapbook. Remind the class that God's choice to preserve these images for us in His Word tells us that these snapshots are important. After groups have completed the scrapbook assignment, ask a representative of each group to move to another group and tell why his or her group chose to include their photos.

After the discussions wind down, debrief your class by asking the following questions:

1. What do you think the Lord is teaching about His nature when He says, "Wist ye not that I must be about my Father's business?" (v. 49)? Why did God include that question to Jesus' parents in the Bible?

2. What clues do you see in this text that Mary and Joseph were struggling with Jesus' identity as God's Son, yet also as their own son?

3. Why do you think God also included in the Bible the phrase "and was subject unto them" (v. 51)? What is God teaching us about the nature of Jesus' humanity and divinity?

## Into Life

Tell the class that Jesus, at age 12, was already beginning to focus on His life's mission. He hints of that in verse 49 when He mentions "my Father's business." Suggest that we too must identify our life purpose or mission. Ask, "What do you think is the purpose of humans? Why do we exist? Why did God create us?" Tell them to share their answers by choosing one of the two activities below (reproduce these on handouts). Allow the class to work in the teams formed earlier. Display Genesis 1:26-31 and Micah 6:8 for the groups to refer to.

*Option #1 (less difficult):* What is the purpose of humans? Post your answer for all to see. After you note this purpose statement, list at least three reasons why your group thinks this.

Next, have each person in your group talk about God's specific purpose for his or her own life. What evidence do you have that leads you to believe this purpose actually is of God?

*Option #2 (more difficult):* What is the purpose of humans? Write a single-sentence answer to the question by creating an acrostic using the word *Purpose*. Start the acrostic with "We Propose that humans . . . " The statement will then use the rest of the letters of the word *Purpose*.

Next, have each person in your group talk about God's specific purpose for his or her own life. What evidence do you have that leads you to believe this purpose actually is of God?

Allow groups to share their answers. Then close the lesson by thanking God for this reminder to keep life focused on our mission.

# Let's Talk It Over

*The questions on this page are designed to promote discussion of the lesson by the class and to encourage application of the lesson Scriptures. The answers provided are only discussion starters. Let your class talk it over from there.*

**1. What traditions or customs associated with the transition to a new year do you observe in your family? Do any of these help serve to pass Christian faith from one generation to the next? If not, how can you do better?**

Many families have seasonal traditions that are very important to them. Easter and Christmas are obvious "big" days on the calendar in this regard. Many traditions associated with these are widely replayed, while others are more personalized and distinctive to individual families. Fewer significant traditions seem to be associated with the transition to the new year, however.

Perhaps you can begin some kind of New Year's Day "time passes" tradition for yourself or your family. This may involve a reflection on what you and your loved ones did for Christ in the past year and what you may do for Him in the year ahead, should He tarry in His return. Everyone could offer a brief reflection along these lines in connection with a New Year's Day dinner, for example.

**2. If you had been there, what do you think you would have heard 12-year-old Jesus talking about? What insights from His lips would have astonished the temple crowd? What sayings of Jesus still astonish you today?**

The timing of the visit to Jerusalem may have shaped the conversation Jesus had with the doctors in the temple. Modern Passover celebrations often include a ritual in which the youngest child present asks, "Why is this night different from all other nights?" We see this echoed in Exodus 12:26, 27: "When your children shall say unto you, What mean ye by this service? That ye shall say, It is the sacrifice of the Lord's passover."

Thus we can easily imagine a rabbi discussing with the young Jesus the meaning of the just-completed Passover. Jesus' answer, coming through the lips of a child but from the soul of the author of the Passover, likely gave the listeners much to talk about!

**3. What challenges do parents face when their children put serving God ahead of following the parents' desires? How do those challenges differ in Christian and non-Christian families?**

Christian parents desire that their children develop their own, individual relationships with God. Sometimes, though, the fruits of that relationship lead the children in directions that the parents would not have chosen. Parents may want their grown children to remain near; God may be calling them to a faraway mission field. The parents may long for grandchildren; God may be calling the adult children to remain single and celibate. Parents may desire Ivy League credentials and material success for their offspring; God may be calling them to a life of sacrifice.

The above deals with children who have grown to adulthood. The issue of minor children allowing their desire to serve God to take priority over parental expectations (as we see in 12-year-old Jesus) is somewhat different. Conflict is much more likely when parents do not share their child's heart for God.

**4. Mary "kept . . . in her heart" the details of Jesus' birth and youth. What memories do you treasure, ponder, or savor? What does this say about your own spiritual maturity?**

Jesus said, "Where your treasure is, there will your heart be also" (Matthew 6:21; Luke 12:34). We could also say, "Whatever is primary in your heart is what you treasure above all." The treasure that is above all is the fact that God sent His Son to die in our place (John 3:16, 17). Your learners will have unique stories concerning how God has rescued and transformed them.

**5. Do the aspects of personal growth describing Jesus' life give us a model for spiritual growth in our own lives? Why, or why not?**

To increase in "wisdom and stature, and in favor with God and man" can be summed up as maturing *mentally, physically, spiritually,* and *socially.* Each area is essential in becoming a mature, well-rounded person. Also, the areas are interrelated. For example, poor physical health can make it hard to concentrate mentally, function socially, or remain focused spiritually. As creatures of flesh and spirit, we are integrated in such a way that when one part is wounded the rest struggles. Think of some ways your church can assist people in growing in these four ways.

# Inspired to Love

DEVOTIONAL READING: Psalm 37:1-11.

BACKGROUND SCRIPTURE: Luke 6:27-36.

PRINTED TEXT: Luke 6:27-36.

### Luke 6:27-36

27 But I say unto you which hear, Love your enemies, do good to them which hate you,

28 Bless them that curse you, and pray for them which despitefully use you.

29 And unto him that smiteth thee on the one cheek offer also the other; and him that taketh away thy cloak forbid not to take thy coat also.

30 Give to every man that asketh of thee; and of him that taketh away thy goods ask them not again.

31 And as ye would that men should do to you, do ye also to them likewise.

32 For if ye love them which love you, what thank have ye? for sinners also love those that love them.

33 And if ye do good to them which do good to you, what thank have ye? for sinners also do even the same.

34 And if ye lend to them of whom ye hope to receive, what thank have ye? for sinners also lend to sinners, to receive as much again.

35 But love ye your enemies, and do good, and lend, hoping for nothing again; and your reward shall be great, and ye shall be the children of the Highest: for he is kind unto the unthankful and to the evil.

36 Be ye therefore merciful, as your Father also is merciful.

GOLDEN TEXT: Love ye your enemies, and do good, and lend, hoping for nothing again; and your reward shall be great, and ye shall be the children of the Highest.—Luke 6:35.

## God's Call to the Christian Community
### Unit 2: Inspired by God's Call
(Lessons 6-9)

## Lesson Aims

After participating in this lesson, each student will be able to:

1. List several specific acts of love that Jesus commanded in this text.

2. Compare the acts of love in lesson aim #1 with the mercy and love of God.

3. Treat one "enemy" in the coming week with the kind of love of which Jesus spoke.

## Lesson Outline

INTRODUCTION
    A. My Rights and My Wrongs
    B. Lesson Background
 I. WHAT TO DO (Luke 6:27-31)
    A. General Principles of Love (vv. 27, 28)
    B. Concrete Examples of Love (vv. 29, 30)
    C. Golden Rule of Love (v. 31)
II. WHY TO DO IT (Luke 6:32-36)
    A. Proper Motive (vv. 32-34)
        *Without Reward*
    B. Proper Attitude (vv. 35a, 35b)
        *Love Your Enemy*
    C. Proper Example (vv. 35c, 36)
CONCLUSION
    A. What Does Love Look Like?
    B. Prayer
    C. Thought to Remember

## Introduction

### A. My Rights and My Wrongs

I know a couple who obviously love each other, but they bicker a lot. Usually a visitor gets drawn into the argument with comments like, "Does your husband watch TV as much as mine?" Before there's time for a response, the grinning husband chimes in, "Do you nag your husband as much as my wife does?" It's just the pattern they have established.

But recently their small group studied *Boundaries*, a popular book written by Henry Cloud and John Townsend. On my most recent visit, I noticed a distinct change in their tone. Instead of their usual bickering, they were heard to say, "You're not hearing my *no*," and "You don't

respect my boundaries." So far so good—but not good enough!

They had come to understand the concept that we are to appreciate the needs of others. But they use this understanding only to have their own needs met. Each is concerned that giving too much to the other means being left with nothing. Each wonders, "If I take care of his or her needs, who will take care of mine?" It's important to have healthy boundaries. But how much should we protect our own interests, and how much should we look out for the interests of others?

Our world is full of messages about "our rights"—as employees, as women or men, as Christians. While our world teaches, "Watch out for yourself because no one else will," Jesus has a different message.

### B. Lesson Background

This week's passage is an excerpt from Jesus' Sermon on the Plain (Luke 6:17-49). The sermon is dominated by a beatitude section (Luke 6:20-38) that is very similar to that in Matthew 5. It is important to consider the background of the sermon as a whole in order to develop a context for our passage today.

After His baptism (Luke 3:21) and temptation (Luke 4:1, 2), Jesus returned to Nazareth. There He announced the fulfillment of Isaiah 61:1, 2 (Luke 4:18, 19). News about Him spread rapidly, and He began to perform miracles to affirm His identity (Luke 4:31-41). Then He selected His disciples. He further affirmed His identity in debates with the Pharisees and by healing people (Luke 5).

Luke 6:1-11 begins to show us that Jesus' understanding of the law was different from that of the Pharisees with whom He debated. Jesus deliberately did things on the Sabbath that certain Pharisees believed to be unlawful. Jesus informed the Pharisees that their understanding of the law was the reverse of what it should be.

This is important because the sermon in Luke 6:20-49 presents the proper way to think about how God expects us to live. Somewhere along the way, religious leaders had begun to teach that godly behavior was based in following minute details of the law. Jesus announced that the details must fit within a bigger picture (compare Luke 11:42).

As Jesus and His apostles came down from a mountain, they were met by a large crowd of people (Luke 6:12-19). They tried to get close to Jesus—to hear Him, touch Him, and be healed by Him. Although the sermon was "in the audience of the people" (Luke 7:1), we find that Jesus turned and directed His sermon toward the disciples (Luke 6:20). The sermon presented the way to think about the law and what it meant to follow and honor God. Those disciples eventually ended up being leaders of the church. So how did Jesus instruct them on how to live before God?

# I. What to Do
## (Luke 6:27-31)

### A. General Principles of Love (vv. 27, 28)

**27a. But I say unto you which hear, Love your enemies.**

The dominant ethical command in the New Testament is to *love* (Matthew 22:36-40). Modern Christians have numerous ethical issues about which to be passionate: abortion, homosexuality, and stem-cell research are just three. It is troubling, though, for Christians not to be at least as passionate about the rigorous discipline of love.

Love is often considered to be a romantic idea, fit for weak and emotional people. But this sort of thinking ignores the fact that love is "the bottom line" of Christian behavior: the Christian walk begins with love; other ethical ideals follow after that. First John 4:20 is an important text here. In John's view, to fail to love one another is to fail to love God.

As we read through the New Testament's perspective on love, we are alerted to the fact that the kind of love in view is not primarily an emotion. "My little children, let us not love in word, neither in tongue; but in deed and in truth" (1 John 3:18). Love in the New Testament is the practice of self-sacrifice!

The truth is, though, that some are not willing to engage in the sort of self-sacrifice the New Testament stresses. Perhaps we are willing to do some work for someone or give money to a godly ministry in a way that's not too inconvenient. The New Testament, though, sees a love that goes beyond this. The New Testament sees a love that

is characterized by allowing one's own needs to be subordinate to the needs of others, even if they despise you (compare Philippians 2:3).

The most difficult form of love required of us is the type of love Christ displayed in His own life. He loved people who hated Him, ignored Him, and did not even know Him. But in practice, how is it possible to love an enemy? To get us started on answering this, we must first get away from the notion that *love* and *like* are the same thing. That is, we must not confuse the command to love with an emotional experience. To love someone is to be willing to sacrifice for that person.

Before we move on, we should pause to note that Jesus' command to *Love your enemies* is nothing new. See Exodus 23:4, 5 and Proverbs 25:21. [See question #1, page 176.]

**27b. Do good to them which hate you.**

The normal response to someone who hates you is to hate him or her right back. If people do nasty things to us, we naturally are not very likely to respond by doing things that are genuinely in their best interest! But the life of Jesus provides an example of how love-as-sacrifice reveals itself. By commanding us to *do good to them which hate you,* Jesus is asking us to sacrifice our feelings and indignation on the altar of obedience to Him.

We must be careful to note that Jesus is not saying, "Don't hate them back." He is requiring us to go beyond not hating—actually to go so far as to do good for them! Further, the underlying language suggests that Jesus is not talking about just one act of kindness. Rather, He is referring to an entire way of life that is characterized by doing good to those who hate us, as difficult as this may be to implement.

Jesus' command goes against certain elements of the culture of His day. For example, the "Rule of the Community" that is part of the Dead Sea Scrolls calls for love of "all the sons of light" and hatred of "all the sons of darkness."

**28. Bless them that curse you, and pray for them which despitefully use you.**

The phrase *despitefully use you* refers to abusive treatment. We're still dealing with the same kind of enemy we saw in verse 27, but now Jesus shifts the focus from their attitude to their behavior toward us. Interestingly, in the previous verse we were told to confront hateful attitudes with a good action; here we are commanded to confront hateful behavior with prayer and blessing. That is, Jesus requires us to go even further now and bring an action of love into our private thought world. This speaks to the importance of our inner orientation. [See question #2, page 176.]

---

### How to Say It

ASCETICISM. uh-*see*-tuh-seh-zum.
CAESAREA. Sess-uh-*ree*-uh.
GRECO-ROMAN. *Greh*-ko *Row*-men.
JUDAISM. *Joo*-duh-izz-um or *Joo*-day-izz-um.
NAZARETH. *Naz*-uh-reth.
PHARISEES. *Fair*-ih-seez.
SANHEDRIN. *San*-huh-drun or San-*heed*-run.
THESSALONIANS. *Thess*-uh-*lo*-nee-unz
   (strong accent on *lo; th* as in *thin*).

## B. Concrete Examples of Love (vv. 29, 30)

**29. And unto him that smiteth thee on the one cheek offer also the other; and him that taketh away thy cloak forbid not to take thy coat also.**

The idea in this and the following verse is contrary to the cultural ideal today that we should demand that others observe our personal rights. Once again Jesus is calling us to have a sacrificial attitude. We are commanded to surrender our instinctive reaction toward an enemy for an entirely different response.

Some commentators suggest that the idea here is more of how to respond to religious persecution than to criminal mistreatment. We note, however, that both Jesus and Paul responded sharply when they were struck in the face as acts of religious persecution (John 18:22, 23; Acts 23:2, 3).

Paul noted that the attack against him was in violation of the law. After some dialogue, Paul eventually humbled himself before the Sanhedrin (Acts 23:5). Paul also used the Roman legal system to protect himself from persecution (Acts 22:25; 25:10-12). Clearly, applying Jesus' command as He intends will require much study and prayer! See the next verse.

**30. Give to every man that asketh of thee; and of him that taketh away thy goods ask them not again.**

The commands of Jesus seem severe, don't they? We may ask ourselves how the behavior proposed in this verse is even possible! Is Jesus saying that if someone asks me for my home and all of my possessions, then I am to give it all away with a smile to boot?

Keep in mind that Jesus is further developing the idea of love. In so doing, He is saying that our attitude toward our possessions, our sense of entitlement, should not get in the way of our ability to exhibit Christian love. Christian love cannot work in a context where we privilege ourselves over others.

We may note in passing that to give away our homes and possessions to others merely because they ask may violate 2 Thessalonians 3:10 in that our actions may reward laziness. Such giveaways may also violate 1 Timothy 5:8 if we lose the means to provide for our own families.

## C. Golden Rule of Love (v. 31)

**31. And as ye would that men should do to you, do ye also to them likewise.**

In Jesus' day, there are two forms of this rule floating around: a negative form and a positive form. The negative form is something like, "don't do bad things to others lest others do bad things to you." This form is popular in both Judaism and in the wider Greco-Roman world of the first century.

Jesus stresses the positive form of the Golden Rule. This is the less common but not unknown form at the time. The positive form has a different function: it shifts the focus from self to others. The negative form says, "Keep yourself safe by not stirring up trouble"; the positive form that Jesus uses says, "The way you treat others should be based on how you would like to be treated."

That Jesus uses the less common form demonstrates that He is not just tossing around a popular cliché. Furthermore, the positive form of the Golden Rule reflects the values Jesus has been developing throughout His sermon. In particular, it reflects the idea that our actions toward others cannot be based on how we have been treated so far. Again, we see a reflection of the sacrificial attitude that is required by Christian love. [See question #3, page 176.]

## II. Why to Do It
## (Luke 6:32-36)

### A. Proper Motive (vv. 32-34)

**32-34. For if ye love them which love you, what thank have ye? for sinners also love those that love them. And if ye do good to them which do good to you, what thank have ye? for sinners also do even the same. And if ye lend to them of whom ye hope to receive, what thank have ye? for sinners also lend to sinners, to receive as much again.**

There is an obvious repetition in the structure of these verses as they repeat ideas from earlier parts of the sermon: *love* (v. 27), *do good* (vv. 27, 31), *give/lend* (v. 30). Each of the verses before us contains the phrase *what thank have ye?* This means something like "why should you get any recognition for doing that?" Returning love for love, good for good, and stuff for stuff is what *sinners* themselves are very capable of doing. That's just natural. But Christians are to go above and beyond this.

When Jesus commands us to live according to the Golden Rule, we should be careful to note that He does not promise that people will respond in kind. The rule is a command from our Lord to act toward others in a specific way, regardless of their response. It is, therefore, not based on a desire to make our lives easier. The single point in these three verses is that the Golden Rule is a norm for *our* behavior and lifestyle. As such, the way we implement this rule is not dependent upon the actions of those whom we are called to love. [See question #4, page 176.]

### WITHOUT REWARD

Servers in restaurants know that the better service they provide, the bigger tip they should receive. We provide Christmas gifts for our mail carriers because packages are left (and will continue to be left) carefully inside our screen doors. It is always a temptation to do things for others with the expectation that they will respond by doing something special for us.

Basil of Caesarea (AD 329–379) set a different example. As an early leader of Eastern Orthodox monasticism, he saw many monks practice lives of extreme self-denial (asceticism). But he thought it was to little purpose other than self-satisfaction. So Basil decided to point monasticism toward a great measure of service outreach with no thought of intrinsic rewards.

As a result, some monasteries became hospitals and took in the sick. Others became educational centers. Many monasteries sent their monks out into the fields to gather the town crops at harvesttime, then return to the monastery and refuse any payment for their work.

Jesus encourages us to give without expectation of receiving in return. Such is the essence of true Christian service. Did Basil of Caesarea understand this better than we do today?   —J. B. N.

### B. Proper Attitude (vv. 35a, 35b)

**35a. But love ye your enemies, and do good, and lend, hoping for nothing again.**

Jesus repeats the threefold theme of *love . . . , do good, and lend.* Tying these to *hoping for nothing* highlights once more a major idea of our passage: don't focus on yourself.

It is tempting for us to agree with Jesus that genuine Christian love does not seek any benefit beyond the opportunity to act in love. We could nod our heads in affirmation and then turn to the next verse. But if we stop and think about how Jesus repeats this idea, and if we reflect also upon the fact that love is the dominant ethic in the New Testament, then perhaps we ought to pause to investigate our own intentions carefully.

In all honesty, are we able to act in a way that is self-sacrificing? Can we act in the interests of others with *no* expectation of anything in return? Can we act with no expectation of thank-you cards or pats on the back? God knows our hearts! [See question #5, page 176.]

Visual for Lesson 7

*Point to the military uniform as you ask, "How should love for enemies show itself in wartime?"*

### LOVE YOUR ENEMY

Dirk Willems was an Anabaptist living in Holland in 1569. The Anabaptists were a persecuted religious minority under the Spanish rulers, who were still trying to enforce a Roman Catholic monopoly in the country. Willems was thrown into prison to await trial as a heretic. The prison diet was inadequate, and Willems lost a considerable amount of weight. Knowing his life was at stake, he made a rope out of knotted rags and lowered himself out of an upper window. Then he ran!

A prison guard saw Willems and pursued. Willems was able to cross over a frozen pond safely; his lightweight, emaciated body did not break through the thin ice. But his pursuer, much heavier, broke through the ice. He tried to get out on his own but was unsuccessful.

Willems heard the man's cries. But Willems knew that if he tried to help the pursuer, he most likely would be caught again. He could not let the man drown. So he returned and helped the man to safety. Then the guard promptly hauled Willems back to prison. Shortly thereafter he was burned at the stake for his "heresy" of being an Anabaptist.

Dirk Willems exemplified exactly what Jesus was talking about. Willems loved his enemy to the extent that it cost him his own life. Jesus' words are easily acknowledged, but rarely implemented. Dirk Willems is a marvelous exception.
—J. B. N.

**35b. And your reward shall be great, and ye shall be the children of the Highest.**

Here are the ultimate benefits of the kind of love that Jesus has in mind. The stated benefits are a part of a worldview that Jesus is presenting in this sermon. Jesus clearly is stressing that the ability to love others in a self-sacrificial manner is an important component of our eternal reward. This kind of love is a vital part of our identity as *the children of the Highest.*

Thus Jesus' sermon presents the idea that the motivation for living a certain kind of life is not based on "what we can get out of it" in the here and now. Even so, isn't the motivation of an eternal reward at least somewhat selfish in and of itself? The next passage answers this.

### C. Proper Example (vv. 35c, 36)

**35c. For he is kind unto the unthankful and to the evil.**

God's character is our ultimate example. Our desire to please Him is our ultimate motivation. The character of God is to love all people, even those who are *unthankful* and *evil.*

Jesus introduces this point so that we can understand that the way we're being called to live our lives is not arbitrary. Rather, it is a life that imitates our heavenly Father. So here we have the motivation for achieving the objectives Jesus laid out for us in the earlier part of the sermon.

**36. Be ye therefore merciful, as your Father also is merciful.**

We could restate this as, "Since you have benefited from the Father's mercy, who are you to be unmerciful to others?" That is, the command refers to a kind of behavior (being *merciful*) and a way to measure that behavior (as God *is merciful*).

This idea is repeated elsewhere in the Gospels. Consider the Parable of the Unmerciful Servant in Matthew 18:21-35. Jesus uses the parable to show that God can be endlessly merciful, but that a failure to reflect the very mercy we ourselves are shown is to encounter the wrath of God.

Through all of these verses, the underlying principle is that everything we have is a result of God's love and mercy to us. Thus we are in no position to be unloving, ungracious, or selfish. To do so is to reject God outright.

## Conclusion

### A. What Does Love Look Like?

Think of the person you like least. This can be someone you know personally or an infamous public figure. Why do you dislike or fear that person? What would it mean to love him or her as Jesus desires?

This brings us to another question: What does love really look like? It's hard to say, especially when we consider the kind of love Jesus spoke about. Is there such a thing as a loving quarrel? Can a bouquet of flowers be given in hate? Jesus seems to teach that the motive is the deciding factor, not necessarily the action itself. If we argue with an alcoholic sibling in order to convince him that he needs help, it becomes an action of love. If we present an expensive gift in order to be seen as more generous than other guests at the party, it is far from the act of love it would seem to be (compare Matthew 6:1-4).

The love of a mother seems to be a perfect example of the kind of love that sacrifices at each turn. From the moment of conception, she gives over her very body to the needs of the child. The act of bringing her child into the world is one of extreme pain.

As the child grows, the requirement for sacrifice grows, moving the mother to forego sleep to care for him in sickness and to put aside her embarrassment when he causes a scene in a store. In these daily choices, a mother shows her selfless love. Jesus calls us to exhibit that same kind of love, not only to those we hold dear, but also to strangers, even to those who hurt and hate us.

### B. Prayer

Our loving Father, thank You for exhibiting true love to us through Jesus. Please help us to love as He loved because that kind of love is so difficult. In Jesus' name and by His love we pray, amen.

### C. Thought to Remember

Love doesn't always *feel* good,
but love always *is* good.

### Home Daily Bible Readings

**Monday, Jan. 7**—Trust in the Lord (Psalm 37:1-11)

**Tuesday, Jan. 8**—Love Your Neighbor (Leviticus 19:17, 18)

**Wednesday, Jan. 9**—Love Your Enemies (Luke 6:27, 28)

**Thursday, Jan. 10**—Absorb Injustice (Luke 6:29, 30)

**Friday, Jan. 11**—Set the Standard (Luke 6:31)

**Saturday, Jan. 12**—Expect Nothing in Return (Luke 6:34-36)

**Sunday, Jan. 13**—Posterity for the Peaceable (Psalm 37:35-40)

# Learning by Doing

*This page contains an alternative lesson plan emphasizing learning activities.*
*Classes desiring such student involvement will find these suggestions helpful.*

## Into the Lesson

Ask two people in advance to prepare a skit that will introduce this lesson. The actors will portray a husband (John) and wife (Mary). The scene will be a dinner-table conversation. John will tell Mary about a sale he had made, but was not present to write it up. A coworker wrote up the sale and put his own name on the sales slip to claim the commission.

John vents his anger and frustration at the dinner table. Mary concludes her comfort by reminding John that Jesus says we must love our enemies. John's response: "Yeah, right! It's absolutely impossible to love that jerk!"

Make the transition to Bible study by asking, "Is that kind of love really impossible as John suggests? Or is it possible to love our enemies? Today, we'll address those questions as we look for practical applications to this difficult assignment from the Lord."

## Into the Word

Ask your minister or another speaker to make a video presenting the Lesson Background material that is printed in the lesson commentary. Of course, the speaker may add greetings and encouragement to the class during the video presentation. Play the video to the class. Next, read the printed text (10 verses) aloud for the class. Then ask some or all of the following discussion questions. (These questions are also printed in the optional student book.)

1. What are the types or descriptions of enemies that Jesus chooses as illustrations in this passage? *(Make a list on the board of students' answers; those answers should draw from the following half-verses: 27b, 28a, 28b, 29a, 29b, 30b.)*

2. What are some practical demonstrations of loving your enemies cited by Jesus? *(Again, make a list on the board of learners' answers; those answers should draw from the following verses and half-verses: 27b, 28a, 28b, 29a, 29b, 30, 31, 35.)*

3. Since the kind of love that Jesus describes in the text is not an emotion, how would you define or describe it?

4. What are some of the obvious benefits to the kind of love at issue in the previous question?

5. What are some possible motives for practicing this kind of love?

6. What are some of the obstacles to expressing this kind of love to those who have been unloving toward us?

7. What are some suggestions you would give for developing a discipline to express this kind of love? What habits, emotions, or attitudes need to be developed? *(List the suggestions separately. You will need this list later in the lesson.)*

## Into Life

*Option #1:* Divide the class into "application teams" of three or four. Display this phrase: *Role Play, Mime, or Cartoon.* Each team is to choose one of these methods to demonstrate or illustrate the discipline of showing love to enemies. The demonstration or illustration must represent realistic life situations. Tell them to work quickly because they have only eight minutes to prepare.

Allow each team to share or present its work. Small classes will be able to share each team's presentation. Larger classes may choose to have pairs of teams show their work to one another.

*Option #2:* Divide the class into "application teams" of three or four. Give each team a piece of poster board and a marking pen. The purpose of these teams is to identify and list the names of persons who have practiced and modeled Jesus' command to love our enemies.

First, each team is to identify at least one person from the Bible, other than Jesus, who demonstrated loving his or her enemies. Then each team is to name one person from history (other than Bible characters) who demonstrated this kind of love.

Finally, each team member is to name one person from his or her personal experience who has demonstrated such a love; if someone thinks it best not to list the name of an individual, he or she may substitute the word *unnamed.* Then have each team share its findings with the rest of the class or with one other team.

*Concluding Activity:* Ask learners to review the list of suggestions from question #7. Ask, "Which one will be the most helpful to you in developing the skill of expressing love for enemies?"

Ask each learner to write his or her choice on an index card. Each learner can hold it while praying for that skill during the closing prayer time.

# Let's Talk It Over

*The questions on this page are designed to promote discussion of the lesson by the class and to encourage application of the lesson Scriptures. The answers provided are only discussion starters. Let your class talk it over from there.*

**1. How do the enemies we face today compare and contrast with the enemies of Jesus' time? What are some ways you have shown love to your enemies?**

Christians in some parts of the world today face enemies as ruthless as those who nailed Jesus to the cross. Satan's operatives are still deadly. Although some societies give freedom and protection to Christians, more Christians are being persecuted today than at any other time in history.

Even in countries with freedom of religion, Christians constantly face challenges from opponents. The opposition comes on social issues, from academics who dismiss the value of faith, and from politicians who seek popularity at the expense of values. This is hardly surprising, though, since Jesus promised that if He were persecuted, His disciples would be as well.

**2. What are some specific ways that we can "do good to them which hate" us and "bless them that curse" us?**

Trying not to hate our enemies can be a challenge. Actively blessing them, though, seems hardly reasonable. And, of course, it is *not* reasonable in a worldly sense. You will seldom hear God suggest that we follow a reasonable course as the world understands the word *reasonable.*

That being said, we admit that overcoming negative feelings with grace and love is never easy or natural. We may need to begin by blessing in small ways. Refusing to speak ill of another is a good thing. Looking for good things to say about him or her is better. Honest praise to his or her face is better yet. A gift of some kind may improve the relationship.

**3. Who among those you know is best at living out the Golden Rule (v. 31)? What do you see in that person's life that demonstrates this?**

Truly selfless people stand out. Even in the church, theirs is a rare breed. "Golden-Rule lives" are marked by generosity and gentleness. Gracefulness contrasts so sharply with the way of this world that those who truly live for others make an unforgettable impression.

We need to be careful of attempting to reach this ideal love through its negative: "do not do to others what you would not have them do to you." Jesus' example and His command show an active love: be a blessing to others. The Golden Rule does not simply mean we avoid harming others. It insists on a more assertive approach, one that looks for the opportunity to give.

**4. In the twenty-first century, what does loving, doing good for, or giving to people who can return the favor look like? How does that contrast with Jesus' example?**

Secular publications have plenty of ideas on how to use a "network" of people to exchange career-building favors! Yet Jesus exchanged Heaven for a manger. He released His grip on equality with God to be bound by a physical body. He muted the songs of angels to hear the mocking of the soldiers, the cursing of the thief, the rejection of the people, the denial of Peter, and the betrayal of Judas. He embraced the thorns, the whips, and the cross for us. Which of us can return the favor to Him?

There is no way to pay Jesus back for what He has given us. Perhaps we can say that Jesus has asked us to "pay it forward." Visiting an AIDS patient in the hospital, spending time with a prisoner in jail, or volunteering in a nursing home will probably not be rewarded by an approving public. Sometimes it may not even be appreciated by other church members. It will be seen by God and honored by Him.

**5. Without mentioning names, when was the last time you helped someone who absolutely could not repay you? How have you found your motivation to be different when you helped others who could return the favor from when you helped others who could not?**

Jesus warned His listeners during the Sermon on the Mount to do their good deeds in secret so that God, who sees in secret, would reward them (Matthew 6:4). The trade-off was quite clear: good deeds done for the reward would be rewarded, but only in the expected fashion. If someone did good deeds for public acclaim, then the public would reward that person. If someone did good deeds for God's pleasure, then God would reward him or her.

# Inspired to Pray

**Devotional Reading: Psalm 28:6-9.**

**Background Scripture: Luke 11:1-13.**

**Printed Text: Luke 11:5-13.**

### Luke 11:5-13

5 And he said unto them, Which of you shall have a friend, and shall go unto him at midnight, and say unto him, Friend, lend me three loaves;

6 For a friend of mine in his journey is come to me, and I have nothing to set before him?

7 And he from within shall answer and say, Trouble me not: the door is now shut, and my children are with me in bed; I cannot rise and give thee.

8 I say unto you, Though he will not rise and give him, because he is his friend, yet because of his importunity he will rise and give him as many as he needeth.

9 And I say unto you, Ask, and it shall be given you; seek, and ye shall find; knock, and it shall be opened unto you.

10 For every one that asketh receiveth; and he that seeketh findeth; and to him that knocketh it shall be opened.

11 If a son shall ask bread of any of you that is a father, will he give him a stone? or if he ask a fish, will he for a fish give him a serpent?

12 Or if he shall ask an egg, will he offer him a scorpion?

13 If ye then, being evil, know how to give good gifts unto your children; how much more shall your heavenly Father give the Holy Spirit to them that ask him?

**Jan 20**

---

Golden Text: I say unto you, Ask, and it shall be given you; seek, and ye shall find; knock, and it shall be opened unto you.—Luke 11:9.

---

## God's Call to the Christian Community
### Unit 2: Inspired by God's Call
#### (Lessons 6-9)

## Lesson Aims

After participating in this lesson, each student will be able to:

1. Summarize Jesus' teaching on asking, seeking, and finding.

2. Give some examples of the kind of things he or she should and should not ask of God.

3. Create a prayer list of five things or people that he or she will lift up consistently and persistently before God in prayer.

## Lesson Outline

## Introduction

### A. Asking and Seeking

Imagine going to your bank manager to ask for a loan. You sit at his desk and open the conversation with, "You probably won't want to give me a loan. I know you're pretty tight-fisted. In fact, I've heard you never grant loans—especially not to people like me." In spite of your somewhat insulting tone, he continues with the usual process and asks you to present your proof of income. You respond, "Oh, I didn't bother to bring any papers with me, since I expected you probably wouldn't be interested in giving me the loan anyway."

Do you think you'd get the loan? I imagine not; in fact, it would be natural for the flabbergasted bank manager to ask why you even bothered to come to his office if you had no hope that he would give you a loan. Leaving the bank, you tell yourself, "I knew he wouldn't give me the loan," as you blame the manager's hard-heartedness. But would you be right in that assessment of his motives?

When we approach God with a request, how do we assess His motives? Do we assume He's looking for a reason to give us as little as possible? Do we neglect even to approach Him when we sense a need because we think He doesn't care? As we'll see today, when it comes to dealing with the one who knows our hearts, motives are as much a factor as the specifics of the request.

### B. Lesson Background

The passage for today's lesson is the final component of the larger teaching section of Luke 10:25–11:13. In this section, three different events give rise to Jesus' description of characteristics of those who wish to follow Him. In the first, Jesus is approached by a lawyer and is asked how one could inherit eternal life (Luke 10:25-37); that question gives rise to the Parable of the Good Samaritan. The second is the situation of Martha fussing about Mary (Luke 10:38-42); that gives rise to Jesus' pronouncement that the good disciple seeks Jesus above all else.

The third section (Luke 11:1-13) contains our passage for today (11:5-13). In this section Jesus' disciples asked Him how they should pray (11:1). Jesus responded by offering a "model prayer." Then He offered further teachings on the nature of prayer, the teachings with which our lesson is concerned.

Before proceeding, we should take stock of the model prayer, since today's lesson extends from it. The model prayer of Luke 11:2-4 is also located in Matthew 6:9-13 in a fuller form, although the points overlap. In Matthew 6:5-7, Jesus criticizes prayers that are meaninglessly repetitive. He stresses that such repetition is unnecessary since God already is aware of our needs before we pray (Matthew 6:8).

It is this last comment that ties the model prayer as presented in Matthew to this prayer as presented in Luke. In fact, the point of our lesson today is essentially the same as that made in Matthew 6:8: God is already present in our lives, knowing our needs before we pray. Prayer is, on one level, an affirmation of our awareness of God's presence in our lives. The content of this kind of prayer is our need, which God already knows.

# I. Friend's Request
## (Luke 11:5-8)

### A. Confident Expectation (vv. 5, 6)

**5, 6. And he said unto them, Which of you shall have a friend, and shall go unto him at midnight, and say unto him, Friend, lend me three loaves; for a friend of mine in his journey is come to me, and I have nothing to set before him?**

Today, not many of us would have the nerve to take a trip and show up unannounced at a friend's door in the middle of the night! Ancient customs of hospitality are different from ours, however. Thus a person on a *journey* might drop in unannounced, especially since in the first century there is no telephone, e-mail, or text messaging with which to do the advance announcing! Such a drop-in visitor might need food, and there are no all-night diners or convenience stores at the time. Thus the need to knock on a neighbor's door *at midnight* to ask for bread.

The willingness of the needy neighbor to go to his friend's house to ask for food suggests that he is confident that there will be a positive outcome to the request. He has good reason for this confidence because hospitality is a part of the fabric of the culture. So, based on what is "normal," he expects that the nearby *friend* will oblige (Romans 12:13; 1 Peter 4:9).

Jesus thus is speaking in terms the audience can appreciate. Furthermore, the fact that Jesus opens the parable with the phrase *which of you* brings this story to the level of actual experience. That is, Jesus is using a situation with which He expects them to be able to relate personally. As with other parables, Jesus forces His audience to confront a personal choice; those who hear Him have experienced this situation in one form or another. [See question #1, page 184.]

### B. Reluctant Friend (v. 7)

**7. And he from within shall answer and say, Trouble me not: the door is now shut, and my children are with me in bed; I cannot rise and give thee.**

The response, in short, is "Go away, we're asleep!" And let's be honest: we are not surprised at this response in this situation. [See question

---

**How to Say It**

IMPORTUNITY. im-per-*too*-nuh-tee.
PHILIPPIANS. Fih-*lip*-ee-unz.
SAMARITAN. Suh-*mare*-uh-tun.

---

#2, page 184.] However, while we may consider this as somewhat "normal," Jesus actually is using this as an example of ungracious behavior. Having just offered us the example of the model prayer—that we may pray to God for our needs (Luke 11:2-4)—Jesus now implicitly contrasts an ungracious attitude to God's graciousness. [See question #3, page 184.]

### C. Ultimate Response (v. 8)

**8. I say unto you, Though he will not rise and give him, because he is his friend, yet because of his importunity he will rise and give him as many as he needeth.**

The word *importunity* refers to an urgent request or begging. Some may think that this verse means that if we badger God long enough, then He will give us whatever we ask for. To think along this line is to labor under a very dangerous assumption!

Let's do a comparison with the Parable of the Persistent Widow (Luke 18:1-8). That parable describes a widow who keeps asking a wicked judge for relief that he is unwilling to give. However, because she keeps asking and asking, he finally relents: "Yet because this widow troubleth me, I will avenge her, lest by her continual coming she weary me" (Luke 18:5).

If we leave the text there, we may assume that the point is *persistence pays off.* But as we read on, we find that this is not the point at all. Jesus goes on to explain the parable—and it's always helpful to listen to Jesus' own explanations of His parables before we make our own interpretation! Jesus explains that *in contrast* with the wicked judge, God will respond quickly with His justice (Luke 18:6-8). He will not keep putting people off as the wicked judge does.

The point of the verse in front of us is that Jesus is drawing a contrast between ungracious behavior and the way God acts toward us. This is made clearer in our passage as we read along; the point is that if an ungracious friend will eventually live up to his needy neighbor's confidence, how much more so can we expect our heavenly Father to do so.

We have characterized this part of our lesson using the idea of *confidence.* It is important for us, therefore, to draw the connection between *confidence* and *persistence.* Our ultimate interpretation of this passage will be that because of who God is, we can trust that our prayers will be answered. That kind of trust in God leads us to a certain kind of expectation. We observe this kind of confident expectation in the needy neighbor; it lies behind his persistence.

Persistence here is an expression of confidence; the abnormal behavior is not that of the needy neighbor, but that of the reluctant friend. On the basis of this reluctance, Jesus now goes on to make a point about how we can trust God to respond properly in contrast with the reluctant friend.

### A CONFIDENT REQUEST

Some years ago I was the interim dean of our seminary. That meant, among other things, that all applications for admission to the school came across my desk for approval. One request came from a potential student who did not have a grade point average that was sufficient to qualify for admission. It wasn't even close. It was easy to turn down her application.

But then the admission department contacted me. "This girl really wants to come," the admission officer said. I explained that her grades were too low. She would never survive graduate school—it was a waste of her money and our time.

The admission counselor contacted the girl and then called me back. "She really wants to come," he insisted. I explained again. "But she really wants to come." In a moment of weakness, I said, "OK, but tell her we think it's a mistake. We can't give her any financial assistance. We'll be glad to take her money, but we think she should stay home and not waste her money on tuition, books, and living expenses here."

But she really wanted to come. So she came. Yet to conclude merely that "persistence paid off" is to look at things superficially. Her persistence was an expression of her confidence. That confidence proved to be well founded three semesters later when she made the dean's honor roll. She ultimately finished two graduate degrees with us. She turned out to be a good student with a compassionate nature, a great sense of humor, and a real desire to learn and serve the Lord. Do you approach your service for God with confidence that He will help you?      —J. B. N.

## II. Ask and Receive
## (Luke 11:9, 10)
### A. What to Do (v. 9)

9. And I say unto you, Ask, and it shall be given you; seek, and ye shall find; knock, and it shall be opened unto you.

When the statement *Ask, and it shall be given you* is read in context, the emphasis shifts away from ourselves and toward God. The result is that we ask because we have confidence that

God will give. The two statements that follow, which deal with seeking and knocking, are parallel to this one. Thus we are to be confident that when we ask, *seek*, or *knock* that God indeed will respond.

### B. Why to Do It (v. 10)

10. For every one that asketh receiveth; and he that seeketh findeth; and to him that knocketh it shall be opened.

God is always faithful to respond appropriately to our needs. But let's be honest: are we sometimes too proud to ask God (or anyone else) for help? Do we think we always should try to meet our own needs without God's help? If our answer to these questions is *yes*, then we may have a problem with pride.

Perhaps we think that the old saying, "God helps those who help themselves," is a biblical truth. Actually, it is a quote from Benjamin Franklin's *Poor Richard's Almanack* of 1733 (page 81). The notion expressed in this saying is tied in with the early American ideal of "rugged individualism." Yet God expects us to ask Him for our daily bread (Luke 11:3).

Asking requires faith, and God honors faithful people. Jesus is the one who provides a way for us to have confidence that our requests will be heard and fulfilled. We should be wary, however, of the notion that we are the ones who have to get God moving on things, assuming that God won't act unless we push Him.

An important point in this and the previous verse is that a specific kind of person is in view here. Recall that today's lesson text occurs within a long teaching section that deals with how Jesus' disciples are to think and behave. Thus when Jesus refers to people who ask, seek, and knock, He is referring to the kind of person who has the sort of relationship with God that Jesus has been describing all along.

In other words, these verses are directed to the kind of people who ask, seek, and knock while having the right kind of motives and goals. This means that the person who asks to win the lottery is not the kind of person Jesus is talking about (compare James 4:3). [See question #4, page 184.]

## III. Giving Father
## (Luke 11:11-13)
### A. Earthly Illustration (vv. 11, 12)

11. If a son shall ask bread of any of you that is a father, will he give him a stone? or if he ask a fish, will he for a fish give him a serpent?

The question about *bread* and *a stone* does not appear in the earliest Greek manuscripts of the Gospel of Luke. But it does appear in Matthew 7:9, so we are confident that it is a genuine part of Jesus' teaching. All parents have had the experience of their children asking to receive food. The questions that Jesus asks challenge His audience to think through a certain issue in light of their own experiences with their families.

**12. Or if he shall ask an egg, will he offer him a scorpion?**

The proper response is obvious. That is just the point: the degree to which the right response is obvious is the degree to which we can be confident in placing our trust in our heavenly Father, who meets our needs.

### B. Heavenly Reality (v. 13)

**13. If ye then, being evil, know how to give good gifts unto your children; how much more shall your heavenly Father give the Holy Spirit to them that ask him?**

That Jesus refers to His audience as *evil* does not imply that He is speaking to opponents. Luke 11:1 suggests, rather, that He is addressing His disciples. Jesus is sketching a broad contrast between humans and God. Compared to God, we all are evil (Romans 3:10-18, 23).

Thus, Jesus employs a lesser-to-greater argument: if we ordinary mortals are capable of being nice to our children, then God is all the more capable! And if we ordinary mortals are capable of being gracious to our friends, even after a period of ungraciousness (vv. 5-8, above), then God's capabilities for graciousness cannot be doubted.

That Jesus points to *the Holy Spirit* as that which God will give us when we pray alerts us to an important fact: Jesus is not referring simply to bettering our material lives through prayer. A popular perception of God says that if you want a bigger car or a better house, all you need to do is ask for it in faith. This theory carries the assumption that God promises us health and wealth. It is a "name it and claim it" view of the gospel.

But there is no such promise in the New Testament. Human expectation of entitlement is just that. Remember that Jesus is teaching us how true disciples understand the nature of God; Jesus is not teaching that we can get from God all we want simply by virtue of persistence.

So, does all this mean that God is not at all concerned about our material situation in life? In next week's lesson, we will see Jesus draw attention to this very issue. We are also instructed by Matthew's version of today's lesson text. Having

Visual for
Lesson 8

*Use this visual to start a discussion of right and wrong motives in asking, seeking, and knocking.*

presented an example of how not to think about prayer (Matthew 6:7), Jesus says that the true disciple understands that the heavenly Father "knoweth what things ye have need of, before ye ask him" (Matthew 6:8).

The point of the contrast in Matthew is to highlight the difference between how pagans pray and how God expects a believer to pray. The fact that God knows what we need before we pray is to mark the way a Christian prays. True disciples pray for what they need, realizing that God already knows their needs. He knows the distinction between what we really need and what we only think we "need."

Luke's account takes this even further by pointing to the giving of the Holy Spirit as being the result of prayer; that is, Jesus frames the issue of need mainly in terms of our relationship with God. The lives of true disciples are focused on serving God. True disciples see that fact as the basis for their prayers.

Moreover, true disciples are confident that God will indeed supply all that they need. Later, Paul will make the point that material possessions are valuable to him insofar as they assist him in his service to God (Philippians 4:11-18). Moreover, Paul's idea of *need* is defined within one's relationship to Jesus Christ. Thus Paul states "my God shall supply all your need according to his riches in glory by Christ Jesus" (Philippians 4:19).

Jesus teaches us that prayer is something to pursue in godly confidence. Doing so reflects our relationship to God through Jesus Christ as we seek greater faithfulness as His disciples. [See question #5, page 184.]

## GOOD AND BETTER GIFTS

I have a friend who often had to do without things in his youth, although he was not raised in poverty. When he got married and became a father, he determined that his children would not have to go without as he had. Educated and trained as an engineer, he had enough income so that his family did not suffer any deprivation. He was never overly extravagant, but his sons had plenty of toys when they were young, cars when they got older, and all the benefits of his well-intentioned benevolence.

When the sons got married and set up their own housekeeping, they tended to continue the practice of their earlier years. Whenever they saw something they wanted, they bought it, often using credit. The habit of a lifetime was difficult to break. One son finally realized he was in over his head when his credit-card indebtedness reached $30,000.

Jesus says our heavenly Father knows how to give good gifts, just as earthly fathers do. But sometimes earthly fathers go too far. If we stop and think about it, it is undoubtedly a good thing that God does not give us everything we ask for. We could easily become smug, spoiled, satiated, and self-satisfied.

God gives us whatever we really need, but not all that we want. In the process He demonstrates that He is a better Father than earthly fathers. He sustains us, but He also keeps us aware that earthly gadgets don't bring us lasting happiness. Only His grace can do that.          —J. B. N.

# Conclusion

## A. My Goodness!

A friend of mine who is a Bible college professor told me of a certain classroom experience she had had. One day she started the lesson by asking the class to respond to the question, "Are you confident of your salvation?"

She was astonished to find only a few of the 20 students responded in the affirmative. Why the doubt? Perhaps many hesitated to say *yes* for fear of appearing to be prideful. No spiritually mature Christian would dare think, "I'm so good that God couldn't possibly deny my entry into Heaven." Such an approach to salvation focuses on our goodness, not His.

Perhaps the same kind of hesitation shows up in our prayer requests at times. Many of us are aware of the pridefulness of the "name it and claim it" kind of prayers. So we take our prayers too far in the other direction in an attempt to avoid that error.

The result may be that we approach God in a tentative, hesitant way. We may question whether we "deserve" the good things that we request. Such an approach turns the focus away from God and onto ourselves. Avoiding the sin of pride is always a good thing. But being overly self-conscious and introspective in this area brings us right back to the problem of focusing on self!

If we understand just how much God loves us and just how good and generous He is, our thoughts of our own worthiness (or lack thereof) will not be the main issue in our prayers. A tried-and-true prayer format is summed up in the acronym *ACTS*. This stands for *adoration, confession, thanksgiving,* and *supplication* as a series of steps to follow when praying. Notice that *supplication* (which means asking humbly for something) comes last. The first three steps refer to praising God for who He is, acknowledging the things that hinder our relationship to Him, and recognizing what He has already done for us. If we go through those three prayer-steps first, then our supplications are more likely to be offered with right motives.

## B. Prayer

Our good and generous Father, we trust that You love us because of Your own goodness, not ours. Help us to ask for those things You want for us and to trust that You will grant them to us. Even as we pray, we know that You will answer in accord with Your perfect will. By Jesus' generous work we pray, amen.

## C. Thought to Remember

God helps those who *forget* themselves.

## Home Daily Bible Readings

**Monday, Jan. 14**—Answered Prayer (Psalm 28:6-9)

**Tuesday, Jan. 15**—Teach Us to Pray (Luke 11:1-4)

**Wednesday, Jan. 16**—A Friend's Request (Luke 11:5-8)

**Thursday, Jan. 17**—Ask and Receive (Luke 11:9-12)

**Friday, Jan. 18**—Persistent in Prayer (Luke 18:1-17)

**Saturday, Jan. 19**—God's Gift of the Holy Spirit (Luke 11:13; Acts 2:1-4)

**Sunday, Jan. 20**—Give Thanks to the Lord (Psalm 106:1-3)

# Learning by Doing

*This page contains an alternative lesson plan emphasizing learning activities.*
*Classes desiring such student involvement will find these suggestions helpful.*

## Into the Lesson

In the week before this lesson, make a video that surveys 7 to 10 people. Ask for their responses to this question: "What does prayer mean to you?"

You may choose to call church members and video their responses at their homes or conduct this survey at another midweek church meeting or small-group gathering. However, the best survey would be of people on the street. You will probably discover a wide variety of responses.

To introduce today's lesson, tell the class of your survey and play the video responses. Make the transition to Bible study by telling the class that people have varied ideas about the purpose and function of prayer. Many of them are correct. Yet most of us need a clearer definition of prayer's power and purpose.

A variant of the above activity is to ask one of your class members to take some of your learners to the side as they arrive for class. Even a hallway can serve as a videotaping area. Have the videographer ask the same question: "What does prayer mean to you?" Continue taping people's responses right up to the time class begins. Then play the video for the entire class.

## Into the Word

Divide the class into study groups. The instructions for supplies needed and the task of each group is as follows:

*Group #1.* Give this group one piece of poster board, a marker, and a photocopy of the Lesson Background and the commentary on verses 5-8. Provide the following instructions: "Your task is to read the Lesson Background and the commentary on verses 5-8. Then write out the model prayer (vv. 2-4) and be ready to explain its place in today's study. Also be ready to explain verses 5-8 to the class."

*Group #2.* Give this group a photocopy of the Introduction and of the commentary on verses 9, 10. Provide the following instructions: "Read the commentary on verses 9 and 10. Then read the Introduction. Your task is to quickly prepare and deliver a skit for the class built on the loan request illustration. Then have a group member explain to the class how this skit illustrates verses 9 and 10."

*Group #3.* Give this group one piece of poster board, a marker, and a photocopy of the commentary on verses 11-13. Provide this list of questions:

1. How do verses 11-13 clarify or illustrate the intent of verses 9 and 10?
2. What does Jesus mean when He calls His listeners "evil"?
3. What is Jesus' lesson or challenge to us in these verses?

Provide also the following instructions: "Read the commentary on verses 11-13. Then write the following questions on the poster board, discuss the questions, and list your conclusions. One of your group members will share your responses with the rest of the class."

## Into Life

Ask the discussion questions listed below. While asking and discussing the first question, circulate throughout the room as you give each person a colored self-adhesive circle of one-half inch or one inch in diameter. Such circles are commonly available at office supply stores and the stationery section of discount stores. Your church office may have them in supply as well. The circles will be used at the end of the lesson. The discussion questions are as follows:

1. Why does this passage not teach us that God will give us absolutely *everything* we ask at any time of our lives?
2. Since *ask, seek, knock* does not mean that God will grant us absolutely everything we ask at any time of our lives, then what does it mean?
3. In terms of persistence, confidence, and motivation, what is Jesus teaching us about prayer? What general truths jump out at you? (List their answers on a large piece of poster board.)

Next, say, "Now, make this lesson personal. Look at the answers we've just listed. Which truth or lesson especially touches you today? Bring your adhesive circle over to the poster board and place it right next to the truth you've just selected."

Close the class by placing the poster on the floor or a table in the center of a prayer circle. With heads bowed, give each of your learners a chance to express a prayer of thanks for the truths listed.

# Let's Talk It Over

*The questions on this page are designed to promote discussion of the lesson by the class and to encourage application of the lesson Scriptures. The answers provided are only discussion starters. Let your class talk it over from there.*

**1. What have been your experiences in asking favors from friends? How did the responses affect your friendships? How have you grown spiritually as a result?**

Many who live in the United States value traits such as "rugged individualism" and a do-it-yourself spirit—perhaps more so than many other countries. Yet most of us appreciate (or at least don't mind) being asked to help. It is nice to be needed. Certainly that can be abused, and there are those whose dependency damages relationships. In general, though, a true friendship will be strengthened by living in a relationship that can give and receive favors. We can't do favors for God, of course, but He stands ready to help us—if we can swallow our pride and ask.

**2. In what ways have you found God to be different from the one who said, "Trouble me not"?**

People can suffer from "compassion fatigue." Aid workers notice that if there are multiple natural disasters in a year, the response diminishes with each succeeding tragedy unless there are special circumstances. Even when our response begins strong, over time our resources become committed elsewhere and our attention turns away. Although the needs may not be any less, eventually we stay in bed and let people knock on the door for a while.

When you read this, Hurricane Katrina will have moved from the front page of the newspaper to a footnote in the history textbooks—that is, unless you live in the parts of the Gulf Coast of the U.S. that were devastated by the storm. For you, the repercussions of Katrina still confront you. For the rest of us, maintaining that level of attention is difficult at best.

God could not be more different. His grace never ends, His mercy never ceases. "His compassions fail not. They are new every morning: great is thy faithfulness" (Lamentations 3:22, 23).

**3. Is this an issue of (a) the friend being ungracious as opposed to God being gracious or (b) the friend reacting "normally" as opposed to God reacting in a way that is "better than normal"? What's the difference, or is there any real difference? Justify your answer.**

When we get to verses 11-13, alternative *b* will definitely be in view. But in verses 5-8, the answer is not so clear. One difference between the two sections is the hesitation we see on the part of the sleepy friend in verse 7 that we don't see on the part of the father in verses 11-13.

If we interpret the grumpy hesitation as ungraciousness, then we would tend to think alternative *a* to be true for verses 5-8. But if we see that kind of hesitation as more "normal" than "ungracious," then we would go for *b*. Perhaps Jesus is teaching *a* for verses 5-8 and *b* for verses 11-13 to cover all bases.

**4. Why do you think people fail to ask God?**

You may have met people who feel that they cannot ask God for anything until they have exhausted their own resources. God says just the opposite: ask for His help first! Some people feel they are too sinful to expect a response from God. If that were true, then no one could come to God. Some of us do not like to let go of control. When we ask God to take care of something, that means He will do it in His way!

**5. Was there ever a time when you "gave up" on prayer? What happened? How did you turn this around?**

Some of us have been hurt by what we considered to be unanswered prayer. So we gave up on asking God for anything. Biblically, we may understand that God answers prayer with *yes, no,* or *not yet.* But personally we find that the *no* and *not yet* answers hurt.

Yet sometimes we can look back and see God's wisdom in the *no* answers. For example, that relationship you prayed for never became a marriage, but the one you later met became a true soul mate. Or that healing that you prayed for but did not get taught you a new kind of grace and gave you a new depth of compassion.

The prophet Jeremiah—certainly no stranger to sorrow!—exclaimed, "When I cry and shout, he shutteth out my prayer," and "Thou hast covered thyself with a cloud, that our prayer should not pass through" (Lamentations 3:8, 44). Yet he still prayed. God did not show Jeremiah all the answers in his lifetime, and the same applies to us.

# Inspired to Trust

January 27
Lesson 9

DEVOTIONAL READING: **Psalm 31:1-5.**

BACKGROUND SCRIPTURE: **Luke 12:22-34.**

PRINTED TEXT: **Luke 12:22-34.**

### Luke 12:22-34

22 And he said unto his disciples, Therefore I say unto you, Take no thought for your life, what ye shall eat; neither for the body, what ye shall put on.

23 The life is more than meat, and the body is more than raiment.

24 Consider the ravens: for they neither sow nor reap; which neither have storehouse nor barn; and God feedeth them: how much more are ye better than the fowls?

25 And which of you with taking thought can add to his stature one cubit?

26 If ye then be not able to do that thing which is least, why take ye thought for the rest?

27 Consider the lilies how they grow: they toil not, they spin not; and yet I say unto you, that Solomon in all his glory was not arrayed like one of these.

28 If then God so clothe the grass, which is today in the field, and tomorrow is cast into the oven; how much more will he clothe you, O ye of little faith?

29 And seek not ye what ye shall eat, or what ye shall drink, neither be ye of doubtful mind.

30 For all these things do the nations of the world seek after: and your Father knoweth that ye have need of these things.

31 But rather seek ye the kingdom of God; and all these things shall be added unto you.

32 Fear not, little flock; for it is your Father's good pleasure to give you the kingdom.

33 Sell that ye have, and give alms; provide yourselves bags which wax not old, a treasure in the heavens that faileth not, where no thief approacheth, neither moth corrupteth.

34 For where your treasure is, there will your heart be also.

**Jan 27**

GOLDEN TEXT: Fear not, little flock; for it is your Father's good pleasure to give you the kingdom.—Luke 12:32.

## God's Call to the Christian Community

Unit 2: Inspired by God's Call

(Lessons 6-9)

## Lesson Aims

After participating in this lesson, each student will be able to:

1. Identify some physical and spiritual treasures listed in today's text.

2. Interpret what it means to receive the kingdom in light of his or her need to trust God.

3. Describe how he or she will trust God more fully for one of the items listed under Lesson Aim #1.

## Lesson Outline

INTRODUCTION

    A. Adornment or Burden?

    B. Lesson Background

 I. DON'T WORRY (Luke 12:22-26)

    A. What Not to Worry About (v. 22)

    B. Why Not to Worry (vv. 23, 24)

    C. Where Worry Doesn't Lead (vv. 25, 26)

    *Body Building*

 II. TRUST GOD (Luke 12:27-31)

    A. Simple Example (v. 27)

    B. Gracious God (v. 28)

    C. What the Pagans Do (vv. 29, 30)

    D. What You Should Do (v. 31)

III. DON'T FEAR (Luke 12:32-34)

    A. God's Pleasure (v. 32)

    B. Our Responsibility (v. 33)

    *No Thieves*

    C. End Result (v. 34)

CONCLUSION

    A. Physical Means, Spiritual End

    B. Prayer

    C. Thought to Remember

## Introduction

### A. Adornment or Burden?

Once upon a time there was a wealthy king. He sat in his palace on his throne of solid gold, dressed in the finest silk and furs, and wept. He wept because he didn't have a crown.

Oh, he had a plain little thing, of course. But it wasn't the kind of crown befitting a king of his stature. And so he set off on a journey to find the most exquisite jewels in the world in order to transform his plain crown into the grandest ever seen.

First his journey took him to Burma for the purest rubies. Once there, he piled hundreds of rubies onto his plain crown. Then he set his camel toward Russia. There the king acquired the finest emeralds, also heaping them onto his crown. Finally, he turned toward South Africa to find the largest diamond in the world.

The king's camel eventually brought him to the jeweler who could provide that diamond. The king's eyes lit up when he saw the enormous jewel. The end of his mission in sight, he balanced it on the very top of his bulging crown.

The king then proudly climbed onto his camel to set off for home, the king's neck straining under the weight of the fantastic headpiece. But once atop the poor beast, there was a swooshing sound as camel, king, and crown disappeared into the desert sands, never to be seen again. The adornment had become a fatal burden!

A nice children's fantasy, isn't it? But when we think of all the people today who sink under the burden of many worldly "adornments"—including the burdens of debt and worry—it may not be such a fantasy after all!

### B. Lesson Background

Our lesson text occurs within one of the major teaching sections in Luke's Gospel, namely Luke 12:1–13:21. It is set during Jesus' later Judean ministry. This particular teaching section follows a segment that notes increasing friction between Jewish leaders and Jesus.

Many Jewish religious leaders (Pharisees, scribes, etc.) had become very hostile toward Jesus. Just prior to today's text, Luke presents Jesus' teaching against some Pharisees (Luke 11:37-54). Jesus' main criticism was that they were hypocritical, having evil intent on the inside while posturing godliness on the outside (examples: Luke 11:39, 44).

Hypocrisy presents us with two problems. First, it is simply dishonest since it involves pretending to be something that one is not. Second, and worse, it assumes that God looks only on the surface when evaluating a person's activities. Thus after Jesus left the Pharisees (11:53), He warned His disciples to be wary of the leaven of the Pharisees, "which is hypocrisy" (12:1).

This transition is important to note because it is the basis of the theme throughout the section Luke 12:1–13:21. That is, Jesus' primary point throughout is for His disciples to grasp the difference between the present world and the Father's spiritual kingdom. If the disciples were capable of placing their values in the latter, then the temptations and "adornments" of the present world—which Jesus' enemies loved so much—would not shake them from their future with the Father.

Thus, the point is to not fear the threats or temptations of this world, because God has far greater power. In this way, Jesus prepared His disciples for the difficulties they would face as leaders of the church (Luke 12:11, 12). The Parable of the Rich Fool (12:13-21) also deals with attachments to this world. Today's lesson further develops this theme.

# I. Don't Worry
# (Luke 12:22-26)

## A. What Not to Worry About (v. 22)

**22. And he said unto his disciples, Therefore I say unto you, Take no thought for your life, what ye shall eat; neither for the body, what ye shall put on.**

The word *therefore* links our passage to the Parable of the Rich Fool in Luke 12:13-21. But Jesus now shifts the focus away from the desire to amass wealth and toward the general concern of having sufficient material possessions. This problem is more widespread than the one faced by the rich fool; we may not be inappropriately attached to wealth as such, but we likely have a strong attachment to a "regular" comfortable life.

The challenge to *take no thought for your life* is startling! Is Jesus speaking in an exaggerated way to achieve a shocking effect? Or does He mean precisely what He says? When our instinct is self-preservation, how can we *not* care for our own lives?

The parallel verse at Matthew 6:25 is helpful. Whereas Luke has recorded the verse before us right after the Parable of the Rich Fool, Matthew has recorded it directly after the teaching that a person cannot serve two masters. This is summarized as, "Ye cannot serve God and mammon" (Matthew 6:24). Obviously, Matthew and Luke see Jesus' idea the same way. The rich fool of

---

### How to Say It

CORINTHIANS. Ko-*rin*-thee-unz (*th* as in *thin*).

JUDEAN. Joo-*dee*-un.

PHARISEES. *Fair*-ih-seez.

PHILIPPIANS. Fih-*lip*-ee-unz.

SOLOMON. *Sol*-o-mun.

THESSALONIANS. *Thess*-uh-*lo*-nee-unz (strong accent on *lo; th* as in *thin*).

---

Luke 12:13-21 puts his material life above God. In Matthew 6:19-24, material well-being either rules in your life or God does; both cannot rule at the same time.

Thus in referring to one who takes *no thought for . . . life,* Jesus has in mind the kind of person who should prefer Heaven over earth. This is the true disciple. The question now becomes this: How we can embrace Jesus' command in a meaningful way? The challenge is to investigate our lives to figure out the nature of our attachments to this world. As we shall see, the issue is a matter of our salvation (compare John 12:25).

We may conclude that Jesus is not calling us to rid ourselves of earthly attachments altogether, but to rid ourselves of spiritually unhealthy ones. If we had "no attachments" to the material world in an absolute sense, we could not function! Thus, our challenge is to determine whether we are being spiritually honest in the way we approach our material possessions. (Such wrongheaded attachments not only involve stuff that we *already* own, but also things that we *want* to own.)

## B. Why Not to Worry (vv. 23, 24)

**23. The life is more than meat, and the body is more than raiment.**

When we focus on our material needs, we negate an important reality: the *life* of a true disciple extends beyond the physical to the eternal. The fact is, though, that we are a combination of both physical and spiritual. Thus Jesus does not say we should totally ignore food and clothes. These are important, but they deal only with the physical aspects of life. We are to see such things as physical means to spiritual ends. If we make them the point of life, then we subordinate our spiritual life to the physical (compare Philippians 3:19).

Paul argues in 1 Corinthians 6:19, 20; 7:23 that Christians must understand themselves to have chosen to relinquish "ownership" of their bodies. That is, with the blessing of salvation comes the sacrifice of our worldly interests. The body belongs to the Lord. To use the body to achieve worldly interests at the expense of spiritual ones is to reject Christ's sacrificial purchase of body and spirit. [See question #1, page 192.]

**24. Consider the ravens: for they neither sow nor reap; which neither have storehouse nor barn; and God feedeth them: how much more are ye better than the fowls?**

In the overall context of this teaching section, Jesus instructs the disciples how to live according to God's interests while still being in this world.

Because the world is hostile to God's interests (see John 15:18, 19), true disciples will experience a conflict of interests while living for Him on this fallen planet. Thus Jesus arms the disciples with a way to understand God. The ability to fend off the anxiety that leads us to latch onto this world's interests lies in appreciating how much God cares for us (see also Psalm 147:9).

### C. Where Worry Doesn't Lead (vv. 25, 26)

**25. And which of you with taking thought can add to his stature one cubit?**

This should be a no-brainer. The height *(stature)* that each of us ends up with as we approach adulthood is beyond our control. It is genetically programmed. Some try injections of human growth hormones to help their short children grow taller, but with very limited success. Even then, mere worry doesn't add to the child's height. So why should we worry about anything that's beyond our control? That is exactly Jesus' point!

#### BODY BUILDING

We live in a time when many are trying to alter their shape. Some want to increase their shape, most want to reduce it. I have a friend who is beginning to lift weights so that he can "bulk up" and show off some real muscle when he wears T-shirts in the summer.

On the other hand, I met a man recently who said that two years ago he weighed 538 pounds. After weight reduction surgery, he lost over 300 pounds. Diet fads are big business, and the public spends billions of dollars every year to try to lose weight.

While we may try to put on or lose weight, nothing practical can be done to increase one's height. Better nutrition over the last century has apparently increased average heights, but a person cannot "think" or even "work" himself or herself into a taller stature. So we repeat the point of the commentary: Why should we worry about anything that's beyond our control?    —J. B. N.

**26. If ye then be not able to do that thing which is least, why take ye thought for the rest?**

*That thing which is least* refers to the adding of stature of verse 25. The phrase *the rest* is probably a reference to "other concerns of this world." With these phrases, Jesus concludes the point from the previous verse: since anxiety does not work in terms of the issues of verses 24 and 25, why be anxious about anything else? How much better it is to focus on our eternal lives through service in the kingdom of God! Thus Jesus

continues to teach His disciples how to think of the eternal while living in the physical world.

## II. Trust God
## (Luke 12:27-31)

### A. Simple Example (v. 27)

**27. Consider the lilies how they grow: they toil not, they spin not; and yet I say unto you, that Solomon in all his glory was not arrayed like one of these.**

Jesus continues to make His same point. The splendor of *Solomon* is noted in 1 Kings 10:14-29 and the parallel account 2 Chronicles 9:13-28. The glory of what he created for himself does not compare with the glory that God creates in simple *lilies,* however. The importance of this fact is demonstrated in the next verse.

### B. Gracious God (v. 28)

**28. If then God so clothe the grass, which is today in the field, and tomorrow is cast into the oven; how much more will he clothe you, O ye of little faith?**

Anxiety is fruitless because it fails to grasp who God is and what we mean to Him. True disciples, therefore, are not anxious since they trust God to care for them.

Jesus simply says that we need only to consider God's ability to sustain the world around us to confirm God's ability to sustain us. Since He does sustain the world, and we are worth more than plants, then to be anxious is to forget God's love for us. The problem is that of having *little faith*. At its heart, this is an unwillingness to let go of this world and cling to God. [See question #2, page 192.]

### C. What the Pagans Do (vv. 29, 30)

**29. And seek not ye what ye shall eat, or what ye shall drink, neither be ye of doubtful mind.**

This verse summarizes the previous section, restating that we ought not to focus on things that give rise to anxiety. Jesus' statement here prepares the disciples to consider what they *should* concern themselves with (v. 31, below). We cannot allow ourselves to be anxious about even the small things of our physical lives, since this reveals a lack of trust in God.

**30. For all these things do the nations of the world seek after: and your Father knoweth that ye have need of these things.**

Jesus likens anxiety about daily needs to the things done by those who don't know God *(the nations of the world)*. He then contrasts that mind-set to reality: God does know what you need in order to live. We can trust that since God does know what we need, He is able to provide.

### D. What You Should Do (v. 31)

**31. But rather seek ye the kingdom of God; and all these things shall be added unto you.**

Up until now, Jesus has been telling us what to avoid doing. Now He reveals what we should do. This verse can be taken several ways, especially if read out of context. In context, the command to *seek ye the kingdom of God* is contrasted with the things that Jesus has been warning us about: material benefit and blessing.

If we busy our lives exclusively with physical concerns, we shift our attention away from that which is most important. In so doing, we risk our relationship with God. The point, though, is not about whether or not we get material needs, but on where we look for our values. When we look at the effort we put into life, is it spent securing spiritual blessings or material blessings?

We should also caution that Jesus is not teaching that true disciples will always have a guarantee of food and water. Faithful Christians die of starvation and thirst. This has been so since Jesus' time. Yet if God wants us to continue to live on this earth and serve His kingdom, then He will enable us to do so through His provision of life's necessities.

Kingdom-seeking is profoundly more important than worrying about material needs in any case. A lifestyle focused on God's kingdom does not place much value in the world's material concerns. This is an extremely difficult concept for those who live in materialistic, consumer-driven cultures. But this doesn't change what Jesus is saying; it just throws things into sharper contrast. [See question #3, page 192.]

## III. Don't Fear
## (Luke 12:32-34)

### A. God's Pleasure (v. 32)

**32. Fear not, little flock; for it is your Father's good pleasure to give you the kingdom.**

The hope of the future is brought to bear upon the concerns of the present. If we focus on God's promises for the future, then we are able to deal with problems in the present—problems that can prevent us from reaching that future reality. To live in anxiety is to fail to grasp who God is and how much we matter to Him.

If, however, we do grasp who God is and how much He loves us, then He is sure to give to us the kingdom. If we can embrace the truth of Jesus' teaching here, then we have all we need

Visual for Lesson 9

*Point to this visual as you introduce question #2 on page 192.*

to make the leap from a life governed by material concern to a life governed by our eternal membership in the kingdom of God. In doing so, we make sure of our salvation and participation in kingdom blessings.

### B. Our Responsibility (v. 33)

**33. Sell that ye have, and give alms; provide yourselves bags which wax not old, a treasure in the heavens that faileth not, where no thief approacheth, neither moth corrupteth.**

Jesus clarifies the underlying exhortation from the previous verses. We can summarize the verse in contemporary language: "Let go of this temporary world and grab hold of the eternal."

The idea of selling what we have is consistent with what Jesus teaches elsewhere (compare Luke 18:22). Jesus' ministry exhibits a concern for the material needs of the poor, and today it may be through our hands that their needs are met as we *give alms* (compare 1 John 3:17). This leads us to conclude that material needs are understood by Jesus to be basic to life. Continual effective living for God does require that basic needs be met. [See question #4, page 192.]

### No Thieves

The problems of modern urban living are hard to escape. In a city where I once lived, our home was burglarized twice. Several items of value were stolen, as well as personal items of little worth but of great nostalgic significance. I was very irritated that people had done this to us. I wished for a return to the olden days of trust and security, when a person's belongings were safe—days when people would never lock their houses.

But then I realized that perhaps those golden-olden days were not always so safe. Crime has always been a problem. This has been true whether in the year 1900, 1800, 1500, or earlier. In the days of the Roman Empire, many places simply were not safe—either for life or property. That's why Jesus could easily call attention to the issue.

But crime is not a problem in Heaven since there is no sin there. Neither are there any moth-eaten bags that fail to safeguard what they're intended to protect. If we know all this to be true, then why are we still so fascinated with our earthly possessions?     —J. B. N.

### C. End Result (v. 34)

**34. For where your treasure is, there will your heart be also.**

Here it is helpful to consider the comments made to the rich young ruler later in Luke 18:18-22. The man seems to be good disciple-material since he claims to have kept the law. The man asks how to have eternal life. Jesus replies that adherence to the external requirements of discipleship must be accompanied by releasing his attachment to material things. Ultimately, the man fails to have salvation because of an unspiritual attachment to earthly possessions.

Many today make the same error. What gives value to our behavior is the intention of our hearts. Being a "good" person, going to church, and praying do not count as acts of discipleship if they are products of a *heart* that is attached to the material world. Thus Jesus challenges the man: Are you a true disciple?

A disciple's inner life is oriented toward the interests of God's kingdom rather than material concerns. Our lesson concludes with this basic principle. Jesus stresses that attachment to the material world is not a small choice, but a matter of our own salvation. Both those who are and those who are not able to let go of material concerns know where their hearts lie. We should keep this in mind the next time we begin to fret over our pension plans, Social Security, IRAs, and 401(k)s! [See question #5, page 192.]

## Conclusion

### A. Physical Means, Spiritual End

One of the dangers we face when we discuss material issues is to think that Jesus' cautions apply only to the superwealthy, such as Donald Trump. Biblically, though, "rich" includes a certain mind-set. The "rich man" in the Bible is the one who relies on wealth more than on God. The modern Christian who lives in a prosperous Western democracy is certainly not immune from this danger!

We know that our lives shouldn't revolve around acquiring the latest car and the finest clothing. But how should we, as Christians, approach material interests? In a way, it would be easier to live in a hut and wear an old sack than to figure out how to have a three-bedroom home, two cars, and a closet full of nice clothes while not actually caring much for those possessions.

However, Jesus doesn't require us to run away from our lives, but to make choices daily that honor Him. We are faced with the challenge of working to provide for our daily needs (2 Thessalonians 3:10) without placing too much value on those things for which we work so hard.

So—how can we be members of an affluent culture without being wrapped up in our material possessions? Is it possible to see a house as a spiritual thing? Perhaps, if one fills it regularly with those who need a roof or a meal. Is it possible to "sell all" and live in a cave yet still be attached to the world? Perhaps, if you do so in order to call the world's attention to yourself and your piety. Only you and God can judge where your treasure really lies.

### B. Prayer

Our Father, You have given us so much. Help us use Your gifts for You. Help us to see how we can use finite things for eternal good. In Jesus' name we pray, amen.

### C. Thought to Remember

An eternal perspective
is the cure for materialism.

---

## Home Daily Bible Readings

**Monday, Jan. 21**—Trust God (Psalm 31:1-5)

**Tuesday, Jan. 22**—Valuable to God (Luke 12:22-24)

**Wednesday, Jan. 23**—Worry Won't Help! (Luke 12:25, 26)

**Thursday, Jan. 24**—Clothed by God (Luke 12:27, 28)

**Friday, Jan. 25**—God Knows Your Needs (Luke 12:29-31)

**Saturday, Jan. 26**—Receive the Kingdom (Luke 12:32-34)

**Sunday, Jan. 27**—Trust God, Not Princes (Psalm 146:1-7)

# Learning by Doing

*This page contains an alternative lesson plan emphasizing learning activities.*
*Classes desiring such student involvement will find these suggestions helpful.*

### Into the Lesson

As learners enter the classroom, give each a piece of paper with one of the following four words printed in large letters vertically on it: *WEALTH, WORRY, TREASURE,* and *TRUST.* Print these instructions on the top of each handout page: "Please make an acrostic out of the word listed below. You may choose to use the letters in the acrostic to begin a word, end a word, or serve as one of the other letters of a word. However, the words you choose for the acrostic should describe or define the word assigned."

Learners may begin the assignment immediately. However, be sure to allow latecomers a few minutes to build their acrostics at least partially. Then ask for volunteers to share one acrostic for each word. Make the transition to Bible study by telling the class that the four words you distributed point to key concepts in today's study. The principles behind them were contemporary when Jesus spoke of them, and they continue to speak to us today.

### Into the Word

Before class, affix seven pieces of poster board to the walls of your learning area. Each poster board is to have one of the following seven headings:

1. Thinking About Life (vv. 22, 23)
2. Raving About Ravens (v. 24)
3. Stretching Our Stature (vv. 25, 26)
4. Lilies and Kings (vv. 27, 28)
5. Pagan/National Goals (vv. 29-31)
6. Ahhh, Peace! (v. 32)
7. Sell? Really? (vv. 33, 34)

Depending on class size, appoint a study team or an individual for each poster. Give each team a marker for writing on its poster. (Make sure the posters are thick enough that the ink doesn't bleed through onto the wall.) You may also choose to give each team a photocopy of the lesson commentary of the verse or verses assigned to that team.

Ask the teams to study the assigned verses and commentary. The teams are to make notes on the posters of key points in their assigned texts. They should focus on applying Jesus' teaching to modern life.

After completing the project, each team or individual will explain its conclusions to the class. (A similar activity is included in the optional student book.)

### Into Life

Try to make time to do all three of the following activities. Each is unique and important in applying today's text. Depending on the size of your class, you may choose to use small groups. (Activities similar to #1 and #2 are also included in the optional student book.)

*Activity #1: Discussion Questions: Interpretations and Applications.* What does Luke 12 tell us about how Christians should approach material possessions? How can Christians "provide . . . bags which wax not old" (v. 33)? How can Christians exist in an affluent society without being wrapped up in material possessions?

Illustrate your answer to each question with a specific, real-life application. Also, give examples of Christians who are living these principles out daily.

*Activity #2: Getting Personal.* Ask each learner to reread today's text, looking for a word or phrase that stretches or challenges his or her life priorities or lifestyle. Ask learners to circle their words and phrases either mentally or physically. Then ask each person to jot his or her word or phrase on an index card, followed by a brief note about how he or she will try to be like the ideal expressed by the word or phrase.

*Activity #3: Looking Outward.* Tell your class that the principles about material possessions in this passage apply not only to individuals, but also to groups such as your class. Ask your learners to discuss class-project ideas that demonstrate material unselfishness.

As an example, mention the possibility of your class serving as a work crew to help someone in a way that costs the class money or material assets, not just time. This may involve handyman projects around someone's house or automobile maintenance.

List the ideas on the board as they are presented. You may wish to use a brainstorming format: not allowing discussion until after many ideas are offered. Then ask the class to decide on a project and appoint leaders to spearhead it.

# Let's Talk It Over

*The questions on this page are designed to promote discussion of the lesson by the class and to encourage application of the lesson Scriptures. The answers provided are only discussion starters. Let your class talk it over from there.*

**1. Why do some people obsess over things like fashion or cuisine? How can we help them see how foolish that is?**

If this life is all that we have, then there is really no compelling reason to choose an eternal, spiritual priority over an earthly priority. Putting the pleasures of the senses into a lower priority is coherent only if those pleasures will be replaced by something better. In fact, if there is no eternal life, then life's purpose is whatever you want it to be (1 Corinthians 15:32).

To serve the living God means that one's earthly life is but the opening chapter of an endless book. To write that chapter without any view of the subsequent chapters will yield a life of confusion, missed opportunities, and shallow infatuations. If, however, we appreciate the weight of eternity, then this life takes on a meaning that makes itself known only in light of the reality of Heaven.

**2. Why do you think some Christians worry, despite Jesus' promise that God will take care of us? How can we help lift one another out of his or her worries?**

Some try to justify worry, calling it "concern" or some such. Jesus is very clear, though: worry comes from a lack of faith. And faith means focusing on Jesus. When Peter started to walk on the water, he was successful until he took his eyes off of Jesus (Matthew 14:25-31). The same is true in our lives: when we keep our eyes fixed on Jesus, we have no reason to worry.

It may be impossible, though, to stop worrying solely through force of will. Most of us cannot simply decide, "I will not worry anymore." Successfully battling worry requires approaching the problem from different directions. Praying alleviates much worry, as we surrender problems to the one best able to deal with them. Study of Scripture, especially study of God's faithfulness to His people, can ease one's mind. Accountability to someone who can remind us of God's commands and God's commitment is valuable.

**3. How do you recognize those who seek the kingdom of God? How will others recognize you as someone who is seeking the kingdom of God?**

Someone who is seeking the kingdom of God makes a difference in lives. Sometimes we hear a concern expressed that "we can be so heavenly minded that we are no earthly good." That is impossible. Someone who is truly heavenly minded, someone who is seeking the kingdom of God, is showing God's love to others (see 1 John 4:20). Kingdom-seekers are difference-makers.

**4. How would you respond if someone at church suddenly sold everything she owned and gave the money to the poor? Why would you respond that way?**

For most of us, that kind of "hard core" obedience to Luke 12:33; 18:22 would be surprising—perhaps even alarming. Although there were certainly disciples who did just that during and after Jesus' time, context does not require that this be seen as a universal command to be taken in an absolute, literalistic sense.

What *is* universal is that Jesus has called and continues to call people to selfless generosity toward the poor. This involves sacrificial giving (Mark 12:43, 44). Surrendering the temporary blessings of this world to store up for the eternal treasures of Heaven is not foolish. It is the best investment a person can ever make.

**5. When you look at your own life, what tells you where your heart and your treasure are truly located?**

When measuring a life, three barometers are quite useful in determining where a person's heart is. The first is *time:* how do I spend it? The second indicator is *money:* again, how do I spend it? The third indicator is *talent* or *giftedness:* where do I focus my creativity?

None of these is fully indicative by itself. Nor is there only one right way to spend time, money, or talent. The mother devoting her life to a developmentally challenged child may be no less "heavenly treasured" than the missionary in the jungle. When we look at our own lives, though, we usually know whether we are spending time, money, and talent in the right way and for the right purpose. Through the study of God's Word and prayer, we can all determine where our treasure truly lies.

# Called to Labor

DEVOTIONAL READING: Psalm 78:1-4.

BACKGROUND SCRIPTURE: Luke 10:1-20.

PRINTED TEXT: Luke 10:1-12, 17-20.

### Luke 10:1-12, 17-20

1 After these things the Lord appointed other seventy also, and sent them two and two before his face into every city and place, whither he himself would come.

2 Therefore said he unto them, The harvest truly is great, but the laborers are few: pray ye therefore the Lord of the harvest, that he would send forth laborers into his harvest.

3 Go your ways: behold, I send you forth as lambs among wolves.

4 Carry neither purse, nor scrip, nor shoes: and salute no man by the way.

5 And into whatsoever house ye enter, first say, Peace be to this house.

6 And if the son of peace be there, your peace shall rest upon it: if not, it shall turn to you again.

7 And in the same house remain, eating and drinking such things as they give: for the laborer is worthy of his hire. Go not from house to house.

8 And into whatsoever city ye enter, and they receive you, eat such things as are set before you:

9 And heal the sick that are therein, and say unto them, The kingdom of God is come nigh unto you.

10 But into whatsoever city ye enter, and they receive you not, go your ways out into the streets of the same, and say,

11 Even the very dust of your city, which cleaveth on us, we do wipe off against you: notwithstanding, be ye sure of this, that the kingdom of God is come nigh unto you.

12 But I say unto you, that it shall be more tolerable in that day for Sodom, than for that city.

. . . . . . . . . . . .

17 And the seventy returned again with joy, saying, Lord, even the devils are subject unto us through thy name.

18 And he said unto them, I beheld Satan as lightning fall from heaven.

19 Behold, I give unto you power to tread on serpents and scorpions, and over all the power of the enemy; and nothing shall by any means hurt you.

20 Notwithstanding, in this rejoice not, that the spirits are subject unto you; but rather rejoice, because your names are written in heaven.

Feb
3

GOLDEN TEXT: Therefore said he unto them, The harvest truly is great,
but the laborers are few: pray ye therefore the Lord of the harvest,
that he would send forth laborers into his harvest.—Luke 10:2.

God's Call to the
Christian Community
Unit 3: Responding to God's Call
(Lessons 10-13)

## Lesson Aims

After participating in this lesson, each student will be able to:

1. Summarize the mission of the 70.

2. Compare and contrast Jesus' sending of the 70 with modern mission work.

3. Give greater support to the evangelistic and missionary efforts of his or her church in one specific way.

## Lesson Outline

INTRODUCTION
 A. Twenty-First Century Mission Strategy
 B. Lesson Background
 I. SENDING OF THE SEVENTY (Luke 10:1, 2)
 A. Preparing the Way for the Lord (v. 1)
 B. Working the Harvest for the Lord (v. 2)
 *Lost Harvest*
 II. TESTING OF THE SEVENTY (Luke 10:3-12)
 A. Traveling in Faith (vv. 3, 4)
 B. Partnering in Peace (vv. 5-7)
 C. Blessing When Received (vv. 8, 9)
 *Eat What Is Served*
 D. Denouncing When Rejected (vv. 10-12)
 III. REJOICING OF THE SEVENTY (Luke 10:17-20)
 A. Victory over Demons (v. 17)
 B. Victory over Satan (vv. 18-20)
CONCLUSION
 A. Experiencing God's Call to Service
 B. Prayer
 C. Thought to Remember

## Introduction

### A. Twenty-First Century Mission Strategy

The work of the church in the nineteenth and twentieth centuries was marked by a great interest in foreign missions. To be a missionary in that era often was a life commitment—a commitment to be trained for service, to leave one's home country, and to take up permanent residence in a foreign land.

The risky nature of these ventures was shown in the requirement of some missionary agencies for their people to take caskets with them when they went out. This was because of the high likelihood that they would die on the mission field. Yet there are many success stories from this era, and nations such as South Korea and the Philippines, as well as many African countries, were left with a permanent Christian witness.

Christian missionary endeavors boomed after World War II, as military veterans came home with a clear understanding of the need for the gospel in foreign lands. As new technology emerged, it was often incorporated into mission work. This included airplanes to reach remote regions and radio broadcasts to penetrate areas closed to missionaries. Later came computers to assist with Scripture translation as well as e-mail and Internet access.

When we speak of *missions* in a technical sense, we mean more than occasional or random opportunities to share the gospel. *Missions* is intentional, strategic, cross-cultural evangelism. It does not happen accidentally. Crossing cultural boundaries to bring the gospel to others requires planning.

One of the most dynamic developments in Christian missions in the last few years is the rise of short-term missionary trips. These have allowed Christians with little training or experience to travel abroad and engage people with the gospel. Admittedly, some short-term mission trips are more productive than others (as is also the case with long-term missions). But the short-term trips have brought a renewed excitement in many congregations concerning the need for worldwide evangelism. Some believers who would never be candidates for full-time mission work have experienced spiritual growth in ways that may not have happened otherwise.

Today's lesson is about a mission trip. It was *intentional*, because it came from Jesus' directives. It was *strategic* because it involved advance planning and sought to accomplish a larger goal. It may have been even a little *cross-cultural* in that the missionaries were going to places where they were not known. (We do not know if those whom Jesus sent out ventured into non-Jewish environments.)

We may be surprised, though, to realize that this was a short-term missions project. Perhaps some of these disciples became "career" missionaries at a later date, but probably most did not. Yet as is true with short-term missions today, the participants engaged in important tasks.

### B. Lesson Background

Luke 9:51 begins a new section of Luke's story of Jesus. Here we are told that, "When the time was come that he should be received up, [Jesus] steadfastly set his face to go to Jerusalem." So Jesus and His group departed from Galilee to visit the holy city.

Some commentators refer to this section (which extends from Luke 9:51 to 13:21) as "the later Judean ministry." Within it we find many great teachings of Jesus (example: The Good Samaritan, Luke 10:30-37) as well as His interactions with some interesting people (example: Mary and Martha, Luke 10:38-42).

As we know, it was in Jerusalem that Jesus fulfilled His earthly destiny: the cross. His arrival in the Jerusalem precincts to fulfill that vital part of God's plan (which would be His final trip to Jerusalem) did not happen until Luke 19:29, some 10 chapters later. At least part of the reason Jesus sent out the 70 disciples (Luke 10:1) was to prepare the way for that final trip.

Earlier, Jesus had initiated a similar "sending out" project that was limited to the 12 chosen disciples (Luke 9:1-6). They had been sent out with the authority to cast out demons, the power to heal diseases, and the responsibility of preaching the gospel. The word used to describe the act of sending in Luke 10:2 is related to the word *apostle*. Indeed, when they returned from their mission, the 12 were called *apostles*, for they had been sent out (Luke 9:10).

# I. Sending of the Seventy (Luke 10:1, 2)

## A. Preparing the Way for the Lord (v. 1)

**1. After these things the Lord appointed other seventy also, and sent them two and two before his face into every city and place, whither he himself would come.**

Occasionally, the Gospel accounts give us a glimpse of the fact that Jesus was accompanied by a large band of followers. Here we learn of at least 70 disciples, beyond the initial 12 apostles, whom Jesus chooses for special service.

The alert reader may notice that some English translations have 72 rather than 70, both here and at Luke 10:17. This is because both the numbers 70 and 72 are found in old copies of Luke.

Both 70 and 72 are significant numbers in the Bible. The number 70 is associated with God's timing in years (see Genesis 11:26; Daniel 9:2) and with the number of Israel's elders (Exodus 24:1). The number 72 is 12 multiplied by half a 12. The number 12 is significant because of the previous mission of the 12 in Luke 9:1-10.

There is more strategy involved here than first meets the eye. The large group of 70 is paired up and sent to specific places that Jesus plans to visit *(whither he himself would come)*. Thus they, in some sense, prepare those places for Jesus' arrival. [See question #1, page 200.]

## B. Working the Harvest for the Lord (v. 2)

**2. Therefore said he unto them, The harvest truly is great, but the laborers are few: pray ye therefore the Lord of the harvest, that he would send forth laborers into his harvest.**

*The harvest* is the multitude of potential believers who have not yet heard the good news about Jesus. The *Lord of the harvest* is not someone who controls who believes and who does not. Rather, He is God, to whom those who believe owe their allegiance.

The *laborers* are no more than that. They are not building their own empires or reputations. They are working for the Lord of the harvest, God, and bringing glory to Him (compare John 4:35). [See question #2, page 200.]

### LOST HARVEST

I once worked with a church located in the heartland of the American Midwest. While I was there, the senior minister told me a story that he had heard. It seems that a windmill salesman had passed through that farming area in the early part of the nineteenth century. This was long before the days of electrification, and windmills provided the power to draw the needed water. The windmill salesman was quite skilled; he took hundreds of orders.

Unfortunately, the factory he worked for could not produce enough windmills to keep up with his orders. So they fired him. Unwilling to make the adjustments necessary to meet demand, they

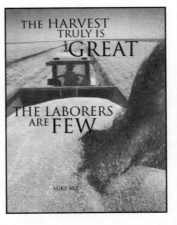

Visual for Lesson 10

*Point to this visual as you introduce question #2 on page 200.*

found it easier simply to get rid of the successful salesman who was putting such pressure upon their factory schedule. A great "harvest" thus was lost!

We chuckle at such shortsightedness. Couldn't the factory simply have added more workers, putting on a second shift? We may ask the same question about the church. Christ still needs messengers to convey the good news about His kingdom.                                    —J. B. N.

## II. Testing of the Seventy
## (Luke 10:3-12)

### A. Traveling in Faith (vv. 3, 4)

**3. Go your ways: behold, I send you forth as lambs among wolves.**

No missionary endeavor is without glitches. Such glitches cause participants to be tested in their patience and their faith. Jesus seems to be designing the mission of the 70 to ensure that such testing will take place.

The metaphor *lambs among wolves* indicates that the 70 will be people of peace thrown against violent opposition. Jesus does not raise up an army of warriors to do battle with physical weapons. They are defenseless in this respect.

**4. Carry neither purse, nor scrip, nor shoes: and salute no man by the way.**

A *purse* is a small leather bag to hold coins; thus the 70 are to go without money. A *scrip* is a larger shoulder bag, made of cloth or leather, that holds general traveling accessories, such as a change of undergarments. *Shoes* are probably sandals; Jesus prohibits any of the 70 from taking along an extra pair. They must travel light. [See question #3, page 200.]

To *salute* involves stopping and talking with a person going the opposite direction. The teams are to stick to their purpose and not dilly-dally along the way. Jesus gave similar instructions to the 12 apostles when He sent them out earlier (Luke 9:3; compare 2 Kings 4:29).

### B. Partnering in Peace (vv. 5-7)

**5, 6. And into whatsoever house ye enter, first say, Peace be to this house. And if the son of peace be there, your peace shall rest upon it: if not, it shall turn to you again.**

To say *Peace be to this house* is to offer a blessing (Hebrew *shalom*) upon a household. This means to ask for God's prosperity to rest upon the family in question. If the man of the house is a *son of peace,* a fellow "lamb" seeking God, then this blessing will *rest* on the household. If the householder rejects the team, however, there is

no harm done because the blessing will be withheld by God to *turn to you again.*

**7. And in the same house remain, eating and drinking such things as they give: for the laborer is worthy of his hire. Go not from house to house.**

The teams are to accept with graciousness whatever meals are provided. The idea that *the laborer is worthy of his hire* does not mean that if the home offers low quality food and drink, then that is all the laborers are worth. The quality of ministry is not measured by the level of compensation. Instead, the assumption is that those who minister should have their physical needs taken care of by those to whom they minister (compare 1 Corinthians 9:6-14; 1 Timothy 5:18).

The instruction *go not from house to house* is similar to the directive given to the 12 in Luke 9:4. "Staying put" will help eliminate the distraction of always seeking better accommodations.

### C. Blessing When Received (vv. 8, 9)

**8. And into whatsoever city ye enter, and they receive you, eat such things as are set before you.**

When accepting hospitality, we should be careful not to offend because of our personal pickiness (compare 1 Corinthians 10:27). What may seem unappetizing to you may be considered an expensive delicacy to others. Hospitality is a reciprocal relationship, involving courtesy on both sides. Ultimately we must trust God to provide our daily bread (Matthew 6:11, 25, 26).

### EAT WHAT IS SERVED

One health condition I have is a tendency for cholesterol buildup, even when the cholesterol numbers themselves are in the normal range. The result has been two experiences with angioplasty to open up some coronary arteries. A further result is that I am now on a diet restricted in saturated fats. I can live with it easily. I have lost some weight, and in general I feel fine.

However, I also go to East Europe each summer to teach some classes in a mission situation. To my dismay, I have discovered that most people in that area do not understand the meaning of the phrase *low-fat diet.* Sausage, cheese, and other foods high in cholesterol and saturated fats are standard fare.

So I have a dilemma. The people want to honor me as their guest, and they serve me their finest—things I should not eat. For me to refuse would be to insult them.

So I go ahead and eat. I try to be careful, but when a low-fat meal is not possible, I just indulge (moderately). I figure that I am in East Europe for the Lord's business, so the ball is in His court. If He can turn water into wine, He can turn saturated fat into fiber. One night I was served a five-layer torte. I mentally said, "Thank You, Jesus," and I ate it. See 1 Timothy 4:3-5.      —J. B. N.

**9. And heal the sick that are therein, and say unto them, The kingdom of God is come nigh unto you.**

As with the mission of the 12, the 70 are given power over disease (compare Luke 9:1). In the Jewish villages of Jesus' day, this is seen as a sign of God's visitation. This is most clearly demonstrated in the person of Jesus himself (see Luke 11:20), who plans to visit these villages.

### D. Denouncing When Rejected (vv. 10-12)

**10, 11. But into whatsoever city ye enter, and they receive you not, go your ways out into the streets of the same, and say, Even the very dust of your city, which cleaveth on us, we do wipe off against you: notwithstanding, be ye sure of this, that the kingdom of God is come nigh unto you.**

If a team is rejected *(receive you not)* by a village, that team is to waste no time there. Symbolically, the team members are to shake the *dust* of that place from their feet, indicating that they had received absolutely nothing from the residents (compare Acts 13:51; 18:6). In such a case, the arrival of *the kingdom of God* will not be good news because the villagers rejected the ministry of the 70. [See question #4, page 200.]

**12. But I say unto you, that it shall be more tolerable in that day for Sodom, than for that city.**

The ancient city of *Sodom* is infamous both for its immorality and for its lack of common hospitality (see Genesis 18:20, 21; 19:5; Ezekiel 16:49, 50). Jesus promises here that that vile city will receive more mercy on the Day of Judgment than the villages that reject the 70 and their mission! (Compare Matthew 10:15; 11:24.)

## III. Rejoicing of the Seventy (Luke 10:17-20)

### A. Victory over Demons (v. 17)

**17. And the seventy returned again with joy, saying, Lord, even the devils are subject unto us through thy name.**

This mission is for a limited time and includes a planned report-back session. This will be a time for the teams to share their experiences and relate them to Jesus as He continues to plan His itinerary in His travel toward Jerusalem.

Whatever the levels of success, the teams return *with joy.* They have received personal blessing from this experience. The thing that amazes them the most, though, is the reception they had received from *the devils* (demons) they had encountered. Those evil spirits had recognized the delegated authority of Jesus in the 70. The devils had been driven out.

### B. Victory over Satan (vv. 18-20)

**18. And he said unto them, I beheld Satan as lightning fall from heaven.**

Some see this verse as a reference to a prehistoric event, namely the rebellion of *Satan* in *heaven* and his expulsion to earth. However, this interpretation has more in common with John Milton's *Paradise Lost* than with the information we have in the Bible. The Bible has little information about the origin of Satan and his authority on earth (compare Job 1:6, 7; 2:1, 2; John 12:31; Revelation 12:8, 9).

Jesus' comment indicates that He sees the success of the 70 as a grave blow to the power of Satan. The prince of demons had been able to operate freely in some of the villages, but he is now being fenced in by the power of the coming kingdom of God. The claims of the gospel and the power of Jesus' name are always threats to the people and places controlled by Satan.

Many missionaries today experience unexpected spiritual resistance to their work. In such cases we must believe that the Holy Spirit is more powerful than evil spirits, which are controlled by Satan (compare Acts 13:6-12; 16:16-18).

**19, 20. Behold, I give unto you power to tread on serpents and scorpions, and over all the power of the enemy; and nothing shall by any means hurt you. Notwithstanding, in this rejoice not, that the spirits are subject unto you; but rather rejoice, because your names are written in heaven.**

The truth that Jesus' missionaries will be protected from the poison of snakebites is shown when Paul survives such an attack (Acts 28:3-6). This is not a blanket promise that those who preach the gospel will never suffer physical harm, even death. The history of missions is full of accounts of martyrs for the cause of Jesus.

---

### How to Say It

CORINTHIANS. Ko-*rin*-thee-unz (*th* as in *thin*).

EZEKIEL. Ee-*zeek*-ee-ul or Ee-*zeek*-yul.

JERUSALEM. Juh-*roo*-suh-lem.

SAMARITAN. Suh-*mare*-uh-tun.

SHALOM (Hebrew). shah-*lome*.

Ultimately, though, physical well-being is not of paramount importance. The greatest danger comes from God's authority to consign souls to Hell (Luke 12:5). When we are believers and thus assured that we are not headed for Hell, we truly can say in faith, "nothing can hurt me." Even in the times of greatest trial, we should find joy in knowing that our *names are written in heaven,* in the Lamb's book of life (Revelation 21:27). There is nothing Satan can do to take this away from us. [See question #5, page 200.]

# Conclusion

### A. Experiencing God's Call to Service

Experiencing and understanding God's call to service is one of the most perplexing issues facing church members. Most assume that "calls of God" are reserved for career preachers, missionaries, etc. Yet we are all called to be faithful and to serve God as the Bible teaches us. This is a universal call, and we should rejoice in it. The more specialized calls to ministry come to relatively few believers. This does not make them elite or specially privileged. It just means they are chosen by God for certain tasks.

I have spent a quarter of a century preparing people for the various ministries of the church. At the same time, I have preached in over 150 local churches. These experiences have caused me to observe two great tragedies.

First, I have found people in ministry positions who were never called by God to be in that ministry. This has caused them to doubt their vocation, act in a tentative manner, and generally cause damage to the people they work with. Ministry training alone does not make a minister.

Second, I have encountered Christians—some who were in their twilight years—who knew they were called by God into ministry *but did not respond to the call.* Such people may have been successful in business and may have lived rich, productive lives. But they have lived regretfully, knowing in their hearts that God intended them to be preachers or missionaries.

In counseling many people through the process of evaluating God's call to ministry, I have found two principles that seem always to apply. First, if God is calling you to ministry, the call does not go away. It is not a one-time invitation. It is not the stirring of the heart at an emotional moment that disappears after a good night's sleep. If God is calling you to be a missionary, for example, that desire will be etched on your heart until the day you die.

Second, if God is calling you to ministry, you will never be satisfied doing anything else. If you are called to be a preacher, circumstances may require you to take a job selling cars or delivering mail at particular points in your life. But you will not be happy doing just that. Your call will cause your heart to yearn for the ministry to which God has appointed you.

Participation in limited ministry experiences is a good way to explore a possible call to ministry. Many churches organize short-term mission trips. Have you ever considered going along on one of these? Such an experience may help you explore the possibility of God's call. Even if God is not calling you to be a career missionary, perhaps He intends that you become an annual mission-trip participant. Maybe He has some other plans for you. In all things, however, we should be guided by Scripture and open to the leading of God's Holy Spirit.

### B. Prayer

Lord of the harvest, many years have passed since Jesus sent out the 70, but not much has changed. We still see a great harvest of souls waiting, with few workers for it. We pray that You would raise up laborers to work the fields of the unsaved, whether in foreign countries, another city, our own neighborhood, or even in our own families. We pray that each of us will find a way to be part of this army of evangelists. We pray this expectantly, looking forward to Your blessing and our rewards in Heaven. We pray in the name of our master, Jesus Christ, amen.

### C. Thought to Remember

A few dedicated workers
can accomplish much for Jesus.

## Home Daily Bible Readings

**Monday, Jan. 28**—Instruct the Believers (Psalm 78:1-4)

**Tuesday, Jan. 29**—The Twelve on a Mission (Luke 9:1-10)

**Wednesday, Jan. 30**—The Seventy Go in Pairs (Luke 10:1-3)

**Thursday, Jan. 31**—Travel Lightly in Peace (Luke 10:4-7)

**Friday, Feb. 1**—Proclaim God's Kingdom (Luke 10:8-12)

**Saturday, Feb. 2**—They Returned with Joy (Luke 10:17-20)

**Sunday, Feb. 3**—See God's Work (Psalm 66:5-12)

# Learning by Doing

*This page contains an alternative lesson plan emphasizing learning activities.*
*Classes desiring such student involvement will find these suggestions helpful.*

## Into the Lesson

Read an account (or show a very brief video) of a missionary relating how he or she developed an interest in that area of Christian service. The best way to obtain such a testimony is probably via direct e-mail contact with a missionary. You may be able to obtain missionary e-mail addresses from your church office. Make the transition to Bible study by saying, "Today's lesson text shows us how Jesus called and trained missionaries during His time on earth."

*Alternative:* From the video *End of the Spear,* play the scene where the missionaries are killed. Make the transition to Bible study by saying, "Martyrdom is the ultimate sacrifice that a missionary may be called to make. Of course, there are also other sacrifices. When Jesus called disciples to a short-term mission trip, He cautioned about the sacrifices they would make."

## Into the Word

Tell your learners that they will teach portions of the lesson to the entire group. Four teams of 2 to 5 people each are ideal. For classes smaller than 8, double up the tasks; for classes larger than 20, assign the same task to more than one team. Each team is to answer questions about an assigned section of today's text and share its findings with the entire class.

Give each team enough copies of its assignments for each person to have a copy (see below) plus one photocopy of the lesson commentary on its assigned passage. Team 3 will also need a poster board and a marker. (This activity is also in the optional student book.)

*Team 1: The Two-Man Teams (v. 1).* 1. Why did Jesus send out the new missionaries in teams of two? 2. What value do you see in this team approach? 3. What does this model say to missionary endeavors today, if anything?

*Team 2: The Pep Talk (vv. 2-4):* 1. Why did Jesus use the metaphor, "Lambs among wolves"? 2. What does this metaphor teach missionaries today, if anything? 3. What was the purpose of traveling light? 4. Why did Jesus make the comment about not saluting anyone?

*Team 3: The Approach to the Villages (vv. 5-12):* 1. What general principles do you find that someone going to the mission field could apply today? (List these on the poster board.) 2. How would you rephrase this text to be instructions for twenty-first century missionaries?

*Team 4: Missionary Reports (vv. 17-20):* 1. Given that the reports of the missionaries implied a successful and encouraging trip, why do you think Jesus tempered their celebration by saying that they should focus on their eternal reward? 2. What is the meaning and modern application of Jesus' promise in verse 19?

Allow the teams to report their conclusions.

## Into Life

Before class, affix four poster boards to different walls of the room. Write one of these four headings on each poster: *Short-Term Mission Trips, Long-Term Missionaries, Community Outreach Strategies, My Personal Mission Field.* Assign a team to sit near each poster. Distribute these instructions:

*Short-Term Mission Trips Team*: Make two columns on your poster board. List in the first column the blessings of taking short-term mission trips. In the second column, list a few challenges of these trips. Be ready to share ways to encourage church members to participate in such trips.

*Long-Term Missionaries Team:* List the names of some missionaries supported by your church or mission board, or list the names of one or more famous missionaries of the past. Then list reasons why those mission works are (or were) important. (Note: This task requires a certain level of knowledge that not everyone in the class may have; you should assign members to the team with this fact in mind.)

*Community Outreach Strategies Team:* List some ways your church can reach individuals and families in your area with the good news of Jesus. Be ready to tell the class how and why the chosen strategies would be effective.

*My Personal Mission Field Team:* Each person in your group is to identify one person or group of persons he or she would like to introduce to Jesus. After each such identification, all other group members are to discuss various ways or approaches that could be successful.

Ask one person from the group to summarize his or her team's conclusions to the class.

# Let's Talk It Over

*The questions on this page are designed to promote discussion of the lesson by the class and to encourage application of the lesson Scriptures. The answers provided are only discussion starters. Let your class talk it over from there.*

**1. What is the value in conducting ministry in teams today?**

The book of Acts shows us frequent instances of kingdom workers laboring together in teams. Working in teams provides several benefits. One benefit is protection. This protection might be physical protection for those working in hostile environments. Working in teams also can provide protection against charges of moral impropriety if set up to do so. Teamwork establishes accountability.

People working together in teams can also provide encouragement to each other. One person going out alone to conduct visitation for the church may get cold feet and decide not to go. Knowing someone else is going along provides some much needed confidence. Working in teams also provides the chance for a person seasoned in the task of visitation to be a mentor to a novice.

**2. How can you and your church fulfill the prayer request of Jesus for more laborers?**

One of the best ways to pray in the will of God is to pray the prayers of Scripture. Christians who gather to share prayer concerns are often good at praying for physical needs while neglecting the most important need of all: the need for Jesus.

We can help answer a prayer for the Lord to send forth workers into the harvest field by being involved in the answer. We can be alert to those whom we feel might answer this call. We can encourage them as well as pray for them. And as we pray for new workers to be sent forth, we can also pray for those who are already laborers in the harvest field. This requires a personal knowledge of missionaries and their needs.

**3. How does living in a materialistic society hinder the work of the gospel of Christ?**

The things of the world are alluring, and Christians are not immune. Some may refuse to go on short-term mission trips unless they can "travel heavy," taking along their creature comforts. In one case, a young woman decided against going on such a trip because there wouldn't be any way to plug in her hair dryer!

The desire to "travel heavy" through life is to put personal comfort ahead of passionate commitment to bring people into the kingdom of God. A desire for the things of this world causes many to look for jobs that pay the most rather than for ministries that serve Christ. Sometimes young people who desire to go into Christian service are discouraged from doing so by parents or school counselors because they are told that they can make more money in other occupations. At times we would rather spend our money on bigger buildings for our worship comfort than on outreach to the lost.

**4. How should we respond when our message is not accepted?**

One thing we must be careful *not* to do is overstay our welcome. Sometimes what people may need is simply some time alone to process the message they have heard. In this we need not pester, but instead pray. Replacing a condemning spirit with a caring spirit is important.

Another thing we can do is keep our eyes open for a more opportune season. There are "seasons of the soul." These are times when people may be going through some tough situations, such as the death of a loved one, the loss of a job, or other life events that may make them more open to our caring concern. They may be more open to the message of Christ as we support them.

**5. In what ways have you rejoiced in right things? How have you made progress in this area over the years?**

We should be careful that our standards of rejoicing are those of God. We make a mistake if we rejoice simply in numbers, whether in church attendance or financial giving. Though numbers are important in that they demonstrate more souls, sometimes the desire for numbers may cause us to dilute the true teaching of the Word of God to achieve those numbers.

We do right to rejoice when our church buildings serve the purposes for which they were built. To be fascinated with beautiful buildings for other reasons is a mistake. This problem is not new; see Jeremiah 7:4; Mark 13:1, 2; John 11:48.

# Called to Repent

DEVOTIONAL READING: **Psalm 63:1-6.**

BACKGROUND SCRIPTURE: **Luke 13:1-9.**

PRINTED TEXT: **Luke 13:1-9.**

### Luke 13:1-9

1 There were present at that season some that told him of the Galileans, whose blood Pilate had mingled with their sacrifices.

2 And Jesus answering said unto them, Suppose ye that these Galileans were sinners above all the Galileans, because they suffered such things?

3 I tell you, Nay: but, except ye repent, ye shall all likewise perish.

4 Or those eighteen, upon whom the tower in Siloam fell, and slew them, think ye that they were sinners above all men that dwelt in Jerusalem?

5 I tell you, Nay: but, except ye repent, ye shall all likewise perish.

6 He spake also this parable; A certain man had a fig tree planted in his vineyard; and he came and sought fruit thereon, and found none.

7 Then said he unto the dresser of his vineyard, Behold, these three years I come seeking fruit on this fig tree, and find none: cut it down; why cumbereth it the ground?

8 And he answering said unto him, Lord, let it alone this year also, till I shall dig about it, and dung it:

9 And if it bear fruit, well: and if not, then after that thou shalt cut it down.

**Feb
10**

GOLDEN TEXT: I tell you, . . . except ye repent, ye shall all likewise perish.—Luke 13:3.

## God's Call to the Christian Community
### Unit 3: Responding to God's Call
#### (Lessons 10-13)

## Lesson Aims

After participating in this lesson, each student will be able to:

1. Tell what Jesus said about repentance in light of tragedy and the need to bear fruit.

2. Articulate the biblical connections between sin, repentance, and spiritual fruit.

3. Address one area of his or her life in which repentance and/or the bearing of more fruit is needed.

## Lesson Outline

INTRODUCTION
   A. Repentance in the Bible
   B. Lesson Background
I. SIN, TRAGEDY, AND REPENTANCE (Luke 13:1-5)
   A. Pilate and the Galileans (vv. 1-3)
   B. Siloamites and the Tower (vv. 4, 5)
     *Comparing Sins*
II. REPENTANCE, FRUIT, AND PATIENCE (Luke 13:6-9)
   A. Tree with No Fruit (v. 6)
   B. Owner and His Patience (vv. 7, 8)
   C. Fruit of Repentance (v. 9)
     *Expectations*
CONCLUSION
   A. The Causes of Tragedy
   B. Prayer
   C. Thought to Remember

## Introduction

### A. Repentance in the Bible

"If I have offended anyone by what I did, I'm sorry." In today's world, we often hear this type of apology. While this may be sincere, these words express no regret or remorse for the *actions* that offended. The only regret is that someone *was* offended. This is a far cry from apologizing by saying, "I'm sorry for what I did. It was wrong, and I regret my actions and the damage they have caused. Will you forgive me?" The difference between these two kinds of apologies is *repentance.*

Repentance is a major topic throughout the Bible. Sin is rebellion against God; it is disobedience to His will and commands. Because God is merciful, His primary reaction to our sin is not to punish immediately, but to call for repentance. A constant refrain of God's Old Testament prophets was, "Turn ye again now every one from his evil way, and from the evil of your doings" (Jeremiah 25:5).

A prayer of Solomon describes the first step in repentance: "We have sinned, and have done perversely, we have committed wickedness" (1 Kings 8:47). Repentance begins with recognition of sin. We should not assume that we can determine what is sin by our feelings. The Bible contains many clear statements as to what constitutes sinful behavior.

A second aspect of repentance is to experience a deep-seated sense of sorrow and regret for our sin. This is much more than regret at being caught or sorrow that comes as a result of disastrous sin. It is, rather, a soul-searching realization that our rebellious actions and attitudes constitute a slap in the face of our loving Father in Heaven. Paul describes this as sorrow "after a godly manner" (2 Corinthians 7:9).

A third aspect of repentance is replacing sinful actions with righteous actions. "If the wicked turn from his wickedness, and do that which is lawful and right, he shall live thereby" (Ezekiel 33:19). John the Baptist called this the fruit of repentance (Matthew 3:8). True repentance will have tangible results in our lives.

The New Testament uses two concepts to express the idea of repentance. The first is the idea of a change in thinking processes, a renewal of mind (see Romans 12:2). A second way of expressing the idea of repentance is to use the metaphor of the physical act of turning around. The principle is that we cannot be chasing sin and pursuing God at the same time. Paul expressed both of these ideas when he reported that the Gentiles had repented and turned to God (Acts 26:20).

In our world today, repentance seems to be a sadly lacking and increasingly rare commodity. Today's lesson gives us insights into the high level of importance that Jesus placed on repentance. As His followers, we should hear His words carefully.

### B. Lesson Background

Today's passage from Luke is set during what has been called "the later Judean ministry" of Jesus. Combining Luke 10:1–13:21 with John 7:11–10:39 will give us the fullest picture we can have of this particular facet of Jesus' work. The Gospels of Matthew and Mark do not record Jesus' work during this period.

A theme of Jesus in the two chapters immediately preceding Luke 13 is the need for spiritual preparedness. He taught the necessity for living lives of light, not darkness (Luke 11:35). He exhorted the crowds to realize that they could not hide sin from God (12:2, 3). He warned of the sin that could not be forgiven (12:10). He promised strength and words from the Holy Spirit in the time of trials before the religious authorities (12:11, 12). He illustrated the folly of a man who cared more for his wealth than for his soul (12:16-21). He instructed His followers to be ready for any coming crisis (12:35).

There is no more significant aspect to spiritual preparation than repentance. The fruitful spiritual life cannot be found without consistent self-examination and purging of sinful attitudes. We cannot love sin and God at the same time; He will not stand for it. God is a jealous God (Deuteronomy 4:24), one who will have nothing to do with the devotion of His people to fictitious gods.

Jesus understood the preaching of repentance to be at the core of His ministry (see Luke 5:32; 24:47). The thirteenth chapter of Luke contains important teaching on repentance. Here we find the words of our Savior on this matter, a man who needed no repentance because He was without sin.

# I. Sin, Tragedy, and Repentance (Luke 13:1-5)

When a great tragedy occurs, is it God's punishment for sin? Is catastrophe God's way of bringing people to repentance? These are two very different questions. The assumptions behind them are the focus of this section.

## A. Pilate and the Galileans (vv. 1-3)

**1. There were present at that season some that told him of the Galileans, whose blood Pilate had mingled with their sacrifices.**

The phrase *at that season* does not refer to the parts of the annual calendar such as spring or summer. It means, rather, "at that time." Thus this message comes from some of those who are accompanying Jesus on His way to Jerusalem (but they are not necessarily His disciples).

They relate the report of a recent atrocity in Jerusalem, where the Roman governor, Pontius *Pilate*, had slaughtered some Jewish *Galileans* within the sacrificial areas of the temple. Pilate is known to have little hesitation in using Roman military personnel to crush any resistance to his rule.

The incident is offensive in two ways. First, the brutality of a Roman massacre of Jews is a reminder of the fact that the Jews are not free; they are captives in their own land to the Roman overlords. Thus it is a political outrage. Second, the fact that the incident took place within the temple is a sacrilege, possibly involving the presence of Gentiles (the Roman soldiers who did the killing) in forbidden parts of the temple. Thus, it is also a religious outrage.

**2. And Jesus answering said unto them, Suppose ye that these Galileans were sinners above all the Galileans, because they suffered such things?**

Jesus responds by turning the focus from the perpetrator (Pilate) to the victims *(these Galileans)*. Jesus wants His listeners to consider why this incident happened. Were the victims more sinful than the general population, thus deserving of God's punishing wrath? Were the Romans being used as an instrument of God's justice? The issue thus ceases to be a political question. It is now a doctrinal question.

**3. I tell you, Nay: but, except ye repent, ye shall all likewise perish.**

Jesus answers His own question. He tells the audience that this is not a matter of the level of sinfulness found among the massacre victims. All men and women are sinners. All unrepentant sinners will eventually perish, for the only eternal reward for sin is death (Romans 6:23). [See question #1, page 208.]

## B. Siloamites and the Tower (vv. 4, 5)

**4. Or those eighteen, upon whom the tower in Siloam fell, and slew them, think ye that they were sinners above all men that dwelt in Jerusalem?**

Visual for Lesson 11

*Have this visual on display as you ask your learners about spiritual U-turns they have made.*

Jesus now moves to another incident: the collapse of a certain *tower* in *Jerusalem* that had killed 18 people. We have no other details about this tragedy. Some theorize that this tower was part of the wall of the city near the pool of *Siloam*. This pool is located about 600 yards south of the temple precincts in Jesus' day. Jesus' point is that the tower catastrophe was not God's way of punishing its victims.

The mention of Siloam brings out an interesting connection to the story of the man born blind that is found in John 9. This event is in the past as Jesus now speaks. Some in the crowd may know that this man was healed when he washed in the pool of Siloam (John 9:7). The disciples of Jesus thought this man's blindness was the result of sin (John 9:1, 2). Jesus did not accept their "sin causes blindness" conclusion there. And He does not tolerate the "sin causes catastrophe" argument here. [See question #2, page 208.]

**5. I tell you, Nay: but, except ye repent, ye shall all likewise perish.**

The language of this verse is identical to Jesus' statement in Luke 13:3, above. The point is the same: sin is not a comparison game where we attempt to point fingers at who is the worst. The need for repentance is universal. The alternative is eternal death. As Paul phrased it, "death reigned" (Romans 5:14) because of the widespread nature of unforgiven sin and unrepentant sinners. [See question #3, page 208.]

### COMPARING SINS

Humans seem to have such a knack for making biased comparisons and drawing self-justifying conclusions! The fictional Henry Higgins in *My Fair Lady* reveals this trait nicely when he sings, "Why Can't a Woman Be More Like a Man?" In the song he admits that men have their minor flaws, but when all is said and done, it is men who should be imitated by women and not the reverse.

That kind of comparison makes for a humorous movie script, but it is deadly when it evolves into a game of comparing sins. We all know of people who we think commit more sins than we do. The temptation is both to count their sins and to rank-order those sins (on a scale of *mild* to *horrible*). The end result of this comparison game is to conclude that we personally are "not really that bad." Won't God be gracious to us because we are such nice people?

Jesus' words confront those guilty of such smug self-satisfaction. Instead of self-justifying comparisons, we need the constant reminder to *repent*. We are all sinners. And the penalty for all

unrepented sin is eternal destruction. The best time to repent is always *now*.     —J. B. N.

## II. Repentance, Fruit, and Patience (Luke 13:6-9)

If personal tragedy and pain are not God's ways of punishing sin, then why do we suffer? Does God ever use our misfortunes to accomplish His purposes? These are the questions that Jesus now explores in His Parable of the Barren Fig Tree.

### A. Tree with No Fruit (v. 6)

**6. He spake also this parable; A certain man had a fig tree planted in his vineyard; and he came and sought fruit thereon, and found none.**

It may seem confusing to find *a fig tree* in a *vineyard* rather than an orchard, but we should not be surprised. Farmers in the ancient world plant several kinds of crops to guard against disaster if a single crop fails. Planting several crops also provides a variety of food for their own families.

The language here does not imply that the farmer himself *planted* the fig tree, but simply that he owned a vineyard where a fig tree had been planted, perhaps by a previous owner. This may be a single tree intended to produce figs for the farmer's family, whereas the surrounding grapevines produce grapes to be sold.

Vineyards are planted in patches of ground that are especially fertile. A fig tree will "use up" the ground where at least one grapevine (and perhaps more) can be cultivated. Thus, the farmer is anxious to gauge the productivity of his tree. We see this concern as he comes to seek *fruit thereon*.

### B. Owner and His Patience (vv. 7, 8)

**7. Then said he unto the dresser of his vineyard, Behold, these three years I come seeking fruit on this fig tree, and find none: cut it down; why cumbereth it the ground?**

A *dresser* is a hired laborer or servant charged with the care of the *vineyard*. His task is to maximize the field's productivity. As we will learn, he is well acquainted with the unproductive *fig tree* and has faith in its potential for bearing fruit.

Some who read this lesson will know far more about fruit trees than this lesson writer does! I can say this much, though. Flanking the entrance to my driveway are two apple trees, one on each side. They are of different (but unidentified) varieties. Some years they both produce fruit. Some years neither one produces fruit.

Some years the west tree produces fruit and the east tree doesn't (or vice versa). Why is this? I don't know.

When neither tree had more than a couple of apples in one particular year, I contemplated replacing them with ornamental cherry trees. I decided to wait, though, and the next year they each had a bumper crop. But to wait for *three years*? No way! After three years of no apples, I would declare them lost causes.

**8. And he answering said unto him, Lord, let it alone this year also, till I shall dig about it, and dung it.**

The one tending the vines and the tree (the "dresser") pleads for his tree. He offers to carefully *dig about it* (aerate the soil) and *dung it* (fertilize it). We are not told why, but we see something that can only be described as love in his care for the barren fig tree.

This imagery helps unfold the meaning of the parable. The owner of the vineyard and the tree is God himself, the Lord God of Israel. The barren fig tree is the nation of Israel; this reminds us of Isaiah's parable of the vineyard, which casts Israel as the field that produces an unacceptable crop (Isaiah 5:1-7). The one tending the tree is Jesus.

In context, the owner (God) had shown extraordinary patience with his unproductive tree (Israel), tolerating three years of failure. The standard procedure is to remove the tree after the second year of no fruit. But now the dresser (Jesus) pleads for a fourth year. He desperately hopes his tree (Israel) will begin to bear fruit that is pleasing to God (compare Luke 6:44). [See question #4, page 208.]

## C. Fruit of Repentance (v. 9)

**9. And if it bear fruit, well: and if not, then after that thou shalt cut it down.**

The owner agrees to give the tree one more year, one last chance. The stakes are high, though. If there is no *fruit* for a fourth straight year, the tree will be cut down. It will have little potential use except as firewood (compare Luke 3:9). Although fire is not mentioned here, Jesus' hearers know that this is the inevitable result for unproductive fruit trees.

In the Old Testament, Israel's lack of repentance resulted in the national disaster of the destruction of Jerusalem and the captivity in Babylon (see Zechariah 7:8-14). A second destruction, this one by the Romans, will occur in AD 70, only some 40 years after Jesus tells this parable. Sadly, the tree of Israel will indeed be cut down.

The application to individuals is obvious. There is no question but that God is incredibly patient with His unrepentant sons and daughters (compare Nehemiah 9:30). God wants all to come to repentance (2 Peter 3:9). God's *patience*, however, is not the same thing as *permanent tolerance*. God awaits our repentance. God watches for evidence (fruit) of our changed, repentant hearts. Yet at some point, at a time determined by God alone, this period of patience will end. This will seem sudden and unexpected to us, like a "thief in the night" (2 Peter 3:10). If we ignore repentance, we will not be ready for this "day of the Lord." [See question #5, page 208.]

### EXPECTATIONS

Figs are one of the earliest domesticated fruits. Secular records from about 2500 BC refer to figs, as do some of the earliest narratives of the Old Testament. The Spanish brought figs with them when they established a mission at San Diego in 1769. The most common variety of fig was called the *Mission* because of its association with the Spanish missions in California. More variety in figs eventually arrived, including the *Sari Lop*, from Smyrna, Turkey.

But early attempts to grow the Sari Lop in California were a failure. The trees, for some reason, did not produce. As a result, many of the trees were torn up and disposed of as worthless. But some people were not willing to give up on the newcomer. As later discovery proved, it was an issue of pollination. Once that was figured out, the Sari Lop trees were a great success in California (www.nafex.org/figs.htm).

We like reading success stories! But it is safe to assume that if the pollination issue could not

---

### How to Say It

BABYLON. *Bab*-uh-lun.

DEUTERONOMY. Due-ter-*ahn*-uh-me.

EZEKIEL. Ee-*zeek*-ee-ul or Ee-*zeek*-yul.

GALILEANS. Gal-uh-*lee*-unz.

ISAIAH. Eye-*zay*-uh.

JEREMIAH. Jair-uh-*my*-uh.

NEHEMIAH. *Nee*-huh-*my*-uh (strong accent on *my*).

PONTIUS PILATE. *Pon-shus* or *Pon*-ti-us *Pie*-lut.

SILOAM. Sigh-*lo*-um.

SILOAMITES. Sigh-*lo*-uh-mites.

SOLOMON. *Sol*-o-mun.

ZECHARIAH. *Zek*-uh-*rye*-uh (strong accent on *rye*).

have been resolved with the Sari Lop, then the patience of the orchard owners would have run out. A tree that bears no fruit is not worth the space it takes up in the orchard and is certainly not worth the caretaker's time. Does this warning sink in?     —J. B. N.

## Conclusion

### A. The Causes of Tragedy

Why do bad things happen to good people? Some may think that Christians should be entitled to a special, protective relationship with God that exempts us from personal pain and tragedy. Yet the people of Christ's church live with heartbreak on a continual basis. The joy of childbirth is changed into the grief of crib death. A family's normal existence is shattered by a drunk driver. Financial stability is lost due to unemployment. The list goes on.

A few years ago, a good friend's house was destroyed when a windstorm caused a tree in his neighbor's yard to fall on it. Fortunately, no one was hurt, but there was no way he could have foreseen or avoided this accident. He is a fine person, a leader in his church, a faithful husband, and a wonderful father. Why did this happen to his family?

When we evaluate such tragedies, there are two big mistakes we are likely to make. First, some believe that God causes such events as direct punishment for some type of hidden sin. Today's lesson is a rebuttal to this way of thinking. We are all sinners. If God were constantly punishing sin with tragic consequences, we should be suffering the unspeakable on a daily basis. To believe that God immediately punishes sin with

pain is to misunderstand His patient desire for us to repent.

Second, some think that God is unable to prevent our misfortunes and doesn't really care about our suffering. It is easy to feel abandoned when we are in the deepest abyss of sorrow or fear. But this also misunderstands the nature of God. God is sovereign, the master of the universe. Nothing is beyond His control. God is loving, the Father who sacrificed His own Son for us. He will not abandon us in the time of trial (see Deuteronomy 4:31).

In the end, we may not completely understand the *why* of tragedy, except to remember that we live in a sinful, rebellious, and imperfect world. There is no simple answer, because sin can have both direct and collateral damage to our lives.

Is it possible, however, to understand that God sometimes *uses* tragic events to bring people to repentance? Almost all people will eventually suffer in a way that rocks them to their emotional core. Will we respond by shaking our fist in anger at God? Or will we better understand our utter dependence on Him and turn our wayward hearts toward home? Will we accept the reality of life's pain and turn to the one who gives comfort and perfect peace (Isaiah 26:3)?

Yes, we cry when our friend dies because it hurts us deeply. But we must hold on to our eternal hope (Titus 1:2). We are to be in constant self-examination for those actions and attitudes that separate us from the one who will comfort us the most. This is the fruit of repentance.

The words of the prophet Joel are particularly eloquent for bringing this lesson to a close: "Rend your heart, and not your garments, and turn unto the Lord your God: for he is gracious and merciful, slow to anger, and of great kindness" (Joel 2:13).

### B. Prayer

Merciful Father, we confess our lack of repentance. We confess that there are areas in our lives that we have not totally allowed to come under Your control.

Most of all, we confess that Your patience with us is far more than we deserve. Your mercies are everlasting. Your steadfast love endures forever. Through Your power and presence, give us hearts of repentance and grant to us the capacity to produce fruit in our lives. We pray this in the name of the one who bore the guilt of our sins on the cross, Jesus Christ, amen.

### C. Thought to Remember

God awaits life-changing repentance.

## Home Daily Bible Readings

**Monday, Feb. 4**—My Soul Is Satisfied (Psalm 63:1-6)

**Tuesday, Feb. 5**—Turn from Your Ways (Matthew 3:1-6)

**Wednesday, Feb. 6**—Jesus Calls for Repentance (Mark 1:14, 15)

**Thursday, Feb. 7**—Repent or Perish (Luke 13:1-5)

**Friday, Feb. 8**—Bear Fruit of Repentance (Luke 13:6-9)

**Saturday, Feb. 9**—Paul Calls for Repentance (Acts 26:19-23)

**Sunday, Feb. 10**—Choose God's Way (Psalm 1)

# Learning by Doing

*This page contains an alternative lesson plan emphasizing learning activities.*
*Classes desiring such student involvement will find these suggestions helpful.*

## Into the Lesson

Give each of the first eight learners who arrive a letter-sized sheet of paper with one of the following words printed on it in bold lettering: *Except, ye, repent, ye, shall, all, likewise, perish.* Ask the learners to work together to unscramble the words to make a well-known Scripture statement. If necessary, they may look in Luke 13:1-9 to find these words.

Ask your learners to display the words by standing in front of the class in the correct order. Tell the class that this verse is part of the thrust of today's lesson. The lesson deals with two major issues: God's expectations of His followers and the problem of bad things happening to people thought to be good.

## Into the Word

*Activity #1.* Give each student an index card with one of these letters printed on it: *R, E, P, E, N, T.* Also write the word *repent* vertically down the center of the board.

Tell the class that together you will build an acrostic of this word. Give these directions: "For the letter you have received, identify a descriptive word in today's text that characterizes issues of repentance. The letter assigned to you may be any part of the word you choose. An example: You may use the word *sinners* for the letter *R.* Then be ready to tell why you selected that word." (For classes larger than six students, repeat the letters. A similar activity is found in the optional student book.)

As students report their chosen words, write the words on the board as part of the acrostic. Start by writing one word for each letter. After each letter has an associated word, go back and write additional words beside the appropriate letters. Be sure each student explains why he or she chose each word.

*Activity #2.* Early in the week, recruit two people to participate in research-and-report activities. The task of the learner delivering *report A* is to help the class understand the concept of *repentance.* The learner is to read ahead of time Luke 13:1-9 and a photocopy of the lesson Introduction. Then the learner is to prepare a brief presentation for the class. This presentation should use visuals to help the class grasp (1) the

different kinds of repentance found in everyday apologies and (2) the steps in the process of biblical repentance.

Introduce this segment of the lesson by telling your learners that the class needs some background on the word *repentance* as used in the Bible. Then allow your presenter to explain the results of the research.

*Activity #3.* The second learner you recruited (see above) will deliver *report B.* This report will help the class understand why bad things happen to people thought to be good. The learner doing this research is to read ahead of time Luke 13:1-9 and a photocopy of the lesson's Conclusion. Then he or she is to prepare visuals to help the class understand (1) the issue and (2) the big mistakes people often make in coming to grips with this issue.

Before *report B* is delivered, read aloud Jesus' statement in verses 1-4 from today's text. Explain that these words raise the question that some ask about why bad things happen to people thought to be good. After *report B,* you may wish to conclude this part of the lesson by asking class members to identify and pray for people who have experienced tragedies in their lives.

## Into Life

State: "Let's talk about bearing fruit and repentance. If the church is to bear fruit, where do you think our church does well? And where does it need to repent (change directions) and focus more of her energy?" You may wish to write these questions on the board. (Similar questions are included in the optional student book.)

While the class discusses the question, circulate throughout the room, distributing index cards. Say, "We will now focus on our personal lives. Each person is to identify an area of life where he or she feels a need to bear more fruit for the kingdom of God. Some ideas may include more time in service, winning a family member, or having a stronger testimony at work."

Ask your learners to write just one word on the top of the index card that will remind them of this need. Then they are to write a prayer thanking God for patience as they grow and for increased commitment to the task they have identified.

# Let's Talk It Over

*The questions on this page are designed to promote discussion of the lesson by the class and to encourage application of the lesson Scriptures. The answers provided are only discussion starters. Let your class talk it over from there.*

**1. What are some areas in which we as individuals need to repent? What about as a church? What will happen when we do?**

All of us have prideful habits in our lives that need correcting. Repentance has to happen for pride to give way to humility.

For some, the things of this world have become the driving force for living. To turn from these requires that we trust the promise of Scripture that when we seek first the kingdom of God, He will provide our needs (Matthew 6:33). As individuals and as the church, prejudice and racism may be sins that call for repentance. Gossip needs to be replaced with gracious speech. The list here is potentially quite long!

Remember that Jesus cursed a fig tree for failing to bear fruit (Mark 11:12-14, 20, 21). Jesus also threatened to remove the light of an unrepentant church (Revelation 2:4, 5).

**2. What is the danger of seeing all tragedies as direct punishments for sin? How do we correct this problem?**

At any one time, hurricanes, earthquakes, tornadoes, tsunamis, floods, and mudslides may be happening somewhere in the world. To see these as direct punishments from God for particular sins was the error of Job's friends. Natural disasters are a general result of Adam's sin.

It is arrogant for us to think we know the mind of God in all situations. When tragedies strike, infants, Christians, and unbelievers are all subject to harm. How are we to go about determining whom God is and is not punishing when that happens? Another danger is that we may begin to think that a lack of tragedy in our own lives indicates that we have no sin for which to be punished. In this case, pride can set in.

**3. What are we often tempted to do instead of repenting? How do we overcome this?**

Repentance concerns admission of sin in our lives. But sometimes we would rather not think of the things we do as sin. Therefore we come up with creative ways to avoid seeing ourselves as sinning.

Sometimes we try to justify the sin. That is, we come up with a good reason for why we did

something (compare 1 Samuel 15:12-21). At other times we blame others for the sins we commit (compare Exodus 32:22-24). Still other times we claim that we are victims of a misunderstanding.

We also may try to bargain with God and with ourselves, asserting that a relatively "minor" sin should not really be considered a sin. In other cases, we simply try to work our way back into favor with God instead of repenting. All of these approaches are inadequate to restore a broken relationship with the Father.

**4. What can we learn about the vinedresser (Jesus) that should serve as a model for us as we interact with those caught in lives of sin?**

The vinedresser had a heart of compassion and concern. As we deal with those caught in sin, we can demonstrate an attitude of love and care. The vinedresser asked the Lord of the vineyard for permission to work. We too can seek God as we work with those in sin. We do not approach them with our own strength, but in the power of the Lord.

We also can provide some "cultivation" in the life of the person for whom we have concern. This may include holding them accountable and offering holy alternatives. We can pray for them and with them, study God's Word together, and offer words of encouragement as ways to foster spiritual productivity.

**5. In what ways do you bear fruit to demonstrate that you truly have repented? Or is it prideful to point out your own fruit? Why, or why not?**

Repentance is not just something that is done in the heart and mind of the believer. Repentance is seen in outward actions. Scripture speaks of showing fruit that demonstrates repentance (Matthew 3:8; Luke 3:8). Some fruit is produced in private (Matthew 6:1-4); some is produced openly for all to see (Matthew 5:16).

If we commit a sin against a person, we can demonstrate repentance by going to that person and apologizing. If the sin against the other person has meant the loss of something belonging to him or her, we can make restitution (Exodus 22:1-4; Luke 19:10).

# Called to Be Humble

February 17
Lesson 12

DEVOTIONAL READING: **Psalm 25:1-10.**

BACKGROUND SCRIPTURE: **Luke 14:1-14.**

PRINTED TEXT: **Luke 14:1, 7-14.**

### Luke 14:1, 7-14

1 And it came to pass, as he went into the house of one of the chief Pharisees to eat bread on the sabbath day, that they watched him.

. . . . . . . . . . . .

7 And he put forth a parable to those which were bidden, when he marked how they chose out the chief rooms; saying unto them,

8 When thou art bidden of any man to a wedding, sit not down in the highest room; lest a more honorable man than thou be bidden of him;

9 And he that bade thee and him come and say to thee, Give this man place; and thou begin with shame to take the lowest room.

10 But when thou art bidden, go and sit down in the lowest room; that when he that bade thee cometh, he may say unto thee, Friend, go up higher: then shalt thou have worship in the presence of them that sit at meat with thee.

11 For whosoever exalteth himself shall be abased; and he that humbleth himself shall be exalted.

12 Then said he also to him that bade him, When thou makest a dinner or a supper, call not thy friends, nor thy brethren, neither thy kinsmen, nor thy rich neighbors; lest they also bid thee again, and a recompense be made thee.

13 But when thou makest a feast, call the poor, the maimed, the lame, the blind:

14 And thou shalt be blessed; for they cannot recompense thee: for thou shalt be recompensed at the resurrection of the just.

Feb
17

GOLDEN TEXT: For whosoever exalteth himself shall be abased; and he that humbleth himself shall be exalted.—Luke 14:11.

## God's Call to the Christian Community
### Unit 3: Responding to God's Call
(Lessons 10-13)

## Lesson Aims

After participating in this lesson, each student will be able to:

1. Identify the marks of humility and lack of humility in today's text.

2. Paraphrase Jesus' illustration of the banquet for the twenty-first century.

3. Make a plan to meet a need without expectation of repayment.

## Lesson Outline

INTRODUCTION
    A. Awarding Ourselves
    B. Lesson Background: Jesus' "Reputation"
    C. Lesson Background: Symbol and Shame
  I. HUMILITY THROUGH WATCHING JESUS (Luke 14:1)
 II. HUMILITY THROUGH CHOICE (Luke 14:7-11)
    A. Seeking Honor (vv. 7-9)
      *Pride and Place*
    B. Seeking Humility (vv. 10, 11)
III. HUMILITY THROUGH SERVICE (Luke 14:12-14)
    A. Self-Serving Banquet Host (v. 12)
    B. Other-Serving Banquet Host (vv. 13, 14)
      *Delayed Compensation*
CONCLUSION
    A. Lives of Service
    B. Prayer
    C. Thought to Remember

## Introduction

### A. Awarding Ourselves

Across the street from my office is a small business that started as a trophy shop. For years it supplied the community with bowling statuettes, trophies for Little League, and engraved paraphernalia for sports tournaments.

Recently, though, it has become an awards business, supplying companies with plaques, engraved paperweights, and other gear to be used as motivational tools for employees. This part of the business is based on the belief that ongoing praise for employee performance will result in higher levels of sales, service, and profits.

That this approach is often effective serves as a commentary on our world today. We have become a society that craves recognition and praise. We value being honored. This is not new or unusual. What is sad, though, is that this overshadows the satisfaction that comes from humble service to others.

One can rarely surf the channels of cable television these days without encountering some type of awards show. Awards are given by academies. Honors are bestowed by virtue of the people's choice. The voting is often controversial, and this just adds to the appeal of the show. Some wags think that we'll eventually see *The Awards Show Channel*, where those who like this type of programming will be able to watch it continually!

Our fascination with watching others receive awards is related to another strong trend in today's world: rewarding ourselves. One commercial for a builder of expensive houses says that we should purchase one of their homes "because life has its rewards." It is the oldest marketing trick in the book: getting us to believe that we *deserve* to be rewarded (or to reward ourselves).

Should Christians participate in this practice of self-indulgent rewarding? If we do good things and end up being recognized and honored, isn't that a positive thing? Are we less than whole if we are not praised? Today's text reveals the teachings of Jesus on this subject.

### B. Lesson Background: Jesus' "Reputation"

Luke 14 is set within a period of time that some call "the later Perean ministry" of Jesus. Luke 13:22–19:28 is the most comprehensive of the four Gospel accounts in documenting this period of time. In Luke 14, Jesus stopped for Sabbath-day dinner at the home of an unnamed Pharisee, an important religious leader in his community. As we read the chapter, we realize that this was not a simple matter of hospitality. The Pharisee and his comrades were testing Jesus.

Two years earlier, Jesus had challenged the Pharisees on two important points. First, He had been willing to share meals with people the Pharisees saw as unacceptable (see Luke 5:30). Second, Jesus had shown that laws regarding the keeping of Sabbath were not to be understood absolutely (see Luke 6:2). More recently, Jesus had denounced the practices of the Pharisees and other religious leaders in no uncertain terms (Luke 11:37-52).

As a result, the Pharisees began "to provoke him to speak of many things: laying wait for him, and seeking to catch something out of his mouth, that they might accuse him" (Luke 11:53, 54).

The Pharisees had labeled Him as a Sabbath-breaker, one who followed the Jewish law in a careless, casual manner (see Luke 13:14). In short, they saw Jesus as one who ran with a bad crowd and had no respect for the law.

### C. Lesson Background: Symbol and Shame

Two hallmarks of the ancient world are important for putting today's lesson in context. The first is the symbolic power of table fellowship. Today we might sit in a fast-food restaurant and "share" a meal with anyone who sits nearby. We don't know of their character, and we don't care. But for the Jews of Jesus' day, to eat with someone signified tacit approval of that person and his or her behavior.

By contrast, to refuse to eat with someone was a sign of disapproval and rejection of that person. Jesus' willingness to eat with some disreputable characters was both a source of consternation for the Pharisees and a sign of His acceptance of those people (see Luke 15:1, 2; 19:7).

Second, people in the ancient world were very mindful of the concept of *shame*. Today it is hard to find a person concerned about shame. The media parades shameless public leaders and celebrities in front of us daily. Many behaviors once thought shameful now pass as normal. The recognition received for outrageous public behavior is seen as a positive thing—"a good career move"—for some celebrities.

But in the tight-knit communities of Jesus' day, to be shamed had long-term consequences. If a shameful act were exposed, the shame would fall upon the entire family and perhaps upon an entire village (compare Matthew 1:19; Luke 13:17). To act purposely in a shameful manner was unthinkable. Avoidance of shame was every bit as strong a motivation as the quest for honor. This understanding of shame and honor is a key to understanding Jesus' Parable of the Wedding Banquet.

## I. Humility Through Watching Jesus (Luke 14:1)

**1. And it came to pass, as he went into the house of one of the chief Pharisees to eat bread on the sabbath day, that they watched him.**

The exact location of the event that is about to unfold is not specified. All we know for sure is that it occurs at the home *of one of the chief Pharisees*, probably a well-known leader and teacher (compare Luke 11:37). The Pharisees were a "lay" movement, meaning they all had other professions and did not make their living

from being Pharisees. Some lived in small, out-of-the-way places.

Jesus has been invited to this man's house for a *sabbath day*. This is a banquet-style meal with many guests. Luke lets the reader know that this meal is not intended to honor Jesus or to hear Him teach. It is a contrived situation where the Pharisees watch Jesus closely. In other words, they are testing Him in order to find a flaw. [See question #1, page 216.] This may be "payback" for the recent event where they had been shamed by Jesus (Luke 13:17 or John 10:22-39). But instead of finding an inconsistency in Jesus' words and actions, they are about to learn a powerful lesson in humility.

## II. Humility Through Choice (Luke 14:7-11)

### A. Seeking Honor (vv. 7-9)

**7. And he put forth a parable to those which were bidden, when he marked how they chose out the chief rooms; saying unto them.**

To choose *the chief rooms* speaks to the strict traditional codes when it comes to seating at such a banquet. The head of the household (in this case the chief Pharisee of v. 1) is the host; he takes a seat at the center of the head table.

The place of greatest honor is the seat that is at the host's right hand. The honor associated with other seats is in relationship to a seat's distance from the host. This is partly based on the assumption that the most important conversations and the best food are found in proximity to the host.

The Jews of Jesus' day do not really sit in chairs at a table as we do. They instead recline on low benches or couches around a table. They use their left arms to prop themselves up, thus freeing their right hands to take food from common bowls or platters. The places of least honor may not be around the table at all, but involve sitting on the floor.

The most foundational meaning of the word *parable* is "comparison." Here, Jesus does not tell a story-parable, but gives a comparison between the jockeying for position around the table and

---

### How to Say It

DEUTERONOMY. Due-ter-*ahn*-uh-me.
PEREAN. Peh-*ree*-un.
PHARISEES. *Fair*-ih-seez.
PHILIPPIANS. Fih-*lip*-ee-unz.
QUID PRO QUO. kwid-pro-*kwo*.

God's call in people's lives for humility in actions and service.

The guests have *rooms* in the sense of "room at the table," not as places of lodging. There must be some controversy over seating arrangements for Jesus to notice and make comments. Perhaps a guest of great honor has arrived unexpectedly and late, causing a chain reaction of demoting people to less honorable seats.

In any case, there is some type of scrambling for seats based on individual desire for respect (compare Matthew 23:6). Jesus seizes upon this mini-chaos as a teaching opportunity. [See question #2, page 216.]

**8. When thou art bidden of any man to a wedding, sit not down in the highest room; lest a more honorable man than thou be bidden of him.**

The host is master in his own home, and he has unquestioned authority to determine seating order. This is his opportunity to honor those whom he wants to honor and, perhaps, dishonor those whom he thinks are taking advantage of his hospitality. It undoubtedly will be embarrassing to be bumped from one of the most honorable seats! [See question #3, page 216.]

**9. And he that bade thee and him come and say to thee, Give this man place; and thou begin with shame to take the lowest room.**

Losing a seat of honor may involve more than just "going down a level." For example, if there were a banquet with 50 guests and the host determined that the guest in seat #3 did not deserve that much honor, it does not mean that that guest would be pushed down to seat #5 or #8. It may mean that that guest would be sent to the *lowest* place: seat #50—probably a seat on the floor. This would be a public indignity and an opportunity for laughter and derision from the more honored guests. It would be a moment of *shame* not quickly forgotten.

### PRIDE AND PLACE

The American Civil War provides numerous illustrations of human characteristics—some good, some bad, many somewhere in between. An interesting study in contrasts is that of the personal demeanors of Generals George A. Custer and Ulysses S. Grant.

Custer graduated from West Point in 1861 and was immediately sent off to war. He went through the ranks of second lieutenant to major general in less than four years. When he assumed command of his brigade in 1863, he was dressed in a showy uniform of black velveteen, gold braid from his elbow to his wrist, a blue sailor shirt with silver stars sewn on, and a red necktie. He was never accused of humility.

By contrast, General Grant was never accused of flamboyancy. Also a West Point graduate, he served in the Mexican War of 1846–1848, left the army, but came back in 1861. Victorious in several battles in the western theater, he came east in 1864 and ultimately forced Robert E. Lee to surrender in 1865. At the surrender, Grant wore the mud-splattered uniform of a private, with shoulder straps the only indication of his rank.

Custer dressed to impress; Grant (who later became president) cared only to succeed. Custer wanted to be noticed; Grant wanted only to win. If they both had been invited to a wedding banquet in the first century, one wonders who would have pushed up to the head table and who would have drifted to the back.     —J. B. N.

## B. Seeking Humility (vv. 10, 11)

**10. But when thou art bidden, go and sit down in the lowest room; that when he that bade thee cometh, he may say unto thee, Friend, go up higher: then shalt thou have worship in the presence of them that sit at meat with thee.**

Jesus presents an alternative scenario of being asked to move up from a common seat to a place of honor. Yet what Jesus is teaching is nothing new; see Proverbs 25:6, 7.

We may imagine a host looking around and seeing humble Bob in the corner, sitting on the floor. The host may think, "That Bob is a solid guy; he deserves better." He then calls Bob publicly to sit next to him, and thereby honors him in the eyes of everyone present. Rather than embarrassment and snickers from the other guests, they are thinking, "Bob is a lucky guy. I wish I were sitting where he is." They give *worship* to Bob in the sense of respect and honor.

**11. For whosoever exalteth himself shall be abased; and he that humbleth himself shall be exalted.**

Moses taught Israel that the one who exalts *himself* has done so by forgetting God (Deuteronomy 8:11-14). If praise and honor are rightly given to God, we have no right to take them upon ourselves. God will shame the one who seeks honor at God's expense (see Psalm 35:26).

The flip side of this is that God is not unmindful of people who live lives of intentional humility. There is no need to toot our own horn to get God's attention for our humble deeds of service (compare Matthew 23:12; Luke 18:14).

We may ask ourselves what it means to seek humility. Is this just a sick way of attempting to receive honor through self-abasement? No. True humility is not concerned with honor at all. No task is too degrading. No person is unimportant. No personal pleasure is so enticing that it cannot be postponed or lost. Service motivated by humility has its own rewards.

## III. Humility Through Service (Luke 14:12-14)

### A. Self-Serving Banquet Host (v. 12)

**12. Then said he also to him that bade him, When thou makest a dinner or a supper, call not thy friends, nor thy brethren, neither thy kinsmen, nor thy rich neighbors; lest they also bid thee again, and a recompense be made thee.**

Jesus now directs His attention to the banquet host, the unnamed chief Pharisee *(him that bade him).* Jesus draws the man's attention to four groups that are typical guests at social meals: *friends* (social peers, often those someone has grown up with), *brethren* (immediate family members), *kinsmen* (extended family members), and *rich neighbors* (those who may be able to offer financial benefits).

There is nothing inherently wrong with entertaining these people. Rather, Jesus finds fault with the motive for hospitality: the expectation of *recompense* (repayment of some type). Such a *dinner* is not a lavish social event given for the enjoyment of all who attend. It is, rather, a calculated attempt to obligate the attendees. In the future, they must bless the host in some way.

### B. Other-Serving Banquet Host (vv. 13, 14)

**13, 14. But when thou makest a feast, call the poor, the maimed, the lame, the blind: and thou shalt be blessed; for they cannot recompense thee: for thou shalt be recompensed at the resurrection of the just.**

Jesus now offers a markedly different foursome of potential guests for a private *feast.* Why not invite those who are seen as social misfits and outcasts? Why not make up the guest roster from the village's *poor, maimed, lame,* and *blind*?

No socially respectable person like the chief Pharisee would consider allowing such people into his banquet hall. If this were the entire guest list, then the host would even have to place a *poor* or *maimed* person in the place of honor at his right hand!

Jesus uses somewhat exaggerated language here to make a point. He is not saying that we can never feel right about having a family dinner unless we include some homeless people. His point is that we should not consider ourselves to be practicing true hospitality if we serve only

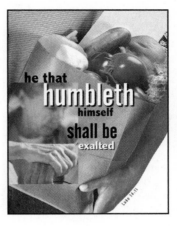

Visual for Lesson 12

*Use this visual as a discussion starter on ways to serve those who can't repay us.*

those who can return the favor. Service that is pleasing in God's eyes is service that helps those who cannot help us in return.

To do this is necessarily a humbling process. We are willingly acting as servants for those who may be many rungs beneath us on the social ladder. It is not a false humility, but a practical, legitimate humbling of oneself in favor of the needs of other people. It is to be judged by one thing: can those whom you are serving repay *(recompense)* you? Are you expecting to get some tangible benefit out of this act? Or are you willing to wait and meekly trust God to reward your selflessness? [See question #4, page 216.]

"You scratch my back, and I'll scratch yours" is a common ethic. The fancy term for this is *quid pro quo* (literally, "something for something"). In this way of doing business, there is no such thing as a gift without strings attached. The idea is that if I do something that benefits you, you can be sure that I will expect a benefit in return. [See question #5, page 216.]

While this may be a necessary part of the normal conduct of business, Jesus does not teach this to His disciples as a way to treat others. Is a man truly a generous host if he expects his generosity to be repaid? Is a woman actually practicing humility if she expects her service to be recognized and honored?

The Bible teaches that there will be reward and honor in Heaven (see Matthew 5:12; 6:20; 1 Peter 4) and hints that there will be levels of reward (Luke 19:11-19). We do not understand this fully, and we must caution ourselves to remember that we are not granted eternal life in Heaven on the basis of our works. However, we can take hope in the promise that God does not overlook our dedication to service and humility. He has plans to reward us appropriately at the *resurrection of the just.*

### DELAYED COMPENSATION

Frank Capra's 1946 film *It's a Wonderful Life* is a classic, often seen on TV during the Christmas season. It tells the story of George Bailey, who has given up his dreams in order to run the family-owned lending institution. When thousands of dollars are misplaced and his business is about to be shut down, George considers suicide because his life apparently has been so worthless.

Then Clarence, George's guardian angel, intervenes. Clarence shows him how the entire town would have been different in George's absence. Rather than being worthless, George's life has been a blessing to the town. One thing leads to another, and many friends give him money. Even the crusty bank examiner, moved by the town's love for George, puts his own money into the hat.

The fictional George Bailey was a selfless "giver." In the end he experienced a reward that he could not have imagined. Our heavenly Father is willing and able to reward us in the end. Any blessings we have been denied on earth will be compensated in ways that we surely cannot now imagine!                —J. B. N.

## Conclusion

### A. Lives of Service

Have you ever been surprised to find out that certain people have led secret lives of service? Have you ever noticed what unexpected things you learn at memorial services?

## Home Daily Bible Readings

**Monday, Feb. 11**—Prayer of Humility (Psalm 25:1-10)

**Tuesday, Feb. 12**—Jesus Heals on the Sabbath (Luke 14:1-6)

**Wednesday, Feb. 13**—Disgraced at a Banquet (Luke 14:7-9)

**Thursday, Feb. 14**—Exalted Though Humble (Luke 14:10, 11)

**Friday, Feb. 15**—The Guest List (Luke 14:12-14)

**Saturday, Feb. 16**—A Life of Humility (Ephesians 3:1-10)

**Sunday, Feb. 17**—Tending the Flock with Humility (1 Peter 5:1-5)

In my city I recently learned that the prominent owner of a car dealership had been taking one afternoon a week to read stories to critically ill patients at our children's hospital. He had done this for over 30 years. Another time I became aware that a coworker of mine, a single professional woman, had been funneling her money to needy college students. Over the years, she gave away thousands of dollars anonymously, even though her salary was minimal.

While visiting a certain church, I learned that its quiet but steady head usher had passed away that month. The preacher of the church told me that this man had faithfully come early every Sunday morning to turn on the furnace and warm up the building. He then had stayed to hand out bulletins to those entering the sanctuary. He was a very quiet, shy man, but he had found a way to serve without drawing attention to himself. He had done this for nearly 50 years.

Acts of generosity and service that are designed to garner public attention can do a great deal of good. However, Jesus teaches us that such behavior ultimately is self-serving, and we should not expect God to reward us for them. Nor should we expect to be rewarded by those we serve. Service driven by a humble spirit will persevere, even in the face of ingratitude. True, a thank you makes this path easier to travel, but even this reward should not be expected.

Our greatest example of a humble servant is Jesus himself. Paul tells us that before Jesus' incarnation, He shared equality with God the Father. Yet Jesus did not consider this something to be hoarded or protected. Instead, Paul writes, Jesus assumed a human likeness, the form of a servant. Although a rightful king, Jesus humbled himself and went to the cross obediently, taking on the sins of the world as a sacrifice (Philippians 2:5-8). The result of this is God's exaltation of Jesus above all others (Philippians 2:9). Although we will not be exalted in this way, God promises to reward us too—if we choose the life of a humble servant.

### B. Prayer

Lord, give us hearts that seek to serve without a desire for honor or recognition. Give us hearts that are satisfied with the pleasures of doing Your will and receiving praise from You. Give us hearts that are humble and pliable to Your will. We pray this in the name of the great servant, Jesus, Your Son, amen.

### C. Thought to Remember

God honors humble service.

# Learning by Doing

*This page contains an alternative lesson plan emphasizing learning activities. Classes desiring such student involvement will find these suggestions helpful.*

## Into the Lesson

Before class prepare the front and back of four poster boards. On the front side, each poster board will have identical headings over three columns. Over the first column on each write *Chosen last (or nearly last) for . . .* Over each of the second columns write *Why?* Over each of the third columns write *I Felt . . . .* Write one each of these headings on the backs of the posters: *Practicing Humility at Church, Practicing Humility at Home, Practicing Humility at Work, Practicing Humility in the Community.*

When you are finished, each poster will read the same on the front, but differently on the back. Affix the posters to the wall. Be sure to place them far enough apart to allow several people to view and work on the posters simultaneously. Large classes may need more poster boards, in multiples of the four described.

As learners enter the room, hand each a marker. Encourage each person to write one answer in each of the three columns. Each learner is to identify an activity from childhood for which he or she was chosen last (or nearly last) and the associated feelings. (A similar activity is included in the optional student book.)

To begin the class, review a few of the remarks listed on the posters. Then tell the class it is natural not to want to be last. There is prestige and honor in being chosen first. Even in adult years, we desire the honor of being seated at "the head table." Jesus, however, uses this instinct to teach a lesson in how He prefers us to behave and how to think of others.

## Into the Word

Deliver a brief lecture from the Lesson Background. Outline your mini-lecture in the following way:

I. The Context
II. The Symbolic Power of the Table
III. The Sense of Shame and Honor

You may wish to write this outline on the board as you speak.

Next, read today's printed text aloud before asking the following questions. 1. What character trait is Jesus teaching us for 2008? *(expected answer: humility).* 2. What is humility? Define or describe it. 3. What behavior does humility often inspire in life? *(expected answer: service).* 4. If we were to throw a banquet like Jesus described in verse 13, whom would we invite, and how could we fulfill Jesus' wishes literally? *(if needed, give an example of a banquet for nursing home residents who seldom get out; rent vehicles capable of transporting the handicapped).* 5. Why do you think humility is important? 6. Why does Jesus encourage this trait and behavior?

## Into Life

Ask your class to think back to a Christian memorial service or funeral service. What specific traits and behaviors were mentioned about the deceased? What stories or testimonials do you remember from the memorial services?

List on the board the traits or behaviors mentioned by class members. If your learners need an example, tell the story from the lesson Conclusion of the quiet, shy man who served by faithfully coming to church early every Sunday to warm up the building and hand out bulletins. This life of service was remembered after he died.

After listing these traits and behaviors, ask learners to recall how often service to other people, the community, and the Lord are mentioned and valued at Christian funerals and memorial services. We as the Lord's people value what He values. Worldly measures of success are seldom mentioned at Christian funerals and memorials.

Next, turn over the four poster boards used in the Into the Lesson segment and reaffix them to the wall. Ask class members to move among the posters, writing practical ideas for demonstrating humility in each context. For example, "parking at the very back of the church parking lot" is an act of humility because it allows others to park closer to the door. (A similar activity is included in the optional student book.)

Quickly review a few of the ideas written on the posters. Then ask each learner to select something on the lists that he or she has seldom or never done before and commit to doing it. To conclude the lesson, ask the class members to do a "neighbor nudge" and share what they have chosen to do to demonstrate humility this week. Ask your learners to form pairs to pray for one another in closing.

# Let's Talk It Over

*The questions on this page are designed to promote discussion of the lesson by the class and to encourage application of the lesson Scriptures. The answers provided are only discussion starters. Let your class talk it over from there.*

**1. In what ways are people watching us as Christians? Why are they watching? How do you conduct yourself with these realizations in mind?**

The old question is, "If you were accused of being a Christian, would there be enough evidence to convict you?" Those who may be deciding whether to make a decision to follow Christ may watch Christians to see what difference Christianity is really making in their lives. Skeptics may watch in the hopes of catching us in a failure.

All may watch to see how we respond when we go through trials and hard times. They are looking to see if our responses to these situations in life are consistent with the faith we profess. Faith that falters in these times is not faith worth emulating.

**2. In what ways have you been guilty of jockeying for position at work and at church? How have you made progress in correcting this problem?**

One of the ways we set up "the chief rooms" for ourselves is by putting others down. We can heap praise on some to curry their favor, especially if the person is of "higher standing."

We jockey for position in the church by desiring the more upfront and visible roles, rejecting roles that require behind-the-scenes service. The solution begins with remembering that God knows our motives.

**3. What are some ways that higher and lower seats present themselves in modern culture? Do you find it harder to take the lower seat instead of the higher seat? Why, or why not?**

There are many kinds of higher and lower seats in modern culture. We may think in terms of preferred parking spaces (even at church). Think also of first-class airline seats, box seats at ball games, and preferred seating at concerts. We often have it within our power to gain better seating through the expenditure of extra money. Ostentatious displays in this regard announce to the world that we've "arrived."

Pride motivates us to want more and better things, including positions for self. Voluntarily taking the lower seat requires humility. But the world sees humility as a sign of weakness. We don't often praise and reward those who are willing to descend the ladder of success, only those who climb it. We also don't like the lower seat because it is often inconvenient.

Try this: the next time your church has a potluck, make a point of being last to go through the serving line. The people you meet who also are at the end of that line may be the most spiritually mature people you will ever talk with!

**4. What are some practical ways we can care for the poor and needy? What cautions are we to be aware of?**

Giving money directly to a poor person is rarely a good idea. It is better to give the person what he or she actually needs. So instead of giving money to buy food, give the food itself. A benevolence program that is well thought out and "intentional" is better than a stopgap program that is improvised as needs arise. See cautions in 2 Thessalonians 3:10 and 1 Timothy 5:3-11.

Remember that the reason we give is to benefit the person who is in need, not to be recompensed later somehow. Giving to meet needs may have to be sacrificial at times; this will involve giving more than mere leftovers and hand-me-downs. Also, some giving may be in terms of time and demonstration of genuine concern.

**5. How can we guard against seeking *quid pro quo* in our lives or in the church?**

Many do good deeds in anticipation of receiving the same treatment in return. Yet we do not like to see this in the world of politics. We abhor political cronyism. But the same thing can happen in the workplace, in families, and in the church.

Churches can be guilty of trying to attract influential people for what they can bring in terms of money or influence (compare James 2:1-7). Church-planting strategies have, at times, been directed toward the more economically advanced areas because of the financial considerations. Sometimes there have been those who wanted positions in the church, so they catered to wishes of others for the purpose of garnering votes for this position. The solution to this problem begins with confession of wrong motives.

# Called to Be a Disciple

Devotional Reading: Psalm 139:1-6.

Background Scripture: Luke 14:25-33.

Printed Text: Luke 14:25-33.

### Luke 14:25-33

25 And there went great multitudes with him: and he turned, and said unto them,

26 If any man come to me, and hate not his father, and mother, and wife, and children, and brethren, and sisters, yea, and his own life also, he cannot be my disciple.

27 And whosoever doth not bear his cross, and come after me, cannot be my disciple.

28 For which of you, intending to build a tower, sitteth not down first, and counteth the cost, whether he have sufficient to finish it?

29 Lest haply, after he hath laid the foundation, and is not able to finish it, all that behold it begin to mock him,

30 Saying, This man began to build, and was not able to finish.

31 Or what king, going to make war against another king, sitteth not down first, and consulteth whether he be able with ten thousand to meet him that cometh against him with twenty thousand?

32 Or else, while the other is yet a great way off, he sendeth an ambassage, and desireth conditions of peace.

33 So likewise, whosoever he be of you that forsaketh not all that he hath, he cannot be my disciple.

Golden Text: Whosoever doth not bear his cross, and come after me, cannot be my disciple.—Luke 14:27.

## God's Call to the Christian Community
### Unit 3: Responding to God's Call
#### (Lessons 10-13)

## Lesson Aims

After participating in this lesson, each student should:

1. Identify some marks of disciples that set them apart from non-disciples.

2. Compare and contrast the cost of discipleship in the first century with the cost in the twenty-first century.

3. Give up one habit, belief, or possession that is distracting him or her from full discipleship.

## Lesson Outline

INTRODUCTION
   A. Leaders and Followers
   B. Lesson Background
  I. COMMITTING OUR ESSENTIALS (Luke 14:25-27)
   A. Our Relationships (vv. 25, 26)
     *Family or Discipleship?*
   B. Our Freedom (v. 27)
 II. ESTIMATING THE EXPENSE (Luke 14:28-33)
   A. Completing a Project (vv. 28-30)
   B. Winning a War (vv. 31, 32)
   C. Living a Life of Discipleship (v. 33)
     *Cost and Benefit Analysis*
CONCLUSION
   A. The Cost of Discipleship
   B. Prayer
   C. Thought to Remember

## Introduction

### A. Leaders and Followers

"Lead, follow, or get out of the way!" That old slogan may seem trite, but it is based on a great truth in organizations: many people are neither leaders nor followers. They are uncommitted, uninvolved, and disinterested in the success of the institution. Sadly, this is true in many churches. Churches may have qualified leaders, but not enough committed followers to move forward.

The leader-follower relationship requires two elements. First, there must be a leader, the one in front. Second, there must be a follower, someone not in front, but moving in the same direction as the leader. This simple model means that *following* describes a relationship of subservience.

Followers yield themselves to the direction of the leader. It also means that following requires a living relationship. We do not talk about one rock following the lead of another rock in a rock garden. If nothing is moving, then there is no leader-follower relationship.

A central demand of Christianity is that we be followers of Jesus. This does not imply that we are on some kind of group tour. And it is much more than being a member of a certain family. To follow Jesus is an individual, personal choice. It is both a life commitment and a daily decision.

Because Jesus is not a physical presence in our lives, following Him is an act of faith. We believe in Him; therefore we follow Him. To do this is to acknowledge Him as our Lord and Master. To follow Jesus is to be His disciple. Jesus leads us all. We in the church submit ourselves to the lordship of Jesus. It is His church—He paid for it with His blood (1 Corinthians 6:20).

But Jesus also calls some in the church to act as leaders on His behalf. Effective, vibrant churches have committed leaders and followers. Ineffective churches have a large percentage of bystanders, those who choose neither to lead nor to follow. Such churches become like the rock garden. They may have people in place, but nothing ever changes. No progress is ever made.

This is why *discipleship* is such a crucial issue for the church. The church is to be made up of followers (disciples) of Jesus. They are committed to making more disciples. To do this is to carry out the Great Commission of Matthew 28:19, 20.

### B. Lesson Background

Church folks are very familiar with the term *disciple*. When we study the New Testament, we quickly encounter the disciples of Jesus. Some of these are later described as *apostles*, and their names are familiar to us: Peter, John, Andrew, etc. It is easy to assume, therefore, that *disciple* is the title of some type of specially qualified follower of Jesus.

To go no further than this is to misunderstand who a disciple was in the world of Jesus. In Jesus' day, the term *disciple* was drawn from the type of educational system they practiced. A disciple was simply the student of a chosen teacher. The teacher in Jesus' Jewish world was known as a *rabbi*. In the New Testament, this term is used many times as a title for Jesus (example: John 3:2). A rabbi had students who followed him and learned from him.

There were other traveling rabbis (teachers) at that time besides Jesus. John the Baptist was also called *rabbi* and had disciples (John 3:26; compare Matthew 9:14). The *King James Version* often renders words for teacher or rabbi as "master" (see Matthew 10:24). This reflects an older usage in English, a time when a teacher might be called a schoolmaster.

There is a question as to who chose the disciples in the ancient world. Some believe that disciples were hand-selected by the teacher (that is, "by invitation only"). Others think that potential disciples attached themselves to a teacher by mutual agreement, but that the initial contact was made by the student.

Both ways probably were used. Paul was sent at a young age to study under the famous Jerusalem rabbi Gamaliel (Acts 22:3). This was probably the result of Paul's father's choice and Gamaliel's agreement.

While this relationship existed, Paul was Gamaliel's disciple. The Gospels show Jesus inviting individuals to discipleship with the simple call, "Follow me" (example: Luke 5:27). We also see a time when disciples of Jesus were offended by His message and chose to follow Him no longer, thus ending the teacher-disciple relationship (see John 6:66).

Luke 14 is part of Jesus' "later Perean ministry." The chapter opens with a challenge to Jesus for healing a man on the Sabbath. Such incidents became occasions for Jesus to give instructions to His disciples and to the crowds. In today's lesson, Jesus addresses the crowds with teachings on the nature of discipleship.

# I. Committing Our Essentials
## (Luke 14:25-27)
### A. Our Relationships (vv. 25, 26)

**25. And there went great multitudes with him: and he turned, and he said unto them.**

Here we see that the traveling group is more than just Jesus and His original 12 disciples. To be *with him* does not necessarily mean these are all followers of Jesus. Yet that does not prevent Jesus from seizing the opportunity to do a little teaching.

In the verses that follow, Jesus begins His teaching by noting two conditions for following Him. According to Jesus, failure to meet either one of these conditions means that a potential follower "cannot be my disciple." [See question #1, page 224.]

**26. If any man come to me, and hate not his father, and mother, and wife, and children, and brethren, and sisters, yea, and his own life also, he cannot be my disciple.**

This seems to be a very hard saying. Is Jesus truly, literally commanding His disciples to *hate* their closest family members? Is a follower of Jesus required to despise one's *own life* in a very literal sense as well?

A key to understanding today's lesson is to appreciate a practice in speaking and writing known as *hyperbole*. Hyperbole is a technique widely used in the ancient world. It is still used often today. Hyperbole is defined as "deliberate exaggeration for the purpose of emphasis." Therefore, hyperbole should not be taken literally.

For example, one may say, "He talks on his cell phone constantly." We would not understand this to mean, "He uses his cell phone every second of every day." What this means is, "He uses his cell phone a lot—much more than most people." Hyperbole thus is not intended to be deceptive. Those who use hyperbole make their point by using a deliberate exaggeration that they expect people to recognize as such.

Jesus uses hyperbole frequently. Sometimes this is very easy to detect. For example, Jesus did not really think that people walked around with literal beams (planks of wood) stuck in their eyes (Luke 6:41, 42). To take such statements literally is to misunderstand what Jesus says. In other places, though, identifying hyperbole is not as easy. Today's lesson offers some statements of hyperbole, and this verse is one of them. We must be careful to understand such statements as Jesus intends.

To take the verse before us literally is to miss the nature of discipleship. What Jesus is stressing is that His disciples cannot have divided loyalties (compare Luke 16:13). He or she cannot play the role of disciple only when it is convenient. Commitment to Jesus demands that a disciple will choose to follow Him in even extreme circumstances. If someone is forced to choose

---

### How to Say It

AMBASSAGE. *am*-buh-sij.

DEUTERONOMY. Due-ter-*ahn*-uh-me.

DIETRICH BONHOEFFER. *Dee*-trick *Bon*-huh-fur.

GAMALIEL. Guh-*may*-lih-ul or Guh-*may*-lee-al.

HYPERBOLE. high-*per*-buh-lee.

JERUSALEM. Juh-*roo*-suh-lem.

JULIUS CAESAR. *Joo*-lee-us *See*-zur.

MONASTICISM. mah-*nas*-tuh-si-zum.

PEREAN. Peh-*ree*-un.

RABBI. *rab*-eye.

between obeying Jesus or obeying his or her *father and mother*, then that person must choose Jesus (compare Deuteronomy 33:9; Matthew 10:37, 38). If the demands or expectations of our spouses would lead to violation of our commitment to Jesus, then we must choose Jesus.

This is not a call to abandon family relationships as a part of Christian discipleship. Christians can still be the best husbands, sisters, sons, and mothers possible. We can still love our families and cherish our relationships. But we cannot allow family loyalty to override our devotion to Jesus and His teachings.

Sadly, some new believers are forced to make this very choice. To be the only Christian in one's family may result in enormous pressure to compromise one's faith or to live a life of conditional discipleship. Right here is where the fellowship and support of the church becomes vital to successful discipleship. [See question #2, page 224.]

### FAMILY OR DISCIPLESHIP?

Anthony (AD 251–356) is considered to be the father of monasticism—a way of life characterized by voluntary poverty and solitude. He sold the family farm he had inherited from his parents, gave away the proceeds, and went to the desert to become a monastic hermit.

Anthony's activities became typical for many of the monks who followed him, monks who became known as *the Desert Fathers*. These monks lived alone in individual mud huts, content to spend their time in prayer and contemplation. They abandoned all semblance of family life and all association with family members. These early monks took the words of Jesus literally in this regard.

One exception, however, was a monk named Abraham. He had a brother who died, leaving an orphan daughter. Abraham took the 7-year-old girl and placed her in an outer room in his cell, communicating with her only through a small window. With the passage of time, he taught her in the ways of monasticism—a life of prayer, praise, and self-restraint.

The monk Abraham did the right thing in providing for his young orphaned niece. But in so doing, we must conclude that he violated a literal interpretation to "hate" family members. One wonders how he reconciled the conflicting ideals!                                    —J. B. N.

### B. Our Freedom (v. 27)

**27. And whosoever doth not bear his cross, and come after me, cannot be my disciple.**

As with verse 26, this saying also ends with *cannot be my disciple*. In this case Jesus uses an even more enigmatic image to portray discipleship: carrying *his cross*. We should remember that the cross at this point in time is not a Christian symbol suitable for jewelry. Rather, it symbolizes the execution of a criminal. A Roman cross represents death. What does Jesus intend by this startling declaration? Does He mean that all true disciples will be asked to give up their lives for the sake of Jesus?

To be a Christian martyr is to die for one's faith in Jesus. When forced to choose between either death or renouncing Christ, the Christian chooses death. Martyrdom is a sad yet noble part of the history of the church. But this verse does not teach that we are less than true disciples if we are not slaughtered for the faith.

This is clarified when we compare the verse with Luke 9:23. There, Jesus equates taking "up his cross daily" with denying oneself (compare Matthew 16:24; Mark 8:34). We die to self when we accept Jesus' call to discipleship. As Paul puts it, we are crucified with Him and He now lives in us, taking control of our lives (Galatians 2:19, 20).

## II. Estimating the Expense (Luke 14:28-33)

### A. Completing a Project (vv. 28-30)

**28. For which of you, intending to build a tower, sitteth not down first, and counteth the cost, whether he have sufficient to finish it?**

Jesus continues His address to the crowds by using some simple analogies to illustrate the *cost* of discipleship. The first one involves a building project. A *tower* is some kind of commercial building, perhaps a guard tower for a valuable vineyard or olive orchard. It is intended to enhance or protect the revenue of the owner in some way.

Many of us have witnessed construction projects that began well, but then languished with half-built edifices that served no one. The cause may have been lack of funds to finish the building. This is why a bank will not lend money for new construction unless it is sure there will be *sufficient* money to complete the project. A half-completed building is of no use to anyone. It costs a lot of money with no return on the investment. [See question #3, page 224.]

**29, 30. Lest haply, after he hath laid the foundation, and is not able to finish it, all that behold it begin to mock him, saying, This man began to build, and was not able to finish.**

There can be several community reactions to an unfinished construction project, but Jesus chooses this one: ridicule. In Jesus' day, no one would be overly concerned about the ugliness or waste of the failed construction. Instead, neighbors would immediately reflect on the foolishness of a builder who underestimated his final costs and ran out of money.

Despite centuries of hard lessons in this regard, this still happens. In the 1970s, a well-known televangelist began to build a very expensive office tower. His ministry went bankrupt before it was finished. [See question #4, page 224.]

How foolhardy it is to make a commitment without counting its cost! If one signs a contract to buy a house without any idea how it will be paid for, disaster probably will follow. If one joins a club but can never attend its meetings and cannot afford to pay its dues, expulsion is inevitable. Discipleship is not bought and sold like a commodity, but it has a great cost. This cost must be taken into account before the commitment is made.

### B. Winning a War (vv. 31, 32)

**31. Or what king, going to make war against another king, sitteth not down first, and consulteth whether he be able with ten thousand to meet him that cometh against him with twenty thousand?**

Jesus' second analogy for the cost of discipleship involves warfare strategy. History tells us that the number of troops is not always the most important factor in winning battles. For example, Julius Caesar was known to have won important battles with armies that were smaller than those of his enemies. Even so, the rule of thumb for wartime is "the more troops available, the better." Most generals are leery of engaging another army with equal forces. To wage war with an army outnumbered two to one is extremely risky. The likely outcome is not just defeat, but the total annihilation of the smaller army.

**32. Or else, while the other is yet a great way off, he sendeth an ambassage, and desireth conditions of peace.**

The wise king knows when he has no hope for victory. In such circumstances, the best course of action is to seek favorable terms for surrender by sending *an ambassage* (a delegation). With his own army intact, he will still pose a threat to the more powerful king, so he may be given some concessions. But if he fights the battle and loses his army, he will be in no position to expect favorable terms. The terms will be dictated to him.

Visual for Lesson 13

*Use this visual to review the unit themes of the quarter and how our 13 lessons fit together.*

### C. Living a Life of Discipleship (v. 33)

**33. So likewise, whosoever he be of you that forsaketh not all that he hath, he cannot be my disciple.**

The point of the analogies in verses 28-32 is that there is a personal cost involved in Christian discipleship. In the verse before us, Jesus again uses hyperbole to reinforce His point. By *forsaketh . . . all,* He does not mean that anyone who becomes a Christian must liquidate all personal assets, give the proceeds to the church, and take a vow of poverty. Rather, the idea is that to be Jesus' disciple, you must love Him more than any material wealth or possession.

In the final analysis, we cannot let our attachments to anything hinder our obedience to Jesus and His demands on our lives. These attachments may include families, personal ambitions, investments, and new cars. Jesus comes first. [See question #5, page 224.]

COST AND BENEFIT ANALYSIS

Otto von Bismarck (1815–1898) was a statesman who united northern Germany into a confederation under Prussian control in the 1860s. But he wanted southern German states to join as well. He decided that one way to make this happen was to maneuver the French into declaring war on Prussia. The southern German states would then join Prussia against this aggressive move, and Bismarck would have his united Germany.

France became a hapless tool in this plan. Spain offered her throne to a German prince, and the French protested. One thing led to another, and the French declared war in 1870. The

Prussian army then overwhelmed the French in a series of battles, in one event even capturing Emperor Napoleon III. The Prussians ended up besieging Paris, which experienced several months of famine.

In the ensuing peace agreement, France had to pay hefty war reparations, and she lost most of the provinces of Alsace and Lorraine. France paid a high price to initiate a war she was ill prepared to fight; losing that war cost even more.

The cost of discipleship is itself very high. But this is a struggle that we *cannot* lose as long as we remain faithful. The reward at the end will be worth any price we pay now. Yet Jesus wants us to count the cost in advance nonetheless. When we do, we are less likely to lose heart during those times when that cost seems high. —J. B. N.

## Conclusion

### A. The Cost of Discipleship

Does the cost of following Jesus ever become too great? Are we willing to let Jesus be Lord in some area of our lives but not in others? The Gospels teach that the earliest disciples of Jesus gave up *everything* to follow Him (see Mark 10:28; Luke 5:11).

To be a disciple of Christ means that we may be asked to give up ownership of the most private and precious things we have. This means that anything and everything is on the table, especially material possessions and relationships. To hold back in any area means we have not totally yielded to Jesus' lordship, and we are not truly His disciples (Matthew 16:24; Mark 8:34; Luke 9:23).

Jesus does not want people to commit to being His disciples without understanding the depth of that commitment. Discipleship must be more than "try it, you'll like it." Jesus is looking for fully devoted followers.

One of the great martyrs of the twentieth century was a German minister named Dietrich Bonhoeffer (1906–1945). During the rise to power of the Nazis in Germany, Bonhoeffer published an important book entitled *The Cost of Discipleship* (1937). In this he challenges Christians to understand that being a follower of Jesus requires full commitment of one's life under any circumstance.

A few years later, Bonhoeffer had these principles put to the test. He was arrested by the Gestapo (the Nazi secret police) for treason and sent to a concentration camp. There he ministered to his fellow prisoners under extreme pressure. His commitment to Jesus allowed him to go to his own execution calmly, secure in his relationship with his Lord.

Jesus' teachings in today's lesson offer us the opportunity to reexamine our commitment to Him. Would an outsider describe you as a disciple of Jesus Christ? Does anyone look at your life and see a fully devoted follower of Christ? What or who is more important to you than your relationship with Jesus? Such questions of self-reflection are important in our attempts to evaluate our commitment.

In Revelation 3:16, Jesus offered a different type of comment on this same issue: the lukewarm church or Christian will be spewed from His mouth. This is a comment about discipleship and commitment. Jesus is not pleased with those who serve Him a little. He does not seek our lukewarm commitments. He desires men and women to be His disciples who will count the cost of commitment and then pay the price—whatever the price.

### B. Prayer

God, our Father, You have demonstrated Your commitment to us by sending Your Son to pay the price for our sins. You have asked us, through Jesus, to be committed to You and obedient to Your will.

This is not always easy, Father. May You continue to bless our desire to seek and follow Your will. May our lives continue to be conformed to Your will by the power of Your Word and Your Holy Spirit. We pray this in the name of our master, Jesus Christ, amen.

### C. Thought to Remember

Full commitment still required!

## Home Daily Bible Readings

**Monday, Feb. 18**—You Know Me (Psalm 139:1-6)

**Tuesday, Feb. 19**—Conditions of Discipleship (Luke 14:25-27)

**Wednesday, Feb. 20**—First, Count the Cost (Luke 14:28-33)

**Thursday, Feb. 21**—The Rich Ruler's Response (Luke 18:18-25)

**Friday, Feb. 22**—Rewards of Discipleship (Luke 18:28-30)

**Saturday, Feb. 23**—First Disciples Called (Luke 5:1-11)

**Sunday, Feb. 24**—Saul Called to Be a Disciple (Acts 9:1-6, 11-16)

# Learning by Doing

*This page contains an alternative lesson plan emphasizing learning activities.*
*Classes desiring such student involvement will find these suggestions helpful.*

## Into the Lesson

Write the following two headings on the board: *Volunteer Activities* and *Sacrifices Made*. Begin class by asking your learners where they have volunteered their time for service. What are the causes, secular or Christian, for which they have served without pay? Expect answers such as tutoring learners, being a mental health advocate, or teaching Sunday school. List responses in the first of the two columns.

Next, ask, "What are some of the things you gave or sacrificed for these causes or organizations?" List responses in the second column. After completing this exercise, ask the learners, "Why did you make these sacrifices or commitments?" Encourage discussion. Expect answers that affirm that the sacrifices were important to the causes.

Make the transition to Bible study by reminding learners that the word *disciple* comes from the word *discipline*. Jesus' cause is the greatest of all causes. And He has disciplines He expects of us, His disciples.

## Into the Word

Use the commentary to deliver a very brief lecture that you outline this way:
  I. Following Jesus Is Expected
  II. Discipleship Defined
  III. Hyperbole
Write the outline on the board as you speak. Then divide the class into three or more study teams. Give each team a photocopy of the lesson commentary of the passage assigned to that team and a copy of its assignment (below). Some teams will duplicate the assignments if you use more than three teams. Also, give teams B and C poster board and markers. (Questions similar to those below are also in the optional student book.) Team assignments are as follows:

*Team A:* Read Luke 14:25-27 and the lesson commentary on these verses. Discuss the following questions and be ready to report your answers. 1. Are Jesus' commands in verses 26 and 27 to be taken literally or to be considered as hyperbole? Why do you think so? 2. What is the lesson Jesus wants us to learn in terms of "hating" our families? Give an example. 3. What does it mean to "bear his cross"? Explain and illustrate.

*Team B:* Read Luke 14:28-33 and the lesson commentary on these verses. Then compare and contrast the cost of discipleship in the first century with the twenty-first century. Make two columns on the poster board and jot your comparisons and contrasts in the columns. Be ready to explain your conclusions to the class.

*Team C:* Read Luke 14:25-33. Then read the lesson commentary notes on verse 33. After reading those notes, identify some marks of disciples of Jesus that set them apart from non-disciples. Decide how you will summarize these to the class. One idea is to make two columns headed "Disciple" and "Non-disciple" on the poster board. List characteristics and behavior traits (or lack thereof) in the columns.

Allow each group to report its conclusions.

## Into Life

*Brainstorming.* Tell the story of Dietrich Bonhoeffer from the Conclusion of the lesson commentary. Then ask, "What characteristics or behavior patterns should an outsider see in fully devoted followers of Jesus Christ?" As the class members brainstorm answers, note these on the board.

Next, remind your learners that Jesus intends this lesson to be personal to each of us. He calls us to examine our commitment and walk as His disciples or followers continually.

*Getting Personal.* Ask each class member to identify one of the behaviors or characteristics from the brainstorming activity that he or she would like to develop or improve for Jesus' sake. Then ask each to write an acrostic prayer using the word *DISCIPLE* stating a commitment or asking for help. Show this example from a person who wishes to quit swearing:

> **D**ear Lord,
> **I** want to quit
> **S**wearing. As your
> dis**C**iple
> **I**
> **P**romise that I
> wil**L** try to honor You
> in my sp**E**ech.

(You can find this activity in the optional student book as well.)

# Let's Talk It Over

*The questions on this page are designed to promote discussion of the lesson by the class and to encourage application of the lesson Scriptures. The answers provided are only discussion starters. Let your class talk it over from there.*

**1. How does Jesus' approach to the multitude differ from the response some churches have toward large crowds? What can churches do better to follow Jesus' example?**

Sometimes churches and preachers get caught up in believing that a large crowd equals effectiveness and success. Crowds are considered a sign that God is blessing the work. This may be the case, but sometimes the crowds are the result of a spellbinding leader or a slick production.

When the crowds arrive, some churches seek to cater to them in order to keep them. Yet Jesus did not mind making the crowds uncomfortable. He sought followers who were committed, not necessarily comfortable (see John 6:66). It is imperative that church leaders continually evaluate their motives and teaching to be sure people are not being manipulated and that doctrine is not being sacrificed.

**2. What are some things you need to "hate" in order to follow Jesus?**

We live in a world that offers plenty of enticements that can impede spiritual growth. Too much overtime on the job to afford certain possessions will hinder spiritual progress. The entertainment industry offers a steady stream of theatrical releases for our "must see" amusement. A variety of sports and hobbies demands time. These are things we may love to do, but they may be things we need to "hate" so that we can pursue our first love: our relationship with God.

**3. Why are there many Christians who seem not to have counted the cost of discipleship? How has the church contributed to this problem? How can the church contribute to a solution?**

In consumer-driven cultures, it's easy for people to "shop around" to find a church that caters to their desired level of commitment. This is to misunderstand the nature of discipleship. Discipleship is not something we tack onto our lives as time and interest allows. Discipleship, rather, is a whole-life perspective.

Churches may give the impression that quality or quantity of service does not really matter much in a relationship with Christ. Thus Christian service is rendered halfheartedly, and discipleship is shallow. When we present a view of discipleship that centers on "easy believism" or "accept Christ and all your needs will be supplied," then we cater to selfishness, not discipleship.

The solution begins by understanding what Jesus really did for us on the cross. When we grasp that, we are then in a position to realize what Jesus is really saying about discipleship.

**4. What is an area in your life that you have not been "able to finish"? What about in the life of your church? What have you learned from these experiences?**

Many possibilities of Christian service seem noble and inviting at first. But when we get into the task, we find it to be difficult. As a result, we leave the job undone.

Perhaps you shared the gospel with a neighbor who needs the Lord, but he or she asked a question that you were unable to answer right away and you felt like a failure. As a result, you did not go back to that person. Some churches have been challenged to support benevolence projects in the community. But the early excitement was replaced by boredom or apathy later on, and the task was abandoned.

The solution begins with the church's leadership. Whatever tone the leaders set will be picked up on by many in the church. Continuing excitement and dedication to the task begets the same.

**5. What is one habit, belief, or possession that is distracting you from full discipleship to Jesus? How can your fellow class members help you overcome this problem?**

Our lives can fall into patterns and routines that, if not monitored, can become ruts. These ruts seem innocent at first glance, but they can become detriments to spiritual growth.

For example, reading the newspaper to keep up with current events is a good thing. But there is a lot of trivial information in the newspaper that just takes up time to read and sift through. This time would be better used reading God's Word. Perhaps you can ask a brother or sister in Christ to hold you accountable as you make this change.

# Spring Quarter 2008

## God, the People, and the Covenant

### (Chronicles, Nehemiah, Daniel, Haggai, and Luke)

### Special Features

### Lessons

#### Unit 1: Signs of God's Covenant

#### Unit 2: The Covenant in Exile

#### Unit 3: Restoration and Covenant Renewal

## About These Lessons

A contrarian is someone who chooses to "go against the grain," often doing the opposite of what the world expects. We will meet some contrarians this quarter. Perhaps we will meet ourselves in the process.

Mar 2

Mar 9

Mar 16

Mar 23

Mar 30

Apr 6

Apr 13

Apr 20

Apr 27

May 4

May 11

May 18

May 25

# Quarterly Quiz

*The questions on this page may be used in several ways: as a pretest at the beginning of the quarter; as a review at the end of the quarter; or as a review after each lesson. The questions are based on the Scripture text of each lesson* (King James Version). **The answers are on page 232.**

## Lesson 1

1. In Jerusalem, David housed the ark of the covenant in an old temple. T/F *1 Chronicles 15:1*

2. David decreed that the only people allowed to carry the ark of the covenant were _____. *1 Chronicles 15:2*

## Lesson 2

1. God reminded David that he had been called from the lowly position of a _____ in order to be king of Israel. *1 Chronicles 17:7*

2. Which prophet told David that the house of the Lord would be built by David's son? (Elijah, Nathan, Micaiah?) *1 Chronicles 17:15*

## Lesson 3

1. Who chose Solomon to be king after David and to build the temple? (David himself, Nathan the prophet, the Lord God?) *1 Chronicles 28:5*

2. David reminded Israel that in order to continue to dwell in the promised land, they must keep and seek all the Lord's commandments. T/F *1 Chronicles 28:8*

## Lesson 4

1. What two things were noted about Solomon's posture at the temple dedication? (choose two: head covered, kneeling, eyes closed, arms folded, head bowed, hands lifted) *2 Chronicles 6:13*

2. Jesus opened the minds of the disciples after the resurrection so that they would understand the _____. *Luke 24:45*

## Lesson 5

1. What was Josiah's reaction when the book of the law was read? (wept mightily, tore his clothes, broke his staff?) *2 Chronicles 34:19*

2. At the end of his life, Josiah turned away from the Lord. T/F *2 Chronicles 34:33*

## Lesson 6

1. Daniel was given the ability to interpret visions and dreams. T/F *Daniel 1:17*

2. Nebuchadnezzar found that Daniel and his friends were wiser and had more understanding than what group? (magicians and astrologers, the king's sons, exiles from Greece?) *Daniel 1:20*

## Lesson 7

1. When Shadrach, Meshach, and Abednego said, "But if not," it indicated what? (they could not win, they were not sure God would save them, they had made a mistake?) *Daniel 3:17, 18*

2. Shadrach, Meshach, and Abednego were stripped naked before being cast into the fiery furnace. T/F *Daniel 3:21*

## Lesson 8

1. Daniel was willing to sacrifice his life in order to be able to _____. *Daniel 6:10*

2. What did King Darius hope would happen to Daniel in the den of lions? (quick death, slow death, God would save him?) *Daniel 6:16*

## Lesson 9

1. By studying the writings of _____, Daniel learned about 70 years of desolation. *Daniel 9:2*

2. For Daniel, the possibility of God answering his prayer was based on the continuing righteousness of the people. T/F *Daniel 9:18*

## Lesson 10

1. Haggai said that the people were storing their wages in bags with holes. T/F *Haggai 1:6*

2. Failure to finish the temple had resulted in drought and crop failure. T/F *Haggai 1:9, 10*

## Lesson 11

1. What did Nehemiah want to do in Jerusalem? (rebuild the temple, drive out foreigners, rebuild the walls?) *Nehemiah 2:8*

2. The people's response to Jeremiah was, "Let us rise up and _____." *Nehemiah 2:18*

## Lesson 12

1. Tobiah claimed that a cat could break down the wall the Jews were building. T/F *Nehemiah 4:3*

2. Nehemiah and his people finished their project of rebuilding in _____ days. *Nehemiah 6:15*

## Lesson 13

1. Ezra read to the people from the book of the law of _____. *Nehemiah 8:1*

2. What two titles are given to Ezra in Nehemiah 8? (choose two: prophet, scribe, priest, prince, governor, wise man) *Nehemiah 8:1, 2*

# Our Covenant Relationship with God

*by Joe M. Sprinkle*

THE WORD *COVENANT* is no longer used much in common speech, but it is a very important word in the Bible. A covenant is an agreement between two parties. One way of organizing our Bible doctrine is through considering the various covenants between God and His people: the implied covenants at creation and with Adam after the fall, the covenant with Noah, the Abrahamic covenant, the covenant through Moses, the Davidic covenant, and the new covenant inaugurated by Jesus Christ.

The word *covenant* relates to the terms for the two parts of our Bible: Old Testament and New Testament. *Testament* is another word for *covenant.* Old Testament refers to books written after the older, Mosaic covenant was established. The New Testament refers to books written after Christ established the new covenant.

Whenever one sees the word *covenant,* one should think of the word *relationship.* Covenants establish and regulate relationships. The marriage covenant establishes a relationship between a man and a woman. It is accompanied by vows that establish the boundaries within which that relationship is to be conducted. So also the covenants between God and His people establish a relationship between them. The terms of the covenants guide the conduct within that relationship. Just as the partners of the marriage covenant are to be faithful to their vows, the people of God are to be faithful to their covenant with their Lord, who in turn faithfully keeps His covenant promises.

The glorious message of the Bible is that God took the initiative to establish a personal relationship between himself and His people. The lessons of this quarter focus on one of God's covenant relationships. The lessons will show how during the monarchy God's covenant was symbolized by the ark of the covenant, how covenant promises were fulfilled in Solomon's temple, and how the covenant was renewed under Josiah after years of neglect.

The lessons will discuss God's special covenant with David, whose promise of an eternal dynasty finds its ultimate fulfillment in Jesus Christ. We will see how during the Babylonian exile Daniel and his friends sought to be uncompromisingly faithful to the covenant despite a hostile, pagan environment.

Finally, we will discover how, after the exile was over, the prophet Haggai, the governor Nehemiah, and the priest Ezra sought to help God's people make their covenant relationship with God a priority and commit themselves to restoring and renewing their commitment to follow God's Word.

### Unit 1. March
### Signs of God's Covenant

These lessons focus on three kings (among many) during the time of the monarchy: David, Solomon, and Josiah.

**Lesson 1: The Ark Comes to Jerusalem.** The ark of the covenant was a symbol of God's presence among His people. David brought the ark to Jerusalem with great pomp, ceremony, and loud music to restore this symbol to its proper place of prominence in Israel's worship. In our worship under the new covenant, the Lord's Supper is the greatest symbol of God's presence among His people.

**Lesson 2: God Makes a Covenant with David.** One of the most important covenants in the Bible is God's covenant with David. In this covenant God promised to make David's name great and to establish his throne forever. Despite the lack of faithfulness to God's covenant on the part of David's descendants, God kept His covenant promises by raising up Jesus Christ. Upon His death, resurrection, and ascension, Jesus fulfilled the promise to David by assuming David's throne.

**Lesson 3: God Calls Solomon to Build the Temple.** Part of the Davidic covenant involved David's son building God's house (1 Chronicles 17:12). Solomon was called by God to fulfill this prediction. We too must seek to find the work to which God has gifted and called us to further His kingdom.

**Lesson 4: God Fulfills His Promises.** Solomon went on to build and dedicate the temple. This is an example of how God keeps His covenant promises. In the New Testament Jesus identifies himself as the replacement for the earthly temple. God and the Lamb will be our temple in the heavenly Jerusalem (Revelation 21:22).

**Lesson 5: Josiah Renews the Covenant.** Sometimes covenants are broken and relationships need to be restored. This was the case with ancient Judah when God's Word was ignored and forgotten. When the book of the law was redis-covered in the days of Josiah, that king repented and sought to have the Jewish people recommit themselves to learning God's Word and following God's covenant. Similarly, God's Word can come to be neglected and forgotten today. With biblical illiteracy growing in the church, we too need to rededicate ourselves to mature Bible study.

## Unit 2. April
## The Covenant in Exile

These lessons focus on heroes of faith dur-ing the Babylonian exile: Daniel and his three friends Shadrach, Meshach and Abednego.

**Lesson 6: Holding to Convictions.** Daniel and his friends remained faithful to the covenant while in exile by maintaining a distinctive diet in con-formity with their Jewish convictions. To main-tain their identity as God's people, they had to be visibly distinct from the Babylonians among whom they lived and by whom they were being educated. Today also Christians must maintain a visibly distinct way of life in order to be wit-nesses to the world.

**Lesson 7: Taking a Stand.** Shadrach, Meshach, and Abednego were given a choice: violate Israel's covenant with God by worshiping Nebuchadnezzar's statue or be burned to death in a furnace. They said no to idolatry and were willing to die for their convictions, though God honored their faithfulness by saving them. Like-wise we should take a stand and say no to things contrary to our Christian convictions even when it hurts—or kills.

**Lesson 8: Refusing to Compromise.** Conspira-tors tricked King Darius into passing a decree condemning to death anyone who prayed to a god or man except Darius for a period of 30 days. The idea was to entrap Daniel, whom they knew prayed to God daily.

Upon hearing this decree, Daniel refused to compromise. He was condemned to be eaten by lions as a result, though God saved him. Chris-tians today may have to choose between their faith and their jobs, family, or social standing.

**Lesson 9: Praying for the People.** Prayer is an essential element for remaining in a covenant relationship with God. Daniel's prayer for his people is still a great example of how to pray.

## Unit 3. May
## Restoration and Covenant Renewal

The lessons for May focus on three key figures after the exile who inspired renewed obedience to God's covenant: the prophet Haggai, the gover-nor Nehemiah, and Ezra the priest.

**Lesson 10: Setting Priorities.** Haggai shamed his fellow Jews who had returned from Babylo-nian exile for making personal comfort and luxury their priority rather than rebuilding the temple. Just as the covenant had warned in Deuteronomy 28, disobedience meant forfeited blessings. But with the help of good leaders, God's people can put aside selfishness. When we do, we make God's priorities our priorities.

**Lesson 11: Following a Visionary Leader.** Nehe-miah was a courageous and godly leader. Out of concern for God's people and zeal for God's covenant, Nehemiah took risks. He stepped out on faith in order to restore God's work among his people. Who will be a Nehemiah for the year 2008?

**Lesson 12: Finishing the Task.** Nehemiah's most visible act of restoring God's work in Judah was rebuilding the walls of Jerusalem, the city of God. But this work provoked the opposition of regional governors Sanballat and Tobiah. They threatened Nehemiah with an invasion if he continued building. Through prayer and stead-fast resolve, Nehemiah overcame his opponents and completed the walls. The church is still able to overcome opposition and do great things for God.

**Lesson 13: Renewing the Covenant.** Ezra the priest assisted Nehemiah the governor in fur-thering God's work by reading and explaining God's Word (the law) to the people. The people responded with worship and a renewed com-mitment to obey God's covenant, as evidenced by their reinstitution of the Feast of Tabernacles. God's Word is still essential for bringing about revival.

## Who Will Be Faithful?

God was faithful to His covenant people Israel during the monarchy, during the exile, and after the exile. David, Solomon, Josiah, Daniel and his friends, Haggai, Nehemiah, and Ezra each played a role in helping Israel be faithful to God's covenant. They helped maintain symbols of God's covenant relationship, they set faith-ful examples, and they exhorted others to obey God's covenant. They were exemplary (despite stumbles by some) in living out God's covenant relationship.

The new covenant has given the church a wonderful and special relationship with God through Jesus Christ. May the actions and words of these Old Testament characters in this quar-ter's lessons continue to inspire God's people to maintain, deepen, and restore their new-cov-enant relationships with their Lord.

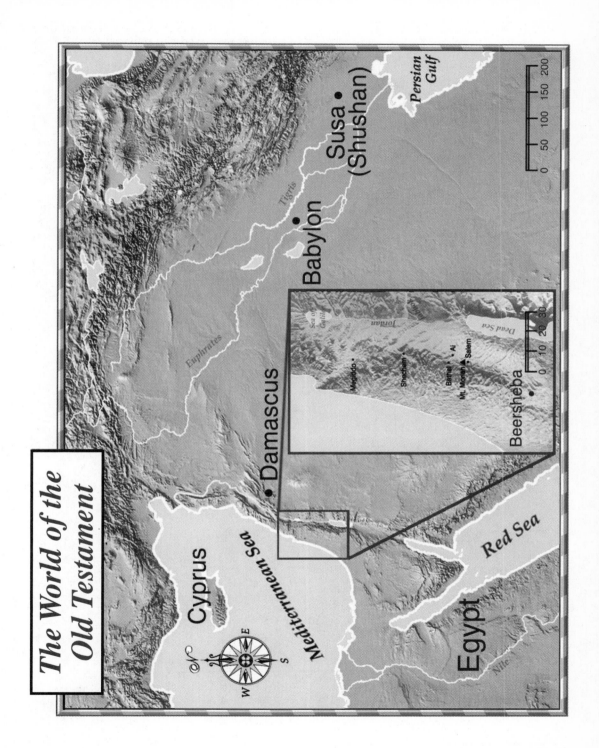

*The World of the Old Testament*

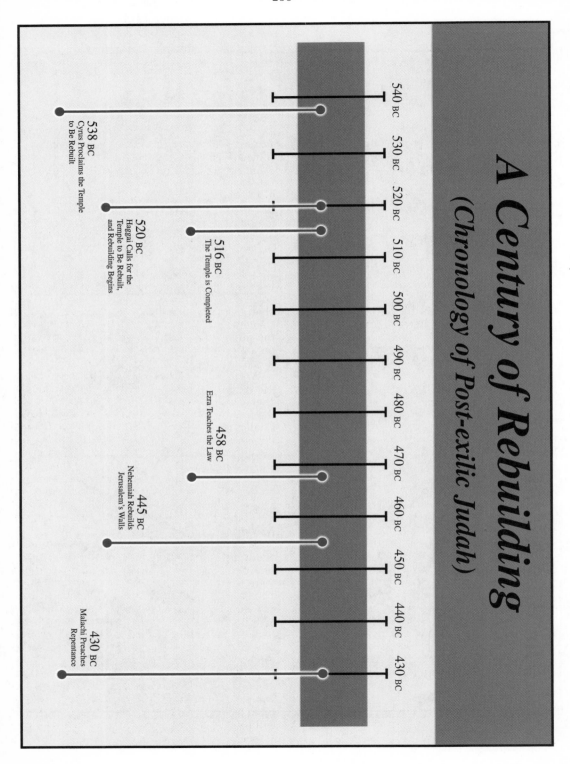

# A Century of Rebuilding

*(Chronology of Post-exilic Judah)*

540 BC
530 BC
520 BC
510 BC
500 BC
490 BC
480 BC
470 BC
460 BC
450 BC
440 BC
430 BC

**538 BC**
Cyrus Proclaims the Temple to Be Rebuilt

**520 BC**
Haggai Calls for the Temple to Be Rebuilt, and Rebuilding Begins

**516 BC**
The Temple is Completed

**458 BC**
Ezra Teaches the Law

**445 BC**
Nehemiah Rebuilds Jerusalem's Walls

**430 BC**
Malachi Preaches Repentance

# Variety Is the Spice of Teaching

## Involving All the Senses

### by Charlotte Mize

TEACHING IS AN ENORMOUS but rewarding responsibility. Many people are fearful of becoming teachers because teachers bear a greater accountability (James 3:1). However, there are also admonitions for followers of Christ to mature spiritually to the point where they can teach others (Titus 2:3; Hebrews 5:12). God honors those who teach (Romans 10:15).

### Better Teaching, Greater Learning

What is your view of yourself as a teacher? Do you see yourself as a facilitator or a door opener? When a kindergarten teacher begins to show her class how to read, she doesn't read all of the material to them. She allows them to struggle with the letters, the sounds, the words, and finally the sentences. She provides a learning experience where children can develop their own skills. The teacher is the guide and the role model, but she does not do all the work for the child.

Adults need a similar environment—an environment that allows them to mature in their faith. It is your job as teacher to create such an environment. You provide the gift (lesson), but you don't unwrap it entirely for your learners. You allow them the excitement of discovery.

A phrase that has stuck with me from my early days of teaching is this: "There is no teaching without parallel learning, and there is no true learning without a change in behavior." Of all the methods utilized to impart God's Word, *the lecture method* is probably the least effective at bringing about behavioral changes. The reason may be that lecture uses only one of the learner's five senses: hearing. A challenge for teachers is to find ways to use more than one of the five senses.

For example, merely talking about the ark of the covenant can be abstract and dull. Seeing a picture of the ark brings some interest. Making a model of the ark based on God's instructions to Moses (Exodus 25) for **Lesson 1** will involve even more senses. (Use simple materials to keep the model-building manageable within the time available.)

For **Lesson 2**, you can challenge each class member to write some kind of brief contract (covenant). This can be a sales contract or a neighborhood watch pact. A key point is that the

expectations of all parties should be clear. For **Lesson 3,** the class can research Solomon's temple and bring samples of the building and decorating materials (or pictures downloaded from the Internet, if samples are hard to come by).

**Lesson 4** can involve a dramatic monologue to reenact Solomon's prayer of dedication of the temple. Thinking about Josiah's renewing of the covenant in **Lesson 5**, one application activity is to have your class brainstorm what a rededication ceremony for your church would involve.

Don't overlook the importance of visualization and role-playing; these can affect the subconscious. For **Lesson 6,** you can write a very short three-act play to involve the entire class in Daniel's story of standing up for what is right in the midst of persecution. A parallel play based on a modern situation would allow your learner to see how the lesson applies today.

Write the fiery **Lesson 7** on learners' hearts as well as on their minds with active, intense visualization. Have a reader dramatically speak the lesson text while everyone has eyes closed. Challenge learners to hear, feel, see, and smell the atmosphere of that episode as they visualize the progression.

In **Lesson 8** you can compare the lions' den of Daniel's persecution with the Roman persecution of Christians. Then you can share modern stories of persecution of Christians. The Voice of the Martyrs web site (www.persecution.com) can provide you some good material.

Daniel prays for the people in **Lesson 9**. This would be a good time for a real-life experience. The class can select a section of town where there is much evil and pray for the people there. The best involvement would be to go to the area, but an alternative would be for the class to divide into groups in the classroom to pray using Daniel's prayer as a pattern. The prayer certainly should include confession for not doing more as a church to reach that area for Christ.

For **Lesson 10,** cut out articles and advertisements from a week's worth of newspapers. As you pass them around for discussion on how to avoid being influenced by worldly priorities, you will be engaging the eyes, the ears, and the sense of touch.

**Lesson 11** offers an opportunity to invite some of your church leaders to share with the class their vision for how to improve the church facilities to reach more for Jesus. You can arrange for those leaders to take your class on a walking tour of the church facility either during class or later. Class members may find themselves motivated to volunteer for a service activity during the ensuing week to further that vision.

The subject matter of **Lesson 12** offers a good opportunity to receive reports from those who volunteered for a service activity in connection with Lesson 11. For **Lesson 13,** think of a way to arrange your classroom space that parallels the arrangement during Ezra's reading of the law. As your learners stand to hear, a prepared volunteer can read the Ten Commandments (Deuteronomy 5:1-21) or the Beatitudes (Matthew 5:1-13).

Trying to reproduce Ezra's high platform indoors is probably neither feasible nor safe. But something that allows the speaker to stand safely at least a few inches off the floor can add to the dramatic effect. Some of your learners should be prepared to respond *amen, amen* and adopt the various postures noted in Nehemiah 8:6. The people weren't passive when Ezra read the law!

### Don't Forget the Overall Theme

All of these lessons deal with the concept of *covenant* in one way or another. It is vital for teacher and learner to understand what is involved in a covenant, since this involves understanding how various relationships work.

To introduce this series of lessons, ask your class to try to think of some human interactions that involve a covenant or agreement, either formally or informally. How are those similar to God's covenant with us? How are they different?

If your learners need help, you can offer modern examples of covenants such as business contracts and marriage vows. You can also point out that covenant implies some kind of agreement between at least two parties, although the parties may not be equals in terms of being in the same peer group. The words *treaty, pact, accord,* or *contract* may be more familiar to your learners than the word *covenant.*

If your learners need more examples from you, you can mention that parents use covenants (contracts) with their children to define expected behavior and what rewards and punishments are included. God understands the need His children have for covenant. The Bible is the story of the unfolding of God's covenants with His people throughout history. Throughout the 13 weeks, review often the concept of covenant so

that the overall theme does not get lost in individual stories.

Your learners also need to know that covenants demand faithfulness on both sides. God is faithful. His children must grow in their faithfulness. God made a covenant with His chosen nation, Israel. God remained faithful to all His promises in both reward and punishment. His nation was not faithful and thus often suffered the punishment.

However, God also made provision for restoration. The church, unfortunately, has been unfaithful at times. Like the nation of Israel in the Old Testament, we sometimes need restoration. Restoration is available through Jesus' sacrifice and payment for our sin (1 John 1:9).

Human-to-human agreements will end, but our new covenant with God is everlasting. Even when we fail, the covenant continues. This is the only eternal agreement. It is reassuring to know that God's covenant will never fail. As you develop each lesson with the Davidic covenant in mind, make sure that your learners also realize that the new covenant in Jesus is *our* hope.

### Don't Be Afraid to be Creative

Finding creative ways to allow learners to discover God's truth is a challenge. Start by asking yourself, "How can I involve as many of the five senses as possible in my next lesson?"

The advance planning needed to do this may seem to be too time-consuming. At first it will take additional time to prepare an effective learning environment thoughtfully. But with practice this becomes easier, even second nature. The results will be gratifying. And don't forget that we've done some of the work for you in the Learning by Doing activities!

### Answers to Quarterly Quiz on page 226

**Lesson 1**—1. false. 2. Levites. **Lesson 2**—1. shepherd. 2. Nathan. **Lesson 3**—1. the Lord God. 2. true. **Lesson 4**—1. kneeling, hands lifted. 2. the Scriptures. **Lesson 5**—1. tore his clothes. 2. false. **Lesson 6**—1. true. 2. magicians and astrologers. **Lesson 7**—1. they were not sure God would save them. 2. false. **Lesson 8**—1. pray. 2. Daniel's God would save him. **Lesson 9**—1. Jeremiah. 2. false. **Lesson 10**—1. true. 2. true. **Lesson 11**—1. rebuild the walls. 2. build. **Lesson 12**—1. false. 2. 52. **Lesson 13**—1. Moses. 2. scribe, priest.

# The Ark Comes to Jerusalem

DEVOTIONAL READING: **Psalm 150.**

BACKGROUND SCRIPTURE: **1 Chronicles 13, 15.**

PRINTED TEXT: **1 Chronicles 15:1-3, 14-16, 25-28.**

### 1 Chronicles 15:1-3, 14-16, 25-28

1 And David made him houses in the city of David, and prepared a place for the ark of God, and pitched for it a tent.

2 Then David said, None ought to carry the ark of God but the Levites: for them hath the LORD chosen to carry the ark of God, and to minister unto him for ever.

3 And David gathered all Israel together to Jerusalem, to bring up the ark of the LORD unto his place, which he had prepared for it.

· · · · · · · · · · ·

14 So the priests and the Levites sanctified themselves to bring up the ark of the LORD God of Israel.

15 And the children of the Levites bare the ark of God upon their shoulders with the staves thereon, as Moses commanded, according to the word of the LORD.

16 And David spake to the chief of the Levites to appoint their brethren to be the singers with instruments of music, psalteries and harps and cymbals, sounding, by lifting up the voice with joy.

· · · · · · · · · · · ·

25 So David, and the elders of Israel, and the captains over thousands, went to bring up the ark of the covenant of the LORD out of the house of Obed-edom with joy.

26 And it came to pass, when God helped the Levites that bare the ark of the covenant of the LORD, that they offered seven bullocks and seven rams.

27 And David was clothed with a robe of fine linen, and all the Levites that bare the ark, and the singers, and Chenaniah the master of the song with the singers: David also had upon him an ephod of linen.

28 Thus all Israel brought up the ark of the covenant of the LORD with shouting, and with sound of the cornet, and with trumpets, and with cymbals, making a noise with psalteries and harps.

---

GOLDEN TEXT: David gathered all Israel together to Jerusalem, to bring up the ark of the LORD unto his place, which he had prepared for it.—1 Chronicles 15:3.

## God, the People, and the Covenant
Unit 1: Signs of God's Covenant
(Lessons 1-5)

## Lesson Aims

After participating in this lesson, each student will be able to:

1. Describe the sequence of events that David initiated to bring the ark of God to Jerusalem.

2. Compare and contrast the worship practices of ancient Israel with worship practices today.

3. Determine one way to worship with greater enthusiasm in private or corporate worship experiences.

## Lesson Outline

INTRODUCTION
  A. Symbols of God's Presence
  B. Lesson Background
  I. ARRANGEMENTS FOR THE ARK (1 Chronicles 15:1-3)
    A. David's Preparations (v. 1)
    B. Levites' Task (v. 2)
    C. Israel's Gathering (v. 3)
 II. BRINGING OF THE ARK (1 Chronicles 15:14-16)
    A. Sanctification (v. 14)
    B. Transportation (v. 15)
      *The Right People for the Job*
    C. Authorization (v. 16)
III. WORSHIPING BEFORE THE ARK (1 Chronicles 15:25-28)
    A. Ark Retrieved (v. 25)
    B. Sacrifices Offered (v. 26)
    C. Linen Worn (v. 27)
    D. Joy Evident (v. 28)
      *"A Way to Glorify God"*
CONCLUSION
    A. Worshiping in the Presence of God
    B. Prayer
    C. Thought to Remember

## Introduction

### A. Symbols of God's Presence

I once visited a certain church to conduct a Bible study. The building was functional, practical, and not "showy." But eight stained-glass windows in the sanctuary overwhelmed me with their messages. On the left were four Old Testament symbols: the tree of life, a rainbow with Noah's ark, a burning bush, and a pillar of fire. On the right were four New Testament symbols: a stable (for Jesus' birth), a cross, an empty tomb, and a dove descending. The impact of these eight beautiful windows has never left me.

These symbols clearly communicate God's presence or promise. As long as Adam and Eve had access to the tree of life, they could live forever in God's presence. Every time we see a rainbow, it reminds us of God's promise never to flood the earth again. Moses knew he was in God's presence when he approached a burning bush. The pillar of fire was a clear demonstration of God's presence in the midst of the Hebrew people.

On the New Testament side, the symbols are just as powerful. The stable symbolizes that the Word of God became flesh. The cross has always been a symbol of God's promised forgiveness. Of course, without the empty tomb of the resurrection there would be no salvation for the world; the resurrection assures us that God is still here. Finally, the dove is a symbol of God's Spirit, which is present within every Christian. Today's lesson focuses on another important symbol of God's presence for Old Testament believers: the ark of the covenant.

### B. Lesson Background

The ark of the covenant was ancient Israel's most precious symbol of God's presence. The construction of the ark is recorded in Exodus 37:1-9. That happened in about 1446 BC. Within the ark of the covenant eventually were placed the testimony, a gold jar of manna that the Israelites had gathered during their time in the wilderness, and Aaron's budded rod (Exodus 40:20; Hebrews 9:4).

Four gold rings were fastened to the ark. Poles were inserted through these rings for transporting it. The ark was never to be carried in any way other than by Levites with those poles on their shoulders (Exodus 25:13-15; 37:5; 1 Chronicles 15:2, 15). Since the ark was top-heavy, using a cart to carry it was dangerous (1 Chronicles 13:7-10). Indeed, the top cover itself (called *mercy seat* or *atonement cover*) was made out of gold—an extremely heavy substance (Exodus 25:17).

The ark of the covenant symbolized the throne of God (see 1 Samuel 4:4; 2 Samuel 6:2; 2 Kings 19:15; 1 Chronicles 13:6; Psalm 80:1; 99:1). Perhaps more precisely, the space between the cherubim on the atonement cover represented the "footstool" of God (see 1 Chronicles 28:2; Psalm 99:5). Atonement for sin was made by sprinkling the blood of bulls and goats before the mercy seat (Leviticus 16:11-16). The importance of the ark of the covenant to the Hebrew people cannot be overstated!

After the ark was built and placed in the tabernacle, it stayed with the Israelites throughout their wilderness wanderings. Eventually it was placed in Shiloh, about 30 miles northeast of Jerusalem, after the conquest of the promised land (Joshua 18:1). Through an unusual series of events, the ark ended up in a private residence, where it remained in obscurity for some time (1 Samuel 4:4–7:2). The tabernacle that had housed the ark was located elsewhere at that time, separated from the ark (1 Chronicles 16:39; 21:29; 2 Chronicles 1:3, 13). It was under these conditions that David sought to bring the ark to Jerusalem and place it within a specially prepared tent (1 Chronicles 13:5; 15:1).

Today's background texts of 1 Chronicles 13 and 15 must be understood as part of a literary unit, namely chapters 13–17. This unit brings us to an important stage in the establishment of Jerusalem as both a political and religious center for the newly united kingdom under King David. This stage began when David brought the ark to Jerusalem (chapter 13) and concluded when God gave His promise concerning David's dynasty (chapter 17; see Lesson 2).

By the time David became king, more than 400 years had elapsed since the ark of the covenant had come into being. First Chronicles 13 recounts the first attempt at bringing the ark to Jerusalem. That attempt ended in failure. Someone, either David or the priests, made a serious mistake by appointing the wrong people to move the ark (1 Chronicles 15:13a).

Another mistake was in transporting the ark in the wrong manner (1 Chronicles 15:13b). The result was a tragedy that halted the process (2 Samuel 6:1-7; 1 Chronicles 13:1-10). David was despondent: "How shall I bring the ark of God home to me?" (1 Chronicles 13:12b; compare 2 Samuel 6:9). For three months the project languished until everyone, including David, recognized that God had blessed the household of Obed-edom, where the ark was housed temporarily (1 Chronicles 13:13, 14).

The author of Chronicles arranged his material to show that David's first major decision and act as king of a united Israel was to bring the ark to Jerusalem. Our printed text picks up the story of King David's second attempt at this project.

# I. Arrangements for the Ark (1 Chronicles 15:1-3)

## A. David's Preparations (v. 1)

**1. And David made him houses in the city of David, and prepared a place for the ark of God, and pitched for it a tent.**

The *city of David* is, of course, Jerusalem. Before David attempts to bring up *the ark,* he improves that city's infrastructure in certain ways (*made him houses;* see also 2 Samuel 5:9-11; 1 Chronicles 14:1). This is entirely appropriate, as the population of Jerusalem probably numbers only around 2,000 at the time in an area of no more than 12 acres.

Part of this city-improvement plan involves preparing *a place for the ark of God.* We are not certain where this is, but it is likely the highest place in the area, later to be known as Mount Zion (see Psalm 132:13). Today one observes the Dome of the Rock mosque close to that location.

With the tabernacle still located in Gibeon, David must devise a special *tent* for the ark (2 Samuel 6:17; 1 Chronicles 16:1, 39; 21:29). We may speculate that the tent is patterned in some way after the tabernacle. The tabernacle proper will not be brought to Jerusalem for many years (2 Chronicles 1:6, 13, 5:5).

When God revealed instructions to Moses for building the tabernacle and its furnishings (Exodus 25–31:11; 35:4-40), the ark of the covenant was the first article to be described (Exodus 25:10-22). It was the most important item because it was precisely between the two cherubim on top of the ark where God met with Moses and gave His commands for the Israelites (Exodus 25:22; Numbers 7:89). [See question #1, page 240.]

### B. Levites' Task (v. 2)

**2. Then David said, None ought to carry the ark of God but the Levites: for them hath the LORD chosen to carry the ark of God, and to minister unto him for ever.**

---

## How to Say It

CHENANIAH. Ken-uh-*nee*-uh.

CHERUBIM. *chair*-uh-bim.

EPHOD. *ee*-fod.

GIBEON. *Gib*-e-un (G as in *get*).

LEVITES. *Lee*-vites.

MELCHIZEDEK. Mel-*kiz*-eh-dek.

OBED-EDOM. *O*-bed-*ee*-dum.

PHILISTINES. Fuh-*liss*-teens or *Fill*-us-teens.

SHILOH. *Shy*-low.

UZZAH. *Uz*-zuh.

ZECHARIAH. *Zek*-uh-*rye*-uh (strong accent on *rye*).

David's statement *none ought to carry the ark of God but the Levites* seems to be reflected in Deuteronomy 10:8; 18:1-5. A certain violation of this rule contributed to the death of Uzzah that marked the first attempt to move it (1 Chronicles 13:7-10; 15:13). Even though he seems to have been a Levite, he apparently was not one of the lawful ones to transport the ark, considering the improper manner in which the first attempt was made (see Numbers 7:1-9, especially v. 9). That mistake involved both *how* as well as *who* in moving the ark. [See question #2, page 240.]

### C. Israel's Gathering (v. 3)

**3. And David gathered all Israel together to Jerusalem, to bring up the ark of the LORD unto his place, which he had prepared for it.**

This is a good summary of all that David originally tried to do regarding the first attempt to bring the ark *to Jerusalem* (1 Chronicles 13:1-5). This second gathering is thus a natural continuation of this all-important project. In 1 Chronicles 15:4-12, 17-24 (not in today's text), the author gives details regarding whom *all Israel* includes.

## II. Bringing of the Ark (1 Chronicles 15:14-16)

### A. Sanctification (v. 14)

**14. So the priests and the Levites sanctified themselves to bring up the ark of the LORD God of Israel.**

A good description of what it means to sanctify oneself can be found in Exodus 19:10-15. For the priests and *Levites* it means at least washing the body, changing clothing (to fine linen; see 1 Chronicles 15:27), and abstaining from sexual relations. Since Levites have to stay away from the common and the profane, then fasting and prayer may be part of the process, but this is not certain (see also Exodus 29; 30:17-21; 40:30-32; Leviticus 8:5-36). [See question #3, page 240.]

### B. Transportation (v. 15)

**15. And the children of the Levites bare the ark of God upon their shoulders with the staves thereon, as Moses commanded, according to the word of the LORD.**

We have already mentioned that the issue of transporting *the ark of God* includes issues of both *who* and *how*. Perhaps those who initially put the ark on a cart in 1 Chronicles 13:7 were ignorant of the implications of Exodus 25:10-15; 37:1-5. *The Levites* must carry the ark by putting its *staves* (poles) *upon their shoulders*. The rings for the poles are a permanent part of the ark for

this very purpose. No one is to touch the ark on penalty of death (again, see 2 Samuel 6:6-8; 1 Chronicles 13:9-11; 15:13).

### THE RIGHT PEOPLE FOR THE JOB

You may have seen the following humorous description of what happens as we age: "A very weird thing has happened. A strange old lady has moved into my house. I have no idea who she is, where she came from, or how she got in." The piece goes on to describe how, when the writer looks in the mirror, the stranger is hogging the view and obscuring the writer's youthful face and body. The stranger puts things in places where the writer can't find them and turns the TV down low so it can't be easily heard.

Most of us over "a certain age" have seen that stranger in the mirror. The person in the mirror is no longer "the right person"—that youthful person we imagined we would be for the rest of our lives.

Being "the right person" is important in many areas of life. That seems to have been the case when the ark was being moved. The first time it was moved, apparently the right people weren't carrying it and/or they had gone about it in the wrong way. That provides a lesson for us: being the person *God* wants us to be for carrying out His work is more important than who *we* would like to be.

God chose Levites for holy tasks; today, He chooses Christians for the holy tasks of the church. He uses His Word and our life experiences to prepare us for the work He has called us to do. Those wrinkles and gray hairs can be the evidence that God has been at work in us for a long time, preparing us to do things reserved for those of greater spiritual maturity.     —C. R. B.

### C. Authorization (v. 16)

**16. And David spake to the chief of the Levites to appoint their brethren to be the singers with instruments of music, psalteries and harps and cymbals, sounding, by lifting up the voice with joy.**

---

### VISUALS FOR THESE LESSONS

The visual pictured in each lesson (example: page 237) is a small reproduction of a large, full-color poster included in the *Adult Resources* packet for the Spring Quarter. The packet is available from your supplier. Order No. 392.

With the ark in Jerusalem, the city will become a center for worship. Hence the need for musicians and *singers* from among *the Levites.* [See question #4, page 240.]

To this end David delegates *the chief of the Levites to appoint* those with such abilities to sing and to play musical instruments (see 1 Chronicles 15:17-24, not in today's text; see also 2 Samuel 6:5). The three mentioned instruments—namely, *psalteries* (lyres), *harps,* and *cymbals*—are three of the most common listed in the Chronicles (1 Chronicles 16:5; 25:1, 6; 2 Chronicles 5:12; 29:25). Nehemiah 12:27 lists these important instruments as they came to be used hundreds of years later.

## III. Worshiping Before the Ark (1 Chronicles 15:25-28)

### A. Ark Retrieved (v. 25)

**25. So David, and the elders of Israel, and the captains over thousands, went to bring up the ark of the covenant of the LORD out of the house of Obed-edom with joy.**

God had blessed Obed-edom's household over the three months that *the ark of the covenant* was in his *house* (1 Chronicles 13:14). This fact gives courage to David to make a second attempt at bringing the ark to Jerusalem (2 Samuel 6:12). In 1 Chronicles 14, the author indicates that God also is blessing David in all that he does. So *with joy* David and all the leaders of Israel go to Obed-edom's house to *bring up* the ark to the high hill above David's palace. Things are looking up!

### B. Sacrifices Offered (v. 26)

**26. And it came to pass, when God helped the Levites that bare the ark of the covenant of the LORD, that they offered seven bullocks and seven rams.**

This verse tells us about the sacrifices that are made at the beginning of this trip. First Chronicles 16:1 tells us about offerings made as the trip concludes. Second Samuel 6:13 adds to the richness of the imagery.

### C. Linen Worn (v. 27)

**27. And David was clothed with a robe of fine linen, and all the Levites that bare the ark, and the singers, and Chenaniah the master of the song with the singers: David also had upon him an ephod of linen.**

At first glance, *David* may appear to be improperly dressed, for he is wearing garments reserved for *Levites*, especially the *ephod of linen.* This is a tightly fitted white undergarment that

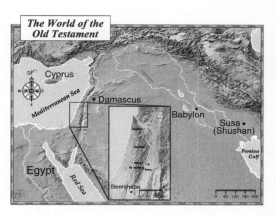

*The World of the Old Testament*

Visual for Lesson 1. *Keep this map displayed the entire quarter to give your learners a geographical perspective.*

is sleeveless. It usually comes down only to the hips. It is worn by those serving at the tent of meeting (see 1 Samuel 2:18; 22:18).

In a sense, David is acting in a priestly mode in bringing the ark into Jerusalem as he offers sacrifices and blesses the people (1 Chronicles 16:2). His actions are not without precedent when we consider Psalm 110 and the "priest-king" Melchizedek (also see Genesis 14:18-20). It is possible we are viewing David, in a sense, as a priest-king (compare Zechariah 6:9-15; also see Acts 2:29, 30, which refers to David as a prophet).

### D. Joy Evident (v. 28)

**28. Thus all Israel brought up the ark of the covenant of the LORD with shouting, and with sound of the cornet, and with trumpets, and with cymbals, making a noise with psalteries and harps.**

Ancient Israelite worship music is culturally different from what is called "contemporary worship" today. But there is one thing the two have in common: they are both loud (compare Ezra 3:13; Nehemiah 12:43; Psalm 150). The louder the better! By the use of percussion, wind, and string instruments, the gathering crowd of Israelites and their gifted musicians make a tremendous joyful noise to the Lord.

We may be able to imagine how loud this worship is by counting the number of musicians in 1 Chronicles 15:19-22. There we see three musicians on cymbals, eight on psalteries (lyres), and six on harps. The number of singers is unknown. But 1 Chronicles 15:5-10 reveals hundreds of Levites to be present, all singing. [See question #5, page 240.]

### "A WAY TO GLORIFY GOD"

A few years ago, having someone's house "flocked" or "flamingoed" was a popular method by which churches raised money for missions or other congregational projects. A church member would give perhaps $25 to the project, and a crew would place 50 plastic pink flamingoes on another member's front lawn. That person then would have to pay the same amount to have the awful-looking things removed or placed on another member's lawn.

One church in Florida used this idea to raise $1,200 for outreach projects such as feeding and clothing the poor. At one time they had a month-long waiting list for their flightless flock. The coordinator of the project said, "It's a way to glorify God. It's good for the church and good for the community."

What do you think of this method of raising money for the Lord's work? Love it or hate it, it certainly was creative! One Christian's idea of what glorifies God can be different from another's. This is certainly true of our worship music. Some Christians don't like any instrumental music at all; others believe a pipe organ is best; others—most often young people, it seems—would be happy listening to David's worship band making a loud noise. (Some older Christians might say that's *all* it was!) The main challenge is to make our worship become a more heartfelt and meaningful way to glorify God. Remember: He is our audience.    —C. R. B.

## Conclusion

### A. Worshiping in the Presence of God

The ancient Israelites rejoiced greatly, for they had placed on Zion the symbol of God's presence that was initiated by God himself. The ark itself symbolized God's throne, or at least His footstool. The status of the Israelites as God's people was based in large part on their receiving and keeping the Ten Commandments, located within the ark. God's gracious provision for His people during the wilderness wanderings was symbolized by a jar of manna, also within the ark. The God-given leadership of Moses and Aaron was signified by Aaron's budded rod, within the ark as well.

For the Christian, the greatest physical symbol of God's presence is found in the Lord's Supper. Jesus said, "This is my body, which is broken for you." To symbolize His shed blood Jesus said, "This cup is the new testament in my blood: this do ye, as oft as ye drink it, in remembrance of me" (1 Corinthians 11:24, 25). The Gospel of John makes it clear that God's spiritual presence today is His own Holy Spirit (John 16:5-15; compare Acts 5:32; Ephesians 1:13).

Look around you the next time you worship with fellow believers. What symbols of God's presence do you see? Certainly the cross is a good one. The Bible, as the revelation of God's Word, is another. But keep looking! Some of the greatest symbols of God's presence are all around you. These are the men and women who worship alongside us. God has created every human being in His image (Genesis 1:26, 27). It is we and not the animals who can reflect who God is in love, graciousness, and compassion (compare Psalm 111:4, 5).

More vital symbols of God's presence are the hungry we feed, the thirsty to whom we give drink, the strangers we welcome, the naked we clothe, the sick we look after, and the prisoners we visit. Jesus himself said, "Inasmuch as ye have done it unto one of the least of these my brethren, ye have done it unto me" (Matthew 25:40b). God is present in those we serve.

### B. Prayer

Our Father, whenever we partake of the bread and cup, may we see Jesus as He is in all His love and compassion for us. May we discern the unity of the body of Christ, the church. Help us to see Christ in those we serve. Take away all selfishness and greediness in our hearts. May we reflect Your righteousness, generosity, and compassion as Your image-bearers. Be glorified in Your people. In Christ we pray, amen.

### C. Thought to Remember

Rejoice in the symbols of God's presence.

## Home Daily Bible Readings

**Monday, Feb. 25**—Let Everything Praise the Lord (Psalm 150)

**Tuesday, Feb. 26**—The Ark of God (1 Chronicles 15:1-3, 11-15)

**Wednesday, Feb. 27**—Music, Joy, and Celebration (1 Chronicles 15:16-24)

**Thursday, Feb. 28**—Bringing the Ark of the Covenant (1 Chronicles 15:25-29)

**Friday, Feb. 29**—Ministering Before the Ark (1 Chronicles 16:1-6)

**Saturday, Mar. 1**—A Psalm of Thanksgiving (1 Chronicles 16:7-36)

**Sunday, Mar. 2**—Worship Before the Ark (1 Chronicles 16:37-43)

# Learning by Doing

*This page contains an alternative lesson plan emphasizing learning activities.*
*Classes desiring such student involvement will find these suggestions helpful.*

## Into the Lesson

Collect in advance pictures of the following from magazines or the Internet: A. a diploma or cap-and-gown for graduation; B. a TV; C. wedding rings; D. a hard hat; E. balance scales; F. a football; G. a piggy bank; H. a recreational vehicle.

If you have large pictures of each, label each one with its letter and display them together on a wall of your classroom. If you have smaller pictures, put them on a single piece of paper with their letters; give each learner a photocopy.

Distribute these instructions (but don't distribute the answers): For each activity or institution listed below, identify a common symbol from the images displayed. 1. Savings; 2. Justice; 3. Education; 4. Work; 5. Marriage; 6. Vacation; 7. Recreation; 8. Entertainment. *Answers: 1, G; 2, E; 3, A; 4, D; 5, C; 6, H; 7, F; 8, B.* Have volunteers share their answers and discuss other symbols that could have been used.

Next, display or distribute images of these Christian symbols: A. a lion; B. a dove; C. a cross; D. a fish; E. Noah's ark. Explain to your class that each of these symbols was used by the early church to represent some special person, event, or doctrine of Scripture.

Ask your students to match those symbols with these possible answers: 1. The Holy Spirit; 2. Baptism; 3. Jesus (two answers); 4. Forgiveness of sin. *Answers: 1, B (Luke 3:22); 2, E (1 Peter 3:18-21); 3, A & D (Revelation 5:5; the Greek word for fish, ichthus, was used by Christians as an acrostic for "Jesus Christ, Son of God, Savior"); 4, C (1 Peter 2:24).*

Once again, have volunteers share their answers and discuss other symbols the early church used. Then tell your class that today's lesson involves ancient Israel's most precious symbol of God's presence.

## Into the Word

From the Lesson Introduction and Lesson Background, develop a brief lecture to explain the symbolism of the ark of the covenant, its importance to the Hebrew people, and the historical background of today's lesson.

Then ask three learners to read these verse sections aloud, one volunteer per section: 1 Chronicles 15:1-3, 14-16, 25-28. After a section is read, use the lesson commentary and the questions below to discuss it. (The questions are reprinted in the optional student books.)

*First Chronicles 15:1-3:* Where would David most likely have prepared a place for the ark in Jerusalem? Why were the Levites the only ones allowed to carry the ark?

*First Chronicles 15:14-16:* What was involved in the process by which a priest sanctified himself? Why did the priests carry the ark on their shoulders?

*First Chronicles 15:25-28:* Who normally wore linen robes? (See 1 Samuel 2:18.) What did David's robe signify? (See Zechariah 6:9-15.) How do you imagine the worship sounded, according to verse 28? Why were the Israelites so joyful?

## Into Life

Divide your learners into small groups for the two exercises below. If your class is small, you can do the exercises as a class. The first exercise is printed also in the optional student book. If you don't use that resource, distribute copies of the instructions below.

*Exercise #1: Their Worship, and Ours.* Ask someone in your group to read aloud Psalm 150. Based on what you have heard in today's text (including 1 Chronicles 16:1, 2) and in Psalm 150, make a list of similarities and contrasts between worship practices in ancient Israel and in our congregation today. Answers should be organized into the following categories: 1. Types of worship activities; 2. Types of musical instruments used (if any); 3. Things for which God is praised; 4. Religious symbols used; 5. Involvement of the congregation.

After groups finish their work, discuss their conclusions as a class. When you address the fifth category, ask your learners how they think your congregation compares with Israel in its enthusiasm in worship. Discuss the benefits and possible problems of that level of enthusiasm.

*Exercise #2: Passionate Praise.* Within your small group, discuss ways to use more Christian symbolism in our worship services. Brainstorm several ways to make your worship more enthusiastic. Be prepared to share your answers with the class.

# Let's Talk It Over

*The questions on this page are designed to promote discussion of the lesson by the class and to encourage application of the lesson Scriptures. The answers provided are only discussion starters. Let your class talk it over from there.*

**1. What symbols have you found to be helpful in reminding you that God is near? Under what circumstances can a symbol be harmful?**

For some people, wearing a cross or a dove on a necklace or lapel is helpful. Others like to have religious artwork on their walls. Still others listen to Christian music to keep themselves focused on God. While some may disapprove of the practice, many young Christians have tattoos with Christian symbols or slogans. The list of possible symbols is nearly endless.

Symbols become harmful when we allow ourselves to become enamored with the symbol itself rather than that to which the symbols should point: God. The ancient Jews got into trouble when thinking of the temple as something of a good-luck charm (Jeremiah 7:4).

**2. What was a time when one of your plans failed because of poor execution even though your heart was in the right place? How did you grow spiritually as a result of that experience?**

David had the right heart in both of his attempts to move the ark. Yet 1 Chronicles 13 demonstrates a good idea with poor execution. The happy ending of the 1 Chronicles 15 account shows that David learned from his mistake. As his son Solomon observed, "He that refuseth instruction despiseth his own soul: but he that heareth reproof getteth understanding" (Proverbs 15:32).

Whenever we draw near to God, we must do so on His terms. A sincere heart is important, but people can be sincerely wrong. Zeal must be based on knowledge (Romans 10:2). Popular thinking is sincere in believing that there are many roads to God, but Jesus taught differently: "I am the way, the truth, and the life: no man cometh unto the Father, but by me" (John 14:6).

**3. What can we do to prepare ourselves for drawing near to God?**

People have different practices that help them focus on God and filter out distractions. A time of sharing these tips can be mutually beneficial. Some Scriptural precepts include quieting one's body and mind (Psalm 46:10); making peace with others (Matthew 5:23, 24; 1 Peter 3:7); prayerfully

examining ourselves (1 Corinthians 11:27-29); choosing to live in obedience to God's commands (Proverbs 15:29; 1 Peter 3:12); and approaching God with a worshipful, thankful attitude (Psalm 100).

**4. Which songs bring you into a worshipful state of mind? Why?**

Music can unite our hearts in worship. Sadly, however, different tastes in music styles become points of division in some churches. Some folks like to stick only with their old favorites. Yet many psalms speak of singing "a new song" to the Lord (Psalms 33:3; 40:3; 96:1; 98:1; 144:9; 149:1). New songs will be sung in Heaven (Revelation 5:9; 14:3). But whether we sing new songs or old, we are to "serve the Lord with gladness: come before his presence with singing" (Psalm 100:2).

**5. First Chronicles 15:25-28 describes an all-out worship celebration. What would an all-out worship celebration look like today? How would we know if such a celebration had gone "too far"? Or is it even possible to go "too far"? Explain.**

We see in 2 Samuel 6:14 a fuller description of David dancing "before the Lord with all his might." He expressed unbridled joy as he led the procession to bring the ark to Jerusalem. Psalm 150 gives us a description of uninhibited praise that includes dancing. Yet at least one person thought David had gone too far as he "shamelessly uncovereth himself" (see 2 Samuel 6:16, 20). Concerns about "what people might think" can prevent us from worshiping freely.

Differing opinions over styles of worship have caused conflict in churches. Fuel is added to the fire when labels are used (examples: those who don't like "traditional" worship call it *dead;* those who don't like "contemporary" worship call it *mindless emotionalism*). Romans 14 is important to consider in this regard. While we will not always agree, we must accept each other. It's fine to hold strong convictions (Romans 14:5), but we must do so with respect and consideration for God's other servants. God is more concerned about worship that is "in spirit and in truth" than He is about particular styles (John 4:23, 24).

# God Makes a Covenant with David

DEVOTIONAL READING: **Psalm 78:67-72.**

BACKGROUND SCRIPTURE: **1 Chronicles 17.**

PRINTED TEXT: **1 Chronicles 17:1-4, 6-15.**

### 1 Chronicles 17:1-4, 6-15

1 Now it came to pass, as David sat in his house, that David said to Nathan the prophet, Lo, I dwell in a house of cedars, but the ark of the covenant of the LORD remaineth under curtains.

2 Then Nathan said unto David, Do all that is in thine heart; for God is with thee.

3 And it came to pass the same night, that the word of God came to Nathan, saying,

4 Go and tell David my servant, Thus saith the LORD, Thou shalt not build me a house to dwell in.

· · · · · · · · · · · ·

6 Wheresoever I have walked with all Israel, spake I a word to any of the judges of Israel, whom I commanded to feed my people, saying, Why have ye not built me a house of cedars?

7 Now therefore thus shalt thou say unto my servant David, Thus saith the LORD of hosts, I took thee from the sheepcote, even from following the sheep, that thou shouldest be ruler over my people Israel:

8 And I have been with thee whithersoever thou hast walked, and have cut off all thine enemies from before thee, and have made thee a name like the name of the great men that are in the earth.

9 Also I will ordain a place for my people Israel, and will plant them, and they shall dwell in their place, and shall be moved no more; neither shall the children of wickedness waste them any more, as at the beginning.

10 And since the time that I commanded judges to be over my people Israel. Moreover I will subdue all thine enemies. Furthermore I tell thee, that the LORD will build thee a house.

11 And it shall come to pass, when thy days be expired that thou must go to be with thy fathers, that I will raise up thy seed after thee, which shall be of thy sons; and I will establish his kingdom.

12 He shall build me a house, and I will stablish his throne for ever.

13 I will be his father, and he shall be my son: and I will not take my mercy away from him, as I took it from him that was before thee.

14 But I will settle him in mine house and in my kingdom for ever: and his throne shall be established for evermore.

15 According to all these words, and according to all this vision, so did Nathan speak unto David.

---

GOLDEN TEXT: I have been with thee whithersoever thou hast walked, and have cut off all thine enemies from before thee, and have made thee a name like the name of the great men that are in the earth.—1 Chronicles 17:8.

*God, the People, and the Covenant*
Unit 1: Signs of God's Covenant
(Lessons 1-5)

## Lesson Aims

After participating in this lesson, each student will be able to:

1. List the most important features of God's covenant with David.

2. Compare and contrast God's covenant with David and with God's covenant with Christians.

3. Suggest one specific way to demonstrate that he or she is living under the covenant promised to David and fulfilled in Christ.

## Lesson Outline

INTRODUCTION
    A. Covenant Making
    B. Overview of Old Testament Covenants
    C. Lesson Background
  I. WHAT DAVID NOTICES (1 Chronicles 17:1, 2)
    A. King's Noble Desire (v. 1)
    B. Prophet's Rash Response (v. 2)
 II. HOW GOD REACTS (1 Chronicles 17:3, 4, 6-8a)
    A. Historical Review, Part 1 (vv. 3, 4, 6)
    B. Historical Review, Part 2 (vv. 7, 8a)
III. WHAT GOD PROMISES (1 Chronicles 17:8b-14)
    A. David's Name (v. 8b)
    B. Israel's Security (vv. 9, 10a)
      *What a Difference in Covenants!*
    C. David's Dynasty (vv. 10b-14)
      *A Different Kind of Dynasty*
IV. WHAT NATHAN DOES (1 Chronicles 17:15)
CONCLUSION
    A. Keeping Covenant with God
    B. Prayer
    C. Thought to Remember

## Introduction

### A. Covenant Making

When I was growing up, I had a second cousin who was like a brother to me since I had no brother and only one sister. We were the same age and played together as often as we could. When we were in about the third grade, we made a covenant with one another. We even pricked our fingers to "exchange" our blood in this special relationship. (We had seen Indians do this in the movies.)

What was our covenant? *To never get married!* We announced this covenant to all family members and to as many others as we could. This, of course, was in our prepuberty days, and girls were our natural enemies. We held each other accountable to the covenant for a number of years. But eventually we broke the covenant. Charles married after he had graduated from high school, and I married at the end of my graduate studies. No one was surprised that we broke our covenant.

Western culture has a problem with the term *covenant*. We know what a *contract* is, but the word *covenant* has fallen into disuse for the most part. Also, the concept of living under a covenant relationship (such as marriage) is antiquated and unthinkable to many because of secular cultural influences. It is no wonder that even many Christians in Western democracies have a difficult time understanding the concept of covenant as the Bible presents that idea. But try we must.

### B. Overview of Old Testament Covenants

A *covenant* is an agreement between two parties in which various promises, obligations, and conditions are expressed or implied. The terms of the covenant depend on the parties and their interests. Many covenants in the Bible are between people. These include covenants of friendship (example: 1 Samuel 18:3; 20:8), the institution of marriage (example: Malachi 2:14), and agreements between rulers or authority figures (example: Genesis 21:27; 31:44; 1 Kings 15:19). The latter includes agreements in which the more powerful ruler may dictate terms to the weaker (example: 1 Samuel 11:1, 2).

The above examples are interesting, but it is the covenants that God has made with His people that we want to focus on. Some think that the first covenant in the Bible is found in Genesis 1 and 2—what has been called *the Edenic covenant*. Here God is seen to obligate humans to have dominion over the earth. One prohibition is given: "But of the tree of the knowledge of good and evil, thou shalt not eat of it" (Genesis 2:17).

*The Adamic covenant* follows in Genesis 3. There God promises to bring some form of hope in the midst of curses for disobedience to the provisions of Genesis 2:17 in the Edenic covenant. "And I will put enmity between thee and the woman, and between thy seed and her seed; it shall bruise thy head, and thou shalt bruise his heel" (Genesis 3:15).

The third covenant has been called *the Noahic covenant*. Noah and his sons were blessed by God and told to, "Be fruitful, and multiply, and replenish the earth" (Genesis 9:1). They were given dominion over all living things upon the earth, even the flesh of animals for food. Capital punishment for murder was instituted to acknowledge the sanctity of human life (9:6). The sign of the rainbow assured Noah and his family that God would never again flood the earth (9:15, 16).

The fourth covenant is *the Abrahamic covenant*. God promised to Abraham land of his own, seed that would become a great nation, and blessing (both materially and spiritually) by God's presence. Somehow all peoples of the earth were to be blessed through Abraham (Genesis 12:1-3). This promise was confirmed by the slaughter of animals (Genesis 15:9-21). God obligated himself to the promise of land, seed, and blessing. Abraham's part was to be faithful to God's instructions. The sign of this covenant was to be in the flesh of every male descendant of Abraham (Genesis 17:11-14).

The fifth covenant in the Bible is called *the Sinaitic covenant* or *the Mosaic covenant*. God had delivered the Israelites from Egypt, and at Mount Sinai He bestowed a special position to Israel (Exodus 19:5, 6a). A key part of obeying God's voice was the obligation to keep the Ten Commandments (Exodus 20:1-17). Blessings and curses were pronounced, depending on the Israelites' behavior (Leviticus 26).

After the rebellion of the Israelites in the desert, Moses renewed this covenant as he prepared to die on Mount Nebo (Deuteronomy 32–34). The entire book of Deuteronomy is patterned in the shape of a covenant renewal treaty. See also Joshua 8:30-35; 24; 1 Samuel 12; and Nehemiah 8–10.

The prophet Jeremiah spoke of "a new covenant" because Israel had broken the Sinaitic covenant time and again throughout her history (see Jeremiah 31:31-34; Hebrews 8:8-12). But before that new covenant came into being, God instituted *the Davidic covenant*, the subject of today's lesson.

---

### How to Say It

ABRAHAMIC. Ay-bruh-*ham*-ik.
ADAMIC. Uh-*dahm*-ik.
DAVIDIC. Duh-*vid*-ick.
EDENIC. E-*den*-ik.
JEBUSITES. *Jeb*-yuh-sites.
MOSAIC. Mo-*zay*-ik.
NOAHIC. No-*ay*-ik.
PHILISTINES. Fuh-*liss*-teens or *Fill*-us-teens.
SINAITIC. Sin-ee-*at*-ik.

---

### C. Lesson Background

According to 2 Samuel 5 and 6, David ultimately became king over a united Israel. This happened approximately 1000 BC. After conquering the Jebusites and their city of Jerusalem, David made that city the capital of the newly united kingdom. Then he defeated the Philistines (2 Samuel 5:17-25). Afterward, he brought the ark of the covenant into Jerusalem and placed it on Mount Zion under a tent (last week's lesson). This move made Jerusalem both the political and religious capital of the kingdom.

The author of Chronicles, writing much later than the author who writes the parallel account in 2 Samuel, used a combination of psalms to illustrate David's attitude of thanksgiving: compare Psalm 105:1-15 with 1 Chronicles 16:7-22; Psalm 96 with 1 Chronicles 16:23-33; and Psalm 106:1, 47, 48 with 1 Chronicles 16:34-36. It is at this point in the Chronicles account that God made His eternal promise to David—today's text.

## I. What David Notices (1 Chronicles 17:1, 2)

### A. King's Noble Desire (v. 1)

**1. Now it came to pass, as David sat in his house, that David said to Nathan the prophet, Lo, I dwell in a house of cedars, but the ark of the covenant of the LORD remaineth under curtains.**

Apparently *Nathan* is a court *prophet* who lives in Jerusalem. As such, he has ready access to King *David*. The parallel account of 2 Samuel 7 also mentions Nathan.

David conveys to Nathan his embarrassment at his personal surroundings of a beautiful cedar palace (see 2 Samuel 5:11; 1 Chronicles 14:1) in contrast with the mere tent covering he has provided for *the ark of the covenant* (1 Chronicles 16:1). The implication of David's statement of contrast is his desire to build a better, more permanent structure for God's ark. [See question #1, page 248.]

### B. Prophet's Rash Response (v. 2)

**2. Then Nathan said unto David, Do all that is in thine heart; for God is with thee.**

We may be inclined to think of the great men of old, such as the Old Testament prophets, as superspiritual. They are indeed very holy, yet they can still make mistakes. What we see here is that Nathan's line of thinking is the same as David's. *Nathan* also equates his own thoughts with the will of God. As a result, Nathan replies *do all that is in thine heart; for God is with thee.* This statement proves to be rash, as the next verse shows. Nathan jumps the gun. [See question #2, page 248.]

## II. How God Reacts
## (1 Chronicles 17:3, 4, 6-8a)

### A. Historical Review, Part 1 (vv. 3, 4, 6)

**3, 4. And it came to pass the same night, that the word of God came to Nathan, saying, Go and tell David my servant, Thus saith the LORD, Thou shalt not build me a house to dwell in.**

That very *night,* before anything can be done to advance David's dreamed-of building project, *the word of God* comes *to Nathan* in a vision (see v. 15, below). God gives specific words to Nathan to relate to *David.* What God has to say is rather lengthy, as we shall see.

The first sentence of God's communication is quite pointed: *Thou shalt not build me a house to dwell in.* The unmistakable effect of this declarative statement is the negation of David's desire.

**6. Wheresoever I have walked with all Israel, spake I a word to any of the judges of Israel, whom I commanded to feed my people, saying, Why have ye not built me a house of cedars?**

Verse 5 (not in today's text) emphasizes the fact that God has dwelt in a tent ever since the exodus, some 400 years in the past by this time. Yet tents are not durable over such a long period. Materials wear out due to normal wear and tear, exposure to the elements, and destruction by insects. This realization is undoubtedly part of David's desire to improve this situation. Yet has God ever said a word to any of Israel's leaders throughout their history about wanting *a house* to dwell in? [See question #3, page 248.]

We should pause to note a certain play on words in Hebrew that occurs throughout this chapter. So far the Hebrew word for *house* has had two meanings: *house* as in "palace" (v. 1) and *house* as in "temple" (vv. 4-6). In verse 10 (below), it will take on a third meaning. This is a major literary device both here and in 2 Samuel 7.

### B. Historical Review, Part 2 (vv. 7, 8a)

**7. Now therefore thus shalt thou say unto my servant David, Thus saith the LORD of hosts, I took thee from the sheepcote, even from following the sheep, that thou shouldest be ruler over my people Israel.**

God, through Nathan, reminds *David* of his humble beginnings. David, the youngest of eight brothers, had been a shepherd boy in Bethlehem (1 Samuel 16:1-12). He had not been allowed even to fight alongside his brothers in battle (1 Samuel 17:14, 15, 28). [See question #4, page 248.]

By divine providence David killed Goliath, the Philistine hero. This was an important milestone in David's road to kingship. David's days as a shepherd with a sling and staff had prepared him for killing the Philistine giant. Those same shepherd days also prepared him to be king over God's people. The word *shepherd* could be used to describe the role of kings (see Isaiah 44:28; Ezekiel 37:23, 24; Zechariah 11:16). The word also describes God (Psalm 80:1) and Jesus (Hebrews 13:20; 1 Peter 2:25; 5:4).

**8a. And I have been with thee whithersoever thou hast walked, and have cut off all thine enemies from before thee.**

God's presence with David has been constant. Passages such as 1 Samuel 16:13; 17:45-47; 23:2, 14; 24:10; 26:12; 30:23; 2 Samuel 5:10, 23-25; 6:21 bear this out. In this David is unlike his predecessor King Saul. The Spirit of the Lord was with Saul for a while, but eventually departed from him (1 Samuel 16:14; 18:12).

## III. What God Promises
## (1 Chronicles 17:8b-14)

### A. David's Name (v. 8b)

**8b. And have made thee a name like the name of the great men that are in the earth.**

The terminology we see here reminds us of God's covenant promise to Abraham: "and make thy name great" (Genesis 12:2). The fact that it is God who has made David's name great is also reflected in the parallel passage of 2 Samuel 7:9. Ancient rulers get themselves in serious trouble when they assume that their greatness is due to their own efforts rather than to God (see Daniel 4:28-33; Acts 12:19b-23). David does not tread this path!

### B. Israel's Security (vv. 9, 10a)

**9, 10a. Also I will ordain a place for my people Israel, and will plant them, and they shall dwell in their place, and shall be moved no more; neither shall the children of wickedness waste them any more, as at the beginning, and since the time that I commanded judges to be over my people Israel. Moreover I will subdue all thine enemies.**

God is now bringing to fullness His promise of Genesis 15:13-21 to Abraham: that *Israel* is to find a peaceful *place* in her own land. The word *ordain* suggests "to put, place, or set." (The *King James Version* uses *appoint* for the same Hebrew word in the parallel passage of 2 Samuel 7:10.) All *the children of wickedness* (Israel's *enemies*) will be subdued, just as God has subdued and will continue to subdue all of David's personal enemies.

The time of the judges (about 1380 to 1050 BC) had seen great oppression of God's people because of unfaithfulness. In God's ideal plan, this shall be no more! Indeed, Israel is to be planted as a vine in an orchard (see Psalm 80:8-11; Isaiah 5:1-7; Jeremiah 2:21; Ezekiel 19:10-14; compare John 15:1-5).

### What a Difference in Covenants!

Police in Klamath Falls, Oregon, uncovered a bizarre covenant in February 2005. A man had been using the Internet to entice people to participate in a mass suicide that was to take place on Valentine's Day of that year. The plan was for participants to commit suicide while logged onto the Internet with others who had agreed to do the same.

Fortunately, the pact was discovered before it could be acted upon. Someone alerted authorities after learning that a woman planned to kill her children before committing suicide. The man who tried to set up the mass suicide had been promoting his "suicide ideology" for several years.

The covenants God has made with His people come from His loving heart, not from a twisted mind. His covenants are for our benefit. He has no hidden agenda. His covenants have promised life, not death. They have been offered to people with ears to listen and hearts to respond. God's promise to David is a vital precursor to the new covenant we have in Christ. Through Christ, we share in God's promise to David.     —C. R. B.

### C. David's Dynasty (vv. 10b-14)

**10b, 11. Furthermore I tell thee, that the LORD will build thee a house. And it shall come to pass, when thy days be expired that thou must go to be with thy fathers, that I will raise up thy seed after thee, which shall be of thy sons; and I will establish his kingdom.**

Within the phrase *the Lord will build thee a house* we see the third meaning of *house* that we mentioned in the commentary to verse 6 (above). This word now signifies the dynasty of David. David is promised that his sons shall reign in his stead after his death. A dynasty of Davidic sons will rule over God's people. God himself will build this house (dynasty).

### A Different Kind of Dynasty

What image does the word *dynasty* bring to your mind? In some countries, people may think of a powerful family that rules (either with benevolence or oppression) for generation after

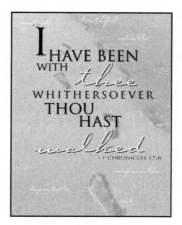

Visual for Lesson 2

*Turn this visual into a discussion question: "What was a time when God was with you?"*

generation. Sports fans may speak of *a dynasty* when a particular team wins two championships in a row. Americans over the age of 35 may recall the tawdry TV show of the 1980s named *Dynasty*. The show involved schemes and feuds for wealth and power in an oil-rich family. In this respect, that TV program portrayed people much like many to be found in real-life political dynasties.

The producers of that program seem to have zeroed right in on the darker side of human nature. The public's taste for the schemes that made the characters of *Dynasty* rich and strong is seen in the fact that there are still Web sites devoted to the various episodes and characters in the program. Power-at-any-cost can be a strong fantasy.

When God promised David a dynasty, He had something *much* different in mind! God, not any man, created that dynasty. David himself was the first king in the dynastic line, and his son Solomon was the second. But by far the greatest and ultimate Son in the royal line would be Jesus. His kingdom is one of righteousness, a far cry from the political and TV-show kingdoms of this world. Our righteous lives demonstrate whose kingdom we are subjects of.     —C. R. B.

**12. He shall build me a house, and I will stablish his throne for ever.**

We know from the way that history unfolds that the *he* in this verse refers to one of David's sons—namely, Solomon. He is the one who will build for God a *house* (temple); the delay of building the temple from the time of David to the time of Solomon thus will be more than 30 years. In the passage of time, God will establish Solomon's kingdom *(his throne)* too (see 1 Kings 2:46b; 8:15-21; 9:5; 10:4-9, 23-25).

**13, 14. I will be his father, and he shall be my son: and I will not take my mercy away from him, as I took it from him that was before thee: but I will settle him in mine house and in my kingdom for ever: and his throne shall be established for evermore.**

The phrase *I will be his father, and he shall be my son* is adoption terminology (compare 2 Samuel 7:14; Psalm 2:7; 2 Corinthians 6:18). God, as the ruling Father, has adopted this person as a son to be ruler with His approval.

The word *mercy* should be understood to signify "covenant love" or "covenant loyalty." God will not take away His covenant love or covenant loyalty from David or his descendants as He took it away from Saul (the first king). [See question #5, page 248.] Note that the author of Chronicles leaves out mention of possible punishment if any of David's sons should sin against God as we see in 2 Samuel 7:14b. This does not mean that the author of Chronicles is ignorant of that. Rather, he wishes to present Solomon in the best possible light (see Lesson 3).

Note also that the author of Chronicles emphasizes God's part in this covenant promise by saying *mine house* and *my kingdom* rather than "thine house" and "thy kingdom," as we see in 2 Samuel 7:16. It is a dynasty, a kingdom, a throne that will be established forever at the initiative of God (compare also Psalm 89:3, 4, 20-37). While some may think that this never happened, ultimately God does fulfill this promise as He does with all His promises (see Luke 1:32, 33).

## Home Daily Bible Readings

**Monday, Mar. 3**—God Chose David (Psalm 78:67-72)
**Tuesday, Mar. 4**—No House for God (1 Chronicles 17:1-6)
**Wednesday, Mar. 5**—God's House for David (1 Chronicles 17:7-10)
**Thursday, Mar. 6**—A House of Ancestors (1 Chronicles 17:11-15)
**Friday, Mar. 7**—Great Deeds of God (1 Chronicles 17:16-19)
**Saturday, Mar. 8**—A House of Israel (1 Chronicles 17:20-22)
**Sunday, Mar. 9**—The House of David (1 Chronicles 17:23-27)

## IV. What Nathan Does
## (1 Chronicles 17:15)

**15. According to all these words, and according to all this vision, so did Nathan speak unto David.**

*Nathan* is faithful in delivering *this vision* to *David* word for word. While these are joyful *words* to deliver, Nathan will later have to be the bearer of bad news for David (2 Samuel 12:1-12). Nathan will live long enough to be the prophet to anoint David's son Solomon as king (1 Kings 1:34).

# Conclusion
## A. Keeping Covenant with God

It is clear that there were all kinds of covenants in the world of ancient Israel. But one of the greatest covenants was God's covenant of an eternal promise to David that his throne would be forever. It was an unconditional promise in the sense that God would somehow fulfill His promise regardless of the behavior of David's descendants.

History tells us that David's royal descendants did sin—grievously. God did punish those descendants, even to the point of cutting off the Davidic dynasty for a long while (see 2 Samuel 7:14; 1 Chronicles 28:7 [next week's lesson]; Psalm 89:19-49). Many years later, a Davidic Son would appear to whom God would give David's throne (see Luke 1:32, 33). Thus this promise was fulfilled at Jesus' resurrection and ascension to God's right hand (see Acts 2:33-36; 13:34).

Just as God is a covenant-keeping God for His people, we need to be a covenant-keeping people for God. Those who accept Christ and follow the biblical plan of salvation enter into God's new covenant. We need to renew our commitment to that covenant daily. Every step we make, every word we speak, every breath we take is to be made in light of our covenant with God. May we keep covenant with God!

### B. Prayer

O Lord God of covenants, may we keep Your new covenant in Christ as You have kept all covenants with us in the past. May we live up to the great name *Christian* that You have given to us. In Christ's great name, amen.

### C. Thought to Remember

Keeping covenant with God should be our first priority.

# Learning by Doing

*This page contains an alternative lesson plan emphasizing learning activities.*
*Classes desiring such student involvement will find these suggestions helpful.*

## Into the Lesson

Say to your learners, "Imagine that you are part of a building committee in charge of negotiating with a contractor to construct a new addition to the church facilities. Your committee must draft a contract between the church and the builder that is fair to both parties. What would be some of the key elements of that contract?"

As learners share the answers, record their responses on the board for the whole class to see. Some of the key elements would include the names of the parties to the contract, a definition of terms, the terms of payment, the scheduled completion of the project, and provisions for correcting problems in the building.

When you have compiled a sizable list, tell your class that God has made a number of special contracts or "covenants" with people in the Bible. Today's lesson deals with one of those covenants: the one between God and David.

## Into the Word

Using the Lesson Introduction, review briefly the various covenants that led up to the Davidic covenant. Then use the commentary to explain the first five verses of today's lesson text.

Just before moving into a consideration of 1 Chronicles 17:6, distribute copies of the following true-false quiz (the quiz is also printed in the optional student book). Say, "Read 1 Chronicles 17:6-15 to find the correct answers."

T F 1. God promised to treat King Solomon differently from how He treated King Saul.

T F 2. God had not yet commanded Israel to build a permanent structure for Him.

T F 3. God promised to build David a beautiful palace.

T F 4. God promised David that one of his sons would build the temple.

T F 5. God never claimed to have made David famous.

T F 6. God promised to establish the throne of David's son forever.

T F 7. God reminded David of his humble beginnings before God made him king of Israel.

T F 8. Part of God's promise to David was that Israel would be a nomadic people forever, continually moving from place to as they did under Moses.

*Answers: 1. T (v. 13); 2. T (v. 6); 3. F (v. 10, the promise was to create a dynasty of David's descendants); 4. T (vv. 11, 12); 5. F (v. 8); 6. T (v. 12); 7. T (v. 7); 8. F (v. 9).* Go over the correct answers as a class.

Inform your learners that distinct sections may be discerned in Old Testament covenants. Distribute handouts that list those sections as follows (or direct attention to the optional student book, where the list is reproduced):

*1. The historical prologue:* a review of events leading up to the covenant under consideration.

*2. The stipulations:* statements of the terms of the covenant, including what God promises to do for those who obey them.

*3. The sanctions:* warnings against breaking the covenant and a description of penalties for doing so.

*4. The oath:* a pledge to keep the covenant.

Next, divide your learners into small groups. Ask groups to scan 1 Chronicles 17 and 28:2-10, then write a brief summary of what the Davidic covenant included in terms of the four features. When you review their answers, you will find that section one is covered in 17:1-7; 28:2, 3; section two in 17:7-14; 28:4-9; section three in 28:9; section four in 17:23-27.

(To allow more time for the Into Life segment, you can put the answers on the handouts before you distribute them. This will allow you to summarize them quickly, skipping the small-group research at this point.)

## Into Life

Remind your class that we live under the new covenant, mediated by our Lord Jesus Christ. Ask your small groups to study and summarize each of the following Scriptures, then categorize them under the four covenant section headings of *prologue, stipulations, sanctions,* and/ or *oath:* Matthew 28:18-20; John 3:14-18; Acts 2:38; 1 Corinthians 11:23-26; Galatians 3:23–4:7; Ephesians 2:8-10; 1 Timothy 6:11-14; Hebrews 1:1-3; 3:1–4:1; 6:13-20; 9:13-15; 10:19-31.

When groups have finished their work, discuss findings as a class. Ask for volunteers to suggest specific ways to demonstrate that one is living under the covenant promised to David and fulfilled in Christ.

# Let's Talk It Over

*The questions on this page are designed to promote discussion of the lesson by the class and to encourage application of the lesson Scriptures. The answers provided are only discussion starters. Let your class talk it over from there.*

**1. How does the quality of the furnishings in your home compare with the quality of the furnishings in the church building where you worship? If the quality of the furnishings in your home is nicer, what can you do to correct the imbalance?**

David was uncomfortable with the fact that his home was nicer than the housing for the ark. Do we have a conscience like David's? Does it bother your conscience to donate your old microwave oven to the church when you get a new one for your house?

David's passion for God is clearly felt in various psalms. When we "catch" David's passion as our own, our priorities will fall in line. Godly priorities will please Him and help us prepare for our eternal home. As Jesus reminds us, "Lay up for yourselves treasures in heaven, where neither moth nor rust doth corrupt, and where thieves do not break through nor steal" (Matthew 6:20).

**2. What was a time when you spoke out but later had to "eat your words"? How did you grow spiritually as a result?**

Nathan gave David the go-ahead to build God a temple; then God corrected Nathan's rash remark. Yet Nathan was given the opportunity to pass the correct instructions to David. We don't have it within our power to be perfect with every word and act. Fortunately for us, God works with and through imperfect people. Think about Moses, who spoke rashly when he should have known better (Numbers 20:10-12; Psalm 106:33). The apostle Peter also spoke rashly at times (example: Luke 9:33), yet God still could use him as a powerful witness.

Learning to be "swift to hear, slow to speak" (James 1:19) will put the brakes on much of our rash talk. Taking to heart Proverbs 13:3; 21:23 will help. When we do speak rashly, it is vital that we accept God's correction. That correction may come directly from God's Word or from a spiritually mature acquaintance (see Proverbs 12:1).

**3. God made it clear that He did not need a house. So how is it possible to give something back to the one who owns all things and gives us all things? How do you do this in your own life?**

God is self-sufficient. He needs nothing from us (Psalm 50:9-12). Yet obedience is what God desires from us. He will not force obedience from us; He wants us to give it willingly. "If ye love me, keep my commandments" (John 14:15).

Our obedience takes many forms. Prayer, worship, offerings, and benevolence are surely on the list of things we can give God. Although God didn't "need" a house, He accepted one from Solomon. God will accept things from us too.

**4. God reminded King David of his lowly shepherding days. What are some ways that God has guided you up to this point in your life?**

God gave His Spirit to David (1 Samuel 16:13) and developed a shepherd into a mighty king. God gives us His Spirit as well (Acts 2:38). He will develop us also, if we are faithful and willing (Matthew 13:12; Ephesians 4:15; 2 Peter 3:18). The experiences in our lives that seem to be inconsequential or menial may very well end up being God's training ground as He prepares us for future kingdom responsibilities. God likes to work through human weakness (1 Corinthians 1:26-29; 2 Corinthians 12:7-10).

**5. How do you react to the fact that God wants you to be a covenant partner with Him in the new covenant?**

Covenants, commitments, contracts—today it seems that there are as many of these as there are people looking for loopholes in them. This theme is the staple of fictionalized courtroom drama and the lives of real-life sports superstars.

How thankful we can be to know that God takes His covenants seriously (Hebrews 6:13-20)! He neither has nor seeks loopholes. We also may be thankful that God's covenant with us is not a parity covenant. This means that the new covenant does not require as much from us as it does from Him (see Matthew 26:28).

Our part is to accept His gracious offer (Acts 2:38; Ephesians 2:8-10; etc.). Although Jesus alone paid the cost for our salvation, our choosing to accept His covenant offer means we must reject living our own self-led ways. In that respect, it is costly on our end (Matthew 16:24, 25). But the cost is worth it (Mark 10:29-31).

# God Calls Solomon to Build the Temple

March 16
Lesson 3

DEVOTIONAL READING: Psalm 132.

BACKGROUND SCRIPTURE: 1 Chronicles 28.

PRINTED TEXT: 1 Chronicles 28:5-10, 20, 21.

### 1 Chronicles 28:5-10, 20, 21

5 And of all my sons, (for the LORD hath given me many sons,) he hath chosen Solomon my son to sit upon the throne of the kingdom of the LORD over Israel.

6 And he said unto me, Solomon thy son, he shall build my house and my courts: for I have chosen him to be my son, and I will be his father.

7 Moreover I will establish his kingdom for ever, if he be constant to do my commandments and my judgments, as at this day.

8 Now therefore, in the sight of all Israel the congregation of the LORD, and in the audience of our God, keep and seek for all the commandments of the LORD your God: that ye may possess this good land, and leave it for an inheritance for your children after you for ever.

9 And thou, Solomon my son, know thou the God of thy father, and serve him with a perfect heart and with a willing mind: for the LORD searcheth all hearts, and understandeth all the imaginations of the thoughts: if thou seek him, he will be found of thee; but if thou forsake him, he will cast thee off for ever.

10 Take heed now; for the LORD hath chosen thee to build a house for the sanctuary: be strong, and do it.

. . . . . . . . . . . . . .

20 And David said to Solomon his son, Be strong and of good courage, and do it: fear not, nor be dismayed, for the LORD God, even my God, will be with thee; he will not fail thee, nor forsake thee, until thou hast finished all the work for the service of the house of the LORD.

21 And, behold, the courses of the priests and the Levites, even they shall be with thee for all the service of the house of God: and there shall be with thee for all manner of workmanship every willing skilful man, for any manner of service: also the princes and all the people will be wholly at thy commandment.

---

GOLDEN TEXT: Take heed now; for the LORD hath chosen thee to build a house for the sanctuary: be strong, and do it.—1 Chronicles 28:10.

*God, the People, and the Covenant*
Unit 1: Signs of God's Covenant
(Lessons 1-5)

## Lesson Aims

After participating in this lesson, each student will be able to:

1. Summarize David's charge to Solomon.

2. Compare and contrast the attitudes and behavior David challenged Solomon to display with the attitudes and behaviors the New Testament commands for Christians.

3. Encourage one other person in the coming week to be strong in Christian faith and service.

## Lesson Outline

INTRODUCTION
  A. Chosen for a Specific Task
  B. Lesson Background
  I. DAVID'S PRONOUNCEMENTS (1 Chronicles 28:5-7)
  A. Solomon Chosen to Be King (v. 5)
  B. Solomon to Build the Temple (v. 6)
  C. Solomon's Reign to Be Conditional (v. 7)
    *The Big If*
 II. DAVID'S CHARGES (1 Chronicles 28:8-10)
  A. Charge to the People (v. 8)
  B. Charges to Solomon (vv. 9, 10)
III. DAVID'S EXHORTATIONS (1 Chronicles 28:20, 21)
  A. Regarding Character (v. 20)
  B. Regarding Workers (v. 21)
    *Creating Something Beautiful*
CONCLUSION
  A. Making a Difference in the World
  B. Prayer
  C. Thought to Remember

## Introduction

### A. Chosen for a Specific Task

One day my dad decided to add a bedroom and porch to the back of our small house. It was a good idea, because my sister and I were reaching our teenage years, and we needed separate bedrooms.

The only problem was that Dad was not a builder. He was a very good sawmiller and mechanic, but he was not a builder. Yet we could not hire people to do such work because we were poor by the standards of America in the 1950s. So we did it ourselves.

When we were finished, it looked good. But the first substantial rain proved all visual satisfactions to be false security. That roof never stopped leaking. So Dad covered the entire back part of the roof with tar, tar, and more tar. That finally stopped the water leaks, but in really hot weather it leaked tar!

Neither my dad nor I ever became builders in the fullest sense of that word. Today I can safely say that God has called me to be a teacher and preacher, and I try to utilize every facet of my abilities in those directions. It is very satisfying. The few times I have tried to remodel our house have ended in frustration. So now whenever I have such a project to do, I hire others to do it. I know my limitations and my calling.

King David recognized that God had called him to carry out certain tasks, but the task of building the temple was reserved for his son Solomon. King David's limitation was not (unlike mine) one of skill, but one of divine restriction (last week's lesson). David thus encouraged his son to complete the task of building the temple. David had an important calling to fulfill, but building the temple was not part of that calling.

### B. Lesson Background

In the first two lessons of this quarter, we have seen our texts from 1 Chronicles paralleled in 2 Samuel. But today's lesson text from 1 Chronicles 28 has no parallel in 1 Kings 1–2, where we would expect to find such a parallel if it existed. The reason seems to be that the author of Chronicles had a particular interest in recording the beginnings of the temple that the author of Kings did not have. We see much emphasis in Chronicles on the skilled craftsmen who participated in this project.

God had chosen Solomon to see this task through (see 1 Chronicles 28:5, 6, 10; 29:1). No other person was to launch this project. Even though David wanted to build the temple and had collected materials for it, God forbade him because he had been a man of war and had shed blood (1 Chronicles 28:3).

David undoubtedly was aware of the divine choices that God had made through the centuries. Judah had been elevated above his brothers (see Genesis 49:8-10), and David himself had been elevated above his own brothers as well (1 Chronicles 28:4). In a sense, Solomon was elevated above his father, David, in being privileged to build the temple. The temple had to be built by a man of peace, which is the meaning of Solomon's name. Solomon's lengthy reign was characterized by peace (1 Kings 4:24, 25).

# I. David's Pronouncements
## (1 Chronicles 28:5-7)
### A. Solomon Chosen to Be King (v. 5)

**5. And of all my sons, (for the LORD hath given me many sons,) he hath chosen Solomon my son to sit upon the throne of the kingdom of the LORD over Israel.**

David had six *sons* born from six different wives during his seven and one-half years in Hebron (2 Samuel 3:2-5; 1 Chronicles 3:1-4). When David made Jerusalem his capital, he took more concubines and wives, and more children were born (2 Samuel 5:13-16; 1 Chronicles 3:5-9; 14:3-7).

Indeed, God gave David *many sons.* But of all these it is *Solomon* (who is not David's firstborn) who is chosen to sit on David's *throne.* This is a major theme in this text.

David is very conscious of God's promise to him of an everlasting dynasty (see 2 Samuel 7:16; 1 Chronicles 28:4a). David was overwhelmed by this promise when it was given many years before (2 Samuel 7:18-29). It is through the Davidic dynasty that God chooses to accomplish His plan for the world. Somehow God's reign in Heaven is to be expressed through this *kingdom* on earth.

So God's throne in Heaven and the Davidic throne on earth are interconnected. The author of Chronicles uses an unusual phrase to communicate this idea: *the throne of the kingdom of the Lord over Israel.* This throne is "a faithful witness in heaven" (Psalm 89:37); and even though one day God will "cast [David's] throne down to the ground" (Psalm 89:44), He will never take away His promise concerning David's everlasting dynasty.

Perhaps David may think that Solomon is the "Lord" to sit at God's right hand until all his enemies are made a footstool for his feet (see Psalm 110:1; compare 1 Kings 5:3). We now know that only Jesus fulfilled and fills that role and position (see Luke 1:32, 33; Hebrews 5–7).

---

### How to Say It

DAVIDIC. Duh-*vid*-ick.
DEUTERONOMY. Due-ter-*ahn*-uh-me.
GERSHON. *Ger*-shun.
KOHATH. *Ko*-hath.
LEVITES. *Lee*-vites.
MERARI. Muh-*ray*-rye.
SHALEM (Hebrew). *shay*-lem.
SHALOM (Hebrew). shah-*lome*.

---

### B. Solomon to Build the Temple (v. 6)

**6. And he said unto me, Solomon thy son, he shall build my house and my courts: for I have chosen him to be my son, and I will be his father.**

Even though the author of Chronicles does not mention it, there has been a long and bitter struggle among David's sons to attain the kingship. It took great court intrigues to have *Solomon* anointed king (see 1 Kings 1–2).

It was by divine direction that David announced Solomon as his successor (1 Chronicles 22:5-13) and the future builder of the temple that David himself so much wanted to build (1 Chronicles 22:7, 8). The wording *chosen him to be my son, and I will be his father* emphasizes Solomon's election by God. It also emphasizes an adoption by God in terms of kingship (compare 2 Samuel 7:14a). [See question #1, page 256.] The verse before us essentially is a covenant statement to reveal a special relationship between God and Solomon, the son of David.

The word *house* signifies "temple." The addition of the word *courts* (as in "courtyards") will be important to the future pilgrims who will arrive in Jerusalem to celebrate the festivals. They will savor the moment when they enter into the courts of the temple (see Psalm 84:2; 100:4; Isaiah 62:9).

### C. Solomon's Reign to Be Conditional (v. 7)

**7. Moreover I will establish his kingdom for ever, if he be constant to do my commandments and my judgments, as at this day.**

This verse is an echo of the original promise in 2 Samuel 7:13-15. But the author of Chronicles decides not to mention the potential punishment of 2 Samuel 7:14b: "If he commit iniquity, I will chasten him with the rod of men." Even without this, however, the author of Chronicles emphasizes the conditional nature of Solomon's reign by using the little word *if.* If Solomon will obey God's commands, then *his kingdom* (dynasty) will last *for ever* (compare 1 Chronicles 22:12, 13).

At the time Chronicles is written centuries after the time of Solomon, there is no Davidic king on a throne in Jerusalem. By that time the remnant in Jerusalem knows the conditional nature of the Davidic dynasty because of the destruction of Jerusalem by the Babylonians in 586 BC. The people will hold out hope that God will restore Israel's fortunes by an anointed one like David to bring about a return to the golden age of David. Surely God will fulfill His promise to David that his kingdom will be forever!

History proves that Solomon became disobedient toward the end of his life. As a result, the

Davidic dynasty suffered. That little word *if* packs a big punch!

Before we move on, we should stress also the unconditional element that we brought out in last week's lesson. In the course of time, God places Jesus on David's throne in a spiritual sense (Luke 1:32, 33). God does this despite the sinful behavior of David's descendants.

### THE BIG *IF*

*Operation Overlord* marked a turning point in World War II. That was the code name for the Allied invasion of Europe, which took place on June 6, 1944. The success of that operation contributed greatly to the eventual defeat of the Nazis.

Several factors helped the invasion succeed. First, General Eisenhower, Supreme Allied Commander, gambled on a break in the weather. Second, Allied planes dropped bombs well north of the invasion area in an attempt to deceive the Germans into thinking the invasion would come elsewhere. Third, Allied airborne troops delayed German reinforcements so the seaborne invasion would have time to establish a beachhead. *If* the weather improved and *if* the deception worked and *if* the delaying action went as planned, *then* the invasion might succeed. It did.

But what if any one of those *ifs* had fallen through? It is much more likely that the invasion would have failed, with history taking a different turn. *If* is such a little word, but it has profound implications. Most of us have played the "what if?" game with ourselves, if not with others.

David's instruction to Solomon was, in effect, "Serve God with a faithful heart. *If* you do, then you will be blessed; but *if* you do not, then God will turn away from you." The principle still stands. *If* is a big word, isn't it?    —C. R. B.

## II. David's Charges
## (1 Chronicles 28:8-10)

### A. Charge to the People (v. 8)

**8. Now therefore, in the sight of all Israel the congregation of the LORD, and in the audience of our God, keep and seek for all the commandments of the LORD your God: that ye may possess this good land, and leave it for an inheritance for your children after you for ever.**

Those whom David addresses are listed in 1 Chronicles 28:1. In short, they are Israel's leaders and bravest warriors. David concludes his address to them by presenting two witnesses to his words: *all Israel the congregation of the Lord* and *God* himself. The people are charged to obey the Lord's *commandments* in order to *possess this*

*good land, and leave it for an inheritance* for their descendants permanently. This charge bears a strong resemblance to that given by Moses centuries before (Deuteronomy 32:46, 47).

By the time Chronicles is written, Judah has lost her territory once, and only a remnant populates the land. The people have to learn the hard way that disobedience means the loss of land, just as predicted (see Deuteronomy 31:14-18). For the ancient Israelites, keeping the land is always conditioned on obedience.

### B. Charges to Solomon (vv. 9, 10)

**9. And thou, Solomon my son, know thou the God of thy father, and serve him with a perfect heart and with a willing mind: for the LORD searcheth all hearts, and understandeth all the imaginations of the thoughts: if thou seek him, he will be found of thee; but if thou forsake him, he will cast thee off for ever.**

David charges *Solomon* to *know . . . the God of thy father.* To know God is a covenant concept (see Jeremiah 22:16; Hosea 6:6; Philippians 3:8-10). To know God is to serve Him faithfully in covenant relationship. Solomon is to do this with *a perfect heart.* The Hebrew word for *perfect* is *shalem,* which can also be translated "whole" or "complete." This may be a play on Solomon's name, which is similar to *shalom*—meaning "peace." The words *shalem* and *shalom* look the same without vowels, which is how Hebrew is written. The idea of *a perfect heart* is a favorite of the author of Chronicles (see 1 Chronicles 12:38; 29:9, 19; 2 Chronicles 15:17; 16:9; 19:9; 25:2).

When we add heart to *mind,* we see that Solomon is being charged to know and serve God with every fiber of his being. This is equivalent to the command, "And thou shalt love the Lord thy God with all thine heart, and with all thy soul, and with all thy might" (Deuteronomy 6:5).

The fact that God can search all human hearts and minds, understanding even the imaginations of our thoughts, is remarkable from a human standpoint. For God, however, it is reality. That is why God alone is our judge. For that we should be thankful (see Psalm 139:4).

The charge to Solomon here could become a motto for all: "If we seek God, then we will find Him; but if we forsake Him, then He will cast us off." No great task can be done *for* God unless one first comes to terms *with* God himself. [See question #2, page 256.] One must *know* the Lord first before one can *serve* faithfully. The building of the temple—indeed, the success of Solomon's entire reign—is contingent upon a personal and covenantal relationship with God by Solomon.

**10. Take heed now; for the LORD hath chosen thee to build a house for the sanctuary: be strong, and do it.**

The Hebrew word for *take heed* is sometimes translated *behold* in the *King James Version* (examples: Deuteronomy 1:21; 11:26). It is like saying, "Be alert to God's call upon your life!"

God is the one who has *chosen* Solomon *to build* a temple on Mount Zion. The pages of Scripture tell us that it is not an easy life to be handpicked by God. God calls His servants to all kinds of tasks, but this temple-building task for Solomon is a major challenge. And so David charges his son to *be strong, and do it.* Don't we all need someone to provide this kind of encouragement at times? [See question #3, page 256.]

## III. David's Exhortations (1 Chronicles 28:20, 21)

### A. Regarding Character (v. 20)

**20. And David said to Solomon his son, Be strong and of good courage, and do it: fear not, nor be dismayed, for the LORD God, even my God, will be with thee; he will not fail thee, nor forsake thee, until thou hast finished all the work for the service of the house of the LORD.**

Solomon has heard this before in a private setting before David (see 1 Chronicles 22:13). Now the exhortations are given to Solomon in public.

The kind of public assembly taking place is described in 1 Chronicles 28:1. The nature of this assembly may be compared with that of other assemblies after Israel becomes a monarchy (see 2 Samuel 5:1; 1 Kings 8:1) and after the exile (see Ezra 10:1, 5; Nehemiah 8:1; 9:1). The exhortation *be strong and of good courage* is very similar to those found in Joshua 1:6, 7, 9, 18.

One of the covenantal promises that Solomon receives is that of the presence of God himself. He will be there to strengthen and inspire Solomon. Solomon has been chosen for a huge task, and it cannot be done alone. God must be with him. God will see the task to its completion and beyond. [See question #4, page 256.]

### B. Regarding Workers (v. 21)

**21. And, behold, the courses of the priests and the Levites, even they shall be with thee for all the service of the house of God: and there shall be with thee for all manner of workmanship every willing skilful man, for any manner of service: also the princes and all the people will be wholly at thy commandment.**

We have already mentioned that 1 Chronicles 23–26 is a listing of all those who will participate

Visual for
Lesson 3

*Point to this visual as you ask, "What was a time when God strengthened you for your work?"*

in the building and maintenance of the new temple. The *priests and Levites* are especially important in this regard.

The author of Chronicles gives some interesting statistics and information concerning the Levites. Only those 30 years old or older are counted, and they number 38,000. Of these, 24,000 are to supervise the construction of the temple while 6,000 are to be "officers and judges." The gatekeepers will number 4,000. Another 4,000 are to play musical instruments as part of a praise orchestra (1 Chronicles 23:3-5).

Organizationally, the Levites are divided into three groups corresponding to the sons of Levi: Gershon, Kohath, and Merari (1 Chronicles 23:6-23). They will be in charge of the service of the temple of the Lord upon its completion (1 Chronicles 23:24-32). For the origin and history of the Levites, see Genesis 29:34; 46:11; Exodus 6:16-25; Numbers 1:47-53; 3:5–4:49; 8:5-26; 35:1-5; etc. Duties in the temple include singing (1 Chronicles 15:16, 17; 25:1-7), oversight of the treasuries (26:20-28), and various other things (26:29-32).

We should recall that while all priests are Levites, not all Levites are priests. Priests are defined in terms of descent from Aaron's sons Eleazar and Ithamar (Exodus 6:23; 28:1; Numbers 3:2-4). David had given the priests an organizational structure (1 Chronicles 24:1-19).

All these people are to be at the disposal of Solomon, especially *every willing skilful man.* Just as God provided Spirit-filled men to build the tabernacle (Exodus 31:1-11), so God now provides such skilled and willing laborers for the awesome task at hand (see 1 Kings 5–6). Just as God showed Moses the plans for building the tabernacle (Exodus 25–30), so now David shows Solomon the plans for building the temple; it is a plan inspired by the Spirit of God (1 Chronicles 28:11-19). What Solomon must do now is execute the plan.

### CREATING SOMETHING BEAUTIFUL

*Question:* What is the most complex piece of handmade machinery in the world? *Answer:* A grand piano. Both the question and the answer come from Miles Chapin's book *88 Keys: The Making of a Steinway Piano* (New York: Clarkson Potter, 1997).

The construction of a grand piano takes several years. Little wonder, since each one has 12,000 parts, including "tiny levers, springs, pins, screws, knobs, plates, bushings, bearings, hinges, and flanges," to use Chapin's words. The process involves more than 500 craftsmen who possess skills in mechanical engineering, cabinetmaking, wood finishing, and metallurgy.

This complexity makes a grand piano begin to sound like Solomon's temple. The process needed to create both amazes us. People in Solomon's day were given the opportunity to use their gifts and skills to create something of great beauty, and everyone had to work together in harmony. Carrying out the ministries of the church also involves many people and their spiritual gifts coming together. What is your part?                —C. R. B.

## Conclusion

### A. Making a Difference in the World

Solomon had a rare calling: to be ruler over God's people and to build a temple of staggering size and quality. It's safe to say that God will not call anyone today to repeat this role since the church is not ruled by earthly kings, and it is our bodies, not structures of stone, that serve as temples (1 Corinthians 6:19; 2 Corinthians 6:16; Ephesians 2:19-22). [See question #5, page 256.]

Even so, God still calls us to serve by using the spiritual gifts He has granted (Romans 12:4-8; 1 Corinthians 12; Ephesians 4:11-13). When we recognize what our spiritual gifts are, then we are able to move forward in serving God in specific areas.

However, some people become frustrated when they discover that they are unable to make a living doing what God has called them to do. In other words, they must work at a job in order to make an income that allows them to do what they feel called to do. That situation may be a sign that they have misinterpreted what they thought to be their calling; on the other hand, it may be a sign that even though they have correctly interpreted their calling, God wants them to "go slow" for a while—perhaps to allow time for growth in patience and maturity.

Let me encourage you to listen to God's calling as you discover your spiritual giftedness. When you do, you will find a need in the world you can fill for Christ. Even in retirement, many senior citizens have been given new life by finding such a calling and fulfilling it.

If you wish to make a great contribution to the kingdom of God, first you must have a spiritually healthy attitude concerning who and whose you are. As a child of God, you should have no problem accepting yourself as God's most prized treasure (compare Exodus 19:5).

Second, you need to realize that great achievements require great struggle. Third, expect that great struggle will yield discouragement at times. That is what forces us to lean on God's Spirit to accomplish the task. No one can accomplish great tasks alone. That thought has kept me in the fray when giving up would have been easy. Choose now to make a difference for Christ in the world.

### B. Prayer

Our Father, creator of the earth, the great builder of this universe, use us in Your kingdom to accomplish Your will. For whatever You have called us to do, equip us, motivate us, and give us assurance that You are with us in the task of Your calling. Help us to make a great contribution to Your kingdom. In Jesus' name, amen.

### C. Thought to Remember

Expect God's help.

## Home Daily Bible Readings

**Monday, Mar. 10**—God's Promise to David (Psalm 132:1-12)

**Tuesday, Mar. 11**—God Chose Solomon (1 Chronicles 28:1-5)

**Wednesday, Mar. 12**—David Advises Solomon (1 Chronicles 28:6-8)

**Thursday, Mar. 13**—Wholehearted and Willing (1 Chronicles 28:9, 10)

**Friday, Mar. 14**—David's Plan for the Temple (1 Chronicles 28:11-19)

**Saturday, Mar. 15**—God Is with You (1 Chronicles 28:20, 21)

**Sunday, Mar. 16**—For God's Chosen (Psalm 132:13-18)

# Learning by Doing

*This page contains an alternative lesson plan emphasizing learning activities.*
*Classes desiring such student involvement will find these suggestions helpful.*

## Into the Lesson

Prepare the following two lists on a sheet of paper; make a copy for each learner. Down the left side, list the occupations *policeman, judge, physician, teacher,* and *minister.* Down the right side, list the character traits or skills of *honesty, courage, wisdom, patience, faith, logic,* and *humor.*

At the bottom of the sheet, print "Which character traits are *E* (for essential), *H* (for helpful), or *U* (for unnecessary) to be successful for each occupation listed?" Distribute copies as your learners enter the classroom (or ask them to turn to the same exercise in the optional student books).

Learners can work on this activity in small groups. Notice that the 5 occupations multiplied by the 7 character traits or skills means that there will be 35 answers. To make this activity go faster, you may wish to assign only one occupation to be evaluated per group.

After a few minutes, call on volunteers to share and explain their opinions. Ask what other traits would be essential for each profession. Tell your class that today's lesson will allow comparing and contrasting the attitudes and behavior David challenged Solomon to display with the attitudes and behaviors the New Testament commands for Christians.

## Into the Word

Use the Lesson Background and the commentary on 1 Chronicles 28:5-7 to familiarize your learners with today's text. Then divide your class into pairs to work on the following exercise. (This exercise is also printed in the optional student book.)

*Solomon's Mission, and Ours.* With your partner, study 1 Chronicles 28:5-10, 20, 21 to review the task assigned to Solomon and the character traits he would need to complete that task. Then give brief answers to these questions:

1. What condition did Solomon have to meet in order for God to bless and maintain Solomon's kingdom forever? What conditions do Christians meet in order to be part of God's eternal kingdom?

2. Who would be a witness to make sure Solomon kept God's commandments? Who is our witness in keeping God's commandments?

3. What do you think David meant when he said Solomon should serve God "with a perfect heart and with a willing mind"? How can we have such a heart and mind today?

4. Why would Solomon need strength and courage to complete the temple? In what way do we need strength and courage to complete the work on the temple of our bodies (1 Corinthians 6:19; 2 Corinthians 6:16; Ephesians 2:19-22)?

5. Who was to assist Solomon in his work? Who assists us in ours?

After your pairs complete their assignments, review their findings with the entire class. What similarities did they see between the duties of Solomon and the duties of Christians? What essential traits would each need to complete their ministries?

## Into Life

Make a transition by asking about the character traits and skills that are essential for missionaries to accomplish their tasks. Write these questions on the board:

1. How are the traits missionaries need to accomplish their tasks different (if at all) from the traits needed by non-missionary Christians?

2. What is our congregation doing to develop the traits that people will need before going to the mission field?

3. What more could each of us be doing to develop the traits and skills that people will need before going to the mission field?

Turn your attention to the lesson conclusion. The author says a Christian desiring to make a contribution to the world for God's kingdom needs one thing and should expect two other things. Write these on the board:

*1. A spiritually healthy attitude*
*2. An expectation of struggle*
*3. An expectation of*
*discouragement*

Discuss each of these points with the class. If the discussion is slow getting started, use these questions as prompts: How do we know when we have a spiritually healthy attitude and when we don't? How do we grow through struggle? Does *expectation* mean the same as *looking forward to it*? Why, or why not?

# Let's Talk It Over

*The questions on this page are designed to promote discussion of the lesson by the class and to encourage application of the lesson Scriptures. The answers provided are only discussion starters. Let your class talk it over from there.*

**1. Solomon had an important task, as did each of the workers involved in the temple's construction and maintenance. What work has God called you to do? If you have not discovered how you can contribute to the kingdom work, what can you do to discover your role?**

We see in Ephesians 2:10 that God has designed us to fulfill a purpose for His kingdom. If you are seeking your niche in the body of Christ, pray. God has given us His Holy Spirit to guide us. Ask God to show you. Then watch for His response. But don't just sit around doing nothing while you wait for that response. Get involved in one of your church's ministries. The successes or roadblocks you encounter may be part of God's response.

If it doesn't seem like God has given you anything big to do, do the small things around you with great gusto. Your faithfulness in smaller tasks may lead to an opportunity to expand your responsibilities. "He that is faithful in that which is least is faithful also in much" (Luke 16:10).

**2. Why do you think that our relationship *with* God is more important than our work *for* God? Or is it our work *for* God that reveals the quality of our relationship *with* God? Explain.**

David was careful to give Solomon not only his *work* assignment, but also his *life* assignment. It is easy to get caught up in tasks and lose track of how far we're drifting from God.

Jesus had harsh words for those who had plenty of (seemingly) good works, but whose relationship with God was all wrong (Matthew 15:8; 23:1-36). First Corinthians 13 shows that improper hearts and motives can invalidate talents and accomplishments. "For thou desirest not sacrifice; else would I give it: thou delightest not in burnt offering. The sacrifices of God are a broken spirit: a broken and a contrite heart, O God, thou wilt not despise" (Psalm 51:16, 17).

**3. What was a time when you encouraged someone else to a service in God's kingdom? What was a time when someone encouraged you to a kingdom task? How did things turn out?**

Part of David's God-given work was to pass along the charge of building God's temple to Solomon. Nehemiah encouraged many people to help build a wall. Jesus gave final charges before his ascension (Matthew 28:19, 20; Acts 1:8).

The apostle Paul gave personal, one-on-one charges to Timothy and Titus (1 Timothy 6:11-21; 2 Timothy 3:10–4:5; Titus 1:5; etc.). Much of Paul's writings consist of charges to entire churches. The author of Hebrews encourages us all to "consider one another to provoke unto love and to good works" (Hebrews 10:24).

**4. There is a saying, "God doesn't call the equipped; He equips the called." Do you agree with this saying? Why, or why not?**

We may find ourselves disagreeing with the saying when we're looking at our weakness as an excuse for not doing something! Yet Scripture and church history are filled with unlikely "heroes of the faith." Don't ever feel too small to accept God's call on you (Exodus 4:10-12; Jeremiah 1:6-10; 1 Corinthians 1:26-29). As has been said, "You can never be too small for God to use, only too big."

**5. What are some things you can do to create and maintain a proper home for God's Spirit in the temple of your body?**

Solomon was called to build God's temple of wood and stone. From 1 Corinthians 6:19 and Ephesians 2:19-22, we know that for Christians our bodies are God's temples; the body is home to the Holy Spirit. Living a life of holiness is a key (1 Peter 1:15, 16).

A. W. Tozer states, "To God our thoughts are things. Our thoughts are the decorations inside the sanctuary where we live. . . . If you would cultivate the Spirit's acquaintance, you must get hold of your thoughts and not allow your mind to be a wilderness in which every kind of unclean beast roams and bird flies. You must have a clean heart." A major part of having a clean heart is monitoring what we allow our eyes to dwell on (see Psalm 101:3).

The Bible is packed full of instructions on how to maintain holiness in behavior. For example, 1 Corinthians 6:18 tells us to us to flee from sexual immorality, while verse 20 tells us to honor God with our bodies.

# God Fulfills His Promises

**DEVOTIONAL READING: Psalm 135:1-5.**

**BACKGROUND SCRIPTURE: 2 Chronicles 6; Luke 24.**

**PRINTED TEXT: 2 Chronicles 6:12-17; Luke 24:44-49.**

### 2 Chronicles 6:12-17

12 And he stood before the altar of the LORD in the presence of all the congregation of Israel, and spread forth his hands:

13 For Solomon had made a brazen scaffold, of five cubits long, and five cubits broad, and three cubits high, and had set it in the midst of the court: and upon it he stood, and kneeled down upon his knees before all the congregation of Israel, and spread forth his hands toward heaven,

14 And said, O LORD God of Israel, there is no God like thee in the heaven, nor in the earth; which keepest covenant, and showest mercy unto thy servants, that walk before thee with all their hearts:

15 Thou which hast kept with thy servant David my father that which thou hast promised him; and spakest with thy mouth, and hast fulfilled it with thine hand, as it is this day.

16 Now therefore, O LORD God of Israel, keep with thy servant David my father that which thou hast promised him, saying, There shall not fail thee a man in my sight to sit upon the throne of Israel; yet so that thy children take heed to their way to walk in my law, as thou hast walked before me.

17 Now then, O LORD God of Israel, let thy word be verified, which thou hast spoken unto thy servant David.

### Luke 24:44-49

44 And he said unto them, These are the words which I spake unto you, while I was yet with you, that all things must be fulfilled, which were written in the law of Moses, and in the prophets, and in the psalms, concerning me.

45 Then opened he their understanding, that they might understand the Scriptures,

46 And said unto them, Thus it is written, and thus it behooved Christ to suffer, and to rise from the dead the third day:

47 And that repentance and remission of sins should be preached in his name among all nations, beginning at Jerusalem.

48 And ye are witnesses of these things.

49 And, behold, I send the promise of my Father upon you: but tarry ye in the city of Jerusalem, until ye be endued with power from on high.

---

GOLDEN TEXT: These are the words which I spake unto you, while I was yet with you, that all things must be fulfilled, which were written in the law of Moses, and in the prophets, and in the psalms, concerning me.—Luke 24:44.

*God, the People, and the Covenant*
Unit 1: Signs of God's Covenant
(Lessons 1-5)

## Lesson Aims

After participating in this lesson, each student will be able to:

1. Restate Solomon's words of dedication and Jesus' words of challenge.

2. Compare and contrast the promises of God recognized by Solomon with the promises of God affirmed by Jesus.

3. Tell how he or she would explain the fulfilled promise of Christ's death and resurrection to an unbeliever.

## Lesson Outline

INTRODUCTION
    A. Promises
    B. Lesson Background I: 2 Chronicles 6
    C. Lesson Background II: Luke 24
  I. SOLOMON'S PRAYER (2 Chronicles 6:12-17)
    A. Place and Audience (vv. 12, 13)
    B. Praise and Recognition (vv. 14, 15)
    C. Request and Review (vv. 16, 17)
      *Keeping Promises*
 II. JESUS' PRESENCE (Luke 24:44-49)
    A. Prophecy and Fulfillment (vv. 44, 45)
    B. Proclamation and Witness (vv. 46-49)
      *Useless Curiosities*
CONCLUSION
    A. The Temple and Jesus' Resurrection
    B. Prayer
    C. Thought to Remember

## Introduction

### A. Promises

People have been known to make promises they didn't keep. When people do keep promises, especially to us personally, it makes us trust them more. The same is true for God. The God we worship is a promise-keeping God. The Scriptures declare that God has kept every promise He ever made and continues to do so. But what about promises we make to God?

I remember making a bold promise to God once. It happened when I was about eight years old. My father was an alcoholic, and our family suffered the usual consequences. My mother was often frustrated with the weekend drinking bouts, and arguments continued throughout the evening on a regular basis. One night my father hit my mother and slammed her against the bedroom wall so hard it shook the house. I saw it happen.

Feeling helpless and hopeless, I ran out of the house to the back lot and jumped into the middle of briars and thistles. There in my "wilderness" surroundings in the middle of the night I prayed. I was not a Christian at the time, but I prayed this prayer anyway: "God, if you are there, please don't let my dad hit my mom again. I will give you my life if you will do this." That was perhaps a rather brazen offer to make. But to my knowledge my parents never fought like that again, although it would be another 13 years before my father would conquer his alcoholism.

Does this kind of bargaining mean anything to God? I felt I had made a promise to God. And if God answered my prayer, I was certainly obligated to keep my promise. He did, and I did! I did not become a Christian until age 14, but my experience at age 8 was the beginning of my life dedicated to full-time Christian ministry. May we all keep our promises. God sure does!

### B. Lesson Background I: 2 Chronicles 6

Today's text of 2 Chronicles 6:12-17 closely follows the parallel of 1 Kings 8:22-26. A broad look at 2 Chronicles 6 reveals three separate addresses. First, Solomon prayed to God (2 Chronicles 6:1, 2). Solomon did this again as he faced the temple, acknowledging God as present in "the thick darkness" (compare Exodus 19:9, 16; 20:21; Deuteronomy 4:11; 5:22).

Second, Solomon turned from facing the temple toward the congregation in order to bless them (2 Chronicles 6:3-11). The content of this blessing was to praise God for fulfilling His promises to David (see v. 10, a major theme of this chapter). Solomon, David's son, had become king over David's house, the fulfillment of one promise. Another promise was fulfilled when God allowed Solomon to build the temple (vv. 10, 11).

Third, Solomon resumed his prayer to God as he stood on a specially built platform (v. 13) before the altar in the courtyard. Much of today's text is in this third section, with the dedication occurring in about the year 959 BC. The focus is on gratefulness for promises kept and anticipation of the keeping of promises in the future.

### C. Lesson Background II: Luke 24

Luke 24 is the resurrection chapter of that Gospel. Here Luke records an appearance of Jesus that is not included in the other Gospel accounts: that of the resurrected Lord to Cleopas and his friend (vv. 13-35) as they walked seven miles from Jerusalem to Emmaus.

Before today's text from Luke 24 opens, Jesus taught those two disciples from Scripture that the Messiah had to suffer before He entered into His glory (Luke 24:26, 27). After recognizing Jesus during the breaking of the bread (vv. 30, 31, 35), they reported their encounter to the disciples in Jerusalem.

Jesus then appeared to them while they were all together. They were so amazed and disbelieving that Jesus resorted to eating a piece of broiled fish in their presence to convince them that His resurrection was real (vv. 41-43)! No doubt the group had experienced this type of meal with Jesus many times before His crucifixion. This is where the second part of today's lesson picks up. Talk about a promise kept!

# I. Solomon's Prayer (2 Chronicles 6:12-17)

## A. Place and Audience (vv. 12, 13)

12, 13. **And he stood before the altar of the LORD in the presence of all the congregation of Israel, and spread forth his hands: for Solomon had made a brazen scaffold, of five cubits long, and five cubits broad, and three cubits high, and had set it in the midst of the court: and upon it he stood, and kneeled down upon his knees before all the congregation of Israel, and spread forth his hands toward heaven.**

As our text begins, we see Solomon in the third posture that he takes in this ceremony of dedicating the temple of God. (See Lesson Background I for a description of the first two postures.) It is logical to presume that Solomon is in the temple's outer court where the people are, yet he has oriented himself toward or *before the altar.*

### How to Say It

CLEOPAS. *Clee*-uh-pass.
DAVIDIC. Duh-*vid*-ick.
DEUTERONOMY. Due-ter-*ahn*-uh-me.
EMMAUS. Em-*may*-us.
EZRA. *Ez*-ruh.
GABRIEL. *Gay*-bree-ul.
JERUSALEM. Juh-*roo*-suh-lem.
NEHEMIAH. *Nee*-huh-*my*-uh (strong accent on *my*).
PENTECOST. *Pent*-ih-kost.
SOLOMON. *Sol*-o-mun.

Why the altar? Because it is the place where sacrifices are made and forgiveness is to be found. The need for forgiveness is a major theme of the prayer to follow in 2 Chronicles 6:22-39 (not in today's text).

The parallel account of 1 Kings 8 does not mention this *brazen scaffold.* It is an interesting touch added by the author of Chronicles. Converting the *cubits* to modern measurements, the platform is seven to eight feet square and four to five feet high.

The use of platforms for special occasions is attested to in other cultures of the ancient Near East. The purpose of this platform is for Solomon to be seen by the crowd (compare Nehemiah 8:4, 5). This allows the full impact of the occasion to have its effect on the people when Solomon kneels with his hands outstretched toward *heaven* (compare Exodus 9:29, 33; Ezra 9:5; Job 11:13; Psalm 44:20). The setting is dramatic.

The parallel account of Solomon's prayer in 1 Kings 8:22-61 makes for an interesting comparison. That account begins by noting Solomon to be standing; much later, it notes that Solomon rises from where he has been kneeling (v. 54). Thus at some point Solomon has moved from standing to kneeling during his prayer. But the 1 Kings 8 account by itself does not allow us to know exactly when Solomon makes that transition. The account in 2 Chronicles 6 fills that gap: Solomon kneels right at the point we see in 2 Chronicles 6:13, which comes between verse 22 and verse 23 of 1 Kings 8.

## B. Praise and Recognition (vv. 14, 15)

14. **And said, O LORD God of Israel, there is no God like thee in the heaven, nor in the earth; which keepest covenant, and showest mercy unto thy servants, that walk before thee with all their hearts.**

In the *King James Version* (as in many other translations), the word LORD as rendered in capital letters reflects the Hebrew word *Yahweh.* The stately phrase *Yahweh, God of Israel* occurs three times in our printed text (2 Chronicles 6:14, 16, 17). The exact phrase *there is no God like thee* is found in the Bible only here and in the parallel of 1 Kings 8:23. A similar idea (though not the exact wording) occurs in Deuteronomy 4:39; 2 Samuel 7:22; and elsewhere.

Thus does Solomon introduce his praise to God for being a covenant-keeping God. When God keeps a covenant with His people, He shows covenant loyalty to them. [See question #1, page 264.] To keep the covenant going, God forgives sins against Him; without this forgiveness the covenant would collapse; thus, the idea of "covenant love" and "covenant loyalty" has the idea of *mercy* built in. Yet even with God's mercy expressed to us in forgiveness, He still expects us to walk *before* Him *with all* [our] *hearts.*

**15. Thou which hast kept with thy servant David my father that which thou hast promised him; and spakest with thy mouth, and hast fulfilled it with thine hand, as it is this day.**

It is on the basis of covenant-faithfulness and mercy that God kept His promise to *David* to allow his son Solomon the task of building the temple (see 2 Chronicles 6:8, 9). Solomon also anticipates that God will keep His promise that the Davidic dynasty will be forever (compare 1 Chronicles 17:12-14, 23, 24; 22:10; 28; 2 Chronicles 6:10; 13:5; 21:7; 23:3). Solomon thus interprets the completion of the temple and his enthronement as king over Israel as a continuing fulfillment of God's past promises. [See question #2, page 264.]

### C. Request and Review (vv. 16, 17)

**16. Now therefore, O LORD God of Israel, keep with thy servant David my father that which thou hast promised him, saying, There shall not fail thee a man in my sight to sit upon the throne of Israel; yet so that thy children take heed to their way to walk in my law, as thou hast walked before me.**

Solomon now looks to the future of the Davidic dynasty. He petitions Yahweh not to *fail* (literally, "cut off") the dynastic line. The fact that the author of Chronicles is writing many years after the apparent "cutting off" of David's line in 586 BC makes this request all the more significant.

## Home Daily Bible Readings

**Monday, Mar. 17**—Praise for God's Goodness (Psalm 135:1-5)

**Tuesday, Mar. 18**—Dedication of the Temple (2 Chronicles 6:1-11)

**Wednesday, Mar. 19**—Solomon's Prayer (2 Chronicles 6:12-17)

**Thursday, Mar. 20**—Pray Toward This Place (2 Chronicles 6:18-31)

**Friday, Mar. 21**—Repent and Pray (2 Chronicles 6:36-39)

**Saturday, Mar. 22**—God's Promise Remembered (2 Chronicles 6:40-42)

**Sunday, Mar. 23**—God's Promise Fulfilled (Luke 24:44-49)

Solomon, speaking in about 959 BC, knows that the promise of an enduring dynasty is conditional in a sense. That is, the people as well as the king are to *take heed to their way to walk in my law* (see also 1 Chronicles 28:7). The Hebrew word translated *keep*, used to refer to God's keeping His promises to David, is the same Hebrew word that challenges the Israelites to *take heed* of God's law.

Interestingly, the parallel passage 1 Kings 8:25 lacks the phrase *to walk in my law* that the author of Chronicles includes. While Solomon prays for God's promise of an eternal dynasty, the author of Chronicles can hope only for a Davidic Messiah to come in the future. For the author of Chronicles, writing centuries before Christ, the promise is still to be fulfilled. This author has seen how badly the people have sinned in rejecting God's law.

### KEEPING PROMISES

General Douglas MacArthur (1880–1964) uttered one of the most famous promises in American history. When Japanese forces overran Allied troops in the Philippines in 1942, President Roosevelt ordered MacArthur to withdraw. MacArthur publicly vowed, "I shall return."

The tide of the war eventually turned, and the Philippines were liberated. As Supreme Commander of Allied forces in the Southwest Pacific Area, MacArthur accepted the Japanese surrender on September 2, 1945. Historians still debate the character of MacArthur in certain regards. He could be flamboyant and arrogant at times. But no one can doubt that he kept his promise.

When Solomon dedicated the temple, he placed the focus where it belonged: on God's faithful fulfillment of His promises. There is no debating the character of God on this matter—He takes His promises seriously and exhibits no flaws in doing so. This fact is both a blessing and a challenge. We are blessed to serve a God who is faithful to His people. We are also challenged by this fact to replicate that divine characteristic in our own lives. Can others count on us for that kind of integrity? —C. R. B.

**17. Now then, O LORD God of Israel, let thy word be verified, which thou hast spoken unto thy servant David.**

Solomon certainly wants God's promise to be *verified,* that is, "come true." This is similar to David's own request in 2 Samuel 7:25-29. The verification can come only as each succeeding king takes his place on the throne of Israel and as each king remains faithful to God's law.

The fact that most of the Davidic kings end up being unfaithful to God according to His law may leave the author of Chronicles wondering how God will fulfill His promise that David's dynasty will last forever. Yet the author of Chronicles hopes for the future. Christians know that God has fulfilled this important promise through the person and work of Jesus the Christ. [See question #3, page 264.]

## II. Jesus' Presence
## (Luke 24:44-49)

### A. Prophecy and Fulfillment (vv. 44, 45)

**44, 45. And he said unto them, These are the words which I spake unto you, while I was yet with you, that all things must be fulfilled, which were written in the law of Moses, and in the prophets, and in the psalms, concerning me. Then opened he their understanding, that they might understand the Scriptures.**

Solomon reigned between about 970 and 930 BC. Thus we jumped forward almost 500 years to reach the day of the author of Chronicles, whether the author was Ezra or someone else. Now we jump almost another 500 years to Jesus' day in the first century AD. How grand is the sweep of history!

After Jesus' resurrection from the dead, He appeared to various people. In the text before us, Jesus stands in the presence of His apostles *(them)* in their hiding place. Luke has prepared us for verse 44 by reporting at the beginning of his Gospel what the angel Gabriel said to Mary: "The Lord God shall give unto him the throne of his father David: and he shall reign over the house of Jacob for ever; and of his kingdom there shall be no end" (Luke 1:32b, 33). That time has come!

Here Jesus reminds His stunned disciples how everything written about Him had to be *fulfilled.* [See question #4, page 264.] The prophecies cover the entire Hebrew Scriptures, described here as *the law of Moses, . . . the prophets, and . . . the psalms.* These three designations sum up the totality of the Hebrew Bible, which we call the Old Testament.

Today, our Bibles arrange the Old Testament in a 5-12-5-5-12 format. This means that there are, in order, 5 books of law, 12 books of history, 5 books of wisdom literature, 5 books by "major" prophets, and 12 books by "minor" prophets. But that is not the arrangement of Jesus' day, although the text then and now is the same. The first-century Jews use the simpler arrangement of law, prophets, and psalms. The designation *psalms* is used rather loosely to signify all the in-

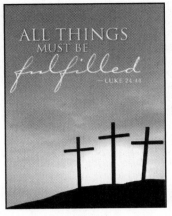

Visual for
Lesson 4

*Use this visual to introduce discussion question #4 on page 264.*

spired Old Testament books that are not properly classified as books of law or prophets.

Other New Testament passages refer to what the law and the prophets say about Christ (see John 1:45; Acts 28:23; Romans 3:21). Jesus uses the Psalms extensively to refer to himself during His ministry (examples: compare Matthew 21:16 with Psalm 8:2; Matthew 21:42 with Psalm 118:22, 23; Mark 15:34 with Psalm 22:1; and Luke 20:42, 43; 22:69 with Psalm 110:1).

### B. Proclamation and Witness (vv. 46-49)

**46, 47. And said unto them, Thus it is written, and thus it behooved Christ to suffer, and to rise from the dead the third day: and that repentance and remission of sins should be preached in his name among all nations, beginning at Jerusalem.**

The disciples had had great trouble with Jesus' teaching about His going to Jerusalem to suffer and die (see Matthew 16:21-23; Mark 8:31, 32; Luke 18:31-34). But surely Jesus had spoken to them of the suffering servant of Isaiah 53! (Compare Luke 22:37, which quotes Isaiah 53:12.) Jesus' teaching had included the other servant songs of Isaiah (compare Matthew 12:18-20 with Isaiah 42:1-4; Acts 13:47 with Isaiah 49:1-6; etc.). Such texts include Jesus' teaching about *repentance and remission of sins* and Messiah's mission to the Gentiles *(all nations).* And Jesus is unlikely to have left out Isaiah 25 and 26 when discussing His own resurrection (compare John 2:22)!

**48. And ye are witnesses of these things.**

We see the fact of Jesus' resurrection confirmed again in Acts 2:25-28, where the apostle Peter uses Psalm 16:8-11 as an argument for the resurrection of Jesus. Peter was a witness to this fact of history. Peter acknowledges his own status as witness by saying this of David: "Therefore being a prophet, and knowing that God had sworn with an oath to him, that of the fruit of his loins, according to the flesh, he would raise up Christ to sit on his throne; he, seeing this before, spake of the resurrection of Christ, that his soul was not left in hell, neither his flesh did see corruption. This Jesus hath God raised up, whereof we all are *witnesses*" (Acts 2:30-32).

In an early cleansing of the temple, Jesus had encountered the authorities (John 2:13-18). They had demanded a miraculous sign from Him to establish His authority for doing what He did. The sign Jesus offered was unexpected: "Destroy this temple, and in three days I will raise it up" (John 2:19).

The Jews were astonished by this, for the only temple they were familiar with was still being built after 46 years (John 2:20)! Yet Jesus had been talking about himself (John 2:21)—the place of God's dwelling, "the Word . . . made flesh" (John 1:14). From the beginning of Jesus' ministry, His resurrection was uppermost in His mind. The disciples had been witnesses of all this, although full comprehension was delayed.

### USELESS CURIOSITIES

Susanne Kaplan has studied landscape architecture. So it's no wonder that she finds intriguing what a former owner of her house did to the front yard. Buried there is what Kaplan calls her "little history museum." It is actually a bomb shelter, built in 1961.

A 30-foot spiral stairway leads down to a room that holds 8 bunk beds, a generator, bathroom, and kitchen. The shelter is typical of thousands that were built during the nuclear war scares of the 1960s—the Cold War era.

Kaplan, like many other homeowners with similar shelters in their yards, is unsure what to do with it. She finds it claustrophobic, and the spiral staircase makes it difficult to use as storage space. Many owners say theirs are havens for vermin and are nothing more than useless curiosities.

Jesus also spent time in an underground space. The fact that Jesus' tomb is empty is a vital fact of Christianity. But the fact God has not chosen to preserve it for us demonstrates that it too is a useless curiosity (wherever it is). Why look for Jesus in a place where He is not to be found?

The gospel message of Jesus' resurrection brings with it the important fact that *all* graves eventually shall lose their usefulness! The Law, the Prophets, and the Psalms had all pointed toward this truth, but the gospel message finally made it clear.　　　　　　　　　　　—C. R. B.

**49. And, behold, I send the promise of my Father upon you: but tarry ye in the city of Jerusalem, until ye be endued with power from on high.**

With Christ's resurrection comes the fulfillment of Old Testament prophecies. However, a more recent *promise* remains to be fulfilled at the time Jesus speaks the words of verse 49. It is the promise of the Spirit (see John 14:15-31).

Just a short time later, on the Day of Pentecost, the apostles indeed will *be endued with power from on high* (Acts 2). After Pentecost, each Christian becomes a witness to the power of the indwelling Holy Spirit as well as a witness to the God who keeps promises (Acts 2:38, 39). [See question #5, page 264.]

## Conclusion

### A. The Temple and Jesus' Resurrection

The concept of *temple* is one of the most important images for the church's mission in the world today. The Old Testament temple was a symbol of covenant made, kept, and broken. God was pleased to put His glory in Solomon's temple (1 Kings 8:11; 2 Chronicles 5:14). Because of the sins of God's people and their kings, God withdrew His glory (Ezekiel 10). The temple was destroyed in 586 BC. Ezekiel envisioned a perfect temple for the future (Ezekiel 40–48).

Jesus visited the temple that Herod was building and called it "my father's house" (John 2:16). But He also identified himself as the temple, the place of God's dwelling (John 2:19-21). With the arrival of Jesus on earth and His subsequent resurrection, the promise of God's new covenant became reality (Jeremiah 31:31-34; Hebrews 8:8-12; 10:16, 17). The question now is, will we keep that covenant or will we break it? Will we learn lessons from Old Testament history about the faithfulness of God and the tendencies of sinful human nature?

### B. Prayer

Our Father, thank You for fulfilling all Your promises to us in Jesus our Lord. We anticipate our own resurrection because You have raised Him from the dead. Teach us to live the resurrected life each and every day. In Christ's powerful name, amen.

### C. Thought to Remember

God makes promises. God keeps promises.

# Learning by Doing

*This page contains an alternative lesson plan emphasizing learning activities.*
*Classes desiring such student involvement will find these suggestions helpful.*

## Into the Lesson

Distribute copies of the following quiz as your learners arrive. (The quiz is also printed in the optional student book.) Ask learners to match each famous promise with the person who made it. Then decide if the promise was kept or broken.

*Promises*: 1. "I shall return." 2. "Whether you like it or not, history is on our side. We will bury you." 3. "Read my lips: No new taxes." 4. His "last territorial demand" in Europe would be the Sudetenland. 5. "The Jets will win [Super Bowl III] on Sunday, I guarantee it."

*Promise Makers*: a. Adolf Hitler, 1938; b. Douglas MacArthur, 1942; c. Nikita Khrushchev, 1956; d. Joe Namath, 1969; e. George H. W. Bush, 1988.

*Answers*: 1. b. Kept. MacArthur led American troops back to the Philippines in 1944; 2. c. Broken. Far from burying capitalism, Soviet Communism collapsed in 1991. 3. e. Broken. In 1990, President Bush signed into law a major tax increase. 4. a. Broken. After that 1938 promise, Hitler went on to attempt the conquest of all of Europe. 5. d. Kept. Namath led the New York Jets to victory in Super Bowl III.

Discuss the quizzes together. Tell your class that today's lesson deals with some of God's greatest promises fulfilled through Solomon in the Old Testament and Jesus in the New.

## Into the Word

Use the Lesson Background to introduce today's text. Then divide your class into small groups; give each a copy of the questions below. Each group will study 2 Chronicles 6:12-17 and Luke 24:44-49. (Answers are in parentheses, but do not distribute those. The questions also appear in the optional student books.)

1. Where was Solomon in Jerusalem when he prayed in the presence of all Israel? *(before the altar of the Lord)*

2. According to David, what two things set God apart from false gods? *(He keeps His covenants and He shows mercy to His servants)*

3. The condition upon which God keeps His covenants is what? *(the people walk before Him with all their hearts)*

4. What promise did God make to David? *(an enduring dynasty)*

5. Jesus said which sections of the Old Testament contained prophecies about Him? *(the Law of Moses, the Prophets, the Psalms)*

6. Jesus commanded the disciples to preach what message? *(repentance and remission of sins)*

7. The disciples were to wait in Jerusalem until they received what? *(power from on high)*

Use the questions and answers to guide your discussion of today's text. Follow each answer by asking, "Why is this important?"

## Into Life

Make, photocopy, and distribute copies of the following two-column chart. Down the left-hand side of the page, put the entries that are under the heading *Promise That Messiah Would*. Down the right-hand side, put the entries that are under the header *As Fulfilled in Jesus*. Make each entry on the left-hand side exactly even with its counterpart on the right-hand side.

### Promise That Messiah Would . . .

1. come from Judah
2. begin ministry in Galilee
3. preach the good news
4. enter the temple
5. be a prophet
6. die for our sins
7. rise from the dead
8. conquer death for us
9. preserve David's dynasty
10. be a light to the Gentiles

### . . . As Fulfilled in Jesus

1. Micah 5:2; Matthew 2:3-6
2. Isaiah 9:1, 2; Matthew 4:12-17
3. Isaiah 61:1; Luke 7:22
4. Malachi 3:1; Matthew 21:12, 13
5. Deuteronomy 18:15; Acts 3:22, 23
6. Isaiah 53:4-6; 1 Peter 2:24, 25
7. Psalm 16:8-11; Acts 2:30-32
8. Isaiah 25:8; 1 Corinthians 15:54, 55
9. 1 Chronicles 22:10; Luke 1:32, 33
10. Isaiah 49:6; Acts 26:23

Allow for a time of reaction to the chart. Ask your learners to suggest ways to use this chart as a resource for explaining Christ to unbelievers. Encourage your learners to keep the chart in their Bibles for that purpose.

# Let's Talk It Over

*The questions on this page are designed to promote discussion of the lesson by the class and to encourage application of the lesson Scriptures. The answers provided are only discussion starters. Let your class talk it over from there.*

**1. Do most people you deal with "keep covenant" in doing what they say they will do, or is that more the exception than the rule? How does (or how should) this affect you?**

Our experiences can color our outlook. If we experience a continuing succession of broken promises, we can grow cynical easily, distrusting everyone. On the other hand, if we are surrounded by the kind of people who always keep their promises, we can become naïve in thinking that everyone else does too.

Ultimately, we can control no one's actions but our own. God expects us to keep our promises (see Numbers 30:2; James 5:12). We serve a promise-keeping God, and in this light we "hold fast the profession of our faith without wavering; for he is faithful that promised" (Hebrews 10:23).

**2. In what ways has God protected and provided for you?**

Caution: this question can yield some very emotional answers! Yet it is healthy to recall God's past faithfulness to us. Answers may run the gamut from the mundane to the miraculous.

Be aware that one person's example of God's faithfulness can seem trivial to another. Often it is timing, prayer, and circumstances that may help a person sense God's involvement in a way that a "secondhand" hearer cannot perceive. To probe deeper, ask, "How did you know that that was really God's intervention and not random coincidence?" after each example is offered.

**3. After reviewing God's faithfulness with question #2, it is appropriate to affirm our faith in God's promises to us. Which promises do you cling to on a daily basis? Which fulfillments do you anticipate most? Why?**

Answers will fall into two categories: "the here and now" and "in eternity." Concerning the latter, the return of Jesus should be at the top of every Christian's list of anticipated fulfillments (1 Thessalonians 4:13-18). Your learners may also mention eternal life (John 3:16), God's rest (Hebrews 4:1), and a new home with God (2 Peter 3:13).

For "the here and now," your learners may cling to the promises of the continuing indwelling of the Holy Spirit (Acts 2:38, 39), God's presence (Hebrews 13:5), having physical needs met (Matthew 6:25-34), having a way to avoid sin (1 Corinthians 10:12, 13), and continuing forgiveness of sins (1 John 1:9).

**4. Jesus opened His followers' minds to the Scriptures. What was a time when you had an "Aha!" moment in God's Word?**

The apostles had the promise that the Holy Spirit would guide them in all truth (John 16:13). The Holy Spirit still allows us to hear God's voice (Hebrews 3:7-11). When we read our Bibles, we are reading the testimony of the Holy Spirit (Hebrews 10:15). The gospel comes to us via the Holy Spirit (1 Peter 1:12). It makes sense to conclude, then, that the Holy Spirit will play an important part in our "Aha!" moments as we study God's Word.

Naturally, we should pray for the Spirit's help in understanding when we study or meditate on the text of Scripture. Hand in hand with that prayer should come good study techniques. When striving to understand a passage in the Bible, it helps to read verses, paragraphs, and chapters surrounding the passage for context. It can also be helpful to refer to other Scriptures. This practice is called letting Scripture interpret Scripture. Study Bibles often list passages dealing with similar themes.

**5. How will you be a witness to the power of the Spirit within you this coming week?**

In the past, God chose various ways to make His presence known. These included a burning bush (Exodus 3), a pillar of cloud (Exodus 33), an audible voice at night (1 Samuel 3), an audible voice in a storm (Job 38:1), and dreams and visions (Daniel 1:17; Acts 2:17). Jesus lived on earth as God in the flesh, which was the ultimate picture of the invisible God (John 1:14; 14:9).

Today we give evidence to the world that God is present with us as we demonstrate the fruit of His Spirit: "love, joy, peace, long-suffering, gentleness, goodness, faith, meekness, temperance" (Galatians 5:22, 23). The challenge is to think of some ways to move those nine from abstract ideas to concrete action.

# Josiah Renews the Covenant

DEVOTIONAL READING: Psalm 119:25-40.

BACKGROUND SCRIPTURE: 2 Chronicles 34.

PRINTED TEXT: 2 Chronicles 34:15, 18, 19, 25-27, 29, 31-33.

## 2 Chronicles 34:15, 18, 19, 25-27, 29, 31-33

15 And Hilkiah answered and said to Shaphan the scribe, I have found the book of the law in the house of the LORD. And Hilkiah delivered the book to Shaphan.

. . . . . . . . . . .

18 Then Shaphan the scribe told the king, saying, Hilkiah the priest hath given me a book. And Shaphan read it before the king.

19 And it came to pass, when the king had heard the words of the law, that he rent his clothes.

. . . . . . . . . . .

25 Because they have forsaken me, and have burned incense unto other gods, that they might provoke me to anger with all the works of their hands; therefore my wrath shall be poured out upon this place, and shall not be quenched.

26 And as for the king of Judah, who sent you to inquire of the LORD, so shall ye say unto him, Thus saith the LORD God of Israel concerning the words which thou hast heard;

27 Because thine heart was tender, and thou didst humble thyself before God, when thou heardest his words against this place, and against the inhabitants thereof, and humbledst thyself before me, and didst rend

thy clothes, and weep before me; I have even heard thee also, saith the LORD.

. . . . . . . . . . .

29 Then the king sent and gathered together all the elders of Judah and Jerusalem.

. . . . . . . . . . .

31 And the king stood in his place, and made a covenant before the LORD, to walk after the LORD, and to keep his commandments, and his testimonies, and his statutes, with all his heart, and with all his soul, to perform the words of the covenant which are written in this book.

32 And he caused all that were present in Jerusalem and Benjamin to stand to it. And the inhabitants of Jerusalem did according to the covenant of God, the God of their fathers.

33 And Josiah took away all the abominations out of all the countries that pertained to the children of Israel, and made all that were present in Israel to serve, even to serve the LORD their God. And all his days they departed not from following the LORD, the God of their fathers.

---

GOLDEN TEXT: The king stood in his place, and made a covenant before the LORD, to walk after the LORD, and to keep his commandments, and his testimonies, and his statutes, with all his heart, and with all his soul, to perform the words of the covenant which are written in this book.—2 Chronicles 34:31.

## God, the People, and the Covenant
### Unit 1: Signs of God's Covenant
#### (Lessons 1-5)

## Lesson Aims

After participating in this lesson, each student will be able to:

1. Tell what Josiah did upon learning of the discovery of the book of the law in the temple.

2. Explain why humility is necessary to be in a right relationship with God and His law.

3. Make a public or private renewal of his or her commitment to obey Jesus.

## Lesson Outline

INTRODUCTION
  A. Mending a Broken Relationship
  B. Lesson Background
 I. PROGRESS OF REFORM (2 Chronicles 34:15, 18, 19)
  A. Finding the Book of the Law (v. 15)
  B. Reading the Book of the Law (v. 18)
  C. Tearing of the King's Robe (v. 19)
    *Rekindling the Spark*
 II. DELAY OF CURSES (2 Chronicles 34:25-27)
  A. Reasons for the Curses (v. 25)
  B. Reaction of the Lord (vv. 26, 27)
III. RENEWAL OF COVENANT (2 Chronicles 34:29, 31-33)
  A. Public Calling (v. 29)
  B. Public Recommitment (vv. 31, 32)
    *"I Pledge Allegiance . . ."*
  C. Public Purge (v. 33)
CONCLUSION
  A. Renewing the Covenant
  B. Prayer
  C. Thought to Remember

## Introduction

### A. Mending a Broken Relationship

When I became a Christian at age 14, I knew I had entered into a covenant relationship with God through Jesus Christ. I believed that relationship was sustained by the power of God's Spirit abiding in my life, though I had no means of biblically analyzing the relationship at such a young age.

At age 18 I found myself working at a service station in East Point, Georgia, in 1961. The Civil Rights movement was gaining momentum in the Deep South, and Southern whites who were in businesses that served the public were on edge, fearful of an all-out rebellion. The owner of the service station, the father of a good friend of mine, had given me a job as a gesture of kindness. He was essentially a decent man. But like many Southerners, he held a racial prejudice that considered whites to be superior.

After I had worked for almost three months, my boss trusted me with running the station whenever he went to the bank to deposit money. On one occasion, he said to me as he was leaving, "Don't let any blacks use the whites-only restroom." African-Americans only were allowed to use the same restroom the workers used, which also remained dirty most of the time!

Almost as soon as he left, a large Cadillac pulled into the station. A young black family emerged, and the father asked me to "fill it up with high test." In the process, the mother gathered her two young children to take them to the restroom.

Without thinking or searching my conscience, I parroted my boss's warning and told them they couldn't use the whites-only restroom. Immediately I knew I had made a serious mistake. The father ordered me to stop filling the tank with gas. He paid me for the gas I had put in to that point, and then the parents rushed their children into the car and sped off.

Why did I have to be so morally weak? I had sinned against God as well as against that family. I fell on my knees underneath the canopy of the station and prayed out loud to God, "O God, forgive me! Take this vile prejudice from my heart forever and never let me be a part of this sinful system again. Give me opportunities to make it up to this family that I have greatly harmed. I beg You, in Jesus' name."

From that day on I dropped the racial prejudice that had been instilled in my life by my parents and my culture from the time I was a child. God tested me on many occasions, giving me many opportunities to help African-Americans who faced formidable roadblocks as they sought an education through a Bible college or a place of service among the churches.

Only after many years of faithful service and direct obedience to God's will in this area of my life could I feel that I had mended a broken relationship with God. Some people seem to require a stunning confrontation with the reality of sin to be obedient fully to the will of God as revealed in His Word. I think that is what happened to King Josiah.

## B. Lesson Background

Second Chronicles 34 is the story of the reforms of godly King Josiah. Josiah ruled the southern kingdom of Judah from about 640 to 609 BC. Josiah's two predecessors, namely Manasseh and Amon, were evil. Their evil permeated Judah for nearly 60 years. This meant that Josiah had a lot of work to do to turn things around spiritually for his nation.

Second Chronicles 34 offers us interesting parallels to 2 Kings 22 and 23. It is important to study both accounts for the fullest picture. Some information that the author of Chronicles gives us is unique, not being mentioned in 2 Kings 22 and 23. One such piece of information is that in the eighth year of Josiah's reign (about 632 BC) he began to seek after "the God of David his father" (2 Chronicles 34:3a). Perhaps the preaching of Zephaniah of the time had some influence upon the young Josiah (age 16). The ministry of the prophet Jeremiah, which began about 626 BC (see Jeremiah 1:2), may have had some influence as well. Another piece of information in 2 Chronicles but not 2 Kings is that Josiah began to purge the land of idolatry when he was 20 years old (2 Chronicles 34:3b).

Before today's lesson text opens, those accounts tell us that we are in the eighteenth year of King Josiah's reign (2 Kings 22:1, 3; 23:23; 2 Chronicles 34:1, 8), with the king at age 26. At that time he undertook to repair the temple, since it had not been attended to during the reigns of previous kings. Throughout the story one can perceive the author's emphasis on the Levites' part in the repairs (2 Chronicles 34:9, 12, 13, 30; absent from 2 Kings).

After Josiah began his reform in Jerusalem and Judah, he moved into the northern territory. Then, "he returned to Jerusalem" (2 Chronicles 34:6, 7). That holy city is the setting for today's lesson.

# I. Progress of Reform
## (2 Chronicles 34:15, 18, 19)

Josiah sought to repair the temple in his eighteenth year as king, as noted above. In the process of paying money to the workers and their overseers, "Hilkiah the priest found a book of the law of the Lord given by Moses" (v. 14).

### A. Finding the Book of the Law (v. 15)

**15. And Hilkiah answered and said to Shaphan the scribe, I have found the book of the law in the house of the LORD. And Hilkiah delivered the book to Shaphan.**

We may be amazed to read that *Hilkiah*, a priest, has *found the book of the law* in the temple. Isn't that where it's supposed to be? And how can such an important thing ever get "lost"?

The answers lie in the neglect of decade after decade by evil Kings Manasseh and Amon. Whatever godly priests continued to exist during their evil reigns probably were inclined to hide such a precious document from destructive hands. As most of us know to our embarrassment, we can be so good at hiding something for "safekeeping" that we end up forgetting where we hid it!

Another issue also presents itself: Exactly which book is this? Many scholars think that it is probably the book of Deuteronomy. There are several facts to support this conclusion. First, the phrase "the book of the covenant" in 2 Chronicles 34:30 can fit the entirety of the book of Deuteronomy since it is in the form of a covenant renewal treaty. (We also recognize, however, that the phrase "the book of the covenant" is used in Exodus 24:7, most likely to describe the material included in Exodus 20–23.)

Second, the emphasis in Deuteronomy 12 on worship in one place is consistent with Josiah's reform methods. Third, the purging of the land of pagan cultic places is found also in Deuteronomy 12. This could make a big impression on Josiah, since that is exactly what he is doing even before the book of the law is found.

Fourth, the reference to "curses" in 2 Chronicles 34:24 could point to the extended curses spelled out in Deuteronomy 27:9-26; 28:15-68. Fifth, the celebration of the Passover in 2 Chronicles 35 is similar to the commands of Deuteronomy 16:1-8.

A final argument that Deuteronomy is the book that is found is its emphasis that keeping the land depends on obedience to the covenant. Reading Deuteronomy 29 alone would be enough to cause Josiah to rend his clothes in anguish in this regard (compare 2 Chronicles 34:19, below).

### How to Say It

AMON. *Ay*-mun.
HILKIAH. Hill-*kye*-uh.
JEHOIAKIM. Jeh-*hoy*-uh-kim.
JEREMIAH. Jair-uh-*my*-uh.
JERUSALEM. Juh-*roo*-suh-lem.
JOSIAH. Jo-*sigh*-uh.
MANASSEH. Muh-*nass*-uh.
SHAPHAN. *Shay*-fan.
ZEPHANIAH. Zef-uh-*nye*-uh.

## B. Reading the Book of the Law (v. 18)

**18. Then Shaphan the scribe told the king, saying, Hilkiah the priest hath given me a book. And Shaphan read it before the king.**

*Shaphan* is part of the group given responsibility to repair the temple (2 Chronicles 34:8). As a *scribe*, Shaphan naturally has a keen interest in this book. So *Hilkiah the priest* delivers the book to him in order to get it to King Josiah as quickly as possible. We may speculate that Shaphan reads the entire book of Deuteronomy to *the king*.

## C. Tearing of the King's Robes (v. 19)

**19. And it came to pass, when the king had heard the words of the law, that he rent his clothes.**

To rend or tear one's *clothes* is to communicate remorse, humility, and repentance (see Isaiah 36:22; 37:1). [See question #1, page 272.] King Josiah already has been busy ridding the land of the trappings of idolatry. The anguish that Josiah now demonstrates shows that his heart truly matches those actions. He instinctively knows that outward reform in terms of smashed pagan idols will not necessarily mean inward reform or true repentance on the people's part. [See question #2, page 272.]

We may note here in passing that Josiah's reaction is in marked contrast to the later reaction of King Jehoiakim (Josiah's son). Evil Jehoiakim will exhibit a brazen contempt for the Lord's message that comes through Jeremiah by cutting up the prophet's scroll, casting it into the fire, and refusing to tear his robes (Jeremiah 36:22-24).

### REKINDLING THE SPARK

Everett and Pauline Carl got married the first time in 1936. They eloped to Arizona where it was legal for 17-year-olds to get married. But after 12 years of marriage and three daughters, Everett and Pauline allowed financial problems to sink their marriage, so they divorced. Each married someone else. Years later, both their spouses died.

The daughters then planned a family cruise and invited their widowed parents. Everett and Pauline accepted the invitation, and aboard ship the old spark of romance was rekindled. Just after the cruise ended, the couple remarried, having divorced 56 years earlier.

The story of God's people is somewhat parallel to that of the Carls. The Bible often uses the marriage analogy to describe the relationship between God and Israel. However, God divorced northern Israel after she let her fascination with other gods lead her astray (Jeremiah 3:8). God

eventually turned away from southern Judah for the same reason (Ezekiel 23:18). But as Josiah was repairing the neglected temple, the lost book of the Law was found, and the relationship with God was rekindled, at least temporarily.

"The Book" still tells us of God's continuing love. Though we might wander, the relationship can be rekindled if we will return to God. May the church continue to present herself as the bride of Christ in all her purity!　　　—C. R. B.

# II. Delay of Curses (2 Chronicles 34:25-27)

Josiah's anguish moves him to action: he sends Hilkiah and a delegation to inquire of Huldah the prophetess, who lives in Jerusalem (vv. 20-22, not in today's text). Her response is not reassuring: the curses of the book will indeed fall upon the people and the land (v. 24, not in today's text). The reason why is given next.

## A. Reasons for the Curses (v. 25)

**25. Because they have forsaken me, and have burned incense unto other gods, that they might provoke me to anger with all the works of their hands; therefore my wrath shall be poured out upon this place, and shall not be quenched.**

The people are violating the key prohibition in Deuteronomy: they are following *other gods* (see particularly Deuteronomy 13). This mind-set has become ingrained in the people over a period of nearly 60 years since evil King Manasseh (Josiah's grandfather) began to reign (2 Chronicles 33:1-9). Burning incense as an act of worship is reserved for the one true God (Exodus 30:1-10; 40:26, 27; Luke 1:9). The prophet Jeremiah, whose ministry overlaps the reign of King Josiah, also speaks out on this issue (Jeremiah 1:16; 7:9; 11:13; etc.).

Hundreds of years before, God promised to pour out His *wrath* should His people follow fictitious gods (Deuteronomy 5:7-9; 6:14, 15; 8:19, 20; 31:16-21). God's wrath, which will result in the destruction of Jerusalem, is 36 years away, given the time frame of the verse before us. [See question #3, page 272.]

## B. Reaction of the Lord (vv. 26, 27)

**26, 27. And as for the king of Judah, who sent you to inquire of the LORD, so shall ye say unto him, Thus saith the LORD God of Israel concerning the words which thou hast heard; Because thine heart was tender, and thou didst humble thyself before God, when thou heardest his words against this place, and against the inhabitants**

**thereof, and humbledst thyself before me, and didst rend thy clothes, and weep before me; I have even heard thee also, saith the LORD.**

The wrath of God that is coming upon the land is certain (see 2 Kings 21:10-15; no parallel in 2 Chronicles). But now the prophetess Huldah speaks personally of Josiah, *the king of Judah,* in light of that certainty. Because Josiah is sensitive *(tender)* to God's Word, God has *heard.* The Lord notices godly humility yet today (James 4:6; 1 Peter 5:5, 6).

## III. Renewal of Covenant (2 Chronicles 34:29, 31-33)

In verse 28 (not in today's text) Huldah prophesies that Josiah will go to the grave "in peace" and that his eyes will not see any of the evil coming upon the land and the people. This prophecy may give Josiah a bit of false hope, for he may interpret it to mean that he will live a full life and that disaster is not near. Little does he realize that he will live only another 13 years.

Josiah will die in 609 BC because of a questionable decision to engage the Egyptians in battle (see 2 Chronicles 35:20-25). He goes to his grave "in peace" in the sense that Judah is still a viable nation at the time. Truly Josiah's eyes will not see the destruction of the land because he will die early. What irony the prophetess speaks! Josiah reigns for 31 years (640–609 BC), but lives only 39 years (being born about 648 BC).

### A. Public Calling (v. 29)

**29. Then the king sent and gathered together all the elders of Judah and Jerusalem.**

The *elders* represent all the leadership *of Judah and Jerusalem.* Verse 30 (not in today's text) sketches this gathering further as including "all the men of Judah, and the inhabitants of Jerusalem, and the priests, and the Levites, and all the people, great and small."

The parallel account in 2 Kings 23:2 mentions prophets instead of Levites, so both groups are included. Both the authors of Kings and Chronicles want to emphasize that all the leadership is there with a huge crowd of people, which includes both "small and great."

### B. Public Recommitment (vv. 31, 32)

**31. And the king stood in his place, and made a covenant before the LORD, to walk after the LORD, and to keep his commandments, and his testimonies, and his statutes, with all his heart, and with all his soul, to perform the words of the covenant which are written in this book.**

The *place* where Josiah stands is beside a pillar (see the parallel in 2 Kings 23:3). In Hebrew the word for *place* (here) and the word for *pillar* (used in 2 Kings 23:3) have the same consonants but different vowels.

To make *a covenant* may involve sacrificing an animal, although this is not explicitly stated. Perhaps animal sacrifices are not needed for this ceremony. In any case, the king shows his leadership qualities by setting a public example. Further, Josiah will see to it that many animals are sacrificed during his renewal of the Passover celebration, also in this same year (2 Chronicles 35:1-9). Other covenant renewal ceremonies can be found in Joshua 8:30-35; 24; 1 Samuel 12; and Nehemiah 8–10.

**32. And he caused all that were present in Jerusalem and Benjamin to stand to it. And the inhabitants of Jerusalem did according to the covenant of God, the God of their fathers.**

It is not just Josiah who renews a commitment *to the covenant* while the others remain spectators. No, Josiah causes the people to recommit themselves as well. [See question #4, page 272.]

The mention of *Benjamin* adds a bit of color to the narrative that is not found in the parallel of 2 Kings 23:3. Benjamin has always been considered to be a part of Judah as opposed to the northern kingdom of Israel (in exile by his time). Thus Benjamin belongs to the southern tribes (compare 2 Chronicles 25:5; 34:9; Ezra 1:5; 4:1; 10:9).

"I PLEDGE ALLEGIANCE . . ."

Americans are flag-wavers. After the 9/11 terrorist attacks, people who hadn't flown an American flag in years hoisted the Stars and Stripes in

Visual for Lesson 5. *Start a discussion with this visual as you ask, "What steps can you take this week to renew your life in Christ?"*

pride and defiance. Flags flew on poles and radio antennae; they were pasted in windows and painted on the roofs of buildings.

Patriotic symbols were seen everywhere. Much was made in the media about a "rebirth of patriotism." Yet Americans also can be fickle. It wasn't too long before many of the flags came down and people went back to life as usual.

One U.S. senator said that patriotism should be a love of ideals—the values that inspire the nation. A love of godly ideals was what inspired Josiah to lead his people in renewing their pledge of allegiance to God and His covenant. For centuries the people of God had vacillated between serving God and serving idols. The captivity of northern Israel in 722 BC and the Assyrian invasion of 701 BC probably were something like "9/11 experiences" for Judah: first came alarm, then resolve, and then it was back to business as usual.

The text in front of us shows the people once again pledging their allegiance to God. Yet again it wouldn't last. Their attention would again drift elsewhere. Times change, but human nature doesn't seem to!                                   —C. R. B.

### C. Public Purge (v. 33)

**33. And Josiah took away all the abominations out of all the countries that pertained to the children of Israel, and made all that were present in Israel to serve, even to serve the LORD their God. And all his days they departed not from following the LORD, the God of their fathers.**

This is a summary statement by the author of Chronicles of all that Josiah does to bring reform to the people of God. [See question #5, page 272.] It also functions as what is called an *inclusio*

## Home Daily Bible Readings

**Monday, Mar. 24**—Revive Me (Psalm 119: 25-32)

**Tuesday, Mar. 25**—Josiah Seeks God's Way (2 Chronicles 34:1-7)

**Wednesday, Mar. 26**—A Big Discovery (2 Chronicles 34:8-18)

**Thursday, Mar. 27**—Josiah Repents (2 Chronicles 34:19-21)

**Friday, Mar. 28**—God Hears Josiah (2 Chronicles 34:22-28)

**Saturday, Mar. 29**—The Covenant Renewed (2 Chronicles 34:29-33)

**Sunday, Mar. 30**—Teach Me (Psalm 119:33-40)

since it comes full circle where the story of Josiah began: "And [Josiah] did that which was right in the sight of the Lord, and walked in the ways of David his father, and declined neither to the right hand, nor to the left" (2 Chronicles 34:2).

This speaks highly for a young king who follows two of the most wicked kings ever to rule the southern kingdom of Judah. Unfortunately, Josiah will not live very long. His reforms and renewal will turn out to be "too little, too late," as subsequent events show.

## Conclusion

### A. Renewing the Covenant

I have taught for over 30 years, in two Bible colleges. My emphasis in all my Bible classes has been *teach the people!* How will they ever know the Lord without a mature and full knowledge of His Word?

There is a desperate need in our churches for renewal. We can change worship styles or add programs to help our churches grow, but what we absolutely need is greater biblical literacy.

Only a recommitment to God's Word as divine revelation can avert a coming disaster. Submission to the Word's authority in terms of obedience is vital. Churches are in danger of losing their heritage, identity, and roots. We have whole generations that know little of the Bible, and what little they know is often misinterpreted. A fresh discovery of the Word of God can mend broken relationships with God as well as with others. It is possible to become (again) "a people of the Book"!

One person can make a difference in the life of a congregation by encouraging a recommitment to Bible study. This will take time and effort, but mature study over a long period of time will make all the difference. Let us seek to restore our covenant relationship with God through a renewed effort to understand God's Word.

### B. Prayer

Our Father, you have revealed to us Your will through holy Scripture and through Your Son, the incarnate Word. Forgive us for breaking covenant with You. Today we renew our covenant with You. Help us to walk in Your ways with all our heart, soul, and strength. May Your Word bring renewal to our lives so that our relationship with You will be restored. In Jesus' name, amen.

### C. Thought to Remember

Renewal always begins with repentance.

# Learning by Doing

*This page contains an alternative lesson plan emphasizing learning activities.*
*Classes desiring such student involvement will find these suggestions helpful.*

## Into the Lesson

Make and distribute copies of this quiz for your learners to work on as they arrive. (The quiz also appears in the optional student books.) Learners are to match each famous discovery with the date when it was made.

1. Bedouin goatherds discover the Dead Sea Scrolls; 2. James Marshall discovers gold at Sutter's Mill, Coloma, California; 3. Columbus discovers the new world; 4. Marie Curie discovers radium; 5. Heinrich Schliemann discovers the ruins of the city of Troy, in Turkey; 6. Searchers discover the wreck of the Titanic; 7. William Harvey discovers the human circulatory system; 8. Alexander Fleming discovers penicillin; 9. Francis Crick, James Watson, Rosalind Franklin discover the structure of DNA; 10. Hilkiah, the Jewish priest, discovers the book of the law.

A. 622 BC; B. 1492; C. 1628; D. 1848; E. 1870; F. 1898; G. 1928; H. 1947; I. 1953; J. 1985.

*Answers: 1. H; 2. D; 3. B; 4. F; 5. E; 6. J; 7. C; 8. G; 9. I; 10. A.*

After you have graded the quizzes together, ask which items on the list were discovered only after having first been "lost" or forgotten. (Items 1, 5, 6, and 10 can fit this description in various senses.) Use this fact to lead into today's lesson, which deals with #10.

## Into the Word

Use the Lesson Background to prepare a brief introduction of the events that led up to the discovery of the book of the law, where today's text begins. Briefly review 2 Chronicles 33 as you explain how Josiah's grandfather (Manasseh) and father (Amon) had led Judah into idolatry.

Next, divide your class into small groups of three to five. Give each group copies of the following two activities (or direct them to the same activities in the optional student books). Ask your groups to follow the instructions printed on the exercises.

*Exercise #1—Recipe for National Revival.* Josiah's great reform program in 2 Chronicles 34 had four steps to it: (1) research the law (vv. 15, 18, 20-25); (2) repent of past sins (vv. 19, 26-28); (3) renew the covenant with God (vv. 29-32); and (4) remove pagan influences from society (v. 33). Write a brief summary of Josiah's actions under each of the four steps. Be prepared to share results with the rest of the class.

*Exercise #2—Prescription for Church and Personal Revival.* How can we apply Josiah's reform program to ourselves? What New Testament passages will help us do so?

After about 10 minutes, have volunteers share their answers. Responses for Exercise #1 may look something like this: 1. When Josiah heard the Word read, he sent the priests to the prophetess Huldah to learn what the Lord wanted them to do; 2. Josiah tore his robes as a sign of repentance for Judah's failure to keep the law; therefore, God promised to spare Josiah from the disaster He would bring on Judah; 3. Josiah brought all the people together to pledge themselves to keep the covenant God made with their ancestors; 4. Josiah had idols removed from the land, so Judah could focus on serving God.

Responses for Exercise #2 may look something like this: 1. Research the Word (1 Corinthians 10:11; 2 Timothy 3:16, 17; etc.); 2. Repent of past sins (2 Corinthians 2:5-11; Revelation 2:5, 16; etc.); 3. Renew the covenant with God (1 Corinthians 11:23-32; etc.); 4. Remove pagan influences from oneself and from the church (1 Corinthians 5; 10:7-10, 14-21; Colossians 3:5; etc.).

## Into Life

Make a transition by saying, "Now that we've worked through a recipe and a prescription, let's try to see how this could apply today."

*Modern Revival.* Say, "Imagine that you are the spiritual advisor to a political leader. Your job is to help him or her bring moral or spiritual reform to the people. Keeping in mind the constitutional rules governing the interaction of religion and government in our society, what changes or actions would you recommend in terms of Josiah's *Four Rs* reform program?"

Have groups brainstorm their ideas and then share them with the class. Ask, "How difficult would it be to carry out these reforms?"

*Alternative activity: Interview with a Reformer.* Have one of your learners take the role of a TV reporter who is interviewing a modern-day Josiah, who is trying to reform society. Recruit in advance the two who will play these roles so they can work up a dialogue beforehand.

# Let's Talk It Over

*The questions on this page are designed to promote discussion of the lesson by the class and to encourage application of the lesson Scriptures. The answers provided are only discussion starters. Let your class talk it over from there.*

**1. Josiah tore his clothes as a way to express his grief over sin. What might a Christian do today when confronted with national or personal sin?**

Weeping is an ageless expression of grief that seems to cut across all social and cultural boundaries. Weeping indicates a sorrowful heart. This reaction to sin matches Joel 2:13: "Rend your heart, and not your garments, and turn unto the Lord your God: for he is gracious and merciful, slow to anger, and of great kindness."

If we stray, we can return to God. Coming back to God is a matter of sincere, heartfelt desire for God over self and sin. After his horrific sin regarding Bathsheba, King David recognized that "the sacrifices of God are a broken spirit: a broken and a contrite heart, O God, thou wilt not despise" (Psalm 51:17).

**2. What was a time when you set out to improve an area of your life, only to discover that you were in worse shape than you had originally thought? How did you react to the discovery? How did you grow spiritually as a result?**

Josiah was already involved in God-pleasing reform activity when the book of the law was found. The book helped Josiah see just how far from God the nation had fallen. When we approach our Holy God, we become more acutely aware of how far from holy we are. When the prophet Isaiah saw the Lord, he was immediately aware of his own "unclean lips" (Isaiah 6:5). This is not said as a discouragement, but as an acknowledgment of our sinful condition and need for grace. The Lord took care of Isaiah's unclean lips (Isaiah 6:6, 7), and He can take care of ours too.

God is pleased when we choose to repent (2 Peter 3:9). As long as we are alive and in control of our will, it is not too late. We are never too far away to turn to Him. The Lord even accepted back evil King Manasseh after an unholy reign of several decades (2 Chronicles 33:10-13). Through abiding in Christ, we can grow in our ability to make better choices (Philippians 1:9-11).

**3. Most of us are very comfortable discussing God's love. On a scale of 1 (low) to 10 (high),** what is your comfort level when discussing God's anger? Explain.

God is indeed love (1 John 4:8, 16). Yet God is also "a consuming fire" (Deuteronomy 4:24; Hebrews 12:29). He "is angry with the wicked every day" (Psalm 7:11). Even now, "the wrath of God is revealed from heaven against all ungodliness and unrighteousness of men, who hold the truth in unrighteousness" (Romans 1:18).

Although the punishment foretold in today's lesson was for Old Testament Israel, a day of judgment is still to come (Hebrews 9:27). God's wrath is a part of the Christian message. For those who choose Christ, there is no need for fear (Romans 8:1).

**4. What practical advice would you offer a new believer to help him or her draw closer to God?**

Getting back on track with God always begins with repentance. Realizing this, we may be poor judges of our personal walks. Comparing ourselves to others is not helpful (Galatians 6:4). Having a clear conscience is important (Hebrews 13:18), but that is not proof of godly living (1 Timothy 4:2; Titus 1:15).

A solution is to have Christian friends who will pray for us (1 John 5:16). Unfortunately, many believers feel more comfortable praying for each other's physical needs than spiritual issues. We must recall Jesus' model prayer and not neglect to pray, "And lead us not into temptation, but deliver us from evil" (Matthew 6:13).

**5. As Josiah removed abominations from the land, so we too must "take out the trash" in our lives in order to renew our walk with God. How do you do this in your own life?**

Answers will be highly personal. If pornography is a person's sin of choice, discontinuing cable TV or Internet access may be necessary for renewal. If pride is our problem, we must cease promoting ourselves (even if only to ourselves) and focus on the glory of God; taking on "lowly" tasks that others shun may help. Mark 9:43-48 discusses cutting off one's hand if it causes sin. While this may be exaggerated language (hyperbole), God makes His point clear: remove whatever you need to in order to keep from sinning.

# Holding to Convictions

DEVOTIONAL READING: **Psalm 141:1-4.**

BACKGROUND SCRIPTURE: **Daniel 1.**

PRINTED TEXT: **Daniel 1:8-20.**

**Apr 6**

### Daniel 1:8-20

8 But Daniel purposed in his heart that he would not defile himself with the portion of the king's meat, nor with the wine which he drank: therefore he requested of the prince of the eunuchs that he might not defile himself.

9 Now God had brought Daniel into favor and tender love with the prince of the eunuchs.

10 And the prince of the eunuchs said unto Daniel, I fear my lord the king, who hath appointed your meat and your drink: for why should he see your faces worse liking than the children which are of your sort? then shall ye make me endanger my head to the king.

11 Then said Daniel to Melzar, whom the prince of the eunuchs had set over Daniel, Hananiah, Misha-el, and Azariah,

12 Prove thy servants, I beseech thee, ten days; and let them give us pulse to eat, and water to drink.

13 Then let our countenances be looked upon before thee, and the countenance of the children that eat of the portion of the king's meat: and as thou seest, deal with thy servants.

14 So he consented to them in this matter, and proved them ten days.

15 And at the end of ten days their countenances appeared fairer and fatter in flesh than all the children which did eat the portion of the king's meat.

16 Thus Melzar took away the portion of their meat, and the wine that they should drink; and gave them pulse.

17 As for these four children, God gave them knowledge and skill in all learning and wisdom: and Daniel had understanding in all visions and dreams.

18 Now at the end of the days that the king had said he should bring them in, then the prince of the eunuchs brought them in before Nebuchadnezzar.

19 And the king communed with them; and among them all was found none like Daniel, Hananiah, Misha-el, and Azariah: therefore stood they before the king.

20 And in all matters of wisdom and understanding, that the king inquired of them, he found them ten times better than all the magicians and astrologers that were in all his realm.

GOLDEN TEXT: Daniel purposed in his heart that he would not defile himself
with the portion of the king's meat, nor with the wine which he drank:
therefore he requested of the prince of the eunuchs
that he might not defile himself.—Daniel 1:8.

> *God, the People, and the Covenant*
> Unit 2: The Covenant in Exile
> (Lessons 6-9)

## Lesson Aims

After participating in this lesson, each student will be able to:

1. Describe how and why Daniel, Hananiah, Mishael, and Azariah avoided self-defilement.

2. Explain how the example of Daniel, Hananiah, Mishael, and Azariah is helpful to Christians as they face challenges from an ungodly culture.

3. Make a plan to resist one unholy cultural trend.

## Lesson Outline

INTRODUCTION
   A. Maintaining Identity
   B. Lesson Background
 I. FAITHFULNESS TO GOD (Daniel 1:8-13)
   A. Daniel's Request (v. 8)
   B. Official's Resistance (vv. 9, 10)
     *Those Who Are Different*
   C. Daniel's Insistence (vv. 11-13)
II. FAITHFULNESS FROM GOD (Daniel 1:14-20)
   A. God Grants Success (vv. 14-16)
   B. God Grants Blessing (v. 17)
   C. God Grants Witness (vv. 18-20)
     *"You Can't Fight City Hall"*
CONCLUSION
   A. Learning from Daniel and Friends
   B. Prayer
   C. Thought to Remember

## Introduction

### A. Maintaining Identity

In 2005, a new church sought to rent space in a certain public school building. There was nothing unusual about this fledgling church. Countless churches have rented similar facilities for identical purposes. Yet after this church secured a contract, the news went public and the response was startling.

Based on pure speculation, the church was accused of being a terrorist organization seeking to infiltrate the school system to plant bombs in students' desks. The church was required to pay for a security guard to protect school premises from potential terrorist activity. As I write this, a legal battle is being waged over whether it is appropriate for this church, or any other, to rent state-owned facilities.

Christians increasingly are deemed a threat to societal progress. Being Christian is indeed challenging when Christianity is not the norm. For many, these developments seem new and unnerving. But God's people have held minority status quite often throughout history. Scripture has much to say about what it takes to protect our identity in hostile cultures. In Daniel 1, we learn that this requires costly intentional effort. God empowers such effort and blesses those who remain committed to Him.

### B. Lesson Background

Working through Kings David and Solomon, God built Israel into a mighty nation. Israelites occupied an impressive stretch of land, they were ruled by their own kings, and smaller nations paid tribute to them. By the end of Solomon's reign (about 930 BC), the Israelites had come a long way since the Egyptian bondage of some 500 years previous.

But prosperity went to their heads. The Israelites began worshiping the gods of other nations, mistreating the poor, and trusting human power rather than God. The Israelites, whom God called to be distinct from other nations, became like the nations they dispossessed. Through prophets, God warned His people that He would punish them if they refused to reform their ways. The Israelites did not repent permanently, so God used the Assyrians and the Babylonians to conquer His people.

Jerusalem was quite a distance from Babylon—some 900 miles. For the Babylonians to maintain control of the territory of Judah was a challenge. The Babylonians could establish a large military presence in Judah, but the costs would be high and soldiers undoubtedly were needed elsewhere in the empire.

So King Nebuchadnezzar of Babylon chose a different strategy: he crippled Judah's ability to revolt by relocating the most educated and skilled Jews. This way the king of Babylon could benefit from their abilities while the Jews who were left behind would lack the leadership to rebuild. The word we normally use for such forced relocation is *exile*.

In Daniel 1:1-7, we learn that Daniel, Hananiah, Mishael, and Azariah were among those gifted Jews who were taken into exile (about 605 BC). Being of royal blood, they were selected to serve in Nebuchadnezzar's royal court in

Babylon. Such service required preparation. So for three years these men were given the finest education Babylon could offer.

Yet such an education raised questions for exiled Jews. How much could they immerse themselves in Babylonian culture before they ceased being Jews? How could they survive among the pagans without becoming just like them? As recent events have taught us, these questions apply not only to ancient Jews, but also to modern Christians. Let us therefore pay careful attention to the answers of Scripture.

## I. Faithfulness to God (Daniel 1:8-13)
### A. Daniel's Request (v. 8)
**8. But Daniel purposed in his heart that he would not defile himself with the portion of the king's meat, nor with the wine which he drank: therefore he requested of the prince of the eunuchs that he might not defile himself.**

Our text begins with Daniel's heartfelt conviction that eating *the king's* rations will lead to defilement. It is not clear, however, what it is about the king's royal food that may *defile* Daniel. Jewish law forbids eating certain kinds of *meat,* but other kinds are perfectly acceptable. *Wine* is not forbidden (Numbers 6:20; 18:12; 1 Samuel 1:24; Psalm 104:14, 15; etc.), although it is spoken of in negative terms when excess is involved (Isaiah 28:7; 5:11, 22; Proverbs 20:1).

Daniel may be avoiding food and drink associated with pagan temple offerings and thus idolatry (compare 1 Corinthians 8). But under this theory, the vegetarian alternative he proposes in verse 12 would be equally suspect since flour is also offered to pagan idols.

Perhaps Daniel thinks it inappropriate to eat festive food such as meat and wine during Israel's

time of exile—a time of Jewish mourning. This suggestion, however, does not account for Daniel's concerns about defilement. Another theory is that Daniel refuses to be dependent upon a foreign ruler; however, he does not reject extensive training or later appointments to high positions in the king's court.

One further possibility should be considered. Daniel knows that even in exile the Jews need to maintain a distinct identity. They cannot simply blend in with the surrounding cultures. To adopt every and all foreign practices is to defile themselves and forsake their Jewishness. Daniel knows, however, that one can learn about the ways of other people without accepting those ways. That's probably why he doesn't object to learning the Babylonian language and literature (v. 4).

Food, however, is different in light of God-given dietary laws for Old Testament Jews. The Jews had been set apart by diet. Daniel has to make choices regarding what will compromise his Jewish identity and what won't. To compromise on the food issue will mean that he and his friends are becoming full-fledged Babylonians rather than Jews that happen to live in Babylon.

Regardless of the specific reason for his decision, Daniel is not content to keep his conviction to himself. He sticks his neck out and tells the king's official that he wishes to avoid being defiled by the king's food. What a bold statement! Daniel publicly declares that the king's chosen food is unacceptable. [See question #1, page 280.]

### B. Official's Resistance (vv. 9, 10)
**9. Now God had brought Daniel into favor and tender love with the prince of the eunuchs.**

The official can respond in more than one way. A mild response would be to demote Daniel. If delicacies enjoyed by the king's closest attendants are not acceptable to Daniel, then perhaps he should join lower-level servants who eat lesser food. More severely, an underling who insults the king's graciousness can be executed. Yet neither of these fates befalls Daniel because *God had brought Daniel into favor* with this particular official.

**10. And the prince of the eunuchs said unto Daniel, I fear my lord the king, who hath appointed your meat and your drink: for why should he see your faces worse liking than the children which are of your sort? then shall ye make me endanger my head to the king.**

Although the official does not respond harshly, neither does he immediately grant Daniel's request. Instead, he expresses fear that his own life will be at risk should he agree to Daniel's plan.

---

### How to Say It
ABRAHAM. *Ay*-bruh-ham.
ASSYRIANS. Uh-*sear*-e-unz.
AZARIAH. Az-uh-*rye*-uh.
BABYLON. *Bab*-uh-lun.
BABYLONIANS. Bab-ih-*low*-nee-unz.
EGYPTIAN. Ee-*jip*-shun.
HANANIAH. Han-uh-*nye*-uh.
JUDAH. *Joo*-duh.
MISHAEL. *Mish*-a-el.
NEBUCHADNEZZAR. *Neb*-yuh-kud-*nez*-er (strong accent on *nez*).
SOLOMON. *Sol*-o-mun.

Perhaps the king will notice a difference in appearance between those who abstain from the food he supplies and those who don't. The official thus makes what appears to be a compelling case for why Daniel's suggestion should be denied.

A person of lukewarm convictions would eat whatever the king sets before him. A bold Jew would go one step further and venture a request like we see in verse 8. But only the most conscientious Jew would persist in his request after being rebuffed like Daniel is here in verse 10.

### THOSE WHO ARE DIFFERENT

The Netherlands has a long-standing reputation for cultural "tolerance." The freewheeling drug and sex culture of the late twentieth century seemed to indicate the nation could tolerate anything and still flourish. However, large numbers of Muslim immigrants who settled there did not assimilate into the prevailing culture. The Muslim ghettos became breeding grounds for unrest and, many feared, potential terrorism.

One fearful response has been legal repression, such as outlawing Muslim attire. Similar concerns and responses can be found throughout the world as migration increases in the twenty-first century.

Such circumstances may help us to understand better the situation in which Daniel and his friends found themselves. The Babylonian king, like modern governments, was wary of a cultural minority in his land. As Christianity becomes or remains a minority religion in many lands, we may find ourselves under increasing suspicion as well. The question for Christians is, how will we present ourselves to a culture that is hostile to the truth of Christ?     —C. R. B.

### C. Daniel's Insistence (vv. 11-13)

**11. Then said Daniel to Melzar, whom the prince of the eunuchs had set over Daniel, Hananiah, Misha-el, and Azariah.**

*Hananiah, Misha-el, and Azariah* were introduced earlier in Daniel 1:6. Now we learn that they too share Daniel's convictions. The words "now among these" in verse 6 indicate that other Jews besides these four are also in the king's palace. But they apparently make different choices about diet and Jewish identity. We are not told that God judged these other Jews, but as the story unfolds it is clear that God blesses the most conscientious.

**12, 13. Prove thy servants, I beseech thee, ten days; and let them give us pulse to eat, and water to drink. Then let our countenances be looked upon before thee, and the countenance of the children that eat of the portion of the king's meat: and as thou seest, deal with thy servants.**

Daniel does not give up. Since the official is nervous about the future physical appearance of these four, Daniel proposes a test. He requests *water* instead of wine and seed-bearing plants *(pulse)* instead of meat. This diet resembles what God gave humans to eat in the Garden of Eden (Genesis 1:29) and corresponds to what many nutritionists recommend today.

We must be careful, however, not to read too much into such connections. In Genesis 9:3, God granted that humans also could eat meat. We also should be mindful that what it means to look healthy differs from culture to culture. In modern Western cultures, a slim figure is a sign of health, and a vegetarian diet is one way for overweight people to trim down. In ancient cultures, however, a slim figure may indicate poverty while plumpness indicates the presence of a robust diet and the wealth necessary to have it. [See question #2, page 280.]

## II. Faithfulness from God (Daniel 1:14-20)

### A. God Grants Success (vv. 14-16)

**14, 15. So he consented to them in this matter, and proved them ten days. And at the end of ten days their countenances appeared fairer and fatter in flesh than all the children which did eat the portion of the king's meat.**

Here we see God's hand at work in two ways. First, as in verse 9, the official continues to have a favorable view of Daniel. So when Daniel boldly yet respectfully counters the official's reservations, the official does not receive it as an affront to his authority, but as an idea worth trying. [See question #3, page 280.]

Second, it may be that God blesses these four so they will gain more weight than their peers. Experience teaches us that under normal circumstances those who drink water and eat vegetables lose weight, whereas those who eat meat and drink wine tend to gain. But the exact makeup of the diet, which is unknown to us, may result in the opposite here.

**16. Thus Melzar took away the portion of their meat, and the wine that they should drink; and gave them pulse.**

The king's official is now comfortable enough to remove their portions of *wine* and *meat* altogether. Perhaps for a while he has set these items alongside their vegetables just for show. If so, this procedure is no longer necessary, since the superior appearance of the four Jews now testifies to the validity of their diet. Thus is removed any threat to the official's life.

## B. God Grants Blessing (v. 17)

**17. As for these four children, God gave them knowledge and skill in all learning and wisdom: and Daniel had understanding in all visions and dreams.**

God's blessings do not end with the favor and health of *these four*. God does not bless them for mere survival. He wants to bless them with abundant life. Such blessing is central to God's promise to Abraham (Genesis 12:1-3) and covenant with Israel (Deuteronomy 28:1-14).

Such blessing, however, comes with conditions. God's people have to serve God alone and follow His instructions diligently. If not, they will experience curses (Deuteronomy 28:15-68). This is why Jerusalem is destroyed in 586 BC (less than 20 years in the future from the time of the incident we are considering now).

Judah's failure to honor God's Word is the reason these four young Jews now find themselves serving a foreign king in Babylon. The book of Daniel teaches us, however, that even in exile God wishes to bless those who remain true. [See question #4, page 280.]

## C. God Grants Witness (vv. 18-20)

**18. Now at the end of the days that the king had said he should bring them in, then the prince of the eunuchs brought them in before Nebuchadnezzar.**

The time period in view with the phrase *at the end of the days* is not the 10-day test we saw earlier, but the three years of training introduced in verse 5. All the trainees are brought before King *Nebuchadnezzar*, not just the four Jews we have been talking about.

**19. And the king communed with them; and among them all was found none like Daniel, Hananiah, Misha-el, and Azariah: therefore stood they before the king.**

*The king* spends time with his new recruits, interviewing them and selecting them for various administrative posts. Like his official, Nebuchadnezzar is impressed with *Daniel, Hananiah, Misha-el, and Azariah*. They are therefore given high positions near the king himself; that's what *therefore stood they before the king* signifies.

**20. And in all matters of wisdom and understanding, that the king inquired of them, he found them ten times better than all the magicians and astrologers that were in all his realm.**

God has so blessed Daniel and his rookie friends that they are vastly superior to the king's

Visual for
Lessons 6 & 7

*Point to this visual as you ask, "What kind of temptation gives you the most trouble?"*

veteran counselors. Those other counselors are described in such a way as to highlight the source of their so-called wisdom. Unlike Daniel and his friends, who owe their *wisdom* to the one true God, these rivals rely on various tricks and the movements of the stars. (Sound familiar?)

This verse is the starting point for two themes that become increasingly important as the book of Daniel moves along. First, God blesses His people, not just for their own sake, but for the sake of the nations. His will is that all nations worship Him. God has exalted these Jews in Nebuchadnezzar's eyes because He wants Nebuchadnezzar to exalt God in the eyes of all Babylon. This begins to happen in chapter two. [See question #5, page 280.]

Second, we will see that when God's people are exalted in foreign lands, foreigners are not pleased. Imagine how the native Babylonians feel as their positions of power and influence fall under the supervision of Jewish outsiders! Competition and jealousy will arise, and this will pose an additional threat to God's people.

### "You Can't Fight City Hall"

"You can't fight city hall" is an old sentiment. It is uttered by those who are frustrated with government practices.

Take, for example, the doctrine of *eminent domain*, which says government may condemn private property for a greater public good. The U.S. Supreme Court ruled in 2005 that a city could exercise eminent domain even in cases where a private developer would profit substantially if it were to result in an enhancement of local tax revenues. The high court said this could be done even if the property were not blighted (one of the usual reasons for exercising the doctrine).

This was a case of fighting city hall and losing. But some people decided to continue fighting anyway. Since Justice David Souter had agreed with the majority opinion, someone proposed to use the doctrine to take Justice Souter's farmhouse and turn it into the *Lost Liberty Hotel* with a *Just Desserts Café* on the premises. It was probably a tongue-in-cheek gesture, but it demonstrated frustration with what was perceived to be bureaucratic arrogance.

The four Hebrews in today's lesson decided to "fight city hall," and they won! Of course, it was with God's help, not that of a lawyer. God honored their trust in Him and caused them to be elevated to prominent positions in Babylon's government. The "good guys" don't always win in the way the world defines winning. The most important thing is to make sure you're on God's side of the issue before the battle starts. —C. R. B.

## Conclusion

### A. Learning from Daniel and Friends

In adopting an alternative diet, Daniel and his friends reminded themselves daily that they were different from the Babylonians. Remaining God's people meant remaining visibly distinct from the nations.

Christ said that His followers are not of the world, but are sent into it as ones who are set apart (John 17:14-19). We live in the world (1 Corinthians 5:10); yet the apostle Paul cautions us not to be yoked with unbelievers, but to come out and be separate from them (2 Corinthians 6:14-18). The separation is not one of physical isolation, but of maintaining a pure spiritual identity. According to James, pure religion entails, in part, keeping oneself unstained by the world; those who befriend the world become God's enemies (James 1:27; 4:4).

Peter ties these themes together with Israel's Old Testament witness by referring to Christians as strangers in this world (1 Peter 1:1, 17; 2:11) and calling us to be holy as God is holy (1:14-17). So while the cross of Christ has removed barriers between believers—whether of race, gender, age, ability, or social status—our distinctively holy way of life continues to set us apart from those who do not believe. We must never forget, however, that this difference is not for difference's sake. We are different for the sake of witness, so that others may be drawn to God (1 Peter 2:9).

The nonbelievers we know at work, at school, and in our neighborhoods should notice that we are different. If this is not clear to them, then perhaps we, like Daniel and his friends, need a symbolic reminder of our unique identity. They chose diet as their reminder, but that won't work today (see Mark 7:17-19). So we choose other ways to remember and announce our set-apart status. Some wear certain rings to remind themselves of the need for sexual purity. Some wear WWJD bracelets. Others wear necklaces with crosses. Some remove the TV from being the focal point of the living room.

Christians do such things because they believe that symbolic practices can be meaningful if used properly. When Jesus washed His followers' feet, He did not significantly improve hygiene in Palestine. Nor did He change the way kings and governors rule. Rather, He created a symbol for His disciples so they would not forget that leadership in His kingdom is not about worldly power, but about service. How will you remember your unique identity in Christ this week?

### B. Prayer

We thank You, God, for setting us apart. We thank You for calling us to the adventure of following You. This adventure is never dull and always entails making tough yet life-giving choices. Empower us the way You empowered Daniel and his friends to make the right decisions. Forgive us when we have preferred simply to blend in. Give us the courage to stand out so that You may use our witness to draw others unto You. In Jesus' name, amen.

### C. Thought to Remember

Make your unique identity in Christ known.

## Home Daily Bible Readings

**Monday, Mar. 31**—A Prayer for God's Support (Psalm 141:1-4)
**Tuesday, Apr. 1**—God's House Besieged (Daniel 1:1, 2)
**Wednesday, Apr. 2**—The King's Plan (Daniel 1:3-7)
**Thursday, Apr. 3**—Daniel's Resolution (Daniel 1:8-10)
**Friday, Apr. 4**—The Ten-Day Test (Daniel 1:11-14)
**Saturday, Apr. 5**—Four Fine Young Men (Daniel 1:15-17)
**Sunday, Apr. 6**—Tested and True (Daniel 1:18-21)

# Learning by Doing

*This page contains an alternative lesson plan emphasizing learning activities.
Classes desiring such student involvement will find these suggestions helpful.*

## Into the Lesson

Display the phrase *The Cultural Dilemma of the Godly.* Also display these two scrambled words: AADEIILMSST and ACDEFIINST.

Let your class ponder the possibilities for a time. If they need some help, write A_____ED and S_____ED on the board. If they still struggle, give them the second letter of each or the third letter from each end. *ASSIMILATED* and *SANCTIFIED* are the words. Briefly note that the godly person always has a choice: either to be assimilated or to be sanctified in relation to his or her culture—to go along or to stand apart, to disappear or to be conspicuously holy.

## Into the Word

Daniel was a man of conviction and action. Ask your class to look at Daniel 1:8-20 to identify the verse or verses where Daniel did each of the following as you read them aloud. Provide paper and pen for this activity and the next. Possible answers are noted in italics. Allow alternate responses if there is a reasonable explanation.

1. Daniel challenged *(v. 8).*
2. Daniel understood *(v. 17).*
3. Daniel excelled *(v. 19).*
4. Daniel led *(v. 8).*
5. Daniel endeared himself *(v. 9).*
6. Daniel impressed *(v. 15).*
7. Daniel dieted *(v. 12).*
8. Daniel purposed *(v. 8).*
9. Daniel requested *(v. 8).*
10. Daniel wagered *(v. 12).*

Note that when the king questioned Daniel and his friends, he found them superior to all the advisors in his kingdom. Say, "I'm going to question you to see how superior your knowledge is. Use the entirety of Daniel 1 to answer the following questions."

1. How did Daniel and his friends end up in Babylon?
2. What valuable objects had the king also brought from Jerusalem—objects that would play an important role in another story given in Daniel 5?
3. What type of young men did the king choose for his government-training program?
4. What was the curriculum of the young men's program?
5. How long did the academic program last?
6. What names did Ashpenaz give to the four young men from Judah?
7. What did Daniel find offensive about the king's planned regimen?
8. Why was the official hesitant to permit Daniel's request?
9. How long did the four young Jews have to demonstrate the effects of a special diet?
10. What was the "secret" of the young men's success in physical health and mental acumen?
11. On what basis did the king make his final judgment regarding the men to be appointed to places of administrative leadership?
12. How much better and brighter did the king find the Hebrew men to be in comparison to his other advisors?
13. How long did Daniel remain in a position of authority in Babylon?

Let learners respond in writing as you read the questions or as you reveal them on an overhead. At the end, go back and have learners respond orally. They should be able to note verses where the answers are found.

## Into Life

Prepare and duplicate strips of paper having a row of 10 1-inch circles. Put the letters *GP* in each of the first 5 circles; put the letters *SC* in each of the other circles.

Give seven strips of circles to each learner, one for each day of the week ahead. Explain that the GP stands for *God's Person* and the SC stands for *Society's Child.*

Say, "That is the choice we all have daily: being God's person and living life in holiness or being society's child and resembling the culture around us. Carry a new strip of paper for each day of the week. As you catch yourself obviously being either *God's Person* or *Society's Child*, mark off an appropriate circle. At the end of the week, do a bit of biblical introspection regarding how you did. Make a commitment to God to look more like His person than simply another child of our wayward society."

Go back to the two words with which you started today's class: *ASSIMILATED* and *SANCTIFIED*. Point out the relationship of these words to this closing activity.

# Let's Talk It Over

*The questions on this page are designed to promote discussion of the lesson by the class and to encourage application of the lesson Scriptures. The answers provided are only discussion starters. Let your class talk it over from there.*

**1. In what ways have you sought to avoid defiling yourself with the things of this world? How can you do better?**

The world is filled with various pleasures by which people can be drawn away from God and into sin. To stand against these temptations demands effort on the part of God's people. Instead of seeing how close we can get to sin without falling, the teaching of Scripture is to flee at the first sight of temptation (1 Corinthians 6:18; 1 Timothy 6:11).

The first step in being able to flee is training oneself to recognize what should be fled from. The entertainment industry promotes a distorted view of sex, marriage, and personal relationships. Talk show hosts promote an arrogance that demeans others. As a result, people think this is an appropriate way to act. Because of these unholy influences, what one views or listens to should be monitored continually.

**2. What are some areas in which you can prove your faithfulness as well as demonstrate the faithfulness of God?**

Sadly, Christians often fall into the patterns of this world, and then adopt the world's "solutions" when those patterns "don't work." Divorce statistics for Christians are no better than those of non-Christians. Church leaders allow themselves to fall prey to adultery or Internet pornography. Christians spend beyond their means; as a result they are not able to support adequately the work of the kingdom of God. They may adopt the world's solution of declaring bankruptcy to get out of their mess.

Fear and anxieties plague many Christians. Often these problems are not dealt with by the power and grace of God, but rather in the world's ways through sinful worry, substance abuse, and anger toward God. When we respond in this way, we are undermining the very faith we claim. This makes God seem to be inadequate to take care of our needs.

**3. How can partnerships be of value when making spiritual commitments today?**

Daniel and his friends entered into their agreement as a group. Doing so enabled them to draw strength from one another during the 10 days of proving themselves. One person seeking to do this alone could easily fail. But "a threefold cord is not quickly broken" (Ecclesiastes 4:12).

There is spiritual strength in numbers. Perhaps that's why the author of Hebrews says, "Not forsaking the assembling of ourselves together, as the manner of some is; but exhorting one another: and so much the more, as ye see the day approaching" (Hebrews 10:25). Growing in faith and remaining faithful is enhanced when others hold us accountable, encourage us, and even rebuke us when we stray from the way of truth.

**4. What are some ways that God has blessed you beyond what you have asked or imagined?**

In Ephesians 3:20, the apostle Paul states that God can bless us beyond what we can ask or think is possible. God did this for Daniel and his friends. He continues to do so today in the lives of His people as individuals and in the church as a whole.

God is an abundant giver. Jesus says that He came to give abundant life (John 10:10). But it is important to see in this story of Daniel and his friends that the blessing came after faith was exercised, not before. Often we want to see God give the blessing before we move forward. We often prefer to walk by sight, not by faith.

**5. How can our faith influence our actions and thereby influence the course of history?**

We often feel we have very little if any influence upon the world. We say, "I am just one person. What difference can one person make?" But the influence of the one, coupled with the influence of another, can start a giant movement of faith.

Christians who work together can covenant to seek to be an influence for Christ in their workplace. Others of faith may take notice, "come out of hiding," and join in the process. After a while the atmosphere of the workplace can be changed for the better because someone was willing to take a stand. Consider how you can form a network with another Christian at work or in your community to become this positive influence for Christ.

# Taking a Stand

DEVOTIONAL READING: **Psalm 121.**

BACKGROUND SCRIPTURE: **Daniel 3.**

PRINTED TEXT: **Daniel 3:10-13, 16-18, 21, 24-26.**

### Daniel 3:10-13, 16-18, 21, 24-26

10 Thou, O king, hast made a decree, that every man that shall hear the sound of the cornet, flute, harp, sackbut, psaltery, and dulcimer, and all kinds of music, shall fall down and worship the golden image:

11 And whoso falleth not down and worshippeth, that he should be cast into the midst of a burning fiery furnace.

12 There are certain Jews whom thou hast set over the affairs of the province of Babylon, Shadrach, Meshach, and Abednego; these men, O king, have not regarded thee: they serve not thy gods, nor worship the golden image which thou hast set up.

13 Then Nebuchadnezzar in his rage and fury commanded to bring Shadrach, Meshach, and Abednego. Then they brought these men before the king.

. . . . . . . . . . . . .

16 Shadrach, Meshach, and Abednego, answered and said to the king, O Nebuchadnezzar, we are not careful to answer thee in this matter.

17 If it be so, our God whom we serve is able to deliver us from the burning fiery furnace, and he will deliver us out of thine hand, O king.

18 But if not, be it known unto thee, O king, that we will not serve thy gods, nor worship the golden image which thou hast set up.

. . . . . . . . . . . . .

21 Then these men were bound in their coats, their hose, and their hats, and their

other garments, and were cast into the midst of the burning fiery furnace.

. . . . . . . . . . . . .

24 Then Nebuchadnezzar the king was astonished, and rose up in haste, and spake, and said unto his counselors, Did not we cast three men bound into the midst of the fire? They answered and said unto the king, True, O king.

25 He answered and said, Lo, I see four men loose, walking in the midst of the fire, and they have no hurt; and the form of the fourth is like the Son of God.

26 Then Nebuchadnezzar came near to the mouth of the burning fiery furnace, and spake, and said, Shadrach, Meshach, and Abednego, ye servants of the most high God, come forth, and come hither. Then Shadrach, Meshach, and Abednego, came forth of the midst of the fire.

**Apr
13**

---

GOLDEN TEXT: If it be so, our God whom we serve is able to deliver us from the burning fiery furnace, and he will deliver us out of thine hand, O king. But if not, be it known unto thee, O king, that we will not serve thy gods, nor worship the golden image which thou hast set up.—Daniel 3:17, 18.

---

*God, the People, and the Covenant*
Unit 2: The Covenant in Exile
(Lessons 6-9)

## Lesson Aims

After participating in this lesson, each student will be able to:

1. Retell the story of Shadrach, Meshach, and Abednego and the fiery furnace.

2. List some challenges that believers face in which they are threatened with harm if they do not go along with popular thinking or behavior.

3. Take a stand against one ungodly law or cultural practice.

## Lesson Outline

INTRODUCTION
    A. Learning to Say *No*, Part 1
    B. Lesson Background
  I. RESISTANCE (Daniel 3:10-13)
    A. King's Decree (vv. 10, 11)
    B. Jews' Refusal (v. 12)
      *Scapegoats*
    C. King's Rage (v. 13)
 II. FAITHFULNESS (Daniel 3:16-18)
    A. Jews' Persistence (v. 16)
    B. Jews' Resoluteness (vv. 17, 18)
      *The Pressure of a Profane Culture*
III. DELIVERANCE (Daniel 3:21, 24-26)
    A. Jews' Punishment (v. 21)
    B. King's Astonishment (vv. 24, 25)
    C. God's Praise (v. 26)
CONCLUSION
    A. Learning to Say *No*, Part 2
    B. Prayer
    C. Thought to Remember

## Introduction

### A. Learning to Say *No*, Part 1

Not long ago, a television cartoon mocked the popular Christian animation series *Veggie Tales*. A friend alerted me to this spoof because of its sick portrayal of the Christian faith. I will not go into all the details, but imagine the cast of *Veggie Tales*—now called the *Religetables*—looking at pornographic material, killing infidels during the crusades, hanging innocent "witches" in Salem, molesting children, etc., while singing pious songs with their cute veggie voices.

Sadly, this warped depiction of Christianity (or at least parts of it) is the image many non-believers have of Christian faith. Yet it should not surprise us that unbelievers would portray Christianity in this light. The name of Christ has been slandered from the beginning. What is surprising, however, is how common it is for Christians to enjoy watching programs that routinely belittle Christ and His church.

This incongruity reveals the inability of many Christians to say *no* to various activities. We may feel justified in participating in it as long as we do not let its bad parts affect us. We fear that saying *no* to such activities will make us appear to be puritanical legalists.

This line of reasoning may sound valid, but is it? In Daniel 3, three young Jews faced a similar question. Their answer is instructive.

### B. Lesson Background

Last week we learned that Hananiah, Mishael, and Azariah were among the young Jewish nobles who were taken into exile during the early days of Babylonian domination of Judah. Daniel 1:7 notes the change of their names to Shadrach, Meshach, and Abednego. Following Daniel's lead, they boldly stood out by choosing their own diet over the king's rations. God honored their stance by exalting them in the king's court and kingdom.

The situation changes in Daniel 3. Independent of Daniel's leadership, these young men face a new challenge. King Nebuchadnezzar erected a giant statue approximately 90' high and 9' wide. Bizarre dimensions notwithstanding, this monument to human greatness, like the tower of Babel in Genesis 11, was a farce in God's eyes.

In Nebuchadnezzar's eyes, however, this statue played a critical role in the stability of his empire. He had relocated droves of foreigners to his capital city, and it was necessary to keep everyone on the same page. Nebuchadnezzar needed to make it clear that there was only one law, one king, and one empire—and that it all revolved around him. This is why he sent a decree to "people, nations, and languages" that when the king authorized the imperial music to play, they all had to worship the statue (Daniel 3:4, 5).

Failure to comply meant fiery execution. The statue was a symbolic reminder that the Babylonian kingdom was undivided despite its diversity. From an earthly, imperial perspective, it all made perfect sense. But from a godly perspective, it was riddled with problems. In today's text we see how three faithful Jews handled this situation.

# I. Resistance
## (Daniel 3:10-13)

In verses 8, 9, certain Babylonians (Chaldeans) approach Nebuchadnezzar to remind him of a decree he has established. Yet their agenda is not merely informative. They intend to accuse God's people of violating this decree.

### A. King's Decree (vv. 10, 11)

**10. Thou, O king, hast made a decree, that every man that shall hear the sound of the cornet, flute, harp, sackbut, psaltery, and dulcimer, and all kinds of music, shall fall down and worship the golden image.**

What a diversity of musical instruments! Stylistically, it is worth noting that much of Daniel 3 consists of lists of related but distinct items and people, many repeated several times (Daniel 3:3-5, 7, 10, 12-16, 19-23, 26-30). Repetition is a trademark of Hebrew storytelling. The repetition produces a poetic feel with a certain cadence.

We may be curious about the exact form the *golden image* takes. Is it an image of the king himself? a Babylonian god? some other national or religious symbol? In chapter two, Daniel tells Nebuchadnezzar that he, the king, is the golden head of a statue that he has dreamed about. So perhaps his inflated ego has prompted him to build a golden statue of himself.

On the other hand, the accusations against the Jews in this chapter are that they will not heed the king, serve his gods, or worship the statue (vv. 12, 14, 18). Is this list intended to indicate different, distinct offenses, or does the list merely indicate different aspects of the one offense of not bowing to the statue? Again, the text is silent.

Not identifying the precise nature of the statue may be the author's way of saying that what matters most is that the king's decree is violated. What is at stake is the king's authority to dictate what his citizens must do, even if it violates their faith convictions. [See question #1, page 288.]

**11. And whoso falleth not down and worshippeth, that he should be cast into the midst of a burning fiery furnace.**

The penalty for disobedience is severe indeed! But what is the nature of this *furnace*? We do not know for sure, but it may be made of metal and shaped like a beehive with an open top out of which smoke can escape. Additionally, it probably has some kind of side door for removing ashes and monitoring the burning process. Another theory is that it is made of brick and shaped like a tunnel with a similar access door on the side.

### B. Jews' Refusal (v. 12)

**12. There are certain Jews whom thou hast set over the affairs of the province of Babylon, Shadrach, Meshach, and Abednego; these men, O king, have not regarded thee: they serve not thy gods, nor worship the golden image which thou hast set up.**

The accusers finally get to the point. The very ones whom Nebuchadnezzar has *set over* his affairs refuse to *serve* the king's *gods* and *worship the golden image*. This verse does not help us discern if the image is associated with the gods, but it is abundantly clear that failure to serve the gods and honor the image is interpreted as a failure to regard the king. The charge is insubordination; the evidence behind the charge involves both gods and the statue.

This passage bookends the denunciation that begins in Daniel 3:8. Verse 8 specifies that the accusers are Chaldeans (natives of Babylonia), and the accused are Jews. (This point is obscured by the *New International Version*, which identifies the accusers as "astrologers"—a possible but less likely translation.) Then, in verse 12, the accusers highlight the fact that the king has set Jews over the affairs of Babylon. The repeated use of these terms suggests that "the locals" are jealous. (We probably see jealousy also in Daniel 6:1-5.) After all, the Babylonian natives have long served loyally, and now these immigrants have been elevated to positions higher than theirs.

So now it is payback time. When the accusers inform the king how these foreigners are ignoring his decree, he will surely punish them and return the locals to their rightful positions of power and influence. [See question #2, page 288.]

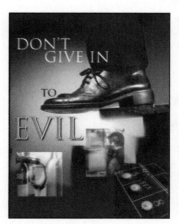

Visual for
Lessons 6 & 7

*Continue last week's discussion: "What kind of temptation gives you the most trouble?"*

### SCAPEGOATS

Finding scapegoats to explain whatever is wrong has a long history. It started in the Garden of Eden (see Genesis 3:12). Modern politicians are especially adept at this. Is the economy in trouble? It's because of the policies of the other political party. Is there too much crime? It's because the previous administration did not crack down on "those people" who are different from us—in skin color, religion, etc.

Name a trouble spot anywhere in the world, and someone can name a scapegoat for why things are the way they are. For Hitler, it was the Jews; for many Arab countries, it's America; in the case of natural disasters in the U.S., blame FEMA. The list goes on.

For Nebuchadnezzar's advisers, the problem to be solved was personal. They were loyal Chaldeans, but their king had placed capable Jews in positions of authority. Those Jews had taken jobs that the Chaldeans probably thought belonged to them. So "they played the race card," and the king fell for it. (We will see this same problem play out in next week's lesson.) The nature of their charge was almost beside the point—it was a convenient launching point for an attempt at payback. It still happens.                    —C. R. B.

### C. King's Rage (v. 13)

**13. Then Nebuchadnezzar in his rage and fury commanded to bring Shadrach, Meshach, and Abednego. Then they brought these men before the king.**

The accusers' plan succeeds, and *Nebuchadnezzar* takes the offense personally. He may have taken a lot of flak already for his decision to exalt foreigners, and now it blows up in his face. Nebuchadnezzar has been gracious in offering these foreigners education, food, and positions. They have every reason to be grateful, but in Nebuchadnezzar's mind they respond with ingratitude.

## II. Faithfulness
## (Daniel 3:16-18)

Although Nebuchadnezzar is furious, he does not act rashly. He invites Shadrach, Meshach, and Abednego in and allows them to explain themselves. He gives them a second chance (Daniel 3:14, 15, not in today's text).

### A. Jews' Persistence (v. 16)

**16. Shadrach, Meshach, and Abednego, answered and said to the king, O Nebuchadnezzar, we are not careful to answer thee in this matter.**

The phrase *we are not careful to answer thee in this matter* in the antique English of the *King James Version* may sound curious to modern ears. It means something like "there is no need for us to offer a defense of our actions." In short, the three Jews are responding with a firm *no* to the second chance they are being offered. The force of this *no* needs to be felt by Christians today.

We may note that the king's request is not as drastic as it could be since he is not asking these Jews to stop worshiping their own God altogether. He is "merely" asking them to make a certain addition to their worship practice. Is this not the least they can do to pay him respect?

Yet the modern habit of rationalizing questionable practices is nowhere to be found in Shadrach, Meshach, and Abednego. They know that the God of Israel is not to be worshiped alongside other gods. God has no equal, and He will not tolerate being treated as such (Deuteronomy 4:35, 39). [See question #3, page 288.]

Any action that grants uncontestable allegiance to a sovereign other than God is idolatry. That's what bowing before the statue would do. It is one thing to work for the king and show him the basic respect that is due to those in authority. It is another thing entirely to acknowledge someone or something as a rival to God.

Today, respect also is due to presidents, governors, bosses, ministers, elders, and parents (Mark 7:10; 1 Timothy 5:17). But they do not have blanket permission to lead in such a way that they eclipse God. The prophet Jeremiah commanded the Jews to submit to the Babylonian Empire (Jeremiah 27), and the apostles taught Christians to submit to the Roman Empire (Romans 13:1; 1 Peter 2:13-17). But God's people are never to interpret such commands as unconditional support for any and all actions of earthly rulers (example: Acts 4:18-20).

### B. Jews' Resoluteness (vv. 17, 18)

**17, 18. If it be so, our God whom we serve is able to deliver us from the burning fiery furnace, and he will deliver us out of thine hand, O king. But if not, be it known unto thee, O king, that we will not serve thy gods, nor worship the golden image which thou hast set up.**

These three Jews express faith in *God* in two ways. First, they acknowledge that God is *able to deliver* them from both the *fiery furnace* and the *king* who thinks he has absolute power. They do not worship a weak god or a distant god who is unable to intervene in events on earth. They worship Israel's God, who has proven His ability and who desires to work for the good of those who love Him (Deuteronomy 7:9; Romans 8:28). So too Christians today rightly pray for God's intervention. Those who seek to live on their own strength, to muscle their own way out of the tough spots in life, and to avoid faith decisions that require divine assistance have marginalized Father, Son, and Holy Spirit.

Second, these three Jews are firm in their worship of God to the point that they refuse to bow, whether God chooses to intervene or not. God's nonintervention is a strong possibility. In His larger plan, God does not always choose to intervene, as the deaths of Urijah (Jeremiah 26:20-23) and James (Acts 12:1, 2) establish.

Yet true believers are those who faithfully serve God regardless of the negative consequences they may suffer. Christians continue to die for their faith in many parts of the world. Others have lost jobs, housing, and other necessities. Unfortunately, there are also those who claim to be Christians who show that they actually are idolaters because of the compromises they make for the sake of pride, position, property, popularity, or power.

### THE PRESSURE OF A PROFANE CULTURE

Ginny Foster spent $10,000 four years ago on T-shirts and bumper stickers that expressed opposition to the deluge of dirty language that surrounds us. Talk about trying to resist culture! Sadly, she gave up the project within two years, saying she no longer had the fire within her to fight this battle. After she appeared on a Showtime TV show, her Web site received hundreds of e-mails full of abusive curses.

Americans do indeed live in a profane culture. An Associated Press opinion poll found that 74 percent encounter profanity frequently or occasionally, while 59 percent admit to cursing a few times a month. Listen carefully and you may

even hear profanity among Christians. Certain profane words are so commonly used that those who *really* want to curse may soon have to come up with some new terms!

This is just one of many ways secular culture affects (and infects) godly people. Shadrach, Meshach, and Abednego set a good example by being careful not to compromise with the pagan culture in which they lived. We each may be tempted to sin in different ways, but watchfulness is a trait all Christians should cultivate.

—C. R. B.

## III. Deliverance (Daniel 3:21, 24-26)

Verses 19 and 20 (not in today's text) tell us that Nebuchadnezzar will not accept *no* for an answer. So the three are to be executed in a furnace heated to seven times its normal level. Some of the king's strongest men are assigned the task of binding Shadrach, Meshach, and Abednego.

### A. Jews' Punishment (v. 21)

**21. Then these men were bound in their coats, their hose, and their hats, and their other garments, and were cast into the midst of the burning fiery furnace.**

The three Jews are threatening the unity of the king's empire. If Nebuchadnezzar allows them to walk free, he will appear to be weak and indecisive. So the king has to honor his decree and toss them into the fire. Not only that, but he decides to make an example of them by cranking the fire up so high that the men who throw them in die for coming so close (v. 22, not in today's text).

It is interesting to note what kind of religion the Babylon Empire is willing to tolerate. In Daniel 2:47, Nebuchadnezzar acknowledges Israel's God as the God of gods. Presumably this means that it is OK for Jews to worship their God while others worship Babylonian gods. Nebuchadnezzar thus appears to be a tolerant religious pluralist. His subjects can worship whatever and whomever they wish as long as they remain devout citizens who do what is asked of them. This includes "adjusting" one's religious beliefs when the king deems it necessary. Worship of any deity who authorizes worshipers to deny the king's policies is not acceptable. [See question #4, page 288.]

### B. King's Astonishment (vv. 24, 25)

**24, 25. Then Nebuchadnezzar the king was astonished, and rose up in haste, and spake, and said unto his counselors, Did not we cast**

---

### How to Say It

ABEDNEGO. Uh-*bed*-nee-go.
AZARIAH. Az-uh-*rye*-uh.
BABYLON. *Bab*-uh-lun.
BABYLONIA. Bab-ih-*low*-nee-uh.
CHALDEANS. Kal-*dee*-unz.
HANANIAH. Han-uh-*nye*-uh.
MESHACH. *Me*-shack.
MISHAEL. *Mish*-a-el.
NEBUCHADNEZZAR. *Neb*-yuh-kud-*nez*-er (strong accent on *nez*).
SHADRACH. *Shay*-drack or *Shad*-rack.
URIJAH. Yu-*rye*-juh.

three men bound into the midst of the fire? They answered and said unto the king, True, O king. He answered and said, Lo, I see four men loose, walking in the midst of the fire, and they have no hurt; and the form of the fourth is like the Son of God.

As Shadrach, Meshach, and Abednego believe, God is able to spare them. Moreover, God actually does spare them from the flames. It is a miracle that the men are walking around alive and well.

Our only clue as to how all this happens is the fourth person, this *Son of God,* who walks among the flames. We should not assume that this fourth person is an Old Testament appearance of Jesus, although we cannot rule out this possibility. The description *Son of God* is given from the perspective of Nebuchadnezzar, not from one of the devout Jews.

In Old Testament times, the phrase *son(s) of God* sometimes refer to people, but also can refer to an angel (examples: Genesis 6:2, 4; Job 1:6; 2:1; 38:7). This is the most probable reading of our verse. God may be sending an angel to comfort these Jews or to provide a sign to the king and his counselors. Either way, God gets the king's attention!

### C. God's Praise (v. 26)

**26. Then Nebuchadnezzar came near to the mouth of the burning fiery furnace, and spake, and said, Shadrach, Meshach, and Abednego, ye servants of the most high God, come forth, and come hither. Then Shadrach, Meshach, and Abednego, came forth of the midst of the fire.**

It is a mystery how the king can draw close enough to the fire to speak over the roaring flames without being consumed like the men who threw Shadrach, Meshach, and Abednego in! His message nonetheless is communicated, and the Jews walk out unharmed. Not a hair is singed, and their garments bear no scent of smoke according to verse 27. When God delivers, He does so in a convincing manner!

Nebuchadnezzar is certainly convinced. He refers to the Jews as *servants of the most high God.* This praise culminates in a royal decree that protects those who worship Israel's God (Daniel 3:29). The point is clear: God is indeed the most high God, and His will always prevails in the end. Those who worship Him alone do so with this ultimate end in sight, regardless of short-term suffering. [See question #5, page 288.]

# Conclusion

### A. Learning to Say *No,* Part 2

Shadrach, Meshach, and Abednego teach us that it sometimes is necessary to say *no* even when an activity can be rationalized. They could have bowed out of gratitude for the king's generosity to them. They could have bowed to preserve their influential positions in order to use them to do good for other people. They could have bowed for the sake of their witness, lest Jews gain a bad reputation for being uptight, intolerant, narrow-minded, or unpatriotic.

There were many seemingly good reasons why they could have participated in compromising actions under the pretense that they were not affected by them and were not exchanging Israel's God for the gods of Babylon. Yet these Jews knew better. They knew that no action leaves one unaffected, and that one's willingness to compromise means one has already begun worshiping a lesser god. Their ability to say *no* was their witness, and their story continues to be told because they risked it all to remain faithful. The same is true of Daniel—but that's next week's lesson.

### B. Prayer

Most high God of Shadrach, Meshach, and Abednego, please make us like them. Teach us to be obedient to You, especially when it hurts. Help us to say *no* when our actions would betray You. Convict us when saying *no* is necessary, because we are so skilled in explaining our way out of saying it. Make us like Jesus, whose *no* to Satan's wiles made possible Your *yes* for us on Calvary's cross. In Jesus' name, amen.

### C. Thought to Remember

True worshipers of God
are willing to suffer for saying *no.*

---

## Home Daily Bible Readings

**Monday, Apr. 7**—God's Protection Forevermore (Psalm 121:1-4)

**Tuesday, Apr. 8**—King Nebuchadnezzar's Golden Statue (Daniel 3:1-7)

**Wednesday, Apr. 9**—The Refusal to Worship the Statue (Daniel 3:8-15)

**Thursday, Apr. 10**—Brought Before the King (Daniel 3:16-23)

**Friday, Apr. 11**—Not a Hint of Fire (Daniel 3:24-27)

**Saturday, Apr. 12**—A New Decree (Daniel 3:28-30)

**Sunday, Apr. 13**—God Will Keep You (Psalm 121:5-8)

# Learning by Doing

*This page contains an alternative lesson plan emphasizing learning activities.*
*Classes desiring such student involvement will find these suggestions helpful.*

## Into the Lesson

Cut a large *NO* from poster board. Affix the two letters to the wall near the entrance where learners arrive. Put *No* on large, colorful sheets of paper and display them randomly throughout the room. To begin, ask, "Is it possible for a person to have too many *no's*?" and "Do most people say *no* too much or too little? Why do you think so?"

If a church music leader can provide it for you, play the song "Know When to Say No" from the children's musical *It's Cool in the Furnace* (© Word Music, 1973). This musical deals with the early chapters of Daniel.

## Into the Word

Recruit three good oral readers. Label them Shadrach (S), Meshach (M), and Abednego (A). Tell the class these three are going to recall the events of today's lesson text. The class's task will be to give verse numbers to the remembrances in terms of Daniel 3, where each idea appears.

Give each reader the statements below. Verse numbers are indicated here, but they should not be included in the reading. The readers can move straight through the list, taking turns as indicated (the statements are already randomized). Allow verse answers after each "remembrance."

S: "I remember our stand: 'even if we must die, we will not worship idols.'" *(v. 18)*

M: "I remember being marched to the furnace fully clothed." *(v. 21)*

A: "I remember how angry King Nebuchadnezzar became at us." *(v. 13)*

S: "I remember the accusations of our enemies." *(v. 12)*

M: "I remember the first foot I stepped out of that furnace, never looking back." *(v. 26)*

A: "I remember being thrown into the fire . . . and receiving no harm!" *(v. 21)*

S: "I remember the king's astonishment when he saw us walking in the fire unscathed." *(v. 24)*

M: "I remember the day we were assigned government responsibilities." *(v. 12)*

A: "I remember our expression of faith in God's ability to save us." *(v. 17)*

S: "I remember hearing the king calling our names and crying, 'Come out!'" *(v. 26)*

M: "I remember all the instrumental music, a regular symphony." *(v. 10)*

A: "I remember the fear produced by the threatened punishment of fire." *(v. 11)*

S: "I remember when the king signed the decree regarding the golden statue." *(v. 10)*

M: "I remember when our heavenly friend materialized with us in the fire!" *(v. 25)*

*Optional activity: Making a Choice.* Reproduce the following multiple-choice quiz. Distribute for learners to work on individually or in pairs. (The quiz also appears in the optional student book.)

1. The stimulus for worshiping the king's statue was (A) appearance of the full moon, (B) sunrise, (C) sound of musical instruments; 2. The penalty for failing to obey the king's decree was (A) being thrown to the lions, (B) being burned alive, (C) being beheaded; 3. Shadrach, Meshach, and Abednego were accused of two disobedient acts: ignoring the king's authority and (A) not worshiping the golden image, (B) stealing from the king's treasury, (C) praying to the God of Heaven; 4. Nebuchadnezzar's attitude when he heard of the disobedient Jews was (A) violent rage, (B) disbelief, (C) forgiveness; 5. Shadrach, Meshach, and Abednego affirmed God's ability to save them, but (A) dared the king to try to kill them, (B) expressed doubt that God would save them, (C) affirmed their faith in God even if He did not save them; 6. The three were thrown into the furnace with (A) copies of their Bible scrolls, (B) copies of the king's decree, (C) all their clothes on; 7. When Nebuchadnezzar looked into the furnace, he saw (A) nothing but flame, (B) the three men praying, (C) a fourth man walking with the three thrown in.

*Answers: 1. C; 2. B; 3. A.; 4. A; 5. C; 6. C; 7. C.*

## Into Life

Say to the class, "Laws are still being written that make life difficult for the person of God. Some are laws that forbid; some are laws that permit. What are some of those laws that you find yourself bumping up against?"

Make a quick list as learners give answers. Ask the class to explain how each complicates their lives and witness. Ask also for ideas for resolving the complications. (The optional student book lists examples such as gambling, abortion, homosexuality, the sale of alcoholic beverages, etc., as complications to life.)

# Let's Talk It Over

*The questions on this page are designed to promote discussion of the lesson by the class and to encourage application of the lesson Scriptures. The answers provided are only discussion starters. Let your class talk it over from there.*

**1. In what ways does our culture challenge us to bow down to "golden images"? How do we resist?**

The images or gods we are challenged to bow down to in the world today are not statues made of gold, silver, or wood (unless one lives somewhere other than a Western democracy). But there are other things we are challenged to bow to either instead of or in addition to bowing before God.

Sometimes it is bowing to other people, such as in a culture of hero worship. Others worship their country; they will stand and cheer approvingly when they hear their national anthem, but sit unmoved when a great song of faith is sung. For others, the "image" they worship is the corporate ladder; when decisions must be made between Christian service and a job, the job wins every time. Resistance begins with recognition of the danger.

**2. Have you ever been accused of something by people who had a devious intent or a hidden agenda? How did things turn out? How did you grow as a result?**

To be falsely accused outright is bad enough. To have our actual godly behavior slandered by someone who has a devious intent or a hidden agenda can be worse! In Revelation 12:10, Satan is called "the accuser of our brethren." We remember from the book of Job that Satan's accusation was that Job's godly behavior sprang from wrong motives.

Often the desire is to strike back by accusing the one who accused us or by seeking revenge. Peter has a better right idea: "Having your conversation honest among the Gentiles: that, whereas they speak against you as evildoers, they may by your good works, which they shall behold, glorify God in the day of visitation" (1 Peter 2:12).

**3. When have you been guilty of rationalizing actions to avoid being harmed or to avoid doing God's will? How have you grown spiritually through repentance of your shortcomings in this regard?**

The lure to fit into society or a peer group is strong. Though we must be in the world to be salt and light, the temptation is to take on the ways of the world. In doing so, we rationalize that we are identifying with others in order to reach them. We may put ourselves into a potentially compromising situation in thinking that we are there to be a witness and influence. But if that is an area of weakness for your life, you may end up being influenced toward evil.

**4. How should Christians respond in the face of a pluralistic culture?**

We begin by realizing that pluralism as a basic tenet is not evil; it is simply the realization that diversity exists and that people should not be persecuted for their diversity. But when pushed, especially in the area of religion, pluralism becomes a politically correct attempt to shame people into seeing different religious viewpoints as equally valid.

This means that the Christian needs to be convinced of his or her beliefs. We remember that Jesus said: "I am the way, the truth, and the life: no man cometh unto the Father, but by me" (John 14:6). In dealing with those who don't believe this, we must have patience. Scripture challenges the Christian in this area with these words: "But sanctify the Lord God in your hearts: and be ready always to give an answer to every man that asketh you a reason of the hope that is in you, with meekness and fear" (1 Peter 3:15).

**5. What are some "fiery furnaces" from which God has delivered you?**

We should begin by realizing that the normal stresses and strains of life are not all to be categorized as "fiery furnaces." Perhaps we can say that a fiery furnace experience is something that has the potential to result in a very great loss depending on the stand we take.

God allows His people to go through times of trial so that our faith can be strengthened (James 1:2-4). Pressures to conform to group norms are around us every day. For example, a certain corporate culture may expect those who work in the accounting department to go along with shady accounting practices. Those who refuse can experience a fiery furnace of demotion or dismissal.

# Refusing to Compromise

April 20
Lesson 8

DEVOTIONAL READING: **Psalm 119:57-64.**

BACKGROUND SCRIPTURE: **Daniel 6.**

PRINTED TEXT: **Daniel 6:4-7, 10, 16, 19, 21, 22, 25, 26.**

### Daniel 6:4-7, 10, 16, 19, 21, 22, 25, 26

4 Then the presidents and princes sought to find occasion against Daniel concerning the kingdom; but they could find none occasion nor fault; forasmuch as he was faithful, neither was there any error or fault found in him.

5 Then said these men, We shall not find any occasion against this Daniel, except we find it against him concerning the law of his God.

6 Then these presidents and princes assembled together to the king, and said thus unto him, King Darius, live for ever.

7 All the presidents of the kingdom, the governors, and the princes, the counselors, and the captains, have consulted together to establish a royal statute, and to make a firm decree, that whosoever shall ask a petition of any God or man for thirty days, save of thee, O king, he shall be cast into the den of lions.

· · · · · · · · · ·

10 Now when Daniel knew that the writing was signed, he went into his house; and, his windows being open in his chamber toward Jerusalem, he kneeled upon his knees three times a day, and prayed, and gave thanks before his God, as he did aforetime.

· · · · · · · · · ·

16 Then the king commanded, and they brought Daniel, and cast him into the den of lions. Now the king spake and said unto Daniel, Thy God whom thou servest continually, he will deliver thee.

· · · · · · · · · ·

19 Then the king arose very early in the morning, and went in haste unto the den of lions.

· · · · · · · · · ·

21 Then said Daniel unto the king, O king, live for ever.

22 My God hath sent his angel, and hath shut the lions' mouths, that they have not hurt me: forasmuch as before him innocency was found in me; and also before thee, O king, have I done no hurt.

· · · · · · · · · ·

25 Then king Darius wrote unto all people, nations, and languages, that dwell in all the earth; Peace be multiplied unto you.

26 I make a decree, That in every dominion of my kingdom men tremble and fear before the God of Daniel: for he is the living God, and steadfast for ever, and his kingdom that which shall not be destroyed, and his dominion shall be even unto the end.

**Apr 20**

---

GOLDEN TEXT: Now when Daniel knew that the writing was signed, he went into his house; and, his windows being open in his chamber toward Jerusalem, he kneeled upon his knees three times a day, and prayed, and gave thanks before his God, as he did aforetime.—Daniel 6:10.

*God, the People, and the Covenant*
Unit 2: The Covenant in Exile
(Lessons 6-9)

## Lesson Aims

After participating in this lesson, each student will be able to:

1. Retell the story of Daniel and the lions' den.

2. Explain why Daniel could not pray with the window closed, and compare that with situations in which Christians must take their faith public in spite of opposition.

3. Give thanks to God for the strength to resist idolatrous practices and trends.

## Lesson Outline

INTRODUCTION
    A. Dream Job?
    B. Lesson Background
  I. OFFICIALS TRAP DANIEL (Daniel 6:4-7)
    A. Officials Scheme (vv. 4, 5)
    B. Officials Manipulate (vv. 6, 7)
 II. DANIEL REMAINS FAITHFUL (Daniel 6:10)
    *Spiritual Technicalities*
III. GOD DELIVERS DANIEL (Daniel 6:16, 19, 21, 22)
    A. Darius Is Reluctant (v. 16)
    B. Darius Is in a Hurry (v. 19)
    C. Daniel Is Alive! (vv. 21, 22)
    *Tempting or Trusting?*
IV. DARIUS HONORS GOD (Daniel 6:25, 26)
    A. What Everyone Must Do (vv. 25, 26a)
    B. Why Everyone Must Do It (v. 26b)
CONCLUSION
    A. Faith on Hold
    B. Prayer
    C. Thought to Remember

## Introduction

### A. Dream Job?

"Thank you for applying at Dream Job, Inc. I'm sure you've read our literature and are familiar with our six-figure salary and deluxe benefits package. Having reviewed your application, we believe you are the one best qualified for this job. There are only a few minor wrinkles to iron out.

"In your application you expressed a strong desire not to work on Sundays. Unfortunately that is one of our busiest and most profitable days, so we've put you down to work Sunday every other week. You also expressed a desire to be home on Wednesdays by 7:00 PM to attend Bible study. Typically we knock off work by 5:30 PM, so that should not be a problem—but your desire does raise a red flag for us. We want to be sure you are not one of those people who hang crosses in the office, give Bibles to coworkers, and starts prayer groups over lunch.

"Now don't get us wrong, we have no problem with people who are Christians privately; we simply ask all our workers to check their faiths at the door. You can worship whomever you wish before and after work, but in our facilities we do not say words like *Jesus, church, grace,* and *salvation.* I am sure you understand. Did I mention we provide free child care?"

Should a Christian accept an offer like this? Is it appropriate to suspend one's faith temporarily for "the greater good" of one's family or country? The familiar story of Daniel and the lions' den can help form answers to such questions.

### B. Lesson Background

In Daniel 5 we learn that there has been a regime change. The Babylonian Empire, which carried many Jews into exile, has come to an end. The famous handwriting on the wall of Daniel 5:25-28 predicted that collapse. The year was about 539 BC.

With this change in regime came a new foreign policy. The Persians believed in sending exiled people home and helping them reestablish their old ways of life. That included religious practices and local governance. As long as those being resettled maintained the peace and paid regular tribute to the Persians, they could govern themselves somewhat independently.

Not all Jews accepted this invitation to go home. Daniel apparently was among these. In fact, Daniel seemed to be prospering even more under Persian rule. We learn in Daniel 6:1-3 that Daniel proved superior to all others as Darius the Mede began appointing local rulers. Daniel was on the verge of becoming second-in-command.

Daniel's status as an exile from a distant land probably strengthened his position. As the new regime settled in, the leaders probably wanted to avoid having Babylonian sympathizers occupying positions of power that could be used as a launching pad for revolt. Perhaps Darius sought to appoint Daniel over such rulers because Daniel could be trusted to keep them in line and would not be swayed by bribes. In any case, the local rulers felt threatened by the prospect of Daniel's promotion (Daniel 6:1-3). So they sought to do away with him.

# I. Officials Trap Daniel
## (Daniel 6:4-7)
### A. Officials Scheme (vv. 4, 5)

**4. Then the presidents and princes sought to find occasion against Daniel concerning the kingdom; but they could find none occasion nor fault; forasmuch as he was faithful, neither was there any error or fault found in him.**

Daniel's rise to power means less power for everyone else. An uncorrupt boss also means less chance of getting away with graft. So whether due to racism, jealousy, greed, or expectation of "entitlement," the local rulers are determined to eliminate Daniel. Their obstacle is Daniel's impeccable character. He is a man above reproach.

**5. Then said these men, We shall not find any occasion against this Daniel, except we find it against him concerning the law of his God.**

What a compliment! *These men* know that Daniel will not compromise when it comes to faith. His weak spot (to their way of thinking) is not pride, power, or prosperity, but devotion to God's laws. This chapter offers a picture of laws at battle. Whose law is final, God's or Persia's?

An important question for us to ask is how Daniel earned such a reputation to this point. What personal practices send such a clear message about his priorities? What patterns of speech communicate his single-minded commitment? Could people say the same thing about us that Daniel's enemies say about him? If not, why not?

### B. Officials Manipulate (vv. 6, 7)

**6. Then these presidents and princes assembled together to the king, and said thus unto him, King Darius, live for ever.**

Notice that these men do not appoint a representative to advocate their case before *the king*. Instead, they join *together* to flex their numerical

---

### How to Say It
ABEDNEGO. Uh-*bed*-nee-go.
BABYLONIAN. Bab-ih-*low*-nee-un.
DARIUS. Duh-*rye*-us.
JERUSALEM. Juh-*roo*-suh-lem.
KIEV. *Kee*-ef or *Kee*-ev.
MESHACH. *Me*-shack.
NEBUCHADNEZZAR. *Neb*-yuh-kud-*nez*-er (strong accent on *nez*).
SHADRACH. *Shay*-drack or *Shad*-rack.
SOLOMON. *Sol*-o-mun.
ZOROASTRIANISM. Zor-eh-*was*-tree-eh-nih-zem.

---

muscle. They begin their act of deceit by complimenting the king and promoting his well-being by wishing him long life. There is nothing out of the ordinary about such an address in royal settings (1 Kings 1:31; Nehemiah 2:3; Daniel 2:4; 3:9; 6:21), so the king's suspicions are not raised.

**7. All the presidents of the kingdom, the governors, and the princes, the counselors, and the captains, have consulted together to establish a royal statute, and to make a firm decree, that whosoever shall ask a petition of any God or man for thirty days, save of thee, O king, he shall be cast into the den of lions.**

Now these men falsely claim that *all* rulers have endorsed their idea for a *decree* that is to state that no one may *ask a petition of any God or man for thirty days, save of thee, O king.* It is obvious that Daniel—who is one of those rulers—has neither seen nor approved it. Thus the idea for such a decree is set before the king with great cunning: it appeals to the king's ego while being a threat only to those whose faith will force them to violate it.

Notice that the proposed decree does not ask the citizens to deny their faith outright or to change their way of life permanently. It merely will instruct people to modify temporarily one practice—that of making requests—and to do this only for a brief period of time. Even so, it will be a symbolic reminder that whatever human or divine being the king's subjects normally petition for daily sustenance, the king is their ultimate source of well-being. This one-month hiatus is designed to affirm the priority of the king over all other benefactors. [See question #1, page 296.]

It is also important to note the nature of royal decrees in Persia. The Persians pride themselves on ruling humanely. They do not go about torturing subjects to keep them in line, but generously provide for their well-being. The famous Cyrus Cylinder, made of baked clay, sets forth religious tolerance, abolition of slavery, and freedom of choice as hallmarks of Persian rule.

Yet the Persians still need to maintain order and respect. So they establish a strict legal system. All royal decrees are *firm* and cannot be broken—not even by the king. This policy not only deters potential law-breakers but also limits corruption among the officials. Since the king himself keeps these laws, the officials may not bend them for selfish gain. Esther 3 records a Persian edict for the destruction of the Jews. That order could not be rescinded, even by the king himself. But the king could issue a separate decree to allow the Jews to defend themselves.

## II. Daniel Remains Faithful
## (Daniel 6:10)

**10. Now when Daniel knew that the writing was signed, he went into his house; and, his windows being open in his chamber toward Jerusalem, he kneeled upon his knees three times a day, and prayed, and gave thanks before his God, as he did aforetime.**

*Daniel* can protect himself in various ways. One possible strategy is secrecy. He can shut his *windows* and pray privately. Or he can leave his windows open but alter his posture so others will not be able to tell he is praying (example: praying silently in bed at night).

A third potential strategy is simple abstinence from prayer for the 30 days. Daniel can merely acknowledge Darius's divine appointment as governor and submit to his authority (compare Romans 13:1-7). After all, Daniel is not being asked to deny God out-and-out. The Law of Moses does not require Jews to pray *three times a day*. So Daniel can take the month off and make up for it next month. As wise as Daniel is, he easily can find some kind of "faith loophole" to keep the king's decree without technically violating God's decrees. [See question #2, page 296.]

Yet another potential strategy is political change. Daniel can use his favor with Darius to expose the agenda of the officials and undermine the law (as in Esther 8:5-8) they have forced into effect. Daniel resists this temptation as well. Instead of viewing persecution as an ill to be avoided, he sees it as an opportunity for witness. How will the Persian world ever learn that there is a God in Heaven worth serving wholeheartedly

if His followers do not publicly live out His claim on their lives?

So Daniel goes home and kneels by his *open* window. We may be tempted to fault Daniel here in light of Jesus' teaching that people should not pray publicly in order to be seen (Matthew 6:5, 6), but that would be a mistake. The kind of public prayer Jesus is condemning is one that is self-serving and hypocritical. Daniel is neither of those. He is displaying his faith publicly with right motives (compare Matthew 5:14-16).

The practice of praying three times daily is not commanded in Scripture, although it is reflected in Psalm 55:17. The practice likely develops independently as a method for Jews in exile to remind themselves of their identity. Facing Jerusalem while praying in captivity was a practice predicted by Solomon centuries before (see 1 Kings 8:46-53). Solomon asked God to answer the prayers of His people should they ever be in that situation. This is the best context for understanding Daniel's prayer.

### SPIRITUAL TECHNICALITIES

Human endeavors have sets of rules by which they operate. These rules contribute (or should contribute) to the betterment of society. For example, neighborhood associations have their CC&Rs—covenants, conditions, and restrictions —to protect property values.

Each sport naturally has its own set of rules as well. One unusual rule was established by a Houston-area amateur softball league: a player who hits a home run is *out*. The reason for the rule was that just past the outfield fence were some expensive houses that were getting their windows broken by home runs. Most of the players agreed that the rule was necessary.

But it seems that where there is a rule there is also a "rules lawyer" who will try to find a way around the rule through a technicality. Sadly, there are rules lawyers in Christianity too. They think, "Here's a loophole; I can still do this and be a Christian." That was not Daniel's approach. He simply asked himself, "What is the best way to act to demonstrate faithfulness to God?" —C. R. B.

## III. God Delivers Daniel
## (Daniel 6:16, 19, 21, 22)

### A. Darius Is Reluctant (v. 16)

**16. Then the king commanded, and they brought Daniel, and cast him into the den of lions. Now the king spake and said unto Daniel, Thy God whom thou servest continually, he will deliver thee.**

Visual for Lesson 8. *Point to this visual as you say, "But I thought the art of compromise was a good thing! What do you think?"*

Daniel 6:11-15 (not in today's text) shows us the conspirators going to *the king* to tattle on Daniel. After doing all he can do to spare Daniel's life, Darius's commitment to his decree requires him to throw Daniel to the *lions.*

It is interesting to note that the means for capital punishment have changed since the incident involving the fiery furnace in Daniel 3. This may reflect a different religious practice. By this time the Babylonian empire of Nebuchadnezzar has fallen to the Persians. According to Zoroastrianism, the official religion of Persia, fire is sacred. That being the case, it may be inappropriate to use it for executions.

Note also the king's address to Daniel. First, he acknowledges that Daniel serves his God *continually.* In other words, the king knows that Daniel is unwilling to put his faith on hold temporarily. If God is a God worth praying to, then He is a God worth praying to without ceasing (compare 1 Thessalonians 5:17).

Second, the king holds out the possibility that Daniel's God may come to Daniel's rescue. Perhaps he has heard about Daniel's miracle diet (chapter 1), the fiery furnace involving Daniel's friends (chapter 3), and/or Daniel's ability to interpret revelations from God (chapters 4 and 5). It is also possible to take these words sarcastically: the king may be mocking Daniel for foolishly thinking his God can save him. But the king's sympathy toward Daniel throughout this chapter makes this unlikely. [See question #3, page 296.]

### B. Darius Is in a Hurry (v. 19)

**19. Then the king arose very early in the morning, and went in haste unto the den of lions.**

After a night of sleeplessness and fasting (v. 18, not in today's text), the king heads straight to the lions' *den* to see how Daniel has fared. This seems to indicate a certain level of faith on Darius's part. He does not send a cleanup crew to deal with Daniel's remains; rather, he has a glimmer of hope that Daniel has survived.

### C. Daniel Is Alive! (vv. 21, 22)

**21. Then said Daniel unto the king, O king, live for ever.**

Daniel's first words in this narrative are remarkable. Like Darius's officials in verse 6, he wishes *the king* long life. Despite the fact that it was the king who had thrown him to his anticipated death, Daniel pays him respect. In disobeying the king's decree, Daniel does not wish the king ill. Rather, Daniel rightly believes that the best way to honor the king is to show him that God alone is to be feared. Daniel rejects the lie

that says that the best way to honor the king is to follow him blindly wherever he leads.

Likewise, the best way for Christians today to honor our rulers is by disallowing them to compromise our faith for some supposed "common good." We realize that we are to obey our governing authorities (Romans 13:1-7). But we also realize that obedience has its limits (Acts 4:19; 5:29). Christians realize that they ought not give governing authorities a "blank check" to rule as they please, and we rightly critique unbridled patriotism. But it is also wrong to swing in the complete opposite direction and become antiauthority or anticountry. Daniel teaches us to give proper respect within limits. He exemplifies 1 Peter 2:17: "Fear God. Honor the king."

**22. My God hath sent his angel, and hath shut the lions' mouths, that they have not hurt me: forasmuch as before him innocency was found in me; and also before thee, O king, have I done no hurt.**

Once again *God* is the source of deliverance. Previously, God had sent an *angel* to protect Shadrach, Meshach, and Abednego (Daniel 3:25). Now we see that God also sent an angel to protect Daniel by shutting *the lions' mouths* (compare Psalm 91:9-13; Hebrews 1:14). In so doing, God affirms Daniel's innocence. And in his innocence, Daniel can truly claim to have done the king no harm.

It can never be said of God's people that they are doing what is wrong toward others when they remain faithful to Him. Others may perceive it as wrong, and we may suffer because we refuse to defy God. But it is always in the long-term interest of all parties for God's people to remain faithful to Him. This does not mean that the innocent will always survive. According to Hebrews 11:32-40, Israel's hall of fame includes both those who escaped death at the hands of enemies and others who died courageously. [See question #4, page 296.]

TEMPTING OR TRUSTING?

It is said that history repeats itself. Sometimes it does, sometimes it only comes close. An example of the latter happened at the municipal zoo in Kiev, Ukraine, on June 5, 2006. While visitors swarmed the zoo, a man lowered himself by rope into the lion enclosure. He took off his shoes and shouted to the crowd, "God will save me, if He exists." Then he walked toward the lions. A lioness knocked him down and killed him.

There are significant differences between the man in the Kiev zoo and Daniel in Darius's den of lions. For one thing, Daniel was not there because he decided to be; the same cannot be said for the man in Kiev. Also, Daniel was not mentally unbalanced; the man in Kiev may have been.

The most important difference, however, was motive. Daniel had no doubts about God's existence. Daniel knew God would do what was right regardless of the consequences for him personally. Daniel was not challenging God to prove His existence. Is Daniel's faithfulness ours as well?

—C. R. B.

## IV. Darius Honors God (Daniel 6:25, 26)

### A. What Everyone Must Do (vv. 25, 26a)

**25, 26a. Then king Darius wrote unto all people, nations, and languages, that dwell in all the earth; Peace be multiplied unto you. I make a decree, That in every dominion of my kingdom men tremble and fear before the God of Daniel.**

*God* uses Daniel's witness to make a believer out of *Darius.* Thus Darius sets forth a new *decree,* this one legislating *fear* of Daniel's God.

### B. Why Everyone Must Do It (v. 26b)

**26b. For he is the living God, and steadfast for ever, and his kingdom that which shall not be destroyed, and his dominion shall be even unto the end.**

On the one hand, the king's decree is an incredible statement about Israel's God. God has proven His existence and power by intervening on Daniel's behalf. He has proven that He is *steadfast* by defending His people despite the fact that their land was conquered and they remain under foreign control. Since this heavenly king does not depend upon the well-being of His

people in their land for His power, His *dominion* can never end.

Of course, this decree does not necessarily reveal an understanding by Darius that every earthly ruler is subject to Israel's God. Also, Darius seems to be ignorant of the fact that faith cannot be legislated. A decree cannot change a person's innermost beliefs. Earthly kings may come close to understanding God's ways, but often they don't quite get it! [See question #5, page 296.]

## Conclusion

### A. Faith on Hold

Christianity once met with widespread appreciation in the Western world. That time, however, is over. Christians are being asked daily to choose between their faith and their jobs, social standing, etc. We began this lesson by asking whether Daniel could teach us anything about whether it is ever appropriate to suspend our faith temporarily. To put faith on hold at the king's request is to fear the king more than God.

However, while thinking about how to honor Christ in the secular workplace, we should recall that Daniel went home before he offered his prayer for all to see. Daniel didn't take some kind of "in your face" stance while at work in the king's palace. Your boss has the right to tell you, "Please take that picture of Jesus off your cubicle wall." The boss has the right to say what can and cannot happen on company property, within the bounds of law and decency. Few, if any, companies have a policy against bowing one's head in prayer over a meal eaten in the company cafeteria! Openly witnessing for Christ is still possible in many situations in Western democracies.

May we continue to demonstrate by the choices we make that we worship the same God whom Daniel worshiped.

### B. Prayer

Living God, thank You for giving us Your laws and showing us abundant life through Christ. Thank You for making us a people whose spiritual prosperity does not depend on the ebbs and flows of the nations among which You have scattered us. Make us, like Daniel, a people who never hide our faith nor justify retreat with clever arguments. Instead, may we shine like stars in the universe. In Jesus' name, amen.

### C. Thought to Remember

True followers of Christ never suspend their faith.

## Home Daily Bible Readings

**Monday, Apr. 14**—Prayer and Commitment (Psalm 119:57-64)
**Tuesday, Apr. 15**—An Honest Leader (Daniel 6:1-4)
**Wednesday, Apr. 16**—A Dishonest Plot (Daniel 6:5-9)
**Thursday, Apr. 17**—The King's Distress (Daniel 6:10-14)
**Friday, Apr. 18**—The Charge Stands (Daniel 6:15-18)
**Saturday, Apr. 19**—Daniel Trusted in God (Daniel 6:19-23)
**Sunday, Apr. 20**—The Living God (Daniel 6:24-28)

# Learning by Doing

*This page contains an alternative lesson plan emphasizing learning activities.*
*Classes desiring such student involvement will find these suggestions helpful.*

## Into the Lesson

Check your local library to see if you can borrow a sound effects disc that includes the sound of a roaring lion. You can also find this sound effect on the Internet. Have the sound playing as learners arrive.

Before class, give the following monologue to one of your learners to practice in advance. Introduce the monologue by saying, "We are fortunate to have a translation of the lion's roars, for this is none other than one of the lions that wanted to eat Daniel but could not!"

*Monologue:* "Grrrood morning! My name is Grrregory. Once I thought I was grrrroing to have a tender politician for dinner, Daniel by name. But just when I grrrowled in delight, lockjaw set in. And my paws began to feel like tree trunks, anchored to the grrrround. Oh, the frustration! Oh, the disappointment. It was grrrawful!

"All night long, there sat a juicy meal looking like *he* was saying grrrrace. The next thing I knew, I heard the voice of the king. My food jumped up—something I couldn't do—and was pulled out of our den, leaving us starved for protein and calcium. But that diet was soon provided by the king once again."

Say, "Well, that gets us to the end of our story, but we need to start at the beginning."

## Into the Word

Ask the class to offer text support for each of the following generalizations as you read them aloud. (This activity is also included in the optional student book.) Possible ideas and verse numbers are given in parentheses, but these should not be included in your reading.

*Generalizations:* 1. Faith, to be true faith, must be expressed. *(Daniel prayed, no matter what, in full view of his accusers, v. 10.)* 2. Sometimes the godly person must be disagreeable; he must disagree with sin. *(Though Daniel knew the law was in place, he prayed anyway, v. 10.)* 3. It is possible to sound religious and patriotic with ulterior, sinful motives. *(The political leaders suggested a religious devotion to the king, but their intention was to see Daniel dead, vv. 4-7.)* 4. Anyone, even a pagan king, can believe in the power and mercy of God. *(Darius expressed confidence that Daniel's God could save him, v. 16.)* 5. Respect

for authority is a necessity if one would be godly. *(Authority is by God's design, and Daniel greeted the king respectfully even after the king sent him to a night surrounded by lions, v. 21.)* 6. Never look for other explanations when it is obvious God did it. *(Daniel credits God for his salvation, v. 22.)* 7. A personal claim of innocence is always appropriate . . . if one is innocent! *(Daniel reaffirms his innocence after being rescued, v. 22.)* 8. Even when people in authority agree on a matter, their decision does not necessarily make it right. *(Many officials colluded for the law proposed to the king, but it's still a bad, even immoral, law, vv. 4-7.)* 9. Capital punishment is the discretionary choice of a government, but death for praying hardly fits the crime. *(Governments, by God's design, are responsible for punishing evildoers, in ancient Persia as today, but God expects appropriate penalties for lawbreakers, vv. 7, 16.)* 10. A servant of God must never let fear overwhelm faith, for fear denies God's power, love, and grace. *(Fear of grisly death would not even give Daniel pause regarding his worship practices, v. 10).*

## Into Life

Ask your class to consider the issues below. Say, "Most of us are tempted at times to put our faith on hold by certain events and circumstances. Rate the following as occasions you personally are challenged to leave your faith on hold. Use a scale of 0 to 4, with 0 meaning *not tempted to put faith on hold at all* and 4 for *a real temptation to put faith on hold.* (These are included in the optional student book.)

___You are offered free tickets to a very popular and thought-provoking R-rated movie known to be filled with nudity and sexual activity.

___The office Christmas party has a reputation for drunkenness and crudity. The boss says, "We'll see you there!"

___Your professional association is having its annual convention in Las Vegas. The keynote speaker is someone you have always wanted to hear, but the hotel is best known for its vices.

___You are asked to judge the creative products at a community arts and crafts show. Several of the participants are good friends and fellow church members.

# Let's Talk It Over

*The questions on this page are designed to promote discussion of the lesson
by the class and to encourage application of the lesson Scriptures. The answers
provided are only discussion starters. Let your class talk it over from there.*

**1. How does our culture ask us to suspend our faith temporarily? How have you resisted doing so?**

Hostility to Christian faith can take various forms. A Christian may be expected to go along with deceptive business plans for the sake of the company. Sales people are at times instructed in ways of bending the truth to close the deal. Accountants may be asked to "cook the books" to show a profit where none exists so stockholders will be pleased. (Remember Enron?)

Some companies support various charitable organizations that are involved in practices that violate a Christian's conscience; the workers are asked to be "team players" as they make contributions to support those organizations. Companies have been known to conduct "diversity training," in which employees are taught to accept homosexual lifestyles. No one is allowed to speak against it; attendance is required.

In each of these situations the Christian is asked to suspend his or her beliefs and principles. Having a "faith buddy" to stand alongside you can make you stronger to take your stand.

**2. What are some "faith loopholes" you have used to try to avoid being honest about your beliefs with others? How have you learned to avoid using such loopholes?**

Because of fear of what someone might say, we may make excuses for not living out our faith. Though praying before a meal is not a command of Scripture, it is a regular practice in many Christian homes. But when out in public, many Christians do not do so. Choosing not to pray before a meal is not necessarily a sin. Yet to shy away from praying because someone looking might make fun of us is to use a loophole. Sometimes secret prayer is appropriate (Matthew 6:5, 6), but sometimes it is not; motive is all-important.

Sometimes we may be asked to participate in an activity when we have already committed ourselves to something with the church. We may feel embarrassed to say that we have a church commitment, so we simply say we already have plans. Saying that in and of itself is not a sin. But if we do so simply because we fear rejection, then we have used another loophole.

**3. What are some ways that God may use the demonstration of your faith for good?**

Jesus said, "By this shall all men know that ye are my disciples, if ye have love one to another" (John 13:35). Jesus also said, "Herein is my Father glorified, that ye bear much fruit; so shall ye be my disciples" (John 15:8). "Invisible fruit" is a problem! See Matthew 5:14-16; 7:17.

Referring back to the loopholes discussed in the previous question, God may use your response that you are involved in a church activity as an open door for future discussions on matters of faith with someone. Scripture presents ways in which our demonstrations of faith can have positive effects.

**4. Why is it important that we testify before others of God's deliverance?**

There is a saying about our activity of witnessing: "Share your faith—use words if necessary." That seems like a clever sound bite until we realize that *actions* (the demonstration of our faith discussed in the previous question) open the door for *words*.

Some people demonstrate very fruitful lives in their love for others, but they are not necessarily prompted to do so out of love for God. Therefore we set ourselves apart by speaking of our faith. When we have victories over special problems, people may ask how we made it. Sharing a testimony of faith helps us to remember that it was not by our might but by God's blessing that victory was achieved. Doing this also keeps us humble.

**5. How are some in positions of authority today guilty of domesticating God's law or making Christianity into a subset of national life? How should we react when we see this happening?**

Some politicians will resort to any means to gain the favor of voters. They may try to play on the concerns of Christian people and use Christian language when courting Christian votes. But then they will turn and seek to appease another group whose views are totally opposed to Scripture. Exhorting the nation to pray at specific times plays well to those lacking spiritual discernment (Hosea 14:9; Philippians 1:9, 10).

# Praying for the People

DEVOTIONAL READING: Psalm 130.

BACKGROUND SCRIPTURE: Daniel 9.

PRINTED TEXT: Daniel 9:1-7, 17-19.

### Daniel 9:1-7, 17-19

1 In the first year of Darius the son of Ahasuerus, of the seed of the Medes, which was made king over the realm of the Chaldeans;

2 In the first year of his reign, I Daniel understood by books the number of the years, whereof the word of the LORD came to Jeremiah the prophet, that he would accomplish seventy years in the desolations of Jerusalem.

3 And I set my face unto the Lord God, to seek by prayer and supplications, with fasting, and sackcloth, and ashes:

4 And I prayed unto the LORD my God, and made my confession, and said, O Lord, the great and dreadful God, keeping the covenant and mercy to them that love him, and to them that keep his commandments;

5 We have sinned, and have committed iniquity, and have done wickedly, and have rebelled, even by departing from thy precepts and from thy judgments:

6 Neither have we hearkened unto thy servants the prophets, which spake in thy name to our kings, our princes, and our fathers, and to all the people of the land.

7 O Lord, righteousness belongeth unto thee, but unto us confusion of faces, as at this day; to the men of Judah, and to the inhabitants of Jerusalem, and unto all Israel, that are near, and that are far off, through all the countries whither thou hast driven them, because of their trespass that they have trespassed against thee.

. . . . . . . . . . . .

17 Now therefore, O our God, hear the prayer of thy servant, and his supplications, and cause thy face to shine upon thy sanctuary that is desolate, for the Lord's sake.

18 O my God, incline thine ear, and hear; open thine eyes, and behold our desolations, and the city which is called by thy name: for we do not present our supplications before thee for our righteousnesses, but for thy great mercies.

19 O Lord, hear; O Lord, forgive; O Lord, hearken and do; defer not, for thine own sake, O my God: for thy city and thy people are called by thy name.

---

GOLDEN TEXT: Now therefore, O our God, hear the prayer of thy servant, and his supplications, and cause thy face to shine upon thy sanctuary that is desolate, for the Lord's sake.—Daniel 9:17.

---

## God, the People, and the Covenant
### Unit 2: The Covenant in Exile
### (Lessons 6-9)

## Lesson Aims

After participating in this lesson, each student will be able to:

1. List the elements of confession and supplication in Daniel's prayer.

2. Explain why confession is an important prerequisite to supplication in prayer.

3. Write an intercessory prayer that includes adoration, confession, and supplication elements.

## Lesson Outline

## Introduction

### A. Learning How to Pray

We know that prayer is central to healthy faith. The New Testament instructs us to pray (example: Romans 12:12). It also provides examples of people who made prayer a priority. Jesus left the crowds to speak to His heavenly Father (Matthew 14:23). The apostles were committed to prayer (Acts 6:4), as was the earliest church (Acts 2:42).

Sometimes, however, we are curious about what people actually said while praying because we find ourselves wondering about what to say when we pray. Jesus' model prayer (Matthew 6:9-13) and unity prayer (John 17:20-26) are great places to start. Luke 22:42 and Acts 1:24; 7:59 provide more examples of the specific content of prayers in the New Testament. But the nature of those particular prayers, given the situations in which they were offered, may leave us hungering for even more insight.

The Old Testament is extremely helpful in this regard. The book of Psalms contains a rich supply of prayers that cover a wide range of topics and situations. In addition, the narrative portions of the Old Testament contain many lengthy prayers. By studying how our ancestors in faith prayed through their situations, we can learn how to pray in the situations we face.

Think about Daniel's situation. In his lifetime, Daniel had seen God begin to fulfill His promises for His people, but this fulfillment caused Daniel to be confused. Part of the confusion and distress concerned the length of time involved in fulfillment, as we shall see. Many of us experience the same thing in our lives and the lives of our churches—things just (to our understanding) take too long!

So how do we go about praying when we long for God to intervene and "hurry up" to finish the good work He began in our lives? Daniel's prayer in chapter 9 is a helpful place to start.

### B. Lesson Background

Daniel, a Jew, served as a captive in the king's palace in a foreign land. Daniel spent most of his life there, from about 606 BC (Daniel 1:1) until at least 538 BC (1:21). More than one foreign ruler esteemed him highly (2:46-48; 5:29; 6:1, 2). More importantly, Daniel was highly esteemed by God (9:23; 10:11, 19).

Daniel 1–6 focuses on key events in the lives of four Jewish men who remained faithful to God while exiled in Babylon. Daniel 7–12 focuses on the future from Daniel's perspective, particularly how God was to restore His people after subduing those who had oppressed them. We are concerned with how Daniel responded to the plight of his people and how his prayer can teach us to pray.

## I. Cause for Concern
## (Daniel 9:1-3)

### A. The Time (v. 1)

**1. In the first year of Darius the son of Ahasuerus, of the seed of the Medes, which was made king over the realm of the Chaldeans.**

This verse supplies the first clue as to why Daniel is praying the prayer that begins in verse 4 (below). That clue is the year and what it signifies. During Darius's *first year*, the *Chaldeans* (also called Babylonians) are defeated by the Persians. That is 539 BC. Subsequently, the Jews are released from exile to return to their land.

It need not concern us that historical research has identified Cyrus—not *Darius*—as the ruler who took over the realm of Babylon (2 Chronicles 36:22, 23; Ezra 1; Isaiah 44:28; 45:1, 13). Cyrus did not reign alone.

Daniel 6:28 may imply that Darius and Cyrus reigned right alongside one another. Under this theory, Darius (also known as Gubaru) is thought to lead the Persian army that captures Babylon in 539 BC, and Cyrus, his king, rewards him with a regional kingship. Another theory is that Daniel 6:28 implies that Darius and Cyrus are two names for the same person.

## B. The Insight (v. 2)

**2. In the first year of his reign, I Daniel understood by books the number of the years, whereof the word of the LORD came to Jeremiah the prophet, that he would accomplish seventy years in the desolations of Jerusalem.**

This verse provides a second clue concerning why Daniel prays the prayer that follows: Daniel's prayer is prompted by his reading of *Jeremiah the prophet*. The specific prophecy in question is presented briefly in Jeremiah 25:11, 12 and more extensively in Jeremiah 29:10-14. According to this prophecy, Babylon's domination ends after 70 years, and God's people return from captivity to experience peace and prosperity.

But why mention this prophecy in light of the first year of Darius's reign? The answer is found in 2 Chronicles 36:22 and Ezra 1:1-4. The context of these two passages indicates that Cyrus's takeover of Babylon has already occurred in

fulfillment of Jeremiah's prophecy as we read the text before us. That being the case, one may assume that Daniel's prayer to follow will be one of praise and thanksgiving. At last, mighty Babylon has fallen! Now God's people can be restored! But this is not how Daniel prays, as we shall see.

## C. The Reaction (v. 3)

**3. And I set my face unto the Lord God, to seek by prayer and supplications, with fasting, and sackcloth, and ashes.**

Before our text gives us the actual content of Daniel's prayer, the author is careful to note Daniel's state of mind: Daniel is in distress. The actions he takes before praying have something to teach us about how to approach God.

Apparently, Daniel is aware of a problem. At this point, we don't really know what the problem is. We'll have to dig into Daniel's prayer below to discover that. But whatever it is, Daniel begins by setting his *face unto the Lord God*. Daniel does not remain fixated on the problem. He can stare at Jeremiah's prophecy until he turns blue in the face, but focusing only on the problem (whatever it is) is not going to help. He must turn to God.

So Daniel turns to God in order *to seek by prayer and supplications*. This shows us Daniel's great faith in God's willingness and ability to act. Then Daniel supports his prayers with behavior. Daniel is not simply paying lip service to God. He demonstrates his concern through the self-denial of fasting. The *sackcloth* and *ashes* demonstrate that Daniel truly grieves. We may compare these signs of mourning with passages such as Nehemiah 9:1; Esther 4:3; and Psalm 35:13.

In our day, sackcloth and ashes are not staples of mourning practices in the Western world. But throughout the ages Christians have remained committed to *fasting*, that is, abstaining from food or other activities to focus on God (Acts 13:2, 3; 14:23). Indeed, there are countless symbolic gestures by which we can convey to God that our prayers are sincere. [See question #1, page 304.]

### DOING OUR PART

Half a century of rule by the atheistic Communist Party left China with a serious ethical gap. China has embraced capitalism to an extent, but without the Christian perspective that provides the ethical structure that keeps Western capitalism in check. The result is an epidemic of corruption in China. Increasing numbers of both government and business personnel are being prosecuted for graft, bribery, extortion, and even murder.

## How to Say It

AHASUERUS. Uh-haz-you-*ee*-rus.
BABYLONIANS. Bab-ih-*low*-nee-unz.
CHALDEANS. Kal-*dee*-unz.
CYRUS. *Sigh*-russ.
DARIUS. Duh-*rye*-us.
GABRIEL. *Gay*-bree-ul.
GUBARU. Goo-*bahr*-roo.
JEREMIAH. Jair-uh-*my*-uh.
LEVITICUS. Leh-*vit*-ih-kus.
MEDES. Meeds.
PHILIPPIANS. Fih-*lip*-ee-unz.

Another sobering trend in China is a widespread loss of the respect for the elderly that had been a hallmark of Chinese culture. The government has started publicly shaming—even imprisoning—people who neglect their aged parents.

Godly people do not need the threat of punishment to force them into doing right. This was certainly true of Daniel. He was concerned about his fellow Jews. He pled with God for the prophecies of national restoration to be fulfilled. Then he did what he could to confirm his seriousness: he donned sackcloth and ashes and began fasting. The situation was beyond Daniel's control, yet he took the steps he could to show God where his heart was. Small gestures are yet significant today.                          —C. R. B.

## II. Confession of Sin
## (Daniel 9:4-7)

### A. Judah's God (v. 4)

**4. And I prayed unto the LORD my God, and made my confession, and said, O Lord, the great and dreadful God, keeping the covenant and mercy to them that love him, and to them that keep his commandments.**

Daniel demonstrates that he truly knows the God to whom he is praying: he is praying to *the Lord,* the God of Israel. He is praying to the God who beckons us to petition Him, but who is also worthy of being feared. This God holds life and death in His hands, so we dare not address Him flippantly. [See question #2, page 304.]

Even so, this *dreadful God* is gracious. He keeps His *covenant* with His people and shows them *mercy.* Here Daniel helps us understand two

aspects of God that we may have difficulty holding alongside one another. Daniel does not shy away from either attribute, but prays to the God who is both gracious and dreadful simultaneously.

This is the God we must fear as we seek His mercy—the God whose mercy we must seek even when we fear Him most. These attributes are not somehow in competition with one another inside of God. Rather, they reflect the unique nature of the God we serve.

God demonstrates His mercy especially to those who *love Him* and *keep his commandments.* We should not think of commandment-keeping as an outdated Old Testament principle that has somehow been superseded by grace. In John 14:15, Jesus says, "If ye love me, keep my commandments." See also 1 John 2:3; 3:22, 24; 5:3; Revelation 12:17; 14:12.

### B. Judah's Sin (vv. 5, 6)

**5. We have sinned, and have committed iniquity, and have done wickedly, and have rebelled, even by departing from thy precepts and from thy judgments.**

Instead of offering a prayer of thanksgiving for fulfillment of Jeremiah's prophecy, Daniel begins by confessing sin (here and in v. 6). The sinner's proper response to God is confession. We remember that the Babylonian captivity had come about because of sin. Daniel realizes that Judah's restoration is to be accomplished by repentance.

It is important to note how Daniel identifies with the sin of the people. We know from prior accounts that Daniel is a man of exceptional character and devotion to God. Yet Daniel knows that God's people rise and fall together. So he prays *we have sinned* because he knows something important about God's purpose in the world. [See question #3, page 304.]

In forming the nation of Israel, God was not trying to create merely a bunch of righteous individuals. Rather, He was creating a holy society. The laws He gave were not only about personal piety, but also about social justice and communal witness. The Israelites are to bear witness to God's purposes in all aspects of their lives. If Israel produces only a few righteous individuals, then it fails. The communal life of God's people must shine like stars in the sky (Daniel 12:3; Philippians 2:15). But Daniel knows that his fellow Jews have failed in this regard, and he does not consider himself to be above them.

**6. Neither have we hearkened unto thy servants the prophets, which spake in thy name to our kings, our princes, and our fathers, and to all the people of the land.**

## Home Daily Bible Readings

**Monday, Apr. 21**—The Assurance of Redemption (Psalm 130)

**Tuesday, Apr. 22**—Preparing to Pray (Daniel 9:1-3)

**Wednesday, Apr. 23**—A Righteous God (Daniel 9:4-10)

**Thursday, Apr. 24**—God's Response to Sin (Daniel 9:11-14)

**Friday, Apr. 25**—Hear, O God (Daniel 9:15-19)

**Saturday, Apr. 26**—A Word Gone Out (Daniel 9:20-23)

**Sunday, Apr. 27**—God's Strong Covenant (Daniel 9:24-27)

Daniel also knows that Judah has had every chance to remedy the situation of unholiness. God has not left Israel alone to slip into sin without realizing it. God has sent *prophets* to warn them. These prophets went to all strata of society, from king to commoner, to communicate God's message. But neither the northern kingdom of Israel nor the southern kingdom of Judah heeded them. [See question #4, page 304.]

## C. Judah's Lot (v. 7)

**7. O Lord, righteousness belongeth unto thee, but unto us confusion of faces, as at this day; to the men of Judah, and to the inhabitants of Jerusalem, and unto all Israel, that are near, and that are far off, through all the countries whither thou hast driven them, because of their trespass that they have trespassed against thee.**

As Daniel wraps up the confession part of his prayer, the contrast between God and His people comes into sharp relief. God is righteous, and all His people are (or should be) ashamed of themselves because they have sinned.

We can now summarize the features of Daniel's confession. First, Daniel knows to whom he is praying. Second, Daniel knows how he stands in relation to God. Third, Daniel knows he must pray not only for himself but also for others. Fourth, Daniel accepts responsibility for the sin of God's people, not just for his own. Fifth, Daniel confesses sin to God, neither hiding nor ignoring it. Sixth, Daniel acknowledges that the sin of *Judah*, *Jerusalem*, and *Israel* has a history. Part of that history is God's consistent warning.

These six features have obvious application to our prayers today. Having established all six, Daniel is in the right frame of mind to make his request.

### AN OPEN SHAME

The secular world was delighted just a few years ago when the child abuse scandal rocked the Roman Catholic Church. Similar crimes take place in secular society, but the fact that they were taking place in a religious institution made the news especially "juicy."

Perhaps the more important aspect of the crime was the fact that the church stonewalled when accusations were made. *The Boston Globe*, right in the Catholic Church's backyard, so to speak, reported, "For decades church leaders kept horrific tales of abuse out of the public eye through an elaborate culture of secrecy, deception, and intimidation" (www.boston.com).

The world was appropriately shocked, and the church hierarchy *should* have been. As months went by, more stories began leaking out. Gradually, the harsh glare of publicity forced the church to confess its corporate sin of covering up the private sins of some of its priests.

The Catholic Church's difficulties with this sin demonstrate how hard it can be to confess sin, especially when the confession needs to be a public one. Daniel's confession in his prayer was done privately, but he was praying on behalf of the Jewish people, whose unholiness was "an open shame." Are there other open shames in the body of Christ that the church overlooks? —C. R. B.

# III. Petition for Help (Daniel 9:17-19)

## A. Introduction of Petition (v. 17)

**17. Now therefore, O our God, hear the prayer of thy servant, and his supplications, and cause thy face to shine upon thy sanctuary that is desolate, for the Lord's sake.**

Verses 8-16 (not in today's text) offer Daniel's lengthy recounting of the sins of God's people. The wrap-up of the prayer is verses 17-19. These two segments build upon one another in ways that involve repetition.

Central to Daniel's request is that God *hear* and respond. Daniel knows that God does not have to heed his petition. God is not obligated. His people have practically disowned Him, and He warned them long ago that disobedience on their part would result in rejection on His part (Leviticus 18:28; Deuteronomy 28:15-68).

But Daniel also knows that God is merciful and will listen to his earnest prayer. So he asks for a response. He petitions God to show favor upon God's own *sanctuary* for God's own *sake*.

A cynic may read this passage as slick salesmanship on Daniel's part: Daniel wants something from God, so Daniel presents his request as if God is the one who stands to gain. A better reading, however, is that Daniel is acknowledging what has been true all along: the temple sanctuary belongs to God, but the people have acted as if it were theirs to do with as they pleased. Similarly, they forget that they exist to fulfill God's purposes in the world, not their own. The future of the Jewish people depends on their recognizing this. [See question #5, page 304.]

## B. Basis of Petition (v. 18)

**18. O my God, incline thine ear, and hear; open thine eyes, and behold our desolations, and the city which is called by thy name: for we do not present our supplications before thee for our righteousnesses, but for thy great mercies.**

Daniel intensifies his petition in two ways before submitting its basis. First, he asks God not only to *hear* his request but also to see for himself the *desolations*. Second, Daniel draws God's attention specifically to *the city* of Jerusalem. This city, like the temple, is attached to God's *name*. Forgetting this fact led to Judah's demise (1 Kings 11:36; 2 Kings 23:27).

Daniel comes before God knowing that Judah is empty-handed in terms of righteousness. Nothing Judah has done or will do can earn God's favor. Daniel cannot appeal to Judah's holy accomplishments as bargaining chips. The ultimate basis of Daniel's appeal is God's *great mercies*. It can be ours as well.

### C. Urgency of Petition (v. 19)

**19. O Lord, hear; O Lord, forgive; O Lord, hearken and do; defer not, for thine own sake, O my God: for thy city and thy people are called by thy name.**

Daniel concludes his prayer with a sense of urgency as he entreats God four times. He asks God to *hear, forgive,* and act, doing these quickly *(defer not)*. Notice that Daniel does not make his petition because the Jews are weary of their affliction or worthy of intervention. Rather, Daniel asks God to act because God has an important mission for His *people* to accomplish, and God's reputation in the world is connected to that people.

God took a risk by attaching His *name* to Israel. By their actions His name is either lifted high or dragged through the mud. In closing his prayer by drawing attention to God's name, Daniel acknowledges that the Jewish people now remember (or should remember) why they

Visual for Lesson 9. *How has prayer changed the lives of your learners? Point to this visual as you ask for examples.*

exist. Their task is to be eager to live up to their namesake.

# Conclusion

### A. Daniel's Prayer Answered

While Daniel was still praying, God sent the angel Gabriel to answer the prayer (Daniel 9:20-27). In short, Gabriel told Daniel that the punishment had been multiplied by 7. So instead of being restored fully after 70 years, God's people were to be restored after "seventy weeks" (or "seventy sevens"). There is some debate over how to interpret this number, but we can at least say that it involved the distant future from Daniel's perspective. This was not an arbitrary punishment by God. In Leviticus 26:18, God warned Israel that He would punish her sevenfold for disobedience.

### B. Daniel's Prayer Applied

We are to remind ourselves, as Daniel did, that God's purposes for us are not complete. Though the power of sin was defeated on the cross, it still rears its ugly head in our lives. Christ is the fulfillment of our hope, but we await a day to experience the fullness that God has in store for us in the heavenly Jerusalem.

Until then, we can follow Daniel's lead in prayer. We draw near to God not only in speech but also in action. Fasting and signs of contrition can help as we own up to individual and corporate sins, confessing them to God and one another. We must renounce all thoughts of entitlement, as if God were obligated to answer our prayers to our liking. We must commit ourselves to Him and remain true to His purpose for us in this world, for it is the Christian who bears the name of Christ. We were saved not for comfort or pleasure, but for God's mission for the church.

Daniel prayed like this, and God answered him. Let us pray likewise.

### C. Prayer

O God who hears our prayer, teach us to pray like Daniel. Like him, we are often baffled by Your timing. We cannot see the big picture, and we get hung up on the details. Please give us the faith to wait for You. We confess to You our sins, we submit to You our unworthiness, and we call upon Your mercy. Hear us when we pray, for Your name's sake and for the sake of Your world, in Jesus' name, amen.

### D. Thought to Remember

Petition God humbly and urgently.

# Learning by Doing

*This page contains an alternative lesson plan emphasizing learning activities.*
*Classes desiring such student involvement will find these suggestions helpful.*

## Into the Lesson

As learners arrive, hand each a copy of the following list of Bible references and directions: "The Bible records many great prayers. Look up these references and figure out who is praying and what the occasion is for each." Genesis 18:23-32; Exodus 32:11-13; 1 Samuel 2:1-10; 1 Kings 8:22-53; 1 Kings 18:36, 37; Nehemiah 1:5-11; Psalm 51; Psalm 73; Daniel 9:4-19; Matthew 6:9-13; Acts 4:24-30; Ephesians 1:15-23.

As an alternative and less time-consuming approach, simply give one reference to each learner along with the same directions. As you discuss these prayers, ask your learners if they see any patterns.

## Into the Word

Reproduce and distribute the following list of statements. (They are also printed in the optional student book.)

Say, "Daniel's prayer and the prelude to his prayer in Daniel 9 reveal much about God. List a verse from today's text that reveals the truth of each of the following." You may have your learners work in pairs or small groups if you wish.

1. The God of Daniel and the God of today knows the future: ___.
2. The God of Daniel and the God of today can provide for human needs: ___.
3. The God of Daniel and the God of today is the Lord: ___.
4. The God of Daniel and the God of today welcomes repentance: ___.
5. The God of Daniel and the God of today is great and dreadful: ___.
6. The God of Daniel and the God of today keeps His covenants: ___.
7. The God of Daniel and the God of today shows mercy: ___.
8. The God of Daniel and the God of today reveals His expectations: ___.
9. The God of Daniel and the God of today is offended by sin: ___.
10. The God of Daniel and the God of today has expressed His will for human behavior: ___.
11. The God of Daniel and the God of today sends spokesmen to speak to His people: ___.
12. The God of Daniel and the God of today can hear the prayers of His people: ___.

13. The God of Daniel and the God of today can give or withhold blessings: ___.
14. The God of Daniel and the God of today sees our condition: ___.
15. The God of Daniel and the God of today answers prayer because He is good, not because we are: ___.
16. The God of Daniel and the God of today can forgive: ___.
17. The God of Daniel and the God of today can be claimed as "my God": ___.
18. The God of Daniel and the God of today gives His name to His children: ___.

*Possible answers:* 1. verse 2; 2. verse 19; 3. verse 4; 4. verse 3; 5. verse 4; 6. verse 4; 7. verse 18; 8. verse 6; 9. verse 5; 10. verse 6; 11. verse 6; 12. verse 17; 13. verse 18; 14. verse 18; 15. verse 18; 16. verse 19; 17. verse 19; 18. verse 19. Accept other answers with reasonable explanations.

## Into Life

Make a transition by asking your learners to look at the attributes and actions of God from the exercise of the Into the Word segment. Ask, "How do the truths you see here and in Daniel's prayer affect your own prayer life?" Discuss.

*Alternative:* Reproduce and distribute the list of questions below. (These are also printed in the optional student books). Say, "A common Christian affirmation is that prayers should include (among other things) adoration, confession, and supplication. This may suggest to us not only content but also sequence. Consider the following questions."

1. Should adoration of God precede personal confession? Why, or why not?
2. Should adoration of God precede supplication for needs? Why, or why not?
3. Should confession of personal weakness precede asking for God's help? Why, or why not?
4. Should supplication be the last concern in our prayers? Why, or why not?
5. Is this sequence the way you usually pray? Why, or why not?
6. What changes do you need to make to your prayer life, if any?

Depending on the time that is available, have your learners work in pairs, small groups, or as a class.

# Let's Talk It Over

*The questions on this page are designed to promote discussion of the lesson by the class and to encourage application of the lesson Scriptures. The answers provided are only discussion starters. Let your class talk it over from there.*

**1. What are some specific areas of your life where you need to set your face on the Lord and pray? How can you support these prayers with action?**

A mistake Christians often make is thinking that prayer is reserved just for "the big issues" of life. But God desires that we take all of our cares to Him. Parents may have special concerns for their children and want to trust them into God's hands and seek God's guidance upon them. But that prayer needs to be accompanied with godliness on the part of the praying parents as well as training the children in the ways of the Lord.

Financial difficulties are a concern to take to the Father. But we may also need to learn to be better stewards of what God has already blessed us with and make better decisions in the way we budget. We pray for the salvation of others, but we need to actively share our faith with those for whom we are praying.

**2. Are there ever times when you approach God with less than proper reverence? How do you keep this from happening?**

As we pray, we must never forget the one to whom we are praying. We are guilty of being flippant in our prayers when we fail to approach God with the reverence He is due or with the awe we should feel.

Ecclesiastes 12:13 reminds us that when all is said and done the end of all things is to "Fear God, and keep his commandments: for this is the whole duty of man." Arrogance is seen when we demand things of God instead of seeking His will. Psalm 63:1-5 reveals that our greatest longing should be for the Lord's presence in our lives. This kind of prayer leads us to seek to glorify God and not to exalt self.

**3. Are there specific sins you need to confess to God? Do you need to confess these sins to others? How will you get started doing this?**

Intellectually, we know that God knows all things, even our sins. But some still think they can hide sin from God. It may be shame or it may be pride that keeps us from specifically mentioning sins we struggle with to God. Also, pride or shame will cause us to fail to confess our sins to others. At times pride will cause some to think they have no sin, which in itself is a sin according to 1 John 1:8 because saying this involves lying. But the teaching of Scripture is that we take care of our sin issues with others before we come to God (see Matthew 5:24).

**4. Why do Christians find it hard at times to listen to God's servants?**

A premise of the sixteenth-century Protestant Reformation involved the idea of personal interpretation. Many have taken that to mean that everyone has the right to interpret the Scriptures for himself or herself. As a result, people feel they don't really have to listen to those who have studied and prepared messages because "what they say is just their opinion."

But the real significance of that reformation premise is that everyone has a *duty* to interpret the Bible, seeking to understand its meaning as the original authors intended. When we walk this path, we reject the idea that truth is relative to the individual. We can then listen to sermons and Sunday school lessons with humility, seeking truth from the speaker or teacher (Acts 17:11).

**5. How can you and your church pray more effectively for the Lord to bless His work?**

Too often the prayers of the people of God are very general. We may simply pray for God to bless all the missionaries or to bless all those for whom it is our duty to pray.

A means to more effective prayer is to be more knowledgeable about those things for which we pray. Then we can pray specifically about these matters. Maintaining a prayer list is one way of accomplishing this. Churches can do their part to make the people aware of specific needs of missionaries and others for whom the church is praying.

Another means to more effective praying is to be consistent and persistent in our prayers. We can swallow our pride and be open in asking for others to pray with us and for us about specific matters instead of just announcing that we have an unspoken request. Notice in Colossians 1:9; 1 Thessalonians 5:25; and 2 Thessalonians 3:1 how Paul spoke of (and requested) praying for one another.

# Setting Priorities

DEVOTIONAL READING: Psalm 84:1-4.

BACKGROUND SCRIPTURE: Haggai 1; Ezra 5 .

PRINTED TEXT: Haggai 1:1-10, 12-15.

### Haggai 1:1-10, 12-15

1 In the second year of Darius the king, in the sixth month, in the first day of the month, came the word of the LORD by Haggai the prophet unto Zerubbabel the son of Shealtiel, governor of Judah, and to Joshua the son of Josedech, the high priest, saying,

2 Thus speaketh the LORD of hosts, saying, This people say, The time is not come, the time that the LORD's house should be built.

3 Then came the word of the LORD by Haggai the prophet, saying,

4 Is it time for you, O ye, to dwell in your ceiled houses, and this house lie waste?

5 Now therefore thus saith the LORD of hosts; Consider your ways.

6 Ye have sown much, and bring in little; ye eat, but ye have not enough; ye drink, but ye are not filled with drink; ye clothe you, but there is none warm; and he that earneth wages, earneth wages to put it into a bag with holes.

7 Thus saith the LORD of hosts; Consider your ways.

8 Go up to the mountain, and bring wood, and build the house; and I will take pleasure in it, and I will be glorified, saith the LORD.

9 Ye looked for much, and, lo, it came to little; and when ye brought it home, I did blow upon it. Why? saith the LORD of hosts. Because of mine house that is waste, and ye run every man unto his own house.

10 Therefore the heaven over you is stayed from dew, and the earth is stayed from her fruit.

. . . . . . . . . . .

12 Then Zerubbabel the son of Shealtiel, and Joshua the son of Josedech, the high priest, with all the remnant of the people, obeyed the voice of the LORD their God, and the words of Haggai the prophet, as the LORD their God had sent him, and the people did fear before the LORD.

13 Then spake Haggai the LORD's messenger in the LORD's message unto the people, saying, I am with you, saith the LORD.

14 And the LORD stirred up the spirit of Zerubbabel the son of Shealtiel, governor of Judah, and the spirit of Joshua the son of Josedech, the high priest, and the spirit of all the remnant of the people; and they came and did work in the house of the LORD of hosts, their God,

15 In the four and twentieth day of the sixth month, in the second year of Darius the king.

May
4

---

GOLDEN TEXT: Go up to the mountain, and bring wood, and build the house; and I will take pleasure in it, and I will be glorified, saith the LORD.—Haggai 1:8.

## Lesson Aims

After participating in this lesson, each student will be able to:

1. Describe how the cultural, economic, and religious climate in Haggai's day worked against the rebuilding of the temple.

2. Give a modern example of misplaced priorities that is parallel to the situation of Haggai's day.

3. Suggest a plan to correct one misplaced priority in order to obey God more fully.

## Lesson Outline

INTRODUCTION
   A. Priorities
   B. Lesson Background
 I. TEMPLE NEGLECTED (Haggai 1:1-4)
   A. Context (v. 1)
   B. Rationalization (v. 2)
     *"I Simply Haven't Had Time"*
   C. Confrontation (vv. 3, 4)
 II. BLESSINGS FORFEITED (Haggai 1:5-10)
   A. Thinking It Through, Part 1 (vv. 5, 6)
   B. Thinking It Through, Part 2 (vv. 7-10)
III. WORK STARTED (Haggai 1:12-15)
   A. People's Obedience (v. 12)
   B. Lord's Favor (v. 13)
   C. Everyone's Work (vv. 14, 15)
     *Waking Up*
CONCLUSION
   A. Our Priorities or God's?
   B. Prayer
   C. Thought to Remember

## Introduction

### A. Priorities

There is not enough time in life to do everything that we would like to do, and some things in life are crucial to do, like it or not. For example, if we put off paying our electric bill long enough, the utility company will shut off the power. Paying that electric bill becomes an increasingly high priority as time goes by.

So how does a busy person make sure that the most important things actually get done? One efficient way is to write out a priority list. Of the things that could be done today, what is the most important one? That goes at the top of the list. Then come the second, third, and fourth most important items, and so on.

Once the list is made, one goes down the list and tries to accomplish as many items as time allows. Those things that cannot be accomplished then go on the next day's list. Low priority items at the bottom of the list may never get done, but this system makes sure that the most important things do get done.

But many times I do not operate in this efficient way. I start not with what is most important, but with what I want to do—no matter how trivial. I desperately need to pay the bills, but I watch the news or surf the Internet instead. As a result, some things that absolutely needed to be done that day may have failed to get done. The problem was that my priorities in action did not correspond with the real priorities in my life.

The same problem comes in the spiritual life. The Christian should have the things of God as a priority in life. But all too frequently other matters, both important and trivial, crowd out the things of God. The book of Haggai reminds us that we need to make God and His service our priority.

### B. Lesson Background

Solomon began to build the temple around 966 BC. After its completion, it stood for nearly four centuries as the grand religious monument of Solomon's reign.

The temple replaced the tabernacle as Israel's focal point for worship. The Israelites came to the temple for three annual feasts (Deuteronomy 16:16). Standing as the symbolic dwelling place of God in the midst of His people, the temple had a fond place in the hearts of pious Israelites. For example, in Psalm 84:1-4 the psalmist expresses some sentimental jealousy for the sparrows that built nests in the temple's structure, longing like them to remain always in its courts.

But a catastrophe befell the temple during the reign of Zedekiah. In 586 BC the Babylonians devastated Jerusalem. The temple was looted and burned (2 Kings 25). The period that followed is known as *the Babylonian exile*, a time in which large numbers of Jews were deported from Judah to live in Babylon.

The exile came to an end shortly after Cyrus, king of Persia and Media, conquered Babylon in 539 BC. In late 539 or early 538 BC, Cyrus issued a decree allowing Jews who so wished to return to Judah and rebuild the temple (Ezra 1:1-4). About 50,000 went back.

The Jews who returned from exile were eager to take advantage of Cyrus's decree and rebuild the temple. They succeeded in rebuilding the altar and began once again to conduct sacrifices (Ezra 3:1-6). They even succeeded in laying the foundations for a new temple (Ezra 3:7-13), but opposition forced a halt (Ezra 4:24). As a result, the temple proper remained unfinished for the better part of two decades after Jewish exiles had returned with plans to rebuild it.

After this long time of inactivity, the prophets Haggai and Zechariah preached in the year 520 BC about the need to rebuild the temple (Ezra 5:1, 2). These are the same prophets who wrote the books of the Old Testament that bear their names. The book of Zechariah gives an account of his prophetic encouragement regarding the rebuilding of the temple (see Zechariah 1:16; 4:9). The book of Haggai gives that prophet's perspective on how he preached in this regard and how the people responded to his message.

The book of Haggai consists of four prophetic messages, dating from August to December of 520 BC. Each prophecy begins with the declaration "came the word of the Lord" or "the word of the Lord came" (Haggai 1:1; 2:1, 10, 20). Today's lesson takes us to the first of these four.

# I. Temple Neglected
## (Haggai 1:1-4)
### A. Context (v. 1)

**1. In the second year of Darius the king, in the sixth month, in the first day of the month, came the word of the LORD by Haggai the prophet unto Zerubbabel the son of Shealtiel, governor of Judah, and to Joshua the son of Josedech, the high priest, saying.**

The date of Haggai's first prophecy is very specific as to the year, month, and day of Darius's reign. This particular *Darius* is the third emperor of the Persian Empire; he follows Cyrus and Cambyses to the throne. Darius reigned from 521 to 486 BC. This Darius is not to be confused with the very different King Darius of the book of Daniel.

The *sixth month* in the Jewish religious calendar is called *Elul* (see the exact use of this designation in Nehemiah 6:15). Because the dates of Persian kings are known with certainty, the *second year*, sixth month, and *first day* of Darius converts precisely to August 29, 520 BC.

Shortly after returning from exile, two leaders emerge. The first is *Zerubbabel*, the governor, who is *son of Shealtiel* (compare Ezra 3:2, 8; 5:2). Shealtiel himself is the son of King Jehoiachin. We know this from 1 Chronicles 3:17-19.

That passage says, however, that Pedaiah was Zerubbabel's father rather than Shealtiel. This can be harmonized by realizing that Zerubbabel may have become Shealtiel's son legally through adoption after Pedaiah died (compare Deuteronomy 25:5-10). Zerubbabel is of Davidic descent and, as it turns out, an ancestor of Jesus Christ (Matthew 1:12).

The other leader is *Joshua*, who is the *high priest* (compare Zechariah 6:11). Note that in Ezra 3:2, 8; 5:2, the spelling "Jeshua the son of Jozadak" is slightly different from *Joshua the son of Josedech* here, although this undoubtedly is the same person.

Shortly after returning from exile, Zerubbabel and Joshua led the people in rebuilding the altar of the temple. This allowed renewed sacrifices and celebration of festivals. Nonetheless, the temple itself was not rebuilt (Ezra 3:1–4:5, 24). Haggai addresses the political and religious leaders of Judah to exhort them to finish what they started.

### B. Rationalization (v. 2)

**2. Thus speaketh the LORD of hosts, saying, This people say, The time is not come, the time that the LORD's house should be built.**

Sometimes we try to discern the will of God by circumstances. If we try something and things go poorly, then we may be tempted to think, "This must not be God's will." On the other hand, if things do go well, then we may be tempted to think, "This must be God's will." However, such reasoning may not be a reliable guide to discerning God's will!

The plans to rebuild the temple had not gone well for the returned exiles. They had good plans and good intentions to start (Ezra 3:7-13). But political opposition arose that brought the project to

---

### How to Say It

BABYLONIANS. Bab-ih-*low*-nee-unz.
CAMBYSES. Kam-*bye*-seez.
HAGGAI. *Hag*-eye or *Hag*-ay-eye.
JEHOIACHIN. Jeh-*hoy*-uh-kin.
JESHUA. *Jesh*-you-uh.
JOSEDECH. *Jahss*-uh-dek.
JOZADAK. *Joz*-uh-dak.
PEDAIAH. Peh-*day*-yuh.
SHEALTIEL. She-*al*-tee-el.
ZECHARIAH. *Zek*-uh-*rye*-uh (strong accent on *rye*).
ZEDEKIAH. Zed-uh-*kye*-uh.
ZERUBBABEL. Zeh-*rub*-uh-bul.

a halt (Ezra 4:1-5, 24). Thus the average Jew may well be thinking, "it must not be God's will to rebuild His house at this time." The problem is that this kind of thinking has been going on for more than 15 years! Haggai is anxious to correct this false conclusion. [See question #1, page 312.]

### "I SIMPLY HAVEN'T HAD TIME"

"I decided to quit procrastinating, but I just couldn't get around to starting the project."

Not everyone sees the humor in jokes about procrastination. There are numerous Web sites dealing with procrastination, and one of them carries this blog: "The jokes about procrastination infuriate me. This is not a funny problem—not if you are suffering from true, chronic procrastination."

Procrastination has been defined as "doing something—*anything*—except what one should be doing at the time." As one Web site says, "Procrastination is the grave in which opportunity is buried." Needless to say, procrastination can be a disruptive tendency.

The Jews who had returned from exile may have been procrastinators. However, they may have been suffering from a spiritual problem: they simply didn't care whether God's house ever got rebuilt, as long as their own living conditions were comfortable. Either way, they found it easy to rationalize not doing what God wanted them to do. Surely none of *us* have ever had that problem!
                                   —C. R. B.

### C. Confrontation (vv. 3, 4)

**3, 4. Then came the word of the LORD by Haggai the prophet, saying, Is it time for you, O ye, to dwell in your ceiled houses, and this house lie waste?**

The message of *Haggai the prophet* that follows is probably the same prophecy mentioned in Ezra 5:1. The failure of the Jews to finish rebuilding the temple is quite understandable up to a point. They had indeed made a start with all good intentions. But life undoubtedly was difficult for the Jews when they first returned from exile to begin a new life in Judah. When opposition to rebuilding the temple arises several years before Haggai prophesies, it just becomes easier to let survival take priority.

But most of the returnees are well settled now, a decade and a half after the initial return. It's past time to make God's ruined *house* rather than their own *houses* their priority. Allowing God's temple to remain in ruins is a disgrace and an insult to God. Haggai shames them for this. [See question #2, page 312.]

## II. Blessings Forfeited (Haggai 1:5-10)

### A. Thinking It Through, Part 1 (vv. 5, 6)

**5, 6. Now therefore thus saith the LORD of hosts; Consider your ways. Ye have sown much, and bring in little; ye eat, but ye have not enough; ye drink, but ye are not filled with drink; ye clothe you, but there is none warm; and he that earneth wages, earneth wages to put it into a bag with holes.**

Those who had returned from exile had not prospered materially. Crops of grain for food and grapes for *drink* and flax for clothing had been insufficient to satisfy the needs. Money seemed to disappear, as if leaking from a ripped purse.

Haggai indicates that this is no coincidence. Rather, this is happening because the people are giving no thought to the status of God's house. Apparently, people have been thinking, "Because the economy is bad, we can't afford to build the temple." What they should be thinking is, "The reason the economy is bad is because we haven't built the temple."

Behind Haggai's statement is the teaching of Deuteronomy 28. That passage instructs that God will bless His people if they obey Him, but He will curse them if they disobey. The lack of material blessing among those who have returned from exile is thus a consequence of their failure to obey God's call to rebuild His temple. [See question #3, page 312.]

### B. Thinking It Through, Part 2 (vv. 7-10)

**7, 8. Thus saith the LORD of hosts; Consider your ways. Go up to the mountain, and bring wood, and build the house; and I will take pleasure in it, and I will be glorified, saith the LORD.**

The solution to the disobedience is to repent and obey. In this case that means harvesting *wood* so work on the temple can begin again.

Forests exist in the hill country of Judah in ancient times, but the best wood comes from the mountains of Lebanon (compare 2 Kings 19:23). Solomon had imported cedar and other woods for his temple from there (1 Kings 5:6; 7:2; 2 Chronicles 2:8, 16). The text before us probably implies doing the same for Zerubbabel's temple, since that was the original intent of the returning exiles (Ezra 3:7). Thus the people should *go up to the mountain* in Lebanon to acquire the best wood, as is fitting for God's house. (Alternatively, *mountain* in verse 8 may refer to the temple mount to which wood is to be brought.)

Rebuilding the sacred space of the temple will bring God *pleasure*. Furthermore, the temple will be used to glorify God since it will be a place of worship. Today our bodies are meant to be the temples where God is *glorified* (1 Corinthians 6:19).

**9, 10. Ye looked for much, and, lo, it came to little; and when ye brought it home, I did blow upon it. Why? saith the LORD of hosts. Because of mine house that is waste, and ye run every man unto his own house. Therefore the heaven over you is stayed from dew, and the earth is stayed from her fruit.**

Because people fail to give attention to God's *house* while they are looking to their own houses, God has decided not to bless them materially. In particular, rains have not come in a timely way, so the crops are meager (see also v. 11, not in today's text). But obedience will mean that God will reverse that according to the promises of blessings in Deuteronomy 28.

## III. Work Started
## (Haggai 1:12-15)

### A. People's Obedience (v. 12)

**12. Then Zerubbabel the son of Shealtiel, and Joshua the son of Josedech, the high priest, with all the remnant of the people, obeyed the voice of the LORD their God, and the words of Haggai the prophet, as the LORD their God had sent him, and the people did fear before the LORD.**

The response to prophets in Old Testament times often is not good. Isaiah's audience was blind and deaf to his message (Isaiah 6:9, 10). Jeremiah was beaten and imprisoned (Jeremiah 20:1, 2). But in this case, *all the remnant of the people*—that is, those who have returned from exile, led by the governor *Zerubbabel* and the high priest *Joshua*—respond positively and prepare to rebuild the temple. This response is also recorded in Ezra 5:1, 2, which indicates that the prophet Zechariah supports Haggai in encouraging the Jews in this rebuilding. [See question #4, page 312.]

The people *fear* the Lord in the way that Abraham showed that he feared God. Abraham proved he feared God by demonstrating his willingness to obey God's command to sacrifice Isaac (Genesis 22:12). This kind of fear is the awe or respect for God that leads one to turn from sin and obey His commands no matter what. Those who do not obey God do not in fact fear Him.

### B. Lord's Favor (v. 13)

**13. Then spake Haggai the LORD's messenger in the LORD's message unto the people, saying, I am with you, saith the LORD.**

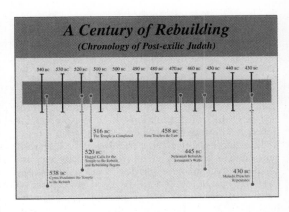

Visual for Lesson 10. *If your learners have personal copies of the* Standard Bible Atlas, *they will find this chart on page 23.*

In response to the people's willingness to build the temple, Haggai conveys God's promise: *I am with you.* What better words can one hear? A sense of God's presence is meant to provide the assurance of God's protection (Genesis 26:24; Isaiah 43:5; Jeremiah 1:8).

Trials and opposition lie ahead. Even after the rebuilding begins, Persian officials will threaten to stop the project (Ezra 5:3-17). But God will see them through to the project's completion (see Ezra 6:13-15; Zechariah 4:8, 9). Christians have a similar assurance of Jesus' presence as we seek to make disciples of the nations and baptize them in His name (Matthew 28:18-20).

### C. Everyone's Work (vv. 14, 15)

**14. And the LORD stirred up the spirit of Zerubbabel the son of Shealtiel, governor of Judah, and the spirit of Joshua the son of Josedech, the high priest, and the spirit of all the remnant of the people; and they came and did work in the house of the LORD of hosts, their God.**

Behind the outward act of beginning to rebuild the temple is an inward, invisible movement of God in the spirits of *the people* and their leaders. God often works through human messengers to stir hearts (example: Acts 2:37). In this case the prophets Haggai and Zechariah are used by God to compel action (again, Ezra 5:1, 2).

Other leaders besides these two prophets are important as well: the political leader *Zerubbabel* and the religious leader *Joshua* the *high priest* put this movement of God's Spirit into the practical effect of temple building. Leaders are still important in the way God stirs His people to action today. [See question #5, page 312.]

### WAKING UP

The First Great Awakening (about AD 1720–1740) came about in reaction to increasing secularism on both sides of the Atlantic Ocean. The secular, rationalistic spirit that preceded the awakening had been itself a reaction to an often-unthinking piety that emphasized emotion more than sound principles of biblical interpretation. So, as usual, the pendulum had swung too far and correction was needed.

The awakening's revitalization of Christian piety had a powerful effect on American culture in the years leading up to the American Revolution. But an educated ministry was needed to teach the large numbers of people turning back to faith, and numerous seminaries for the training of ministers came out of the awakening. We know several of these today as Ivy League colleges. Originally founded as Christian institutions, the Ivy League colleges eventually became secular institutions as the pendulum swung back the other way.

Old Testament Jewish history seems to be all about pendulum swings! As Haggai began to prophesy, the Jews had once again fallen away from God's ideal. However, the prophet's powerful preaching brought renewal, revival, and action. Do you think something similar is taking place today? If not, does it need to? —C. R. B.

**15. In the four and twentieth day of the sixth month, in the second year of Darius the king.**

The date mentioned here can be calculated to be September 21, 520 BC. Thus the work begins only 23 days after Haggai had begun preaching on the need to rebuild the temple (Haggai 1:1, 2). In a little over 3 weeks, things start to turn

## Home Daily Bible Readings

**Monday, Apr. 28**—In God's House (Psalm 84:1-4)

**Tuesday, Apr. 29**—Time to Rebuild the Temple (Haggai 1:1-11)

**Wednesday, Apr. 30**—The Work Begins (Haggai 1:12-15)

**Thursday, May 1**—Rebuilding the Foundation (Ezra 3:8-13)

**Friday, May 2**—Help Rejected (Ezra 4:1-4)

**Saturday, May 3**—The Rebuilding Questioned (Ezra 5:1-5)

**Sunday, May 4**—The Decree of King Cyrus (Ezra 5:6-17)

around. God's people begin the task God wishes for them to undertake. The task will not be easy, since the temple will not be completed until March 12, 515 BC (Ezra 6:15). But God will be with them during those four and one-half years.

## Conclusion

### A. Our Priorities or God's?

Although God is not calling us to build Him a temple of stone and wood, He certainly calls us to worship and serve Him. Often, however, we fail to make God and the things of God a priority in our lives. It is easy to fall into laziness, selfishness, or a life of comfortable self-indulgence.

The book of Haggai reminds us of the need to put God first, not ourselves. It exhorts us to be willing to make the sacrifices and the effort necessary to glorify God and further His work in the world. That sometimes involves the bricks and mortar of building physical buildings, such as churches or housing for the poor. Or it can take the form of building God's spiritual building, the church, by evangelizing and making disciples. Both kinds of work require putting God's priorities above our selfish desires.

For larger tasks on behalf of God, there is also the importance of good leadership. Had the prophets Haggai and Zechariah not stepped up to preach and exhort others to action, no temple would have been built. If the people refused to follow the leadership of their governor, Zerubbabel, and their high priest, Joshua, the temple would not have been built.

Each of us has a role to play. God calls some to lead and others to follow in order that greater works can be accomplished for Him. Part of our setting priorities is determining what God is calling us to do as individuals: to lead or follow others whom God has raised up. Then our priority must be to live out that calling.

### B. Prayer

Lord, help us to set aside our sinful selfishness and make You and Your work in the world a priority in our lives. Like Haggai, help us to encourage others to do Your will, and like the people of his day help us respond to Your exhortations conveyed through others. Raise up leaders with the courage of Haggai, Zechariah, Zerubbabel, and Joshua to help Your church accomplish great things. In Jesus' name, amen.

### C. Thought to Remember

If we do not make God our priority,
He won't make blessing us His priority.

# Learning by Doing

*This page contains an alternative lesson plan emphasizing learning activities.*
*Classes desiring such student involvement will find these suggestions helpful.*

## Into the Lesson

Write this sentence on the board: "First _____, then _____." Ask your class to fill in the blanks. Expect a variety of responses, both serious and humorous. For example, "First the chicken, then the egg"; "First God, then others"; "First wash, then dry"; "First birth, then death"; "First believe, then obey."

Accumulate ideas for a few minutes, and then ask, "Which of our responses are matters of priority rather than simple sequence?" Comment, "Today's study is one of priorities. But sometimes sequence implies priority; for example, giving to Christ's church and her ministries should be first in one's financial planning."

## Into the Word

Display the title *Haggai the Unknown*. Comment: "Haggai is one of those Bible people whose name we barely know. Today our study offers an opportunity to change that, as it focuses on the prophet, his task, and his success."

Prepare 13 large flash cards, each having one of the following nicknames for Haggai. Show them one at a time randomly and affix them to the wall or board as you proceed. Say, "Look at these nicknames for Haggai. Explain how each is an appropriate title for God's prophet." (After each nickname a brief explanation is given in parentheses for the teacher's use; do not put those on the flashcards.)

*Nicknames:* 1. Haggai the One of Two *(he served at the same time as the prophet Zechariah)*; 2. Haggai the Temple Prophet *(his message was largely about restoring the temple)*; 3. Haggai the Easily Dated *(Haggai 1:1 gives a very precise date for Haggai's call to prophesy)*; 4. Haggai the Festive One *(his name means "festive")*; 5. Haggai the Listener *(he spoke only what the Lord told him to speak)*; 6. Haggai the Timekeeper *(his complaint—actually God's—was that the people had lost track of the right time to build the temple: now!)*; 7. Haggai the Challenger *(he came to challenge the people to action)*; 8. Haggai the Observant *(verses 5-7 reveal that God—and Haggai— saw what happens when people ignore God's work)*; 9. Haggai the Financial Adviser *(he knows what happens to money when God is not in the picture; see verses 7, 9, 10)*; 10. Haggai the Obeyed *(verse 12 records the result of his message: the governor and the high priest and the people obeyed)*; 11. Haggai the Comforter *(when the people obeyed, verse 13, Haggai spoke God's great words of comfort, "I am with you")*; 12. Haggai the Effective *(the temple was rebuilt because of the response to his message; see verse 14b)*; 13. Haggai the Hurrier *(verse 15 reports that work began only about three weeks after he started preaching)*.

## Into Life

Make a transition by saying, "Haggai challenges the people to consider their ways. I'd like for you to consider the following questions silently as you carefully think of your own behavior." Make copies of the following list of questions and distribute. (The list also appears in the optional student book.)

1. Are there things your church leadership wants to do but you are standing in the way? 2. Are there repairs and improvements needed in the church property that you would never ignore or delay at home? 3. Are you unsatisfied in your quest for more things? 4. Do you get the feeling your money disappears without explanation? 5. Are you actively seeking to bring God pleasure and glory? 6. Do you ever consider natural disasters, such as famine, to be God withholding His blessing? 7. Do you stand alongside leaders when they listen to God's Word and obey? 8. Do you remind God's people that He is with them when they obey His will?

*Alternative exercise.* Reproduce the following "opposites" on a sheet of paper and distribute copies: *praying/chatting idly; reading about missions/reading about celebrities; studying God's Word/watching TV; corporate worship/recreation; caring for church property/caring for personal property; church giving/luxury spending; teaching God's Word/teaching hobbies; visiting the lonely/going shopping.* Put long lines of dots in place of the slant marks so that the two elements in each pair are on opposite sides of the page.

Say, "Within each pair, which one is a priority? Draw small stick figures along the lines to indicate where you stand. Consider both intent and time spent." (This activity also appears in the optional student book.)

# Let's Talk It Over

*The questions on this page are designed to promote discussion of the lesson by the class and to encourage application of the lesson Scriptures. The answers provided are only discussion starters. Let your class talk it over from there.*

**1. What are some things you have started for the Lord but have not completed? How will you go about making sure you finish?**

Almost everyone has started something that was never finished (compare Luke 14:28-30). On the flesh-and-blood level, it is important to consider the abilities and time one has to finish something. On the spiritual level, we can reevaluate priorities and pray. As we pray, though, we should not be surprised if God sends us Haggais to spur us toward completing our tasks, whether they be short- or long-term pursuits.

**2. What are some personal priorities that you have allowed to displace God's priorities? How do you stay alert to this danger?**

People can get their priorities mixed up, as in the case of those living in Haggai's day. Jesus seemed to be talking about mixed up priorities when He addressed the problem of becoming anxious about basic needs. To allow one's thinking to become consumed by such worries is to show a lack of faith that God is able to provide (Matthew 6:25-34).

Sometimes our priorities are not even *needs* but merely self-centered *desires*. This problem seems all too common in a culture that looks out for self instead of following God and trusting Him to provide. Regular study of the Word of God allows Him to speak to us about priorities.

**3. What causes God to withhold blessings from us today? How do we avoid overspiritualizing in this regard—seeing God blessing or withholding blessing in every action or lack of action on our part?**

The presence of sin must cause us to consider whether trouble in our lives may be God withholding blessings (compare Joshua 7). However, withheld blessings are not always due to sin. It could be a temporary test, such as that of Job. Sometimes what seems to be a withheld blessing may be a matter of God having a different blessing in mind. Consider the case of a child who expresses a desire for a $5.00 toy, but the parents say *no* because they intend to give him a bicycle later.

We also realize that God "maketh his sun to rise on the evil and on the good, and sendeth rain on the just and on the unjust" (Matthew 5:45). This fact should make us cautious about seeing every blessing we receive as an indicator of God's approval on our lives!

**4. What responses can we expect when we share something from God's Word? How do such responses affect our thoughts on whether or not we were "successful"?**

Haggai and Zechariah preached and the people obeyed. Most of the time the Old Testament prophets were not obeyed by a majority of the people. Rejection of God's Word seemed to be the norm.

While building the ark, Noah probably spent decades warning his generation of God's wrath. But Noah saved only himself and his family. Even so, God was well pleased with Noah. In God's eyes, success on our part is not defined in terms of people's positive response, but on our faithfulness to God's call. Jesus said this about salvation: "Enter ye in at the strait gate: for wide is the gate, and broad is the way, that leadeth to destruction, and many there be which go in thereat: because strait is the gate, and narrow is the way, which leadeth unto life, and few there be that find it" (Matthew 7:13, 14).

**5. What do you think made Zerubbabel and Joshua good leaders? How can you follow their example?**

It's been said that to be a good leader one must first be a good follower. That's what we see here. In the instance under consideration, the political leader Zerubbabel and the religious leader Joshua first followed the lead of Haggai the prophet. Zerubbabel and Joshua were humble enough to take counsel from other people, find the counsel good, and act upon it. Proverbs 11:14 says, "Where no counsel is, the people fall: but in the multitude of counselors there is safety."

Once encouraged by the prophets, Zerubbabel and Joshua were no longer going to allow opposition from outsiders to keep them from doing what they knew to be right. They worked for four solid years on a massive building project that was imposing even by today's standards. They were successful leaders.

# Following a Visionary Leader

**DEVOTIONAL READING:** Psalm 137:1-7; 138:1-5.

**BACKGROUND SCRIPTURE:** Nehemiah 1, 2.

**PRINTED TEXT:** Nehemiah 2:1-8, 11, 17, 18.

### Nehemiah 2:1-8, 11, 17, 18

1 And it came to pass in the month Nisan, in the twentieth year of Artaxerxes the king, that wine was before him: and I took up the wine, and gave it unto the king. Now I had not been beforetime sad in his presence.

2 Wherefore the king said unto me, Why is thy countenance sad, seeing thou art not sick? this is nothing else but sorrow of heart. Then I was very sore afraid,

3 And said unto the king, Let the king live for ever: why should not my countenance be sad, when the city, the place of my fathers' sepulchres, lieth waste, and the gates thereof are consumed with fire?

4 Then the king said unto me, For what dost thou make request? So I prayed to the God of heaven.

5 And I said unto the king, If it please the king, and if thy servant have found favor in thy sight, that thou wouldest send me unto Judah, unto the city of my fathers' sepulchres, that I may build it.

6 And the king said unto me, (the queen also sitting by him,) For how long shall thy journey be? and when wilt thou return? So it pleased the king to send me; and I set him a time.

7 Moreover I said unto the king, If it please the king, let letters be given me to the governors beyond the river, that they may convey me over till I come into Judah;

8 And a letter unto Asaph the keeper of the king's forest, that he may give me timber to make beams for the gates of the palace which appertained to the house, and for the wall of the city, and for the house that I shall enter into. And the king granted me, according to the good hand of my God upon me.

. . . . . . . . . . . . .

11 So I came to Jerusalem, and was there three days.

. . . . . . . . . . . . .

17 Then said I unto them, Ye see the distress that we are in, how Jerusalem lieth waste, and the gates thereof are burned with fire: come, and let us build up the wall of Jerusalem, that we be no more a reproach.

18 Then I told them of the hand of my God which was good upon me; as also the king's words that he had spoken unto me. And they said, Let us rise up and build. So they strengthened their hands for this good work.

---

GOLDEN TEXT: I told them of the hand of my God which was good upon me; as also the king's words that he had spoken unto me. And they said, Let us rise up and build. So they strengthened their hands for this good work.—Nehemiah 2:18.

---

## God, the People, and the Covenant
Unit 3: Restoration and Covenant Renewal
(Lessons 10-13)

## Lesson Aims

After participating in this lesson, each student will be able to:

1. Describe how Nehemiah made spiritual, political, and practical preparations for the task of rebuilding Jerusalem's walls.

2. Explain how good preparation is important for getting good results in ministry.

3. Plan a service project following Nehemiah's example.

## Lesson Outline

INTRODUCTION
  A. Taking Risks, Exercising Faith
  B. Lesson Background
 I. SADNESS NOTICED (Nehemiah 2:1-3)
  A. Nehemiah's Position (v. 1a)
  B. Nehemiah's Sadness (vv. 1b, 2a)
    *"Put on a Happy Face"*
  C. Nehemiah's Courage (vv. 2b, 3)
 II. OPPORTUNITY SEIZED (Nehemiah 2:4-8)
  A. King's Question (v. 4a)
  B. Nehemiah's Prayer (v. 4b)
  C. Nehemiah's Request (v. 5)
  D. King's Questions (v. 6)
  E. Nehemiah's Requests (vv. 7, 8)
III. TASK INITIATED (Nehemiah 2:11, 17, 18)
  A. Travel and Rest (v. 11)
  B. Observation and Challenge (v. 17)
    *The Power of Symbols*
  C. Authorization and Reply (v. 18)
CONCLUSION
  A. Christian Leadership
  B. Prayer
  C. Thought to Remember

## Introduction

### A. Taking Risks, Exercising Faith

Most people are aware of the theme parks and movies of the Walt Disney Company. Many are unaware, however, of the difficulties that Walt Disney (1901–1966) faced in achieving his success. When Disney returned from France after World War I, he had a vision of creating a company that would focus on the new art medium of animation. He started a company called Laugh-O-Grams for that purpose. But it went bankrupt in 1923.

Disney then went to Hollywood with only his baggage and twenty dollars to restart his business. His first series of animated short cartoons flopped. He had to borrow money from his brother and set up shop in his uncle's garage to keep his struggling animation business alive. But his business slowly grew. When he invented the character Mickey Mouse, who first appeared on screen in 1928, his company was on its way.

Walt Disney's success came by having a vision and being willing to risk failure. Typically, it is that kind of person who accomplishes great things in business. The same is true in the spiritual life. Those who accomplish great things for God tend to be risk takers (although we may question whether it is proper ever to think of work for God as "risky"). Those who walk by great faith have a vision of what God would have them to do and the courage to attempt things that others would avoid. Nehemiah was that kind of visionary leader.

### B. Lesson Background

Nehemiah, whose name means "the Lord comforts," was a devout Jew who lived in the fifth century BC. That was the period of the Persian Empire. This empire came to prominence when Cyrus conquered Babylon in 539 BC.

Nehemiah served as cupbearer to Artaxerxes I, the Persian king who reigned from 464 to 424 BC in an area that is now southwest Iran. Artaxerxes was the son of the biblical Ahasuerus (Ezra 4:6, also known as Xerxes), who was the husband of Esther. Ahasuerus's kingdom stretched "from India even unto Ethiopia" (Esther 1:1). Artaxerxes I came to the throne after his father was assassinated. As cupbearer to Artaxerxes, Nehemiah had direct, personal access to this powerful Persian emperor.

In November or December of 445 BC, Nehemiah learned from a fellow Jew named Hanani that those who had returned from exile to Jerusalem were in distress. It had been more than 90 years since the first exiles had returned to the holy city, and the place was still a ruin (Nehemiah 1:2, 3). This news, which Nehemiah found surprising, may be a reference to the destruction of Jerusalem by the Babylonians in 586 BC. Yet this was old news by Nehemiah's day. Instead Hanani may have been referring to some more recent catastrophe.

The wider backdrop may be as follows. During the years 460–455 BC, Artaxerxes was involved in putting down a revolt in Egypt. This helps explain why in 458 BC he cooperated with the Jew Ezra (see Ezra 7:1-7; Ezra appears alongside Nehemiah in Nehemiah 8). Artaxerxes gave Ezra permission to appoint magistrates who knew the law of Ezra's God (Ezra 7:25, 26). Artaxerxes perhaps hoped to win support in his western province of Judea by allowing the Jews to incorporate more of their own legal traditions into the local administration of justice. In this way he may have hoped to discourage the Jews from joining Egypt in insurrection.

Ezra 4:8-16 records a letter from certain Persian officials to Artaxerxes reporting that the Jews were rebuilding the walls of "rebellious" Jerusalem, undoubtedly seen as a prelude to revolt. Artaxerxes responded by giving those officials permission to stop that rebuilding (Ezra 4:17-23). It is possible that the Persian authorities not only stopped construction of new walls (Ezra 4:23) but also ended up tearing down Jerusalem's walls that had been rebuilt previously (Ezra 4:12). This state of affairs may be what Hanani and his colleagues described later to Nehemiah (Nehemiah 1:2, 3).

Whatever the cause, Nehemiah began praying and considering over a period of four months what he could do to help his fellow countrymen in Judea (Nehemiah 1:4-11). His prayers culminated in asking God to grant him favorable reception by "this man," meaning King Artaxerxes (Nehemiah 1:11).

# I. Sadness Noticed (Nehemiah 2:1-3)

### A. Nehemiah's Position (v. 1a)

**1a. And it came to pass in the month Nisan, in the twentieth year of Artaxerxes the king, that wine was before him: and I took up the wine, and gave it unto the king.**

---

### How to Say It

AHASUERUS. Uh-haz-you-*ee*-rus.
ARTAXERXES. Are-tuh-*zerk*-seez.
ASAPH. *Ay*-saff.
GESHEM. *Gee*-shem (G as in *get*).
HANANI. Huh-*nay*-nye.
NEHEMIAH. *Nee*-huh-*my*-uh (strong accent on *my*).
SANBALLAT. San-*bal*-ut.
SHUSHAN. *Shoo*-shan.
TOBIAH. Toe-*bye*-uh.
XERXES. *Zerk*-seez.

---

*The month Nisan, in the twentieth year of Artaxerxes the king* is March or April of 444 BC. When we compare this date with Nehemiah 1:1, we see that about four months have passed since Nehemiah heard the news about Jerusalem's distress. Thus Nehemiah has a lot of time in which to think, weep, and pray before his encounter with the king (Nehemiah 1:4-11).

Nehemiah comes before King Artaxerxes in Nehemiah's capacity as cupbearer (Nehemiah 1:11). Cupbearer is an important office (Genesis 40:21; 1 Kings 10:5). According to one ancient Greek writer, the cupbearer tastes the king's wine for poison and guards the royal apartment. Such a trusted person can become a confidant and informal counselor of a king and so can influence the king's decisions. Like Esther in the book that bears her name, God has placed a Jew at the right place and time in order to help His people.

### B. Nehemiah's Sadness (vv. 1b, 2a)

**1b, 2a. Now I had not been beforetime sad in his presence. Wherefore the king said unto me, Why is thy countenance sad, seeing thou art not sick? this is nothing else but sorrow of heart.**

One's face can divulge what a person is feeling. The fact that Nehemiah has *not been beforetime sad in* the king's *presence* means that Nehemiah has been able to disguise his feelings over the past several months—putting on a happy face, as it were. But on this particular day, his anguish over his people's condition shows.

The king seems to show genuine concern over the emotional state of his cupbearer. This may say something about the king's capacity for empathy. It also says something about the character of Nehemiah, that he is the sort of person about whom the king is concerned.

Yet the king may have had another motive for asking his question. A gloomy appearance may be evidence of a plot against the king. The courts of ancient kings are hotbeds of intrigue (1 Kings 16:8-10; Esther 2:21-23). Indeed, the king's own father had been assassinated by a member of the court. So a king has good reason to be suspicious of changes in mood among his servants.

### "PUT ON A HAPPY FACE"

The lyrics to the song "Put on a Happy Face" from the 1960s musical *Bye, Bye Birdie* reflect a deeply ingrained aspect of American culture. There is even a Christian Web site where the words of the song are accompanied by the tune, some cheery animation, and Scripture quotations such as Psalm 35:9, which says "my soul shall be joyful in the Lord."

The pursuit of happiness is one of those "un-alienable rights" mentioned in the U.S. Declaration of Independence. However, one curmudgeon says the phrase is "toxic stupidity entirely unworthy of [its author] Thomas Jefferson." He acknowledges the source of his concern: bleak Christmas celebrations in his childhood when his family got drunk in a futile pursuit of "happiness."

Neither this unhappy person nor Nehemiah would likely be cheered up by the sight of the "happy face" symbol we see so often. However, Nehemiah had a better reason for the anguish of his heart: he was consumed by the knowledge that his people were suffering in the ruined city of Jerusalem. There are times when it is entirely inappropriate to "put on a happy face," in spite of our culture's insistence on it!          —C. R. B.

### C. Nehemiah's Courage (vv. 2b, 3)

**2b, 3. Then I was very sore afraid, and said unto the king, Let the king live for ever: why should not my countenance be sad, when the city, the place of my fathers' sepulchres, lieth waste, and the gates thereof are consumed with fire?**

Nehemiah's apprehension about saying why he is *sad* is not unreasonable. Artaxerxes has the power of life and death. If indeed *the gates* of Jerusalem had been burned in conjunction with a real or imagined revolt against Persian authority (see the Lesson Background), then the showing of sympathy for Jerusalem may be taken by *the king* as treason. Nehemiah is putting his life in jeopardy by discussing this matter with the king.

Courage is not necessarily a lack of fear. Courage means acting bravely in spite of fear. Later Nehemiah's courage will be shown in continuing the work on the wall despite the opposition and threat by the forces of Sanballat, Tobiah, and Geshem (Nehemiah 2:10, 19; 4:7, 8).

We should pause to note that while Nehemiah is courageous, he is no fool. He says nothing of the reasons why Jerusalem's gates came to be burned (whether originally in 586 BC or more recently). Instead he emphasizes the fact that the tombs of his ancestors are in ruins. This fact may tug at the king's emotions. Often the way a matter is presented determines how it is received.

## II. Opportunity Seized (Nehemiah 2:4-8)

### A. King's Question (v. 4a)

**4a. Then the king said unto me, For what dost thou make request?**

Artaxerxes responds by offering a royal favor to help Nehemiah. This is exactly what Nehemiah has been praying for (Nehemiah 1:11). Now it appears that God is granting an answer to his prayer.

### B. Nehemiah's Prayer (v. 4b)

**4b. So I prayed to the God of heaven.**

Before Nehemiah makes his request, he prays. Obviously, this is not a long prayer. Rather, it must be what is sometimes called "an arrow prayer"—a brief prayer shot up to Heaven as fast as an arrow. Such a prayer likely consists of little more than a quick whisper of, "Help me, Lord!"

### C. Nehemiah's Request (v. 5)

**5. And I said unto the king, If it please the king, and if thy servant have found favor in thy sight, that thou wouldest send me unto Judah, unto the city of my fathers' sepulchres, that I may build it.**

Nehemiah's previous prayer in Nehemiah 1:11 culminated in asking God for success before "this man," meaning Artaxerxes. This suggests that Nehemiah already has a plan in mind. He is ready to propose that plan if he ever has opportunity to raise the matter to the king. So when the right time arrives and Artaxerxes offers Nehemiah royal assistance, Nehemiah already knows what to request: he wants to return to *Judah* in order to rebuild Jerusalem.

The boldness of this request should again be emphasized! It was by a royal decree of Artaxerxes in Ezra 4:17-22 that the building up of Jerusalem had been stopped forcibly. [See question #1, page 320.]

### D. King's Questions (v. 6)

**6. And the king said unto me, (the queen also sitting by him,) For how long shall thy journey be? and when wilt thou return? So it pleased the king to send me; and I set him a time.**

Artaxerxes and Nehemiah hash out the details of Nehemiah's leave of absence. The king evidently considers Nehemiah a valuable person in his service, so the king negotiates that Nehemiah will *return* after a certain length of time.

The text does not tell us how Nehemiah replies other than *I set him a time.* But his absence ends up being 12 years (see Nehemiah 5:14; 13:6). His stay probably extends beyond the original estimate!

### E. Nehemiah's Requests (vv. 7, 8)

**7, 8. Moreover I said unto the king, If it please the king, let letters be given me to the governors beyond the river, that they may convey me over till I come into Judah; and a letter unto Asaph**

the keeper of the king's forest, that he may give me timber to make beams for the gates of the palace which appertained to the house, and for the wall of the city, and for the house that I shall enter into. And the king granted me, according to the good hand of my God upon me.

Nehemiah goes on to request *letters* permitting him to travel through the empire. Nehemiah in essence is making himself the governor of *Judah* in asking for travel papers. Such papers will provide the royal permission needed to travel through regions of other *governors.*

Nehemiah knows he will need construction material. So he asks for *timber* to be provided by a certain *Asaph,* the official in charge of *the king's* western *forest.* Asaph is a Jewish name. An earlier Asaph was a Levite musician who wrote several psalms at the time of David (1 Chronicles 16:5; see the superscriptions of Psalms 50; 73–83). The king generously grants Nehemiah's requests. [See question #2, page 320.]

## III. Task Initiated
## (Nehemiah 2:11, 17, 18)

### A. Travel and Rest (v. 11)

**11. So I came to Jerusalem, and was there three days.**

The text does not describe what certainly is an arduous journey of nearly 1,100 miles from Shushan *to Jerusalem.* Naturally, Nehemiah's first priority is to get some rest upon arrival. It is unwise to undertake a great task when one is exhausted. [See question #3, page 320.]

But no doubt Nehemiah already is planning what he will do. After the three-day rest, he obtains an animal to ride. During the night, when no one will recognize him, he inspects the walls around the city (Nehemiah 2:12-16; not in today's text). Thus before he brings up the matter to the local officials, Nehemiah is making plans concerning how best to proceed.

### B. Observation and Challenge (v. 17)

**17. Then said I unto them, Ye see the distress that we are in, how Jerusalem lieth waste, and the gates thereof are burned with fire: come, and let us build up the wall of Jerusalem, that we be no more a reproach.**

After inspecting the walls and formulating his plans, Nehemiah now makes a public announcement. His audience is the priests, nobles, rulers, and "the rest" according to verse 16. Up to this time, they have not been told why Nehemiah has come to Jerusalem. We wonder how shocked the audience must be to hear Nehemiah now exhort

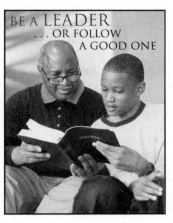

Visual for
Lesson 11

*Point to this visual as you ask your learners to name good leaders they have followed.*

them to join in his great task of rebuilding the walls of Jerusalem.

City walls in ancient times are very important. The most obvious reason is physical security. But there is an important emotional reason too: the city is an object of derision and mockery *(a reproach)* in its current state (compare 2 Chronicles 7:20; Psalm 44:13, 14). Jerusalem is supposed to be the holy city, the site of God's temple. It should be maintained in a way appropriate to this distinction.

We should also note the power of symbols. The biggest danger for the Jews is that of assimilation into the surrounding pagan culture. The successful rebuilding of Jerusalem's walls will be a symbol that God has not forsaken His people.

THE POWER OF SYMBOLS

What is the most important symbol in your life? In a materialistic culture, many things can vie for top symbolic meaning. Luxury cars, yachts, and Rolex® watches can be on such a list.

Many scoff at such symbols of "conspicuous consumption." Yet material symbols are not always bad. Note the challenge Nehemiah presented to his fellow Jews: "Let us build up the wall of Jerusalem, *that we be no more a reproach.*" The important question for us to ask is, "Who was being disgraced?"

Jerusalem with its temple was supposed to be a symbol of God's presence among a certain people of the time. The implication is that the city's disrepair was a symbolic disgrace to the God of the Hebrews as the one true God. When we apply this outlook to the way we "build" our lives for God, we may be embarrassed at our prideful thinking! People will take notice of the symbols with which we surround ourselves, because those symbols indicate what we value. More importantly, God will notice.      —C. R. B.

### C. Authorization and Reply (v. 18)

**18. Then I told them of the hand of my God which was good upon me; as also the king's words that he had spoken unto me. And they said, Let us rise up and build. So they strengthened their hands for this good work.**

Nehemiah rallies the people around him by giving a stirring testimony of how God already has worked providentially in bringing him to Jerusalem. Nehemiah demonstrates that God is behind this plan to rebuild the walls of Jerusalem. This testimony helps inspire the Jews to help with the project. [See question #4, page 320.]

## Conclusion

### A. Christian Leadership

Nehemiah comes across as an ideal leader of God's people. First, Nehemiah was concerned for others. Though he himself was a worldly success, having risen to an important office in the service of the Persian state, he remained concerned about his countrymen who were less well off. When he heard of the distress of his people in distant Jerusalem, he began to look for an opportunity to help. The New Testament likewise calls us to help others (see 1 John 3:17; etc.).

Second, Nehemiah was willing to step out on faith. By showing concern for his people before the Persian king, Nehemiah jeopardized his own rank and privileges. The New Testament calls us to do likewise (see Mark 10:29, 30).

## Home Daily Bible Readings

**Monday, May 5**—A Lament for Jerusalem (Psalm 137:1-7)
**Tuesday, May 6**—Weeping and Fasting (Nehemiah 1:1-4)
**Wednesday, May 7**—Nehemiah's Confession (Nehemiah 1:5-11)
**Thursday, May 8**—Permission to Return (Nehemiah 2:1-10)
**Friday, May 9**—A Secret Inspection (Nehemiah 2:11-16)
**Saturday, May 10**—Determination to Rebuild (Nehemiah 2:17-20)
**Sunday, May 11**—Giving Thanks to God (Psalm 138:1-5)

Third, Nehemiah was willing to make sacrifices. Nehemiah voluntarily stepped down from his position in the royal court and traveled an enormous distance to serve God's people. The New Testament does not call every Christian to travel to a foreign land, but we are to live lives of sacrifice (Mark 12:43, 44; Acts 2:45).

Fourth, Nehemiah was a man of prayer. As a godly Jew, he was concerned about the fact that the holy city of Jerusalem, symbol of God's presence among His people, was in disarray. When his opportunity before King Artaxerxes presented itself, he first sent up an arrow prayer to God. But months of prayer by Nehemiah had prepared the way for his request before the king. And Nehemiah clearly saw that the unfolding opportunity was from the hand of God. Great Christian leaders are people of prayer, even when they are also people of action (Acts 20:36).

Fifth, Nehemiah took time to plan things out. He waited months for just the right time before making a request to the king about rebuilding. When he made the request, he knew just what he needed to ask for because he had thought things through. When he arrived in Jerusalem, he took time to think and plan before speaking to others about his dreams. Planning ahead is not a failure to walk by faith, as Nehemiah's example shows us. Paul's work reveals him to be a man of planning (2 Corinthians 8:16–9:5).

Sixth, Nehemiah knew how to motivate others. He had no power by himself to build the wall of Jerusalem. He needed help and cooperation. But without manipulation he skillfully mobilized the people behind his plan. [See question #5, page 320.] The fact that the community of faith joined him was confirmation that God had in fact raised up Nehemiah for this purpose. Today as then, God does not call all of His people to be super-duper motivational leaders as Nehemiah was. But we all can be good followers. Whether a leader or a follower, the prelude to action is personal holiness (1 Peter 1:13-16).

### B. Prayer

Lord, thank You for godly leaders like Nehemiah who have the vision to see the tasks You would have them do and the courage to carry them out. Help us to have the same kind of passion that Nehemiah had. May we have also Nehemiah's zeal and wisdom to accomplish what You would have us do. In Jesus' name we ask this, amen.

### C. Thought to Remember

God still honors courage.

# Learning by Doing

*This page contains an alternative lesson plan emphasizing learning activities.*
*Classes desiring such student involvement will find these suggestions helpful.*

## Into the Lesson

Display a simple sketch of a block wall, with each block large enough for writing a word or phrase. Across the top of the wall, write *What Does It Take to Build a Wall?* Let learners suggest elements as you write suggestions in the blocks.

Encourage responses to include not only tangible elements (such as bricks and mortar) but also intangibles (such as initiative and planning). (A similar activity is included in the optional student book.) Discuss.

## Into the Word

Use the completed activity above to make a transition into a study of today's text by asking the class to note the ways the named elements formed parts of Nehemiah's plan. For example, Nehemiah secured wood for his task as part of the king's decree (tangible), and Nehemiah surrounded his job with prayer (intangible). Ask your learners also to discuss this question: "How does Nehemiah's procedure reflect the maxim *An ounce of preparation results in a pound of production?*"

After discussing that maxim, say, "Nehemiah did certain things as he demonstrated wisdom in leadership. As I read the following, identify a verse or verses in Nehemiah 1 and 2 that reveal each." (A similar activity is included in the optional student book.)

1. Prayed and planned for months. 2. Revealed his true feelings—had no hypocrisy. 3. Boldly expressed his concerns to the one who could help him do something. 4. Prayed spontaneously for God's help. 5. Agreed to his superior's requests. 6. Stated his requests clearly and thoroughly. 7. Credited God for his successes. 8. Rested before initiating a long and difficult job. 9. Solicited the help of others. 10. Maintained clear-cut goals and noble purposes.

Your learners should easily relate these actions and characteristics to the verses of today's text and other verses in the first two chapters of Nehemiah. *Potential answers: 1. 1:1; 2:1; 2. 2:1, 2; 3. 2:3; 4. 2:4; 5. 2:6; 6. 2:7, 8; 7. 2:8; 8. 2:11; 9. 2:17, 18; 10. 2:17, 18.*

Wrap up this task with this question: "How do you see these actions and attitudes in the lives of contemporary leaders, both in business and in the church?" (To keep the conversation from turning negative, you may wish to ask for positive examples only.)

To highlight Nehemiah's prayer life, say, "The picture of Nehemiah's request and the king who granted it tell us something about the power of prayer. Consider the following list of features of Nehemiah's request and the nature of the responses. Note first how it is seen in today's text; then note how it can characterize our prayer life with God the Father." (A similar activity is included in the optional student book.)

1. Request comes in the midst of faithful service and submission; 2. Request is made to a caring, sensitive superior; 3. Request is made in reverential fear; 4. Request is made only after praise to the one asked; 5. Request is both bold and specific; 6. Request is not selfish, but for the welfare of God's people; 7. Request is graciously granted; 8. The grace involved in the request granted is told to others.

Here are examples of observations your learners may offer: for 1, *Nehemiah earned the king's trust by years of careful performance of his duties, and the more we demonstrate our faith and commitment to God, the more He trusts and honors our petitions;* for 8, *to the people of Jerusalem, Nehemiah revealed the way the king had honored his requests (v. 18), and we need to tell others when God graciously honors our petitions, as a witness to Him.*

Suggest that each learner use these as criteria for evaluating his or her own prayer life.

## Into Life

Distribute a half-page copy of a block wall sketch similar to that used in the introductory activity. Label this one *What Does It Take to Build a Life?*

Say, "Nehemiah was not concerned solely with building a wall. He was concerned about building the lives of his fellow Jews into a strong nation for God. Take this wall home with you this week and reflect on the important components in building one's life to be a part of the church that is able to defend itself from enemies and prepared to assemble for worship in unity." You can suggest that your learners bring their walls back to class next week for a time of sharing.

# Let's Talk It Over

*The questions on this page are designed to promote discussion of the lesson by the class and to encourage application of the lesson Scriptures. The answers provided are only discussion starters. Let your class talk it over from there.*

**1. Why should we take risks for God? Or is it ever proper to think of service for God as risky? Explain.**

Did Nehemiah take a risk in asking the king to allow him to rebuild the walls of Jerusalem? Did Jonathan take a risk when only he and his armor bearer went to fight against an entire Philistine garrison in 1 Samuel 14? To be willing to lose one's life in the service of God is to truly find life (see Luke 17:33).

Men and women of the Bible risked all they had on numerous occasions. As a result, great things were accomplished. These people put their faith and trust in God in a very real way, and they were rewarded. When we step out on faith, we are able to see God's working more clearly; this encourages further steps of faith. From an eternal perspective, to step out on faith is not risky at all since God is in control. From that viewpoint, to fail to step out on faith is the real risk!

**2. With the life of Nehemiah as a guide, what should we do when preparing for a project? Is there anything about Nehemiah's life that should not be used as a guide for today? Explain.**

As soon as Nehemiah recognized a need, he brought the need before the Lord in prayer. He understood the teaching to "commit thy works unto the Lord, and thy thoughts shall be established" (Proverbs 16:3). Before Nehemiah did anything, he prayed, even months before he brought his proposal to the king.

Nehemiah prepared supplies for the task, just as David did in preparation for Solomon's building of the temple (1 Chronicles 22:5). Nehemiah surveyed the damage and determined the extent of the problem. With this information in mind, he organized his people and began the project. Good preparation can be a key to the success of any project. Examples of hasty, ill-conceived plans and actions are seen in Numbers 14:39-45 and 1 Chronicles 17:2.

**3. Why and when is it important to take rest? What have been your experiences (good and bad) in this regard?**

Before Nehemiah began the task of rebuilding the walls, he spent three days resting. God instituted a day of rest for the Israelites to remember both Him and the time when they had been slaves and had no day of rest (see Deuteronomy 5:14, 15).

The human body needs rest in order to recover, heal, and grow. Exhaustion is dangerous, for our spiritual defenses are weaker at that time. Satan chose a time of physical exhaustion for Jesus to tempt Him in the wilderness (Matthew 4:1-11). An exhausted person does not have the energy to begin a project well, let alone complete one.

A well-rested person, on the other hand, has the strength of body and the clarity of mind to take on the Lord's task. To be sure, a sluggard is condemned (see Proverbs 6:9-11; compare Mark 14:37, 38). Yet God's servants need their rest in order to accomplish His work. The modern "24/7" idea of activity is a recipe for disaster.

**4. When have you found it helpful to recall God's dealings from the past?**

It is much easier to trust someone who has proven faithful in the past than to have to trust someone with whom you have had no experience. "But the Lord is faithful, who shall stablish you, and keep you from evil" (2 Thessalonians 3:3). God has been faithful and will continue to be faithful. With the completion of both Old and New Testaments, we can see this much clearer than Nehemiah was able to! But this also means we are more accountable. Such knowledge should be very encouraging in reminding us of the power at God's disposal and His willingness to use that power.

**5. What were the qualities and characteristics in Nehemiah that made him such an effective leader? How can you develop these in your own life?**

Nehemiah had several qualities that can and should be found in godly leaders, as noted in the lesson Conclusion. Finding a spiritually mature mentor will help you to develop some of those qualities. Reading secular books on leadership can help to a point, but these must be used with great discretion.

# Finishing the Task

DEVOTIONAL READING: **Psalm 71:1-6.**

BACKGROUND SCRIPTURE: **Nehemiah 4–6.**

PRINTED TEXT: **Nehemiah 4:1-3, 6-9, 13-15; 6:15.**

### Nehemiah 4:1-3, 6-9, 13-15

1 But it came to pass, that when Sanballat heard that we builded the wall, he was wroth, and took great indignation, and mocked the Jews.

2 And he spake before his brethren and the army of Samaria, and said, What do these feeble Jews? will they fortify themselves? will they sacrifice? will they make an end in a day? will they revive the stones out of the heaps of the rubbish which are burned?

3 Now Tobiah the Ammonite was by him, and he said, Even that which they build, if a fox go up, he shall even break down their stone wall.

· · · · · · · · · · · ·

6 So built we the wall; and all the wall was joined together unto the half thereof: for the people had a mind to work.

7 But it came to pass, that when Sanballat, and Tobiah, and the Arabians, and the Ammonites, and the Ashdodites, heard that the walls of Jerusalem were made up, and

that the breaches began to be stopped, then they were very wroth,

8 And conspired all of them together to come and to fight against Jerusalem, and to hinder it.

9 Nevertheless we made our prayer unto our God, and set a watch against them day and night, because of them.

· · · · · · · · · · · ·

13 Therefore set I in the lower places behind the wall, and on the higher places, I even set the people after their families with their swords, their spears, and their bows.

14 And I looked, and rose up, and said unto the nobles, and to the rulers, and to the rest of the people, Be not ye afraid of them: remember the Lord, which is great and terrible, and fight for your brethren, your sons, and your daughters, your wives, and your houses.

15 And it came to pass, when our enemies heard that it was known unto us, and God had brought their counsel to nought, that we returned all of us to the wall, every one unto his work.

### Nehemiah 6:15

15 So the wall was finished in the twenty and fifth day of the month Elul, in fifty and two days.

GOLDEN TEXT: So built we the wall; and all the wall was joined together unto the half thereof: for the people had a mind to work.—Nehemiah 4:6.

*God, the People, and the Covenant*
Unit 3: Restoration and Covenant Renewal
(Lessons 10-13)

## Lesson Aims

After participating in this lesson, each student will be able to:

1. Describe how Nehemiah overcame opposition in rebuilding Jerusalem's walls.

2. Give an example of faith that overcomes adversity.

3. Make a plan to identify, take charge of, and complete a project or ministry that is facing opposition.

## Lesson Outline

INTRODUCTION
  A. Perseverance Through Opposition
  B. Lesson Background
 I. OPPOSITION (Nehemiah 4:1-3)
  A. Sanballat (vv. 1, 2)
  B. Tobiah (v. 3)
II. Determination (Nehemiah 4:6-9)
  A. Having a Mind to Work (v. 6)
  B. Having a Mind to Hinder (vv. 7, 8)
  C. Having a Mind to Pray and Watch (v. 9)
    *Willingness*
III. VICTORY (Nehemiah 4:13-15; 6:15)
  A. Strengthen the Weak Areas (v. 13)
    *Guns and Butter?*
  B. Remember Whom You Work For (v. 14a)
  C. Remember What's at Stake (v. 14b)
  D. Remember Who's in Charge (v. 15)
  E. Take Note of the Result (6:15)
CONCLUSION
  A. Finishing the Task
  B. Prayer
  C. Thought to Remember

## Introduction

### A. Perseverance Through Opposition

Jason was a young Christian who had a vision to reach youth. He worked hard to organize a rally as a means to bring the gospel to them. His enthusiasm was certainly not lacking as he called others to join him in his vision of winning his peers to Christ.

Although there were many who supported Jason's work and shared in it by giving of their time, finances, and prayers, Jason quickly learned that with any worthy cause comes opposition. Jason heard the comments firsthand. "This is never going to work." "I don't believe anybody will attend, even if it gets organized." Some questioned his integrity—"Jason just wants to be the boss" or "he has to be in the limelight."

After hearing these comments, it didn't take very long for Jason to begin doubting whether he should continue to try to launch this outreach rally. Then came the other disappointments. People said they would help and then would not show up. Rumors spread that the rally had been canceled due to lack of interest. The posters, which had already been mailed out, had the main speaker's name misspelled.

Jason, however, continued to pray. He continued to seek support from those who shared his vision. He pressed forward despite opposition and doubts, and the rally was held as scheduled. There have been many more rallies in Jason's community since that first one, each having some sort of opposition and each being used by the Lord to further His kingdom.

Stories similar to Jason's are being acted out all over the world by God's people, because with every good work of God there are those who will try to stop it. Unfortunately, not all good works end with victory. Many works cease because the worker was not prepared for the opposition—the discouragement was just too much. Today we are going to discover biblical principles that will strengthen us to continue the Lord's work in spite of opposition.

### B. Lesson Background

The Judeans returned from the Babylonian captivity in 3 waves. The first wave, of about 50,000 returnees, was in 538 BC, as led by Sheshbazzar (Ezra 1:1, 11). The second wave, of less than 2,000 men, was led by Ezra 80 years later (Ezra 7:1-9). The third wave was 13 or 14 years after the second. It was led by Nehemiah, although we don't know how many Judeans accompanied him (Nehemiah 2:11).

Although the returned exiles were able to complete the rebuilding of the temple by 515 BC, the walls of the city remained in their ruined state. The walls had been destroyed by the Chaldeans (Babylonians) in 586 BC.

As we saw last week, Nehemiah was the cupbearer of King Artaxerxes of Persia (reigned 464–424 BC). When Nehemiah heard about the condition of the city and its gates, he prayed to God and approached the king to seek permission to return to Jerusalem to rebuild. Artaxerxes granted his request. As God's chosen man, Nehemiah arrived to inspect the ruined walls and lead the people in a campaign to rebuild them.

# I. Opposition
## (Nehemiah 4:1-3)

Nehemiah 3, which occurs between last week's text and today's, shows us Nehemiah and his work crew in action. Great progress is made in building the wall, despite the anger of some neighboring officials. But the opposition is about to kick things up a notch!

## A. Sanballat (vv. 1, 2)

**1. But it came to pass, that when Sanballat heard that we builded the wall, he was wroth, and took great indignation, and mocked the Jews.**

We first meet *Sanballat* in Nehemiah 2:10. He is governor of Samaria. The Samaritans are located just to the north of Judah. They are of mixed origin, composed of the descendants of Israelites who intermarried with foreign colonists brought in by the king of Assyria after the northern kingdom's deportation in 722 BC (2 Kings 17). The Samaritans had offered to help rebuild the temple earlier, but were rebuffed (Ezra 4:1-5). Do we detect some smoldering resentment?

Opposition toward what is good and right starts in the heart. Nehemiah's arrival in Jerusalem to promote "the welfare of the children of Israel" (Nehemiah 2:10) draws Sanballat's initial displeasure. As the work to rebuild the walls proceeds, his displeasure turns to great anger. He does not want the city of Jerusalem to be strengthened, possibly because he wants to be governor of Judea as well as Samaria.

When we are engaged in God's work, we should not be surprised when opposition comes.

---

### How to Say It

AMMONITES. *Am*-un-ites.
ARABIANS. Uh-*ray*-bee-unz.
ASHDODITES. *Ash*-duh-dites.
BABYLONIAN. Bab-ih-*low*-nee-un.
CHALDEANS. Kal-*dee*-unz.
EZRA. *Ez*-ruh.
NEHEMIAH. *Nee*-huh-*my*-uh (strong accent on *my*).
SAMARIA. Suh-*mare*-ee-uh.
SANBALLAT. San-*bal*-ut.
SHESHBAZZAR. Shesh-*baz*-ar.
TOBIAH. Toe-*bye*-uh.

---

The enemies of God will be angry at attempts to build Christ's kingdom (John 15:20; 2 Timothy 3:12). [See question #1, page 328.]

**2. And he spake before his brethren and the army of Samaria, and said, What do these feeble Jews? will they fortify themselves? will they sacrifice? will they make an end in a day? will they revive the stones out of the heaps of the rubbish which are burned?**

As is often the case, opposition includes mocking. Personal attacks on the character of someone who chooses to do what is right are common even today. Here we see Sanballat using a series of rhetorical questions to call into question the character of the workmen.

Sanballat's earlier mocking was intended for the ears of the Judeans themselves, to discourage them directly (Nehemiah 2:19). The same is true here since Nehemiah 4:5 describes the insults occurring "before the builders." But now the mockery is also for the ears of *his brethren and the army of Samaria.* [See question #2, page 328.]

If Sanballat's cronies take his word to heart, they will be emboldened in their opposition. Thus Sanballat's mocking serves not only as an attempt to discourage the Jews, but also as a kind of pep talk to his buddies. "These silly Jews actually think they can carry through with this project with the few resources they have!" The one thing that Sanballat is unable to see is that God is with the Jews, that He is their supply and support.

## B. Tobiah (v. 3)

**3. Now Tobiah the Ammonite was by him, and he said, Even that which they build, if a fox go up, he shall even break down their stone wall.**

The opposition and mockery from *Tobiah the Ammonite* now builds on what we see from him in Nehemiah 2:10, 19. Ammon is to the northeast of Judah. The Ammonites are longtime enemies of the Jewish people.

Faithful workers for God will have not only their character ridiculed, they will also see the work they are doing scorned. That's what we see Tobiah doing here. "What quality of workmanship can this be if even the weight of a mere *fox* will cause their *wall* to collapse?" There is no part of the Lord's work that will not be looked on with contempt by His enemies.

Mocking is one of the easiest things to do and one of the favorite weapons of opposition. If God's worker is not prepared when it happens, it can cut deep. It may leave a broken heart and a crushed spirit that may be difficult to endure (Psalm 89:50; Jeremiah 20:7; etc.).

## II. Determination (Nehemiah 4:6-9)

Between verse 3 (above) and verse 6 (next) is a prayer of Nehemiah against the enemies. We notice in this prayer that Nehemiah directs his reaction to God, not to the enemies. The prayer looks like what we see at Jeremiah 18:23.

### A. Having a Mind to Work (v. 6)

**6. So built we the wall; and all the wall was joined together unto the half thereof: for the people had a mind to work.**

Despite the anger and mocking of their enemies, the Jews continue their work. They get to the point where they have built up *half* the *wall*. Because they have *a mind to work*, they do not allow the attempted distractions to stop them from achieving their mission. They continue to move forward, setting their hearts on completing the work God has given them instead of wallowing in their difficulties.

We can see the value of teamwork as God's people join together in a single-minded work. Everyone does his or her part, and no part of the wall is left undone. Cooperation means that the wall goes up at a rapid pace.

### B. Having a Mind to Hinder (vv. 7, 8)

**7, 8. But it came to pass, that when Sanballat, and Tobiah, and the Arabians, and the Ammonites, and the Ashdodites, heard that the walls of Jerusalem were made up, and that the breaches began to be stopped, then they were very wroth, and conspired all of them together to come and to fight against Jerusalem, and to hinder it.**

Visual for Lesson 12

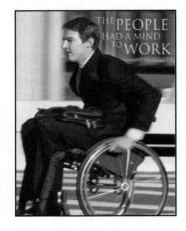

*Use this visual as you discuss verse 6. Ask, "What are some things we allow to distract us?"*

We now see more enemies mentioned, namely *Arabians* and *Ashdodites.* The Arabians probably are to the south, while the Ashdodites are to the east. Counting Samaria and Ammon, Judah is surrounded by enemies!

The progress that Nehemiah and the workers make on *the walls of Jerusalem* does not cause the opposition to cease, but instead makes the opposition even more determined to *hinder* the completion of the project. It has become obvious to *Sanballat* and *Tobiah* that their attempts to discourage through ridicule are not slowing the workers down. So these two increase their efforts by drawing in neighboring people to join their plot to hinder the work by force.

### C. Having a Mind to Pray and Watch (v. 9)

**9. Nevertheless we made our prayer unto our God, and set a watch against them day and night, because of them.**

While the enemy conspires, Nehemiah prepares to face the opposition by combining faith in God with action. The faith and action take the forms of *prayer* and setting *a watch.*

Before Nehemiah does anything else, he seeks God's protection and guidance. (See how Nehemiah prays in Nehemiah 1:5-11; 4:4, 5; 5:19; 6:9b, 14; 13:14, 22, 31.) Having confidence in God's protection and favor does not rule out the obligation that the godly person has to watch out for the traps of the enemy. The Scriptures match together the ideas of watching and praying (see Matthew 26:41; 1 Peter 4:7).

God will protect those who watch as well as pray. It has been said that prayer without watchfulness is presumption and watchfulness without prayer is sinful self-confidence. The two truly work together to enable the worker to keep going in the face of opposition. [See question #3, page 328.]

#### WILLINGNESS

In America's Great Depression of the 1930s, vast numbers of people were desperate for work. So when construction of the Empire State Building began in 1930, some 3,400 men counted themselves fortunate to get jobs. Their bleak circumstances gave them "a mind to work." And work they did: it took only 410 days to complete the task.

The building of the 1,453-foot tower was called one of the most remarkable feats of the twentieth century. It stood as the tallest building in the world until 1972. The building demonstrated what concerted and cooperative human effort could accomplish, a symbol of "what we were capable of," as architectural historian Carol Willis said.

In a sense, Nehemiah was also an architectural historian. His description of the rebuilding of Jerusalem's walls shows us what God's people were able to do in spite of fierce opposition as they toiled together with a common purpose. They were willing to work, they cooperated with others who shared with them in the task, they committed the project to God in prayer, and they watched carefully for anything that might hinder their work.

This is still a good formula for projects that God's people labor to complete. What project is your church attempting that needs this kind of dedication?
—C. R. B.

## III. Victory
## (Nehemiah 4:13-15; 6:15)

The enemy's mocking does not discourage the workers in and of itself. But when the threat of force is added, the people began to lose heart (vv. 10-12, not in today's text). So Nehemiah takes special action to reverse this morale problem.

### A. Strengthen the Weak Areas (v. 13)

**13. Therefore set I in the lower places behind the wall, and on the higher places, I even set the people after their families with their swords, their spears, and their bows.**

Nehemiah shows his shrewdness in military tactics and human nature. He sees certain areas that need to be strengthened, and he does so. He supplies the weapons necessary for defense. Positioning those with weapons *after their families* provides another reason to work and defend the city together.

#### GUNS AND BUTTER?

Earlier, we discussed the construction of the Empire State Building that was part of America's attempt to put people back to work in the 1930s. In 1933, Nazi Germany initiated its own public works program. Government spending increased sixfold in 6 years. Unemployment dropped from 6 million (34 percent) to nearly zero, with 1 million of those being drafted into the military. Many of the newly employed began working on armaments. Thus began the military buildup that led to the tragedy of World War II.

This militaristic approach to recovery from economic depression came to be called "guns, not butter" or sometimes "guns before butter." The idea is that people must forego personal comforts while fighting (or preparing to fight) a

war. Once the war is won, the implied promise is that the good times will roll. But we all know the result of Nazi lies.

When Nehemiah established an armed force, he was not creating an army of conquest that would bring back booty for everyone to enjoy. The arming of the Jews was for defensive purposes only. Their "butter" was the protection of their families (v. 14, below) and a renewed, secure city for the glory of God. And that was "butter enough" for them to keep working!

God still calls His people to work and to vigilance. The distribution of earthly "butter" will not always be what we think is fair. But God's eternal reward will make it all worthwhile.     —C. R. B.

### B. Remember Whom You Work For (v. 14a)

**14a. And I looked, and rose up, and said unto the nobles, and to the rulers, and to the rest of the people, Be not ye afraid of them: remember the Lord, which is great and terrible.**

Any large task can be tiring. There are pressures that cause disappointment and discouragement. It is probable that as Nehemiah looks things over he can see the enemy making preparations to attack. The appearance of the opposition may be overwhelming, with the thought of defending the city and finishing the wall hard to contemplate.

Yet Nehemiah knows that the cure for fatigue, fear, and discouragement is to *remember the Lord, which is great and terrible*. The sight of the enemies may seem great and terrible, but in comparison to the living God, they are not nearly as intimidating. Reminding the people of this truth, Nehemiah tells his workers to *be not ye afraid of them* (compare 2 Kings 6:13-17).

### C. Remember What's at Stake (v. 14b)

**14b. And fight for your brethren, your sons, and your daughters, your wives, and your houses.**

When up against opposition, it is easy to think more about what is happening to us and what it is going to cost us rather than who will be affected by our actions. Here Nehemiah reminds the workers that they are fighting for a noble cause. If these men became too discouraged to fight, their families will be ravaged and destroyed by the enemy. That's motivation!

### D. Remember Who's in Charge (v. 15)

**15. And it came to pass, when our enemies heard that it was known unto us, and God had brought their counsel to nought, that we returned all of us to the wall, every one unto his work.**

The planned surprise attack by Nehemiah's *enemies* is no longer a surprise. So the enemies abandon their plan. It is difficult to assault a fortified position when the defenders are expecting an attack and are prepared to fight back. The sight of God's people standing strong on the partially rebuilt wall, prepared to defend themselves against an attack, is enough to discourage the opposition. [See question #4, page 328.]

Nehemiah's tactics succeed, but he gives credit to God. This is not the first time God has caused His enemies to despair (Exodus 15:14-16; 23:27, 28; Deuteronomy 2:25). The focus of this and other texts is on what God achieves within a community of believers. It is evident that God is working through the people's prayers and actions to protect and strengthen them. Knowing that God is working through them and that He has brought the enemies' plan to nothing leads the Jews to return to *work.* They have confidence in God's protection and provisions.

### E. Take Note of the Result (6:15)

**15. So the wall was finished in the twenty and fifth day of the month Elul, in fifty and two days.**

The enemies said it couldn't be done! "They are too feeble." "It will never work." "If a fox jumps on it, it will break down." When the ridicule doesn't work, the enemies contemplate using force, planning to attack the Jews. Their plan is frustrated and *the wall* is now *finished.* What a hectic 52 *days* it has been! The short time is a testimony to the power of God and the zeal of the workers. [See question #5, page 328.]

*The month of Elul* corresponds with the latter part of August and the beginning of September on our calendar. The year is 444 BC. Nehemiah's

vision has become a reality—and we are less than halfway through the book of Nehemiah at this point!

Despite opposition that comes both from within and without (6:14), Nehemiah never loses sight of his mission and for whom he is working. Nehemiah will continue to seek the guidance of God through prayer. Nehemiah will continue to encourage his fellow workers all the way.

## Conclusion

### A. Finishing the Task

The fruit of the efforts by Nehemiah and the workers brought glory to God (Nehemiah 6:16). The efforts resulted in emotional and physical security for the Judeans. Undoubtedly there was joy at accomplishing a task against tremendous odds (compare Ezra 3:10-13).

We have a wonderful example of godly and devout leadership in Nehemiah. He was a man of prayer who had his heart in God's work. We see Nehemiah engaging in self-denying labor while inspiring others to do the same. He was steadfast in his work, not easily sidetracked. He depended on God and was ready to give Him the glory.

God has called the church to a tremendous task of strengthening its members and taking the gospel to a lost and dying world. It is important that the church be led by people who exemplify the characteristics of Nehemiah. There will be opposition—there always has been—but as God's men and women join together with the same goal in mind, we will be able to accomplish great things for the glory of God.

What has God called you to do? Whatever it is, do not let the size of the task or the amount of time it will take to complete it keep you from setting your heart and hand to it. No job is too big and no problem is too great when we are following God every step of the way. God has called us and equipped us to finish the tasks of the church despite the opposition.

### B. Prayer

Holy Father, thank You for Your faithfulness to Your people and to Your work. Without the assurance of Your love and guidance toward us, we would not be able to stand. Strengthen us to accomplish what You have called each of us to do. Cause our focus to remain on Your great character when we are faced with a difficult task. In Jesus' name, amen.

### C. Thought to Remember

Focusing on God leads to victory.

# Learning by Doing

*This page contains an alternative lesson plan emphasizing learning activities.*
*Classes desiring such student involvement will find these suggestions helpful.*

## Into the Lesson

Wrap several small boxes in gray paper so that the boxes resemble stones (or use brick-colored paper, if available). Each box is to be empty except for the word *GOD* written on a small slip of paper inside. Begin class with the boxes stacked in view of your learners.

Say, "In today's text, the enemies of God's people looked at Nehemiah's wall and were amused. They said, 'You don't even have enough boxes for a good wall!' and 'I could crush those blocks with one hand.'" (Take a small, flimsy box and do so.) "Why, I'll huff and I'll puff and blow the whole thing down!" (Do so.)

Then remark, "But those enemies didn't see what was inside that wall." Hand boxes to several learners and say, "Look inside." Have someone tell what's in the box. Then continue, "Nehemiah's enemies saw only rocks and half-armed soldiers. They never realized that Almighty God was in the project. Today's study is a confirmation of this truth: *When God is in it, expect success!*"

## Into the Word

Prepare half-sheets of paper with one of the following affirmations and verse numbers printed on each. Establish study pairs or small groups; give each pair or group one of the sheets. (If your class is small, give more than one sheet to each group.) Include the following directions on each sheet: "Think about the maxim printed below in two ways. First, what is its relationship to today's Bible text? Second, what is its relationship to godly living in any time and place?" Give the pairs or groups a few minutes, then call for short responses.

*Affirmations and texts:* 1. Evil becomes easier in bad company (vv. 1, 3, 7, 8); 2. A mind to work beats a mind to meddle every time (v. 6); 3. Being armed with prayer may not be enough. Better be armed with practical wisdom too (v. 9); 4. Families that defend together, depend together (vv. 13-15); 5. Realizing that God is against you deflates the boldest mischief (4:15); 6. Anger is a poor foundation for action (vv. 7, 8); 7. Nothing pops the mocker's balloon better than the sharp pin of success (6:15). (These statements are also printed in the optional student book.)

To help impress the class that these were real people in a real struggle, tell them you're going to read some "could-have-been quotes" from the occasion. You want them to identify who would have said it and in what verse of the text. Quotes are given here in random order; the answers, which you should not reveal right away, are in parentheses.

*Could-have-been quotes:* 1. "I'll defend my family and my city!" *(a soldier guarding the lower places, v. 13)*; 2. "It's a poor excuse for a wall!" *(Tobiah, v. 3)*; 3. "God, help us finish!" *(Nehemiah and others, v. 9)*; 4. "Let's push to get it halfway." *(the builders, v. 6)*; 5. "Let's go get 'em!" *(Tobiah, Sanballat, and their allies, v. 8)*; 6. "Silly Jews!" *(Sanballat, v. 2)*; 7. "We're too late!" *(the enemies, 6:15)*; 8. "Why fear men when God is on your side?" *(Nehemiah, v. 14a)*; 9. You can't build a wall out of gravel!" *(Sanballat, v. 2)*; 10. "You're not fighting to defend a wall; you're fighting to defend your family and friends!" *(Nehemiah, v. 14b)*.

You may wish to ask this at the end: "What else do you hear the people of today's text saying?" Let learners respond freely and imaginatively. Some possibilities: "So soon?" *(an enemy at the completion of the wall)* or "Glory Hallelujah!" *(one of the builders on the fifty-second day)*.

## Into Life

Refer to the title of today's study: "Finishing the Task." Say, "Many of the tasks the church needs to accomplish face opposition and simply fizzle out. What are some such projects that fit this description?" Let the class identify some. Possible responses include under-financed building repairs, benevolent projects that some believe unnecessary, and complicated strategies for new church work in what some deem to be "impossible" places. (Caution: the possibility exists for the discussion to become very negative if your church has had recent problems in such areas.)

After a list is suggested, challenge your learners to consider one such unfinished task that they can help complete. Make the matter a prayer emphasis as class is concluded. Consider sending all your learners a postcard or e-mail reminder this week with this simple message: *Finish the Task!*

# Let's Talk It Over

*The questions on this page are designed to promote discussion of the lesson by the class and to encourage application of the lesson Scriptures. The answers provided are only discussion starters. Let your class talk it over from there.*

**1. Why should we expect opposition when working for God? How has God strengthened you to overcome opposition?**

A very real conflict exists between the kingdom of this world and the kingdom of God. Satan (which means "adversary") uses his servants, both demonic and human, to try to interrupt the good that God's servants attempt to do. Since this may happen daily, we need to take precautions daily (Ephesians 6:10-18).

Those who opposed Nehemiah had vested interests in doing so. Christ also faced opposition from those who had vested interests that they were trying to protect: "If we let him thus alone, all men will believe on him; and the Romans shall come and take away both our place and nation" (John 11:48). If what we are doing is important enough for an enemy of the cross to oppose us, sometimes that can tell us that what we are doing is right!

**2. What was a time when you saw mockery succeed in discouraging Christians in their work for God's kingdom? How do we guard against this tactic?**

People have a natural tendency to want to belong, to fit in, to be accepted. Mockery has a tendency to make us think, "I don't fit in, and what I am doing is not valued." The truth is, we are never going to fit in completely (nor should we), for we do not belong here. We are "strangers and pilgrims" in this world (1 Peter 2:11).

If mocking doesn't discourage us completely, it may still serve as a distraction. Distractions are dangerous! When Peter started looking at the distracting waves and wind instead of Christ, his faith faltered (Matthew 14:30). The people of Nehemiah's day were successful because they had a mind for the work and they had a leader of faith who knew how to neutralize distractions.

**3. Are the steps Nehemiah took to overcome ungodly opposition still valid today? Why, or why not?**

Before Nehemiah did anything, he brought the matter before God in prayer. This is still a valid first step when (and before) we face opposition. Next, Nehemiah set watchmen up in preparation for the enemy attack. We can serve as watchmen over our own character, attitudes, or actions; we should not give the enemy a valid reason to accuse us in these areas because of our own carelessness. A failure of vigilance invites disaster (1 Thessalonians 5:6-8; 1 Peter 5:8).

Finally, as Nehemiah did with his people, we can encourage our fellow workers to stand fast in the face of opposition. With God's help, we can be victorious.

**4. What happens when the enemy finds us ready to face opposition? Or is this even possible to predict? Explain.**

In Nehemiah's day, the opposition at first increased in intensity as things went along. But then the opposition faltered when it realized that the Jews were prepared. The opposition eventually ended up demoralized (Nehemiah 6:16).

Ungodly opposition today may give up when it recognizes that we are ready. But sometimes the opposition just gets fiercer, as our modern culture wars reveal. It would be foolish to assume that the opposition will always give up at the first sign of our resistance.

Ultimately, though, the side that serves God wins. "Submit yourselves therefore to God. Resist the devil, and he will flee from you" (James 4:7). What great things could be accomplished for God's kingdom if we were better prepared for the opposition of the enemy when it comes?

**5. What was a time when remembering that God was working through you was an effective tool against opposition?**

Sanballat called the Jews "feeble." He was correct in that assessment! But Sanballat apparently did not realize that God delights in working through human weakness (2 Corinthians 12:9). It is important for us to remember that God works through us so that we may be able to accomplish all things (compare Philippians 4:13).

Remember also that God is the one fighting the battle. The contest between David and Goliath ultimately was between the Lord and Goliath (see 1 Samuel 17:45-47). That contest turned out to be no contest at all. Satan is no match when faced with the power of God.

# Renewing the Covenant

DEVOTIONAL READING: **Psalm 27:11-14;
19:7-14.**

BACKGROUND SCRIPTURE: **Nehemiah 8.**

PRINTED TEXT: **Nehemiah 8:1-3, 5, 6, 13, 14,
17, 18.**

Nehemiah 8:1-3, 5, 6, 13, 14, 17, 18

1 And all the people gathered themselves
together as one man into the street that was
before the water gate; and they spake unto
Ezra the scribe to bring the book of the law
of Moses, which the LORD had commanded
to Israel.

2 And Ezra the priest brought the law before
the congregation both of men and women, and
all that could hear with understanding, upon
the first day of the seventh month.

3 And he read therein before the street that
was before the water gate from the morning
until midday, before the men and the women,
and those that could understand; and the ears
of all the people were attentive unto the book
of the law.

. . . . . . . . . .

5 And Ezra opened the book in the sight of
all the people; (for he was above all the people;) and when he opened it, all the people
stood up:

6 And Ezra blessed the LORD, the great
God. And all the people answered, Amen,
Amen, with lifting up their hands: and they
bowed their heads, and worshipped the LORD
with their faces to the ground.

. . . . . . . . . .

13 And on the second day were gathered
together the chief of the fathers of all the
people, the priests, and the Levites, unto Ezra
the scribe, even to understand the words of
the law.

14 And they found written in the law
which the LORD had commanded by Moses,
that the children of Israel should dwell in
booths in the feast of the seventh month:

. . . . . . . . . .

17 And all the congregation of them that
were come again out of the captivity made
booths, and sat under the booths: for since
the days of Jeshua the son of Nun unto that
day had not the children of Israel done so.
And there was very great gladness.

18 Also day by day, from the first day unto
the last day, he read in the book of the law of
God. And they kept the feast seven days; and
on the eighth day was a solemn assembly,
according unto the manner.

---

GOLDEN TEXT: He read therein before the street that was before the water gate
from the morning until midday, before the men and the women, and those
that could understand; and the ears of all the people were attentive
unto the book of the law.—Nehemiah 8:3.

**May
25**

## God, the People, and the Covenant
Unit 3: Restoration and Covenant Renewal
(Lessons 10-13)

## Lesson Aims

After participating in this lesson, each student will be able to:

1. Retell the event of Ezra's public reading of the law, including preparations made and some results.

2. Explain the importance of reading Scripture in public worship.

3. Plan a program or event that will challenge others to be more regular in Bible reading and study.

## Lesson Outline

INTRODUCTION
    A. The Wonderful Word
    B. Lesson Background
I. FIRST DAY: ATTITUDE OF REVIVAL (Nehemiah 8:1-3, 5, 6)
    A. Assembly Gathers (vv. 1-3)
      *A Word from Beyond*
    B. Assembly Reacts (vv. 5, 6)
II. SECOND DAY: ACTION OF REVIVAL (Nehemiah 8:13, 14, 17, 18)
    A. Leaders Gather Themselves (v. 13)
      *The Search for Understanding*
    B. Leaders Note Requirements (v. 14)
    C. Everyone Builds Booths (v. 17)
    D. Everyone Hears the Law (v. 18)
CONCLUSION
    A. The Effective Word
    B. Prayer
    C. Thought to Remember

## Introduction

### A. The Wonderful Word

A survey of history quickly reveals the great influence the Word of God has had on people and nations. One example is the Old Testament revival under King Josiah (2 Kings 23), which was spurred on by finding and reading the book of the covenant to the king. We also note the time of reform under King Hezekiah, who "clave to the Lord, and departed not from following him, but kept his commandments" (2 Kings 18:6).

The church age has also experienced times of great revival, with expressions of reliance on and obedience to the wonderful Word of God. Many of these revivals pushed themselves forward with slogans such as "the Scriptures alone" and "no book but the Bible."

Just as those who are devoted to the Word will experience revival and continued spiritual growth (2 Timothy 3:14-17), those who neglect the Word will fall into backsliding and spiritual apathy (Hebrews 2:1). As has been said, "Either the Bible will keep you from sin, or sin will keep you from the Bible." The Bible is the reference point for faithful, obedient living. This is because of the nature of its contents and its ultimate author.

Notice some of the things the wonderful Word addresses: the attributes of God, the origin of humanity, the condition of humanity, the way of salvation, the destiny of the unsaved, the destiny of the saved, light for direction, and wisdom for decisions. The Word of God is authoritative and instructive. As has been pointed out, "It is the traveler's map, the pilgrim's staff, the pilot's compass, the soldier's sword, and the Christian's charter."

What a blessing and privilege it is for us to have such a gift of love as the wonderful Word of God! Let us be thankful and attentive to it as we consider how others viewed the Word in centuries past.

### B. Lesson Background

In last week's lesson, we studied Nehemiah's leading of the people in building the wall of Jerusalem. There were serious challenges to overcome. Between the end of that lesson in Nehemiah 6:15 and the opening of today's lesson, we read of more challenges that continued to confront Nehemiah. He had to deal with spies in his midst (Nehemiah 6:17-19). While dealing with those people, Nehemiah had to ensure that the completion of the wall did not mean a return to "business as usual."

Completing the wall was just a start. That wall also needed gates and watchful guards (Nehemiah 7:1-3). Nehemiah also noticed that Jerusalem was underpopulated and there was a problem with a lack of quality housing. "Now the city was large and great: but the people were few therein, and the houses were not builded" (Nehemiah 7:4). So Nehemiah relied on a genealogical list to move toward a solution (Nehemiah 7:5-73; compare Ezra 2). But before that solution was reached (Nehemiah 11:1), some important events intervened.

# I. First Day: Attitude of Revival (Nehemiah 8:1-3, 5, 6)

## A. Assembly Gathers (vv. 1-3)

**1. And all the people gathered themselves together as one man into the street that was before the water gate; and they spake unto Ezra the scribe to bring the book of the law of Moses, which the LORD had commanded to Israel.**

As verse 2 will show us, it's only been about a week since the walls were finished (last week's lesson). Thus the excitement of that accomplishment has not yet worn off. This is a perfect time, then, to read *the book of the law of Moses*. The people are eager to have God's Word brought to them, so they voluntarily gather and ask *Ezra* to read it in their hearing. [See question #1, page 336.]

This is the first time that Ezra is introduced into the narrative of the book of Nehemiah. He came to Jerusalem about 13 or 14 years before Nehemiah to teach and enforce the law of God (Ezra 7–10). Thus he is an old hand at leading public assemblies and dealing with the people. During the time of the exile, God preserved His Word through men like Ezra. As a *scribe*, Ezra not only studies the law of God, but also helps preserve it.

The assembly gathers *before the water gate*, which is probably on the southeast side of the city. The temple and the newly formed walls are in sight as Ezra reads the law of God (see also Nehemiah 3:26; 8:3, 18; 12:37).

**2. And Ezra the priest brought the law before the congregation both of men and women, and all that could hear with understanding, upon the first day of the seventh month.**

The reading of *the law* is to both *men* and *women*. The phrase *all that could hear with understanding* indicates that young people are present too. Everyone needs instruction and encouragement from God's Word! The importance of teaching children was recognized hundreds of years earlier, in the time of Moses (Exodus 12:26, 27).

The wall is finished "in the twenty and fifth day of the month Elul" (Nehemiah 6:15), which is the sixth month of the Jewish religious calendar. The events in the verse before us take place on *the first day of the seventh month*. The year is not given, but the common inference is that it is the same year that the wall is finished. This puts the events of today's lesson beginning about a week after the completion of the wall.

The seventh month is an important festival month. The first day of this month is to be "a

Visual for Lesson 13. *Have this visual on display as you introduce discussion question #1 on page 336.*

sabbath, a memorial of blowing of trumpets, a holy convocation" (Leviticus 23:24). The Day of Atonement is to be observed on day 10 (Leviticus 23:26-32), and the Feast of Tabernacles is to occur on days 15 to 21 (Leviticus 23:33-36). We will see why this is important in this context a bit later.

**3. And he read therein before the street that was before the water gate from the morning until midday, before the men and the women, and those that could understand; and the ears of all the people were attentive unto the book of the law.**

How hungry *the people* are for the Word! *From the morning until midday* is several hours, probably five or six. The desire to seek God is seen in an eagerness to listen for this length of time.

We cannot help but pause and reflect on how indifferent many are who gather for worship today. We must come prepared and eager to hear. If we come expecting nothing, that is probably what we will get. But God blesses the gathering of His people and the instruction of His Word; therefore we should be taking measures to receive the most from His blessings. [See question #2, page 336.]

### A WORD FROM BEYOND

Actress Shirley MacLaine made *channeling* a household word in the 1980s with her book and TV miniseries *Out on a Limb*. MacLaine claimed to speak to a person who had been a contemporary of Jesus. This person "revealed" to MacLaine that she cocreated the world with God, supposedly proving MacLaine's earlier claim that she *is* God! How nice for her self-esteem.

MacLaine is much enamored with a channeler named J. Z. Knight, who claims to speak on a regular basis with a 35,000-year-old Cro-Magnon warrior named Ramtha. Knight fetches up to $1,000 per person at seminars where people hear her mouth Ramtha's insights such as "[we must] open our minds to new frontiers of potential" (http://skepdic.com).

Ironic, isn't it, how people will pay more attention to charlatans such as these than they will to God? Ezra's people were anxious to hear something "from beyond," and they listened eagerly for hours to God's Word!

At least two things stand out in this incident. First, the people sought their message from a trustworthy source: God's law. Second, they had a trustworthy guide who brought God's Word to their attention. What applications can we make to modern life?                    —C. R. B.

### B. Assembly Reacts (vv. 5, 6)

**5. And Ezra opened the book in the sight of all the people; (for he was above all the people;) and when he opened it, all the people stood up.**

Ezra is standing on a wooden platform (v. 4, not in today's text), which elevates him *above all the people*. Thus they are able to hear and see him (compare 2 Chronicles 6:13). Several others are up on the platform with Ezra, including the prophet Zechariah. We do not know what role they play in helping Ezra.

The *book* that Ezra opens is not like a modern book, but is a long strip of parchment rolled on a stick at either end. Such a document is also referred to as a "roll" or "scroll" (Isaiah 8:1; 34:4).

Signifying their reverence for the law that is about to be read, the people rise to their feet. The Jewish custom is to sit when listening (Luke 10:39; Acts 13:14) and to stand while in prayer (Luke 18:11-13), although they occasionally stand to show honor to the person speaking or to the occasion (Job 29:8; Ezekiel 2:1; Matthew 13:2). To stand up is an act demonstrating a willingness to listen, believe, and obey what is about to be heard.

To stand in awe and tremble at God's Word is the proper response for one desiring to know the Lord's will. "But to this man will I look, even to him that is poor and of a contrite spirit, and trembleth at my word" (Isaiah 66:2). God's Word is living, active, and powerful (Hebrews 4:12). It therefore should be opened, read, heard, and heeded with reverence.

**6. And Ezra blessed the LORD, the great God. And all the people answered, Amen, Amen, with lifting up their hands: and they bowed their heads, and worshipped the LORD with their faces to the ground.**

The importance of the Bible is based on the author from whom it comes: *the great God,* the all-wise and sufficient one, the holy and eternal one. His attributes are too many and too great for us to comprehend.

It is an amazing thought to ponder that God has spoken to us. As the psalmist asks, "What is man, that thou art mindful of him?" (Psalm 8:4). Yet the great God has indeed taken the initiative for us to know Him and His will. God has put His thoughts in the form of words, which allows us to grasp them. In the case before us, everyone recognizes the importance of the source of what they are about to hear.

*Ezra* begins by blessing *the Lord.* Leaders of God's people should be the first to recognize the greatness of God and the greatness of the work to which He calls them. Such leaders help the people of God understand their dependence on God. Such leaders also understand that what people need is God. So Ezra brings out the words of God (v. 2), opens the book of God (v. 5), reads the Word of God (v. 3), teaches the Word of God (v. 7), and leads the people in blessing and worshiping God (v. 6).

As a good priest, Ezra's focus is on God. Ezra's intentions are to get others focused on God as well. "For Ezra had prepared his heart to seek the law of the Lord, and to do it, and to teach in Israel statutes and judgments" (Ezra 7:10). The aim of all preachers today should be to set forth God's truth clearly. Faithful exposition of God's Word is the way to bring people to (or back to) God. "Faith cometh by hearing, and hearing by the word of God" (Romans 10:17).

The response of the people is threefold. First is their cry of *Amen, Amen,* which means "truly, truly" (compare Nehemiah 5:13). Second, the people lift *up their hands* to demonstrate need for God and openness to Him (compare Ezra 9:5; Psalm 28:2; 134:2). The third reaction is to bow *their heads* in reverent worship. This bowing is further specified as worshiping *with their faces to the ground* as in Genesis 19:1; Judges 13:20; and 2 Chronicles 7:3; 20:18.

## II. Second Day: Action of Revival (Nehemiah 8:13, 14, 17, 18)

### A. Leaders Gather Themselves (v. 13)

**13. And on the second day were gathered together the chief of the fathers of all the people, the priests, and the Levites, unto Ezra the scribe, even to understand the words of the law.**

The first day had ended with a celebration (Nehemiah 8:12). Now, *on the second day,* the leaders gather to consider what they have heard. When God's Word is heard with an attitude of attentive reverence, it produces a hunger and a thirst for more words of life. So *the chief of the fathers of all the people, the priests, and the Levites* desire *Ezra* to instruct them further.

The humility of the leaders is seen in their desire to search for greater understanding. With the readiness of the people to hear and respond to the words of the law, it is necessary for the leaders to be instructed on how to direct the people. So instead of being content with only what they heard the day before, they press further. They probably want to discern application and learn how they can better instruct those who are under their charge. [See question #3, page 336.]

Revival does not happen without action. And right action cannot take place without understanding. A wise and sincere person does not give up on the search for truth and proper application. When leaders and followers in the church decide to settle for nothing less than to understand and apply the whole counsel of God to the best of their ability, their spiritual growth and the growth of the kingdom will not be in doubt.

### THE SEARCH FOR UNDERSTANDING

Sigmund Freud died in 1939, yet his influence lingers. He is known as "the father of psychoanalysis" because he launched the modern quest for understanding the human psyche.

It is Freud to whom we owe much of our vocabulary for talking about human behavior. If we have trouble admitting to some negative personal trait, we are *in denial.* If we offer lame excuses for an expensive impulse purchase, we are *rationalizing.* Errors in action or word that supposedly are caused by the unconscious mind are

---

### How to Say It

ELUL. *Ee*-lull or *Eh*-lool.

EZEKIEL. Ee-*zeek*-ee-ul or Ee-*zeek*-yul.

EZRA. *Ez*-ruh.

JESHUA. *Jesh*-you-uh.

LEVITICUS. Leh-*vit*-ih-kus.

MOSES. *Mo*-zes or *Mo*-zez.

NEHEMIAH. *Nee*-huh-*my*-uh (strong accent on *my*).

NUN. *None.*

ZECHARIAH. *Zek*-uh-*rye*-uh (strong accent on *rye*).

---

*Freudian slips.* Freud spawned a whole new way of trying to fix personal problems. Where would filmmaker Woody Allen be without him?

In recent years, Freud's method of lengthy self-analysis by expensive therapists has given way to more user-friendly counseling techniques. No one can doubt that the counseling profession has helped multitudes of troubled people. Counseling based on Christian principles has found a place among the ministries offered by many churches.

Ezra was a prophet and a scribe, but perhaps we can think of him as a godly counselor as well. Notice what he did: he led his people to right thinking and right behavior by showing them what God said. Our search for spiritual health will be most successful if we consult the first and greatest psychiatrist: God Almighty!

—C. R. B.

### B. Leaders Note Requirements (v. 14)

**14. And they found written in the law which the LORD had commanded by Moses, that the children of Israel should dwell in booths in the feast of the seventh month.**

The leaders discover that the Jewish people are required to hold a certain *feast* during the *seventh month.* The feast in question is the Feast of Tabernacles (also called Festival of Booths or Feast of Ingathering), and it is to be observed for a week beginning on the fifteenth day of this month (Exodus 23:16; Leviticus 23:33-36; Numbers 29:12-38; Deuteronomy 16:13-15).

On the first day of the observance, the Israelites are to construct *booths* from tree branches. The Israelites are to stay in the booths during the entire festival (Leviticus 23:39-43; Nehemiah 8:15). Dwelling in these booths is to be a reminder of the wilderness wanderings their ancestors had experienced after God had delivered them from Egypt. Jesus attends the Feast of Tabernacles in His day (John 7). [See question #4, page 336.]

### C. Everyone Builds Booths (v. 17)

**17. And all the congregation of them that were come again out of the captivity made booths, and sat under the booths: for since the days of Jeshua the son of Nun unto that day had not the children of Israel done so. And there was very great gladness.**

The leaders learn about the Feast of Tabernacles on the second day of the month (v. 13, above). Since the feast is to start on the fifteenth day, everyone has only 13 days to get the word out and prepare. So the actions of revival continue as the people are obedient to what they have heard from the law of God.

To make the *booths* and stay in them certainly can be considered to be a great inconvenience. But the people have a heart to obey! Their heart is seen in the fact that they celebrate this festival in a way that has not been seen *since the days of Jeshua* (Joshua) *son of Nun,* some 1,000 years before.

To be sure, this festival had been celebrated in various ways since Joshua's time (see 1 Kings 8:2, 65; Ezra 3:4). But this celebration is different somehow. The difference seems to be in the specific connection of the booths with the wilderness wanderings *(that were come again out of the captivity).* What a powerful visual aid of God's providential care!

The verse before us causes us to recall that the purpose of proclaiming, reading, and hearing the Bible is to apply the truth that is uncovered. "But be ye doers of the word, and not hearers only, deceiving your own selves" (James 1:22).

The attitude and actions of the people result in *great gladness.* People who seek to know and do the will of the Lord will experience the joy that comes from knowing and serving the great God. Rejoice in the Lord!

### D. Everyone Hears the Law (v. 18)

**18. Also day by day, from the first day unto the last day, he read in the book of the law of God. And they kept the feast seven days; and on the eighth day was a solemn assembly, according unto the manner.**

The people continue in their obedience as they observe *the feast* for all *seven days* as mandated. They conclude *on the eighth day* with a *solemn*

---

## Home Daily Bible Readings

**Monday, May 19**—Take Courage (Psalm 27:11-14)

**Tuesday, May 20**—The Festival of Booths (Leviticus 23:33-43)

**Wednesday, May 21**—Do Not Appear Empty-Handed (Deuteronomy 16:13-17)

**Thursday, May 22**—Hear the Word (Nehemiah 8:1-6)

**Friday, May 23**—Teach the Word (Nehemiah 8:7-12)

**Saturday, May 24**—Study the Word (Nehemiah 8:13-18)

**Sunday, May 25**—Delight in God's Law (Psalm 19:7-14)

---

*assembly* as required by Leviticus 23:36, 39 and Numbers 29:35-38.

While they are participating in the feast, Ezra continues to *read* and expound *the book of the law of God* daily. This reading reminds us of Deuteronomy 31:9-13. Thus the people continue to receive instruction as they celebrate and worship. [See question #5, page 336.]

## Conclusion

### A. The Effective Word

There is nothing like God's Word, desired and applied, to bring about revival. The result of the reading of the Word in today's lesson was that the people entered into a formal covenant of renewed devotion to the law and service to God. It was signed by Nehemiah, the leaders, the princes, and the priests. They promised to keep the law of Moses, pay their tithes, support the temple, and keep the Sabbath. They bound themselves under a curse to keep this covenant (Nehemiah 9:38–10:39). The people were serious about following God.

As we have seen in this lesson, there are attitudes and actions that will lead to revival and spiritual growth. We too should continue to grow in our knowledge and observance of the Word of God because of the infinite value of the things written in it.

A careful and continuing search of the Bible will produce many great rewards. We will find truths and promises that will encourage and give strength. We will discover instructions to correct wrong thinking and conduct. We will find comfort and joy in knowing true fellowship with God.

If you are in need of restoring your covenant relationship with the Lord, you will find that He is willing and ready to receive you with open arms. Commit yourself to learn from, obey, and worship the Lord as a sign of your renewed relationship with God. You too will experience great gladness in returning to Him.

### B. Prayer

Holy Father, thank You for Your Word. It is powerful and precious. Incline our hearts and wills to it that You would be glorified in our lives and that we would experience the most of Your grace and love. Through Christ we pray, amen.

### C. Thought to Remember

A contrite heart and God's Word
are the starting points for spiritual renewal.

# Learning by Doing

*This page contains an alternative lesson plan emphasizing learning activities. Classes desiring such student involvement will find these suggestions helpful.*

## Into the Lesson

Recruit one of your congregation's best oral readers to stand on a step stool at the beginning of class to read the following series of texts about the marvelous Word of God: Joshua 1:8; Job 23:12; Psalm 119:18, 163; Isaiah 40:8; 55:11; Matthew 24:35; Luke 11:28; John 14:23; Hebrews 4:12; 1 Peter 1:23. Your reader may decide to include surrounding context of personal choice. The order does not need to be in biblical sequence.

At the end say simply, "If all of that is true about God's Word, a person would be foolish to ignore it. Today's text describes an occasion where the people of God listened to the Word of God and then obeyed it. May we be so wise."

## Into the Word

Use the following statements as discussion starters for today's text. Verse numbers are noted in parentheses for the teacher's use. (These statements also appear in the optional student book.)

1. When people gather together in unity to hear the Word of God and to worship, then powerful, life-changing blessings take place *(v. 2)*; 2. Anyone who hungers to know the will of God must go to the Word of God, where His will is revealed *(v. 3)*; 3. Faithful exposition of God's Word is the way to bring people back to God *(v. 6)*; 4. When God's Word is heard with an attitude of attentive reverence, it produces a hunger for more words of life *(v. 13)*; 5. Revival cannot happen without action, and right action cannot take place without understanding *(v. 13)*; 6. The purpose of proclaiming, reading, and hearing the Bible is to apply the truth *(v. 17)*; 7. Because of the infinite value of the Word of God, we should continue to grow in our knowledge and observance of the things written in it, determined to take every advantage of the privileges we have to study God's Word *(v. 18)*.

Next, inform your class that you are going to describe behaviors that reflect positive attitudes, and you want them to note where in Nehemiah 8 the people demonstrated these. The verse numbers noted in parentheses at the end of each statement are for the teacher's use and should not be revealed until the learners have had a chance to answer. The statements below are given randomly.

1. Shouted "Amen! Amen!" *(v. 6)*
2. Stood attentively for hours on end. *(v. 3)*
3. Stood in respect as the book was opened. *(v. 5)*
4. Expected their family heads and national leaders to help them understand. *(v. 13)*
5. Immediately obeyed long-forgotten commands. *(vv. 14, 17)*
(The optional student book also contains an activity with these statements.)

## Into Life

Have one of your better readers make a recording of the lesson background texts for the upcoming summer lessons. (The *King James Version* has no copyright restrictions; for copyrighted versions, seek written permission from the holder of the copyright.) Duplicate the recordings onto audiocassettes or CDs, and give one to each class member.

Provide these directions: "Listen to the recorded texts for the upcoming summer lessons as you are working at home or traveling. Begin a habit of hearing the texts several times before Sunday's study session." Tell your learners that this is a way to begin to give regular and diligent attention to God's Word.

End the lesson by pointing out that the writer of Psalm 119 affirmed his own attitude toward the Word of God in various ways. Reproduce and distribute copies of the following for your learners to initial if they concur (also included in the optional student book).

___ "I delight in thy law" (Psalm 119:70).
___ "Thy word is a lamp unto my feet" (Psalm 119:105).
___ "I will meditate in thy precepts" (Psalm 119:78).
___ "So shall I keep thy law continually" (Psalm 119:44).
___ "My tongue shall speak of thy word" (Psalm 119:172).
___ "I will never forget thy precepts" (Psalm 119:93).
___ "Thy word have I hid in mine heart, that I might not sin against thee" (Psalm 119:11).
___ "At midnight I will rise to give thanks unto thee because of thy righteous judgments" (Psalm 119:62).

# Let's Talk It Over

*The questions on this page are designed to promote discussion of the lesson by the class and to encourage application of the lesson Scriptures. The answers provided are only discussion starters. Let your class talk it over from there.*

**1. How will you show your desire for God's Word today? What will be the outcome when you do?**

The people showed an obvious desire for God's Word. They listened with great eagerness for many hours and then came back to gain more understanding of God's Word. No one expects this exact form of eagerness for God's Word to be repeated today. Yet we can still show our eagerness through a study of the Word during daily quiet times. And public reading (however brief) of Scripture during worship wouldn't hurt!

Perhaps the greatest benefit of desiring God's Word and the righteousness that comes through its pages is found in Matthew 5:6: "Blessed are they which do hunger and thirst after righteousness: for they shall be filled."

**2. What was a time when you were eager for the Word? How did you satisfy your hunger?**

The people in the text listened attentively to God's Word for five or six hours. Considering that many of our church services last only a couple of hours at most, this seems a long time. The people of Ezra's day were starving for God's Word, and so they feasted on it.

Perhaps it has been a while since we as a people have hungered so much that we wanted a feast like that, but God is more than willing to provide such a feast. A common time for such hunger is when a person first becomes a Christian, and the excitement translates into hunger for His Word (see Acts 17:11). The feast of God's Word produced quite a revival in Nehemiah's day; such a revival can happen again.

**3. Do you think it would be a good idea for a person just to read the Bible on his or her own, skipping all the commentaries and instructions from others? Why, or why not?**

Just to sit and read God's Word by oneself is very enlightening! But additional instruction on its meaning can be helpful, particularly when it comes to application. That's why the words you are reading right now are important. A person does not become a physician merely by reading medical textbooks; rather, a person becomes a physician by going to medical school where

expert instruction is available. Expert Bible instruction promotes Christian maturity.

The elders of the people sought out the best teachers they could. They desired for everyone to have more understanding of God's Word. Right actions can be taken only when one has the proper understanding of God's Word. Zeal must be based on knowledge (Romans 10:2).

**4. What part of Scripture have you been guilty of setting aside? What corrective action have you taken (or will you take)?**

The people of Israel had not observed the Feast of Tabernacles as they should have for a very long time. We too can be guilty of neglecting God's Word. At times, we may see parts of God's Word as unimportant, inconvenient, or irrelevant. Yet Deuteronomy 10:13 suggests that God's commands are for our own good. When we neglect following His precepts, we are only hurting ourselves. Neglecting to follow God's Word is like saying, "I know better than God." If there is some part of God's Word that you have been avoiding, today is a good day to change.

**5. Why is continual Bible study so important? What is your track record in this regard?**

The Bible is first of all God's message to us. The mere fact that it is God's Word makes it worthy of continual study. Second, the Bible addresses a variety of topics that are important yet today.

There is so much in Scripture worthy of study that individuals have devoted lifetimes to its study. In the 1,900 plus years since Scripture was completed, people continue to write books about what is found in the Bible. No one can know all that God's Word has to offer, but one can get a lot out of God's Word by continual study. The lives of people in the pages of the Bible provide good and bad examples of behavior and belief (compare 1 Corinthians 10:6).

We easily could add many more reasons for continual Bible study! The end result is that each of us will show ourselves to be "approved unto God, a workman that needeth not to be ashamed, rightly dividing the word of truth" (2 Timothy 2:15).

# Summer Quarter 2008

## Images of Christ
### (Hebrews, Gospels, James)

### Special Features

### Lessons

#### Unit 1: Images of Christ in Hebrews

#### Unit 2: Images of Christ in the Gospels

#### Unit 3: Images of Christ in Us

## About These Lessons

Images are all around us. Some we see clearly and directly. Some we see indistinctly, as distorted reflections. Some are harmful to look at (example: pornography). Some are beneficial to behold (example: Psalm 19:1). No images are more important than those of Christ—this quarter's lessons.

Jun 1
Jun 8
Jun 15
Jun 22
Jun 29
Jul 6
Jul 13
Jul 20
Jul 27
Aug 3
Aug 10
Aug 17
Aug 24
Aug 31

# A Thousand Words

## by Lee M. Fields

I enjoy looking at photographs of my children. I marvel at how they have changed physically over the years, when I would otherwise have forgotten. These photographs record what cannot be written. Yet, they do not record the growth of my children spiritually and emotionally; they do not reveal the more-important inner person that each has become. Words are necessary for that.

This quarter's material treats the theme *Images of Christ* in a powerful way. The images are word pictures. They record sharply the real person and work of Christ. Following images from Hebrews and the Gospels, James presents images to help us put hands and feet to our faith.

### Unit 1: Images of Christ in Hebrews

The book of Hebrews was written to Jewish believers who were undergoing persecution. The author writes to bolster their faith by presenting images of who Jesus really is.

**Lesson 1: God's Son**. Christ is God's unique Son. He is of the same essence as the Father. The very term *Son,* not used of angels, demonstrates Jesus' absolute superiority.

**Lesson 2: Only Intercessor.** How can Jesus be a priest and intercede to God for people? The correct understanding is that Christ's priesthood (reality) is both different from and superior to the Levitical priesthood (shadow).

**Lesson 3: Perfect Redeemer.** Under persecution, the original readers found themselves tempted to abandon Christ. The solution is a contrast of the earthly temple (visible, but shadowy) with the heavenly temple (invisible, but real).

**Lesson 4: Trustworthy Leader.** Christ serves as the best example of endurance under wrongful suffering. Christ's lead teaches that God uses suffering to train His children in holiness.

**Lesson 5: Eternal Christ.** Finally, Hebrews 13 shows us that Christ is eternal and unchanging. This characteristic ought to affect our relationships with other Christians, our commitment to truth, and our praise to God.

### Unit 2: Images of Christ in the Gospels

Each of the next four lessons comes from a different Gospel account. The writers are careful to present accurate pictures of Jesus.

**Lesson 6: Master Teacher.** The exorcism in Luke 4:31-37 shows the authority and power of Jesus over the demons. Luke 20:1-8 offers a pointed lesson about the motives of the Jewish leaders and Jesus' own identity.

**Lesson 7: Powerful Healer.** Mark 1:29-45 shows us Jesus healing not only physically but spiritually. Jesus' power as healer confirms the truth of His message.

**Lesson 8: Exemplary Servant.** John 13:1-20 tells of the washing of the disciples' feet the night before Jesus' crucifixion. If He can do this menial task, how can we not follow His example of serving one another?

**Lesson 9: Promised Messiah.** Matthew 16:13-23 records Peter's great confession. It also gives us a foretaste of the suffering the Messiah had to undergo.

### Unit 3: Images of Christ in Us

Instead of looking at Jesus from the outside as we would watch a movie, James allows us to see Jesus from inside of us, as though we were actors in the movie. It is quite a vista to see Jesus inside us, changing us to be more like Him.

**Lesson 10: Doers of the Word.** When Christ lives in us, the Father is able to help us become more like Him. The presence of Christ will manifest itself in our obedience to God's Word in attitudes, speech, and service.

**Lesson 11: Impartial Disciples.** Christ was no respecter of persons. Neither should we be.

**Lesson 12: Wise Speakers.** James discusses areas in which our speech must be wise. As Christ works in us, may our words be used ever more consistently for the benefit of others.

**Lesson 13: Godly Servants.** James 4:1-12 lists numerous ways that we should be godly servants to others in both attitudes and actions. A condemning judgment of others is a common human fault that Jesus expects us to correct.

**Lesson 14: Prayerful Community.** Finally, James 5:7-18 continues the theme of the previous lesson by teaching the correct approach to handling our desires: patience and prayer. Imagine what the community of Christ would look like if we were as patient and prayerful as Jesus.

In the course of studying these lessons, let us study the word pictures of Jesus. Let us also take before and after photographs of ourselves. As we become more like Him, I dare say we will marvel at the change.

# God's Son

DEVOTIONAL READING: **Proverbs 8:22-31.**

BACKGROUND SCRIPTURE: **Hebrews 1.**

PRINTED TEXT: **Hebrews 1:1-12.**

### Hebrews 1:1-12

1 God, who at sundry times and in divers manners spake in time past unto the fathers by the prophets.

2 Hath in these last days spoken unto us by his Son, whom he hath appointed heir of all things, by whom also he made the worlds;

3 Who being the brightness of his glory, and the express image of his person, and upholding all things by the word of his power, when he had by himself purged our sins, sat down on the right hand of the Majesty on high;

4 Being made so much better than the angels, as he hath by inheritance obtained a more excellent name than they.

5 For unto which of the angels said he at any time, Thou art my Son, this day have I begotten thee? And again, I will be to him a Father, and he shall be to me a Son?

6 And again, when he bringeth in the first-begotten into the world, he saith, And let all the angels of God worship him.

7 And of the angels he saith, Who maketh his angels spirits, and his ministers a flame of fire.

8 But unto the Son he saith, Thy throne, O God, is for ever and ever: a sceptre of righteousness is the sceptre of thy kingdom.

9 Thou hast loved righteousness, and hated iniquity; therefore God, even thy God, hath anointed thee with the oil of gladness above thy fellows.

10 And, Thou, Lord, in the beginning hast laid the foundation of the earth; and the heavens are the works of thine hands.

11 They shall perish; but thou remainest: and they all shall wax old as doth a garment;

12 And as a vesture shalt thou fold them up, and they shall be changed: but thou art the same, and thy years shall not fail.

GOLDEN TEXT: Who being the brightness of his glory, and the express image of his person, and upholding all things by the word of his power.—Hebrews 1:3.

## *Images of Christ*
### Unit 1: Images of Christ in Hebrews
### (Lessons 1-5)

## Lesson Aims

After participating in this lesson, each student will be able to:

1. Describe how the Son is superior to the angels.

2. Tell something about why Jesus' superiority to the angels is important.

3. Prepare a response to a charge that the Son is one of the created angels.

## Lesson Outline

INTRODUCTION
  A. Angels
  B. Lesson Background
I. GOD'S COMMUNICATION (Hebrews 1:1, 2a)
  A. Former Revelation (v. 1)
  B. Latter Revelation (v. 2a)
    *New and Improved*
II. GOD'S SON (Hebrews 1:2b-4)
  A. Son's Inheritance (v. 2b)
  B. Son's Glory and Image (v. 3a)
  C. Son's Work (v. 3b)
  D. Son's Position (vv. 3c, 4)
III. SON'S SUPERIORITY (Hebrews 1:5-7)
  A. Jesus Is the Son (v. 5)
  B. Jesus Is to Be Worshiped (vv. 6, 7)
IV. SON'S POSITION (Hebrews 1:8-12)
  A. Authority (vv. 8, 9)
  B. Permanence (vv. 10-12)
    *Here to Stay*
CONCLUSION
  A. Who's Your Hero?
  B. Prayer
  C. Thought to Remember

## Introduction

### A. Angels

Some folks have an intense fascination with angels. Print and electronic media are filled with stories of angelic visitations. Talk of angels is welcomed, because with angels people can have religious experiences without Jesus Christ.

The problem is that biblical teachings about angels get mixed in with unbiblical ideas. Angel stories are not necessarily bad; angels do exist

and do God's bidding. But angels from God never distract from Him. We must be careful never to leave the master for the servant.

### B. Lesson Background

The book of Hebrews is a bit unusual. It ends with greetings like an epistle (Hebrews 13:20-25), yet the beginning is unlike a normal letter (contrast the opening verses of Hebrews with those of Colossians, etc.). Even so, the author refers to this work as "a letter" in Hebrews 13:22.

Hebrews 1:1-4 is the introduction that contains the starting threads of the key themes of the book. These themes are woven into the fabric of the entire work. Hebrews 1:4, the last verse of this introduction, leads into the author's first point, which actually extends through 2:4.

The original readers of the book of Hebrews were Jewish believers who had been undergoing some persecution (Hebrews 10:32-34). They were tempted to give up true Christianity for something false (10:35-39). Jews of the first century had a pervasive fascination with angels. We see evidence of this in some of the nonbiblical writings that come into being between the Old and New Testaments (called *the intertestamental writings*).

We can almost hear the original readers' questions that prompt our author to write chapter 1: "We know about angels; is Jesus as strong as they? He died; is he powerful enough to save?" The author of Hebrews has clear answers.

## I. God's Communication (Hebrews 1:1, 2a)

### A. Former Revelation (v. 1)

**1. God, who at sundry times and in divers manners spake in time past unto the fathers by the prophets.**

In the past, God communicated indirectly. The Greek word translated *at sundry times* means literally "in the manner of many parts." Considering that the Old Testament is God's revelation through many writers over the course of many centuries, we understand what the author means. *Divers manners* refers to the different ways that God spoke after Moses by various means, such as dreams and visions (Numbers 12:6-9).

The phrase *unto the fathers* refers to Jewish ancestors, the recipients of Scripture. The instrument God used to speak was *the prophets*. Naturally, we think of Isaiah, Jeremiah, etc., as prophets. We expand our understanding when we realize that Moses, Samuel, and David are considered to have been prophets as well (Deuteronomy 18:18; 1 Samuel 3:20; 2 Samuel 23:2-7; Acts 2:30).

## B. Latter Revelation (v. 2a)

**2a. Hath in these last days spoken unto us by his Son.**

This verse makes two contrasts with verse 1. The first is between "in time past" of verse 1 and *in these last days* here. The last days began with the first coming of Christ. We have been living in the last days for two millennia (1 John 2:18).

The second contrast is between "by the prophets" of verse 1 and *by his Son* here. More specifically, this contrast is between the prophets as mere human mouthpieces for God and one who has the quality of divine sonship. When God speaks through His Son, He cannot be more direct! To see Jesus is to see the Father (John 14:9). People who long for more revelation from God need simply to look to the Son. There is no greater nor clearer revelation of God.

### NEW AND IMPROVED

We have all seen the ads for "new and improved" versions of various products. These range from automobiles to can openers, from toothpaste to washing machines.

Producers of computer software are constantly upgrading their products. I have an antivirus package on my computer that gets upgraded frequently. Even books get improved. I have one writing style manual that is currently in its 14th edition. How do they expect us to write in good English if they keep changing the rules?

I often wonder, however, if the result is really improved. The most recent product may indeed be new, but is it improved? And if it is really improved, what does that say about the previ-

ous model? Doesn't that mean that the previous one was inferior? E. S. Ames tells the story about being in his vacation cabin in the Michigan woods and noticing one day the potbellied stove that provided heat for the building. It had a brand name, and then the inscription *Perfection No. 42.* "If it is 'perfection,'" he mused, "then why did it take 42 versions to get to this point?"

Sometimes the more recent products are not really improvements. But sometimes they are. That's what the writer of Hebrews means. God had previously spoken to us through the prophets. But now He has spoken to us through His Son. That's an improvement! —J. B. N.

## II. God's Son (Hebrews 1:2b-4)

### A. Son's Inheritance (v. 2b)

**2b. Whom he hath appointed heir of all things, by whom also he made the worlds.**

Deity is described in seven ways in verses 2, 3. The first two descriptions, here in the second half of verse 2, are related to the actions of God. The last five, in verse 3, are related to the nature and actions of the Son.

First, God appointed the Son as *heir of all things* (compare Matthew 21:38). As God's heir, the Son has divine authority and ownership, far more than any created being. *All things* means everything that exists. In Matthew 28:18, Jesus made known that at that time He had this authority over all.

Second, God created *the worlds* by means of the Son. The Greek word translated as *worlds* usually refers to time, but it is used here to refer to all that goes on or exists in time. Hence, it relates to the universe. The Son not only owns the universe, He was also involved in creating it (John 1:3; Colossians 1:16).

### B. Son's Glory and Image (v. 3a)

**3a. Who being the brightness of his glory, and the express image of his person.**

We now move to the first two of the five descriptions of the nature of the Son. The Father has *glory* of his own, of course. At the same time, the Son also has actual light—*brightness* or radiance. Thus the Son is not reflected light, as we see coming from the moon, but has light himself, as we see from the sun.

Moreover, the Son bears the image of God. The term for *express image* is used of the imprint stamped on coins. *Person* refers to God's real essence or actual being. These two terms make clear that this Son, though distinct as a person

---

### How to Say It

COLOSSIANS. Kuh-*losh*-unz.
CORINTHIANS. Ko-*rin*-thee-unz (*th* as in *thin*).
DAVIDIC. Duh-*vid*-ick.
DEUTERONOMY. Due-ter-*ahn*-uh-me.
HEBREWS. *Hee*-brews.
JEREMIAH. Jair-uh-*my*-uh.
MESSIAH. Meh-*sigh*-uh.
MOSES. *Mo*-zes or *Mo*-zez.
NATHAN. *Nay*-thun (*th* as in *thin*).
SEPTUAGINT. Sep-*too*-ih-jent.
SOLOMON. *Sol*-o-mun.
ZECHARIAH. *Zek*-uh-*rye*-uh (strong accent on *rye*).

from the Father, is of the same divine nature as the Father. Whatever the "stuff" is that makes the Father to be God also makes the Son to be God. The writer of Hebrews could not be clearer. How vital this truth is to the readers! Despite their doubts, they have made the right decision to follow Jesus as the Christ.

### C. Son's Work (v. 3b)

**3b. And upholding all things by the word of his power, when he had by himself purged our sins.**

Third, the Son bears or sustains *all things*. Deuteronomy 33:27 speaks of the arms of God holding the dwelling place of Israel. The Jews refer to God as the one who carries His world, citing Isaiah 46:4, where God will carry His people and deliver them. The Son uses His word to do this; *the word of his power* means "his powerful word," a power that is limited to God alone (2 Corinthians 4:7). The Son's role as sustainer is that which only the divine one can fill.

Whereas the third description of Jesus (above) is of something that continues for all time, the fourth description is that of an occurrence at a specific point in history. The Son brought about the purging, or cleansing, from *sins* when He died on the cross.

Many modern translations do not include the phrase *by himself* because the older Greek manuscripts of the New Testament do not have these words. But the meaning is the same either way: it was the Son (and nobody else) who made the purification through His blood on the cross (Hebrew 9:14).

This fact does not signify that the cleansing is applied to everyone automatically without condition. Rather, the idea is that purging of sin is available through the Son's sacrificial act. [See question #1, page 346.]

### D. Son's Position (vv. 3c, 4)

**3c. Sat down on the right hand of the Majesty on high.**

Fifth, the Son *sat down*. This expression might not catch the attention of those who live in places without kings. This is an official, ceremonial occasion, drawing on Psalm 110:1. The *right hand* of a king signifies a place of honor and prestige (1 Kings 2:19) as well as power for punishment, support, and deliverance (Exodus 15:6; Psalm 18:35; 138:7). The term *the Majesty on high* refers to the Father.

**4. Being made so much better than the angels, as he hath by inheritance obtained a more excellent name than they.**

In all these ways the Son is as superior to the *angels* as His *name* is to theirs. What names? *Son* versus *angel*. Whereas an angel is a created messenger, the Son is the divine, uncreated creator. The difference is infinite. With this lead-in our author moves to the first topic.

## III. Son's Superiority (Hebrews 1:5-7)

### A. Jesus Is the Son (v. 5)

**5a. For unto which of the angels said he at any time, Thou art my Son, this day have I begotten thee?**

In the following argument, the author presents a chain of Scriptures intended to demonstrate truths about the Son's superiority to angels. Our task is to understand each quotation in its original context, then see how the author of Hebrews is using it.

Here in verse 5, the word *he* refers to God. The phrase *Thou art my Son, this day have I begotten thee* is from Psalm 2:7. It is used here to make a vital point: no angel is called *my Son*. That is a title reserved for the unique *Son* of God, as described in verses 1-4. Though the promises made by the Lord in Psalm 2:8, 9 might apply in part to David, they can apply fully only to Jesus.

**5b. And again, I will be to him a Father, and he shall be to me a Son?**

This quotation is from 2 Samuel 7:14. The quotation comes from the passage that is establishing the Davidic covenant. David wished to build a temple for the Lord. Through Nathan the prophet, the Lord explained that He did not need a special house. Instead, the Lord was to establish a house for David.

In 2 Samuel 7:12-16, the Lord says He will raise up David's "seed" and will establish his kingdom. It is that seed who will build His house; the seed, ultimately, is the Lord's Son. King Solomon did build a temple, but it was destroyed. Solomon governed a nation in a golden age, but that kingdom split at the time of his death and eventually ended.

The true fulfillment of the Davidic covenant is in the seed that came after Solomon—the Messiah. The Old Testament teaches this (Jeremiah 23:5; Zechariah 6:12), and the New Testament records this as fulfilled in the first coming of Jesus (Luke 1:32, 33).

In this one verse the author of Hebrews has carefully proven that there is one Son of God. Christ is He, not any angel. [See question #2, page 346.]

### B. Jesus Is to Be Worshiped (vv. 6, 7)

**6a. And again, when he bringeth in the first-begotten into the world, he saith.**

Paul Ellingworth reasons that the expression *bringeth in* refers to Jesus' heavenly enthronement after His resurrection. In this case, *world* would refer not to the earth, but to the heavenly world. This conclusion best fits the context given the following quotes about the actions of angels. *First-begotten* is another term for *Son;* the element "first-" emphasizes the Son's supremacy over creation, picking up from Hebrews 1:1-4.

**6b. And let all the angels of God worship him.**

The location of this quotation is the first issue. Some say it comes from the end of Psalm 97:7, which reads, "worship him, all ye gods" (where *gods* may be used loosely to mean *angels*). However, the wording is not exactly the same as Hebrews.

More likely the author is quoting from Deuteronomy 32:43 in the Septuagint, which is the ancient Greek translation of the Old Testament. Most translations of Deuteronomy 32:43, including the *King James Version*, do not contain the phrase *and let all the angels of God worship him* because the Hebrew text does not have it. Perhaps your edition of the *King James Version* has a footnote at Hebrews 1:6 that explains this.

Deuteronomy 32 is a song that Moses recited before the assembly of Israel about the Lord's judgment on the wicked. In the Septuagint, the song includes a call for the heavens to rejoice and for the angels of God to worship "him." The author of Hebrews identifies the speaker as the Father and *Him* as the Son, the object of worship. In doing this, our author is also attributing to the Son the great deeds of the Lord mentioned in Deuteronomy 32.

The point is clear: since the *angels of God worship* the Son, He is superior to them. [See question #3, page 346.]

**7. And of the angels he saith, Who maketh his angels spirits, and his ministers a flame of fire.**

Visual for Lessons 1, 6, and 10

*Use this visual to open a discussion on the various titles or descriptions of Jesus.*

The author now quotes Psalm 104:4 to define the glorious function of *angels.* They are powerful spiritual beings who are servants of God. To describe them as *a flame of fire* reminds us of passages such as Genesis 3:24 and Exodus 3:2. Our author's point is simply that the angels are servants *(ministers).* They do not have the authority of the Son that we see in the next verse.

## IV. Son's Position (Hebrews 1:8-12)

### A. Authority (vv. 8, 9)

**8, 9. But unto the Son he saith, Thy throne, O God, is for ever and ever: a sceptre of righteousness is the sceptre of thy kingdom. Thou hast loved righteousness, and hated iniquity; therefore God, even thy God, hath anointed thee with the oil of gladness above thy fellows.**

These two verses quote Psalm 45:6, 7. The ancient title to Psalm 45 calls it a "song of loves," or a wedding song. Though Psalm 45:2 may be addressed to an earthly king (and verses 10-15 do seem to celebrate the wedding of an earthly king), the author of Hebrews indicates that some verses are addressed to someone else.

This someone else is "O most Mighty" (Psalm 45:3), who defeats the king's enemies (45:5). Further, Psalm 45:6 addresses this mighty one as God, yet as one who is somehow distinct from God in Psalm 45:7b ("therefore God, thy God"). Who else can this divine and mighty king be but the Son of God? [See question #4, page 346.]

The point is that Jesus' *kingdom* lasts forever. This can be said about no angel, much less about any earthly king.

## B. Permanence (vv. 10-12)

**10-12. And, Thou, Lord, in the beginning hast laid the foundation of the earth; and the heavens are the works of thine hands. They shall perish; but thou remainest; and they all shall wax old as doth a garment: and as a vesture shalt thou fold them up, and they shall be changed: but thou art the same, and thy years shall not fail.**

The author of Hebrews now quotes from Psalm 102:25-27. The key issue is the identity of the speaker of the words recorded here in Hebrews 1:10-12. In the Hebrew of Psalm 102, the speaker throughout the psalm is the psalmist, and the one being addressed is the Lord. But our author uses the word *and* in verse 10 to connect this quotation to the introduction in verse 8: "But unto the Son he saith, [quotes Psalm 45:6, 7] . . . and [quotes Psalm 102:25-27]." Thus our author clearly identifies the speaker as the Father and the addressee as the Son.

Our author does not doubt the superiority of the Son over the angels, and neither should we. The Son is the Lord God. He is the eternal, unchanging creator of all. When we are under crushing pain or stress, we might be tempted to follow something or someone other than the Son. At all times, but especially during dark days, we do well to remember the infinite magnificence of the person and power of the Son. [See question #5, page 346.]

### HERE TO STAY

Ira and George Gershwin comprised one of the greatest duos in American popular music. They were at their peak during the 1920s and 1930s. They wrote numerous Broadway shows, including the musical *Porgy and Bess*. Among the many classic songs they composed are "I Got Rhythm," "Embraceable You," and "Someone to Watch Over Me."

"Our Love Is Here to Stay" also stands tall as one of the best-loved songs of that era. The intent of the song was to declare that although cultural modes, features of the earth, etc., may change, "our love" is eternal. A nice, sentimental thought, but surely containing poetic exaggeration and embellishment.

The writer of Hebrews, however, makes a similar statement. The foundations of the earth and the very heavens shall perish, become old like a garment, and ultimately be folded up and put away. But the Lord God will ever remain the same. All else will change, but His years will not fail. What should this fact lead us to do?—J. B. N.

# Conclusion

## A. Who's Your Hero?

In the 2002 movie *Spiderman*, there is a scene with a girl trapped inside a burning building. The flames are so intense that the police and firefighters are unable to save her. Spiderman, wanted by the police for being a suspected criminal, arrives.

At the scene, Spiderman is arrested. He offers to go get the girl. The policeman, though obligated to hold him, suddenly lets him go. Why? Because only Spiderman is able to help. They need the amazing Spiderman to do what they could not.

But that's fiction, and there is no Spiderman. Yet humans do indeed live in a burning building: death. This is because of sin. We need someone who can rescue us because we cannot overcome or escape on our own. Whom will we trust to do this? A guardian angel? The author of Hebrews has a better answer: trust Jesus! He is stronger than any angel (or any other created being).

Our superhero is the very Son of God. He alone is able to save. He is not a comic book character. He is real.

## B. Prayer

Perfect Father, when fears and doubts about things worldly and unworldly assail us, help us to remember Your Son. He is more than enough! This has always been and always shall be. In Jesus' name, amen.

## C. Thought to Remember

When we listen to Jesus,
we listen to God.

---

# Home Daily Bible Readings

**Monday, May 26**—From the Beginning (Proverbs 8:22-31)

**Tuesday, May 27**—Appointed Heir (Hebrews 1:1-5)

**Wednesday, May 28**—In the Beginning (John 1:1-5)

**Thursday, May 29**—The Firstborn (Hebrews 1:6-9)

**Friday, May 30**—The Work of God's Hands (Hebrews 1:10-12)

**Saturday, May 31**—Full of Grace and Truth (John 1:14-18)

**Sunday, June 1**—Heir of All Things (Hebrews 1:13, 14)

# Learning by Doing

*This page contains an alternative lesson plan emphasizing learning activities. Some of these activities are also found in the helpful student book,* Adult Bible Class.

## Into the Lesson

Display a collection of angel figurines, ceramic and otherwise, in your study space. You may be able to borrow these from a class member who collects them. This will be a useful visual aid as you examine the contrasts between the Son and the angels in today's text. A suggestion in the Into Life section also utilizes these angelic representations.

Use the following "coded" messages to introduce not only today's study but also the first five lessons in this unit of study from the epistle to the Hebrews. Prepare 5 strips of paper, each strip 2½" high. Put creases across each strip 1" up from the bottom. Fill the top 1½" of each strip (from the top edge down to the crease) with the following descriptions, one per strip: *GOD'S SON, INTERCESSOR, REDEEMER, LEADER, ETERNAL.*

Fold up each strip on its crease and tape lightly so that the bottom half of each word is covered. Display each, one at a time. Ask the class to "decipher" the word that is only half seen.

After all are identified, say, "For these next five weeks, we will be looking at texts that reveal images of Christ in Hebrews, lessons that affirm Jesus to be God's Son, our only intercessor, our perfect redeemer, our trustworthy leader, and our eternal Christ." Leave these five posted throughout the five sessions.

## Into the Word

Create ahead of time four sets of 4" by 6" cards: seven cards that each say *NO!;* seven cards with the letters and exclamation *B, E, T, T, E, R, !* (one each per card); five cards with *J, E, S, U, S* (one letter each per card); five cards with *A, N, G, E, L* (one letter each per card).

To begin, post these two labels side by side: *GOD'S SON* and *ANGELS.* Then post the following labels underneath *GOD'S SON:* (1) appointed heir of all things, (2) made the worlds, (3) the brightness of His glory, (4) the express image of His person, (5) upholds all things by the word of His power, (6) purged our sins, and (7) sat down at God's right hand. Turn to the *ANGELS* column. At each line, ask, "Can this be said of any angel?" Post a *NO!* card as each question is answered. After you post all seven, read verse 4 and say, "In every way, the Son is better."

Now have learners read verses 5-7 in unison. Remove the *NO!* cards and post the following labels under *ANGELS:* (1) never referred to as sons, (2) never recorded as calling God "Father," (3) never an object of worship, (4) made by God, (5) simply servants of God to do His bidding.

When all five are in place and related to the text, take your *B-E-T-T-E-R-!* cards put them letter by letter to the left—under *GOD'S SON*—on each line to spell *BETTER!* (If you have the capability, consider preparing the preceding activity as a PowerPoint® presentation.)

Next, divide your class into groups of 5 or 6, or at least 2 groups if you have fewer than 10 learners total. Give each group a set either of the *J-E-S-U-S* cards or the *A-N-G-E-L* cards. Ask your groups to write a statement for each card using the letter in some significant way in the statement. Here are some examples: for *U,* a group could write "I am Jesus; the creation of the universe was in my hands"; for A, a group could write "I am an angel, an ambassador to do my Master's will."

Give the groups time to complete all statements. Then ask them to reveal their decisions to the entire class. As they do, ask, "How do you see that truth in today's text?"

## Into Life

Display one or more angel figurines (see the Into the Lesson idea). Ask the class to keep a tally of angel images and references they see and hear of in the coming week. Say that you will ask for a report at the beginning of next week's study. Suggest they consider why people collect and display angel figures and why they make such remarks as, "I guess my guardian angel was watching out for me" and "I think there are angels everywhere at work."

Some people believe in angels but do not believe in Jesus' sonship. Ask the class, "How could we respond to someone who holds such a belief?" Note that the response should emphasize the superior care, presence, and power of the Son. Anticipate that learners will note some of Jesus' superior attributes in today's text and study. Recommend that they listen for occasions this week in which they can "say a good word about Jesus the Son."

# Let's Talk It Over

*The questions on this page are designed to promote discussion of the lesson by the class and to encourage application of the lesson Scriptures. The answers provided are only discussion starters. Let your class talk it over from there.*

**1. How does (or how should) knowing that your sins have been purged by Christ affect your daily life?**

Some believers want the benefits of Christianity without the responsibilities. They want the forgiveness of sins but do not want to accept the lordship of Christ. But it is important that we see that the power that cleanses our sins is the same power available to direct our lives. It is through the power of the Lord that Christians are able to face the difficulties and obstacles of daily living victoriously.

Second Corinthians 12:9 tells us that this power demonstrates itself in our weakness. The power that created the world, the power that broke the shackles of death, the power that cleanses our sin is the power we have for living.

**2. What significance does (or should) the Father/Son relationship hold for your life in practical ways?**

In this time of broken families, we miss the significance of the value placed on family relationships. Today, children leave home for college and then after graduating locate themselves hundreds of miles away from their family of origin.

This has not always been the case. Historically, extended families worked together and at times even lived together. The son would work with his father and later inherit the family farm or the family business. It was not unusual to see a company called something like *Smith and Sons.* There was a unity of heart and purpose between father and son as they worked.

Those days are gone, by and large, and it's probably wishful thinking to expect that they'll ever come back. Even so, spiritual relationships are the most important things (compare Matthew 3:9; 5:9; 7:11; Romans 8:17; 1 Timothy 1:2; John 17:21; 1 John 3:10; etc.). It takes a lot of work to cultivate such relationships in the church, but it's vital to do so.

**3. What are some ways you have been guilty of failing to worship Christ properly? What have you done to improve?**

The angels were instructed to worship Jesus. Though holding such a high position with God, the angels are still created beings; as such, they are not to receive worship but to give worship.

The angels were created to be spiritual messengers of God. There are great flesh-and-blood messengers of God in the world today. The messenger may be a great preacher of God's Word leading a dynamic and growing church. Or she may be a gifted musician or singer who can lead others in worship to Christ. These people are not to be worshiped, even in the modern sense of being "idolized" as we put them on pedestals. All glory is to go to the Son. We constantly guard against glorifying God's servants, which runs the risk of worshiping and serving created things instead of the creator (compare Romans 1:25).

**4. How do you follow the Lord in loving righteousness and hating iniquity?**

The religious leaders of Jesus' day were more interested in making a show of their religion than in honoring God. They placed burdens on people that exceeded the teachings of the law. We must be careful that we are not "righteous" for impure reasons and that we do not set up a standard of right living that goes beyond God's Word.

Our righteousness comes from Christ (Philippians 3:9). We demonstrate His righteousness in how we treat others, especially the outcasts of society (see James 1:27). Our hatred for iniquity is seen when we refuse to participate in sinful activities.

**5. Why is it important that we see Christ as one who never grows old?**

When we think of someone growing old, we often think of the weaknesses that come with old age. There is the loss of sight and hearing, the loss of energy, and sometimes the loss of creativity. But none of that applies to Jesus. He always hears our prayers. He continues to possess that awe-inspiring power that strengthens and sustains us daily.

There are those who tell the church that we need to make Jesus relevant for our culture today. The fact is that He is already relevant, because the nature He possesses is the nature that transcends generations and cultures. Our task is to make ourselves relevant to Him.

# Only Intercessor

DEVOTIONAL READING: **Jeremiah 31:31-34.**

BACKGROUND SCRIPTURE: **Hebrews 7.**

PRINTED TEXT: Hebrews 7:20-28.

### Hebrews 7:20-28

20 And inasmuch as not without an oath he was made priest:

21 (For those priests were made without an oath; but this with an oath by him that said unto him, The Lord sware and will not repent, Thou art a priest for ever after the order of Melchizedek:)

22 By so much was Jesus made a surety of a better testament.

23 And they truly were many priests, because they were not suffered to continue by reason of death:

24 But this man, because he continueth ever, hath an unchangeable priesthood.

25 Wherefore he is able also to save them to the uttermost that come unto God by him, seeing he ever liveth to make intercession for them.

26 For such a high priest became us, who is holy, harmless, undefiled, separate from sinners, and made higher than the heavens;

27 Who needeth not daily, as those high priests, to offer up sacrifice, first for his own sins, and then for the people's: for this he did once, when he offered up himself.

28 For the law maketh men high priests which have infirmity; but the word of the oath, which was since the law, maketh the Son, who is consecrated for evermore.

GOLDEN TEXT: He is able also to save them to the uttermost that come unto God by him, seeing he ever liveth to make intercession for them.—Hebrews 7:25.

## Images of Christ
### Unit 1: Images of Christ in Hebrews
### (Lessons 1-5)

## Lesson Aims

After participating in this lesson, each student will be able to:

1. Compare and contrast Jesus' priesthood with the Old Testament Levitical priesthood.

2. Explain why it is better for us to live under Jesus' priesthood than under a continued Levitical priesthood.

3. Prepare a response to the assertion that living under the Jewish system is just as good as being a Christian.

## Lesson Outline

INTRODUCTION
   A. "I Am the Greatest!"
   B. Lesson Background
 I. GREATEST IN APPOINTMENT (Hebrews 7:20-22)
   A. Existence of Oath (v. 20)
   B. Priest by Oath (v. 21)
   C. Result of Oath (v. 22)
 II. GREATEST IN DURATION (Hebrews 7:23-25)
   A. Levitical Priests Died (v. 23)
   B. Jesus Lives Forever (vv. 24, 25)
      *Forever*
III. GREATEST IN EXALTATION (Hebrews 7:26-28)
   A. Jesus Is Holy (v. 26)
   B. Jesus Sanctified Himself (v. 27)
      *He Did it Once*
   C. Jesus Is the Greatest (v. 28)
CONCLUSION
   A. No More Dread
   B. Prayer
   C. Thought to Remember

## Introduction

### A. "I Am the Greatest!"

The famous world champion boxer Muhammad Ali is known for many memorable sound bites. But none is better known than his claim to be the greatest boxer of all time. It is impossible to find out whether he was truly better than all those who came before him. Neither is it clear that he could have beaten all the boxers that have come since his heyday. The fact that Ali lost five fights clouds the issue.

This is the way of all humanity; someone will always come along to take your place. The author of Hebrews proves to the reader that Jesus, the Son of God, is different in this respect. Jesus is truly and absolutely the greatest of all eternity. There has been no one before Him who was greater, and there will be no one after. There will be no one to take His place, because there will never be any need for anyone to do so.

### B. Lesson Background

In last week's lesson we learned that the original readers of Hebrews were Jewish believers who were under persecution. As a result, they were beginning to doubt whether faith in Jesus was really better than their previous beliefs. Our author addressed one aspect for his readers by proving from Scripture that Jesus is infinitely better than the angels.

Today's passage falls in the middle of a lengthy discussion covering the priesthood. The larger section includes Hebrews 4:14–10:25; we note the repetition of "high priest" in 4:14 and 10:21, marking off the beginning and ending of this large unit. The Old Testament role of high priest was that of a mediator between God and people to make peace (Hebrews 5:1). It is as though the Jewish believers in Christ were wondering, "Is Jesus' priesthood better than the Levitical priesthood set up in the law of Moses?"

In Hebrews 5, our author began to establish proof of Jesus' superior priesthood by describing the nature of that priesthood. In 5:1-4, the author lists the universal qualities of a priest. In 5:5-10, the author shows Jesus' relation to high priesthood by quoting Psalm 110:4, which compares the Son's priesthood to that of Melchizedek.

The author interrupts the argument at Hebrews 5:11 to warn the readers about falling away. After proving that Melchizedek's priesthood was greater than that of the Levites (the descendants of Abraham, 7:1-10), the author shows that Scripture describes the Son's priesthood as superior even to Melchizedek's (7:11-28). The fact that Jesus' priesthood is superior to even that of Melchizedek is the immediate backdrop to today's lesson (7:13-19).

## I. Greatest in Appointment (Hebrews 7:20-22)

### A. Existence of Oath (v. 20)

**20. And inasmuch as not without an oath he was made priest.**

The words *and inasmuch as* open a sentence that is interrupted by verse 21 and resumed in verse 22. You may notice that your edition of the *King James Version* has the phrase *he was made priest* in italics. This means that the translators found it necessary to add those words to make the meaning clearer. The negative *not without an oath* is a literary way of emphasizing that an oath was involved in making Jesus a priest. The author will finish this thought in verse 22.

## B. Priest by Oath (v. 21)

**21. (For those priests were made without an oath; but this with an oath by him that said unto him, The Lord sware and will not repent, Thou art a priest for ever after the order of Melchizedek.)**

One of the qualities of priesthood the author has already mentioned is that of being called, or appointed, by God (Hebrews 5:4). Although Aaron was called to be a priest by the Lord, all those who were high priests after him succeeded him by birth rather than by a direct call from God. Jesus, the Son, however, was made priest by a direct oath of the Lord. This was predicted in Psalm 110:4, which is quoted here.

Understanding how various words are used in the original context of Psalm 110 requires a bit of patience. In Hebrew, the language in which the Old Testament was written, the personal name of God is *Yahweh*. Most versions render this in English as LORD, with small capital letters. There is a different word that translations render *Lord* or *lord*, which often signifies "master," "owner," or "sir."

When we turn to Psalm 110:1, we see that David (the author) identifies the speaker as "the LORD" and the one being spoken to as "my Lord." The author of Hebrews clearly understands that

in Psalm 110:4 the speaker is still "the LORD" (Yahweh) and the one being spoken to is "the Lord," meaning the Son. *Sware* refers to an oath or vow. The phrase *will not repent* has nothing to do with repenting from any sin, but refers to God's not changing His mind about appointing the Son as high priest.

David quotes the actual words of Yahweh: "Thou art a priest for ever after the order of Melchizedek." The *thou* refers to the addressee. To whom is Yahweh referring? It must refer to the Son, the Messiah, Jesus. Thus, Psalm 110:4 is the oath of God that the Son will be a priest forever. [See question #1, page 354.]

Before we move on, we can pause to note that many translations follow numerous old Greek manuscripts of Hebrews that do not include the words *after the order of Melchizedek* at this point. However, those words definitely occur in the Greek in Hebrews 7:17, so we know the thought is genuine to the author of Hebrews.

## C. Result of Oath (v. 22)

**22. By so much was Jesus made a surety of a better testament.**

With the parenthesis ended, the words *by so much* pick up on what was started in verse 20. The Levitical priests of the Old Testament had no oath to establish their appointment to priesthood, but Jesus did. The difference between having that oath and not is as great as the difference between the old Mosaic covenant and the new covenant in Christ.

The Greek word translated *surety* occurs only once in the New Testament (right here) and only twice in the nonbiblical Jewish works written before the New Testament. However, it is common enough elsewhere. *Surety* may be understood either impersonally or personally. Impersonally, it may be the collateral "thing" that is put up to guarantee repayment of a loan. If the figure of speech is used in this way, Jesus himself is collateral, put up by the Father, who offers the *better testament*.

On the other hand, the word may be used for "a guarantor," meaning the person legally responsible for repayment. If this is the sense here, it means that Jesus is the one responsible to pay for the *better testament* by offering himself.

The latter idea is better, since Jesus' own sacrifice became the payment. The gravity of the role of guarantor is illustrated from the nonbiblical wisdom passage Sirach (Ecclesiasticus) 29:15: "Forget not the friendship of thy surety, for he hath given his life for thee." This is exactly what the Son has done for us—given His life.

---

### How to Say It

AARON. *Air*-un.

ABRAHAM. *Ay*-bruh-ham.

ECCLESIASTICUS. Ik-*leez*-ee-*as*-teh-kus (strong accent on *as*).

EUCHARIST. *You*-kar-ist.

HEBREWS. *Hee*-brews.

JESUIT. *Jeh*-zhu-it.

LEVITES. *Lee*-vites.

LEVITICAL. Leh-*vit*-ih-kul.

LEVITICUS. Leh-*vit*-ih-kus.

MELCHIZEDEK. Mel-*kiz*-eh-dek.

MUHAMMAD ALI. Mow-*hah*-med Ah-*lee*.

SIRACH. *Sigh*-rak.

TRANSUBSTANTIATION. tran-sub-stan-she-*a*-shun.

The *better testament* is the new covenant, or agreement, that God has made with humanity. This covenant is better to the degree that the trustworthiness of God's Son as guarantor is better than that of the earthly, Levitical priests. This is all based on the oath from the Lord himself.

## II. Greatest in Duration (Hebrews 7:23-25)

### A. Levitical Priests Died (v. 23)

**23. And they truly were many priests, because they were not suffered to continue by reason of death.**

The reason the Levitical priests *were many* is that they kept dying. *Were not suffered* means "were not permitted." Death prevented Aaron and his descendants from continuing as priests.

### B. Jesus Lives Forever (vv. 24, 25)

**24. But this man, because he continueth ever, hath an unchangeable priesthood.**

In contrast, the Son abides forever. He is eternal. The author of Hebrews has just made a significant point of this in 7:16. Numbers 35:9-28 lists laws regarding killing and the cities of refuge. If a person kills someone without malice aforethought, the law says that the killer is bound to the city of refuge only until the high priest dies. After that, the person is free to return home without any fear from the kinsman-redeemer. In Hebrews 7:12, our author makes the point that where there is a change of priest, there is necessarily a change in law. Since the Old Testament priesthood with its long succession of priests has been replaced by the new priesthood of Jesus, the old law and priesthood are over and a new law and a new priesthood are in place.

The original audience of Jewish believers can take comfort that Jesus is that new priest. But lest any reader wonder if there is yet another, better priesthood and covenant coming, our author focuses on the words "for ever" in that oath of Psalm 110:4. As a result of His immortality, Jesus has *an unchangeable priesthood.* In this context, Jesus' priesthood is unchangeable in that He has no successors and no need of any. Therefore, there never will be any other priesthood to replace Him. There will never come another covenant to supersede the one of which Jesus is the guarantor.

### FOREVER

People often have different notions of an elapse of time. Some people say, "I'll be ready in a minute," when it actually takes about 10 minutes. "Just a second," someone once told me; I waited for several minutes. I have a dear friend whom I often do things with. But I have learned to double his estimate of time. If he says he will be ready in 10 minutes, I know it will be 20; if he says 15, I know it will be 30.

Children are known to say repeatedly, "Are we there yet?" on car trips. When told that they have not yet arrived, they often say, "It's taking forever!" Indeed, *forever* is another interesting word. In the eighteenth century, the Roman Catholic Church received many criticisms about the Jesuit order because of its alleged political interference in various Catholic countries. Under pressure from several Catholic monarchs, Pope Clement XIV dissolved the Jesuit order "forever" in 1773. However, a new political climate emerged early in the nineteenth century, and the Jesuits were reactivated in 1814—just 41 years after they were dissolved "forever." I suppose that means, then, that "forever" lasts 41 years.

In spite of such variations and unpredictability, there is assurance in knowing that when God says *ever,* He means it. He refers to the new high priest as continuing, ever and ever living. God's assertions will not be changed by a new political climate. They are sure and "forever."     —J. B. N.

**25. Wherefore he is able also to save them to the uttermost that come unto God by him, seeing he ever liveth to make intercession for them.**

Because Jesus is an eternal priest, the guarantor of an eternal, irreplaceable covenant, He alone is able *to save* people. *To the uttermost* means that there is no limit to Jesus' ability to save—neither the depth of sin nor the number of sinners.

The object of Jesus' saving, though, serves as a condition: *them . . . that come unto God by him* means that God turns away no one who comes to Him. But each must come on God's terms. The only way to come to God is through the Son (John 14:6). The Son is able to save all because He lives eternally for the purpose of making eternal intercession (Romans 8:34; 1 John 2:1).

This message strengthened the faith of the original readers (Jewish Christians) as they began to realize the greatness of their Savior and their salvation. But this message is no less valuable today. How many lost people fear coming to God because they doubt that He will forgive them? How many Christians doubt their salvation because they dwell on their sin? Can Jesus save even though we still sin? Yes, Jesus saves now and forever, if we trust in His priestly work. [See question #2, page 354.]

## III. Greatest in Exaltation
## (Hebrews 7:26-28)

### A. Jesus Is Holy (v. 26)

**26. For such a high priest became us, who is holy, harmless, undefiled, separate from sinners, and made higher than the heavens.**

*Became us* is an older way of saying "is fitting for us" or "is suitable to us," as we might say, "That dress is very becoming." The Son is the kind of priest that is suitable to meet our need because of five qualities.

First, He is *holy*. The Greek word translated *holy* is not the usual word referring to God's holiness. The word that the author of Hebrews employs has various uses in the old Greek translation of the Old Testament, depending on context. "Innocent of wrongdoing" is what the author of Hebrews means here.

Second, He is *harmless*. This word occurs in only a few other places in the New Testament. In modern English, it carries the idea of being "without fault" in a moral sense. Third, He is *undefiled*. This means "without blemish." See Hebrews 13:4; 1 Peter 1:4; and James 1:27, which describe other things that are undefiled.

Fourth, the phrase *separate from sinners* does not mean that Jesus has no association with us (see Hebrews 2:11-17), but that He is utterly without sin. [See question #3, page 354.] Fifth, *made higher than the heavens* refers to Jesus' rightful place as divine ruler over the universe (Ephesians 1:20-22; Philippians 2:9-11; 1 Peter 3:22).

### B. Jesus Sanctified Himself (v. 27)

**27. Who needeth not daily, as those high priests, to offer up sacrifice, first for his own sins, and then for the people's: for this he did once, when he offered up himself.**

As priests, both the Son and the Levitical *high priests* had to *offer up sacrifice* for the people. However, before the Levitical high priests could offer sacrifice for the people, they first had to offer sacrifice for their *own sins*. There were two specific occasions when priests had to sacrifice for themselves before they could sacrifice for the people: the annual Day of Atonement (Leviticus 16:6) and the occasions when the anointed priest had sinned (Leviticus 4:3).

However, there is no Mosaic law requiring the priests to sacrifice *daily* for themselves. F. F. Bruce suggests that Leviticus 4:3 is what the author has in mind in using the word *daily*. Leviticus 4:2 talks about sins being committed "through ignorance." Even though they had more knowledge of the law than anyone else, priests

Visual for Lesson 2. *Point to this visual as you ask, "Why is it appropriate to speak of Jesus as a bridge?"*

would need to atone for such unintentional sins. But because the Son is absolutely and completely innocent of anything sinful, He has no need of any of those sacrifices. The Son is a priest who is ever a suitable intercessor on our behalf.

We are all sinful. The best of us is ugly to the core with sin. As intercessors, earthly high priests offered a service to the Old Testament Israelites. But ultimately they were poor representatives for the people, since they were sinful too. What makes the Son exactly suitable as a priest for us is His sinlessness. He is just the one we need to go to the Father on our behalf. [See question #4, page 354.]

#### HE DID IT ONCE

One of the most bitterly disputed issues among the leaders of the sixteenth-century Protestant Reformation was the difference in understanding regarding the Lord's Supper. But the major leaders of that movement all agreed on one thing: they all disagreed with the Roman Catholic understanding. Catholicism taught the doctrine of *transubstantiation*—the idea that the bread and fruit of the vine actually turn into Jesus' flesh and blood at the time of the mass.

This ties in with Catholic teaching that the Lord's Supper is a repetition of the sacrifice of Christ on Calvary. According to this idea, the benefit of the mass comes from offering up Christ again and again to God as a sacrifice for our sins—every time a Catholic priest celebrates the Eucharist. The alleged result is an unending supply of God's grace that comes from the repeated and constant sacrificing of His Son. This also the Protestant leaders rejected.

The writer of Hebrews tells us that Christ is offered up once—not perpetually and not even daily, as the Old Testament high priests offered up their sacrifices. This adds to the foundational theme of Hebrews that Christ is superior in every way to the Old Testament dispensation. Christ's sacrifice was necessary only once.     —J. B. N.

### C. Jesus Is the Greatest (v. 28)

**28. For the law maketh men high priests which have infirmity; but the word of the oath, which was since the law, maketh the Son, who is consecrated for evermore.**

This verse not only summarizes the idea of Jesus' having the greatest perfection, but also the entire first half of the argument begun in Hebrews 4:14: Jesus' high priesthood is superior because of His superior appointment. The kind of *infirmity* that the author of Hebrews has in mind here is both physical (the old priests die) and spiritual (they sin, even the most holy of them). These are the best that the Mosaic law could provide.

*The word of the oath* refers to what God said in Psalm 110:4, quoted in verse 21. Since this oath in Psalm 110 came after the law, it superseded it. Therefore, the Son's priesthood superseded the Levitical priesthood and lasts *for evermore*. The Greek for "for evermore" in verse 28 is identical to the "for ever" in verse 21; so our author is once again drawing from Psalm 110:4.

Under the Old Testament system (to which the original Jewish-Christian readers of Hebrews were tempted to return), the important role of priest as intercessor was carried out by flawed men. The contrast with the high priest Son could not be sharper. All humanity is sinful and in need of someone to make us acceptable to the holy one.

Thanks be to God that He has provided the very kind of intercessor high priest that we desperately need: one who is appointed by the Father himself, one who is immortal with an eternal priestly intercession, and one who is absolutely perfect. The earthly, Levitical priests descended from Aaron had none of those characteristics. [See question #5, page 354.]

# Conclusion

### A. No More Dread

Do you remember a time when you were overcome by a sudden sense of dread? Perhaps it happened when you were young, out on a playground. For some reason, an older, bigger kid threatened you. When he turned his back, you stuck your tongue out at him. But he saw you and came back at you. Sudden dread!

Later as an adult you see in your rearview mirror those flashing blue lights while you are driving. You look down; you are speeding. A ticket means inconvenience, a fine, and higher insurance rates. If you are just barely making ends meet, how will you make it now? Sudden dread!

When we become aware of our sinful standing before God, the only sensible emotion to have is a sense of dread. The realization that our sin against God makes us His enemy ought to give us an overwhelming sense of dread. We puny humans have no chance of standing up against the wrath of the infinitely powerful God of the universe. Our only chance is if we have an intercessor.

Jesus is the only suitable one to stand up for us. If we come to God through the blood of Jesus, we can be saved to the uttermost. Because God himself has appointed the Son to be our eternal, perfect high priest, we can have confidence of being accepted by God. God's acceptance is not based on our own righteousness, but on the perfection and obedience of the Son. We can live our lives today with no dread, no fear.

### B. Prayer

Loving Father, we thank You that You gave us just the right priest, who is really able to remove our sins and make us presentable to You. We offer our thanks in the name of the one who is Your appointee, eternal and utterly perfect, Jesus Your Son, amen.

### C. Thought to Remember

No fear!

## Home Daily Bible Readings

**Monday, June 2**—Preparing for a New Covenant (Jeremiah 31:31-34)
**Tuesday, June 3**—The Old Order of Priests (Hebrews 7:1-3)
**Wednesday, June 4**—King Melchizedek (Genesis 14:17-20)
**Thursday, June 5**—Introduction of a New Order (Hebrews 7:4-17)
**Friday, June 6**—The Permanent Priesthood (Hebrews 7:18-24)
**Saturday, June 7**—Interceding for All Who Approach God (Hebrews 7:25, 26)
**Sunday, June 8**—Perfect Forever (Hebrews 7:27, 28)

# Learning by Doing

*This page contains an alternative lesson plan emphasizing learning activities. Some of these activities are also found in the helpful student book,* Adult Bible Class.

## Into the Lesson

Invite a class member (or someone outside the class) who enjoys drama to prepare and present the following monologue on the Old Testament person Melchizedek. In today's text (and in the whole section of Hebrews related to this subject), Jesus' priesthood is shown to be relatively more like that of Melchizedek than that of Aaron.

Ask your actor to "dress the part," if appropriate ancient dress is available. Otherwise, let your actor wear a big name label around his neck.

### Melchizedek Monologue

"I see you have come to study the one who is the seed of my friend Abraham. Yes, that seed is Jesus; He is my Lord as well as yours. His Father anointed me to His priesthood long before Levi was a twinkle in his earthly father's eyes.

"It was my city of Salem—which you now call Jerusalem—that would one day become the city of the great king. And I don't mean David. My Lord would later sit on the mountain east of my city and bemoan its rejection of His kingship. They never understood how He would or could mediate for them in dying.

"You see that I am shrouded in both priestly garb and kingly regalia. They are both appropriate. Our Lord is both King of kings and high priest of Heaven itself. My own origin and ordination are shrouded in mystery. Can you comprehend the ordination of Christ Jesus to be high priest? Do you understand *forever?*

"Can you fathom the power of an indestructible life? You will hardly understand who I am or whence I came. But that does not matter. Your great high priest, Christ Jesus—understand Him. Understand His offering of His own blood to cover your sins. Who am I, Melchizedek? Only a shadow of the Lord who was and is and is to be. Understand Him. See Him in the words you study today.

"Now, Abraham did not hesitate to provide a tithe of all that he had to me. He knew it would be used only in worship of God Most High. It has always been true. God expects the honor of our gifts—not simply material offerings, but lives. What will you give Him?"

## Into the Word

Prepare and distribute copies of the following word-search puzzle.

```
I E C N O D E V U C T E U Q
R D E L T E S T A M E N T R
R E P A N E V N T S C Y T O
S Q O R I N R N T H T K E P
E U R C E S E S A I O S R R
R E T T E B H N M R S I M C
E R S S T H G R O E E R O I
N A T S A E I T C S E R S C
E J E M A F H E T Y O A T H
S T T B N S L O L T R I O T
N E L I T A E I R E C L E A
R E C E M S A S O R Y R I E
N T E B R D C E S U S O R D
S A C R I F I C E S I N T E
```

Tell your class that the challenge is to find 14 words from today's text. To add excitement, you can have your learners work in small groups or pairs to see which can finish first.

The 14 words to be found are *oath, priest, surety, testament, death, unchangeable, uttermost, holy, higher, daily, sacrifice, once, infirmity, better.* Point out that most verses from today's text have at least one word represented in the puzzle. To add difficulty, do not give your learners the list of 14 words they are to find.

## Into Life

Ask the class, "If we were still living under the Old Testament system of the Levitical priesthood, how would our daily lives be different?" Answers may include the needed trips to a central location for the sacrificial work to be accomplished, the purchase of animals to be offered, the necessity of tithes for support of the priesthood and the worship rituals, the required separation of males and females in worship assembly, and the lesser role each of us would play in the mediation process with God.

Let the group respond freely. Jot answers on the board. Conclude with a simple comment: "Aren't you glad we have Jesus as our high priest, our sacrifice, and our intercessor?" Ask three class members to word prayers of thanksgiving, one each for those three areas of your comment.

# Let's Talk It Over

*The questions on this page are designed to promote discussion of the lesson by the class and to encourage application of the lesson Scriptures. The answers provided are only discussion starters. Let your class talk it over from there.*

**1. What impact does the fact that Jesus is priest forever have on your life? How should that fact help you grow spiritually?**

The thought conveyed in the word *priest* is that of a bridge builder. Old Testament priests were to bridge the gap between people and God. But that system was temporary. Jesus, however, will always be there, building and being that bridge between God and us.

We are often abandoned, either physically or emotionally. Family members move away. Children are abandoned by a parent as the result of divorce. We become accustomed to a particular doctor, then she moves away. Because of these and many other areas where abandonment is common in our society, it is difficult at times to let down our guard to establish a trust relationship. Ultimately, Jesus is the only one who can be fully trusted not to abandon us.

**2. What would you say to a fellow believer who says that he has sins in his life that not even Jesus could forgive?**

One of the ways Satan works to keep us away from Christ is to make us feel that we could never get close to Him. Satan paints Christ as some tyrannical judge, always ready to strike down the sinner. Some preachers seem to focus more on the condemning judgment of God than on the message of redemptive love.

When we feel unworthy, we must realize that we are! That is why Jesus came. We also remember those great saints of old whom we read about in Scripture. There was a liar (Abraham), an adulterer (David), a murderer (Paul), and one who openly denied even knowing Jesus (Peter). We read of prostitutes and swindlers who received the gift of salvation through Christ.

Yet each of these are ones for whom Christ died. These pictures can allow us to live in joy in the knowledge that God accepts us through Jesus no matter how unacceptable we may feel. Salvation is not based on our feelings but on the work of Christ on the cross.

**3. How do you (or should you) respond to the fact that Jesus is "separate from sinners" (utterly without sin)?**

When we understand that Jesus was sinless, yet He died for our sins, it should humble us. This means daily living lives that are characterized by humility. We also will stop trying to do good works in order to earn God's favor because, when we try to do so, we deny the sufficiency of the cross.

As we reflect upon this sinless nature of Christ, we are moved to consider even more deeply how much the Father loves us. All of this should drive us to separate ourselves from sin. We should follow the scriptural admonition to flee from sin by resisting the temptations of the evil one (see James 4:7).

**4. What is the danger of not recognizing the sinfulness of earthly leaders?**

There are spiritual leaders who would hold themselves up as models of spirituality. To follow such a person blindly is dangerous. When we treat earthly leaders as if they were above sin, those leaders can in turn develop an unholy sense of pride.

This does not mean that we are to take the opposite position and find fault and never trust our leaders either. But blindly following leaders who raise themselves up as being above sin and above accountability is one of the things that has led to the formation of various religious cults. Taking the time to be discerning of our leaders and the things they teach is time well spent.

**5. What do you appreciate most about having Jesus as your high priest?**

We know our sins and how far we are from the Father. We know we do not deserve access to the Father. But we also know that Jesus, as the great high priest, is without sin. Not only does He have access to the Father, He is with the Father.

All of our needs are known by the Father because our high priest is there interceding for us. The Father forgives all of our sins because the blood of our high priest has covered them, and Jesus stands as our defense attorney before the Father. Thus we have hope.

All this should result in two things that permeate our daily lives: a feeling of assurance and an attitude of humility.

# Perfect Redeemer

DEVOTIONAL READING: John 4:21-26.

BACKGROUND SCRIPTURE: Hebrews 9:11–10:18.

PRINTED TEXT: Hebrews 9:11-18; 10:12-18.

### Hebrews 9:11-18

11 But Christ being come a high priest of good things to come, by a greater and more perfect tabernacle, not made with hands, that is to say, not of this building;

12 Neither by the blood of goats and calves, but by his own blood he entered in once into the holy place, having obtained eternal redemption for us.

13 For if the blood of bulls and of goats, and the ashes of a heifer sprinkling the unclean, sanctifieth to the purifying of the flesh;

14 How much more shall the blood of Christ, who through the eternal Spirit offered himself without spot to God, purge your conscience from dead works to serve the living God?

15 And for this cause he is the mediator of the new testament, that by means of death, for the redemption of the transgressions that were under the first testament, they which are called might receive the promise of eternal inheritance.

16 For where a testament is, there must also of necessity be the death of the testator.

17 For a testament is of force after men are dead: otherwise it is of no strength at all while the testator liveth.

18 Whereupon neither the first testament was dedicated without blood.

### Hebrews 10:12-18

12 But this man, after he had offered one sacrifice for sins for ever, sat down on the right hand of God;

13 From henceforth expecting till his enemies be made his footstool.

14 For by one offering he hath perfected for ever them that are sanctified.

15 Whereof the Holy Ghost also is a witness to us: for after that he had said before,

16 This is the covenant that I will make with them after those days, saith the Lord; I will put my laws into their hearts, and in their minds will I write them;

17 And their sins and iniquities will I remember no more.

18 Now where remission of these is, there is no more offering for sin.

GOLDEN TEXT: Neither by the blood of goats and calves, but by his own blood he entered in once into the holy place, having obtained eternal redemption for us.—Hebrews 9:12.

## Images of Christ
### Unit 1: Images of Christ in Hebrews
#### (Lessons 1-5)

## Lesson Aims

After participating in this lesson, each student will be able to:

1. Summarize the nature and effects of Christ's sacrifice.

2. Explain how the animal sacrifices of the Old Testament foreshadow the sacrifice of Christ.

3. Write a prayer of gratitude for Christ's sacrifice.

## Lesson Outline

INTRODUCTION
  A. Using Frequent Flier Miles
  B. Lesson Background
 I. ETERNAL REDEMPTION (Hebrews 9:11-14)
  A. Not in the Earthly Tabernacle (v. 11)
  B. Not by the Blood of Animals (vv. 12-14)
    *Quantity and Quality*
 II. ETERNAL INHERITANCE (Hebrews 9:15-18)
  A. New Covenant (v. 15)
  B. Enforceable Will (vv. 16-18)
 III. ETERNAL FORGIVENESS (Hebrews 10:12-18)
  A. Christ Sits at God's Right Hand (vv. 12, 13)
  B. Christ Perfects the Sanctified (v. 14)
  C. Christ Remits Our Sins (vv. 15-18)
    *Hearts and Minds*
CONCLUSION
  A. The Community of the Redeemed
  B. Prayer
  C. Thought to Remember

## Introduction

### A. Using Frequent Flier Miles

Because I fly often, I am careful to get credit for every flight in the various "frequent flier" programs. The system is simple. You accumulate points based on the miles of the flights you take. When you have enough points, you can use them to obtain free tickets or upgrades to first class. When you cash in your points for travel, some programs refer to it as "redeeming" your miles.

Redeeming miles is not always so simple, though. Most airlines restrict the use of mileage programs by having blackout dates. These are high-demand times when the planes will be full

anyway, so airlines hesitate to issue free tickets. Another problem comes when you have many miles accumulated on Airline XYZ, but XYZ doesn't fly to where you want to go. Redeeming frequent flier miles can be a frustrating process.

When the Bible talks about redemption, it intends us to understand something far removed from the imperfect "redemption" programs of modern airlines. To have Christ as our redeemer does not involve unexpected glitches or surprises. The most important difference is that with Christ we have not earned anything we can redeem. He is redeeming us!

### B. Lesson Background

The theme of *redemption* runs throughout the Bible. In the Old Testament it usually has the idea of saving someone from peril. Thus, a *redeemer* is nearly synonymous with a *deliverer*. By delivering the Israelites from the slavery of Egypt, God redeemed them (see Exodus 15:13; Deuteronomy 15:15). On the human-to-human level, the law allowed family property to be repurchased (redeemed) by a kinsman if it had been sold under distress (Leviticus 25:25).

In other places, the Old Testament authors use the concept of redemption to express personal deliverance (see 2 Samuel 4:9; Job 19:25; compare Psalm 19:14). In general, the Old Testament teaches the principle that God redeems those who serve Him (Psalm 34:22).

The later history of Israel saw oppression and exile by foreign nations. In these periods, the Jewish people looked forward to a time when God would redeem them again (see Micah 4:10). This expectation continued into the Israel of Jesus' day. Many Jews looked for deliverance from the hated Romans (see Luke 2:38; 24:21).

While these ideas of national and personal redemption are important themes in the Bible, the social world of the New Testament understood the language of redemption from the context of the institution of slavery. Redemption was related to the concept of ransom (see Mark 10:45). This was the price paid for a slave who was purchased and then set free.

The New Testament often uses slavery or bondage as an image to express spiritual realities. Paul speaks of three great spiritual tyrants: sin, death, and the law. For example, Paul sees us as being servants (slaves) of sin while in the sinful state of unbelief, unable to do genuine acts of righteousness. Faith in Christ saves/redeems us from this slavery, giving us the freedom to serve Christ (see Romans 6:16-19; 8:2). Christ has truly freed us (Galatians 5:1; compare John 8:32).

The book of Hebrews exhibits both an abundant Old Testament background and an awareness of the social structures of the first-century Roman world. When Hebrews speaks of Christ as the redeemer, it draws upon both worlds. The book's original readers looked to God as Israel's redeemer and deliverer in both past and future senses.

The book of Hebrews also understands the realities of the world of freed slaves, with the gratitude and devotion they felt for the one who rescued them. When it comes to sin, we can never redeem ourselves. Our redemption can be purchased only by the blood of the Son of God, our Savior (Colossians 1:14). This is forgiveness and freedom to live as true servants of our Lord.

## I. Eternal Redemption (Hebrews 9:11-14)

The previous sections of Hebrews established Christ as the all-sufficient high priest for the people of God. He is not subject to the failings of the Jewish Levitical priesthood, which amounted to sinful men making continual sin sacrifices for themselves and others. Jesus is presented as the ideal, sinless priest who is not subject to death. Consequently, He will never need to be replaced (see Hebrews 2:17; 7:26-28).

The primary function of the Jewish high priest was to offer sacrifices that would atone for the sins of the nation. These sacrifices were offered at the central place of worship for Israel: first the semiportable tabernacle and then the Jerusalem temple. The author of Hebrews draws upon the image of the tabernacle to explain the nature of Christ's sacrifice for our sins.

### A. Not in the Earthly Tabernacle (v. 11)

**11. But Christ being come a high priest of good things to come, by a greater and more perfect tabernacle, not made with hands, that is to say, not of this building.**

In keeping with his theme of comparing Christianity with the Mosaic covenant, the author uses the ancient tabernacle (rather than the Jerusalem temple) for the point of comparison. The tabernacle was understood to be an earthly representation of the eternal dwelling place of God.

The true tabernacle, however, is in Heaven (Revelation 15:5). God did not dwell in the earthly tabernacle or in the Jerusalem temple (Acts 7:48; 17:24). These merely served as specific locations for the Israelites to perform various offerings for sin. Jesus' work as a high priest was not in Jerusalem, but in Heaven at the *greater and more perfect tabernacle* (compare Hebrews 8:2).

### B. Not by the Blood of Animals (vv. 12-14)

**12. Neither by the blood of goats and calves, but by his own blood he entered in once into the holy place, having obtained eternal redemption for us.**

One of the high priest's duties was to offer an annual sacrifice for the people on the Day of Atonement (Yom Kippur). This involved the sacrifice of a young bull and a goat, plus the sprinkling of their *blood* on the mercy seat within the Holy of Holies, the innermost chamber of the tabernacle (see Leviticus 16:14, 15).

In the Christian system there is no more need for sacrificial animals, because Christ has offered *His own* perfect *blood* for this function. Christ's sacrificial death purchased our *eternal redemption*. [See question #1, page 362.]

#### QUANTITY AND QUALITY

I am always slightly amazed that people have so much difficulty distinguishing between *quantity* and *quality*. In the college classes I teach, I often have students ask if they can turn in "extra credit" work to raise their grade. I always say *no*.

I believe it is not fair to judge some students on the basis of 100 percent of their work and judge others on the basis of 125 percent of their work. Besides, how many *C* papers does it take to raise a grade to a *B*? *C* work should get a grade of *C*; turning in additional work does not raise its quality.

The same principle applies in other areas as well. How many junior high band concerts does it take to equal the quality of a single professional symphony orchestra? How many cans of baked beans does it take to equal an expertly prepared filet mignon? How much blood of bulls and goats does it takes to equal the redeeming value of the blood of the Son of God?

*Quantity* and *quality* are different things. It is Jesus' sinless quality that makes His blood effective for earning our eternal redemption. —J. B. N.

---

### How to Say It

HEBREWS. *Hee*-brews.
ISRAEL. *Iz*-ray-el.
JERUSALEM. Juh-*roo*-suh-lem.
LEVITICAL. Leh-*vit*-ih-kul.
LEVITICUS. Leh-*vit*-ih-kus.
MELCHIZEDEK. Mel-*kiz*-eh-dek.
MICAH. *My*-kuh.
MOSAIC. Mo-*zay*-ik.
MOSES. *Mo*-zes or *Mo*-zez.
YOM KIPPUR. Yom Kih-*pur*.

**13. For if the blood of bulls and of goats, and the ashes of a heifer sprinkling the unclean, sanctifieth to the purifying of the flesh.**

The author now adds *a heifer* (young cow) to the list of sacrificial animals, an animal whose *blood* and *ashes* were also used in a rite of purification for the people of Israel (see Numbers 19:1-10). The author's point is that these animal sacrifices had an effect, even if only a temporary effect. If they had been totally ineffective, then God would not have commanded the people of Israel to use them. This does not nullify the author's main point, however, that the animal sacrifices were short-term fixes offered by earthly priests, who had their own sin problems.

**14. How much more shall the blood of Christ, who through the eternal Spirit offered himself without spot to God, purge your conscience from dead works to serve the living God?**

This verse contains an important indication regarding the nature of Christ's sacrifice. While the author uses the rich imagery of the tabernacle to help us understand this process, he is not saying that there was an actual ceremony in Heaven at which the ascended and glorified Christ entered Heaven's temple.

Christ's offering was done spiritually *(through the eternal Spirit)*. It was done on the physical cross. That was where His perfect *blood* was sprinkled for our purification. Jesus' atoning death was a fulfillment of the intent of the entire sacrificial system of the Old Testament (see Hebrews 12:2). [See question #2, page 362.]

The author now brings this home to the readers. Christ's death makes human actions of sacrificing animals for sin unnecessary *(dead works)*, so any ritualistic behavior has become superfluous. We cannot feel secure by going through the traditional motions of religion. We must *serve the living God*, worshiping Him with our lives of obedience. We don't sacrifice bulls, goats, or heifers. We give the Lord our "sacrifice of praise" (Hebrews 13:15), the full expression of our lives of devotion. [See question #3, page 362.]

## II. Eternal Inheritance (Hebrews 9:15-18)

The Old Testament is a record of covenants—agreements that included promises of future blessings for those who obeyed and served God. We can distinguish specific covenants with Abraham, Moses, David, and others—thus the plural phrase "covenants of promise" (Ephesians 2:12). The authors of the New Testament tend to lump all of the pre-Christ covenants together as the "old covenant" or "old testament." This idea of an old covenant became synonymous with the Scriptures of the Jewish people, what Christians now call the Old Testament (see 2 Corinthians 3:14).

The word translated *covenant* has a dual meaning. It can carry the sense of a binding agreement between two parties. It can also have the sense of a person's will, one's instructions for disposing of possessions after death. When it has this second sense, it may be translated "testament," as it is in the *King James Version* (compare 2 Corinthians 3:6, 14). Here, Hebrews uses both senses in that a new covenant begins with the death of the covenant maker.

### A. New Covenant (v. 15)

**15. And for this cause he is the mediator of the new testament, that by means of death, for the redemption of the transgressions that were under the first testament, they which are called might receive the promise of eternal inheritance.**

A *mediator* is one who brings two sides together into an agreement. Jesus did this by His death. Jesus' sacrificial blood makes possible and begins the *new testament* (see Luke 22:20). The old covenant *(first testament)* is not so much nullified as it is now fulfilled completely.

God redeems His chosen people in an eternal, spiritual way. This is much more important to Him than defeating the national enemies of Israel like the Roman Empire. The Lord has brought about a redemption that frees men and women from the curse of sin and gives them an *eternal inheritance*, meaning eternal life (see John 3:16).

### B. Enforceable Will (vv. 16-18)

**16, 17. For where a testament is, there must also of necessity be the death of the testator. For a testament is of force after men are dead: otherwise it is of no strength at all while the testator liveth.**

Hebrews emphasizes the importance of the death of Jesus. From the context of the Old Testament and its sacrificial system, there had to be a *death* for sins. From the context of a last will and *testament*, the terms of the will are not valid until the *testator* (the one who makes the will) is dead. Then the will comes into *force*.

**18. Whereupon neither the first testament was dedicated without blood.**

Animal sacrifice is a bloody business. Altars are made with drainage systems so that the *blood* can be collected and removed. It has been speculated that the city of Jerusalem in Jesus' day must have had a terrible stench from the continual burning of animal flesh. The smell of spoiling blood is repulsive in and of itself. To the residents of the city, this pervasive odor is a constant reminder of their sin.

We, as Christians, are reminded of this bloody requirement every time we participate of the Lord's Supper. We remember the precious blood of Jesus that was shed for our sins. We should never forget that sin is not forgiven by God without the shedding of blood (Hebrews 9:22).

## III. Eternal Forgiveness (Hebrews 10:12-18)

We Christians know we are saved, but we may forget what we are saved *from*. We are saved from the legitimate consequences of our sin: eternal punishment by God. Unless this sin problem is taken care of in a permanent way, we always live under the threat of the future wrath of God being poured out on us. This section of Hebrews lifts up the eternal nature of our forgiveness through the blood of our Savior, Jesus Christ.

### A. Christ Sits at God's Right Hand (vv. 12, 13)

**12, 13. But this man, after he had offered one sacrifice for sins for ever, sat down on the right hand of God; from henceforth expecting till his enemies be made his footstool.**

The author draws upon the Melchizedek psalm (Psalm 110) once again to help explain the current position of Jesus. Christ has been enthroned with God and now awaits the full submission of all creation to His sovereignty. This is expressed symbolically as having His *enemies* made into a footrest (see Hebrews 1:13; compare 1 Peter 3:22). Even though Christ reigns in Heaven, there is a sense that not all things have become subject to Him just yet (Hebrews 2:8). One thing that remains is the final destruction of death itself (1 Corinthians 15:26).

### B. Christ Perfects the Sanctified (v. 14)

**14. For by one offering he hath perfected for ever them that are sanctified.**

*Sanctified* means to be holy. We are not holy through our own efforts, but because Christ's atoning death has taken away the taint of sin in our lives. The author does not mean that we have eliminated sin from daily life, but that in God's eyes we are *perfected* because our sins are forgiven. We don't need to seek out a temple and slaughter animals as a proxy sacrifice.

### C. Christ Remits Our Sins (vv. 15-18)

**15, 16. Whereof the Holy Ghost also is a witness to us: for after that he had said before, This**

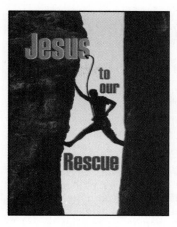

Visual for Lesson 3

*Point to this visual as you ask, "What attitude is necessary on our part to allow Jesus to rescue us?"*

**is the covenant that I will make with them after those days, saith the Lord; I will put my laws into their hearts, and in their minds will I write them.**

The author continues the method of using the Old Testament promises to help the readers understand the wonders of forgiveness in Christ. In this case, the author repeats some of the words of Jeremiah 31, which Hebrews 8 discusses extensively. This should cause us to remember that while the sacrificial system of the old covenant has been superseded in Christ, the Old Testament is still a valid Word of God, a *witness* from the *Holy Ghost*.

This verse serves as a warning against legalism. We do not follow a detailed written code, nor may we impose such a thing on others. Instead, we are controlled by the internal witness of the written Word through the power of the Holy Spirit. We are controlled by the great ethical principles taught by Jesus: to love God fully and to think of others more highly than ourselves. [See question #4, page 362.]

### HEARTS AND MINDS

One of the greatest emperors in ancient history was Justinian, who ruled the Byzantine Empire from AD 527 to 565. He revitalized the empire in numerous ways—reconquering half of the old western Roman Empire, reorganizing the government, and restructuring the army and the finances.

But one of his greatest achievements was codifying the laws of the empire. For centuries, the old Roman Empire had adopted various laws, but it had been a long time since they were organized.

The result was that often various legal enactments contradicted each other. Justinian saw the problems with this and made legal revision a high priority for his reign. The revisions became the basis of law codes for much of the rest of western civilization.

Others have followed Justinian's precedent of organizing (or attempting to organize) laws. Some years ago the U.S. Congress revised the Internal Revenue Code into over a thousand bewildering pages. And that became the problem! The common report is that even agents of the Internal Revenue Service are not consistent in applying the code. All those laws, written on paper, are hard to remember and even more difficult to understand. God has a better plan: He writes the laws of the new covenant on our hearts and in our minds.        —J. B. N.

**17. And their sins and iniquities will I remember no more.**

Under certain circumstances, a bank may be willing to "forgive" a debt through bankruptcy proceedings. But we may rest assured that the unpaid debt is not forgotten. It will be included on credit reports for many years and may make future loans impossible.

The promise in this verse is truly astounding. Through Christ, our *sins* have not just been moved from the *unforgiven* column to the *forgiven* side of the ledger. They have been blotted out completely (see Acts 3:19).

**18. Now where remission of these is, there is no more offering for sin.**

Because of the all-sufficient and eternal nature of our forgiveness through the blood of Jesus, the old sacrificial system (which was so integral to the Judaism of Jesus' day) is rendered redundant and unnecessary. We need not worry about a temple in Jerusalem, for our eternal high priest is in Heaven. His sacrifice for sins has been accepted once for all time. [See question #5, page 362.]

# Conclusion

### A. The Community of the Redeemed

Tradition says that when Roman gladiators entered the Coliseum for their contests, they would address the emperor's box by saying, "We who are about to die salute you!" These brutal men lived their last days with the knowledge that they had survived only to provide a spectacle in their deaths.

A Christian believer's acknowledgement of the Lord should be the flip side of the gladiator salute. Daily we could say, "We who have been rescued from death serve you!" We should celebrate our redemption. We must never forget that our salvation has been accomplished by the sacrificial blood of Jesus, not by our own efforts. We are not part of a team that has developed a successful strategy to avoid the consequences of sin. We are all, individually and as a whole, utterly beholden to Jesus for delivering us from eternal death.

Understanding this has a leveling effect in the church. Some church members may be more prominent and have more authority than other members. Some believers may be more mature in the faith or more learned in the Word than others. Some may have inspiring stories of persecution endured or hardship overcome. But every Christian, young or old, male or female, black or white, rich or poor, has exactly the same status before God. He or she is a sinner who has been granted redemption through the work of our eternal high priest, Jesus Christ.

There is no room for comparisons or boasting here, for we are all equally winners (see Ephesians 2:9). We are a community with a common leader, a common redemption, and a common future. The church is the community of those redeemed from the slavery of sin to live in joyful service to our king.

### B. Prayer

Lord God, who reigns in majesty from Heaven, we offer our thanks for our redemption through Jesus Christ. May we live as people who are not under the threat of punishment, but as those who have been redeemed. We pray this in the name of our Redeemer, Jesus, amen.

### C. Thought to Remember

The perfect Christ perfects us.

## Home Daily Bible Readings

**Monday, June 9**—"I Am He" (John 4:21-26)

**Tuesday, June 10**—Mediator of a New Covenant (Hebrews 9:11-15)

**Wednesday, June 11**—On Our Behalf (Hebrews 9:16-24)

**Thursday, June 12**—Once for All Time (Hebrews 9:25-28)

**Friday, June 13**—A One-Time Sacrifice (Hebrews 10:1-10)

**Saturday, June 14**—For Our Sanctification (Hebrews 10:11-14)

**Sunday, June 15**—Forgiveness Forever (Hebrews 10:15-18)

# Learning by Doing

*This page contains an alternative lesson plan emphasizing learning activities. Some of these activities are also found in the helpful student book, Adult Bible Class.*

## Into the Lesson

Display a grid with the word *ETERNAL* running horizontally. Have three blank spaces above the first *E* and six spaces below (for the word *REDEMPTION*). Have two blank spaces above the *R* and eight spaces below (for the word *FORGIVENESS*). Have seven blank spaces above the *A* and three spaces below (for the word *INHERITANCE*). When completed per the following, you will have on display the outline of today's text: I. Eternal Redemption; II. Eternal Inheritance; III. Eternal Forgiveness.

To fill in the blanks, say to your learners, "Three words will complete this grid and provide an outline of our study today. What letters do you think belong in the blanks? Give me one at a time." As learners suggest letters, fill in the ones that are correct. Continue until all are complete. Note to the class, "Here we have the writer's outline of our study today."

To verify your group's understanding of the concept of redemption, ask them in what ways the term is used today. Expect such responses as "redeeming airline frequent flier miles," "redeeming bonus points at banks or other businesses," and in the sense of someone having "a redeeming quality" that helps cancel out more obvious negative qualities. Introduce the writer's explanation of the concept in the first-century Roman world and thus, in many respects, the New Testament usage.

## Into the Word

Divide your class into two groups, a *Hebrews 9 Group* and a *Hebrews 10 Group* for an antiphonal reading. The readings will be Hebrews 9:11-18 and Hebrews 10:12-18.

Direct the groups to alternate verses: the *Hebrews 10 Group* begins by reading 10:12, then the *Hebrews 9 Group* reads 9:11; the *Hebrews 10 Group* reads 10:13, the *Hebrews 9 Group* reads 9:12; and so forth. Though these texts are not perfectly parallel, reading them in this back-and-forth manner will work, and several interesting pairings will be seen.

Next, give your learners the following list of Bible verses with this direction: "Look up each of these verses and relate each to a specific verse in today's text. Decide which is the best match

for each. You may change your mind as you look up more verses." (This activity may be done as a group activity, or you may allow time for individuals to make matches before the class as a whole looks at decisions.)

*References:* Exodus 27:1, 2; Numbers 19:9; Numbers 27:8-11; 1 Chronicles 6:49; Psalm 110:1; Isaiah 59:20, 21; Jeremiah 31:33; Jeremiah 31:34; Luke 24:46, 47; John 2:19; John 5:36; 2 Timothy 2:21; Hebrews 7:27; 1 Peter 3:22.

Consider these to be appropriate matches: Exodus 27:1, 2 with Hebrews 9:18 (in the sense that the Hebrew worship required an altar for sacrifice; it required blood); Numbers 19:9 with Hebrews 9:13; Numbers 27:8-11 with Hebrews 9:16, 17 (in that it speaks of inheritances being given at the death of a person); 1 Chronicles 6:49 with Hebrews 9:12 (both having to do with entering the Holy of Holies); Psalm 110:1 with Hebrews 10:12; Isaiah 59:20, 21 with Hebrews 9:15; Jeremiah 31:33 with Hebrews 10:16; Jeremiah 31:34 with Hebrews 10:17; Luke 24:46, 47 with Hebrews 10:18 (as both deal with forgiveness of sins by sacrifice); John 2:19 with Hebrews 9:11, 12 (former deals with the heavenly tabernacle, the other with the tabernacle of Christ's body); John 5:36 with Hebrews 10:15 (as each refers to the testimony of the Spirit); 2 Timothy 2:21 with Hebrews 9:14 (both deal with individuals cleansed for service to God); Hebrews 7:27 with Hebrews 10:14 (each emphasizes the once-for-all sacrifice of Christ); 1 Peter 3:22 with Hebrews 10:12.

Learners may make other legitimate matches; ask any who do to explain the relationships they see.

## Into Life

Distribute copies of the following, with a suggestion that your learners fill it in as their personal reflection on the redemptive grace of God.

"Lord, I sold myself to _____; You bought me back at _____. I sold myself for _____; You bought me back in _____. I sold myself by _____; You bought me back by _____. I sold myself too _____; You bought me back with _____. Thank You, Lord, for Your redeeming love in Christ."

Ask one of your learners who prays well publicly to word a concluding prayer of thanksgiving for our redemption in Christ's blood.

# Let's Talk It Over

*The questions on this page are designed to promote discussion of the lesson by the class and to encourage application of the lesson Scriptures. The answers provided are only discussion starters. Let your class talk it over from there.*

**1. Jesus' death on the cross is referred to as the *substitutionary atonement*. What usually comes to your mind when you think of the word *substitute*? How is that different from the idea of Jesus being a substitute?**

We normally think of a substitute as standing in the place of the real thing. A substitute teacher fills in for the regular teacher. Sometimes when something we want from a menu is not available, a substitute is offered. When we think of these substitutes, we often consider them as less than that for which they are a substitute.

But with Jesus, He is a substitute that is superior. Also, when we have substitute teachers or a substitute item in our meal, we may long for the real thing to return. But we are happy to have Jesus as our continual substitute!

**2. Why do some believers find it hard to understand and accept the sacrifice of Christ for their sins? What would you say to someone having trouble in this area?**

In a world where people are more concerned about promoting self and looking out for number one, it is hard to comprehend that one would be willing to sacrifice self for others. People are often more concerned with the idea of "What's in it for me?" than what will benefit others.

We may also find it hard to accept the sacrifice of Christ because we know the depth of our personal sins and how unworthy we really are. Our response to someone having trouble with this can include Romans 5:7, 8: "For scarcely for a righteous man will one die: yet peradventure for a good man some would even dare to die. But God commendeth his love toward us, in that, while we were yet sinners, Christ died for us."

**3. What are some of the "dead works" you have done instead of being involved in active service? How did you put this behind you?**

*Dead works* are things that do not result in or accompany works of active service. Dead works especially include empty rituals. Empty rituals are not heartfelt; they are things we do that amount to little more than formal religious practices.

One example is when we use prayer as a substitute for action (see Exodus 14:15). When we see giving to the church as fulfilling our service, then we are drifting into a "hire it done" mentality. Praying, giving, attending, etc., are not bad things in and of themselves. But when they are used in place of becoming actively involved in service, they become empty rituals. A key is to make a commitment to *be* the church rather merely *belong to* a church.

**4. What gives you confidence in the promise of your eternal inheritance? How do you live out this confidence?**

God is a maker of covenants. He is always faithful to uphold His part in the covenant. Jeremiah 31:31 offers a promise of a new covenant. We see this covenant fulfilled in Jesus Christ.

In a sermon in which Paul preached on how God made promises and covenants with Old Testament saints, we read, "We declare unto you glad tidings, how that the promise which was made unto the fathers, God hath fulfilled the same unto us their children, in that he hath raised up Jesus again" (Acts 13:32, 33). We have personally experienced God's fulfillment of His promise to strengthen and protect His people. Based upon this perfect track record, we can expect God to continue to fulfill His promises. *God is in charge—no matter what* can be the way we live out our lives.

**5. Since our works are not an offering made for the forgiveness of our sins, why bother doing good works? How have you grown in your motives in this regard?**

According to Titus 3:5, we see that God saved us "not by works of righteousness which we have done, but according to his mercy." Trying to work to earn our salvation is an affront to God's grace. Our good works are offered not to gain God's favor, but instead they are performed out of appreciation for the gift of salvation given to us.

The works we do are also a source of personal, spiritual growth. We are simply fulfilling our role that we received when we committed our lives to Christ. Ephesians 2:10 states: "For we are his workmanship, created in Christ Jesus unto good works, which God hath before ordained that we should walk in them."

# Trustworthy Leader

DEVOTIONAL READING: Proverbs 3:5-12.

BACKGROUND SCRIPTURE: Hebrews 12:1-13.

PRINTED TEXT: Hebrews 12:1-13.

### Hebrews 12:1-13

1 Wherefore, seeing we also are compassed about with so great a cloud of witnesses, let us lay aside every weight, and the sin which doth so easily beset us, and let us run with patience the race that is set before us,

2 Looking unto Jesus the author and finisher of our faith; who for the joy that was set before him endured the cross, despising the shame, and is set down at the right hand of the throne of God.

3 For consider him that endured such contradiction of sinners against himself, lest ye be wearied and faint in your minds.

4 Ye have not yet resisted unto blood, striving against sin.

5 And ye have forgotten the exhortation which speaketh unto you as unto children, My son, despise not thou the chastening of the Lord, nor faint when thou art rebuked of him:

6 For whom the Lord loveth he chasteneth, and scourgeth every son whom he receiveth.

7 If ye endure chastening, God dealeth with you as with sons; for what son is he whom the father chasteneth not?

8 But if ye be without chastisement, whereof all are partakers, then are ye bastards, and not sons.

9 Furthermore, we have had fathers of our flesh which corrected us, and we gave them reverence: shall we not much rather be in subjection unto the Father of spirits, and live?

10 For they verily for a few days chastened us after their own pleasure; but he for our profit, that we might be partakers of his holiness.

11 Now no chastening for the present seemeth to be joyous, but grievous: nevertheless, afterward it yieldeth the peaceable fruit of righteousness unto them which are exercised thereby.

12 Wherefore lift up the hands which hang down, and the feeble knees;

13 And make straight paths for your feet, lest that which is lame be turned out of the way; but let it rather be healed.

GOLDEN TEXT: Let us lay aside every weight, and the sin which doth so easily beset us, and let us run with patience the race that is set before us, looking unto Jesus the author and finisher of our faith.—Hebrews 12:1, 2.

## Images of Christ
### Unit 1: Images of Christ in Hebrews
(Lessons 1-5)

## Lesson Aims

After participating in this lesson, each student will be able to:

1. Describe the role and the importance of discipline in the training of an athlete and in rearing a child.

2. Compare and contrast human discipline with God's discipline.

3. Identify one area where he or she needs to submit to divine discipline.

## Lesson Outline

INTRODUCTION
  A. Cheating to Win
  B. Lesson Background
  I. PREPARING TO RUN WITH JESUS (Hebrews 12: 1, 2)
    A. Discarding Our Baggage (v. 1)
    B. Discerning Our Goal (v. 2)
 II. TRAINING TO RUN WITH JESUS (Hebrews 12: 3-11)
    A. Striving Against Sin (vv. 3, 4)
    B. Dealing with Discipline (vv. 5-11)
       *Chastening*
III. HEALING TO RUN WITH JESUS (Hebrews 12: 12, 13)
    A. Adjusting Attitude (v. 12)
       *Encouraging the Weary*
    B. Keeping on Course (v. 13)
CONCLUSION
    A. Practice Makes Perfect
    B. Prayer
    C. Thought to Remember

## Introduction

### A. Cheating to Win

Cheating scandals seem to confront us on a continual basis in the world of professional sports. Baseball players take illegal performance-enhancing supplements to make themselves stronger and faster. Hockey players alter their sticks to give an advantage the rules do not allow. Race car drivers violate their sport's regulations by installing hidden equipment to improve their cars' performance.

Cheating is rampant in other areas of life too. Business leaders "cook the books" to create the illusion of more profit in order to secure bigger performance bonuses. Scientists engage in fraudulent or misleading research in order to make a name for themselves. Students freely admit to cheating on exams, claiming that this behavior is necessary to give them a competitive advantage over other students and thereby gain admission to the best colleges or graduate schools. Too often, people are living under the impression that cheating is the only way to win.

In every area of life, then, society is forced to set up ever tougher enforcement agencies. We must catch those cheaters! We have moved to a cat-and-mouse game in which some say, "I will cheat unless there is a substantial risk of being caught." The onus for cheating prevention is now on those enforcing the rules, not on the cheaters themselves. We have moved a long way from having most participants simply say, "I won't cheat."

All of this is a matter of discipline. A *disciplined* person is one who abstains from cheating and resolves to follow the rules. This person submits to discipline, even when doing things the right way is doing things the hard way. This person is more concerned about living within the rules than questioning the fairness of the rules. True discipline and cheating are incompatible and irreconcilable. In the end, avoiding discipline by cheating is for losers. Winning by cheating is a hollow, empty victory. This lesson looks at some of the key elements of the disciplined life of a Christian, a life where there is no place for cheating.

### B. Lesson Background

Today's lesson text follows one of the most famous chapters in the New Testament, Hebrews 11. That chapter is known as the "Faith Hall of Fame." It is a rehearsal of the lives of several key Old Testament saints, showing how they lived by faith in God. Yet the chapter ends by noting, "And these all, having obtained a good report through faith, received not the promise" (Hebrews 11:39).

The Old Testament faithful could only look ahead to the blessings enjoyed by Christians. The original community receiving the letter to the Hebrews was facing hardship (Hebrews 10:32-34), even persecution. The author of Hebrews did not want his readers to think that they were alone in enduring hardships; the earlier people of God had it rough too. A frequent exhortation in the book is to "hold" or "hold fast" to the precious faith in Christ (see Hebrews 3:6, 14; 4:14; 10:23).

Chapter 12, this lesson's focus, gets down to some of the nitty-gritty details of this "holding fast." Not only will there be hardships imposed on the believers from the outside, there will be hardships that come from God himself. This is the chastening of God. As the author clearly portrays, it is discipline designed for the benefit of the believer. The central principle in this chapter is that such discipline is part of His love.

Discipline could be harsh in the ancient world. The success of the Roman army was built on ruthless discipline within the legions. Apprentices learning a trade were forced to work long hours. Yet there was another side to discipline in this era too. To be a *disciple* meant that you were a student. You had attached yourself to a teacher and allowed him to be your master in all things.

This relationship was more than tutoring once or twice a week. The teacher-disciple arrangement was often a "24/7" situation, where the teacher was in total control of the student's life. This is the way the book of Hebrews pictures the relationship of Christians to God. God is concerned with every aspect of our lives and uses corrective discipline to bring us to advanced levels of godliness and holiness.

# I. Preparing to Run with Jesus (Hebrews 12:1, 2)

At the end of chapter 11, we are told that the great faith heroes of the Old Testament could not be "made perfect" (Hebrews 11:40). This expression was sometimes used of runners who could not finish a race. The author of Hebrews continues this race analogy into chapter 12, now applying it to Christians.

## A. Discarding Our Baggage (v. 1)

**1. Wherefore, seeing we also are compassed about with so great a cloud of witnesses, let us lay aside every weight, and the sin which doth so easily beset us, and let us run with patience the race that is set before us.**

This verse paints a marvelous picture. Imagine the premier running *race* in all the world: the marathon at the Olympic games. A handful of runners, the world's finest, are at the starting line. Thousands of spectators await the starting gun. But this crowd is magnified to perhaps two or three billion people via worldwide television. That would be a great *cloud of witnesses*!

The runners are wearing the barest of essential clothing. They have shed their warm-up suits.

They are not carrying their duffle bags. Some have even shaved their bodies to rid themselves of a tiny amount of weight. Their training has increased their endurance and eliminated excess body fat. They have lain *aside every weight* that might slow them down.

The analogy to the Christian life has to do with personal sin. The author's point is that sin slows us down in our pursuit of godliness. We know the racecourse. We want to finish the race. Sin hinders our success. Unchecked sin in our lives may slow us down, get us off course, or even stop us dead in our tracks. We want to be like Paul, who at the end of his life was able to say, "I have finished my course [race], I have kept the faith" (2 Timothy 4:7). [See question #1, page 370.]

## B. Discerning Our Goal (v. 2)

**2. Looking unto Jesus the author and finisher of our faith; who for the joy that was set before him endured the cross, despising the shame, and is set down at the right hand of the throne of God.**

The text continues the race analogy, now with a slight shift. The author speaks of *Jesus* as the runner, and *the cross* as the race. Jesus was willing to accept the hard things of His run. He was not deterred by *the shame* of His scandalous death, a gruesome execution befitting the worst criminal. He was a *finisher*, not a quitter. In this Jesus has shown us the way, the way of *our faith*, the way we too should run the course of our lives in submission to His leadership.

We also see the great reward Jesus has gained. It is more than an Olympic gold medal or a huge signing bonus for the next season. Jesus has been recognized once and for all by being given a seat *at the right hand of the throne of God.* There is no higher honor available.

# II. Training to Run with Jesus (Hebrews 12:3-11)

The author of Hebrews continues to describe the Christian life in terms of athletic competition. The author uses the metaphor of the oldest competition known to humans: running races.

---

### How to Say It

BARAK. *Bair*-uk.
ENOCH. *E*-nock
JEPHTHAH. *Jef*-thuh *(th* as in *thin).*
MARATHON. *mehr*-uh-thon.

The intent is for us to see this race as a lifelong event, not a short sprint. We run and learn how to run better at the same time. We are in the race of our lives!

## A. Striving Against Sin (vv. 3, 4)

**3. For consider him that endured such contradiction of sinners against himself, lest ye be wearied and faint in your minds.**

Distance runners know that in the race there comes a time when the runner wants to quit. The body screams, "Enough!" Lungs are burning. Legs are rubbery. The runner feels weary, oh so weary! The runner feels *faint*. [See question #2, page 370.]

The race that Jesus ran was made tortuous because of the *contradiction of sinners*, meaning the opposition He received from the leadership of the Jews in His day. He *endured* public denunciations, name-calling, threats of death, attempts to dissuade His disciples from following Him, and eventually arrest and crucifixion. While this atoning death made our salvation possible, the life of Jesus also serves as an example and inspiration to those who follow Him.

**4. Ye have not yet resisted unto blood, striving against sin.**

For the book of Hebrews, to live by faith is *striving against sin*. The life of faith engages in constant struggle against sin, for "whatsoever is not of faith is sin" (Romans 14:23).

The great faith heroes of chapter 11 were surely beset by doubts. They had opportunities to disobey God and serve themselves. The author reminds us that although living the Christian life can be challenging, most of us do not suffer death (resist *unto blood*) in our efforts to resist temptation and avoid falling to sin. Our efforts, no matter how great, will not equal the sacrifices made by our leader, Jesus.

## B. Dealing with Discipline (vv. 5-11)

**5, 6. And ye have forgotten the exhortation which speaketh unto you as unto children, My son, despise not thou the chastening of the Lord, nor faint when thou art rebuked of him: for whom the Lord loveth he chasteneth, and scourgeth every son whom he receiveth.**

A frequent theme in the Old Testament is that God's corrective punishment of Israel is motivated from God's love for Israel (see Deuteronomy 8:5; compare Revelation 3:19). One of the ways in which God is our "Father" is in this matter of discipline. The author uses Proverbs 3:11 to make a point: hardship in life is not a sign of God's disfavor. It may be a manifestation of God's love through corrective discipline. [See question #3, page 370.]

A hard lesson of parenthood is that love for a child is sometimes expressed in the form of discipline. The coddled child who is never told *no* and never experiences parental punishment will be ill equipped to live with the harsh realities of the adult world. Those parents who avoid the painful task of correction and discipline are really thinking more of themselves than of their children.

**7, 8. If ye endure chastening, God dealeth with you as with sons; for what son is he whom the father chasteneth not? But if ye be without chastisement, whereof all are partakers, then are ye bastards, and not sons.**

Sometimes when we are discouraged by the turn of events in our lives, we want to ask, "Where is God in all of this?" The answer is that God may be right in the middle of it. God takes no joy in seeing His children suffer. He is not a masochist. Our pain does not bring Him pleasure. Yet God never abdicates his role as our corrective parent (compare 2 Samuel 7:14).

The author reminds us that we should not fear the hardships that God allows into our lives. We should fear the day when the hardships cease, for that will be the time when we are *not* sons. That will be a day when God truly abandons us, a day when we become God-forsaken. That would be a time when God gives us up to the depraved lusts of our passions (see Romans 1:26, 27).

**9. Furthermore, we have had fathers of our flesh which corrected us, and we gave them reverence: shall we not much rather be in subjection unto the Father of spirits, and live?**

From an adult perspective it is easier to understand that discipline given by our parents was for our own benefit. This principle, however, is not a justification for the cruel, abusive behavior practiced by some parents. Firm and consistent guidelines in the formative years give children the possibility of being self-disciplined as adults.

In the normal course of life, then, we do not hold a grudge against the parent who taught us self-discipline. Instead, we respect that effort, and we are blessed by it. Likewise, we should understand that God's discipline in our lives is motivated by God's concern for us. We give Him the respect He deserves, even in the most trying of times. [See question #4, page 370.]

**10. For they verily for a few days chastened us after their own pleasure; but he for our profit, that we might be partakers of his holiness.**

Discipline by human parents is never perfect. Parents use their best judgment *(after their own pleasure)* when administering discipline. Some parents are too harsh; some are too lenient.

But God's discipline is always just right. The Lord has no need to relieve His frustrations through brutality or abuse. His goal is our perfection, our attainment of *holiness.* On the practical level, holiness is not achieved in one fell swoop. It is more commonly the process of conquering one sinful behavior at a time. In this, God's firm hand of discipline is pushing us along in our faithful, lifelong pursuit of holiness.

**11. Now no chastening for the present seemeth to be joyous, but grievous: nevertheless, afterward it yieldeth the peaceable fruit of righteousness unto them which are exercised thereby.**

One oft-repeated phrase in many disciplines is *no pain, no gain.* We do not become smarter by taking a smart pill. We do not become accomplished musicians by merely buying a guitar. We do not become skilled athletes by watching games on television.

This verse continues the athletic training analogy by saying that our trials are ways in which we are *exercised.* The Greek word behind *exercised* is also the root for our word *gymnasium.* This word is drawn from the athletic terminology of the ancient Greeks. The gymnasium was (and still is) a place where athletes practiced wrestling, did strength-building exercises, and participated in other activities to develop their abilities. Perhaps we can view life as God's gymnasium: the place where we receive ongoing training in our faithful pursuit of holiness, the *fruit of righteousness* (compare James 3:17, 18).

CHASTENING

Some yeas ago, I had a friend who had instructed his son on how to mow the lawn. He showed him all that was to be done—not only cutting the grass, but also trimming around the trees and sweeping up the clippings. For this task, the father promised five dollars (a goodly sum in those days!).

Accordingly, the son cut the grass and swept up the clippings, but he neglected trimming around the trees. When his dad came home and inspected the job, he said that the son had failed to fulfill his assignment and there would be no pay. The son pleaded for the opportunity for a second chance to trim around the trees properly. But his dad refused. Because the job was not done right, there was no financial reward.

The boy was disappointed, but the next time he was asked to mow the grass, he did a thorough job and got paid. In fact, he got so good at it he was soon asked to mow other people's lawns. He worked his way through college by doing yard work. If his dad had let him off the hook on his first assignment, perhaps he never would have learned the lesson of doing a job right the first time. As it was, the father's chastisement resulted in a valuable lesson for the future. Such is true in the Christian life as well.      —J. B. N.

## III. Healing to Run with Jesus (Hebrews 12:12, 13)

The tone changes in this section to one of exhortation. The readers are encouraged not to be deterred by the prospect of God's chastening.

### A. Adjusting Attitude (v. 12)

**12. Wherefore lift up the hands which hang down, and the feeble knees.**

The idea of the athlete in training is continued. Toward the end of a basketball game, coaches remind fatigued players to keep their *hands* up and keep moving their feet when playing defense. Here, the exhortation is to *lift up* hands and *knees.* The underlying idea is that we must grow strong again and not be overcome by weariness. We cannot let fatigue defeat us. We claim God's promise that we may "run and not be weary . . . walk, and not faint" (Isaiah 40:31; compare 35:3).

This is not athletic training advice, however. It is spiritual instruction. We cannot be satisfied with reaching a certain level in our walk with God, or "plateauing." We must continue to employ our hands to work for God. We must stay on our feet and continue our spiritual journey,

Visual for Lesson 4. *Point to this visual as you ask for volunteers to describe some important parts of their faith journeys.*

even if our knees are aching. [See question #5, page 370.]

### ENCOURAGING THE WEARY

Encouraging the discouraged sometimes can be done with gentle words of support; sometimes it has to be done with harsh words of censure. Consider the case of Eddie Rickenbacker (1890–1973).

Rickenbacker was a U.S. World War I Air Corps hero. He was credited with 26 victories, the highest number of any American. After the war he became a pioneer in commercial aviation. During World War II he offered his civilian services to the government, touring air bases and doing public relations work for the military.

He found himself on a tour of bases in the Pacific in October of 1942. Flying west from Hawaii in a B-17, the pilot missed Canton Island, and the plane had to ditch in the Pacific. Rickenbacker and the crew floated on the sea for 24 days, staying alive by eating the occasional fish or captured bird and drinking rainwater.

Rickenbacker became the unofficial encourager of the group, occasionally resorting to browbeating and caustic remarks. He never let them give up. Sometimes he made them hate him, hopefully giving them enough reason to continue to live, if for no other reason than to kill and eat him at the right time.

Throughout the ordeal, Rickenbacker's intention was to "lift up the hands" and strengthen "the feeble knees." Hopefully, our encouragement can be done in ways more polite than some that Rickenbacker had to use! But whatever the method, the ultimate purpose is the eternal rescue of others.

—J. B. N.

---

## Home Daily Bible Readings

**Monday, June 16**—Seek God's Leadership and Discipline (Proverbs 3:5-12)

**Tuesday, June 17**—Endure the Race (Hebrews 12:1-3)

**Wednesday, June 18**—Endure Trials and Discipline (Hebrews 12:4-7)

**Thursday, June 19**—Necessity of Discipline (Hebrews 12:8-11)

**Friday, June 20**—Be Strong and Be Healed (Hebrews 12:12, 13)

**Saturday, June 21**—Be Humble Like Christ (Philippians 2:1-4)

**Sunday, June 22**—Follow Christ's Example (Philippians 2:5-11)

---

### B. Keeping on Course (v. 13)

**13. And make straight paths for your feet, lest that which is lame be turned out of the way; but let it rather be healed.**

The section ends by giving a leadership principle. Why must we continue to work and walk with God? Because there are people following us. There are those who are spiritually disabled, the *lame*, who need a strong leader walking in *straight paths*. If leaders sit down or turn aside, these will never *be healed*.

We should not forget that traveling the paths of righteousness is not a solo journey. There is no place for spiritual selfishness in the church. The spiritually strong are expected to help the weak along the way (see Acts 20:35). Parents will want to make sure their children are walking with the Lord. Teachers should be leading their students to the throne of God. Elders and ministers must never forget the flock they are leading.

## Conclusion

### A. Practice Makes Perfect

We refer to subject areas that are learned or skills that are mastered as *disciplines*. We become accomplished in these areas by watching others who have already mastered the discipline. Sometimes we submit to the tutelage of teachers who are experienced in developing raw ability into proficiency. Whether this be in athletics, music, acting, or writing, no one is a complete "natural" with a full array of inherited skills. Even those with physical gifts and inclinations in a certain area become true masters through disciplined practice.

Why should we think the most important "skill" in the world, living the Christian life, is any different? It likewise is not something we are born with. It is a discipline that we learn by observing our master, Jesus Christ, and by submitting to His teachings. This is not always an easy road, as our lesson today has shown. But eternity will make it all worthwhile.

### B. Prayer

Lord God, we know that our lives are not always journeys of joy. May we not forget that pain and trials are not signs of Your lack of love, and that You will never abandon us. Please help us turn times of trial into opportunities to trust You more. We pray this in the name of our leader in the faith, Jesus Christ, Your beloved Son, amen.

### C. Thought to Remember

Want eternity? Get discipline!

# Learning by Doing

*This page contains an alternative lesson plan emphasizing learning activities. Some of these activities are also found in the helpful student book,* Adult Bible Class.

## Into the Lesson

Prepare colorful labels for each of the following names and groups, all found in the "Faith Hall of Fame" in Hebrews 11: *Abel; Enoch; Noah; Abraham; Isaac; Jacob; Joseph; Moses' Parents; Moses; the Hebrews of the Exodus; Rahab; Gideon; Barak; Samson; Jephthah; David; Samuel; the Prophets.* Post these randomly around your assembly space.

As class begins, ask, "Who can tell me what all these people had in common?" The key responses are "faith in God" and "each is honored as an example in Hebrews 11." If the group hesitates, have someone read Hebrews 12:1 to elicit the responses.

Turn to today's text and say, "Seeing that we are surrounded by such a large number of those exemplifying faith in God, let's talk about our need for their discipline, patience, and perseverance, to follow their example."

## Into the Word

Tell your learners that you are going to present some "Principles of Discipline" based on today's text in Hebrews 12. Ask them to identify verses that justify or contradict the principles you are stating. Suggested verses are given here after each statement, but those should not be read with the statements.

1. Jesus is the ideal example of a disciplined person *(v. 2);* 2. The rigors of discipline hardly ever seem pleasant *(v. 11a);* 3. The good parent will correct and direct the child he or she loves *(v. 7);* 4. Good things result in the life of the disciplined one *(v. 11b);* 5. It is possible that physical and mental weariness will interfere with commitment *(v. 3b);* 6. Opposition is to be expected when one has worthy personal goals *(v. 3);* 7. External discipline should be respected, not rejected *(v. 9);* 8. Discipline from God should be considered punishment, not a matter of holiness demanded *(v. 10);* 9. Those who have achieved success are worthy models for the one trying to do right *(v. 1);* 10. Some parents discipline children for the feelings of power it gives them *(v. 10a).* 11. God is wiser than human parents; He knows what discipline will help us most *(v. 9);* 12. Holding on to old habits makes forming new habits more difficult *(v. 1);* 13. "No pain, no

gain" may be true in the spiritual disciplines as well, but few die in their striving for godliness *(v. 4);* 14. The Christian should consider life to be God's gymnasium, a place to work out in righteousness *(v. 11; see writer's notes);* 15. The one who stays on God's straight path sets an example for the weaker who follow *(v. 13);* 16. When hands flop at one's sides and knees wobble in fatigue, that is the time for extra effort for self or encouragement of others *(vv. 12, 13).*

Today's lesson demonstrates that the discipline in life that characterized the Lord in His journey to the cross will give success to any who follow Him. Give your class the following two lists, one from ideas in the text in Hebrews 12 and one of other biblical texts. Ask students to match the elements in the first with the incidents and/or quotes in the second.

*List A:* 1. The good leader is fully aware of those watching his or her progress with interest and support. 2. The good leader realizes some things have to be left behind in order to make progress. 3. The good leader knows that the example of a successful life is important to those who follow. 4. The good leader can foresee the results of success. 5. The good leader expects opposition, both fair and unfair. 6. The good leader knows that any goal worth pursuing will involve some setbacks and disappointments. 7. The good leader is sensitive to God's correction of his or her plans. 8. The good leader experiences both joy and grief. 9. The good leader stops to help those who flag in the process.

*List B:* a. Matthew 8:19-22; b. Matthew 14:28-32; c. Matthew 16:24-28; d. Matthew 17:1-3; e. Mark 14:35, 36; f. Luke 22:3-5; g. John 6:61-68; h. John 11:33-35, 43, 44; i. Acts 7:55, 56. *Matches:* 1-d, 2-a, 3-c, 4-i, 5-f, 6-g, 7-e, 8-h, 9-b.

## Into Life

Children often know when they deserve and need correction. Likewise, the child of God often knows when correction is needed. Remind your class of these truths.

Suggest that your learners examine themselves and make a commitment of submission to God's discipline in one needed aspect in their lives. This is an area where having an accountability partner can help.

# Let's Talk It Over

*The questions on this page are designed to promote discussion of the lesson by the class and to encourage application of the lesson Scriptures. The answers provided are only discussion starters. Let your class talk it over from there.*

**1. What actions do you plan to take to "lay aside" sins that tempt you?**

Sin has a powerful effect, even on the people of God. Just as we are to repent or turn from sin when we come to Christ initially, so we must continually be in a state of repentance.

Another thing we must do is to refuse to rationalize our sin and instead confess it (1 John 1:9). It is also necessary to avoid situations that would make us especially susceptible to sin. Following the exhortation of James 4:7, we should "submit [ourselves] therefore to God" and "resist the devil." We can also establish a relationship with someone who will hold us accountable in regard to sin.

**2. Why do Christians sometimes find it hard to endure through the hard times? What can be done to help them?**

Western culture places much emphasis on the comforts of life and having conveniences at hand for any purpose. Also, having many options at our disposal makes us think that when a difficulty arises, we can just opt out of that situation and move on.

A mistake that is often made in the church is that when a brother or sister in Christ is going through difficult times, we abandon them instead of being there for them. If they struggle with doubt, we question their faith. If there is a sin they struggle with, we question their commitment to the lordship of Christ. It is in these times that Christians need "to be there," encouraging and teaching instead of criticizing and condemning.

**3. What was a time when you believe you were chastened or rebuked by the Lord? How did you grow spiritually as a result?**

There are various ways in which God may rebuke us. It may be through a messenger such as a preacher or Bible teacher. It may be through a friend who is concerned about our spiritual walk who challenges us, and God uses that to chasten us. As we read Scripture, we may also be rebuked by God as we better understand our sin.

If we try to repress our guilt, God will work on us to convict us of our sin. When God convicts us, we feel the pressure. "Blessed is he whose transgression is forgiven, whose sin is covered. Blessed is the man unto whom the Lord imputeth not iniquity, and in whose spirit there is no guile. When I kept silence, my bones waxed old through my roaring all the day long. For day and night thy hand was heavy upon me: my moisture is turned into the drought of summer" (Psalm 32:1-4; see also Acts 2:37). The pressure God exerts is not to destroy us, but rather to strengthen us for greater service and closer fellowship with Him.

**4. How can you show reverence to God when He corrects your behavior?**

If God chastens us and rebukes us through the words of a preacher, some people get angry with the preacher and leave the church. If a friend chastens us, there is often the tendency to break off the friendship. At times people even forsake God when they feel the pressure of guilt or the sting of rebuke as a result of sin.

But reverence is shown for God and for the servants whom God uses to rebuke us when we respond in love and repentance. A submissive spirit toward God is essential. Paul also speaks of how we are to treat those who are over us in the Lord in 1 Thessalonians 5:12, 13: "And we beseech you, brethren, to know them which labor among you, and are over you in the Lord, and admonish you; and to esteem them very highly in love for their work's sake."

**5. What are some signs that we have reached a plateau in our faith because of spiritual fatigue? How do we correct course?**

Reaching a plateau is a problem that can sneak up on us so gradually that we fail to recognize it. This is true both physically and spiritually. Evidence that this condition is present in a Christian can be seen in a failure to be a witness for God in daily life. Spiritual plateauing is also seen when we resist changes in our spiritual walk as well as in the activities of the church.

Enjoying comfort and sameness over change and progress go hand in hand with a plateaued faith and a plateaued church. Something as simple as failing to maintain our church buildings can be a sign of both physical as well as spiritual fatigue and plateauing.

# Eternal Christ

DEVOTIONAL READING: **Psalm 118:5-9.**

BACKGROUND SCRIPTURE: **Hebrews 13:1-16.**

PRINTED TEXT: **Hebrews 13:1-16.**

### Hebrews 13:1-16

1 Let brotherly love continue.

2 Be not forgetful to entertain strangers: for thereby some have entertained angels unawares.

3 Remember them that are in bonds, as bound with them; and them which suffer adversity, as being yourselves also in the body.

4 Marriage is honorable in all, and the bed undefiled: but whoremongers and adulterers God will judge.

5 Let your conversation be without covetousness; and be content with such things as ye have: for he hath said, I will never leave thee, nor forsake thee.

6 So that we may boldly say, The Lord is my helper, and I will not fear what man shall do unto me.

7 Remember them which have the rule over you, who have spoken unto you the word of God: whose faith follow, considering the end of their conversation.

8 Jesus Christ the same yesterday, and today, and for ever.

9 Be not carried about with divers and strange doctrines: for it is a good thing that the heart be established with grace; not with meats, which have not profited them that have been occupied therein.

10 We have an altar, whereof they have no right to eat which serve the tabernacle.

11 For the bodies of those beasts, whose blood is brought into the sanctuary by the high priest for sin, are burned without the camp.

12 Wherefore Jesus also, that he might sanctify the people with his own blood, suffered without the gate.

13 Let us go forth therefore unto him without the camp, bearing his reproach.

14 For here have we no continuing city, but we seek one to come.

15 By him therefore let us offer the sacrifice of praise to God continually, that is, the fruit of our lips, giving thanks to his name.

16 But to do good and to communicate forget not: for with such sacrifices God is well pleased.

---

GOLDEN TEXT: Jesus Christ the same yesterday, and today, and for ever.—Hebrews 13:8.

## *Images of Christ*
### Unit 1: Images of Christ in Hebrews
### (Lessons 1-5)

## Lesson Aims

After participating in this lesson, each student will be able to:

1. List some of the sacrifices with which the writer of Hebrews says God is pleased.

2. Explain the significance of our giving God the sacrifices mentioned in verse 16 in light of Christ's once-for-all sacrifice.

3. Express one sacrifice of praise for Christ and His work.

## Lesson Outline

INTRODUCTION
  A. The Eternal God
  B. Lesson Background
I. UNCHANGING ACTIONS (Hebrews 13:1-6)
  A. Be Loving (vv. 1-3)
  B. Be Pure (v. 4)
  C. Be Content (v. 5)
    *Without Covetousness*
  D. Be Unafraid (v. 6)
II. UNCHANGING BELIEFS (Hebrews 13:7-14)
  A. What to Embrace (vv. 7, 8)
  B. What to Reject (vv. 9, 10)
  C. What to Remember (vv. 11-14)
III. UNCHANGING WORSHIP (Hebrews 13:15, 16)
  A. Sacrifice of Praise (v. 15)
    *Continual Praise*
  B. Sacrifice of Doing Good (v. 16)
CONCLUSION
  A. The Eternal Jesus
  B. Prayer
  C. Thought to Remember

## Introduction

### A. The Eternal God

Mathematicians use a symbol for infinity that looks like this: ∞. The idea is that if you were to travel around a track shaped like this, you would never reach the end. Instead, you would continue endlessly around the track.

Some religions view eternity in this way, as an endless treadmill from which we never escape. Yet this is not the view of the Bible. The biblical perspective is that eternity is a projection into the future that has no end point. Likewise, eternity looks to the past and sees no beginning point. It is not a repetitive cycle. A prayer of Moses expresses it like this: "Before the mountains were brought forth, or ever thou hadst formed the earth and the world, even from everlasting to everlasting, thou art God" (Psalm 90:2).

Many biblical teachings are tied to this core belief in the everlasting nature of God. God made an everlasting covenant with David that was cemented through Jesus, the Messiah (2 Samuel 23:5). God's mercy toward us "endureth for ever" (Psalm 118:1-4; compare Isaiah 54:8). We, as Christians, are partakers in an "everlasting gospel" (Revelation 14:6).

Therefore, we can take great comfort in the eternal nature of God. God is not like the boss at work who changes his mind on a daily basis. God is not like human governments that rise and fall, come and go. God is not subject to human fads, whims, or trends. As the psalmist wrote about God, "But thou art the same, and thy years shall have no end" (Psalm 102:27). We cannot overestimate the value to us of God's eternal nature.

### B. Lesson Background

The book of Hebrews compares the new covenant of the Christian faith with the old covenant of the Jewish faith. Throughout the book, the author shows that Jesus has inaugurated a new relationship with God that is both a fulfillment of the old covenant patterns and is superior at every point to them. In the final chapter of the book, chapter 13, the author moves to practical matters: relationships between believers. The backdrop of this final section is twofold.

First, there is the strong recognition of the moral expectations that come from the Old Testament. The book of Deuteronomy is an explanation of God's requirements for Israel. Moses uses the image of the Lord as a "consuming fire" (Deuteronomy 4:24) shortly before he gets to the very basics of human relationships: the Ten Commandments (Deuteronomy 5:6-22). Similarly, the author of Hebrews moves from the picture of God as judge to God's expectations for humans in relationship with each other. This may be seen in the admonition of Hebrews 12:29: "For our God is a consuming fire," which comes immediately before today's text.

The second element of background is that of God's eternal nature, found in both Deuteronomy and Hebrews. One of the key standards of God's relationship with His people is that it is more than a temporary arrangement. It is intended to last forever (see Deuteronomy 5:29; 29:29).

# I. Unchanging Actions
# (Hebrews 13:1-6)

The members of the first-century church need to have a good reputation in their communities (1 Timothy 2:2; 3:2). The gospel message will never be heard if Christians are a bunch of bickering malcontents with questionable integrity. The author of Hebrews is well aware of this issue and uses the final section of the book to give practical advice on how to live a Christlike life in the local community.

## A. Be Loving (vv. 1-3)

### 1. Let brotherly love continue.

A hallmark of the Christian community is that Christ's disciples are to be known by their genuine concern for one another. This was commanded by Jesus (John 13:34), and the author of Hebrews reminds the readers that the command has not been rescinded. Jesus set the example in His own life. They were to love each other in the same manner that Jesus had loved them (John 15:12). This *love* of Jesus was strong enough to cause Him to die for His beloved, and we should not be satisfied with any lesser attitude (John 15:13).

So, what does this mean in terms of showing concern for everyone in our church? How do we love the unlovely? How do we act with love toward those who seem to be ornery and mean-spirited? It is not an easy task, and the author does not claim that it is. He simply reminds us to *continue.*

### 2. Be not forgetful to entertain strangers: for thereby some have entertained angels unawares.

The literal meaning of *entertain strangers* here is to "love outsiders." It is the same idea as in verse 1, but now applied to a different group. We are to love our Christian brothers and sisters, and we are to love visitors to our community too.

In the ancient world, there isn't much in the way of accommodations for travelers. To camp out in the public square is dangerous. To stay in an inn or hostelry is to put oneself at the mercy of criminals and to endure filthy, unhealthy conditions. Travelers, therefore, usually stay in private homes. The churches in the various cities are used as a network for providing hospitality for fellow believers. This can become a burdensome task, and there are other places in the New Testament where believers are reminded of their responsibilities in this area (see 3 John 5-8).

The author reminds the readers that there have been instances when the strangers seeking lodging were *angels* traveling incognito (see Genesis 18:2-10). The author of Hebrews is not telling the readers to take care of travelers in the hopes they might get lucky and entertain an angel. Rather, the idea is that caring for strangers may result in unexpected blessings, such as meeting new brothers and sisters and learning from them. [See question #1, page 378.]

### 3a. Remember them that are in bonds, as bound with them.

Being *in bonds* means being in prison. The author does not qualify this in terms of whether the imprisonment is the result of justice or injustice. God still loves those people, and we should too. They should receive support from their brothers and sisters outside (Matthew 25:36; Hebrews 10:34).

Prisons in the ancient world offer little in the way of care for prisoners. To visit a prisoner is more than just for encouragement. It is up to a prisoner's family and friends to bring food and clothes and to dress wounds from floggings or fights. Family might be expected to give money to the jailer in return for a higher level of protection for the prisoner.

### 3b. And them which suffer adversity, as being yourselves also in the body.

The idea of suffering *adversity* likely refers to those in prison. It carries the idea of being tortured. It is not uncommon for prisoners to *suffer* at the hands of brutal and sadistic jailers. This is enhanced by the crude security methods of Roman jails, including heavy manacles and leg irons; these restrictive stocks clamp down on feet and hands. If a fellow Christian is in jail for his faith, the other believers should realize that such a fate could easily be theirs in the future. [See question #2, page 378.]

## B. Be Pure (v. 4)

### 4. Marriage is honorable in all, and the bed undefiled: but whoremongers and adulterers God will judge.

---

### How to Say It

CORINTHIANS. Ko-*rin*-thee-unz (*th* as in *thin*).
DEUTERONOMY. Due-ter-*ahn*-uh-me.
GALATIANS. Guh-*lay*-shunz.
GOLGOTHA. *Gahl*-guh-thuh.
HEBREWS. *Hee*-brews.
ISAIAH. Eye-*zay*-uh.
JERUSALEM. Juh-*roo*-suh-lem.
LEVITICUS. Leh-*vit*-ih-kus.
MOSES. *Mo*-zes or *Mo*-zez.

The traditional *marriage* ceremony includes the well-known statement, "Marriage is an *honorable* estate." There is nothing shameful about being married. But marriages of Christian believers must be protected. Husbands and wives must treat each other with "brotherly love" and show the highest degree of respect for one another.

There is nothing more damaging to a couple's reputation and to the health and longevity of a marriage than to have the marriage *bed* become impure. To engage in sex outside of marriage is not just an act of selfish gratification, it is a disrespectful slap in the face of the marriage partner.

The ancient world of the Greeks and Romans does not hold to these standards. For them, it is not considered dishonorable if a man is a whoremonger (that is, visits prostitutes) or an adulterer (that is, has sex with other men's wives). Loose sexual morality is not to be tolerated within the Christian community of the first century and should not be acceptable today (1 Corinthians 5; Galatians 5:19). [See question #3, page 378.]

### C. Be Content (v. 5)

**5. Let your conversation be without covetousness; and be content with such things as ye have: for he hath said, I will never leave thee, nor forsake thee.**

*Covetousness* relates to materialism, the burning desire to have more possessions. If we have a heart of covetousness, we are in a constant state of jealousy against those who have nicer stuff. To guard against this consuming desire has been a long-standing responsibility of the people of God (see Exodus 20:17; compare Proverbs 21:26).

A deeper motive behind materialism is insecurity: we want more wealth so that we don't have to depend on anyone else. The author reminds the readers that this insecurity is really a lack of faith in God, because God has promised *never* to *leave* or *forsake* us (Deuteronomy 31:8; Joshua 1:5). [See question #4, page 378.]

#### WITHOUT COVETOUSNESS

Some years ago I read of a sales manager who was very successful in challenging his sales representatives to increase their sales. Every year he had an end-of-summer party at his house and invited all his sales reps and their wives. Also every year, he had a new luxurious addition to his home. One year it was a swimming pool. Another year it was a glass-enclosed patio room. Another year it was a backyard barbecuing unit. When the sales reps came over, their wives would *ooh* and *ahh* over the newest feature. It was all part of his plan.

When the party ended and everyone went home, the wives began to "work on" their husbands. "It sure would be nice if we had a _____ like that," they would say. The wives pestered their husbands until they gave in. That meant, of course, that the men would have to push the sales routine even harder to get the money. That's exactly what the sales manager wanted.

By planning on the wives' covetousness, he was successful in keeping his sales reps motivated. Thus they continued to push hard and make more sales, enhancing his own position in the process. Covetousness can be an insidious enemy to our contentment.     —J. B. N.

### D. Be Unafraid (v. 6)

**6. So that we may boldly say, The Lord is my helper, and I will not fear what man shall do unto me.**

If we were to be stripped of all possessions, we would still have the most important thing: our relationship with *the Lord.* No one can ever take this away from us. The author explains that this should embolden us to trust the Lord for all things. If we are being helped or supported by the Lord, we may ask with the psalmist, "whom shall I *fear*?" (Psalm 27:1; compare 118:6).

## II. Unchanging Beliefs (Hebrews 13:7-14)

The foundation of godly relationships within the church is the body of teachings that has been passed on from the apostles. Earlier, the author of Hebrews traced these basic doctrines directly back to Jesus himself (see Hebrews 2:3, 4).

### A. What to Embrace (vv. 7, 8)

**7, 8. Remember them which have the rule over you, who have spoken unto you the word of God: whose faith follow, considering the end of their conversation. Jesus Christ the same yesterday, and today, and for ever.**

These verses have been interpreted two ways. Some think that it is the teaching of the church leaders that doesn't change. In other words, they have taught *Jesus Christ* as Lord and will continue to do so. To be sure, we Christians should follow the teachings of church leaders who *rule over* us. At the same time, we should measure their teachings by the standard of God's Word. There is nothing more central than a focus on Jesus Christ, including His teachings and His sacrificial death and resurrection.

A more common interpretation, though, is that the core of their teaching is the eternal nature of

Christ. In other words, it is Jesus himself who is *the same yesterday, and today, and for ever*. This is a strong statement of the divinity of Jesus.

### B. What to Reject (vv. 9, 10)

**9, 10. Be not carried about with divers and strange doctrines: for it is a good thing that the heart be established with grace; not with meats, which have not profited them that have been occupied therein. We have an altar, whereof they have no right to eat which serve the tabernacle.**

Sometimes we think that false teaching is a new problem in the church. But even the apostles have to deal with teachers who want to introduce false doctrine into the church. For example, within two decades of Jesus' resurrection, a decision is made to condemn the teaching propagated by some that Gentiles are required to be circumcised in order to be saved (see Acts 15:1). Peter warns the church to be on guard for those who bring in "damnable heresies" (2 Peter 2:1).

The author warns against any dependence on *meats,* meaning sacrificial animals. As ceremonial foods, these have no value to the Christian. Our salvation is not tied to the Jewish system of sacrifices but is *established with grace.*

### C. What to Remember (vv. 11-14)

**11, 12. For the bodies of those beasts, whose blood is brought into the sanctuary by the high priest for sin, are burned without the camp. Wherefore Jesus also, that he might sanctify the people with his own blood, suffered without the gate.**

The author draws an interesting contrast between the Jewish sacrificial system and the sacrifice of Jesus. How did the priests dispose of the leftovers—the "holy trash"—of the daily animal sacrifices? The answer is that they were *burned* outside the temple or tabernacle precincts. What seemed holy and special in the ceremony of sacrifice became a common nuisance in the aftermath (see Leviticus 16:27).

The author plays on these disposal practices to illustrate the irony of Jesus' sacrifice. In effect, He was thrown away as being unworthy, but He became the greatest, perfect sacrifice. He was able to *sanctify* us *with his own blood.*

The author includes a historical detail that is only implied in the Gospels: the site of Jesus' crucifixion (Golgotha) was outside the gates and walls of Jerusalem (see John 19:17). This detail was important in determining the location of the Church of the Holy Sepulcher in the fourth century AD and continues to be important for biblical archeologists today.

Visual for
Lesson 5

*Point to this visual as you begin the* Into the Word *section on page 377.*

**13, 14. Let us go forth therefore unto him without the camp, bearing his reproach. For here have we no continuing city, but we seek one to come.**

This is the author's parting shot at those who want to leave the church and return to their Jewish roots. He says, "We must leave the earthly Jerusalem behind." Christians are not tied to the temple and its system of sacrifice for sins. We have forgiveness through the blood of Jesus. We look forward to the perfect city of God, the New Jerusalem that will be established with Christ's second coming (see Revelation 3:12; 21:10; compare Galatians 4:26).

## III. Unchanging Worship (Hebrews 13:15, 16)

The break with the Jewish system has implications for how Christians understand worship. The Jerusalem temple can no longer be a focus for worship, but neither does it need to be.

### A. Sacrifice of Praise (v. 15)

**15. By him therefore let us offer the sacrifice of praise to God continually, that is, the fruit of our lips, giving thanks to his name.**

The author offers us an astoundingly simple yet rich way to worship: *the sacrifice of praise.* We don't have to be in a temple or church building to do this. We don't have to wait for a certain day or hour to begin. Although we are not to forsake "the assembling of ourselves together" (Hebrews 10:25), we can worship God at any time and in any place by pausing to give Him *thanks.* [See question #5, page 378.]

This book has been rich in telling us what we have to be thankful for. We have a wonderful Savior. We have an eternal Father who will never abandon us. We have freedom from the limits of the Jewish system. We have promises that even the greatest heroes of the faith only looked forward to. We are surely blessed.

### CONTINUAL PRAISE

On February 3, 1970, students and faculty of Asbury College in Wilmore, Kentucky, gathered at 10 AM for what they assumed would be a typical chapel service. Instead, revival broke out. The service, originally scheduled for 50 minutes, did not let up for 185 hours.

The meeting was nonstop, 24 hours a day, for that interval. Students and faculty started by giving testimonies and were soon weeping, praying, and singing. Many asked forgiveness from those they had wronged. The meeting was marked by orderliness. Attendees did not become loud, speak out of turn, or fall to the floor in ecstasy.

News of the event soon reached local newspapers and television stations. The revival was highlighted in large cities, some clear across the country. Off-campus people were soon coming to Wilmore to witness and participate in the event.

After the revival had run its course, churches invited speakers from Asbury College to come and talk about the experience. By the summer of 1970 the revival had spread to 130 other campuses and scores of churches, both in America and abroad. One church in Anderson, Indiana, had a spontaneous revival that lasted for 50 nights. The church became so packed that services had to be moved to a school gymnasium for the crowds of up to 2,500 people.

The Asbury experience is obviously not the standard experience. But it is a witness to what can happen when people offer continual praise.
— J. B. N.

## B. Sacrifice of Doing Good (v. 16)

**16. But to do good and to communicate forget not: for with such sacrifices God is well pleased.**

To *communicate* in this context is not referring to verbal communication. It means sharing, in the sense of sharing our possessions. The author finishes this section by reminding the believers that they have a responsibility to perform *good* deeds by taking care of the needy.

God is no longer interested in animal sacrifices. He wants the sacrifice of a humble heart that cares for the less fortunate. It is not enough to listen to the teaching of church leaders and walk around humming praise songs. We must demonstrate our love by assisting our brothers and sisters in their time of need (Hebrews 13:1).

# Conclusion

## A. The Eternal Jesus

Jesus shares God's eternal nature. This is why He can serve as a "high priest for ever" (Hebrews 6:20). This is why His sacrifice for sins is effective forever (Hebrews 10:12). This is why faith in Jesus gives us the promise of eternal life (John 3:15, 16), for Jesus alone has the words of eternal life (John 6:68). If we have named Jesus as Lord (Romans 10:9), we have believed in His eternal nature. Why else would we place our faith in a person who walked the earth 2,000 years ago?

The eternal nature of Jesus should spur us to ongoing praise of His name and into doing good deeds for His sake. We continue His work of caring about the poor and the downtrodden of the earth. If the truth of the eternal reign of Christ makes no impact on our lives, we either have not understood it or have not believed it.

## B. Prayer

Eternal Father, it is beyond our abilities to comprehend Your eternal nature, so we must simply believe it. We have trouble knowing what tomorrow will be, but Your Word says You "inhabiteth eternity." May we offer to You our sacrifice of praise, our humble words of reverence and adoration. We pray this in the name of our Lord Jesus Christ, amen.

## C. Thought to Remember

Jesus Christ doesn't change.
Neither do His expectations.

---

## Home Daily Bible Readings

**Monday, June 23**—Take Refuge in God (Psalm 118:5-9)

**Tuesday, June 24**—Christ as Supreme and Eternal (Colossians 1:15-20)

**Wednesday, June 25**—Show Hospitality and Courage (Hebrews 13:1-6)

**Thursday, June 26**—True Leaders to Imitate (Hebrews 13:7-9)

**Friday, June 27**—Confess Christ's Name (Hebrews 13:10-16)

**Saturday, June 28**—A Leader Who Professes Christ (Philippians 3:12-16)

**Sunday, June 29**—A Leader Looking to Christ Eternal (Philippians 3:17-21)

# Learning by Doing

*This page contains an alternative lesson plan emphasizing learning activities. Some of these activities are also found in the helpful student book, Adult Bible Class.*

## Into the Lesson

Fill your room with as many timepieces as you can accumulate. (Perhaps invite your class members to bring "spare" ones from home.) Include clocks with an audible ticking sound to be plugged in, if not battery powered. Include one old, nonworking clock with the hands removed; post this one prominently.

As class begins, ask, with your hand cupped to your ear, "What is that you hear?" Accept answers, such as "time," "life passing by," and others, but suggest that it is only a man-imposed mechanical sound designed to reflect the measure of that which is truly immeasurable.

Direct the attention of the group to your clock with no hands. Ask, "In what way does this timepiece represent eternity?" Comment on the fact that today's study relates to the eternality of Christ and the necessity of right living while we are still caught by time.

## Into the Word

On a poster board, display this key truth from today's text: "Jesus Christ the same yesterday, and today, and for ever" (Hebrews 13:8). As the learners are watching, write on the poster, *Therefore, I . . .* Lead your class in seeing the implications for Christian living that are a part of the timelessness of Christ's person and power. Ask them to suggest some *therefores* they immediately see. If response is slow, give them an example, such as, "Therefore, I can still believe what He said a long time ago," or "Therefore, I will expect Him to return as He said He would."

Once you have several responses from the class, say, "Look at today's text in Hebrews 13:1-16 and see if you can identify the expected results the writer includes as parts of these truths." Read verses 28 and 29 from chapter 12, and then use a series of questions based on the verses to elicit discussion.

1. "How does our need to continue in love for one another relate to God's character and Christ's constant being?" (v. 1)

2. "How does Jesus' continuing sameness require us to be hospitable to strangers?" (v. 2)

3. "How does Jesus' life and present ministry indicate our need to remember those in bonds and adversity?" (v. 3)

4. "In what sense does Jesus' eternality demand faithfulness and purity in marriage?" (v. 4)

5. "How does God's consistent presence negate the need for covetousness and discontent?" (v. 5)

6. "How is fear inappropriate if Father and Son and Spirit remain constant and true?" (v. 6)

7. "In what way does honoring your leaders show your honor of Christ?" (v. 7)

8. "How does being attracted to 'new' doctrines deny the power and authority of the 'old' Christ?" (v. 9)

9. "In what way does an attraction to the former system of sacrifices minimize the sacrifice that Christ made?" (vv. 9b-12)

10. "How does our shame for the shame of Christ's death dishonor Him?" (v. 13)

11. "In what instances does our focus on either material things or our earthly lives make no sense at all?" (v. 14)

12. "If Jesus were not the same yesterday, today, and forever, why would praising Him with our lips be foolish?" (v. 15)

13. "What does doing good deeds and sharing materially with others have to do with believing Jesus is eternal God, unchanged and unchangeable?" (v. 16)

Help your learners see the relationship between their behaviors as they live within the constraints of time and the unconstrained, eternal person and power of Christ Jesus.

## Into Life

Verses 9-16 of today's text deal with the contrast between the sacrifices of the Old Testament system and the sacrifice of Jesus that is the perfection in the New. Ask the class to identify the specifics of God's work in Christ that are revealed and recalled in this text.

After each is noted, ask a class member to offer a brief prayer of thanksgiving—a sacrifice of praise—for that work. For example, as someone notes the truth that "God will judge," from verse 4, ask a learner to express thanks that God will one day make everything right and just.

As you wind up this activity, suggest that learners copy your list and use items from it this week in their personal times of "sacrifice of praise" with their lips.

# Let's Talk It Over

*The questions on this page are designed to promote discussion of the lesson by the class and to encourage application of the lesson Scriptures. The answers provided are only discussion starters. Let your class talk it over from there.*

**1. What are some blessings you think you may have missed by not practicing hospitality? How have you matured spiritually in this regard?**

Many acts of hospitality that we could do we have turned over to others. We may be practicing a certain form of hospitality when we invite others to go with us to the movies, athletic contests, or concerts, yet it is nearly impossible to interact with others personally in these environments. Thus we have turned over part of our hospitality responsibility to professional entertainers. When we use this as our primary form of hospitality, we miss out on developing meaningful relationships.

Many families in the past were blessed by hosting missionaries or other Christian workers in their homes. Children learned from this practice and were introduced to a broader understanding of the Lord's work and to other cultures. These blessings are missed when we fail to open our homes up to such guests.

**2. What are some practical ways to express sympathy for those in adversity?**

Prisons may be not only physical, but social and economic as well. Many live in the prisons of poverty, illiteracy, and prejudice. The tendency is for those who are blessed to look down on those who are not. The educated might ridicule those who lack education, etc.

Sympathy and empathy should be expressed in words and actions. Those in need are to be approached with a humble realization "that could be me." First Corinthians 13:4 tells us that "Charity suffereth long, and is kind; charity envieth not; charity vaunteth not itself, is not puffed up." Sympathy is expressed in taking time to be with those who are in adversity (see James 1:27).

**3. What can you do this week to help maintain marriage as an honorable institution, even if you're not married?**

Unfaithfulness in marriage is an ever-present problem in society. In many contexts, it has become so commonplace that it is often expected. Maintaining a one-man, one-woman relationship for life is considered by many to be quaint and archaic. That puts pressure on Christians to maintain God's design for marriage.

One way to do this is to fall in love daily with your spouse (if you're married), reminding him or her often of your love. It is necessary to refuse to put yourself in situations where temptations are present. One thing that can lead to unfaithfulness is the use of pornography. Ephesians 5:33 says a man is to "love his wife even as himself" and the wife is to "see that she reverence her husband."

**4. What has caused you to be more covetous than content over the years? How have you made progress in overcoming this tendency?**

Consumer-driven cultures make contentment a hard grace to maintain! Some fail to understand that "godliness with contentment is great gain" (1 Timothy 6:6). The desire to keep up with others in possessions is a driving force for many. One of the things that causes this is pride. We judge our self-worth as well as the worth of others by the accumulation of things.

We fail to be content with what we have when we forget that God has promised to provide for our daily needs. When we expect our possessions to bring us peace instead of God to provide us with peace, we become covetous. Contentment comes when we seek first the things of God, trusting Him to provide for our needs (Matthew 6:33).

**5. What are some of your own sacrifices of praise?**

We think of sacrifices in the context of financial giving. But financial giving can be used as a substitute for true sacrifice. Jesus challenged His followers to give of their material possessions, but also to be sure that their giving included things such as justice, mercy, and faith (Matthew 23:23).

A sacrifice of praise is not dependent on how much one has in regard to money or possessions. All can offer equally in this area of giving to God. A sacrifice of praise is giving of self above all. A sacrifice of praise is seen when we live to honor God and not promote self. Words and actions are the ways we present a sacrifice of praise. Our testimony, both spoken as well as lived out, constitutes a sacrifice of praise to God.

# Master Teacher

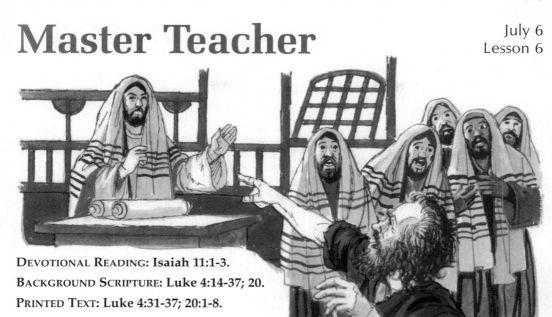

DEVOTIONAL READING: **Isaiah 11:1-3.**

BACKGROUND SCRIPTURE: **Luke 4:14-37; 20.**

PRINTED TEXT: **Luke 4:31-37; 20:1-8.**

### Luke 4:31-37

31 And came down to Capernaum, a city of Galilee, and taught them on the sabbath days.

32 And they were astonished at his doctrine: for his word was with power.

33 And in the synagogue there was a man, which had a spirit of an unclean devil, and cried out with a loud voice,

34 Saying, Let us alone; what have we to do with thee, thou Jesus of Nazareth? art thou come to destroy us? I know thee who thou art; the Holy One of God.

35 And Jesus rebuked him, saying, Hold thy peace, and come out of him. And when the devil had thrown him in the midst, he came out of him, and hurt him not.

36 And they were all amazed, and spake among themselves, saying, What a word is this! for with authority and power he commandeth the unclean spirits, and they come out.

37 And the fame of him went out into every place of the country round about.

### Luke 20:1-8

1 And it came to pass, that on one of those days, as he taught the people in the temple, and preached the gospel, the chief priests and the scribes came upon him with the elders,

2 And spake unto him, saying, Tell us, by what authority doest thou these things? or who is he that gave thee this authority?

3 And he answered and said unto them, I will also ask you one thing; and answer me:

4 The baptism of John, was it from heaven, or of men?

5 And they reasoned with themselves, saying, If we shall say, From heaven; he will say, Why then believed ye him not?

6 But and if we say, Of men; all the people will stone us: for they be persuaded that John was a prophet.

7 And they answered, that they could not tell whence it was.

8 And Jesus said unto them, Neither tell I you by what authority I do these things.

---

GOLDEN TEXT: They were astonished at his doctrine: for his word was with power.—Luke 4:32.

---

> *Images of Christ*
> Unit 2: Images of Christ in the Gospels
> (Lessons 6-9)

## Lesson Aims

After participating in this lesson, each student will be able to:

1. Tell how today's texts reveal Jesus' authority.

2. Compare and contrast the impact of Jesus' authoritative presence in His day with the impact it has today.

3. Identify one area of life where he or she should allow Jesus to have more authority.

## Lesson Outline

INTRODUCTION
    A. Question Authority
    B. Lesson Background
  I. JESUS' ACTION, PEOPLE'S REACTION (Luke 4: 31-37)
    A. Authority (vv. 31, 32)
    B. Recognition (vv. 33, 34)
    C. Command (v. 35)
    D. Amazement (vv. 36, 37)
 II. LEADERS' CHALLENGE, JESUS' RESPONSE (Luke 20:1-8)
    A. Question (vv. 1, 2)
      *At Home?*
    B. Counterquestion (vv. 3, 4)
    C. Response (vv. 5-7)
      *Logic*
    D. Counterresponse (v. 8)
CONCLUSION
    A. Who Has Authority?
    B. Prayer
    C. Thought to Remember

## Introduction

### A. Question Authority

The slogan *Question Authority* may conjure up vague memories of a bumper sticker on the back of a 1960s VW microbus. The slogan may be interpreted as the ravings of an anarchist who cares little for the norms of conventional thought. It may reflect a rebellious spirit that is self-centered and listens only to the voices in one's own head.

But is it ever right to question authority? to stand up to conventional thinking? to challenge the majority view? Albert Einstein (1879–1955)

remarked, "Unthinking respect for authority is the greatest enemy of truth." If someone pounded on your door and demanded entry, it would be the better part of wisdom to question the basis for his or her authoritative demand. If it's the police with a search warrant, the command to open the door requires compliance.

Jesus' voice of authority was accepted by some and questioned by others. But His credentials were available for all honest seekers to examine. Unbelief can start as a matter of evidence. But after the evidence is established, continued unbelief becomes a matter of the heart.

### B. Lesson Background

Luke identifies the beginning of Jesus' Galilean ministry with summary statements in Luke 4:14, 15. The one who had been empowered as God's Son (3:22) and tested concerning the nature of His sonship (4:1-13) now comes to Galilee "in the power of the Spirit" and teaches "in their synagogues."

The scenes comprising Luke 4:14-44 illustrate Jesus' authoritative power and teachings in the "synagogues of Galilee" (see 4:44). In the synagogue in Nazareth (4:16-30), Jesus explained His authoritative powers by identifying himself as one empowered by the Spirit and one who announced the good news of God's saving presence (4:16-20). Those claims resulted in rejection and hostility (4:28, 29).

## I. Jesus' Action, People's Reaction (Luke 4:31-37)

In the next synagogue scene, Jesus has moved about 20 miles northeast of Nazareth to the fishing community of Capernaum. Here His authoritative words and deeds are received more favorably. Unlike the Nazareth experience, where people sought to throw Him off a cliff (4:29), the residents of Capernaum seek Him eagerly (4:42). Yet it is not clear that they grasp Jesus' true identity, although the demons definitely do (4:34).

Throughout Luke's story, the one empowered by the Holy Spirit shatters the tyrannical grip of diabolical forces as the kingdom of God is manifested powerfully. Later, the same power will be extended to the 12 disciples as they are called to participate in Jesus' authoritative mission (9:1).

### A. Authority (vv. 31, 32)

**31. And came down to Capernaum, a city of Galilee, and taught them on the sabbath days.**

Jesus' movement from Nazareth to *Capernaum* is definitely a descent *(came down to)*, since Nazareth is some 1,800 feet above Capernaum. Capernaum is a relatively large fishing village with a population perhaps between 1,000 and 1,500. This site is Jesus' place of residence early in His ministry (Matthew 4:13; John 2:12). Later, Capernaum will be one of the towns singled out for its stubborn refusal to be moved to repentance by Jesus' mighty deeds of power (Matthew 11:20-24).

By custom, male Jews may read from the Scriptures and offer comments in the synagogue on *sabbath days* (see Acts 13:15, 42; 14:1; 17:2). Although the content of Jesus' teaching is not specified, the previous scene in the Nazareth synagogue (4:17-21) is probably a backdrop to Jesus' teaching in Capernaum. We also learn from Luke 4:43 that Jesus preached the kingdom of God. The announcement that God has drawn near to reign over His people surely stirs hearts—one way or another. [See question #1, page 386.]

**32. And they were astonished at his doctrine: for his word was with power.**

Jesus' ongoing teaching is matched by continual amazement at the *power* inherent in His words. Luke connects the authoritative value of Jesus' words to their visible effects. The approach in Mark 1:22 at this point is to contrast Jesus' authoritative words with those of the scribes. Luke, however, chooses to emphasize the inherent power of Jesus' words. What is experienced in Nazareth as "gracious words" (Luke 4:22) is experienced in Capernaum as words of powerful authority. Jesus speaks as one with an awareness of the heart and will of His Father.

### B. Recognition (vv. 33, 34)

**33, 34. And in the synagogue there was a man, which had a spirit of an unclean devil, and cried out with a loud voice, saying, Let us alone; what have we to do with thee, thou Jesus of Nazareth? art thou come to destroy us? I know thee who thou art; the Holy One of God.**

---

### How to Say It

BAAL. *Bay*-ul.
CAPERNAUM. Kuh-*per*-nay-um.
ELIJAH. Ee-*lye*-juh.
GALILEAN. Gal-uh-*lee*-un.
GALILEE. *Gal*-uh-lee.
JUDEA. Joo-*dee*-uh.
NAZARETH. *Naz*-uh-reth.
SANHEDRIN. *San*-huh-drun or San-*heed*-run.
SYNAGOGUE. *sin*-uh-gog.

---

Luke does not provide an explanation of how a demonized man comes to be present *in the synagogue*. Even so, it is clear that the authoritative presence of *the Holy One of God*, who is empowered by the Holy Spirit (Luke 4:14), means the demise of evil forces and the cleansing of the *unclean*. Indeed, the time has come for the tyrannical hold of Satan to be shattered by the advance of God's powerful reign (see Matthew 12:28, 29). While the forces of evil may appear to run rampant, Jesus' exorcisms clearly announce "our God reigns."

The demons immediately recognize Jesus' identity, and the implications are understood in terms of their inevitable destruction. We recall from the testing of Jesus in the desert that Satan recognized Jesus' identity as the Son of God (Luke 4:3, 9).

While humans may dispute the claim, evil cosmic forces have no doubt concerning Jesus' divine nature and authority! This is suggested by the two questions they raise: *what have we to do with thee?* and *art thou come to destroy us?* The first is an idiom that acknowledges that the demons have nothing in common with the holy presence of Jesus. The second concedes their fate and Jesus' judicial power to destroy them.

### C. Command (v. 35)

**35. And Jesus rebuked him, saying, Hold thy peace, and come out of him. And when the devil had thrown him in the midst, he came out of him, and hurt him not.**

This is the first of numerous accounts of miracles in Luke's Gospel. The exorcisms highlight that the Spirit-empowered Jesus exudes a cleansing and liberating power, rescuing humanity from evil forces. Jesus' authoritative rebuke of the demon indicates His refusal to give credence to demonic resistance or protest. Thus with two brief commands Jesus silences the demon and forces him to depart from the man.

As a result, the demon is compelled to release his power and turn the man over to Jesus. This is a concession to Jesus' superior authority. Amazingly, the demon's violent response in throwing the man down results in no injury, for, as Luke says, the act *hurt him not*.

### D. Amazement (vv. 36, 37)

**36. And they were all amazed, and spake among themselves, saying, What a word is this! for with authority and power he commandeth the unclean spirits, and they come out.**

Both Jesus' teaching and deeds of power evoke amazement. [See question #2, page 386.] Like

His authoritative teaching, Jesus' command resulting in the demon's expulsion is recognized as a concrete expression of *power* and *authority*.

The reader knows from Luke 4:14 that Jesus' authoritative power is derived from the Holy Spirit. Jesus' words and deeds can restore, cleanse, and "set at liberty them that are bruised" (Luke 4:18). Luke is careful to link Jesus' authority to both His words and His deeds. Jesus' words are continually validated by the power of His deeds.

**37. And the fame of him went out into every place of the country round about.**

Jesus' *fame* spreads throughout Galilee, even to those regions where He has yet to visit (compare Luke 4:14). The effect of His reputation spreading throughout the area can be seen in Luke 4:40. Later, His fame will spread even farther (Luke 5:15), eventually even "throughout all Judea" (Luke 7:17). Luke will use similar summaries in the book of Acts, his second volume, to describe the growing impact of the early church (see Acts 2:47; 5:11; 6:7; 8:4; 9:31).

But Jesus does not seek the fame of a miracle worker or an exorcist (compare Luke 5:14). His acts of power are almost like parables: they must be interpreted and understood in light of the entire drama unfolding in His ministry. This is why the city of Capernaum stands condemned. Even though the residents are amazed by His deeds of power, they do not interpret those deeds properly. Thus they are not moved to repentance (Matthew 11:23, 24).

## II. Leaders' Challenge, Jesus' Response (Luke 20:1-8)

More than two years have now elapsed since the exorcism of Luke 4. The issue of Jesus' authority surfaces again when He travels to Jerusalem and confronts the city with His staggering claims and deeds. Jesus' actions involving the temple elicit questions from Israel's leadership regarding the nature and source of His authority. We learn from Luke 19:47 that the Jewish leaders are seeking His demise, so the questioning of 20:1-8 has only hostile intentions.

### A. Question (vv. 1, 2)

**1. And it came to pass, that on one of those days, as he taught the people in the temple, and preached the gospel, the chief priests and the scribes came upon him with the elders.**

This is Jesus' final public ministry in Jerusalem before His crucifixion. It appears that Jesus is daily assuming the role of teacher in

*the temple* precincts. His preaching of *the gospel* undoubtedly includes His earlier teaching about God's in-breaking kingdom (compare Luke 4:18, 19, 43; 8:1; 9:6; 16:16). However, the religious leaders are perturbed by Jesus as He assumes a role reserved for those having official standing. They are outraged by this upstart Galilean's presumption to position himself as a teacher in the shadow of Israel's most sacred site.

These leaders, the *chief priests* and *scribes* and *elders*, undoubtedly are members of the Jerusalem Sanhedrin. The Sanhedrin is comprised of 71 members and is the "supreme court" for resolving Jewish legal disputes. They have come to see Jesus as a formidable threat to their leadership authority, and thus this threat must be neutralized.

### AT HOME?

There is an old proverb, "Home is where the heart is." We assume that where a person's emotions are attached marks his or her "real" home. Professional athletes spend a lot of time in arenas and gymnasiums. Devoted mothers spend many hours with their children. Academicians spend time with their books. Religious people spend time in religious activities. All are comfortably "at home" with their primary interests.

The same could be said of Jesus. Early in his Gospel, Luke records Jesus' words, "I must be about my Father's business" (2:49). Jesus came to bring a message of salvation and hope, so He was constantly among the people—preaching, teaching, healing. Whether it was during the Sermon on the Mount, with a crowd along the beach, or with people accompanying Him as He walked from place to place, He was "at home" bringing the gospel to the people.

The religious authorities we see in today's text were "at home" primarily at the temple. But their attachment to it (see John 11:48) was not the same as that of Jesus (see John 2:13-17). Jesus challenges us to reexamine where we are most "at home" and make any and all adjustments necessary (see Luke 14:26; 18:18-30). The religious leaders of His day were not willing to do this. Are we?                    —J. B. N.

**2. And spake unto him, saying, Tell us, by what authority doest thou these things? or who is he that gave thee this authority?**

Jesus' earlier actions in the temple (Luke 19:45, 46) and His assumed role as teacher are enough to alarm the religious leaders. They understand that such actions constitute a claim of authority that openly challenges their own authoritative status.

So the established leaders interrogate Jesus regarding the basis and the source of His *authority.* They understand that Jesus' actions necessitate authorization from a superior source. Yet Jesus has no formal rabbinic or priestly credentials that might warrant His actions and validate His right to teach. So how can He presume to speak with authority about temple proceedings?

The leaders of the Sanhedrin can claim legal and religious jurisdiction as well as their political authorization from Rome. But what does Jesus bring to the table? [See question #3, page 386.] Thus their questions are intended to discredit Jesus by shaming Him before the people. But the result of their questioning undermines their own authority, as we shall see.

### B. Counterquestion (vv. 3, 4)

**3, 4. And he answered and said unto them, I will also ask you one thing; and answer me: The baptism of John, was it from heaven, or of men?**

Notice that Jesus does not challenge the legitimacy of the inquiry. In fact, Jesus will inform His disciples that "the scribes and the Pharisees sit in Moses' seat: all therefore whatsoever they bid you observe, that observe and do" (Matthew 23:2, 3). Obviously a new teacher who calls into question what has been taken for granted in Israel (as Jesus has done) should be investigated. Yet while there is no problem with the religious leaders' questions as such, they are not motivated by an honest pursuit of truth.

So instead of responding directly to their questioning, Jesus counters with a question of His own. He does not do this to be evasive, but to expose the motives behind their inquiry. The ministry of *John* foreshadowed and is in continuity with Jesus' own ministry. Thus an assessment of John is critical to any understanding of Jesus' authority. There are only two options: either John's authority to initiate a cleansing ritual *(baptism)* was divine in origin or it was a mere human invention.

The answer to Jesus' counterquestion will demonstrate where these religious leaders stand. Like Jesus, John (now dead) lacked the sort of credentials they demand; yet he is widely regarded among the people as having had prophetic status. If the leaders interpret John's ministry correctly, then they will have their answer concerning Jesus' authority. But that also means going "on record" in front of everyone listening!

### C. Response (vv. 5-7)

**5, 6. And they reasoned with themselves, saying, If we shall say, From heaven; he will say, Why then believed ye him not? But and if**

Visual for Lessons 1, 6, and 10

*Point to this visual as you ask, "What do these titles and descriptions say about Jesus' authority?"*

**we say, Of men; all the people will stone us: for they be persuaded that John was a prophet.**

The implications of Jesus' question are not lost on the religious leaders. You don't get to be a member of the Sanhedrin by being unintelligent! But their intelligence has limits, since their deliberations indicate that they are more concerned with their own agenda than with truth. [See question #4, page 386.]

Thus the deliberations center not on the spiritual implications of Jesus' question, but upon the earthly consequences of their answer. If they acknowledge that John was backed by divine authority, their hypocrisy will be exposed for not believing and acting upon the implications of John's ministry. John's baptism forms a serious challenge to their authority and their view of God's redemptive purpose (Luke 3:1-20).

On the other hand, if the religious leaders openly repudiate John's baptism, then they run the risk of alienating *the people.* The leaders thus would put themselves in danger of severe retaliation. Their lack of integrity puts them on the defensive.

### LOGIC

We don't normally consider the Bible to be a textbook of logic, but there are numerous examples of pure logic found in its pages. One of the most interesting categories is *the dilemma.* The basic form of a dilemma is this:

1. If A, then B; if C, then D.
2. Either A or C;
3. Therefore, either B or D.

A classic case is found in 1 Kings 18:21. There Elijah confronts the people on Mount Carmel about choosing between the Lord and Baal. The form of his argument is this:

1. If (A) the Lord is God, then (B) serve Him; if (C) Baal is God, then (D) serve him.
2. Either (A) the Lord is God or (C) Baal is God.
3. Therefore, either (B) serve the Lord or (D) serve Baal.

It is presumed that a person cannot serve both the Lord and Baal—one must choose. Sometimes a dilemma is framed in such a way that both options are unpalatable, but it forces us to choose and commit to one idea or the other. This is what Jesus does in Luke 20:5, 6, and the chief priests, scribes, and elders knew it.

1. If we say John's baptism is from Heaven, then why did we reject it? If we say it's from men, then the people will stone us.
2. John's baptism is either from Heaven or men.
3. Either we admit we sinned by rejecting it, or the people will stone us.

They did not like either outcome, so they refused to answer. Jesus then used their unwillingness to answer to justify His own unwillingness to answer the questions as to the origin of His authority. He had caught them on the classic "horns of a dilemma."                    —J. B. N.

**7. And they answered, that they could not tell whence it was.**

Ironically, by their claim of ignorance the religious leaders admit their incompetence to discern spiritual matters! Thus they forfeit their own claim to authority. If they, the religious scholars, cannot determine what is from God and what is of mere human origin in John's case, then how can they possibly stand in judgment concerning Jesus?

What begins as an effort to discredit Jesus results in a self-condemnation of the scholars. They are more concerned about maintaining and protecting their privileged position than they are in recognizing divine intervention. "If we let him thus alone, all men will believe on him; and the Romans shall come and take away both our place and nation" (John 11:48).

### D. Counterresponse (v. 8)

**8. And Jesus said unto them, Neither tell I you by what authority I do these things.**

Notice that Jesus doesn't try to "make nice" with His opponents. He refuses to play their game. The motives of the chief priests, scribes, and elders in asking their question followed by their admitted ignorance concerning the authority of John mean that any further discussion will go nowhere.

Nevertheless, Jesus has implicitly answered their question by connecting His ministry to the divinely authorized ministry of John. While Jesus does refuse a direct response to their question regarding His *authority*, the parable to follow (20:9-18) and subsequent discussions leave no doubt about the nature and source of that authority.

# Conclusion
## A. Who Has Authority?

Jesus' authoritative teachings and deeds cannot be ignored. They must be evaluated in terms of the nature and basis of His authoritative claims. Jesus' claims are validated by His deeds, which point to His divine status. This is the evidence of the miracles (John 14:11).

But such conclusions are determined by a heart that honestly seeks the truth. As we observed with the religious leaders, sometimes a hidden agenda or personal ambitions blunt the force of divine truth. [See question #5, page 386.] The truth of Jesus' authority challenges assumptions that are grounded on earthly foundations. The question we must ask is, "Who has ultimate authority to direct our lives?" The alternatives always have been the same: human authority or divine authority. What is your choice?

## B. Prayer

Father, may Your kingdom come and Your will be done on earth as it is in Heaven. We bow in Your presence and acknowledge that You are our authoritative Lord. We give Your Son the honor and glory forever and ever. In His name, amen.

## C. Thought to Remember

Jesus is God's authoritative Son.

## Home Daily Bible Readings

**Monday, June 30**—Spirit-Anointed Teacher (Isaiah 11:1-3)
**Tuesday, July 1**—Filled with God's Spirit (Luke 4:14, 15)
**Wednesday, July 2**—With Authority (Luke 4:31-37)
**Thursday, July 3**—Blessed Are You (Luke 6:17-23)
**Friday, July 4**—Woe to Them (Luke 6:24-26)
**Saturday, July 5**—Love Your Enemies (Matthew 5:38-45)
**Sunday, July 6**—Authority Questioned (Luke 20:1-8)

# Learning by Doing

*This page contains an alternative lesson plan emphasizing learning activities. Some of these activities are also found in the helpful student book,* Adult Bible Class.

## Into the Lesson

Write the following on the board in large letters: *Teachers Transform Lives!* Point to the poster as you say, "A teacher's transforming power may come through the content of a class, the personality of the teacher, personal exchanges with the teacher, or even just a single comment from the teacher. The transformations teachers bring are seen in changed values, an enlarged vision for the future, career selection, changed behaviors, etc."

Remind the class that influential teachers may surface in a school setting, seminars, churches, or other environments. Then ask for two people to share the names and circumstances of teachers who have been significant influences on their lives or the lives of family members.

Make the transition to Bible study by saying, "The authority of a teacher is foundational to influencing student lives. That's why it is important to view the authority of one who has been called the world's greatest teacher—our Savior. We may be angry with Jesus' antagonists. However, we are blessed by this questioning as we find that our own confidence in His authority soars to new heights."

## Into the Word

Early in the week, ask two students to prepare five-minute presentations for this portion of the lesson. Ask one student to prepare a background for the study; the issue for the presentation is *The Authority of Jesus.* Give him or her a copy of the Lesson Background from the lesson commentary. The student should highlight the issue(s) at stake and the result(s) of each of Jesus' visits. The following outline may be helpful:

    I. Synagogue Scene #1: Nazareth.
    II. Synagogue Scene #2: Capernaum.
    III. Temple Scene: Jerusalem.

The second student will prepare and deliver a presentation on *Demon or Spirit Possession* in the Bible. Give the student copies of articles about demons from Bible dictionaries and Bible handbooks. The presentation should address these questions: "Who or what are demons?" "What do they do or represent?" and "How did they work in human beings in the Bible?"

Introduce the first speaker by telling the class, "First, let's look at the issue of Jesus' authority from circumstances arising in Luke's Gospel. To begin our study I have asked [name of student] to give us some background."

Then distribute photocopies of Luke 4:31-37 and Luke 20:1-8. Read Luke 4:31-37 from it. Students will be asked to write on these copies in a later activity.

Next, introduce the second speaker by saying, "Demon possession is strange to us. Therefore, I have asked [name of student] to give us some background on demon possession."

After the presentation, ask students to underline every word or phrase of Luke 4:31-37 on their photocopies that deals with Jesus' authority. Then ask the following discussion questions:

1. What does your underlining exercise tell you about Jesus' authority?

2. What in this passage seems to give credibility to Jesus' authority?

Then read Luke 20:1-8 from the handout. Again, ask class members to underline every word, phrase, question, or statement that has to do with Jesus' authority. Then, ask the following discussion questions:

1. What does verse 2 refer to when the Jewish leaders mention "these things"?

2. How is the response to Jesus different from the previous passage we studied? Why do you suppose it is so different?

3. What does this say to you about questioning or searching for the source of Jesus' authority?

4. Why do you think Jesus refused to answer their question about His authority?

## Into Life

Ask students how they view the authority of Jesus relative to human authority on these five issues: 1. Sanctity of human life (abortion and embryonic stem cell research). 2. Monetary decisions. 3. Family issues and goals. 4. Career attitudes and values. 5. Life after death.

Ask, "Are there areas that you think Jesus doesn't really care that much about because you think other things 'must be' more important to Him?" After discussion, ask, "What is one area of life where you will allow Jesus to have more authority? How will you pray in this regard?"

# Let's Talk It Over

*The questions on this page are designed to promote discussion of the lesson by the class and to encourage application of the lesson Scriptures. The answers provided are only discussion starters. Let your class talk it over from there.*

**1. If you were to ask "the man on the street" to express his understanding of the kingdom of God, how might he answer? Why is this question important?**

Many think of the kingdom of God mainly as a place "out there" where God lives as absolute ruler. Others stress that the kingdom of God already exists here on earth in some fashion. Still others hold that the kingdom of God is found within the hearts of people (compare Luke 17:21).

Jesus told Nicodemus in John 3 that he could not enter the kingdom of God unless he was born again. The logic is that those who are born again are in the kingdom! If we focus too much on looking around for a physical manifestation of the appearance of God's kingdom, then we risk making the mistake of the disciples in Acts 1:6.

**2. In what ways have you witnessed the power of God at work in people's lives?**

When we mention the phrase *power of God*, people will focus on different things. For example, I remember watching a well-known evangelist on television when I was a child. The adults around me expressed everything from astonishment to disbelief as the evangelist appeared to heal people of their diseases. I don't recall hearing any adult claim that God could not or would not perform a healing miracle; rather, it was a question of whether or not the evangelist could.

But to focus on such debates is to miss a much more important power of God: His ability to transform sinful people into holy people. When a flagrant sinner comes to the Lord and his or her life is completely transformed, it should be easy to see the power of God at work in that life and give God the glory. We should remember that even a person's ability to suffer patiently is a demonstration of God's power (see Colossians 1:11).

**3. The Sanhedrin members who confronted Jesus were clearly more interested in their own credentials than they were in the content of Jesus' message. What are some examples of misplaced priorities in religious circles today?**

Examples of misplaced priorities include bringing in a speaker because of name recognition and his ability to "pack them in" (public credentials) rather than on the content of the message. Congregations make a mistake in selecting leaders based on success in the business world rather than on meeting scriptural qualifications (see 1 Timothy 3:1-13). There is always a danger in allowing ourselves to be impressed by those the world honors rather than those who have shown themselves to be faithful servants of God.

**4. Give an example of a serious spiritual discussion whose major purpose was to "prove a point" rather than arrive at the truth. How did the discussion turn out?**

Use this question with extreme caution! If your church has had problems in this area, you don't want to pour gasoline on smoldering embers. In truth, some of the most intense discussions this writer has ever seen have involved issues that someone was intent on either avoiding or implementing. Some people seek to find in the Bible confirmation for what they are already doing (or failing to do).

The church is not alone in having to struggle with this kind of mind-set. Much of the secular "blogging" we see on the Internet seems to be more concerned with "point scoring" than in pursuing, discovering, and establishing truth.

**5. The religious leaders feigned ignorance rather than answer Jesus' question. How far do people go to "save face" today? When you see others acting in ways to "save face," how do you respond?**

It's human nature: to admit being wrong is hard! Admitting error may involve admitting that the other person is right. But we do have some biblical examples of people who admitted their error. Paul is one (Galatians 1:13, 14). The thief on the cross is another (Luke 23:41). We may assume that Peter admitted his error after Paul confronted him (Galatians 2:11-21). King David confessed his sin after being confronted (2 Samuel 12:1-13; Psalm 51).

An example of one who refused to admit error when confronted is King Saul (1 Samuel 15:20, 21). Will we follow the path he took in making excuses and rationalizing?

# Powerful Healer

DEVOTIONAL READING: Isaiah 61:1-4.

BACKGROUND SCRIPTURE: Mark 1:14-45.

PRINTED TEXT: Mark 1:29-45.

### Mark 1:29-45

29 And forthwith, when they were come out of the synagogue, they entered into the house of Simon and Andrew, with James and John.

30 But Simon's wife's mother lay sick of a fever; and anon they tell him of her.

31 And he came and took her by the hand, and lifted her up; and immediately the fever left her, and she ministered unto them.

32 And at even, when the sun did set, they brought unto him all that were diseased, and them that were possessed with devils.

33 And all the city was gathered together at the door.

34 And he healed many that were sick of divers diseases, and cast out many devils; and suffered not the devils to speak, because they knew him.

35 And in the morning, rising up a great while before day, he went out, and departed into a solitary place, and there prayed.

36 And Simon and they that were with him followed after him.

37 And when they had found him, they said unto him, All men seek for thee.

38 And he said unto them, Let us go into the next towns, that I may preach there also: for therefore came I forth.

39 And he preached in their synagogues throughout all Galilee, and cast out devils.

40 And there came a leper to him, beseeching him, and kneeling down to him, and saying unto him, If thou wilt, thou canst make me clean.

41 And Jesus, moved with compassion, put forth his hand, and touched him, and saith unto him, I will; be thou clean.

42 And as soon as he had spoken, immediately the leprosy departed from him, and he was cleansed.

43 And he straitly charged him, and forthwith sent him away;

44 And saith unto him, See thou say nothing to any man: but go thy way, show thyself to the priest, and offer for thy cleansing those things which Moses commanded, for a testimony unto them.

45 But he went out, and began to publish it much, and to blaze abroad the matter, insomuch that Jesus could no more openly enter into the city, but was without in desert places: and they came to him from every quarter.

GOLDEN TEXT: He healed many that were sick of divers diseases, and cast out many devils.—Mark 1:34.

## Images of Christ
### Unit 2: Images of Christ in the Gospels
### (Lessons 6-9)

## Lesson Aims

After participating in this lesson, each student will be able to:

1. Describe Jesus' early ministry in and around Capernaum.

2. Tell what Jesus' healing ministry reveals to us today about who Jesus is.

3. Articulate one way to share the good news of Jesus' healing presence.

## Lesson Outline

INTRODUCTION
  A. Are Miracles Credible?
  B. Lesson Background
I. JESUS HEALS (Mark 1:29-34)
  A. Peter's Mother-in-law (vv. 29-31)
  B. Town's Sick People (vv. 32-34)
II. JESUS PRAYS (Mark 1:35-37)
  A. Alone (v. 35)
  B. Found (vv. 36, 37)
III. JESUS PREACHES (Mark 1:38, 39)
  A. Desire (v. 38)
    *Sent to Preach*
  B. Action (v. 39)
IV. JESUS HINDERED (Mark 1:40-45)
  A. Request (v. 40)
  B. Response (vv. 41, 42)
  C. Sent (vv. 43, 44)
    *Show a Testimony*
  D. Sought (v. 45)
CONCLUSION
  A. Repentance?
  B. Prayer
  C. Thought to Remember

## Introduction

### A. Are Miracles Credible?

There are many miracle episodes in Mark's story. For some folks, miracles are impossible because they do not conform to known natural laws. Thus the skeptics discount the historical reliability of the Gospels. Skeptics cut away those portions of the story they find offensive to the "reasonable" secular mind. But the miraculous is so embedded in the story line of the

gospel that a radically different picture emerges if the miraculous is removed (see 1 Corinthians 15:13-17).

Jesus' story is a continuation of Old Testament Israel's story. That story looked forward to a time when a compassionate king would reign in righteousness and justice. His reign would result in the oppressed being set free, the eyes of the blind being opened, the ears of the deaf being healed, the lame leaping like a deer, and the mute tongue shouting for joy (see Isaiah 32:3, 4; 35:5, 6; 58:6; 61:1, 2). Jesus embodied that vision as His power and authority were manifested in acts of mercy and compassion to victims of various afflictions.

We caution ourselves that Jesus' miracles must not be misinterpreted. The Jewish authorities admitted that Jesus had miraculous powers, but rather than repent they attributed the source of the miracles to the demonic (Mark 3:22). Cities where Jesus performed many mighty deeds of power were rebuked because His miracles did not result in repentance and recognition of His authoritative status (Matthew 11:20-24).

Jesus had no interest in being perceived as a mere wonder-worker. A theme dominant in Mark's Gospel is Jesus' repeated efforts to deter recipients of His healing powers from speaking publicly about healings (Mark 1:44; 5:43; 7:36). The message of the gospel is primarily "repent" (Mark 1:15), not "come and get your physical problems fixed." Thus the miraculous healings are proof of a greater spiritual reality of the in-breaking kingdom of God. The miracles are to be understood as proof of this (John 14:11).

### B. Lesson Background

Mark, the briefest of the four Gospels, is a book of action. After an introduction of only three verses, the record is that "John did baptize . . . and preach" (Mark 1:4). The action continues at a brisk pace when Mark records only five verses later that "Jesus came." Next we see that "the Spirit driveth" (v. 12) and "Jesus came into Galilee, preaching" (v. 14). The other three Gospels give us more details at various points, but Mark likes to keep the action moving with his condensed style. After the call of the first disciples (1:16-20), Mark records a series of scenes in and around Capernaum (1:21-39). That's where we pick up today's lesson.

Before moving into the lesson proper, we should take note of first-century Judaism as the backdrop of Jesus' healing ministry. Foundational for Judaism is the profound commitment to God as the healer and sustainer of all life (see Exodus 15:26; Deuteronomy 32:39; Isaiah 6:10; Jeremiah

8:15). Sickness and various infirmities are often viewed as signs of God's disfavor resulting from one's sinful condition, although Jesus does not necessarily endorse this view (see John 9:2, 3). The miracles demonstrate the advancement of the kingdom because they demonstrate God's power to accomplish His will.

# I. Jesus Heals
# (Mark 1:29-34)

## A. Peter's Mother-in-law (vv. 29-31)

**29, 30. And forthwith, when they were come out of the synagogue, they entered into the house of Simon and Andrew, with James and John. But Simon's wife's mother lay sick of a fever; and anon they tell him of her.**

Mark gives some clues that the events between verses 29 and 38 take place over a 24-hour period of time. After going "into Capernaum; and straightway on the sabbath day . . . into the synagogue" (v. 21), Jesus and His disciples *were come out of the synagogue*. Events then move forward to the time "at even, when the sun did set" (v. 32), then to "the morning" (v. 35). This movement of the scenes takes the reader from a public gathering in the synagogue (v. 21) to the privacy of a home (v. 29) and ultimately to a "solitary place" where Jesus seeks His Father in prayer (v. 35).

Thus it is clear that the movement from the synagogue (v. 21) to the home of *Simon and Andrew* is intended to continue a recount of events that take place on one particular Sabbath. It appears that Simon and Andrew have moved from Bethsaida (John 1:44) to take up residence in Capernaum. The presence of Simon, Andrew, *James and John* reminds us of their earlier calling (see Mark 1:16-20). We also learn that Peter is married when he is called to follow Jesus (compare 1 Corinthians 9:5).

The fact that Peter's mother-in-law resides with Peter implies that she is a widow with no living sons. In the ancient world, illness is often

### How to Say It

CAPERNAUM. Kuh-*per*-nay-um.
GALILEE. *Gal*-uh-lee.
JUDAISM. *Joo*-duh-izz-um or *Joo*-day-izz-um.
MESSIANIC. mess-ee-*an*-ick.
MOSAIC. Mo-*zay*-ik.
NAZARETH. *Naz*-uh-reth.
NAZARENES. *Naz*-uh-reens.

described in terms of the symptoms (compare John 4:52; Acts 28:8). Leviticus 26:16 and Deuteronomy 28:22 list divine punishment as one cause of *fever*, although there is no indication of such punishment here. The disciples have seen Jesus' power exhibited in the synagogue, and thus they do not hesitate to draw His attention to her condition. [See question #1, page 394.]

**31. And he came and took her by the hand, and lifted her up; and immediately the fever left her, and she ministered unto them.**

In the previous scene, Jesus drove out the demon with an authoritative word (v. 25). Here *the fever* is expelled by Jesus' authoritative touch. There is no need for convalescence, for her cure is instantaneous. Peter's mother-in-law models a fundamental aspect of discipleship by responding to healing with grateful service. [See question #2, page 394.]

## B. Town's Sick People (vv. 32-34)

**32, 33. And at even, when the sun did set, they brought unto him all that were diseased, and them that were possessed with devils. And all the city was gathered together at the door.**

Following the specific healing of Peter's mother-in-law, Mark moves to the broader contours of Jesus' ministry. Jesus' reputation is growing. The interim summaries in Mark 1:39; 3:10-12; and 6:53-56 provide overviews of the scope and impact of Jesus' messianic activity. The way these are told indicates that they are only samples of what is generally characteristic of Jesus' ministry.

While Mark's language *at even, when the sun did set* may sound redundant, it stresses that sunset marks the end of Sabbath and the restrictions associated with it. Thus the people can now bring *unto him all that were diseased, and them that were possessed with devils*.

Notice that Mark makes a distinction between those who are *diseased* and those who are *possessed*. Thus it is not accurate to conclude that ancient people confuse medical conditions such as schizophrenia with demon possession. While occasionally those possessed by demons do exhibit certain forms of physical afflictions (Mark 9:17, 18), it is simply not the case that all people of antiquity attribute every medical condition to demonic possession. See also Mark 6:13 for a clear distinction between the two.

Not only are the conditions distinguished, but also the methods used to remedy the situations are different. Exorcisms are performed with an authoritative command, while healings usually involve Jesus' touch. The note that *all the city* is *gathered together at the door* underscores Jesus' growing popularity. The word has gotten out!

Jesus' healings have important restorative value, socially in addition to physically. The debilitating effects of unclean spirits and the contaminating results of various illnesses have shattered social networks and community involvement (compare Leviticus 13:45, 46). Jesus' healing powers restore people to a valued state.

**34. And he healed many that were sick of divers diseases, and cast out many devils; and suffered not the devils to speak, because they knew him.**

Jesus' ministry of healing is comprehensive. This is indicated by the terms translated *divers diseases*. There are no conditions that Jesus cannot remedy. The only incident where Jesus' power was limited was back in Nazareth (Mark 6:5). But the limitation there was from a lack of faith on the part of the Nazarenes (Matthew 13:58).

We note that the demons are silenced once again (compare 1:25). In this case the reason is given: *because they knew him.* The fact that Jesus is able to silence the demons demonstrates who is really in charge here. It appears that Jesus does not want the demons' knowledge to be revealed, at least at this time. In the Gospel of Mark, Jesus' identity as God's Son is understood only later. Confession by a human that Jesus is "the Son of God" in Mark's Gospel doesn't come until 15:39; a demon makes this confession much earlier (3:11).

Jesus' sonship includes a sacrificial commitment to the will of His Father, and Jesus' identity can be appreciated fully only in the light of His redemptive message. That's a reality no demon can possibly understand.

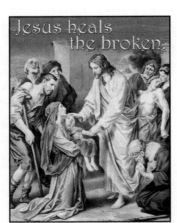

Visual for
Lesson 7

*Point to this visual as you ask, "In what ways has Jesus healed your brokenness?"*

## II. Jesus Prays
## (Mark 1:35-37)
### A. Alone (v. 35)

**35. And in the morning, rising up a great while before day, he went out, and departed into a solitary place, and there prayed.**

The reference to time *(morning . . . before day)* indicates that the 24-hour period begun in verse 21 now comes to a close. The movement is away from the crowds and toward a place of solitude. Before the next phase of His ministry, Jesus needs a time of extended prayer. Mark, unlike Luke, does not record many scenes depicting Jesus' prayer habits. Yet Mark does note often that Jesus retreats from the public arena and the pressure of the crowds (Mark 1:45; 3:13; 6:31, 32, 46; 7:24; 9:2, 30).

It is critical that Jesus remain focused on the will of His Father and not get caught up in the expectations of the crowds. How many popular Christian teachers and preachers today make a mistake in this area?

### B. Found (vv. 36, 37)

**36, 37. And Simon and they that were with him followed after him. And when they had found him, they said unto him, All men seek for thee.**

The disciples, led by *Simon,* embark on an urgent mission in pursuit of Jesus. They are not content to wait until Jesus returns on His own. Apparently, they think that Jesus in His isolation is failing to take advantage of His growing popularity. They would have Jesus accommodate His surge of popularity by returning to Capernaum and building on His newfound fame.

But Jesus has no interest in pursuing the fleeting adulations of the crowds. [See question #3, page 394.] He will not have the plans of other people thrust upon Him. Simon's statement to Jesus is certainly true: *All men seek for thee.* But it apparently is not Jesus' teaching and preaching they want, but His miracles.

## III. Jesus Preaches
## (Mark 1:38, 39)
### A. Desire (v. 38)

**38. And he said unto them, Let us go into the next towns, that I may preach there also: for therefore came I forth.**

Jesus will not be distracted from His divine mission to proclaim the good news of God's kingdom (Mark 1:14, 15). The disciples are invited to accompany Him in His itinerant ministry *(let us go)* that will take Him into the neighboring *towns* and villages. Evidently Jesus' time in prayer has led Him to conclude that it is now time to bring the message to other areas of Galilee. He has not been sent to be a mere local healer or folk hero.

### SENT TO PREACH

John Knox (1513–1572) was the central figure in the Protestant Reformation in Scotland. Probably converted to Protestantism sometime in the 1540s, Knox moved into the castle of St. Andrews in Edinburgh in 1546. Protestant leaders there invited Knox to come among them to preach; he did so realizing that he was putting himself at serious risk.

Indeed, the castle was captured by Catholic forces in 1547, and Knox spent the next 19 months on a prison ship. He was released only at the request of the English government. He served churches in England over the next few years, and it was there that he uttered his famous prayer, "Lord, give me Scotland or I die." His life's interest was to convert the Scots to Protestantism.

Knox later went to the Continent, served in several churches there, and returned permanently to Scotland in 1559. His preaching of evangelical doctrines and his opposition to the Catholic practices of the queen often got him into trouble, but he never wavered from his commitment to preach the truth as he understood it. Preaching the gospel to his people was his life's ambition. Do we have this kind of courage today? —J. B. N.

### B. Action (v. 39)

**39. And he preached in their synagogues throughout all Galilee, and cast out devils.**

What Jesus did in the Capernaum synagogue He now does in *synagogues throughout all Galilee.* Jesus both teaches the message of God's kingdom and reinforces its reality by overthrowing the agents of Satan.

## IV. Jesus Hindered (Mark 1:40-45)

### A. Request (v. 40)

**40. And there came a leper to him, beseeching him, and kneeling down to him, and saying unto him, If thou wilt, thou canst make me clean.**

Following the general description of Jesus' itinerant ministry (v. 39), Mark now focuses on one particular man who makes a request. He is a *leper,* a general term in the ancient world for someone who has some kind of skin disease (not necessarily leprosy in the modern sense).

The priests are charged with determining the severity of such problems along with the neces-

sary course of action (Leviticus 13:1-46; 14:1-32). If the condition is diagnosed as contagious, the afflicted person is excluded from social contact and forced to warn all who come near with the words "unclean, unclean" (Leviticus 13:45, 46).

The banishment is not rooted in a medical concern of spreading infection, but rather in the religious impurity and uncleanness attached to such afflictions. Like touching a corpse, any contact with a leper means religious contamination. [See question #4, page 394.]

The description of the leper's approach to Jesus forms a positive picture of genuine faith and confidence in Jesus' power to remedy the situation. Unlike the scene at Mt. Sinai, where the holiness of God called for the creation of distance between God and the people, God's presence in Jesus does not call for the avoidance of those deemed untouchable.

### B. Response (vv. 41, 42)

**41, 42. And Jesus, moved with compassion, put forth his hand, and touched him, and saith unto him, I will; be thou clean. And as soon as he had spoken, immediately the leprosy departed from him, and he was cleansed.**

The rules for ritual cleanness warn against touching that which is unclean (Leviticus 5:2, 3). Yet Jesus touches those whom others avoid (Mark 1:41; 5:41; 7:32, 33; 8:25). His touch results not in contamination of himself, but in the leper's cleansing.

### C. Sent (vv. 43, 44)

**43, 44. And he straitly charged him, and forthwith sent him away; and saith unto him, See thou say nothing to any man: but go thy way, show thyself to the priest, and offer for thy cleansing those things which Moses commanded, for a testimony unto them.**

After the healing, Jesus emphatically tells the man precisely what he is to do and not do. Three imperatives highlight Jesus' request. The first imperative *See thou say nothing to any man* is intended to counter a misplaced enthusiasm that would draw others to Jesus as a miracle worker.

The second and third imperatives are that the man is to present himself before a *priest* and comply with the Mosaic legislation. This indicates Jesus' respect for the provisions of the law. The procedure also assures that the one formerly excluded from society can now be restored to full communal and spiritual life. We note that the man's healing is not the same as his being declared clean. To be declared clean requires the action of a priest according to Leviticus 14:2-31.

The actions of the leper are also intended as *a testimony unto them*. Probably the pronoun *them* refers to the priests before whom the man will present himself. The leper's sacrifice and healed state are to become powerful witnesses to Jesus' restorative powers. The word out of Galilee will be that God has drawn near in the form of Jesus. [See question #5, page 394.]

SHOW A TESTIMONY

The 1938 film *The Adventures of Robin Hood* was a milestone production. Costing two million dollars, it was the most expensive investment in a film that Warner Brothers had made to that point. The film tells the story of Robin Hood, the legendary nobleman-turned-outlaw, who was trying to save the Saxon peasants from oppression. In one episode, Robin has captured Maid Marian, who was repulsed by the outlaw with his disreputable ways. He tried to tell her that he was working for justice, but she did not believe him.

Then he introduced her to the peasants who were around his camp. For the first time she saw citizenry that was oppressed by Prince John's taxation policies. In contrast, she also saw Robin's kindness to the poor and the outcast. She heard their expressions of gratitude to him. As she returned to the castle, she became a convert to the justice of his cause and fell in love with him as well (after all, it was a Hollywood version).

Actions become a better explanation than words. When Jesus dismissed the healed leper, He told him to show himself to the priests and present the normal offerings required by the Law of Moses. Those were the actions that Jesus wanted to do the speaking and testifying. How do our actions witness for Christ today? —J. B. N.

---

## Home Daily Bible Readings

**Monday, July 7**—Anointed by God (Isaiah 61:1-4)

**Tuesday, July 8**—He Cured Many (Mark 1:29-34)

**Wednesday, July 9**—To Neighboring Towns (Mark 1:35-39)

**Thursday, July 10**—The Word Spread (Mark 1:40-45)

**Friday, July 11**—The Needs for Healing Grow (Mark 2:1, 2)

**Saturday, July 12**—Healed by Faith (Mark 2:3-5)

**Sunday, July 13**—Astonished Beyond Measure (Mark 7:31-37)

---

### D. Sought (v. 45)

**45. But he went out, and began to publish it much, and to blaze abroad the matter, insomuch that Jesus could no more openly enter into the city, but was without in desert places: and they came to him from every quarter.**

Did the man ever go to the priest as Jesus instructed? We don't know. What is clear, however, is that the man disobeyed Jesus' instructions not to tell anyone.

No doubt it would be extremely difficult to contain oneself after experiencing such a remarkable event. Nevertheless, the man's disobedience means that Jesus is hindered from going freely to the towns throughout Galilee, which is His intent (v. 38). Now even *desert places* offer no reprieve from the crush of the crowd.

Certainly Jesus wants the message and power of the kingdom to get out. But the frenzied excitement of the crowds only exalts Him to celebrity status as a miracle worker. Jesus prefers to walk the path of unpretentious service and humility rather than fulfill the aspirations of the crowds.

The episode involving the leper also prepares us for the series of negative responses to Jesus' ministry that we see in Mark 2:6, 7, 16, 18, 24; 3:2, 6. The leper should be a visible witness confronting Israel's leadership with the unprecedented dimensions of Jesus' ministry. But as the scenes comprising Mark 2:1–3:6 indicate, a growing antagonism results in their decision to seek Jesus' destruction.

## Conclusion

### A. Repentance?

Jesus' display of healing powers catapulted Him to instant fame and celebrity status. Yet Jesus showed no interest in seeking the headlines or even remaining in the public eye. The adulation of the crowds rang hollow without their understanding and repentance. In the final analysis, *complete physical healing* plus *no repentance* equals *nothing*. This should cause us to reflect on how we approach Jesus today.

### B. Prayer

Father, please help us to counter the world's definition of power by modeling Jesus' merciful spirit. Empower Your people that we might find the strength to be merciful in an age of brutality. Through Jesus we beseech You, amen.

### C. Thought to Remember

Jesus can heal your spirit,
if you allow Him to.

# Learning by Doing

*This page contains an alternative lesson plan emphasizing learning activities. Some of these activities are also found in the helpful student book,* Adult Bible Class.

## Into the Lesson

Have classroom chairs arranged to accommodate small groups of two to five people as students enter. You will need a minimum of three groups, so construct your group sizes accordingly. Large classes may duplicate the assignments that will be given below. Post the following discussion assignment: *Do you believe in the potential for supernatural physical healings in 2008? Discuss your beliefs.*

After a few minutes of discussion, make a transition to Bible study by saying, "While we usually associate physical healing with prescriptions, doctors, and lifestyle changes, we must recognize that God still has the power to intervene. Otherwise, our prayers at the time of illness and before surgeries are useless. Today we'll view Jesus' supernatural power at work and catch another glimpse of His authority and compassion."

## Into the Word

Give groups copies of the discussion questions below, along with a photocopy of the lesson commentary on the assigned passages. After an appropriate amount of group study time, allow each group to report its findings.

*Group #1:* Read Mark 1:29-34 and answer the following questions:

A. Describe the issues concerning Sabbath activity in this account. What were the potential problems and resolutions?

B. Why do you think Jesus silenced the demons?

C. What does this passage tell you about the nature or character of Jesus?

*Group #2:* Read Mark 1:35-39 and answer the following questions:

A. Describe the setting and events in this passage. Why did Jesus say, "Let us go into the next towns"? What were the implications of that directive?

B. What does this passage tell you about the nature or character of Jesus?

C. What disciplines do you see modeled by Jesus for believers in 2008? Why are they important?

*Group #3:* Read Mark 1:40-45 and answer the following questions:

A. What was the setting of the events? Be sure to discuss the concerns of physical contact with lepers and Jesus' response.

B. Why do you think Jesus commanded the leper to tell no one about his healing?

C. What does this passage tell you about the nature or character of Jesus?

## Into Life

Again, give written copies of assignments to the groups as follows:

*Group #1:* Discuss the lessons we learn from how people react to leprosy and apply them to our reactions to modern afflictions. What do you think are appropriate Christian responses and attitudes toward modern afflictions? How should our reactions differ between contagious and noncontagious afflictions, if at all?

*Group #2:* Remembering our discussion about God's power to intervene in healing in our world, how would you counsel in the following situation? A young wife was reared by Christian parents who disapproved of blood transfusions and allowed only limited doctor's care. The husband is a new Christian. Their one-year-old daughter has certain nonlife-threatening birth defects, and the doctor wants to do surgery. However, the couple is experiencing tensions in deciding how much faith to place in the doctor and how much to place in God's hands.

What Scriptures can you draw upon in counseling this couple? How do you avoid coming across as "a Bible thumper"? How will your counseling be different if this couple seeks you out as opposed to your seeking them out? How do you "counsel" without "giving advice"?

*Group #3:* Remembering our discussion about God's power to intervene in healing in our world, what advice would you give to this couple in their 60s? Both have become Christians in the last couple of months. The husband has been a smoker all of his adult life and has just been diagnosed with lung cancer. Both are frightened as they await the doctor's recommendation for a course of action. They ask you, "Does God really intervene in health issues in today's world?"

How do you respond? What Scriptures can you draw upon in counseling this couple? How would you pray with them?

# Let's Talk It Over

*The questions on this page are designed to promote discussion of the lesson by the class and to encourage application of the lesson Scriptures. The answers provided are only discussion starters. Let your class talk it over from there.*

**1. What limits do people place on their faith in what God can do? How do we go about helping them remove those limitations?**

We all are complex mixtures of belief and unbelief. "Lord, I believe; help thou mine unbelief" we cry (Mark 9:24). As with Martha, we are disappointed when the Lord doesn't do things on our timetable (John 11:21). Sometimes we pray frantic prayers, urging God to "hurry," because time is running out. It can be difficult to surrender our attempts at control and turn our problems completely over to God, trusting that His timing will be perfect. These are good areas to explore in helping people examine their faith limits.

**2. Think of a time when you or a loved one prayed for physical healing. What motivated the request? How was the motivation like or unlike that of those who sought healing from Jesus?**

It is natural and proper to pray for physical healing (James 5:14). The best motive possible is for healing to occur so that the sick person may continue to serve Christ.

We keep a proper perspective when we realize that earthly, physical healing is a temporary fix. We may safely assume that the people whom Jesus raised from the dead died again. The thrust of Jesus' message is heavenly, not earthly (John 3:6, 12). Miraculous healings in the Bible are meant to point to the power of God. That power will take us into His eternal presence.

**3. What are some ways that people try to gain the approval of others? How are those ways like or unlike the way Jesus dealt with crowds?**

Everyone, on some level, wants to "fit in." Peer pressure can be strong. If others make it obvious that they disapprove of our actions, we may be tempted to act differently to regain their approval. Many Christians whose friends and family members are nonbelievers face this problem.

Jesus gives us an excellent example to follow in His steadfast adherence to the Father's will regardless of what others said about Him. Whether it was the Pharisees and Sadducees testing Him (Matthew 16:1) or His own disciple trying to alter the plan (Matthew 16:22), Jesus did not falter in speaking the truth to them. Sometimes Jesus avoided crowds when others preferred that He seek them out (John 7:3-10). At other times He allowed the crowds to stay when others wanted to send them away (Mark 6:36-39). In all these cases, it was the will of the Father, not the will of the crowds, that was Jesus' motive.

**4. How does the church sometimes make it difficult for people to approach God? What can we do to change this?**

The church makes it difficult when her people set up, consciously or unconsciously, unbiblical standards that say, "If you don't meet this standard, then you are contaminated—don't come close." When someone says, "I can't go to church today; I have nothing to wear," the speaker is really saying that his or her clothes do not pass a litmus test of those in the church who focus on attire.

There is an old, familiar story of a minister who dressed in beggar's clothes one Sunday and sat at the front entrance of the church. He noticed with some disappointment that nearly every member who entered made a wide path around him. He shortly entered the pulpit and announced that the membership had just witnessed the subject of his sermon.

**5. The leper was a witness to Jesus' power by the fact that he was known to have been sick, but was healed. What evidence have you seen that Jesus' power is at work in your life?**

People tend to seek cause-and-effect explanations. That was true in Jesus' day (see John 9:2). If we are cured of some sickness, we want to point to a specific drug or a certain treatment that got the job done. Even when it comes to surviving a potentially deadly accident, we like to point to the seat belt, the construction of the car, or something tangible that was responsible for our survival.

If no such explanation is possible, we may say something like, "I was lucky." Yet could not both the explainable and unexplainable be the work of God? Could not the fact that someone was creative enough to invent that seat belt be an act of God? It is a human tendency to credit God with rare occurrences, while giving Him no credit for that which He does on a daily basis.

# Exemplary Servant

DEVOTIONAL READING: Isaiah 53:4-6.

BACKGROUND SCRIPTURE: John 13:1-20.

PRINTED TEXT: John 13:1-20.

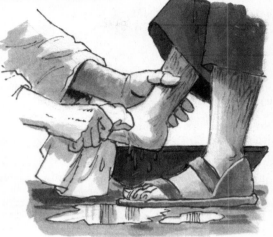

### John 13:1-20

1 Now before the feast of the passover, when Jesus knew that his hour was come that he should depart out of this world unto the Father, having loved his own which were in the world, he loved them unto the end.

2 And supper being ended, the devil having now put into the heart of Judas Iscariot, Simon's son, to betray him;

3 Jesus knowing that the Father had given all things into his hands, and that he was come from God, and went to God;

4 He riseth from supper, and laid aside his garments; and took a towel, and girded himself.

5 After that he poureth water into a basin, and began to wash the disciples' feet, and to wipe them with the towel wherewith he was girded.

6 Then cometh he to Simon Peter: and Peter saith unto him, Lord, dost thou wash my feet?

7 Jesus answered and said unto him, What I do thou knowest not now; but thou shalt know hereafter.

8 Peter saith unto him, Thou shalt never wash my feet. Jesus answered him, If I wash thee not, thou hast no part with me.

9 Simon Peter saith unto him, Lord, not my feet only, but also my hands and my head.

10 Jesus saith to him, He that is washed needeth not save to wash his feet, but is clean every whit: and ye are clean, but not all.

11 For he knew who should betray him; therefore said he, Ye are not all clean.

12 So after he had washed their feet, and had taken his garments, and was set down again, he said unto them, Know ye what I have done to you?

13 Ye call me Master and Lord: and ye say well; for so I am.

14 If I then, your Lord and Master, have washed your feet; ye also ought to wash one another's feet.

15 For I have given you an example, that ye should do as I have done to you.

16 Verily, verily, I say unto you, The servant is not greater than his lord; neither he that is sent greater than he that sent him.

17 If ye know these things, happy are ye if ye do them.

18 I speak not of you all: I know whom I have chosen: but that the Scripture may be fulfilled, He that eateth bread with me hath lifted up his heel against me.

19 Now I tell you before it come, that, when it is come to pass, ye may believe that I am he.

20 Verily, verily, I say unto you, He that receiveth whomsoever I send receiveth me; and he that receiveth me receiveth him that sent me.

GOLDEN TEXT: I have given you an example, that ye should do as I have done to you.—John 13:15.

*Images of Christ*
Unit 2: Images of Christ in the Gospels
(Lessons 6-9)

## Lesson Aims

After participating in this lesson, each student will be able to:

1. Summarize the account of Jesus' washing His disciples' feet.

2. Explain the principle that Jesus established when He washed His disciples' feet.

3. Suggest one practical way to apply the principle above in his or her church.

## Lesson Outline

INTRODUCTION
    A. Understanding Cultural Symbols
    B. Lesson Background
 I.  SPECIAL FEAST (John 13:1-3)
    A. Passover (v. 1)
    B. Prompting (v. 2)
       *Betrayal*
    C. Power (v. 3)
 II.  SYMBOLIC SERVICE (John 13:4-17)
    A. Action (vv. 4, 5)
    B. Interaction (vv. 6-11)
       *You'll Understand Later*
    C. Interpretation (vv. 12-17)
III.  SOBERING DECLARATIONS (John 13:18-20)
    A. Betrayal Is Coming (v. 18)
    B. Belief Is Expected (v. 19)
    C. Ministry Is Transferred (v. 20)
CONCLUSION
    A. Should More Do Humble Service?
    B. Prayer
    C. Thought to Remember

## Introduction

### A. Understanding Cultural Symbols

An early misconception held by the Romans was that Christians engaged in cannibalism. This misunderstanding was based on the "eating of the body" and the "drinking of the blood" of the Lord's Supper. The charge, of course, was unfounded and even a little ironic because the leaders who met in Jerusalem in Acts 15 explicitly forbade the drinking of blood (v. 20).

This issue does illustrate, however, that understanding symbols and symbolic language can be a tricky business. First, one has to understand that something is meant to be a symbol and not to be taken literally. Thankfully, the literary and historical contexts usually provide the information necessary to make this determination.

In today's passage, Jesus washes the disciples' feet. This act of service was viewed as menial by the Greco-Roman culture of the first century. As a task for low-level servants, it was not a job that anyone would embrace voluntarily and eagerly. Yet in so doing Jesus created for the church a symbol of loving service.

### B. Lesson Background

The Passover was one of the great pilgrimage festivals of Jewish antiquity. Its observance recalled God's first deliverance of (what would become) the nation of Israel from slavery (Exodus 12). By Jesus' day, several symbols were used to commemorate the original deliverance: bitter herbs, unleavened bread, etc. Unlike the other Gospel accounts of Jesus' last supper, John's doesn't elaborate on any of these symbols (compare Matthew 26:17-30; Mark 14:12-26; Luke 22:7-23). However, by mentioning the Feast of the Passover, John probably seeks to evoke the symbolic meaning of the total Passover event itself in the light of Christ.

Jesus took two of these symbols—unleavened bread and fruit of the vine—in instituting the Lord's Supper. But that is not the subject of today's lesson. Instead, we will focus on an additional imagery that Christ created on that fateful night: an imagery of service.

## I. Special Feast
## (John 13:1-3)

### A. Passover (v. 1)

**1. Now before the feast of the passover, when Jesus knew that his hour was come that he should depart out of this world unto the Father, having loved his own which were in the world, he loved them unto the end.**

This verse begins the second half of John's Gospel. As such, it serves as an interpretive introduction to this foot-washing passage and also to Jesus' pending death. The first half of John's Gospel deals with Jesus' public ministry. The second half focuses on Jesus' concern for His disciples and His last week and passion.

The drama for Jesus' passion has already been set. The Jewish leaders have conspired to kill Him (John 11:46-53). Jesus has made His triumphal entrance into Jerusalem and predicted His own death (John 12:12-15, 23-33). Now, apart from the noisy crowds, Jesus teaches His disciples privately by performing a simple act of foot-washing. However, this act intends to communicate something profound, as we shall see.

### B. Prompting (v. 2)

**2. And supper being ended, the devil having now put into the heart of Judas Iscariot, Simon's son, to betray him.**

The *supper* we are reading about is the same one indicated in the other Gospel accounts (Matthew 26:17-30; Mark 14:12-26; Luke 22:7-23). We know this because of the similar references to *Judas* (Matthew 26:21-23; Mark 14:18-20; John 13:18 [below]). The Passover meal is an important Jewish ceremony with a defined set of ritual steps or stages. That Jesus would add something to its sequence to wash the disciples' feet shows how important this event is for Him. This is even more evident because usually feet are washed upon entering a household before any meal is served. But in this case the meal is over.

*The devil* here is of course Satan (see John 13:27). The two terms occur in the New Testament about an equal amount of times in the Greek and refer to the same individual. In the Old Testament, the Hebrew word *satan* refers to an adversary or wicked opponent (examples: 2 Samuel 19:22; 1 Kings 11:25). The heavenly being Satan first appears in chapter 1 of the book of Job, where Satan seeks to accuse God's righteous servant Job. Satan opposes God and the salvation He brings to His people (Matthew 13:19-21; John 8:41-44; Revelation 12:9, 17).

A great evil is about to happen: the betrayal of Jesus. Although Satan is the instigator here, he is not ultimately the one in control—God is. God will use this betrayal to advance His greater purposes (see Acts 4:27, 28; etc.). Even though the devil has *put into the heart of Judas Iscariot, Simon's son, to betray him,* this shouldn't be taken to mean that Judas isn't responsible for what is about to happen. Peter acknowledges this in Acts 1:15-25. Even Judas himself eventually comes to realize this (Matthew 27:4, 5).

By deciding to betray Jesus, Judas joins his will with the devil and makes himself one with

---

### How to Say It

CORINTHIANS. Ko-*rin*-thee-unz (*th* as in *thin*).
DEUTERONOMY. Due-ter-*ahn*-uh-me.
EZEKIEL. Ee-*zeek*-ee-ul or Ee-*zeek*-yul.
ISAIAH. Eye-*zay*-uh.
JUDAS ISCARIOT. *Joo*-dus Iss-*care*-ee-ut.

---

him (compare John 6:70, 71). What a contrast this is with what Jesus is about to do!

Incidentally, true followers of Christ should find nothing to fear in this verse. Satan may tempt us, but God has said that He will not allow His people to be tempted beyond what they can handle (1 Corinthians 10:13).

#### BETRAYAL

Benedict Arnold (1741–1801) was an American war hero. He had served with distinction in the French and Indian War and had fought in the Revolutionary War with valor. For his courage in the invasion of Canada, he was promoted to brigadier general. Promotion to major general came in 1777. He led a series of naval battles at Lake Champlain that delayed the British invasion of New York. His actions at the Battle of Saratoga earned the admiration of George Washington as well as the common soldiers.

But Arnold was bitter that he had not received the recognition that he felt he deserved. In addition, he was seriously in debt. As a result, he negotiated with the British to hand over the American fort at West Point, which he controlled. He was to be paid a large bounty and receive an appointment as brigadier general in the British army.

As a result, Benedict Arnold's name has become synonymous in American history with *treason.* The name *Judas* carries similar overtones. The very words *betrayal* and *traitor* carry deep connotations of unpleasantness and disgust. We expect the devil to resist Jesus; we do not expect betrayal from one of His friends. What will eternity say about how your friendship with Jesus turned out?　　　　　　　—J. B. N.

### C. Power (v. 3)

**3. Jesus knowing that the Father had given all things into his hands, and that he was come from God, and went to God.**

Jesus is fully aware of His own status as God the Son and creator (John 1:1-3). He is confidently awaiting glorification. It is with this full awareness that He now undertakes to wash His disciples' feet.

## II. Symbolic Service (John 13:4-17)

### A. Action (vv. 4, 5)

**4. He riseth from supper, and laid aside his garments; and took a towel, and girded himself.**

By removing His outer garment and tying *a towel* around himself, Jesus categorizes himself as a servant.

**5. After that he poureth water into a basin, and began to wash the disciples' feet, and to wipe them with the towel wherewith he was girded.**

In the Mediterranean world of the time, people wear open sandals as they walk along dusty streets. *Feet* thus get dirty quickly. For people to *wash* their own feet is a common practice. Cultural hospitality includes providing water (and sometimes servants) for guests to get their feet clean. This is typical and even somewhat expected (see Luke 7:44).

Perhaps the reason that no one has washed anyone's feet already is that this supper may be taking place in a wealthier, more sanitary part of Jerusalem. This is just a guess. Yet if this is the case, then the need to wash may not be as great as it would be if it were to take place in a less sanitary part of town where animal waste, etc., is present on the streets. In any case, Jesus takes the initiative, availing himself of the opportunity to model an important lesson. [See question #1, page 402.]

### B. Interaction (vv. 6-11)

**6. Then cometh he to Simon Peter: and Peter saith unto him, Lord, dost thou wash my feet?**

To appreciate Peter's astonishment, it is helpful to understand the social dynamics involved. The normal expectation is that foot-washing is to be performed by the lowest-level of servant or slave. In fact, this particular task is thought to be so demeaning that some Jews see foot-washing as a task that is off-limits for male Jewish slaves to perform.

Given these societal taboos, Peter's response *Lord, dost thou wash my feet?* is understandable. If any of the party is going to wash someone else's feet, it should be one of the disciples. *Simon Peter* is well aware of just how far Jesus is humbling himself with respect to normal cultural expectations. [See question #2, page 402.]

**7. Jesus answered and said unto him, What I do thou knowest not now; but thou shalt know hereafter.**

Jesus intends His action to become a symbolic example of humble service in general. The disciples do not yet understand this. But they will understand it *hereafter,* in the future context of Jesus' death and resurrection.

This act of humble service serves as a precursor to Jesus' death on the cross as His ultimate service to humankind. We may pause to note that this is not the first time that people fail to grasp the significance of Jesus' words, nor will it be the last (John 7:37; 12:16; 20:9).

### YOU'LL UNDERSTAND LATER

Some years ago, a friend of mine bought a bicycle for his young daughter. She had outgrown her tricycle, and she desperately wanted a bike. So my friend bought one, complete with training wheels.

His little girl was very happy. She rode her bike all around the yard and the neighborhood. She got comfortable riding that bike because the training wheels saw to it that she never overturned. She often sat still on the bike, keeping her feet on the pedals. The training wheels kept her upright, and she certainly enjoyed the experience.

Then one day my friend took off the training wheels. His daughter was now terrified. She soon discovered she couldn't just sit on the bike any more. Without the training wheels it would fall. Not only that, it was more of a challenge to get going because she had to have a certain amount of speed before the bike would remain upright.

Now she was responsible to get some speed, get on, keep pedaling, and maintain her balance—all at the same time! She almost gave up on the bike, thinking her dad had destroyed her enjoyment of it. But her dad encouraged her, and ultimately she got it all together.

At first she didn't understand why her dad had removed the training wheels. Only later did she realize how much more freedom and enjoyment this gave her. Many things in life are like that. At first we don't understand; the understanding comes later.

—J. B. N.

**8. Peter saith unto him, Thou shalt never wash my feet. Jesus answered him, If I wash thee not, thou hast no part with me.**

We can almost feel the shock of Peter's reply *Thou shalt never wash my feet.* The words *no part with me* is an expression used among Jews for having part in either a physical inheritance, such as land or goods (Numbers 18:20; Deuteronomy 14:27; Luke 15:12), or a spiritual inheritance, bad or good (Matthew 24:51; Revelation 20:6). In this context it is clearly the spiritual that Jesus has in mind. The Lamb of God's blood washes away sin and prepares His disciples to share in His inheritance (John 1:29; 14:2, 3).

**9. Simon Peter saith unto him, Lord, not my feet only, but also my hands and my head.**

Peter is not even grasping the first level of meaning of this foot-washing: an example of loving service. However, Jesus will delay further explaining its first level of meaning until verses 12-17. For now, Jesus will continue to allude to its prefiguring of His loving service of death on a cross.

Whatever the exact cause and nature of Peter's misunderstanding, Jesus is able to use it to develop the discourse in the direction He wants it to go. He is able to take advantage of misunderstandings for this purpose (see John 3:1-5; 4:7-26). [See question #3, page 402.]

**10, 11. Jesus saith to him, He that is washed needeth not save to wash his feet, but is clean every whit: and ye are clean, but not all. For he knew who should betray him; therefore said he, Ye are not all clean.**

Up to this point, Jesus has used what He is doing in the foot-washing to point, in part, toward His coming work of atonement on the cross. Most of the disciples are already *clean* through the word they received (John 15:3). Permanent cleansing will come via the work on the cross. That act of cleansing will never be repeated, nor need it be. True spiritual cleansing will come through both Jesus' word and His sacrifice on the cross.

### C. Interpretation (vv. 12-17)

**12. So after he had washed their feet, and had taken his garments, and was set down again, he said unto them, Know ye what I have done to you?**

Verses 12-17 interpret the significance of the foot-washing, especially at the first level of meaning noted in verse 9, above. The master stoops to perform a slave's task in order to illustrate, by a specific cultural action, a memorable example of general service for His disciples to follow.

**13. Ye call me Master and Lord: and ye say well; for so I am.**

The word *Master* equates to *rabbi* according to John 1:38. Service to one's master or rabbi is considered quite praiseworthy. Jesus affirms the disciples' assessment of Him in this regard.

The word *Lord* takes on different meanings, depending on context. Sometimes it is merely a polite term of respect, such as "sir." The word *Lord* takes on a much deeper meaning after the resurrection (Acts 2:36).

**14. If I then, your Lord and Master, have washed your feet; ye also ought to wash one another's feet.**

Social rank and status are as important and as exaggerated in the ancient world as they are in ours. But Jesus counts that ranking less important than love and service. [See question #4, page 402.] Up to this point in John's Gospel the focus has been on the disciples' relation to Jesus. Now in anticipation of His death, Jesus calls for them to serve one another.

**15. For I have given you an example, that ye should do as I have done to you.**

Some Christians put foot-washing on the same plane as the Lord's Supper and baptism, all three to be practiced on a regular basis. But is that really what Jesus is saying?

By referring to the foot-washing as *an example,* Jesus indicates that He is not just asking for disciples to wash feet. Jesus' historical act is embedded in an arid, dusty culture where this particular kind of humble service is appropriate. It would be less appropriate in other climates. And unlike the Lord's Supper, which according to the other Gospel accounts and 1 Corinthians 11:23-29 was instituted at this last supper, foot-washing is not mentioned again as an established, institutionalized New Testament worship practice. Notice again the word *example.*

The only other time foot-washing is mentioned in the New Testament is in 1 Timothy 5:10. There it is listed as one of several good deeds that characterize certain kinds of widows. It's not that there is anything wrong with washing each other's feet as a reminder of humble service. But humble, loving service to meet others' needs, and not just one's own, is too important to be restricted merely to an occasional act of foot-washing.

**16. Verily, verily, I say unto you, The servant is not greater than his lord; neither he that is sent greater than he that sent him.**

Notice that in verses 13 and 14 Jesus takes the phrase "Master and Lord" (v. 13) and inverts it to "Lord and Master" (v. 14). This places *Lord* at the center of emphasis. He has been building to the verse before us. He wants to emphasize that if their Lord would do such service, so must His servants. What kind of servant would think that he or she was "too good" to do something that

Visual for
Lesson 8

*Use this visual to introduce either question #1 or question #4 on page 402.*

the Lord himself has already done? If Jesus intends to include a deeper level of meaning here, He also may be alluding to His plan to endure the cross (John 18:11; Matthew 26:39; compare Luke 9:23; 14:27).

**17. If ye know these things, happy are ye if ye do them.**

John 13:1 begins what has been called *Jesus' farewell discourse.* It is noteworthy that this discourse begins with an action. True discipleship has to understand God's words, but the disciple hasn't fully learned from Christ until the understanding translates into action. A disciple not only *hears* the Word of God, he or she *does* the things of God (see also Matthew 7:24). Note the importance of keeping the Word in John 8:51; 14:23; 17:6. [See question #5, page 402.]

## III. Sobering Declarations
## (John 13:18-20)

### A. Betrayal Is Coming (v. 18)

**18. I speak not of you all: I know whom I have chosen: but that the Scripture may be fulfilled, He that eateth bread with me hath lifted up his heel against me.**

*Fulfilled* prophecies are proof of God's sovereignty (Ezekiel 24:20-24). The reference here is to Psalm 41:9, which speaks of betrayal by friends. The tragedy of the betrayal is that it is by one who has eaten *bread with* Jesus. Sharing a meal is an activity of friends, not enemies.

### B. Belief Is Expected (v. 19)

**19. Now I tell you before it come, that, when it is come to pass, ye may believe that I am he.**

Jesus' knowledge of the future should help His disciples to continue to *believe* in Him through

this trying time (see John 14:29). Telling the disciples of the forthcoming betrayal proves that the consequent arrest, trial, and crucifixion is not an unexpected development that thwarts the Messiah's intention. Rather, in the providence of God the betrayal will help bring His intentions *to pass.* The disciples need to know that God is still in control throughout the forthcoming events.

*I am he* is a clear allusion to Christ's deity here as it is in John 8:24, 28, 58 (compare Exodus 3:14; Isaiah 43:10). Being a prophet doesn't require that one be God. In fact no one else who spoke God's prophecies was deity. Yet Jesus wants to emphasize His deity here. It is God himself who comes down to offer salvation for all who will believe (John 1:1, 14). It is God's love that motivates Him to do so (John 3:16). It is the God who "is love" (1 John 4:8) who wants His people to reach out and serve each other in love.

### C. Ministry Is Transferred (v. 20)

**20. Verily, verily, I say unto you, He that receiveth whomsoever I send receiveth me; and he that receiveth me receiveth him that sent me.**

Jesus' statement reflects the closeness between God's will and that of Jesus that has already been stated more fully in John 5:19-30 (compare Matthew 10:40). This verse establishes the disciples' forthcoming ministry after Jesus' death. As such, it anticipates their commission in John 20:21. Jesus has the authority of the Father.

## Conclusion

### A. Should More Do Humble Service?

Why don't more Christians take up humble service? Is it the work involved? Work can be hard, but we go to work for pay every day. Is it time constraints? We all could use more time, but we seem to find time for a great many other things. Is it a lack of humility? Is our time just too "valuable" to be bothered with such things? Jesus' time was overwhelmed with His ministry to the people (Matthew 4:23-25; John 6:24; 8:2). But Jesus, out of love, found the time to do even a servant's job. Should we do any less?

### B. Prayer

God, help us to learn to love others and to demonstrate that love in humble service, unconstrained by pride. In the name of our Savior Jesus, amen.

### C. Thought to Remember

Blessed are those whose love
results in service.

---

## Home Daily Bible Readings

**Monday, July 14**—The Suffering Servant (Isaiah 53:4-6)

**Tuesday, July 15**—To the End (John 13:1-5)

**Wednesday, July 16**—Unless I Wash You (John 13:6-11)

**Thursday, July 17**—An Example (John 13: 12-17)

**Friday, July 18**—Whoever Receives Me (John 13:18-20)

**Saturday, July 19**—What Do You Want? (Matthew 20:20-23)

**Sunday, July 20**—Not to Be Served (Matthew 20:24-28)

# Learning by Doing

*This page contains an alternative lesson plan emphasizing learning activities. Some of these activities are also found in the helpful student book,* Adult Bible Class.

## Into the Lesson

Prepare a poster with the heading *The Worst Household Chore Is . . .* Under the heading, make a horizontal list of the following chores: repair plumbing, clean toilets, mow lawn, carry out garbage, scrub floors, change diapers, wash dishes, prepare meals, vacuum floors, wash windows, other (please specify).

As class members enter the room, give each two colored adhesive dots (available at office supply stores or some discount stores). Ask them to vote by placing the dot underneath what they think are the two worst household chores. An alternative is to use colored pushpins if the poster is mounted on a bulletin board.

Make the transition to Into the Word by saying, "The household chores that make lists like this are usually dirty, messy, or thankless jobs. Today, we'll see how Jesus uses a dirty and thankless job to teach a lesson on greatness."

## Into the Word

*Activity #1.* Give each class member a photocopy of today's printed text. Ask learners to listen as you read the text. They are to circle words or phrases that give clues to the nature or character of Jesus.

Then ask your learners to share audibly the words and phrases that they circled. You will write them on the board as they do so. Words and phrases may include "loved His own," "loved them unto the end," "the Father had given all things into His hands," "He was come from God, and went to God," "began to wash the disciples' feet," "Lord," "Master," "given you an example," "servant," etc.

Ask, "What curious question seems to jump out at us in this list of words and phrases?" (Expected response: *Why does the eternal God wash feet?*) Make the transition to the next activity by saying that you're going to unpack some of these words and concepts that teach us so much about God's values and our values.

*Activity #2.* Pose the following questions to the class:

1. What were the cultural or practical issues that led to the practice of washing feet during Jesus' days on earth? Who usually did the service of foot-washing?

2. Why do you think Jesus washed the disciples' feet? What lessons did they learn (or should they have learned)?

3. Is there value in Christians washing one another's feet today? Would you recommend it as a regular or periodic practice? Why, or why not?

4. What twenty-first century practices of humble service could be seen as parallel to the first century practice of foot-washing? *(One possible response: washing one another's cars.)*

5. As Jesus washed the disciples' feet as an example of serving, do you think He belittled His authority or power as the Son of God? Why, or why not? What does this example tell you about Christian vs. secular leadership?

## Into Life

Give poster boards and markers to teams of two to four people. Each team is to make bullet lists in answering these questions:

1. Why is the lesson of servanthood important for Christians?

2. Why is the lesson of servanthood important for the world?

3. What values can you list for acting as a servant? Remember, there will be values both for the servant and for those being served.

Next, your groups are to make lists on the back of the poster boards of ways that Christians can demonstrate servanthood. Assign teams different target groups to serve. Potential areas of focus include the elderly, neighbors, employees, coworkers, neighborhood "latchkey" children, church life. Allow each team to report from each of the above assignments. How will their service differ for Christians and unbelievers?

To make the lesson personal, ask each learner to target someone to encourage in the week ahead by serving that person. Ask learners to share the name of the individual (if appropriate) or the category of that person (elderly Christian, neighbor, etc.) whom he or she plans to serve. Ask learners also to share one or more ideas on how to serve that person.

Groups will close with each member praying for the person to his or her right. If some feel threatened by praying in public, ask for a volunteer from each group to pray for the plans that have just been stated.

# Let's Talk It Over

*The questions on this page are designed to promote discussion of the lesson by the class and to encourage application of the lesson Scriptures. The answers provided are only discussion starters. Let your class talk it over from there.*

**1. In what ways can Christians take the initiative in providing humble service to others?**

It's not unusual to hear the response, "That's not my job!" when someone is asked to provide an act of service. (A similar response that's dressed in religious clothes is, "That's not my area of spiritual giftedness.") Some may say, "Let the government take care of the people who can't pay their bills. That's why I pay my taxes." Yet our Lord calls upon us to be responsive to the cries of those in need (Matthew 25:35-46).

Taking initiative means not waiting to be asked to help. Keeping our eyes open to needs around us and then doing what we can to meet those needs is necessary. A mistake we make when we see someone going through a crisis is to say, "If there is anything I can do, just let me know." Instead, we can open our eyes and see things that can be done—mowing the yard, providing a meal, caring for the children, etc.—then just dive in and do it.

**2. In what areas of your life has Jesus performed a "role reversal" by taking care of your needs?**

The curse and punishment we should have received for sin was borne for us by Christ (Isaiah 53:4-6). Working through His people (the church), Christ continually performs this "role reversal." People go to war in armies and die for their king; with Jesus, the opposite happens.

Sometimes a role reversal will surprise us. We may go to someone to provide encouragement because we are aware of a problem that person is having. But in the process we may discover that the one we go to possesses such a spirit of Christ that he or she ends up encouraging us in ways that we need but have been unwilling to ask for. That's Christ at work!

**3. What was a time in your life when you allowed Jesus to take full control? What brought that on? What was the result?**

Often we try to settle our problems and find solutions on our own in various matters. But try as we might on our own, the problems continue. Finally, we succumb to worry or fear to the point that we are no longer able to function. So we pray and seek the will of God, and things begin to come together. We trust Christ, and the *Aha!* moment occurs.

An old hymn talks about taking our burdens to the Lord and leaving them there. But too often we pray about them, then pick them up and try to handle them on our own. Allowing God full control results in teaching us that God is sufficient for our every need.

**4. Why do we find it hard to follow the example of Jesus when it comes to serving?**

At times we may fail to serve simply because we do not understand what it means to serve. We say we want to serve Christ, and we try to do so by looking for a significant and noticeable way to provide the service. But God puts before us daily opportunities to be faithful by serving in seemingly small ways.

It is by serving faithfully in small ways that we prove ourselves. Then we may be able to serve in the bigger ways. This echoes the teaching of Jesus in Matthew 25:21 where He says to the one who used an opportunity to demonstrate faithfulness, "Well done, thou good and faithful servant: thou hast been faithful over a few things, I will make thee ruler over many things."

**5. What are some things you know that you need to begin to do? When will you start?**

We are not simply to hear the Word, but to do what it says (James 1:22). Faith that is not accompanied by works is a dead faith (James 2:17). There are many tasks that need to be done for the church to fulfill its purpose. Classes need to be taught, widows need to be cared for, the poor need assistance, the hurting need encouragement, and those wrestling with sin need love, support, and perhaps even confrontation.

God may be calling you to one of these tasks, and you've said *no* for too long. Each of us has neighbors or coworkers who need help in some form that we can provide. Many of us need to seek forgiveness from someone we have wronged. In the same way, we need to offer forgiveness to someone who has wronged us. Life will be much more blessed if we do those things we know we should do.

# Promised Messiah

**DEVOTIONAL READING:** Isaiah 43:1-7.

**BACKGROUND SCRIPTURE:** Matthew 16:13-28.

**PRINTED TEXT:** Matthew 16:13-23.

### Matthew 16:13-23

13 When Jesus came into the coasts of Caesarea Philippi, he asked his disciples, saying, Whom do men say that I, the Son of man, am?

14 And they said, Some say that thou art John the Baptist; some, Elijah; and others, Jeremiah, or one of the prophets.

15 He saith unto them, But whom say ye that I am?

16 And Simon Peter answered and said, Thou art the Christ, the Son of the living God.

17 And Jesus answered and said unto him, Blessed art thou, Simon Bar-jona: for flesh and blood hath not revealed it unto thee, but my Father which is in heaven.

18 And I say also unto thee, That thou art Peter, and upon this rock I will build my church; and the gates of hell shall not prevail against it.

19 And I will give unto thee the keys of the kingdom of heaven: and whatsoever thou shalt bind on earth shall be bound in heaven; and whatsoever thou shalt loose on earth shall be loosed in heaven.

20 Then charged he his disciples that they should tell no man that he was Jesus the Christ.

21 From that time forth began Jesus to show unto his disciples, how that he must go unto Jerusalem, and suffer many things of the elders and chief priests and scribes, and be killed, and be raised again the third day.

22 Then Peter took him, and began to rebuke him, saying, Be it far from thee, Lord: this shall not be unto thee.

23 But he turned, and said unto Peter, Get thee behind me, Satan: thou art an offense unto me: for thou savorest not the things that be of God, but those that be of men.

---

GOLDEN TEXT: Simon Peter answered and said, Thou art the Christ, the Son of the living God.—Matthew 16:16.

---

## Images of Christ
### Unit 2: Images of Christ in the Gospels
#### (Lessons 6-9)

## Lesson Aims

After participating in this lesson, each student will be able to:

1. Describe Peter's confession and the circumstances surrounding it.

2. Explain the importance of Peter's confession.

3. Acknowledge Peter's confession to be his or her own.

## Lesson Outline

INTRODUCTION
    A. Who Do People Say Jesus Is?
    B. Lesson Background
 I. PROBING QUESTIONS (Matthew 16:13-15)
    A. Jesus' First Question (v. 13)
    B. Various Wrong Answers (v. 14)
    C. Jesus' Second Question (v. 15)
 II. IMPORTANT ANSWER (Matthew 16:16, 17)
    A. Peter's Belief (v. 16)
    B. Father's Revelation (v. 17)
III. RESULTING PROMISE (Matthew 16:18, 19)
    A. The Rock and the Church (v. 18a)
       *Built on Rock*
    B. The Gates of Hades (v. 18b)
    C. The Granted Authority (v. 19)
IV. NECESSARY MISSION (Matthew 16:20-23)
    A. Important Warning (v. 20)
    B. Dire Prediction (v. 21)
    C. Misguided Rebuke (v. 22)
    D. Stern Response (v. 23)
       *Priorities*
CONCLUSION
    A. Jesus, the Only Savior
    B. Prayer
    C. Thought to Remember

## Introduction

### A. Who Do People Say Jesus Is?

Who do people say Jesus is? The answers vary. That has always been true. And an answer will be heavily influenced by a person's other beliefs. For example, Enlightenment thinkers of the eighteenth century, having discounted miracles, primarily saw Jesus as a commonsense teacher of morality. Some theologians today whose main concern is social justice see in Christ a great liberator of the economic poor, rather than primarily the "poor in spirit."

People tend to make Jesus fit their cultural expectations. The people of the first century AD were no different. It is not that the preceding understandings are totally incorrect. Getting the right answer regarding Jesus' person and work must include an emphasis on what He actually did. The divine revelation we have in the Bible is our starting point in that regard. Our focus on this divine disclosure will help keep us from reducing Jesus to fit our own cultural mold.

### B. Lesson Background

The events in today's lesson take place in the regions of Caesarea Philippi. That city was located in the northeast region of Palestine. The *Caesarea* part of the name was to honor Caesar, the Roman emperor. The *Philippi* part of the name refers to Herod Philip II. Pagan influence is evident in the fact that the city contained a temple for Pan, a Greek nature deity. The area's massive rock cliffs may help suggest the imagery for Matthew 16:18 in today's text. We should be careful not to confuse Caesarea Philippi with the other Caesarea mentioned several times in Acts.

As Jesus and His disciples traveled to the area of Caesarea Philippi in today's lesson, we find Jesus in the third year of His public ministry. Jesus already had performed many miracles and provoked much opposition. It's time for people—or at least the disciples—to come to a conclusion on an important question: Who is Jesus?

## I. Probing Questions (Matthew 16:13-15)

### A. Jesus' First Question (v. 13)

**13. When Jesus came into the coasts of Caesarea Philippi, he asked his disciples, saying, Whom do men say that I, the Son of man, am?**

Having completed the major part of His Galilean ministry (Matthew 4:12–16:12), Jesus is now alone with his 12 disciples. Notice that Jesus does not pose the question *Whom do men say that I, the Son of man, am?* to the crowds. Rather, He asks this question of His disciples in private.

The disciples are allowed to know the deeper realities about Jesus (see Matthew 13:11). Now the time has come to reflect on the various responses to Jesus that His Galilean ministry has evoked. It is time to clarify Jesus' true identity.

The Jewish people of first-century Palestine, including the 12 disciples, have an expectation of a coming Messiah. They also hold certain concepts of what the Messiah will be like. They primarily think of Him in terms of a coming triumphant king, after the model of King David. Further, they think this king will begin His reign on earth by liberating Israel and judging her enemies. If Jesus does not meet those expectations, then who is He?

We can pause to point out that Jesus uses the phrase *the Son of man* to refer to himself more than two dozen times in Matthew's Gospel alone. It is a title with messianic associations, based primarily on Daniel 7:13, 14. Jesus probably favors this title because it is a subtler claim to His messiahship. It is also not as directly tied to, nor limited by, mere earthly kingship. Earlier in His ministry, Jesus could not be too explicit about His messiahship because of misunderstandings about the nature of His kingdom. Claims of kingship also would draw unwelcome attention from the Roman Empire (compare Matthew 27:11).

### B. Various Wrong Answers (v. 14)

**14. And they said, Some say that thou art John the Baptist; some, Elijah; and others, Jeremiah, or one of the prophets.**

The crowds are generally well-disposed toward Jesus. They are amazed by His deeds, but many have no deep understanding or abiding commitment to Him. It is understandable that some think Him to be *one of the prophets* because of His preaching and miracles. But the fact that they do not recognize or acknowledge Him as the Messiah shows in part how successful the Jewish leaders have been in creating doubts about Jesus.

The two Old Testament prophets specifically mentioned are connected with the Messiah. *Jeremiah* predicted Messiah's coming reign (Jeremiah 23:5; 33:15, 16). Discussions about the

---

### How to Say It

ARAMAIC. *Air*-uh-*may*-ik (strong accent on *may*).
BAR-JONAH. Bar-*jo*-nuh.
CAESAR. *See*-zur.
CAESAREA PHILIPPI. Sess-uh-*ree*-uh Fih-*lip*-pie or *Fil*-ih-pie.
CEPHAS (Aramaic). *See*-fus.
ELIJAH. Ee-*lye*-juh.
GALILEAN. Gal-uh-*lee*-un.
GENTILES. *Jen*-tiles.
MACCABEES. *Mack*-uh-bees.
MESSIAH. Meh-*sigh*-uh.
PETRA (Greek). *peh*-trah.
PETROS (Greek). *peh*-tross.

---

importance of Jeremiah appear in the nonbiblical 2 Maccabees 2:1-8; 15:14, 15, written during the time between the Old and New Testaments. The reappearance of *Elijah* is expected to precede the messianic age (Malachi 4:5, 6). Those who think Jesus to be *John the Baptist* may be reflecting Herod's concern (Matthew 14:1, 2).

### C. Jesus' Second Question (v. 15)

**15. He saith unto them, But whom say ye that I am?**

Jesus' follow-up question presses for personal commitment from all the disciples, since the *ye* is plural. The question tests their present level of understanding and faith. Jesus is not interested in mere academic or knee-jerk speculation about who they think He is. The nature of His work demands a more thoughtful and personal response. [See question #1, page 410.]

## II. Important Answer (Matthew 16:16, 17)

### A. Peter's Belief (v. 16)

**16a. And Simon Peter answered and said, Thou art the Christ.**

Combined with Peter's confession, the link of Jesus to Abraham and David in Matthew 1:1 identifies Jesus as the promised Messiah who has come to "save his people from their sins" (Matthew 1:21). This messianic hope began with God's promise to Abraham that through His seed "shall all families of the earth be blessed" (Genesis 12:3; 17:4; 22:18).

God maintained His faithfulness to this promise through Jacob (Genesis 28:14), then through David (2 Samuel 7:12, 16), and then ultimately through Jesus (Galatians 3:8, 16). *The Christ* is the Greek equivalent of the Jewish title *Messiah* (compare John 1:41; 4:25). Both mean "the anointed one." Many psalms and prophecies point to Messiah's arrival and reign (see Psalms 2:7; 110; Isaiah 11; Micah 5:2; Zechariah 9:9). In so doing, they point to Jesus.

**16b. The Son of the living God.**

In a certain sense, Jesus is the obedient *Son of God* whom God wanted Israel to be, but never was because of sin (see Exodus 4:22; Jeremiah 31:9). In a more profound sense, Jesus is the only eternally preexistent Son of God; that is something that has never been true for either Old Testament Israel as a whole or any other human being individually.

There are other clear indications of Jesus' deity recorded in Matthew. For example, Matthew has already identified Jesus as "Immanuel, which

Visual for
Lesson 9

*Use this visual to introduce question #1 on page 410.*

being interpreted is, God with us" (Matthew 1:23). Jesus teaches on His own authority (5:17-20; 21:23-27; 28:18-20; etc.). It is He who will judge humanity (7:21-23). When Jesus forgives sin, He is accused of blasphemy because the Jewish leaders rightly understand that this is the prerogative of God alone (9:2-6). Jesus' enemies recognize clearly who Jesus claims to be (26:63-65). The demonic spirits also testify that Jesus is God's Son (8:29). Only the actual, divine Son of God can live the sinless life that the perfect sacrifice required to redeem humankind (Hebrews 10:11-14).

### B. Father's Revelation (v. 17)

**17. And Jesus answered and said unto him, Blessed art thou, Simon Bar-jona: for flesh and blood hath not revealed it unto thee, but my Father which is in heaven.**

This verse explicitly states that Peter's recognition of Jesus' true identity is because of divine revelation. This fact is also emphasized in this verse by referring to Peter formally as *Simon Bar-jona* coupled with the phrase *flesh and blood.* "Flesh and blood" is a figure of speech used to indicate human beings (see 1 Corinthians 15:50; Ephesians 6:12; Hebrews 2:14).

It is not Peter the mere man who figures this out, but Peter the recipient of the Father's revelation. Peter is *blessed* because he is privileged to receive this revelation and because he expresses it and does not reject it. But how much does Peter really understand at this point? As we will see in Matthew 16:21-23 (below), Peter's understanding of Jesus' divine nature and mission is not yet as deep as it could be.

## III. Resulting Promise
## (Matthew 16:18, 19)

### A. The Rock and the Church (v. 18a)

**18a. And I say also unto thee, That thou art Peter, and upon this rock I will build my church.**

The proper interpretation of this verse has been the subject of much discussion throughout church history. The main issue is to determine to what or to whom *this rock* refers.

*Is the rock Jesus himself?* When we consider this idea, we recall that Jesus refers to himself as the chief cornerstone in Matthew 21:42 (compare 1 Corinthians 10:4; 1 Peter 2:4-8). However, the imagery in the text before us would be rather odd if Jesus were referring to himself as both the foundation *(rock)* of the church and the church's builder *(I will build)* in the same sentence.

We also need to realize that the Bible is flexible in its imagery, depending on what needs to be stressed in various contexts. For instance, Jesus is the builder here, while Paul is "a wise masterbuilder" in 1 Corinthians 3:10, with Jesus as the foundation in 1 Corinthians 3:11. But in Ephesians 2:19, 20, God's household is "built upon the foundation of the apostles and prophets, Jesus Christ himself being the chief corner stone" (compare Revelation 21:14).

This flexibility in figurative language means that the context will determine how words and phrases are to be understood. The context does not seem to require the reader to see Jesus himself as the *rock* in this particular case.

*Is Peter himself the rock?* The word *Peter* is Greek for "rock" or "stone"; in the Aramaic language, the same word is *Cephas,* which we see at John 1:42; 1 Corinthians 1:12; 3:22; 9:5; etc. Those who think Peter himself to be the rock thus see Jesus using a play on words between Peter's name and *this rock.*

This reading seems natural enough, but it has some difficulties. First, there is Peter's mixed historical record. His failings make some think that he is too unreliable to have the church built upon him (v. 23, below; also Matthew 14:31; 26:69-75; Galatians 2:11). Furthermore, Peter's name in the Greek (which is *Petros*) naturally is masculine in gender while the word for *rock* (which is *petra*) is feminine; thus there is a mismatch in the gender of the two words. Some students also see a mismatch in the sizes of a smaller stone *(petros)* and a larger rock *(petra)* in the Greek language.

*Is Peter's confession the rock?* The Bible tells us that confession of Jesus as Savior and Lord is vital to the growth of the church (Matthew 10:32; Romans 10:9; 1 John 4:15; etc.). After denying the Lord before the crucifixion, Peter himself "re-confessed" Christ many times (John 21:15-17; Acts 2:14-40; 4:8-12; etc.). As he did, he was building the church. This leads many students to believe that Peter's confession is the rock upon which Jesus builds His church.

In response, those who think that Peter himself is the rock point out that the play on words between his name and *rock* is unmistakable, despite the fact that one word is masculine and the other is feminine. They also note that any supposed difference in size between a smaller stone *(petros)* and a larger rock *(petra)* in the Greek language becomes meaningless when Peter's Aramaic name *Cephas* is considered; that word is used for both a proper name and a rock without such a distinction.

Before concluding our lengthy discussion of this verse, we point out that this is the first time Matthew uses the word *church* in his Gospel. Jesus himself is the one who inaugurates this community of God's people. They are to be committed to Him and submit to His rule. The church is not an innovation created by His disciples after His death.

### BUILT ON ROCK

Some years ago, I visited the town of Salzburg, Austria, with members of my family. There were many sights to see, including various locations used for the filming of *The Sound of Music*. One of my daughters was particularly interested in the house where Mozart was born. My wife was fascinated by the beautiful floral displays in Mirabell Gardens. My other daughter was interested in the abbey where Maria resided before she became governess to the von Trapp children.

But I must admit, the high point for me (pardon the pun!) was the "High Salzburg" Fortress overlooking the city. The well-preserved fortress, built by the archbishop of Salzburg in 1077, stands atop a rocky hill called, in English, *Monks' Mountain.* I was fascinated to see that the walls of the fortress rest solidly on bare rock. Although the castle is over 900 years old, I saw no evidence of cracks due to settling or shifting. The castle is anchored firmly to the outcropping of rock.

Buildings anchored this way are on the firmest of foundations. Jesus says that the church will be anchored just as firmly. There will be no shifting in the foundation that undergirds God's people.

—J. B. N.

### B. The Gates of Hades (v. 18b)

**18b. And the gates of hell shall not prevail against it.**

Nothing can harm Christ's church! *Gates* can mean "fortifications" as in Psalm 127:5. It doesn't matter how strong those fortifications are, Jesus is stronger. [See question #2, page 410.]

### C. The Granted Authority (v. 19)

**19a. And I will give unto thee the keys of the kingdom of heaven.**

Peter preaches the first sermon after Christ's resurrection. This opens the doors of the church to the Jews first (Acts 2:14-41). Later Peter is the one to open those doors to the Gentiles (Acts 10:34-48) after again receiving and submitting to God's revelation (Acts 10:15, 28; 11:18).

**19b. And whatsoever thou shalt bind on earth shall be bound in heaven; and whatsoever thou shalt loose on earth shall be loosed in heaven.**

This is another one of those passages that has drawn many different interpretations. The binding and loosing have to do with the preaching and teaching of the gospel and the authority inherent in it. Peter has an important role in this, as much of the book of Acts reveals.

This authority is not exclusive to Peter, however. It is also given to church leaders (Matthew 18:17, 18). Peter probably stands as representative here, especially of apostolic authority. We could say that he is "first among equals." The most important thing about this authority is that it is ultimately Heaven's authority. It is only legitimately exercised on earth when it is consistent with all of God's revelation. [See question #3, page 410.]

## IV. Necessary Mission (Matthew 16:20-23)

### A. Important Warning (v. 20)

**20. Then charged he his disciples that they should tell no man that he was Jesus the Christ.**

*Jesus* finds it necessary to withhold this good news to avoid misunderstandings about His messiahship (compare John 6:15). As we learn from the first-century Jewish historian Josephus and Acts 5:36, 37, there were Jewish insurrectionists in and around the time of Jesus who led revolts that were suppressed. Jesus undoubtedly does not want either the people or the Roman Empire to confuse Him with one of those revolutionaries.

We also remember that Herod the Great had attempted to keep this new king from arising (Matthew 2:3-12). When the disciples limit their "God talk" about Jesus at this point in time, it will help ensure that people come to Jesus for the right reasons. Faith, not an expectation of the overthrow of the Romans, is the basis on which people need to approach Jesus.

## B. Dire Prediction (v. 21)

**21. From that time forth began Jesus to show unto his disciples, how that he must go unto Jerusalem, and suffer many things of the elders and chief priests and scribes, and be killed, and be raised again the third day.**

From now on Jesus will use allusions that are less veiled to show His disciples more directly what are the necessary aspects of His mission. It is clear that He is the Messiah (v. 16, above). Now His real redemptive mission as Messiah must also be set forth clearly.

Jesus begins by explaining the sequence of events in the final phase of His earthly ministry. The fact that He *must go* indicates that there is a divine plan behind this imperative. It also signals that Jesus understands that He is fulfilling prophecy (compare Isaiah 42:1 with Matthew 3:16, 17; Isaiah 61:1-3 with Luke 4:18, 19; etc.).

The Messiah's mission must involve suffering (Isaiah 52:13–53:12). It is both ironic and tragic that it is at the hands of the elders, chief priests, and scribes that this suffering comes. These Jewish leaders should be among the ones most open to welcoming Him.

## C. Misguided Rebuke (v. 22)

**22. Then Peter took him, and began to rebuke him, saying, Be it far from thee, Lord: this shall not be unto thee.**

Peter's attempted *rebuke* is a strong one. [See question #4, page 410.] It contrasts sharply with his confession in verse 16 in implying that Peter knows better than Jesus does! The word *began* implies that Jesus does not wait for *Peter* to finish his misguided attempt. Jesus interrupts with a rebuke of His own.

## D. Stern Response (v. 23)

**23. But he turned, and said unto Peter, Get thee behind me, Satan: thou art an offense unto me: for thou savorest not the things that be of God, but those that be of men.**

A very harsh response, indeed! By interfering with God's plan and tempting Jesus to an easier road, Peter, like *Satan* (Matthew 4:8, 9), is making himself into Jesus' adversary. [See question #5, page 410.]

### PRIORITIES

Certain U.S. national parks pride themselves on attracting many tourists. In fact, the more tourists, the more reasonable are the requests for increased governmental funding. Better funding means more financial resources to improve the park, which in turn will attract more tourists.

Unfortunately, some parks have attracted "too many" tourists, and the sheer volume of visitors creates a negative ecological impact. Too many people are walking on the grass, climbing on the rocks, and disrupting the vegetation and wildlife. The result is a park in decline. That will lead to a loss of tourists and a decrease in revenue that could redress the devastation wrought by so many visitors. One suggestion is to make some parks "drive-through only." But the result still will be fewer tourists. Sometimes we don't know enough to set the right priorities!

Peter had the same problem. His priority was to defend Jesus from harm, not realizing that harm was the reason for Jesus' coming into the world. He minded the things of man, not the things of God. This should cause us to be especially prayerful before reaching conclusions about what *is* and *is not* the will of God. —J. B. N.

# Conclusion

## A. Jesus, the Only Savior

In today's world, people look for security in many places. They place their hope in democratic freedom, finances, military security, etc. In effect, these things become false messiahs. But today's lesson makes clear that God has provided only one true Savior: Jesus the Christ.

## B. Prayer

Father, give us grateful hearts to recognize our Savior's love. May we ever confess Jesus as our Messiah. May we renounce our sins to His lordship. It's in His holy name that we pray, amen.

## C. Thought to Remember

Make Peter's confession your own.

## Home Daily Bible Readings

**Monday, July 21**—The Promise of a Savior (Isaiah 43:1-7)
**Tuesday, July 22**—Who Am I? (Matthew 16:13-16)
**Wednesday, July 23**—Tell No One (Matthew 16:17-20)
**Thursday, July 24**—Get Behind Me (Matthew 16:21-23)
**Friday, July 25**—Transfigured (Matthew 17:1-4)
**Saturday, July 26**—Acclaimed (Matthew 17:5-8)
**Sunday, July 27**—Elijah Has Already Come (Matthew 17:9-13)

# Learning by Doing

*This page contains an alternative lesson plan emphasizing learning activities. Some of these activities are also found in the helpful student book,* Adult Bible Class.

## Into the Lesson

As learners enter the room, give each a piece of paper with the heading *Confession* and a subheading *Four Kinds of Confession.* Include the following four kinds of confession as bullets down the left side of the page:

- An act of disclosing one's personal guilt in a crime.
- An act of disclosing one's sins.
- A formal statement of religious beliefs.
- An organized religious body having a common belief system.

Ask learners to work in pairs to think of one or two examples of each of the four kinds of confession. Allow the pairs to share their examples with the class as a whole.

Make the transition to the Into the Word segment by saying, "As you see, the word *confession* has different meanings. Today I'm going to allow you to make a confession. However, I'm not going to tell you what type of confession it is until later, and I won't put you on the spot."

## Into the Word

Before class, put the following identities (real and imagined) of Jesus in bold letters on seven letter-sized pieces of paper, with one name per sheet: *Son of Man, John the Baptist, Elijah, Jeremiah, one of the prophets, Christ, Son of God.* Begin this segment by reading the printed text and asking learners to watch for the identities attributed to Jesus. After the reading, ask people to call out the names or titles as you list them on the board.

*Activity #1: "What's in a name?"* Create four study teams of two to five people each. Teams will interpret the significance of each name and title attributed to Jesus in the lesson. (Smaller classes may make individual assignments.) Give each team a photocopy of the lesson commentary on verses Matthew 16:13-16 and one or more of the appropriate identity signs you prepared earlier. Each team is to prepare a brief report on the names and/or identities assigned.

Team A: *Son of Man,* verse 13. Also give this team a Bible dictionary as a resource. Tell them that the designation *Son of Man* is often listed under *Jesus* or *Christ Jesus.*

Team B: This team has several names to explore from verse 14. Each will require only a very brief report. The names and designations are *John the Baptist, Elijah, Jeremiah,* and *one of the prophets.*

Team C: *Christ,* verse 16.

Team D: *Son of the living God,* verse 16.

Ask each team to report. During the reports, a team member can hold up the appropriate sign displaying the name or designation of Jesus as that name or designation is discussed.

*Activity #2: Mini-lectures and whole-class discussion questions.*

1. What do you think is the significance of Peter's answer in verse 16? Why do we call it *the Good Confession?* Considering 1 Timothy 6:13, is that an appropriate name for it?

2. Using the lesson commentary as a resource, give a mini-lecture on the significance of verses 19b and 20.

3. Tell the class that the lesson commentary on verse 21 makes the following statement, "It is both ironic and tragic that it is at the hands of the elders, chief priests, and scribes that this suffering comes." Ask, "Why would the writer say this is 'ironic and tragic'"?

4. Give a mini-lecture on verse 23.

## Into Life

Remind the learners that one definition of *confession* is "A formal statement of religious beliefs." Peter made his confession. But individuals must decide to accept or reject Jesus as Christ. Many musicians have already done that as they set their feelings about Jesus to music. Brainstorm and list song titles or phrases that make statements about Jesus' divinity. Examples: "Hallelujah! What a Savior" and "He Is Lord."

Remind learners that you promised they would have an opportunity to make a confession. Ask each to write his or her own statement on an index card, answering that probing question, "Who is Jesus?" Give learners a few minutes, then ask for volunteers to read their confessions of faith. Do not put anyone on the spot to read his or her card. After hearing a confession of Jesus' deity, ask how the learner will live out that confession. Have a gracious, low-key reply ready for "non-deity" confessions.

# Let's Talk It Over

*The questions on this page are designed to promote discussion of the lesson by the class and to encourage application of the lesson Scriptures. The answers provided are only discussion starters. Let your class talk it over from there.*

**1. What is the difference between the questions *Who is Jesus?* and *Who is Jesus to you?* How should our understanding of who Jesus is affect our daily living?**

Each person is responsible to determine who Jesus is. Solving that question then determines (or should determine) what role He will play in our lives. This determination needs to be based on the facts of Scripture, not on mere feeling or desire of what one wishes Jesus to be.

The facts are that Jesus is Savior, Lord, king, and the Son of God. Whether or not we allow Him to be those things *to us* is the next issue. As our Savior, we need to know He has taken our sins away and therefore we should forsake sin in our lives. Since He is Lord, we are to be obedient to His commands. Jesus as king requires our submission and loyalty. As the Son of God, Jesus has revealed the Father to us. We are to follow His example as we seek to live for God.

**2. When we see boarded up church buildings, how do we relate that sad fact to Jesus' statement in Matthew 16:18?**

Local churches may close their doors because of a failure to remain faithful to the task (compare Revelation 2:5). Yet "the church universal" continues not only to survive but to thrive. Knowing that the church has survived through wars, persecution, and internal strife gives us confidence that no matter what we may encounter in the life of the church today, she will continue.

Though the world may reject the church, Christ accepts her and sustains her. The demise of the church is a theme that has been echoed by secular thinkers for centuries. The church has been labeled as outdated, irrelevant, ineffective, and useless. Yet the church's continued strength proves all this wrong.

**3. When have you noticed the church struggling with the concept of authority? What is the solution to this struggle?**

The church is influenced regularly by the culture in which her members live. Modern culture is one of power and prestige. Being taught that the person with power gets what he or she wants, people desire power in the church. That, in turn, causes power struggles. Since it is the people with prestige who are honored by the world, the church may put certain folks in positions of authority because of their prestige in the community rather than because of their faithfulness to the Lord. That's a problem.

Another problem is that the idea of being under the authority of another is unwelcome in a culture that emphasizes rugged individualism and the autonomy of self. But the church is one of three spheres of authority that God has established. (The other two are government and the family.) Our continuing struggle is to accept the nature of that authority while rejecting secular authority models for the church.

**4. In what ways are we guilty of rebuking Jesus today? How do we reverse this problem?**

Like Peter, we can confidently proclaim Jesus to be the Christ and the Son of the living God. But we may not understand the implications of that confession. We too can be guilty of contradicting Jesus in both attitude and action.

When Jesus says to us that we should turn the other cheek, our response may be one that says, "But Jesus, You just don't understand how badly that person has mistreated me." In response to Jesus' saying to us that we should seek first the kingdom of God, we instead may seek our own desires. Jesus says that the one who would be great must become a servant, yet we may deny this teaching by expecting people to meet our needs. The effect is to rebuke Jesus by not following His desires.

**5. What are some of the things "of men" that you have valued over the things of God in the past? How did you turn this problem around?**

Our world teaches us to look out for self, to accumulate possessions, and to seek pleasure. As a result, some seek the places of high position or greatest power, even if it means destroying others along the way. We also seek personal freedom, refusing to adhere to the teaching of God's Word on issues of morality and integrity. We may not want anyone telling us what we can or cannot do, not even God. A "long view" of where life is headed is a key to solving this problem.

# Doers of the Word

Devotional Reading: **Psalm 92:1-8.**

Background Scripture: **James 1.**

Printed Text: **James 1:17-27.**

### James 1:17-27

17 Every good gift and every perfect gift is from above, and cometh down from the Father of lights, with whom is no variableness, neither shadow of turning.

18 Of his own will begat he us with the word of truth, that we should be a kind of firstfruits of his creatures.

19 Wherefore, my beloved brethren, let every man be swift to hear, slow to speak, slow to wrath:

20 For the wrath of man worketh not the righteousness of God.

21 Wherefore lay apart all filthiness and superfluity of naughtiness, and receive with meekness the engrafted word, which is able to save your souls.

22 But be ye doers of the word, and not hearers only, deceiving your own selves.

23 For if any be a hearer of the word, and not a doer, he is like unto a man beholding his natural face in a glass:

24 For he beholdeth himself, and goeth his way, and straightway forgetteth what manner of man he was.

25 But whoso looketh into the perfect law of liberty, and continueth therein, he being not a forgetful hearer, but a doer of the work, this man shall be blessed in his deed.

26 If any man among you seem to be religious, and bridleth not his tongue, but deceiveth his own heart, this man's religion is vain.

27 Pure religion and undefiled before God and the Father is this, To visit the fatherless and widows in their affliction, and to keep himself unspotted from the world.

**Aug
3**

Golden Text: Be ye doers of the word, and not hearers only,
deceiving your own selves.—James 1:22.

*Images of Christ*

Unit 3: Images of Christ in Us

(Lessons 10-14)

## Lesson Aims

After participating in this lesson, each student will be able to:

1. Summarize James's teaching on hearing and doing and on making one's religion real.

2. Explain how God's Word should lead to active discipleship.

3. Make a plan to correct one area of life in which he or she needs to move from being a mere *hearer* to being a *doer.*

## Lesson Outline

INTRODUCTION
    A. Gag Gifts
    B. Lesson Background
 I. GIFTS FROM GOD (James 1:17, 18)
    A. The Best Gifts (v. 17)
        *Geostationary*
    B. The Eternal Gift (v. 18)
II. LESSONS FROM A PROVERB (James 1:19-27)
    A. The Proverb (v. 19)
        *Rash Speech*
    B. Controlling Anger (vv. 20, 21)
    C. Hearing God's Word (vv. 22-25)
    D. Controlling Speech (v. 26)
    E. Practical Application (v. 27)
CONCLUSION
    A. Using the Gift
    B. Prayer
    C. Thought to Remember

## Introduction

### A. Gag Gifts

Some gifts are given simply for the fun of the moment. Gag gifts used for a "white elephant" exchange fit this category. Everyone rummages in the basement or attic, goes to the dollar store, or recycles gifts from the last white elephant exchange in order to provide an item that will be the worst (and most hilarious) gift at the party. Bad art, ridiculous hats, and ugly cups—such gifts are worthless in and of themselves.

Other gifts have real, lasting value. The gift talked about in today's passage is foremost of these. In fact, it is the only truly eternal gift.

### B. Lesson Background

The epistle of James was written by James, the brother of Jesus (Galatians 1:19; 2:9). James did not believe Jesus to be the Christ until after Jesus' resurrection (John 7:5; 1 Corinthians 15:7). James was present with those gathered just before the Day of Pentecost (Acts 1:14). By the time of the Jerusalem council in Acts 15, James had emerged as one of the principal leaders of the church. James was noteworthy enough for the historian Josephus to record his murder, which happened in about AD 62.

The epistle of James is his only work in the New Testament. Unlike books from Paul, which often are concerned about the place of Gentiles in the church, James writes primarily to Jewish Christians. They were in a tough situation (James 1:1-3). Some even had fled Jerusalem following the persecution by Herod Agrippa that occurred in the time period of Stephen's stoning and the execution of James, the son of Zebedee (Acts 11:19–12:2 ).

## I. Gifts from God
## (James 1:17, 18)

In the verses preceding those for this lesson (James 1:1-16), James challenges believers to have the kind of mature faith that can stand up to life's disasters and disappointments. He seems worried about their eternal future. He is concerned that many Christians believe—wrongly—that God is tempting them when the opposite is true (1:13). God wants all believers to succeed! In fact, rather than throwing hazards at us, He continually strews our paths with gifts to encourage us as we go.

### A. The Best Gifts (v. 17)

**17. Every good gift and every perfect gift is from above, and cometh down from the Father of lights, with whom is no variableness, neither shadow of turning.**

James describes God in three ways: as the one *from above,* as the *Father of lights,* and as the one with *no variableness, neither shadow of turning.* The first phrase is a common expression of ancient Jews that is based on their understanding of God's location. The second phrase connects God with the creation of light (Genesis 1:3, 14).

This sets the stage for James's third observation. This is an issue of the constancy of God's character, which contrasts with that of people, who are described as "double-minded" and "unstable" in James 1:8. The image *no variableness, neither shadow of turning* brings to mind the lengthening of shadows as created by the interference of the sun's light by buildings and trees. God's character is like a sun that never sets and that has nothing to block its light. With God, it is always high noon. With this correct understanding of God, it is easy to grasp the idea that He wants only the best for us in life. [See question #1, page 418.]

### GEOSTATIONARY

I grew up with the knowledge of satellites as a new science. I still remember the thrill and concern that greeted the news that Sputnik I was in orbit. Of course, we Americans could not let the Russians get ahead of us in the space race, so we soon had our own satellites. They have been increasing in number ever since.

I remember driving out into the country on a summer night in 1960 to watch a satellite moving across the sky. That was the problem with satellites of the time: they moved. There were some advantages to that movement, but the disadvantage was that they didn't give a constant report because their location continually changed.

Since then, a new generation of satellites has arrived—satellites that are *geostationary*. That means they remain in one place over the surface of the earth. This is an improvement over the way the older satellites operate. Because geostationary satellites move in exact synchronous movement with the rotation of the earth, their location and report are constant—they do not vary.

James didn't have geostationary satellites in his day to use to illustrate God's unchanging nature, so James used images of lights and shadows to make his point: with God there is no change. We sinful mortals shift constantly—in our morals, our actions, our priorities, our physical locations, and our attitudes. It is convenient—even vital—to have a point of reference that never changes. That "satellite reference" is the unchanging God.　　　　　—J. B. N.

### How to Say It

EZEKIEL. Ee-*zeek*-ee-ul or Ee-*zeek*-yul.
GENTILES. *Jen*-tiles.
HEROD AGRIPPA. *Hair*-ud Uh-*grip*-puh.
ISAIAH. Eye-*zay*-uh.
JERUSALEM. Juh-*roo*-suh-lem.
JOSEPHUS. Jo-*see*-fus.
PENTECOST. *Pent*-ih-kost.
ZEBEDEE. *Zeb*-eh-dee.
ZECHARIAH. *Zek*-uh-*rye*-uh (strong accent on *rye*).

## B. The Eternal Gift (v. 18)

**18. Of his own will begat he us with the word of truth, that we should be a kind of firstfruits of his creatures.**

As in verse 17 above, this verse first draws on creation ideas from Genesis. The creation of humankind by God's *word* is implied as the absolute best result of all His creation activities.

The major concern of this passage is not to talk about that life-giving word in Genesis, but to use its language as a stepping-stone to talk about God's perfect gift: *the word of truth*. This word gives birth to life of a different order: eternal life.

This birth takes place at the spiritual level and is propelled by a specific word, the message of the gospel. Christians are the *firstfruits* of humanity. This is apparent because (1) the *we* and *us* refer to believers, (2) becoming a Christian is commonly referred to as birth in the New Testament (John 3:3; 1 Peter 1:3), (3) *word of truth* refers to the gospel (see also Ephesians 1:13), and (4) Christians are referred to as firstfruits in Romans 16:5; 1 Corinthians 16:15.

## II. Lessons from a Proverb (James 1:19-27)

At first the following verses don't seem to connect very well to the previous ones. However, 1:22, 23 will again talk about "the word." It can be presumed that this word is the perfect gift, the word of truth from 1:17, 18.

### A. The Proverb (v. 19)

**19. Wherefore, my beloved brethren, let every man be swift to hear, slow to speak, slow to wrath.**

Proverbs are carefully crafted, memorable sayings. This one not only provides a keen perception about the relationship between listening and outbursts of anger, it also provides the framework for the immediate verses that follow. Verses 20, 21 expand on the third part of the proverb, verses 22-25 on the first, and verse 26 on the second. Not only that, the three parts of verse 19 introduce the broad concerns of the entire book of James: correctly hearing the word (chapter 2), the difficulty of controlling the tongue (chapter 3), and the damaging effect angry speech has on the church (chapter 4).

The primary observation of this proverb is that careful attention to what someone else is saying is the gateway to disciplining one's own talk. Then disciplining one's own talk leads to breaking the bad habit of angry, uncontrolled, emotion-laden outbursts. Though every human being occasionally speaks like this, control of this human weakness is a virtue. Such outbursts usually result in our saying things that hurt others whom we really don't wish to hurt.

The teaching of each of the three concerns of this verse is found in the book of Proverbs. Proverbs 5:1, 2; 15:31; 19:20; 22:17, 18; etc., extol the virtue of listening. Proverbs 10:8, 10, 19; 13:3; and 18:2 deal with controlling our speech. Also see Proverbs 12:16; 14:17; 15:18; 16:32; 17:27; 20:3; 29:11, 20, 22.

### RASH SPEECH

When I was a freshman in college, I had not yet learned some of the subtleties of interpersonal communication. On one occasion I asked a fellow student a question about a rather controversial situation. When she began to explain her view on the issue, I immediately realized her opinion was different from mine. So I jumped in, arguing with her. She let me rattle on for a couple of minutes, then she softly observed, "I thought you were asking for my opinion; I didn't realize you just wanted to argue."

I was abashed, but she was right. It was obvious I really didn't care for her opinion; I just wanted to present my own and argue against hers. I learned over the process of time that she was a thoughtful person, quite bright about a lot of things. But at the time I was a presumptuous freshman, more interested in arguing than in intelligent discussion.

First of all, it probably would have been better if I had never initiated a controversial confrontation. But even then it would have been much smoother if I had waited for her to explain her view so we could then calmly discuss our different viewpoints. In other words, it would have been much better for me to be swift to hear, slower to speak. But, of course, I'm the only one who has ever had to learn that lesson the hard way, right?                                    —J. B. N.

## B. Controlling Anger (vv. 20, 21)

**20. For the wrath of man worketh not the righteousness of God.**

The word *wrath* in other contexts can refer to the emotional feelings people have when they are upset. But here it represents the unregulated, hurtful words people shout at others when they are angry. This type of behavior is unacceptable to God.

Angry words that aim to do harm are always wrong. They are vindictive. However, the emotion of anger itself is in many ways a natural, human way of coping with stressful, unfair

things that happen to us in our lives. God himself gets angry (see Zechariah 10:3; Mark 3:5).

The human virtue that is crucial to pleasing God is *control*. How a person deals with his or her anger is the difference between righteous and unrighteous character. A person can use anger as the impetus to solving problems in productive ways. Mean-spirited, emotional outbursts are not helpful to these ends and are therefore displeasing to God. [See question #2, page 418.]

**21. Wherefore lay apart all filthiness and superfluity of naughtiness, and receive with meekness the engrafted word, which is able to save your souls.**

An uncontrolled display of angry words is only one of many unrighteous—and therefore unacceptable—things that people do. By using the word *filthiness*, James pictures people covered in something disgustingly smelly that they need to wash off. With the phrase *superfluity of naughtiness* (meaning "prevalent evil"), the picture switches to that of overgrown weeds that need to be cut back so that righteousness can flourish.

Rather than continue to allow unrighteous behavior (such as angry speech) to dominate our behavior, we are to cultivate the *word* we were given when we believed. That precious gift is the word of truth (1:18, above), the gospel. James pictures this word as a seed that has been planted in the soil of our lives. That seed needs to be nurtured so it will bloom and grow, replacing the weeds of evil and the sinful nature within us. This seed and only this seed enables people to develop the righteous character that God desires.

However, only Christians have received this seed. God has created every human being with a cultivated spot in his or her life to receive this seed, the word of the gospel. However, He does not force anyone to accept it. Rather, each one upon hearing the gospel may accept this seed as a welcome guest into his or her life, just as the believers James is writing about have done (compare Matthew 13:23).

*Meekness*, easily overlooked in verse 21, is a key component for generating the kind of Christian lives that James demands. Certainly, its opposite (namely, arrogance) cannot be present when a person first accepts the gospel, repents of sin, and fully relies on the graciousness of God. [See question #3, page 418.]

Arrogance also impedes the growth of that gospel seed implanted in our lives. Full reliance on God for strength to overcome our unrighteous character is the only way we can become the excellent kind of people God desires. Clearly, the believers James writes to have accepted the implanted word, but they have dampened its growth by their pride. This stands as a warning to us not to do the same.

### C. Hearing God's Word (vv. 22-25)

**22. But be ye doers of the word, and not hearers only, deceiving your own selves.**

The interest now turns to spiritual matters. *The word* mentioned here is still the "word of truth," the gospel planted by God as the eternal gift taking root in the lives of believers.

As most evident in children, there is a big difference between merely hearing and really listening. Poor listening (in terms of "in one ear and out the other") decreases our ability to perform well. Yet we are to be excellent listeners, focusing intently on what God is saying to us through His gospel, which is now a permanent part of our lives. If we listen well, we will perform well. [See question #4, page 418.] Our lives will demonstrate the righteous character that pleases God. We will be *doers* (compare Matthew 7:26).

**23, 24. For if any be a hearer of the word, and not a doer, he is like unto a man beholding his natural face in a glass: for he beholdeth himself, and goeth his way, and straightway forgetteth what manner of man he was.**

What will happen if we refuse to listen attentively to *the word*? Suppose that one morning we look at the face in the mirror and we don't recognize ourselves. We ask, "Is that really me?" What a frightening thought! Something would be terribly wrong if this were to happen. After all, this is our very own face.

Yet, that's what the case would be if we had forgotten what we looked like. Someone who uses a mirror then *straightway forgetteth what manner of man he* is won't recognize himself the next time he uses a mirror. In this case, previously known flaws would go ungroomed.

**25. But whoso looketh into the perfect law of liberty, and continueth therein, he being not a forgetful hearer, but a doer of the work, this man shall be blessed in his deed.**

The mirror analogy applies to the issue of a believer's behavior, or doing. In this the term *word* of verse 23 is replaced by the term *law*. Laws are supposed to be enforceable rules intended to curtail criminal behavior so law-abiding citizens are free from the fear of criminals. Good idea, but whose law is perfect? Not any in human society.

The law at issue here is described as *perfect* and as giving *liberty*. It is that part of the word of truth that God has planted in believers. It is perfect because it is the eternal gift of God (1:17). It provides liberty, or freedom, because it is not like

Visual for Lessons 1, 6, and 10

*Point to this visual as you ask, "How will lifting our eyes to the cross help us control our speech?"*

any normal human law. Rather than an external rule to enforce behavior by punishment, this law (or word) changes people at their core, releasing them to live out God's desires because enacting His word comes naturally. It is the fulfillment of Jeremiah 31:33, "I will put my law in their inward parts, and write it in their hearts."

This *law* is best represented by "Thou shalt love thy neighbor as thyself" (Matthew 19:19). This is a positive principle for determining what God's desire is from one situation to the next. James probably has this in mind because he refers to it in James 2:8 as the royal law. It is the key law instituted by Jesus for the kingdom of God.

### D. Controlling Speech (v. 26)

**26. If any man among you seem to be religious, and bridleth not his tongue, but deceiveth his own heart, this man's religion is vain.**

This verse deepens the importance of the second part of the proverb of James 1:19. The matter of the control of the tongue is underlined in dire, spiritual terms. James draws a straight line that connects this virtue of speech control to the genuineness of one's religious experience *(his own heart),* and then to the validity of the *religion* one claims to be true.

James believes at the very least that any religion worth anything should make its devotees better people in ways that others can observe. As applied to Christianity, the communication of its truth to others is utterly dependent on the way Christians behave. The way we talk is one of the best and easiest ways for people to experience the value of Christianity, not only to them as individuals but also to society at large.

Surprisingly, verse 26 uses the word *religious* like we would today. For the sake of his argument, James views Christianity as one of many religions that people follow. Of course, Christianity is the only completely true religion, since only it incorporates the full, direct revelation from God in Jesus Christ. However, the concern here is not with defending Christianity in terms of its truth claims. Rather, the issue is helping us know that when we fail to control our speech, we exhibit to the world that Christianity has no power to change people for the better.

This is devastating to Christianity. We are to let the implanted word blossom into things like honest, uplifting, and genuine words. Compare Psalm 34:13; 39:1; and 141:3.

### E. Practical Application (v. 27)

**27. Pure religion and undefiled before God and the Father is this, To visit the fatherless and widows in their affliction, and to keep himself unspotted from the world.**

James explicitly extends the observations about the importance of a believer's controlled speech to general behavior. Not only should a valid *religion* affect our speech, it should bring about observable improvements in the way we live our lives.

When this verse speaks of true religion as *pure* and *undefiled,* everyone in the ancient world— Greeks and Jews—would think that what is at issue is ritual sacrifice in a temple. Pure religion in this perspective involves how one goes about selecting the best animals and performing proper prayers and rituals. It is probably shocking to the first readers of James that a connection is made to *widows* and orphans, since they are at the very bottom of life economically and socially.

However, God's consistent concern for their welfare is inscribed in Hebrew law. Deuteronomy 24:17 provides that they should be allowed to take a share from the stored produce of Israel; it warns that anyone who deprives them should be cursed. Prophets condemn Israel for mistreating orphans and widows (Isaiah 1:10-17; Jeremiah 5:28; Ezekiel 22:7; Zechariah 7:10).

This verse emphasizes that believers should *visit* those widows and orphans. This does not imply that merely writing out a check exhibits the behavior that pleases God. Rather, what is at issue is caring enough to be involved personally. This is intended to be an example of many observable behaviors in believers that are the result of the word of truth becoming fruitful in our lives. [See question #5, page 418.]

A second example lies in how believers behave generally. Having cleaned up our lives to allow the implanted word to grow, we no longer want to exhibit behavior that looks like our old lives. To be *unspotted from the world* does not imply that we are to retreat somehow from the world, keeping ourselves apart from unbelievers. Rather, it implies that believers are no longer to be influenced by the ideas and priorities that motivate unbelievers. We are to show them what Christianity looks like "in the flesh." We can't do that if we don't associate with them.

## Conclusion

### A. Using the Gift

Gifts come in all sizes and shapes—and purposes. Blouses, shirts, and ties are to be worn. Cookies and candy are to be eaten. Books are to be read, CDs listened to. Artwork and photos are to be admired. Many gifts are intended to be used and used and used. Tools like drills and screwdrivers fit this category. So do appliances such as can openers, coffee makers, and microwaves.

The gift of salvation is intended to be used too. Its use, however, involves allowing Christ's principle of loving others to transform every word and deed of our lives into object lessons of God's love for men and women everywhere.

### B. Prayer

Author of all good gifts and provider of the gift of life eternal through the gospel, thank You for Your generous demonstration of love toward us. Help us return our love to You by loving others in all we do and say. In Jesus' name, amen.

### C. Thought to Remember

Live out the gift of the gospel in word and deed.

## Home Daily Bible Readings

**Monday, July 28**—The Full Effect of Endurance (James 1:1-4)
**Tuesday, July 29**—Ask in Faith (James 1:5-8)
**Wednesday, July 30**—How to Boast (James 1:9-11)
**Thursday, July 31**—Endure Temptation (James 1:12-15)
**Friday, Aug. 1**—Everything Is from God (James 1:16-21)
**Saturday, Aug. 2**—Blessed in Doing (James 1:22-27)
**Sunday, Aug. 3**—How Great Are Your Works! (Psalm 92:1-8)

# Learning by Doing

*This page contains an alternative lesson plan emphasizing learning activities. Some of these activities are also found in the helpful student book,* Adult Bible Class.

## Into the Lesson

Bring a variety of mirrors to class and place them around the room. Then ask your learners whether they particularly like or dislike mirrors, and why. Expect humorous answers such as, "The mirror is too honest!"

Ask the men, "If you've been shaving all these years, why do you still need a mirror? Don't you know the contours of your own face by now?" Ask the women, "If you've been putting on make-up all these years, why do you still need a mirror? Don't you know the contours of your own face by now?" Expect more humorous answers.

After a few minutes, point out the error in your logic if no one already has: the need for shaving and make-up mirrors isn't an issue of forgetting the contours of our own faces; rather, it's an issue of knowing precisely where to take something off of or put something onto our faces.

Say, "In today's lesson, our Bible author also points out a logic error. The error is being a *hearer* of God's Word and not a *doer* of God's Word. James says that's like someone looking in a mirror, then forgetting what he or she looks like after turning away." Refer to James 1:23-25.

## Into the Word

Next, divide the class into groups of four or five. Provide each group with a blank sheet of paper. Ask your learners to turn the paper so that the longest side is across the top (landscape position). Leaving a 1" margin on each side, have them create three columns labeled as follows: *Verse* (left column, about 1" wide), *Action* (middle column, about 4" wide), and *Reason* (right column, about 4" wide). Instead of handing out blank sheets of paper, you may wish to prepare photocopies of the above to save class time.

Have each group review James 1, looking for the specific ways that James tells his readers to be doers of the word. They are to fill in the chart with the verse reference, the action James describes, and the reason for the action. *Example: Verses: 2, 3; Action: rejoice in temptations. Reason: creates patience.*

After a few minutes of discussion, have each group share its discoveries. If time permits, compile a composite chart on the board that includes each group's findings.

*Optional activity:* One way to learn a passage is to paraphrase it, using modern terminology and examples. Have each student write a paraphrase of James 1. You can offer the following paraphrase as an example for James 1:1. "This e-mail is from James@Jerusalem.org. I want to be known as a servant of God and of the Lord Jesus Christ. I am writing to you my fellow Jews who have been scattered all over the world."

Challenge your learners to capture the meaning without being overly casual or flippant. To keep this activity from dragging out too long, you can assign only one or two verses per learner. After a few minutes, have learners read their paraphrases aloud in sequence.

## Into Life

A week before class, ask learners to visit a nursing home, a hospice situation, or a shut-in during the week. Ask for volunteers to tell about their experiences. If they do not have the opportunity to do this in the week before class, ask for volunteers to discuss a time in the past when they visited one of these places or situations.

A follow-up activity that puts the lesson into practice is for one person to make arrangements for the entire class to visit a caregiving institution. If your church sponsors or supports a specific agency, that can be the first choice. After the visit, discuss a class project that would benefit the residents of that institution.

An alternative is to find a way for the class to help a specific person or family in your congregation who has some special need. When visiting this person or family, don't take "too many" of your class members along lest the ones being visited feel intimidated. These activities provide a practical way for the class to experience the challenge "to visit the fatherless and widows in their affliction" (James 1:27). It is doing what they hear from God's Word.

If you have someone in your church who is experienced in visiting hospitals, nursing homes, etc., you can ask that person to do some visitation role-playing activities with your class in advance of their own visits. This will help keep your learners from making avoidable mistakes or saying and doing inappropriate things during their visits.

# Let's Talk It Over

*The questions on this page are designed to promote discussion of the lesson by the class and to encourage application of the lesson Scriptures. The answers provided are only discussion starters. Let your class talk it over from there.*

**1. Every good thing is from God! Given this fact, what should you thank Him for at this very moment?**

It is so easy to take everyday blessings for granted! Yet can you imagine the disaster we would face if God stepped away from us for even a moment (Colossians 1:16, 17)?

Feeling that we are the source of our own blessings is a problem. When we feel that way, we neglect to consider who gave us our health, our talents, our economy's prosperity, etc. We could spend every moment in giving thanks to God without any risk of overdoing it (1 Thessalonians 5:18).

**2. What situations present the greatest danger for you to speak out inappropriately? What tips have you found helpful for keeping your tongue in check?**

It is quite natural for us to want to lash out when we are hurt. When someone hurts us, perhaps we need to stop and consider the offender. There is a saying: "Hurting people hurt people." Remembering this might help us to stop and listen, rather than react hastily when words or actions cut us.

One Christian writer encourages us not to critique others until we are able to state their position back to them to their satisfaction. That will help keep us from uttering rash words, which have a way of coming back on us. There is truth in this old Irish saying: "Make the words you speak today tender, warm, and sweet, for tomorrow they may be the very words you eat."

We should also realize that we hurt and offend God when we sin. That is true of all sin, whether of word or deed. While we might think our anger is completely justified when we tell someone off, we actually are grieving our Lord who loves that person and died to save him or her. Remember that a fruit of the Spirit in Galatians 5:22, 23 is *temperance* (that is, self-control). If you've surrendered your life completely for God's glory and pleasure, you will deny yourself those unregulated outbursts.

**3. How can an attitude of humility help keep our tempers in check?**

Anger and arrogance are often anchored in self-interest. When we consider others better than ourselves and look out for their interests (Philippians 2:3, 4), we'll have less trouble in this area. Sometimes in disputes, even with others in the family of God, we may feel that we are justified in using any means to make our point because we "know" that our position is right. Yet persuading others is not just a matter of *what* we say but *how* we say it. When we have a healthy dose of humility, we will choose to make our point without impaling anyone on it!

Notice the important mix of virtues in Micah 6:8: "And what doth the Lord require of thee, but to do justly, and to love mercy, and to walk humbly with thy God?" Leaving any of the virtues out is like swimming 90 percent of the way across a lake—you'll still drown.

**4. Have you ever listened to a sermon and thought to yourself, "This is exactly what so-and-so needs to hear"? How can we focus on letting God's Word affect us personally rather than worrying about others?**

We can begin by taking the mote/beam test of Matthew 7:3-5. Because we often are tempted to accuse others to justify our own behavior, we must each be open to God's perspective (1 Corinthians 4:4). We should be willing for God to show us anything in our lives that displeases Him.

Each disciple at the last supper asked *Lord, is it I?* when Jesus informed them that one would betray Him (Matthew 26:22). Each was rightly concerned at somehow having failed the Lord personally. Let us have the same concern.

**5. What keeps us from assisting needy people today? How do we overcome this?**

Most Westerners live in relatively comfortable surroundings. A natural tendency is to avoid traveling near those "seedy" areas where the neediest people live: urban shelters, transient hotels, rundown trailer parks, etc. Thus we may neglect assisting the needy because we simply don't *see* them. Therefore having open eyes is a first step. While short-term mission trips can open our eyes to dire needs in the world, there are many needy people in our own backyards.

# Impartial Disciples

**DEVOTIONAL READING: Matthew 25:31-46.**

**BACKGROUND SCRIPTURE: James 2.**

**PRINTED TEXT: James 2:1-13.**

### James 2:1-13

1 My brethren, have not the faith of our Lord Jesus Christ, the Lord of glory, with respect of persons.

2 For if there come unto your assembly a man with a gold ring, in goodly apparel, and there come in also a poor man in vile raiment;

3 And ye have respect to him that weareth the gay clothing, and say unto him, Sit thou here in a good place; and say to the poor, Stand thou there, or sit here under my footstool:

4 Are ye not then partial in yourselves, and are become judges of evil thoughts?

5 Hearken, my beloved brethren, Hath not God chosen the poor of this world rich in faith, and heirs of the kingdom which he hath promised to them that love him?

6 But ye have despised the poor. Do not rich men oppress you, and draw you before the judgment seats?

7 Do not they blaspheme that worthy name by the which ye are called?

8 If ye fulfil the royal law according to the Scripture, Thou shalt love thy neighbor as thyself, ye do well:

9 But if ye have respect to persons, ye commit sin, and are convinced of the law as transgressors.

10 For whosoever shall keep the whole law, and yet offend in one point, he is guilty of all.

11 For he that said, Do not commit adultery, said also, Do not kill. Now if thou commit no adultery, yet if thou kill, thou art become a transgressor of the law.

12 So speak ye, and so do, as they that shall be judged by the law of liberty.

13 For he shall have judgment without mercy, that hath showed no mercy; and mercy rejoiceth against judgment.

**Aug
10**

GOLDEN TEXT: Hearken, my beloved brethren, Hath not God chosen the poor of this world rich in faith, and heirs of the kingdom which he hath promised to them that love him?—James 2:5.

## Images of Christ
### Unit 3: Images of Christ in Us
### (Lessons 10-14)

## Lesson Aims

After participating in this lesson, each student will be able to:

1. Recount James's admonition to follow the royal law rather than show favoritism.

2. Compare and contrast the effects of following the royal law with what happens when an individual or church does not follow it.

3. Suggest one specific way to implement the royal law more fully in his or her life or church.

## Lesson Outline

INTRODUCTION
    A. A Stain upon Humanity
    B. Lesson Background
 I. UNHOLY DISCRIMINATION (James 2:1-7)
    A. Within the Church (vv. 1-4)
      *Goodly Apparel*
    B. Against the Church (vv. 5-7)
II. ROYAL LAW (James 2:8-13)
    A. Principle for Application (vv. 8-11)
      *No "Respect to Persons"*
    B. Principle for Judgment (vv. 12, 13)
CONCLUSION
    A. At-Risk Christians
    B. Prayer
    C. Thought to Remember

## Introduction

### A. A Stain upon Humanity

The U.S. Declaration of Independence boldly declares "all men are created equal, that they are endowed by their Creator with certain unalienable Rights." By incorporating a biblically influenced view of human dignity, those who wrote this struck a knockout blow against the perceived right of nobility to rule over the faceless hordes of commoners. Yet the writers' own prejudices prevented them from seeing how excluding equal rights and dignity to slaves, women, and others contradicted their bold plan.

Callous disregard for people of different races, tribes, and religious convictions is not just an American problem. It has played itself out against the backdrop of human history and continues today. One need think no further than the Nazi oppression of the Jews or Sunnis versus Shiites in Iraq. The Bible stands firmly against discrimination and prejudicial mistreatment of others for any reason. The lesson today is a key text in this regard.

### B. Lesson Background

Today's text expands on James 1:17-27 (last week) to show how vital it is for Christians to give words and feet to the gospel that is planted in their lives. An embarrassing feature of early Christian gatherings was that the wealthy were given preferential treatment. It is surprising that Christianity attracted any interest at all from the socially advantaged, since first-century Christianity was not a dominant world religion as it is today. By all historical accounts, Christianity was viewed as an obscure sect that attracted an odd assortment of Jews, Gentiles, women, slaves, etc. Christianity did not emerge out of the shadow of Judaism until almost the second century AD.

Though a few people of advantage did attach themselves to Christianity, early Christianity was primarily a religion of people outside of power. "The crowd," the nameless in Jewish society, were the ones who followed Jesus from place to place. He openly and compassionately associated with those "at the bottom": tax collectors, widows, children, lepers, the demon-possessed, Samaritans, Gentiles.

Mary's song at Jesus' birth prophesied the reversal of social positions that He would bring (Luke 1:52, 53). The reversal of position in Jesus' kingdom is addressed in James 1:9-11 and is assumed to be the backdrop to 2:1-13. Here, language similar to Jesus' teaching as found in the Gospels is evident.

## I. Unholy Discrimination (James 2:1-7)

Discrimination and favoritism in the time of James were relative to one's position. This remains true today. People tend to mistreat those below them in the social pecking order and grovel at the feet of people above them. Thus, the vast majority experiences both social mistreatment as well as social superiority. Both are wrong.

### A. Within the Church (vv. 1-4)

**1. My brethren, have not the faith of our Lord Jesus Christ, the Lord of glory, with respect of persons.**

The phrase *respect of persons* describes what people do when they size others up based only on what they can see—the other person's attractiveness, skin color, clothing, house, etc. [See question #1, page 426.] In the Old Testament, the equivalent Hebrew idea is applied to personal relationships as well as to the administration of civil justice. Leviticus 19:15 instructs the people of Israel "Thou shalt not respect the person of the poor, nor honor the person of the mighty" (see also Deuteronomy 1:17; Psalm 82:2; Proverbs 18:5).

Deuteronomy 10:17 explains that God himself is not partial. God's impartiality is foundational to New Testament instruction too. This is clearest in Acts 10:34, 35. See also Galatians 3:28; Ephesians 6:9; Colossians 3:25; Philemon; 1 Peter 2:13-25.

The verse before us bases its appeal for impartial relationships on its readers' *faith* as believers. Their common commitment to Christ makes this obvious. However, the verse draws attention to this by naming *Jesus Christ* specifically, the only mention of that name in this letter other than in James 1:1. He is *the Lord of glory*.

For Jews in the New Testament period, glory has a particular reference to the presence or manifestation of God in all His grandeur. For Christians, glory is associated with the resurrection splendor of Christ. It corresponds with His highest position of exaltation at the right hand of God (Colossians 3:1).

But we should be sure to remember, as 1 Peter 2:21-24 does, that Christ came to His exalted position after abject humiliation, mistreatment, and suffering on the cross. His experience of discrimination was one of being wrongfully convicted, and His position is now reversed! God made Him judge even over those who condemned Him (Mark 14:62; Revelation 1:7).

**2, 3. For if there come unto your assembly a man with a gold ring, in goodly apparel, and there come in also a poor man in vile raiment; and ye have respect to him that weareth the gay clothing, and say unto him, Sit thou here in a good place; and say to the poor, Stand thou there, or sit here under my footstool.**

Verses 2, 3 tell a story of discrimination in the early church. We know it is a hypothetical story because it begins with *if*, yet we could say that it is based on reality. James tells of a person entering a group of believers. The term used for *assembly* is actually the word *synagogue* in Greek, normally expressing the regular gathering of Jews primarily for teaching and prayer.

The problem in this hypothetical event is exaggerated to be sure we "get it." Two men from opposite ends of the social and economic spectrum enter the meeting. One is extremely rich, and the other is very *poor*. One is a *man* of immense influence—perhaps a landowner, nobleman, or politician; the other is someone everyone wants to avoid. One wears a *gold ring*, symbolizing power. He also has an impressive outer cloak, his best of many selections. The other has none of this. He simply comes in "off the street," smelly, unwashed, unkempt. [See question #2, page 426.]

Almost everyone, then and now, would do the same thing James describes with this situation: pander to the rich guy and ignore or insult the smelly guy. The poor man is sent to sit on the floor. The rich man receives a seat of honor. Yet these seating arrangements have nothing to do with character or faith conviction. The host has only looked at the men superficially.

Only a person of extraordinary conviction could possibly treat them the same or even reverse their positions. Yet to do so would model the central tenets of Christianity. In God's kingdom the position of the rich and poor will be reversed. Why not begin having "no respect of persons" in the church now?

### GOODLY APPAREL

In the musical *My Fair Lady*, Alfred P. Doolittle is the charming but irreverent dustman. Often unemployed, he comes to Professor Henry Higgins and asks him for a mere five pounds—that's British currency—in exchange for Alfred's daughter, Eliza. When Higgins offers more, Doolittle refuses. He explains that too much money will only corrupt everything, including himself. Later when Higgins communicates with a wealthy American philanthropist regarding the need for a lecturer on morality, Higgins suggests Alfred P. Doolittle, common dustman.

Doolittle is shocked when he later is informed that the philanthropist has left him a fund guaranteeing an income of 5,000 pounds per year. Just as Doolittle had feared, now everyone comes to him asking for money. His common-law wife

---

**How to Say It**

BEGUINES. *Bay*-genes.
DEUTERONOMY. Due-ter-*ahn*-uh-me.
GENTILES. *Jen*-tiles.
LEVITICUS. Leh-*vit*-ih-kus.
PHILEMON. Fih-*lee*-mun or Fye-*lee*-mun.
SAMARITANS. Suh-*mare*-uh-tunz.
SHIITES. *She*-ites.
SUNNIS. *Sue*-nees.
SYNAGOGUE. *sin*-uh-gog.

demands marriage. All this happens because he has become wealthy and "respectable." He himself has not changed, but his new financial status changes how other people react to him.

When Doolittle had nothing, the wealthy ignored him and the poor treated him as an equal. After ending up with all that money, the poor responded with deference, and the wealthy treated him as an equal. That's a fictional story, but doesn't art often imitate life? Today, people still ignore the Doolittles who are dustmen, but they bow to the Doolittles who have status. Christians dare not embrace such discrimination. —J. B. N.

**4. Are ye not then partial in yourselves, and are become judges of evil thoughts?**

Verse 4 moves beyond the hypothetical scenario to a blunt accusation. It accuses the readers of behaving in ways comparable to the pattern of verse 3. In doing so, they have become *judges of evil thoughts.* See Matthew 7:1.

### B. Against the Church (vv. 5-7)

**5. Hearken, my beloved brethren, Hath not God chosen the poor of this world rich in faith, and heirs of the kingdom which he hath promised to them that love him?**

Verses 5-7 ask four rhetorical questions that assume a *yes* response. They are intended to draw attention to matters that the church already knows but has not applied to the issue of discrimination among themselves.

The first question reminds the church that God remains the champion of *the poor.* This truth assumes the teaching in the Old Testament (examples: Job 34:25-29; Proverbs 14:31). The situation of these poor, who are *heirs of the kingdom,* causes us to think of one of the most memorable sayings of Jesus: "Blessed are the poor in spirit: for theirs is the kingdom of heaven" (Matthew 5:3).

Neither Jesus nor James is suggesting that the poor are somehow automatically saved because of their economic condition. Yet the poor are more inclined than the rich to develop trust in God for His care of them. Despite being at a cultural disadvantage, the poor are at an advantage over the rich when it comes to spiritual development and kingdom potential.

**6. But ye have despised the poor. Do not rich men oppress you, and draw you before the judgment seats?**

Just before asking a second and third rhetorical question, James accuses the church of mistreating *the poor.* If they are treating the poor in any way like the picture in verses 3, 4, then they certainly have *despised* them.

Using questions, James goes on to remind his readers of the social and economic realities of the time. Many of the readers are poor themselves; as such, they surely have experienced the strong arm of exploitation wielded by the *rich* and powerful. Then as now the wealthy have the advantage in court; they know the law, the judges, and the politicians. They own land, and their interests often affect the jobs and development of communities. Thus, they are pictured colorfully as being able to *draw* or drag the poor into court against their will.

What is imagined here is not criminal court, but civil court. There the rich seek debt repayment or seek to extend property rights.

**7. Do not they blaspheme that worthy name by the which ye are called?**

The fourth rhetorical question asks the church to recall that not only do the wealthy exploit them in court, but also by doing so they besmirch *that worthy name by the which* they *are called.* Although His name is not mentioned specifically, there can be no doubt that the name at issue here is *Jesus.* It is possible that the verse thinks of the social harassment or taunting of Christians, but what James is more likely pointing out is the harm done to Jesus' name itself.

This text is written in a social world that contains only two classes of people: poor and rich. Of these, perhaps 90 percent are poor. In today's world, those in the middle class of Western democracies do not consider themselves to be "rich." Yet from the broader standpoint of world economics, they are. Anyone studying these verses must not only consider how he or she is treated by the rich but should also consider that they may well be among those who are exploiting the poor in their culture, whether in business or personally.

## II. Royal Law
## (James 2:8-13)

Our next section shows that discrimination against another person is a violation of the love-for-neighbor principle. Those who violate this principle put themselves at a major disadvantage at judgment, since this is the measure that will be applied.

### A. Principle for Application (vv. 8-11)

**8. If ye fulfil the royal law according to the Scripture, Thou shalt love thy neighbor as thyself, ye do well.**

The *law* of loving one's *neighbor* is found in Leviticus 19:18. Jesus elevated this law to a position above all other laws, except the command to love God (Matthew 22:36-40; Mark 12:28-31). The impact of this teaching on the early church can be observed in the teaching of Paul (Romans 13:9; Galatians 5:14) and in the verses before us, which seek to evaluate behavior based on this principle.

James specifically connects this principle of neighbor love to Jesus' teaching about His kingdom by describing it as *royal*. This law was referred to earlier in James as "the word of truth" (James 1:18) and as "the perfect law of liberty" (1:25). Later it will be called simply the "law of liberty" (2:12). It is the standard that declares judging others to be wrong (4:12). It is a law unlike any other law! [See question #3, page 426.]

**9. But if ye have respect to persons, ye commit sin, and are convinced of the law as transgressors.**

James now takes the microscope of the love-for-neighbor principle and uses it to look at the issue of discriminating against others. Treating others positively or negatively based on superficial cues demonstrates a failure to love them as our neighbors. Within the ethical principles established by Jesus for those in His kingdom, this is blatant *sin*. To discriminate is to break *the law* of Jesus. [See question #4, page 426.]

### NO "RESPECT TO PERSONS"

The Beguines was an interesting social institution of the Middle Ages. There is much about this movement that is not well understood today, but we know enough to form an intriguing picture of them. The Beguines were women who had formed a semimonastic organization. That is, they were not nuns living under vows; they were free to own private property and could leave the group and marry if they wished. Organized first in the Netherlands in the twelfth century, they soon spread to other countries.

Their primary consideration was social works, particularly the care of the poor, the sick, and other needy. In an age of growing urbanization, they normally were associated with urban communities, providing some social relief to those who were caught in the transition from peasantry to urban life, but did not have jobs or skills to provide a decent living. The movement reached its height in the thirteenth century.

The Beguines served a useful function, tending to the needs of a downtrodden portion of the population. They were not respecters of persons and did not discriminate. They were simply women trying to be Christian servants in a changing culture. Do they have anything to teach us today? —J. B. N.

Visual for Lesson 11

*You can use this visual aid to introduce several of the questions on page 426.*

**10. For whosoever shall keep the whole law, and yet offend in one point, he is guilty of all.**

Here James recites a truism that Jewish teachers commonly applied to Jewish law. It is still a valid legal principle. Specific legal regulations generally are grouped under categories. In Jewish teaching, for instance, one can walk only a certain distance on the Sabbath. To go farther than that is to transgress the regulation; but in transgressing the regulation, a person also breaks the law against working on the Sabbath.

The parallel this verse draws is that not to discriminate is a regulation under the broader principle of loving our neighbor as ourselves. Thus to discriminate breaks the *law* of love.

**11. For he that said, Do not commit adultery, said also, Do not kill. Now if thou commit no adultery, yet if thou kill, thou art become a transgressor of the law.**

James offers an example of the truism of verse 10. The Ten Commandments is a unit of law provided in the Old Testament by God (Exodus 20; Deuteronomy 5). Violating 1 of the 10 specific rules makes a person guilty of breaking the wider unit of *law*. The regulations against *adultery* and murder may be chosen as examples because Jesus brought them up himself when He talked with the rich young ruler (Matthew 19:18, 19).

### B. Principle for Judgment (vv. 12, 13)

**12. So speak ye, and so do, as they that shall be judged by the law of liberty.**

*The law of liberty* is the standard by which our lives will be measured. It is a guideline in all things. Although we may tend to think of our lives primarily as a sequence of right or wrong actions, this verse brings the way we talk into the equation.

This is important because people probably have more opportunity to do more harm or good by what they say than by what they do. This verse picks up on an issue that becomes a full-blown concern in James 3. Jesus says in Matthew 15:11 that it is what comes "out of the mouth" that contaminates people.

Both words and behavior will be *judged,* then. But judged for what purpose? Aren't Christians already saved from judgment for their sins by the cross and the grace of God? The New Testament is very clear that although believers escape condemnation through the blood of Christ, they do not escape unevaluated. Second Corinthians 5:10 tells us that this evaluation is to be done by Christ and that everything we have done—our entire lives—will be surveyed. What verse 12 clarifies is that this judgment will include what we say and that it will be based upon Christ's law of liberty, or loving our neighbor.

**13. For he shall have judgment without mercy, that hath showed no mercy; and mercy rejoiceth against judgment.**

In this verse James picks up the teaching of Jesus found in Matthew 5:7: "Blessed are the merciful: for they shall obtain *mercy.*" Within this beatitude is the kernel of Christ's law of neighbor love, but also the threat of judgment. Everyone wants to be given the benefit of the doubt by their coworkers, family, and friends. We need the forgiveness and forbearance of others when we mess up. This need should be the spark that makes us want to do the same for others.

To add to our motivation, this verse develops the beatitude to promise judgment on those who

fail to show mercy, on those who do not live their lives on the basis of Christ's law of love. In His Parable of the Unforgiving Servant, Jesus likewise depicted severe punishment for the man who was forgiven a large debt he owed but would not forgive a smaller one owed to him (Matthew 18:21-35). [See question #5, page 426.]

Verse 13 ends with a proverbial saying that promises safe passage through Christ's seat of judgment for those who live their lives in ways that consciously implement Christ's law of love. They do this by exercising mercy to others. The word *rejoiceth* depicts more than just "getting through." It pictures celebration in the face of anticipated victory, dancing with joy into our eternal reward. If we live our lives under the rule of love, we can enter judgment with supreme confidence that we have pleased Christ and that He will say, "Well done, thou good and faithful servant" (Matthew 25:21).

If we live this way, it also is good news for the people around us. Among other things we won't be showing contempt for those "below" us in the social and economic orders of our culture. Nor will we give undue deference to those "above" us. We will not discriminate on such superficial things, just as God does not. We will be the impartial disciples whom Christ desires.

## Conclusion
### A. At-Risk Christians

The last two verses sound a warning. Whereas Israel was judged on the degree to which they observed the law God gave them through Moses, those who form the church will be evaluated on their implementation of Christ's law for His kingdom. Israel was sent into exile for breaking their covenant with God. What will happen to those in the church? We must look closely at our lives and be fully aware of how well we are loving our neighbor. As Christians, not to live with this principle at the forefront of all our behavioral decisions is to invite God's condemnation.

### B. Prayer

Father of us all, who created us to flourish in the world You made, give us the courage to live out our lives with the unrestricted love You have shown us in Jesus Christ. Enable us to display to the world a community of faith that dignifies all people, even as Christ did. In His name, amen.

### C. Thought to Remember

Uphold the dignity of every person, both inside and outside the church.

## Home Daily Bible Readings

**Monday, Aug. 4**—Sheep or Goats? (Matthew 25:31-46)
**Tuesday, Aug. 5**—Acts of Favoritism? (James 2:1-4)
**Wednesday, Aug. 6**—God's Favored (James 2:5-7)
**Thursday, Aug. 7**—The Royal Law (James 2:8-11)
**Friday, Aug. 8**—The Law of Liberty (James 2:12-17)
**Saturday, Aug. 9**—Faith and Works (James 2:18-20)
**Sunday, Aug. 10**—An Active Faith (James 2:21-26)

# Learning by Doing

*This page contains an alternative lesson plan emphasizing learning activities. Some of these activities are also found in the helpful student book,* Adult Bible Class.

## Into the Lesson

Bring a copy of the U.S. Declaration of Independence to class (easy to find on the Internet). Have someone read aloud just the first two sentences, ending with the words *and the pursuit of happiness*. Discuss the author's view of individual worth that the document proposes. Also discuss who was omitted in this document because of common practices of the time. Answers may include African-Americans (slaves), women (couldn't vote), etc.

Ask, "Why did the author feel—theoretically, at least—that it was important to declare that 'all men are created equal, that they are endowed by their Creator with certain unalienable rights'?" After some discussion time, point out that today's study will show that God has never been a respecter of persons as we have been.

## Into the Word

Before class, write the following Scripture references across the top of 14 sheets of paper, one per paper: Proverbs 14:31; Proverbs 28:3; Matthew 7:1, 2; Matthew 19:24; Acts 10:34; James 2:1; James 2:2-4; James 2:5; James 2:6, 7; James 2:8; James 2:10, 11; James 2:13; 1 John 3:4.

Shuffle the sheets and distribute. Each learner should look up the passage given to him or her and write it out on the paper. Then ask the person with the reference to James 2:1 to read that text. Then ask, "Who has the text closest in meaning to this that is not from James?" Have that person read his or her text. Move through the passages from James 2 in sequence this way. The expected matches are *James 2:1 to Acts 10:34; James 2:2-4 to Proverbs 14:31; James 2:5 to Matthew 19:24; James 2:6, 7 to Proverbs 28:3; James 2:8 to Matthew 22:39; James 2:10, 11 to 1 John 3:4; James 2:13 to Matthew 7:1, 2.*

If you have fewer than 14 students, you can give learners more than one passage each (but give each either texts only from James or only not from James). If considering 14 texts is not practical given the constraints of time, use fewer texts.

*Optional activity #1.* Read the Golden Text, James 2:5. Ask for discussion about why James said that God chose the poor of this world to be rich in faith. Why are the poor more likely to have a strong faith? Why is it difficult for the rich to depend on God's gracious gifts? Passages such as Matthew 19:23, 24 and James 5:1 can enrich your discussion.

*Optional activity #2.* Have some class members pantomime the scene in James 2:2, 3. Select learners who have a flair for the dramatic for this demonstration. You can ask your actors a week ahead of time so they have time to practice.

*Optional activity #3.* Continue paraphrasing the book of James from last week, this time having learners paraphrase James 2. Again, challenge your learners to capture the meaning without being overly casual or flippant.

To keep this activity from dragging out too long, assign only one or two verses per learner. After a few minutes, have learners read their paraphrases aloud in sequence. To extend this learning activity, encourage your learners to paraphrase the entire lesson text each week at home. Comment that this is an excellent way to focus on and understand God's Word.

## Into Life

Assemble your class into four small groups. Ask them to discuss the following sets of questions. Write these questions on the board or make copies of them for each group. Depending on the time available, you can have each group either discuss only one set of questions each or all four sets of questions.

1. What was a time when you felt discrimination directed at you? Do you think you reacted biblically? Why, or why not?

2. With what group of people do you find yourself feeling uncomfortable? Is *lack of comfort* the same as *discrimination*? Why, or why not?

3. Does our congregation show partiality or discriminate? If so, how do we fix this as God would want? What are some specific steps that this church can take to make all people feel welcome here?

4. A secular definition of discrimination is "unequal treatment without a rational basis." Does this definition harmonize with the Bible? Why, or why not?

To wrap up, have one person from each group summarize his or her group's conclusions for the class. Discuss as time allows.

# Let's Talk It Over

*The questions on this page are designed to promote discussion of the lesson by the class and to encourage application of the lesson Scriptures. The answers provided are only discussion starters. Let your class talk it over from there.*

**1. How would you rate your church in having "no respect of persons"? What attitudes or practices should you change to make others feel more welcome?**

Something as subtle as which family gets greeted more quickly and warmly at the door may tip our hand to our prejudices. However, many churches have made a concerted effort to be ethnically and/or economically diverse by examining and changing practices that communicate a lack of acceptance.

We can look to Jesus as the master of loving all kinds of people. The Gospel of Mark tells us He looked at the rich man and loved him (Mark 10:21) and interacted with outcasts (Matthew 9:10-12; John 4). We must strive to do likewise.

**2. What kind of clothing do you choose to wear to church? What motivates your choices? What *should* motivate your choices?**

Some who teach, lead music, or pray from the platform at church dress casually in order to make visitors wearing various clothing styles feel welcome. Some folks always "dress up" for church services because they believe that that is a sign of respect (as in "giving your best to the Master"). The risk is that those who can't dress as well because of limited resources may feel unaccepted.

Whatever level of casualness in our dress, modesty is always a legitimate concern (1 Corinthians 12:23; 1 Timothy 2:9). An important motivation in selecting style of dress is that we not draw attention to ourselves and away from Christ. Discuss motives of economic consideration in addition to motives of "being genuine."

**3. What are some ways we can follow the "royal law" of loving our neighbors as we love ourselves?**

There are many possibilities. Perhaps we can begin with this question: What ministries could our church family initiate that would express love to the needy in our community—those who don't know Jesus, the shut-ins, latchkey children, etc.? Congregations may choose to organize food pantries, ministries to shut-ins, after-school activities for latchkey children, or outreach that helps children with their schoolwork.

These may be new ministries or enhancements to already established community programs. Most larger municipalities have services such as Meals on Wheels, Big Brother/Big Sister programs, etc. A vital consideration is to make sure that all involved know that you are ministering in the name of Christ.

An organized program is not essential for showing God's love. Individuals who pray for opportunities to show kindness to others surely will be blessed with such. How important is this? According to Matthew 25:31-46, it is the way we show our love to Jesus himself!

**4. What kinds of favoritism are there?**

In James 2:9, the specific problem was economic favoritism. Wealth is the most obvious source of power and status, but there are other things in society that may tempt us to favor some people over others. Attractiveness has been called "the universal prejudice." If we find ourselves being less hospitable to those we don't find attractive, we may need to remember that Jesus himself chose to be clothed in an "average" physical body at best (Isaiah 53:2).

Ethnic or nationalistic prejudice can also be a factor. Many communities have populations of immigrants who may lack language skills or more importantly, knowledge of Jesus. Sometimes simply offering to be a "conversation partner" with someone who is learning English can be the easiest way to share your faith.

**5. If showing love and mercy to others is what builds up our "spiritual bank accounts," what words, attitudes, and actions can you change to build up your balance?**

Problem: we tend to judge others by their worst actions while judging ourselves by our best motives. Jesus' point of view is this: "For with what judgment ye judge, ye shall be judged: and with what measure ye mete, it shall be measured to you again" (Matthew 7:2).

Love and mercy often are about giving others the benefit of the doubt. We can do this by believing the best of everyone until the facts demand otherwise, then hold on to hope that God can change them (1 Corinthians 13:4-7).

# Wise Speakers

DEVOTIONAL READING: **Proverbs 15:1-4; 16:21-24.**

BACKGROUND SCRIPTURE: **James 3.**

PRINTED TEXT: **James 3.**

### James 3

1 My brethren, be not many masters, knowing that we shall receive the greater condemnation.

2 For in many things we offend all. If any man offend not in word, the same is a perfect man, and able also to bridle the whole body.

3 Behold, we put bits in the horses' mouths, that they may obey us; and we turn about their whole body.

4 Behold also the ships, which though they be so great, and are driven of fierce winds, yet are they turned about with a very small helm, whithersoever the governor listeth.

5 Even so the tongue is a little member, and boasteth great things. Behold, how great a matter a little fire kindleth!

6 And the tongue is a fire, a world of iniquity: so is the tongue among our members, that it defileth the whole body, and setteth on fire the course of nature; and it is set on fire of hell.

7 For every kind of beasts, and of birds, and of serpents, and of things in the sea, is tamed, and hath been tamed of mankind:

8 But the tongue can no man tame; it is an unruly evil, full of deadly poison.

9 Therewith bless we God, even the Father; and therewith curse we men, which are made after the similitude of God.

10 Out of the same mouth proceedeth blessing and cursing. My brethren, these things ought not so to be.

11 Doth a fountain send forth at the same place sweet water and bitter?

12 Can the fig tree, my brethren, bear olive berries? either a vine, figs? so can no fountain both yield salt water and fresh.

13 Who is a wise man and endued with knowledge among you? let him show out of a good conversation his works with meekness of wisdom.

14 But if ye have bitter envying and strife in your hearts, glory not, and lie not against the truth.

15 This wisdom descendeth not from above, but is earthly, sensual, devilish.

16 For where envying and strife is, there is confusion and every evil work.

17 But the wisdom that is from above is first pure, then peaceable, gentle, and easy to be entreated, full of mercy and good fruits, without partiality, and without hypocrisy.

18 And the fruit of righteousness is sown in peace of them that make peace.

GOLDEN TEXT: Out of the same mouth proceedeth blessing and cursing. My brethren, these things ought not so to be.—James 3:10.

*Images of Christ*
Unit 3: Images of Christ in Us
(Lessons 10-14)

## Lesson Aims

After participating in this lesson, each student will be able to:

1. Restate some of James's illustrations of an untamed tongue.

2. Distinguish between wholesome and unwholesome use of the tongue.

3. Make a plan to improve his or her use of the tongue in one specific way.

## Lesson Outline

INTRODUCTION
  A. A World Full of Words
  B. Lesson Background
I. POWER OF THE TONGUE (James 3:1-5a)
  A. Warning About Judgment (vv. 1, 2)
    *Offending in Word*
  B. Small but Mighty (vv. 3-5a)
II. DANGER OF THE TONGUE (James 3:5b-12)
  A. Capable of Destruction (vv. 5b, 6)
  B. Impossible to Control (vv. 7, 8)
    *Untamed*
  C. Inclined to Evil (vv. 9-12)
III. THOUGHTS ON WISDOM (James 3:13-18)
  A. Wisdom Shown by Life (v. 13)
  B. Wisdom from Below (vv. 14-16)
  C. Wisdom from Above (vv. 17, 18)
CONCLUSION
  A. Be Careful What You Say
  B. Prayer
  C. Thought to Remember

## Introduction

### A. A World Full of Words

Talk fills our lives. Family, friends, coworkers, neighbors, salespeople, teachers, politicians, and preachers knit together the fabric of life with talk. Talk has tremendous impact that often goes unnoticed. We believed in the power of words when were little—that *abracadabra* could bring a rabbit out of a hat and that saying "There's no place like home" could transport a person from Oz to Kansas. But as we grew older and cast aside a "magical" view of words, we seemed to forget that words still have a lot of power.

Most of us utter harmful, dangerous words every day. Our desire to be right, to get ahead, to gain control, to be heard, or to defend ourselves can motivate us to say all kinds of things at the expense of others. Fortunately, with sincere words we can also apologize. However, catching ourselves before we sin with our speech is tough. Still, we can do better, as this lesson will teach.

### B. Lesson Background

The epistle of James sits on the shoulders of a large body of literature that both collects and develops wise sayings to help people succeed. Bible readers will be most familiar with this type of literature, called *wisdom literature*, from reading Proverbs or Ecclesiastes. This style of literature was very popular in the ancient world.

Personal speech habits are one of the most predominant themes of these collections of wisdom. Proverbs 18:21 says, "Death and life are in the power of the tongue: and they that love it shall eat the fruit thereof." Jesus said, "But I say unto you, That every idle word that men shall speak, they shall give account thereof in the day of judgment. For by thy words thou shalt be justified, and by thy words thou shalt be condemned" (Matthew 12:36, 37). Such is the importance of this issue!

After offering a brief warning to be "slow to speak" in James 1:19 and then reinforcing this with the advice in 1:26, James unleashes in chapter 3 his entire arsenal of reasons why the tongue must be controlled. Though it begins as a mandate to teachers in the church, it applies to everyone.

## I. Power of the Tongue (James 3:1-5a)

### A. Warning About Judgment (vv. 1, 2)

**1. My brethren, be not many masters, knowing that we shall receive the greater condemnation.**

The word *masters* refers to teachers. Teachers are highly respected in the ancient world. Given the large number of people entering into the first-century church as new disciples, the importance of having good teachers to guide them in faith, understanding, and behavior is crucial.

Teachers in the first-century church share leadership at the local level with the prophets and apostles (see 1 Corinthians 12:28; Ephesians 4:11). Then as now, however, people sometimes desire to be teachers for the prestige of it without fully recognizing the enormous responsibility involved. James discourages unqualified people from seeking to be teachers with the warning that teachers are under a special scrutiny by Christ. James includes himself as a teacher, indicated by *we,* and accepts this greater risk of judgment he places over all teachers in the church.

The responsibility of nurturing Christian disciples is immense. The fact that this often was not done that well in the first-century church is seen in the New Testament epistles, which address troubling concerns about the influence of false teachers in the churches. This is still a problem today as evidenced by the "Christian" cults that continue to pop up.

**2. For in many things we offend all. If any man offend not in word, the same is a perfect man, and able also to bridle the whole body.**

The primary tool of teachers is the tongue. They talk in order to instruct people. This puts them at risk, because the tongue, or speech, cannot be controlled 100 percent of the time. Only a *perfect* person could stop the sinful tongue every time it is about to do damage. Since no one is perfect, we cannot keep our speech absolutely pure at all times. [See question #1, page 434.]

Good teachers impart the truth from God and are entrusted to nurture their students to growth and maturity with that truth. This is so at all levels of Christian maturity, from nursery age to seniors in the church. Good teachers work hard to prepare and understand what they are teaching and to be sure it is based on Scripture. Bad teachers are sloppy in their preparation and don't work to develop their understanding of Christianity. Their students will not be provided the foundation they need and may become stagnant or may even rebel from their faith. It's no wonder the warning in these first two verses is so threatening!

### OFFENDING IN WORD

A friend of mine was ministering with a church some years ago. His wife, whom he had recently married, was not always discreet in the use of her tongue. Soon after her husband was called to be the minister of that church, the chairman of the elders was showing them the parsonage where they would live. As they walked into the kitchen, she noted the new cabinets and remarked, "Wow, what ugly cabinets. Who chose these?" The cabinets had been chosen by the wife of the chairman of the elders—the very man who was showing them around the parsonage.

On another occasion her husband was at a meeting with the elders, and she became irritated that she had to change yet another one of her infant daughter's diapers. So she marched across the road to the church, walked into the elders' meeting, thrust the baby into her husband's arms, and said, "Here, you take her; it's your turn to change her diaper." Her lack of control over her tongue (which was based in an improper sense of propriety) was a constant impediment to her husband's ministry. It was not long before the elders asked for his resignation.

Indeed, as James states, it is difficult to control the tongue. Someone who has the self-discipline to control his or her tongue can control just about anything. On the other hand, failure to control the tongue can lead to a downfall, in spite of numerous other good qualities.                    —J. B. N.

### B. Small but Mighty (vv. 3-5a)

**3. Behold, we put bits in the horses' mouths, that they may obey us; and we turn about their whole body.**

James now moves on to some poignant examples of the power of the tongue. Once a small bit with bridle is placed properly, a rider can harness a horse's enormous power for the task at hand. This is no less true today.

**4. Behold also the ships, which though they be so great, and are driven of fierce winds, yet are they turned about with a very small helm, whithersoever the governor listeth.**

The second example makes an analogy between the tongue and the rudder *(helm)* of a ship. This analogy is more elaborate than the one involving the horse in verse 3, since James adds the *winds* and the *governor* (ship's pilot). In first-century seafaring, the only source of power for ships (other than muscle power on the oars) is the wind. The rudder is controlled by the pilot on deck. The pilot makes decisions not only about what general direction to go but also how best to negotiate dangerous waters. This is a positive picture only if the pilot knows how to control the ship to its optimum. [See question #2, page 434.]

This picture of the ship is particularly appropriate to accent both the mighty power of the human tongue over the body and the danger of the tongue with a poor pilot. This is the way

---

### How to Say It

CORINTH. *Kor*-inth.

CORINTHIANS. Ko-*rin*-thee-unz (*th* as in *thin*).

ECCLESIASTES. Ik-*leez*-ee-*as*-teez (strong accent on *as*).

EPHESIANS. Ee-*fee*-zhunz.

EPISTLES. ee-*pis*-uls.

GALATIANS. Guh-*lay*-shunz.

MARAH. *Mah*-ruh.

MENAGERIE. meh-*naj*-ree.

verse 5 (next) is able to slip into a negative perspective on the human tongue, which is not so readily possible with the illustration involving the horse and bit.

**5a. Even so the tongue is a little member, and boasteth great things.**

The tongue is portrayed as boasting, one of the many ways people sin when their speech is not under control. Boasting seeks attention to make up for deficiencies. It is a form of lying and deception as it exaggerates the truth or at least the significance of something.

Having set the stage by bringing up the speech sin of boasting, the verses to follow focus on the dangerous threat the tongue poses. For its relatively small size, the tongue is mighty. It can build people up or tear them down. It can launch nations into war or sit them down to peace.

## II. Danger of the Tongue (James 3:5b-12)

### A. Capable of Destruction (vv. 5b, 6)

**5b, 6. Behold, how great a matter a little fire kindleth! And the tongue is a fire, a world of iniquity: so is the tongue among our members, that it defileth the whole body, and setteth on fire the course of nature; and it is set on fire of hell.**

*Fire* is one of the most frightening forces people experience. People in the ancient world are exposed to the ravages of fire more routinely than people who live in modern democracies. Cooking and heating homes with open flame makes house fires more common in the first century.

These verses thus convey the image of the massive destruction that fire is capable of inflicting. Unlike the horse and the ship, whose images are mostly positive, the image turns decidedly negative here. Forest fires always begin at some specific point and then spread wildly. Even today, they are notoriously difficult to stop. And so the human *tongue* through gossip, slander, etc., can sweep through a community just as quickly, just as uncontrollably, and with just as much emotional devastation.

Verse 6 sketches four dimensions of just how corrupt the human tongue is. The first dimension is that the tongue is *a world of iniquity* within a person. This description looks at the tongue as the most evil part of the body—more evil than the hand that steals, for instance. The tongue is the point from which more evil comes forth than anywhere else. It is the "command center" for those despicable sins that are so harmful.

The second dimension of the tongue's destructiveness is its corruption of the rest of the parts

*(members)* of the human body. The tongue that offers someone smooth flattery may be "setting up" the hand to commit theft.

The third dimension of the tongue's destructiveness is the damage it inflicts on society. This is expressed by the use of the phrase *course of nature,* or literally, "wheel of birth." This is a well-known phrase among ancient philosophers for the concept of fate: those external social and cultural forces that affect our lives and over which we have no control. When the sins of speech enter this sphere, then those sins can have devastating results on the lives of people we don't even know.

The fourth dimension of the tongue's destructiveness is its source. This is called *hell,* but that is a roundabout way of referring to Satan. The human tongue is Satan's point of access into our lives—a frightening thought that should make us want to keep that door shut as much as possible.

### B. Impossible to Control (vv. 7, 8)

**7, 8. For every kind of beasts, and of birds, and of serpents, and of things in the sea, is tamed, and hath been tamed of mankind: but the tongue can no man tame; it is an unruly evil, full of deadly poison.**

No longer speaking of the human *tongue* in analogies, these verses label it specifically as hopelessly *evil.* A sad irony in God's creation is detected: people can tame animals, but they can't control their own tongues.

The term *tame* should be taken very broadly, not just in terms of domesticating pets but also in terms of dominating all other living creations (Genesis 1:26, 28; 2:20). The verses before us depict the human tongue itself as a dangerous creature, perhaps the most dangerous. This is the one creature that humans do not seem to rule over. [See question #3, page 434.]

The tongue's description as poisonous makes us think of a snake, an identification made in the Old Testament (see Job 20:12-16; Psalm 58:3, 4; 140:3). However, from the perspective of Genesis 3:1-6 this description connects to the serpent in the Garden of Eden, who deceived Adam and Eve with his conniving words. The result was their being thrust out of the garden.

#### UNTAMED

Wilbert Behn is a self-taught animal tamer. He lives in Aniwa, Wisconsin, where he hosts Behn's Game Farm. Now into his 80s, he still has a menagerie of lions, tigers, and dogs. He opens his shows with an outdoor presentation of performing dogs, leaping and barking, before he moves into his inside arena for the lions and tigers. Visitors are protected by a hurricane fence, but Behn works alone inside the fence.

The animals are trained to respond to music. Behn cracks his whip and lions jump up on barrels. A tiger walks a high-wire. Another large cat jumps through a flaming hoop, snarling menacingly. A tiger falls "dead" at the shot of a pistol loaded with blanks. Behn puts his head in the mouth of a lion. All provide a good show.

Ferocious animals can be tamed, but James says no one can tame the tongue. It's exciting to watch wild animals do tricks under the hands of a daring tamer. How much more useful it would be to see a person in total control of his or her speech! —J. B. N.

### C. Inclined to Evil (vv. 9-12)

**9, 10. Therewith bless we God, even the Father; and therewith curse we men, which are made after the similitude of God. Out of the same mouth proceedeth blessing and cursing. My brethren, these things ought not so to be.**

The next four verses observe some disheartening truths when it comes to the tongue. Though the human tongue can reach its zenith in belting out heartfelt praise for its creator, it reveals the depths of its degradation in its *cursing* the very best of God's creation: men and women created in His image (Genesis 1:27). The fact that verse 10 says this *ought not so to be* holds out a bit of hope that the tongue's evil nature can be controlled with God's help.

**11, 12. Doth a fountain send forth at the same place sweet water and bitter? Can the fig tree, my brethren, bear olive berries? either a vine, figs? so can no fountain both yield salt water and fresh.**

The rhetorical questions acknowledge that we expect certain, predictable things from natural springs and plants. Water that is gloriously drinkable is described with the word *sweet.* (The Greek word behind this gives us our English word *glucose.*) The undrinkable water is *bitter* in the sense of briny or salty. Even today, we know that a natural spring does not produce both kinds of water at once. And we would be quite puzzled to talk to someone who expected to harvest *figs* from his grapevine!

What "harvest" do we expect from our tongues? A dual harvest of both blessing God and cursing others is as improper as expecting both bitter and fresh water to come from the same source. Yet through the power of God's Word the bitter water can become sweet, as when Israel was at Marah (Exodus 15:22-25). [See question #4, page 434.]

Visual for Lesson 12

*Point to this visual as you introduce question #5 on page 434.*

## III. Thoughts on Wisdom (James 3:13-18)

### A. Wisdom Shown by Life (v. 13)

**13. Who is a wise man and endued with knowledge among you? let him show out of a good conversation his works with meekness of wisdom.**

After thinking so much about the tongue with its follies and failures, it is fitting to turn our thoughts to wisdom. Wisdom is what every tongue needs to restrain and guide it.

If asked, each one of us would like to state with confidence, "I am a person who is *endued with knowledge.*" But James wants an answer in the form of our *works* (deeds). A person who does foolish things is not wise.

In the antique English of the *King James Version,* the word *conversation* does not mean "talk." It means, rather, one's entire manner of living (Galatians 1:13; Ephesians 4:22). If a person is wise, his or her lifestyle is *good,* unselfish, helpful. That good lifestyle is the stage on which each individual work is done. Further, it is done with wise *meekness* or humility (compare Matthew 5:5). Now, how wise are you?

### B. Wisdom from Below (vv. 14-16)

**14. But if ye have bitter envying and strife in your hearts, glory not, and lie not against the truth.**

Imagine a popular leader in a certain church. Perhaps he is a handsome man with a ready smile and charming manners. With his pleasant ways and flattering words he wins followers easily, but this fellow is winning them for himself rather than for Christ. His heart is full of *bitter envying* of other leaders. Instead of cooperating with them, he belittles them, their opinions, and their plans. In so doing, he generates *strife* (factionalism) instead of unified fellowship.

James warns such a one to *glory not*—don't brag, don't be proud of yourself and your accomplishments. Speak well of others rather than praising yourself. (This is part of the meekness of v. 13.) Don't exaggerate your own goodness, your own wisdom, your own accomplishments, because when you do, you *lie . . . against the truth.*

**15. This wisdom descendeth not from above, but is earthly, sensual, devilish.**

The *wisdom* that glorifies self is not God-given. It arises out of *earthly* ambition, selfishness, and the prompting of the devil (compare 1 Corinthians 1:20; 2:5, 6). One who asks God for wisdom (Proverbs 2:6; James 1:5) is rewarded with the kind described in verse 17 (below).

**16. For where envying and strife is, there is confusion and every evil work.**

If *envying* and *strife* are prompted by *evil* (v. 15), we can be sure they are not good for us. This kind of disorder infected the church at Corinth (2 Corinthians 12:20). But confusion and *every evil work* please no one but Satan and some victims of his deceit.

### C. Wisdom from Above (vv. 17, 18)

**17. But the wisdom that is from above is first pure, then peaceable, gentle, and easy to be entreated, full of mercy and good fruits, without partiality, and without hypocrisy.**

Paul lists the "fruit of the Spirit" in Galatians 5:22, 23. Here, James lists what may be called the "fruit of *wisdom.*" Wisdom that is pure has no trace of the phoniness that is earthly, sensual,

and devilish. *Peaceable* wisdom will not produce strife, as selfishness and pride often do. A person of *gentle* (considerate) wisdom does not try to overpower others and force opinions on them.

A wise person stands firm for truth and righteousness. In matters of opinion, however, this kind of person is easy *to be entreated.* This means such a person listens to reason and compromises when appropriate. A wise person shows *mercy* by being kind, helpful, and quick to forgive. Wisdom is evident in a person's *good fruits* or deeds to others, especially to fellow Christians (Galatians 6:10). *Partiality* and *hypocrisy* are baser things that have no place in wisdom that is pure.

**18. And the fruit of righteousness is sown in peace of them that make peace.**

Envying and strife provide the soil where confusion grows along with "every evil work" (v. 16). But wise people who make peace find in that peace the soil where they can plant the seeds that grow into the fruit of righteousness, their own and that of others. (See also 2 Corinthians 9:10; Philippians 1:11.)

## Conclusion

### A. Be Careful What You Say

One day I learned an important lesson about being more careful about what I say. While my 10-year-old son was preparing his gear for a Little League baseball game that I couldn't attend, I wanted to send him off with some encouraging words. Jokingly, I said, "Don't hit any home runs tonight, OK?"

Little did I know the positive—and negative—effect this would have on him. After the game, I was both delighted and dismayed when I was told that he hit a ball so far he could have walked to home base, but instead he held up at third and would not budge no matter what the third-base coach said. The coach told me, "He didn't want to break his promise to you."

The power of words goes far beyond what we can imagine at the time we say them. We must be careful and as wise as we can be. We can all do better if we try, and we will make the world a better place for Christ. [See question #5, page 434.]

### B. Prayer

O Lord, who gives us life and breath and the power of speech, help us harness this power to benefit others. In Jesus' name, amen.

### C. Thought to Remember

"For he that will love life, . . . let him refrain his tongue from evil" (1 Peter 3:10).

---

## Home Daily Bible Readings

**Monday, Aug. 11**—The Tongue of the Wise (Proverbs 15:1-4)

**Tuesday, Aug. 12**—With Greater Strictness (James 3:1-4)

**Wednesday, Aug. 13**—Taming the Tongue (James 3:5-9)

**Thursday, Aug. 14**—Purity of One's Words (James 3:10-12)

**Friday, Aug. 15**—Born of Wisdom (James 3:13-16)

**Saturday, Aug. 16**—Sown in Peace (James 3:17, 18)

**Sunday, Aug. 17**—Wise and Pleasant Speech (Proverbs 16:21-24)

# Learning by Doing

*This page contains an alternative lesson plan emphasizing learning activities. Some of these activities are also found in the helpful student book,* Adult Bible Class.

## Into the Lesson

As an attention-getter, bring in lots of pictures of people talking; display them around the room. You can find on the Internet a wide variety of people talking in various situations: on cell phones with friends, in angry confrontations on the street, of parents correcting their children, etc. *Alternative:* make a recording of a few choice minutes of the TV show *The View* and bring it to class for your learners to watch. This show is notable for the four cohosts all talking at the same time and nobody doing much listening.

Ask learners how talk affects their daily lives, both good and bad. Prompt class discussion by mentioning talk radio, 24-hour news programs, sermons, arguments, encouragement from friends and family, sound bites, etc. After a few minutes, ask learners to react to this phrase: *too many words!*

## Into the Word

Ask the class to identify figures of speech and comparisons in James 3. Have one person write them on the board. Ask class members to explain very briefly what each illustrates; tell them that you will go back for fuller analysis later.

Taking the above list in order, discuss each illustration more thoroughly, beginning with the warning regarding teachers. Note that this may not have been listed by the class as a figure of speech. However, it is the first topic listed by James in verse 1 as a use of the tongue.

Divide your class into discussion pairs or five small groups. Give each pair or group a copy of the following list of five passages: Luke 12:48; 1 Corinthians 12:28, 29; 2 Timothy 4:3; Titus 2:3; Hebrews 5:12. Ask groups to discern what is taught about teachers in each passage, and then compare the conclusions with James 3:1.

Each group should formulate a one- or two-sentence summary of the results of the comparison. After groups have finished, have a spokesperson from each group read its summary. (To make this part of the lesson go faster, assign each group or discussion pair only one of the five passages.)

Each of your five discussion pairs or small groups will then analyze one of these five segments from James 3: verses 2-6; verses 7, 8; verses 9-12; verses 13-16; and verses 17, 18. Provide the following written instructions:

*Group #1, James 3:2-6.* Let those in your group who have experience with either horses or ships explain how a small part guides the whole. What parallels are there in modern technology? How do those parallels apply to the tongue? Give personal experiences regarding the destructiveness of fire; how is the tongue like this?

*Group #2, James 3:7, 8.* Who in your group has ever had an exotic or unusual pet? How was that pet tamed? Discuss James's assertion that the tongue cannot be tamed.

*Group #3, James 3:9-12.* Look at the "impossibilities" of verses 11 and 12; paraphrase this using imagery from modern technology. Relate your paraphrase back to verses 9 and 10.

*Group #4, James 3:13-16.* Discuss how the secular world decides who is "wise" and who is not. Compare and contrast that viewpoint with God's view of wisdom.

*Group #5, James 3:17, 18.* Look at the descriptions of wisdom's characteristics in verse 17; then think of some ways to describe secular, earthly wisdom. Compare and contrast your two lists; relate your conclusions to verse 18.

Give each group about 10 minutes to work before you call for conclusions. There is a lot of ground to cover with 18 verses, so keep things moving briskly.

## Into Life

Distribute blank sheets of paper. Have each learner make a list down the left side of places where his or her words will have influence in the coming week. After a few minutes, allow some time for silent prayer about the use of the tongue in those situations.

Finally, ask learners to take their lists home with them. They are to use the lists to make notes during the week of whether the words spoken were beneficial or harmful in various interactions. Encourage learners to have a time of prayer at the end of every day during the week ahead. The prayer will be specifically about words spoken that day and words to be spoken the next day. Also encourage those learners who have chosen to do so to continue paraphrasing James chapter by chapter.

# Let's Talk It Over

*The questions on this page are designed to promote discussion of the lesson by the class and to encourage application of the lesson Scriptures. The answers provided are only discussion starters. Let your class talk it over from there.*

**1. Of the words you heard yesterday, what percentage was helpful? What percentage was neutral? What percentage was negative or hurtful? How do you keep negative or hurtful words from influencing your own speech patterns?**

Proverbs 10:19 affirms, "In the multitude of words there wanteth not sin: but he that refraineth his lips is wise." But before we congratulate those with a naturally quiet nature or who take vows of silence, look at the next verse: "The tongue of the just is as choice silver: the heart of the wicked is little worth" (Proverbs 10:20). While it's better not to speak a bad thought out loud, silence isn't the equivalent of innocence. We must continually examine our hearts, from where thoughts and words originate (Matthew 15:19; Mark 7:21).

**2. What was a time when someone else's words sparked a major decision for you? What was a time when you were surprised with the impact your words had on someone else?**

Words are mighty! We respond to someone's words when we make our decision to live for Christ (Romans 10:14). Unfortunately, many high-impact words are not positive (Proverbs 27:14).

We often judge pleasant, nonconfrontational conversation as "good" and words that evoke sadness or anger as speech to be avoided. That is not always the case. Consider Proverbs 25:11, 12: "A word fitly spoken is like apples of gold in pictures of silver. As an earring of gold, and an ornament of fine gold, so is a wise reprover upon an obedient ear." Paul had to confront Peter's error at one point (Galatians 2:11). Paul's words may not have been pleasant to hear, but they definitely were "fitly spoken."

**3. Since no one can tame the tongue, what hope do we have?**

Galatians 5:22, 23 says that a fruit of the Spirit is temperance (meaning self-control). As we let God's Holy Spirit control and transform our lives, our speech will be seasoned by the other fruit in that passage.

Before the speech can change, the heart must change (Matthew 15:17-19). Don't let the difficulty of the task discourage you from striving to keep your speech in check. Remember, we have heavenly help: "with God all things are possible" (Mark 10:27). Share a Scripture, an anecdote, or an experience that has given you hope that you can improve your speech problem.

**4. What helps you maintain gracious speech under stressful circumstances?**

Sadly, it is all too common for Christians to find themselves leaving Sunday service with a song on their lips only for it to change to words of displeasure toward a fellow driver, a restaurant server, or a family member. Our witness for Christ, our effectiveness for the kingdom, and our peaceful coexistence with the Holy Spirit and with each other are seriously damaged when we forget to season our speech with graciousness (Ephesians 4:29-32; Colossians 4:6). When we think of how we view inconsistencies in other people, we can see the importance of living and speaking consistently ourselves.

**5. What can we do to build in a "critical pause," a "discernment step," into the process of speaking? What will happen when we do so?**

The beauty of communication through writing a letter is that the writer has an opportunity to pause, review the message, and decide whether it is appropriate to send on or not. That's also true of writing e-mail, although that "send" button is just sitting right there waiting to be pressed a little too quickly!

Going back to the first chapter of James's letter, verse 19 gives us sterling advice: "Wherefore, my beloved brethren, let every man be swift to hear, slow to speak, slow to wrath." There are times we could accomplish much more by praying and withholding opinions altogether. But a moment of silence to evaluate the heart's motive and the potential benefit or damage of the message before it gets expressed is always a moment well spent.

Many of us have an intuitive understanding of what others want to hear. And sometimes what folks *want* to hear isn't necessarily what they *need* to hear. Therefore, before we speak it is important to take a moment to reflect on our possible response by asking, "Is this true?" "Is it helpful and kind?" and "Does it need to be said?"

# Godly Servants

Devotional Reading: **Proverbs 3:13-18.**

Background Scripture: **James 4.**

Printed Text: **James 4:1-12.**

### James 4:1-12

1 From whence come wars and fightings among you? come they not hence, even of your lusts that war in your members?

2 Ye lust, and have not: ye kill, and desire to have, and cannot obtain: ye fight and war, yet ye have not, because ye ask not.

3 Ye ask, and receive not, because ye ask amiss, that ye may consume it upon your lusts.

4 Ye adulterers and adulteresses, know ye not that the friendship of the world is enmity with God? whosoever therefore will be a friend of the world is the enemy of God.

5 Do ye think that the Scripture saith in vain, The spirit that dwelleth in us lusteth to envy?

6 But he giveth more grace. Wherefore he saith, God resisteth the proud, but giveth grace unto the humble.

7 Submit yourselves therefore to God. Resist the devil, and he will flee from you.

8 Draw nigh to God, and he will draw nigh to you. Cleanse your hands, ye sinners; and purify your hearts, ye double-minded.

9 Be afflicted, and mourn, and weep: let your laughter be turned to mourning, and your joy to heaviness.

10 Humble yourselves in the sight of the Lord, and he shall lift you up.

11 Speak not evil one of another, brethren. He that speaketh evil of his brother, and judgeth his brother, speaketh evil of the law, and judgeth the law: but if thou judge the law, thou art not a doer of the law, but a judge.

12 There is one lawgiver, who is able to save and to destroy: who art thou that judgest another?

GOLDEN TEXT: Draw nigh to God, and he will draw nigh to you. Cleanse your hands, ye sinners; and purify your hearts, ye double-minded.—James 4:8.

**Aug
24**

## Images of Christ
### Unit 3: Images of Christ in Us
(Lessons 10-14)

## Lesson Aims

After participating in this lesson, each student will be able to:

1. Summarize James's teaching about fighting, humility, and judging others.

2. Explain how fighting, humility, and judging others are related and what impact they have on the church today.

3. Plan a specific way to say or do something encouraging for someone in his or her church.

## Lesson Outline

INTRODUCTION
    A. You've Got a Friend
    B. Lesson Background
I. CREATING ENEMIES (James 4:1-6)
    A. Within the Church (vv. 1-3)
    B. With God (vv. 4-6)
II. CREATING FRIENDS (James 4:7-12)
    A. With God (vv. 7-10)
      *Resist the Devil*
    B. Within the Church (vv. 11, 12)
CONCLUSION
    A. Seeking Forgiveness
    B. Prayer
    C. Thought to Remember

## Introduction

### A. You've Got a Friend

James Taylor's popular song "You've Got a Friend" touches a chord in everyone. We all need friends.

We tend to want lots of friends, to be popular. This kind of casual friendship, however, does not really satisfy our intense longing for deep, lasting friendship—the kind of friendship that is mutual, intimate, unswerving. We will be very blessed to find this kind of friendship in one or two people in the course of our lives.

Today's lesson poses the attractive idea that God wants to be this kind of friend to us. In bonding with God in this way, Christians should be prepared for their lives to be revolutionized with regard to the world and with regard to other believers.

### B. Lesson Background

In James 4:1-12, the epistle's criticism of its audience comes to a climax. James's readers expose the inadequacy of their Christian faith by the mean-spirited way they treat one another in the community of the church. This leads to the demand made in 4:7-10 for repentance and re-commitment to God.

When we look back at what was said earlier in the epistle, we see a carefully laid path to this point. In 3:13-18, the characteristics of true wisdom that come from God are described in contrast to "wisdom" that comes from Satan. This amounts to being a peacemaker who restores community relationships rather than a self-promoter who divides a community. James 4:1-3 accuses the church of being driven by Satan's wisdom, and James 4:4-6 declares that this makes them enemies of God, whom they claim to serve.

In James 4:1-3 the readers are accused of various kinds of harmful speech, probably relating to anger, and in 4:11, 12 they are accused of slander. Concern for such speech sins and lack of control in this area of behavior was developed in 3:1-13 and emphasized in 1:19 and 1:26.

In James 4:4 friendship is held up as the highest expression of relationship with God. Earlier, in 2:23, Abraham was called "the Friend of God." He was God's friend in that he trusted God implicitly. Abraham demonstrated this even to the point of being prepared to sacrifice Isaac, his son of promise. Similarly, James's readers are to demonstrate their trusting relationship with God by living in the way He asks and applying Christ's law of neighbor love to those who hold in common a true faith in Jesus Christ.

## I. Creating Enemies
## (James 4:1-6)

People can hardly claim to be God's servants when they portray attitudes and behaviors that attack other servants of God. To put God's house into such disarray is disgraceful. Those who conduct themselves in this way not only alienate themselves from others, they make any kind of genuine relationship with God impossible.

### A. Within the Church (vv. 1-3)

**1. From whence come wars and fightings among you? come they not hence, even of your lusts that war in your members?**

This verse asks two questions, the second one (with its assumed affirmative response) being the answer to the first. The first question, interestingly, does not ask whether or not the church members are fighting among themselves; James already knows that they are! Rather, James wants to get Christians to probe the reasons *why* they are fighting and to consider the truthfulness of the second question to explain this.

The second question turns the conflict language inward to each individual's private, spiritual war. It challenges Christians to recognize that behavior is determined by whether or not we are able to win the internal *war* with our *lusts.*

The Greek word behind *lusts* comes into English as *hedonism.* This points to a lifestyle that is committed to indulging in worldly pleasures. This passage says that believers have within themselves cravings for these self-indulgent pleasures. If not controlled, this will result in destructive behavior toward the others in the church. [See question #1, page 441.]

**2. Ye lust, and have not: ye kill, and desire to have, and cannot obtain: ye fight and war, yet ye have not, because ye ask not.**

How all this works itself out is startling. *Desire* can lead a person to want something that belongs to someone else. The desire can become so strong that a person will do anything to satisfy it, including *kill.* We can see how this might describe a drug addict or a thief, but how can these verses say such a thing about Christians?

To understand this, it is necessary to look at how closely the Bible equates harmful words with harmful actions. In Matthew 5:21, 22, Jesus teaches that anger that leads to destructive words is equivalent to the anger that leads to murder.

Extremely mean words can be launched against others in the heat of verbal battle: ridicule, insults, cursing, slander. James 3:8 already spoke of the tongue as capable of inflicting death, and this simply follows a trail of horrific images of the tongue in the Old Testament (Job 20:12; Psalm 10:7-10; 64:3; Jeremiah 9:8). Proverbs 12:6 says, "The words of the wicked are to lie in wait for blood." [See question #2, page 441.]

**3. Ye ask, and receive not, because ye ask amiss, that ye may consume it upon your lusts.**

Verses 2 and 3 describe a tension between wanting what does not belong to us (coveting,

as in Exodus 20:17) and simply asking God for what we want. This is a genuine spiritual tension because when we *ask* God for something, we know—regardless of what we ask for—that He wants to give us only what is best for us. He is the giver of good gifts, not bad, as James 1:17 states.

We insult God if we ask Him for something we know to begin with is not good for us or, as in these verses, breaks God's law because it belongs to someone else. The instruction here should be understood to apply to the panorama of situations for which we ask God's help. In each instance, though, we need to remember the holy and good nature of the one to whom we are talking.

### B. With God (vv. 4-6)

**4. Ye adulterers and adulteresses, know ye not that the friendship of the world is enmity with God? whosoever therefore will be a friend of the world is the enemy of God.**

These verses open by addressing the readers in a way that instantly conveys their condemnation in the manner of an Old Testament prophet. Accusations of adultery were reserved for the people of Israel when they had betrayed God by openly cavorting with other gods (Jeremiah 3:20; Ezekiel 23; Hosea 2:2-5).

Ephesians 5:22-33 depicts the church as Christ's bride. We may compare that image with the concern here in James that people who call themselves Christian are conducting themselves in ways that show an intimate relationship with the pleasures of *the world* rather than with the holiness of God.

The public confession of belief in Christ can be understood to be comparable to wedding vows. This confession of Christ is not simply a statement of belief. It is a commitment to a relationship that Christ matches with His own promise of eternal life and the presence of the Holy Spirit. To consort with the world as our soul mate in making decisions about how we are going to conduct our lives is to betray our relationship with Christ. [See question #3, page 441.]

**5. Do ye think that the Scripture saith in vain, The spirit that dwelleth in us lusteth to envy?**

James now offers a *Scripture* quotation whose exact biblical reference is uncertain. This quotation most likely intends to express the intense desire God placed in people that makes us want to have a close relationship with Him. The best Old Testament expressions of this thought are in Psalm 42:1, 2; 84:2.

**6. But he giveth more grace. Wherefore he saith, God resisteth the proud, but giveth grace unto the humble.**

---

### How to Say It

EPHESIANS. Ee-*fee*-zhunz.
EZEKIEL. Ee-*zeek*-ee-ul or Ee-*zeek*-yul.
HEDONISM. *hee*-duh-niz-um.
HOSEA. Ho-*zay*-uh.
JEREMIAH. Jair-uh-*my*-uh.
SEPTUAGINT. Sep-*too*-ih-jent.

The Greek (Septuagint) version of Proverbs 3:34 is quoted as testimony to God's abundant *grace*. It shows that when we come to Him in true humility, even after living in prideful arrogance and self-promotion that insults Him, He will accept us. To have this relationship with God, we must turn our backs on harmful envy and bad attitudes that are part of our lives.

## II. Creating Friends (James 4:7-12)

If people who are God's servants have made enemies among fellow servants in the church, a remedy for their situation exists. This remedy calls first for abject repentance before God. Next comes reformation in how people are treated, with a new emphasis on respect for them as well as respect for God, who created them.

### A. With God (vv. 7-10)

**7. Submit yourselves therefore to God. Resist the devil, and he will flee from you.**

Verses 7-10 contain 10 commands. They demand repentance toward God from the believer who has been behaving like a nonbeliever. Such a backslider has been choosing to be more influenced by worldly attitudes than by the humility God desires. The first command (here) and the tenth command (in v. 10, below) mirror one another in their foundational call for repentance in terms of humble submission to God.

The second command, calling for resisting *the devil,* is the complement to submitting to God. The first step in turning to God has to be turning away from Satan and his unholy influence in our lives. Satan *will flee,* not because of any power we have, but because we are now faced toward

---

## Home Daily Bible Readings

**Monday, Aug. 18**—Understanding and Peace (Proverbs 3:13-18)

**Tuesday, Aug. 19**—Ask Rightly (James 4:1-3)

**Wednesday, Aug. 20**—Yearn for God's Spirit (James 4:4-7)

**Thursday, Aug. 21**—Humble Yourselves (James 4:8-10)

**Friday, Aug. 22**—Do Not Judge (James 4:11-14)

**Saturday, Aug. 23**—Seek God's Wishes (James 4:15-17)

**Sunday, Aug. 24**—Living in the Light of God (Ephesians 5:8-11)

---

God. Satan wants to escape the steady stare of God's goodness and justice.

### RESIST THE DEVIL

A number of years ago, a friend of mine was planting a new church in a western U.S. city. Because the church was unable to pay much of a salary, he also worked as a plumber, a trade he had acquired before he went to Bible college. However, the plumbers' union in that town was controlled by the Mafia. He did not wish to be associated with the Mafia, so he worked as an independent, nonunion plumber.

One day he was visited by men in dark pinstripe suits, who arrived in a new black Cadillac. They asked him to go for a short ride. He agreed, but insisted on driving his own car. The men said it would be healthier for him and his family if he joined the union; otherwise some accident might befall his wife or children.

My friend took this in for a while and then responded in some anger. He said, "I am a minister of the gospel of the Lord Jesus Christ, and I am not afraid of anybody or anything." He started his car and drove back to work. The other men got into their own car and left. He never heard from them again. By taking a firm stand against pressure and trusting in the protection of the Lord, my friend called the Mafia's bluff. They decided he wasn't worth bothering about. My friend had successfully resisted the devil—or at least some of the devil's buddies.     —J. B. N.

**8. Draw nigh to God, and he will draw nigh to you. Cleanse your hands, ye sinners; and purify your hearts, ye double-minded.**

The third command calls for the necessary second step in repentance. Having turned away from Satan toward God, the call to *draw nigh to God* pictures us as taking steps toward Him. God's gracious action of also moving toward us with eyes full of love provides confidence for us to keep going, even to accelerate into His outstretched arms. This picture is worked out marvelously in Jesus' Parable of the Prodigal Son (Luke 15:11-32). [See question #4, page 441.]

The fourth and fifth commands *(cleanse . . . purify)* call for determined action to take real steps to change our lives and attitudes. The call to wash our *hands* pictures our bodies covered with the dirty evidence of our sinful involvement with the world. They must be cleansed in the sense of removing these things from our lives in order for us to be presentable to the loving but holy Father, who is waiting to welcome us into His presence. The call to purify our *hearts* demands that the same thing be done internally. God knows our hearts, so they must be changed in order for us to be near Him.

**9. Be afflicted, and mourn, and weep: let your laughter be turned to mourning, and your joy to heaviness.**

Commands number six *(be afflicted),* seven *(mourn),* eight *(weep),* and nine *(let)* call for various reactions to the sorrow we feel for having betrayed God with our attitudes and actions. If our repentance is genuine and we have truly confronted our sin, this reaction necessarily will be emotional. We should be upset and horrified by what we have done. Speaking of repentance with similar language is both James (later, in James 5:1) and the prophet Joel (in Joel 2:12).

The calling for our reversal of emotions from *laughter/joy* to *mourning/heaviness* parallels what Jesus says in Luke 6:25. It pictures our party life of sinful pleasure and self-indulgence being replaced by our attendance at the funeral of that old life, now dead to us. Will we do this voluntarily, now, before it's too late? Or will it be forced upon us, as in Luke 6:25, after it's too late?

**10. Humble yourselves in the sight of the Lord, and he shall lift you up.**

The tenth command mirrors Proverbs 3:34, quoted in verse 6, above. The tenth command also works with the first command in verse 7 to form bookends for the other 8 commands that develop various components of true repentance. To submit (v. 7) and to *humble* (here) are almost the same thing.

The last half of verse 10 ends this string of harsh commands with a positive, encouraging promise. Now, bowing clean and humble before Him, we will experience God wrapping His arms around us and accepting us fully into His presence to begin our new relationship with Him.

### B. Within the Church (vv. 11, 12)

**11, 12. Speak not evil one of another, brethren. He that speaketh evil of his brother, and judgeth his brother, speaketh evil of the law, and judgeth the law: but if thou judge the law, thou art not a doer of the law, but a judge. There is one lawgiver, who is able to save and to destroy: who art thou that judgest another?**

These verses draw upon two commands in Jesus' teaching: "Judge not, that ye be not judged" (Matthew 7:1) and "Thou shalt love thy neighbor as thyself" (Matthew 19:19; 22:39). The intention is to encourage Christians who have come back to God, after being drawn away to worldly influence, to start over in the way they relate to their fellow Christians. Rather than speaking and

Visual for Lesson 13

*Point to this visual as you introduce question #4 on page 441.*

behaving in unkind and unhelpful ways as before (James 4:1-3), they are now being encouraged to begin a positive approach to relationships.

These verses reason that in order to speak condemningly about someone, we first have judged them in the sense that we have deemed ourselves superior enough to critique various aspects of their lives. Passages such as 1 Corinthians 5 and Titus 1:10-16; 3:10 do authorize a judging function. But those situations are not in view here. Only one being can preside over the law and apply it to sinners, and that is God himself. [See question #5, page 441.]

## Conclusion

### A. Seeking Forgiveness

No one finds it easy to apologize, even when we know we are wrong. It is embarrassing to let down our guard of pride and make ourselves so vulnerable to another person. Yet, if we truly want to be God's servant, we must admit our sinful behavior and attitudes toward others, both to God and the people we have harmed. It is the only way forward into a deeper relationship with God and with others.

### B. Prayer

Lord, convict us today of our worldly attitudes and actions, drive us to our knees before You, and lift us up into Your powerful arms of trust and commitment. We offer our prayer in the name of Your Son, Jesus. Amen.

### C. Thought to Remember

Make sure you know with whom to be friends!

# Learning by Doing

*This page contains an alternative lesson plan emphasizing learning activities. Some of these activities are also found in the helpful student book,* Adult Bible Class.

## Into the Lesson

Say, "People need friends. All of us want approval and appreciation. Even those who seem not to need or want other people in their lives are covering up a real yearning to be accepted. What are some of the ways we try to have others accept us?" Have one class member write responses on the board. The list might include the way we dress, our recreational activities, our memberships in organizations, etc.

At the end of this discussion, ask, "How do these things fit with the well-known idea of *keeping up with the Joneses*?" Continue with these follow-up questions: How much of our time and energy are expended in pleasing others in order to win their approval and friendship? How does this contrast with the amount of time spent developing a friendship with God?

Say, "James lists some very specific attitudes and actions that are ungodly in nature. Let's explore those."

## Into the Word

Divide the class into small groups of three. Ask your groups to complete copies of the following chart that you have prepared ahead of time. Across the top of a sheet of paper, your chart will have these column headers: *Verse, Ungodly Action,* and *Result.* Put several horizontal lines under each heading. Halfway down the page put the following headings: *Verse, Godly Action,* and *Result.* Again draw several lines to be filled in. Instruct each group to use James 4:1-12 to complete the chart.

After groups have had time to fill the blanks, begin a discussion by saying, "What were some of the ungodly actions and results that James mentioned?" When several have been named say, "James also tells how ungodly attitudes can be overcome by godly attitudes. What attitudes will help us be more godly?" Allow discussion. Discuss how this section relates to last week's study on godly wisdom and wisdom from the devil in James 3:13-18.

*Option #1:* If time allows, ask for volunteers to read the following Scriptures: Psalm 33:1-3; 51:1-4; Matthew 5:4; Romans 5:1, 2; Philippians 4:4; 1 Peter 1:3-5. Use these to name other ways that godly attitudes can be developed.

*Option #2:* If some learners are continuing to work on paraphrasing James, ask for volunteers to read their paraphrases of James 4 aloud. Discuss. Ask if this exercise is helping them understand the book of James better. Compliment those who are completing a paraphrase each week and encourage them to finish the project.

If others began writing paraphrases but have faltered, encourage them to resume and complete the assignment. Ask someone who has written each week to express what benefit he or she is gaining from doing it. Remind learners that there is only one more chapter to go.

## Into Life

Line up five people in advance to role-play a conversation in the break room of a large office. Tell four of your actors that they are to criticize a fellow worker who is not present. They do this for a minute or so when a fifth coworker enters the break room unnoticed. The fifth person should listen for 30 seconds, then interrupt the conversation by saying a few nice things about the absent person.

Stop the role playing and ask your learners how they would feel if this scenario involved them in real life; have them put themselves in each of the roles: the critics, the intermediary, and the absent coworker.

Discuss godly and ungodly ways to handle this kind of situation. Ask volunteers to tell about a time when a similar situation happened to them, without using real names. Were they critics, intermediaries, or victims? What emotions were involved? How did the situation turn out? What should they have done differently?

Allow a brief time for silent reflection and prayer. Ask learners to think of times that friendship with the world took priority over friendship with God. Challenge them to think back over today's lesson and make personal application. After an appropriate amount of time, end with a time of silent prayer for confession and restoration with God.

*Optional:* As homework, ask your learners to write a poem or song that is based on James 4:7-10. At the beginning of next week's lesson, ask for volunteers to read or sing the results of their work.

# Let's Talk It Over

*The questions on this page are designed to promote discussion of the lesson by the class and to encourage application of the lesson Scriptures. The answers provided are only discussion starters. Let your class talk it over from there.*

**1. What negative motives do you see in non-believers that have the potential to cause problems between you and your brothers and sisters in Christ? What action will you take to prevent this from happening?**

A key preventative action is to look at our divided loyalties, which is what James calls us to do. While we may want to please God, we also want to please ourselves. This combination can be disastrous within our church families. Our desire to serve may lead us to volunteer, while our pride and desire to be respected can lead us to lord it over those with whom we serve. Or we may be easily hurt or quit when our ideas aren't embraced. The wrong motivation may include feelings of superiority, competitiveness, pride, jealousy, and/or bitterness (James 3:14, 15).

**2. What steps will you take to make sure you are not inflicting pain on other believers? When you cross the line with unkind words, what will you do to initiate the healing process?**

"Lust . . . kill . . . fight." James uses graphic language to expose the harm that believers inflict on one another. As we noted in Lesson 10, hurting people hurt people. We must be doubly careful of what we say when we are hurt or offended. If we find ourselves unable to wish others well when they celebrate victories or to be sad with them in their trials or to live peacefully in day-to-day interactions, then that may be a warning sign that all is not well with us (Romans 12:15, 16).

We must attempt to reconcile with one another as soon as we are aware we have hurt someone. We are not responsible for their response, but God knows our hearts and our efforts (Matthew 5:23, 24).

**3. What are some ways that we cheat on God today? Which of our attitudes or actions indicate that we believe we can be both Christian and one who can sample all the world has to offer? How do we overcome this problem?**

There is fine line between thankfully enjoying a well-prepared meal and gluttony; between appreciating the attractiveness of another person and lusting; between pursuing righteousness wholeheartedly and being prideful at being more righteous than others. Christian service can be either devoted to God or used as a means to gain a reputation for self.

To keep the adversary from gaining a foothold in our lives, we can daily open ourselves up to the Holy Spirit, asking Him to show us those areas where we are moving toward enemy territory (1 Corinthians 4:4). James declares that a double-minded approach to life is unstable (James 1:8).

**4. James is full of action words. What specific steps are you being called to at this time in order to resist the devil and draw closer to God?**

Your learners' comfort level with one another will dramatically affect their willingness to share what God is doing in each of their lives. A teacher who is willing to be transparent and share shortcomings of which the Holy Spirit is convicting him or her will model an openness that may prove to be healing and community-building for the group. This will also set the groundwork for one of next week's key points in James 5:16.

Should your group be open enough to reveal convicted hearts, remember to emphasize the amazing promises God offers. Nothing touches God's heart like true repentance—"and he shall lift you up" (4:10)!

**5. What was a time when a communication of facts turned into slander? How do you keep this from happening?**

Caution your learners not to use real names in their stories. Slander is "false and defamatory oral statements about a person." Sometimes we can slip into slander by sharing things assumed, but not confirmed. We may not intend to do harm, but carelessness can still wreak havoc.

A conversation that starts out, "I love brother Joe, but . . ." may turn out to be anything but loving. Sometimes our tone of voice, facial expressions, or choice of words can color a communication. Our true feelings seem to find a way to seep out of us. Therefore, we should use extreme caution when the conversation turns toward a person with whom we have struggles. Praying for that person will help us adjust our attitude.

August 31
Lesson 14

# Prayerful Community

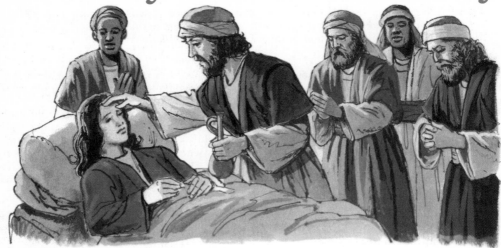

DEVOTIONAL READING: 1 Thessalonians
5:16-22.

BACKGROUND SCRIPTURE: James 5.

PRINTED TEXT: James 5:7-18.

### James 5:7-18

7 Be patient therefore, brethren, unto the coming of the Lord. Behold, the husbandman waiteth for the precious fruit of the earth, and hath long patience for it, until he receive the early and latter rain.

8 Be ye also patient; stablish your hearts: for the coming of the Lord draweth nigh.

9 Grudge not one against another, brethren, lest ye be condemned: behold, the judge standeth before the door.

10 Take, my brethren, the prophets, who have spoken in the name of the Lord, for an example of suffering affliction, and of patience.

11 Behold, we count them happy which endure. Ye have heard of the patience of Job, and have seen the end of the Lord; that the Lord is very pitiful, and of tender mercy.

12 But above all things, my brethren, swear not, neither by heaven, neither by the earth, neither by any other oath: but let your yea be yea; and your nay, nay; lest ye fall into condemnation.

13 Is any among you afflicted? let him pray. Is any merry? let him sing psalms.

14 Is any sick among you? let him call for the elders of the church; and let them pray over him, anointing him with oil in the name of the Lord:

15 And the prayer of faith shall save the sick, and the Lord shall raise him up; and if he have committed sins, they shall be forgiven him.

16 Confess your faults one to another, and pray one for another, that ye may be healed. The effectual fervent prayer of a righteous man availeth much.

17 Elijah was a man subject to like passions as we are, and he prayed earnestly that it might not rain: and it rained not on the earth by the space of three years and six months.

18 And he prayed again, and the heaven gave rain, and the earth brought forth her fruit.

GOLDEN TEXT: Is any among you afflicted? let him pray. Is any merry? let him sing psalms.—James 5:13.

*Images of Christ*
Unit 3: Images of Christ in Us
(Lessons 10-14)

## Lesson Aims

After participating in this lesson, each student will be able to:

1. Summarize James's thoughts on patience and prayer.

2. Suggest a positive outcome if everyone in his or her church made a greater effort to follow James's teaching on patience and prayer.

3. Identify one area of patience or prayer that he or she needs to improve and make a plan for that change.

## Lesson Outline

INTRODUCTION
    A. The Individual and Community
    B. Lesson Background
 I. PATIENCE IN SUFFERING (James 5:7-12)
    A. Until the Lord's Return (vv. 7-9)
    B. Examples of Patience (vv. 10, 11)
    C. Making of Oaths (v. 12)
II. PRAYER OF FAITH (James 5:13-18)
    A. Variety of Circumstances (vv. 13-16)
       *Effective Prayer*
    B. Example of Prayer (vv. 17, 18)
CONCLUSION
    A. Life Together
    B. Prayer
    C. Thought to Remember

## Introduction

### A. The Individual and Community

Americans tend to admire the rugged individualist who doesn't seem to need anyone else in order to prosper. But although lone trailblazers were important in opening up America's Old West, it was the arrival of families who settled into communities that determined the West's future.

Perceptions of Christianity often mirror the individualist model. Christians view themselves to be alone on their spiritual quest to find a deeper relationship with God. However, Christ not only brings us individually into a saving relationship to God, He also brings us into a community. This community is intended to help strengthen our faith. It is also where we exercise our faith in relationship to the needs of others. This lesson encourages us to honor God within the community of the church.

### B. Lesson Background

The epistle of James does not conclude with greetings or a benediction as most New Testament epistles. Rather, it returns to the main themes of its opening—prayer and patience (1:2-8)—while continuing one of its overarching themes of personal speech ethics. The letter's conclusion moves from topic to topic without pointing out specifically how these are connected. This poses the biggest problem for us in James 5:12, as we shall see.

## I. Patience in Suffering (James 5:7-12)

Life supplies many opportunities for believers to demonstrate their confidence in God's fair judgment. This section focuses on the unfair suffering many believers face. It points out their unhealthy tendency to take their frustrations out on one another. It assumes the mistreatment of the poor by wealthy employers (discussed in James 5:1-6). This is a challenge the church faces.

### A. Until the Lord's Return (vv. 7-9)

**7. Be patient therefore, brethren, unto the coming of the Lord. Behold, the husbandman waiteth for the precious fruit of the earth, and hath long patience for it, until he receive the early and latter rain.**

Christians in the earliest days of the church tend to anticipate Christ's return eagerly. His return would mean freedom from the harsh circumstances of their lives; justice would be served on those who oppressed them. The first-century Christians who read this letter also anticipate Christ's return because many of them were alive in AD 30 when He promised He would come back (Acts 1:11). Believers today seem to find it difficult to live with this daily expectation. Nevertheless, patience based on confidence in Christ's return is a trait beneficial for all Christians to develop. [See question #1, page 448.]

The verse before us presents the farmer *(husbandman)* as a positive example of one having the kind of *patience* desirable for Christians. Farmers base their livelihoods on God's provision of proper soil and climate to produce crops. Farmers can go about their daily business confidently because God has demonstrated His trustworthiness to deliver on His promises built into creation (compare Deuteronomy 11:14;

Aug
31

---

### How to Say It

DEUTERONOMY. Due-ter-*ahn*-uh-me.

ELIJAH. Ee-*lye*-juh.

EPISTLES. ee-*pis*-uls.

JEREMIAH. Jair-uh-*my*-uh.

---

Joel 2:23). Christians too need to go about the business of being faithful disciples of Christ in word and deed regardless of the hardships. We can be completely confident that He will return in due season as He said He would.

**8, 9. Be ye also patient; stablish your hearts: for the coming of the Lord draweth nigh. Grudge not one against another, brethren, lest ye be condemned: behold, the judge standeth before the door.**

Christians are to develop lean *hearts* in contrast to the rich who spend their time fattening theirs (5:5). Although difficult times are not fun, they do have the benefit of toughening us up spiritually, making us even better prepared when Christ returns.

Both verses 8 and 9 emphasize the nearness of Christ's coming. The picture of Him being just on the other side of the *door* that leads to His return is drawn from His own teaching in Matthew 24:33 and Mark 13:29. It communicates that He is ready to return, only awaiting the edict of the Father to do so.

As in the teaching in the Gospels, the implication is that believers need to be ready for Him to open that door at any time. This should affect the way we live, especially the way we treat others in the church. See also Romans 13:11, 12; Hebrews 10:25; 1 Peter 4:7. [See question #2, page 448.]

### B. Examples of Patience (vv. 10, 11)

**10. Take, my brethren, the prophets, who have spoken in the name of the Lord, for an example of suffering affliction, and of patience.**

Verses 10 and 11 supply two examples of *patience* for believers to model. One example is general and the other is specific. For the most part, the Old Testament presents *prophets* as people who suffered in the midst of their service as spokespersons for God. The prophets tended to be lone figures who spoke out in opposition to their rulers and the common practices of most people. Because of this, they were not well liked and often had to go about their work amidst threats and mistreatment. Jeremiah is the most detailed in describing his suffering (Jeremiah 7:27; 18:18-23; 20; 26:8-11; 37:16, 21; 38:6), which should be viewed as representative.

**11. Behold, we count them happy which endure. Ye have heard of the patience of Job, and have seen the end of the Lord; that the Lord is very pitiful, and of tender mercy.**

*Job* was not a prophet, but he certainly stands out as the most obvious model of suffering in the Old Testament. Bearing *affliction* of all kinds for no obvious reason, Job discussed the horror of his situation with his friends. Despite much questioning, he stood by his trust in God's goodness and justice and was rewarded by God.

Such blessings await Christians who live steadfastly with faith in Christ, undeterred by life's opposition to our efforts and convictions. The ability to *endure* assumes the connection of this to wisdom in the opening verses of James (1:3-4). [See question #3, page 448.]

### C. Making of Oaths (v. 12)

**12. But above all things, my brethren, swear not, neither by heaven, neither by the earth, neither by any other oath: but let your yea be yea; and your nay, nay; lest ye fall into condemnation.**

Although this verse is grouped under *patience* in this lesson, it might be independent of James 5:7-11 in thought. Most significant is that verse 12 opens with *but above all*. Why is the subject matter of verse 12 (oath-taking) the most important concern of the current line of reasoning?

We answer by realizing that personal speech ethics is a regular theme in James (1:19; 2:12; 3:1-12; 4:1-3, 11). This theme continues in the concluding verses. Not complaining—another issue of speech ethics—is a key component of patience (5:7-11); speaking brings positive outcomes to the church (5:13-18), especially restoring a wayward member (5:19, 20). The issue of oath-taking in 5:12 is part of our speech ethic.

The concern about the importance of honest speech relates to the warning in 5:8, 9 about Christ's coming in judgment. It also seems to be another teaching in James that stems from clear instructions from Jesus: see Matthew 5:33-37; 23:16-22. The restriction against oaths stems from the popular abuse of oath formulas that is so common in first-century Palestine. The use of verbal oaths to guarantee one's word is crucial in the buying and selling of goods and in many other social situations. However, ancient Jews know full well that an oath sworn in the name of God is absolutely binding (Numbers 30:2).

Thus, in practice the ancient Jew avoids oaths in God's name, but uses less holy objects instead. This practice gives them more opportunity to break their oaths. This means that making an *oath* to guarantee honesty is instead being used as a ruse for dishonesty. Neither Jesus nor James wants Christians to have anything to do with such a tainted practice. [See question #4, page 448.]

The restriction of swearing oaths in this verse should not be taken as a modern rule against making oaths in court, for political office, for military service, etc. Those kinds of oaths are not part of the tainted system of Jesus' day, which is routinely used to cover up or justify deceit. The thrust of this verse is that Christians need to be known to be so honest in their character that an oath to prove this is not necessary.

## II. Prayer of Faith
## (James 5:13-18)

A meaningful prayer life is one of the expected outcomes of a deep friendship with God. It is also a necessary component of facing life's difficulties. These final verses in James observe that the spiritual and physical health of the Christian community is the place for the power of prayer to be demonstrated.

### A. Variety of Circumstances (vv. 13-16)

**13. Is any among you afflicted? let him pray. Is any merry? let him sing psalms.**

Prayer is an appropriate and legitimate response to every kind of situation in believers' lives. To this end, the dramatic questions in verse 13 show that prayer should be not only a personal and private response but also a public activity that finds expression by the gathered church. The *you* in this verse is plural, referring to the church. It is fully appropriate, then, that corporate worship be filled with joyful praise to God as well as earnest pleas for His aid and mercy.

**14, 15. Is any sick among you? let him call for the elders of the church; and let them pray over him, anointing him with oil in the name of the Lord: and the prayer of faith shall save the sick, and the Lord shall raise him up; and if he have committed sins, they shall be forgiven him.**

Also part of the prayer activity of the church is attending to members who are facing critical challenges. The fact that we usually *pray* for *the sick* within our worship services reflects this responsibility. [See question #5, page 448.]

However, the responsibility extends more deeply to the leaders of a local church when the sick person's health is at the point where he or she could die. A visit to such a person, whether in the home or in the hospital, is desirable. In today's churches, hospital visitation by the minister is in large measure how this pastoral responsibility of the church is accomplished.

We should not overlook how the physical and the spiritual are related. Ministers or *elders* who visit the sick must make it a priority to give them opportunity to talk about things in their lives they regret, to confess nagging *sins*. This just may be the "medicine" they need to turn the corner on their ailment. Doctors know full well today that a positive emotional/spiritual state can have a decisive impact on a person's recovery.

The *oil* mentioned in verse 14 comes from a common Jewish practice that carries over to the first-century church. In Luke 10:34, oil functions as medicine. Oil is associated with healing in Mark 6:13. Modern medicine has given us healing preparations that are better than oil. However, some still prefer to anoint a sick person with a very small amount of oil. Invoking *the name of the Lord* isn't intended to be a magical incantation. But requesting the Lord's involvement is absolutely vital to the success of the visit.

**16. Confess your faults one to another, and pray one for another, that ye may be healed. The effectual fervent prayer of a righteous man availeth much.**

Here is another important aspect of the congregational prayer life that extends from the forgiveness of sin expressed in verse 15: confession. The opportunity to *confess* sin should be viewed as a form of preventative spiritual medicine.

Some churches handle this rather formally with worship liturgy: worshipers read general prayers of confession. Other churches have no formal way to accomplish this, although the growth of small groups and accountability partners in many churches probably responds to this need. [See question #6, page 448.]

Visual for
Lesson 14

*Point to this visual as you ask, "In what ways have you experienced the power of prayer?"*

Regardless of the purpose of specific prayers, it is vital that believers witness regularly the interaction of God with the needs and joys of their church. *Effectual fervent prayer* enables us to see the power of God at work in our lives.

### EFFECTIVE PRAYER

Wilfrid (634–709) was a leader in the Anglo-Saxon church in the seventh century. A monk, he also became the abbot of a monastery in Ripon in northern England and later was made bishop of York. However, when the Archbishop of Canterbury divided his area up into four separate dioceses, Wilfrid was aggrieved and decided to take his complaint directly to Rome.

He sailed from England in 678, but his ship was driven onto the coast of Frisia. There he was marooned for the winter among a pagan population. He decided to take advantage of this open door and preached to them while awaiting better weather to continue his visit to Rome. His preaching had little success, however, because the people were satisfied with their heathen gods.

Most of the people on the coast made their living by fishing, but there came a time when the fishing was not very successful. One morning Wilfrid accompanied the men to the boats, prayed over the boats, and sent them out. That day the men caught an abundant supply of fish. They decided perhaps the God of Wilfrid was more powerful than their own gods, and thus they were more willing to listen to his preaching. Many accepted Christianity, and this was the beginning of the evangelization of the Netherlands.

Wilfrid's ministry and his commitment to prayer had a great impact on those people. What fervent prayer will you offer today?    —J. B. N.

---

## Home Daily Bible Readings

**Monday, Aug. 25**—Pray Without Ceasing (1 Thessalonians 5:16-22)

**Tuesday, Aug. 26**—The Plight of the Rich (James 5:1-6)

**Wednesday, Aug. 27**—Patience and Endurance (James 5:7-12)

**Thursday, Aug. 28**—Pray for One Another (James 5:13-15)

**Friday, Aug. 29**—The Prayer of the Righteous (James 5:16-18)

**Saturday, Aug. 30**—Stay with the Truth (James 5:19, 20)

**Sunday, Aug. 31**—Prayer for Community Power (Ephesians 3:14-21)

---

### B. Example of Prayer (vv. 17, 18)

**17. Elijah was a man subject to like passions as we are, and he prayed earnestly that it might not rain: and it rained not on the earth by the space of three years and six months.**

*Elijah* is an example of someone who exhibited the power of prayer. Verse 17 underscores that he was not superhuman. Elijah was "a regular guy" whose strong relationship enabled God to do extraordinary things in his life of service to Him, including a miracle of nature.

The passage does not promise that we can all be miracle workers. It does promise, however, that God can and will show His power in our prayer lives if we dedicate ourselves to His service. This involves cultivating a trusting relationship with Him.

Elijah's prayer success offers us three facts not specifically stated in the account of 1 Kings 17–18. First, Elijah *prayed* not only at the end but also at the beginning of the drought. Second, the drought lasted three and a half years. The third fact is in our next verse.

**18. And he prayed again, and the heaven gave rain, and the earth brought forth her fruit.**

Crops flourished after Elijah *prayed again.* Two other powerful prayers in Elijah's service to God are worthy of note: the multiplication of the widow's flour and oil during the drought (1 Kings 17:7-16) and the calling down of fire upon the water-drenched altar in the contest with the priests of Baal (1 Kings 18:16-46).

# Conclusion

## A. Life Together

The virtues of patience, truth, and prayer find their most meaningful expression within our life together as the church. Believers suffer for their convictions and physical afflictions. We struggle with honesty to others and to God. In this context, being a part of a community dealing with similar problems gives us strength and assurance that God is real and that He loves us. Together in Christ we can praise and honor Him meaningfully.

## B. Prayer

"Now unto him that is able to do exceeding abundantly above all that we ask or think, according to the power that worketh in us, unto him be glory in the church by Christ Jesus throughout all ages, world without end. Amen" (Ephesians 3:20, 21).

## C. Thought to Remember

Embrace your Christian community with love.

# Learning by Doing

*This page contains an alternative lesson plan emphasizing learning activities. Some of these activities are also found in the helpful student book,* Adult Bible Class.

## Into the Lesson

Arrange for your congregation's prayer ministry members to visit the class for this lesson. If your church does not have a designated prayer ministry team, request the elders and other leaders to come. Some of your church leaders will have responsibilities that prevent them from attending your class, but bring in as many as possible.

Begin your class with the following illustration: "During an extended time of drought, the mayor of a midsized city proclaimed a day of fasting and prayer to petition God for rain. This proclamation became the subject of a radio talk show where callers were asked to give their opinion of the appropriateness of this action by the mayor." Have your class discuss this statement made by one of the radio show hosts: "Prayer is private and should not be brought into the public arena."

Ask the class to give examples of biblical calls for public prayer and fasting. Does public prayer bring communities together, or is it usually just an exercise in "ceremonial theism"? Considering the church as a community, what part should public prayer play in the life of our congregation? Ask your learners to justify their answers.

## Into the Word

During the above discussion, many may express their personal opinions. Suggest to the class that it is necessary that they look at the Bible to find God's view of prayer, both public and private.

Read James 5:13-20 aloud. Say, "James details a community that prays for one another. About what things does he say we should pray?" As people call out answers, make a list on the board. Also ask for volunteers to look up the following passages that discuss prayer and find answers to add to the list: Genesis 25:21; 2 Samuel 7:18; 24:25; Psalm 51:1, 2; Luke 22:39-42; John 17:15; Philippians 4:6; and Colossians 4:2-4.

These are just a few from a long list of Scriptures referring to prayer. Ask if anyone knows roughly how many times prayer is mentioned in the Bible. *(Answer: over 300 times.)* Have the class find other Scriptures that might add different emphases to your list on the board.

Then say, "Prior to his instructions on prayer, James talks about patience in 5:7-11. Why did the early church need patience?" Allow for discussion. Have one person sum up the story of the prophet Jeremiah. How was he called on to be patient? Have another tell the story of Job. Ask one or more of the following questions (but don't ask more than one question at a time): What did James say about the end of Job's trials? How did God show His tender mercy to Job? How does patience relate to community?

Ask one or two learners to tell of a time of trial in their lives that required patience. Were they more blessed after the trials than before? Explain.

## Into Life

Divide the class into as many groups as you have church leaders and prayer ministry members present. If you have a large number of these guests, you might put two of them with each group. Otherwise, assign one visitor to each group. Have each individual in the group express one personal prayer request to the guest/leader. When all have expressed a need, the guest should pray for each one. If the class is comfortable doing so, have other members of the group put their hands on the one for whom the prayer is offered.

If your church does not have a prayer ministry team, ask if there are people in your class who would like to begin one. In order that it not seem like an overwhelming prospect, suggest that your volunteers make a six-month commitment. At the end of six months, they can evaluate how best to continue.

If your congregation does have a prayer ministry team, take a few minutes for the class to write a note of encouragement and appreciation to them. If most of the prayer ministry team is present, use the opportunity to thank them verbally for the strength and power they bring to the church.

Finally, ask how many students have completed an entire paraphrase of James. Have someone read his or her paraphrase of James 5. Encourage those who began but have not completed this optional assignment to continue the project after this month's study is over.

# Let's Talk It Over

*The questions on this page are designed to promote discussion of the lesson by the class and to encourage application of the lesson Scriptures. The answers provided are only discussion starters. Let your class talk it over from there.*

**1. What is it that makes you stop and think, "Lord, come quickly"? If you utter that in desperation, how can you change your outlook?**

Physical aches and defects might first come to mind. Work stresses may also be high on the list. Some may share ongoing struggles with sin or grief over societal moral decay. Still others may wish for the Lord's rapid return not so much to escape current hardships, but because they envision and long for that place of unmeasured beauty that's beyond our greatest imaginings (Ephesians 3:20). The attitude with which one utters the phrase *Lord, come quickly* can be very revealing!

**2. What counsel would you offer to someone experiencing bouts of annoyance, frustration, or irritation with fellow believers? How do you help him or her resist complaining?**

While author J. R. R. Tolkien describes a certain group as *The Fellowship of the Ring*, the New Testament describes a community that can best be described as *the fellowship of the cross*. The most important thing we have in common with believers is that we all are saved by God's grace. Matthew 6:12 reminds us that the grace that flows from Heaven to us must flow freely from us to others.

Practical methods to disperse a bout of grumbling can include praying until your attitude changes. Also, you can grab a handful of rubber bands and place them on your left wrist. Every time you catch yourself complaining, move one to your right wrist. As you share the meaning of your "bracelets" with others, you'll find that they will help you with accountability.

**3. Whom do you know who is patient in trials? How will you emulate that person?**

Many of your learners know (or know of) individuals whose lives serve as living portraits of patient endurance. One well-known example is Joni Eareckson Tada. She was paralyzed in an accident in 1967, but for decades she has shared her testimony of faith in Christ.

Set the tone by sharing openly yourself. It is often most helpful to share "lessons I learned the hard way and am still learning" rather than relating experiences that send the message "I have arrived."

**4. How do you overcome the temptation to waffle in keeping commitments?**

Some find it easy to agree to things during face-to-face discussions, but then later use the phone or e-mail to back out. Of course, sometimes circumstances force us to back out—we have no choice. But how we go about doing that speaks to our character. Scriptures that speak to the area of keeping commitments include Deuteronomy 23:21-23; Ecclesiastes 5:4, 5; and Acts 5:1-11.

**5. When are you most likely to pray? During what situations are you least likely to pray? Why?**

Frank Laubach (1884–1970) was a missionary to the Philippines and the developer of a literacy program still used worldwide. He became dissatisfied with his spiritual condition during his midlife years. He began questioning whether or not he could actually be in prayer all the time—while operating a machine, while in conversation with someone, while reading, etc. He practiced his "prayer experiments" and encouraged others to do so.

He concluded that when you keep God in your thoughts continually (though it was difficult to do so), everything else in life became easy. Notice that Laubach's idea is quite different from "spare-tire prayers," meaning "for use only in emergencies"!

**6. What qualities should you look for in a person to whom you would confess sin?**

"Discretion" and "the ability to keep confidences" will be popular answers. Many of your learners may also say that it is important to find someone who will love them in spite of their shortcomings—that will be the ideal person to be sought.

Honesty from the one being confided in is also an important quality. While it is tempting for us to try to ease another's pain by downplaying their errors, we must leave them in God's gracious hands and not minimize sin (especially if it is a sin we struggle with as well).